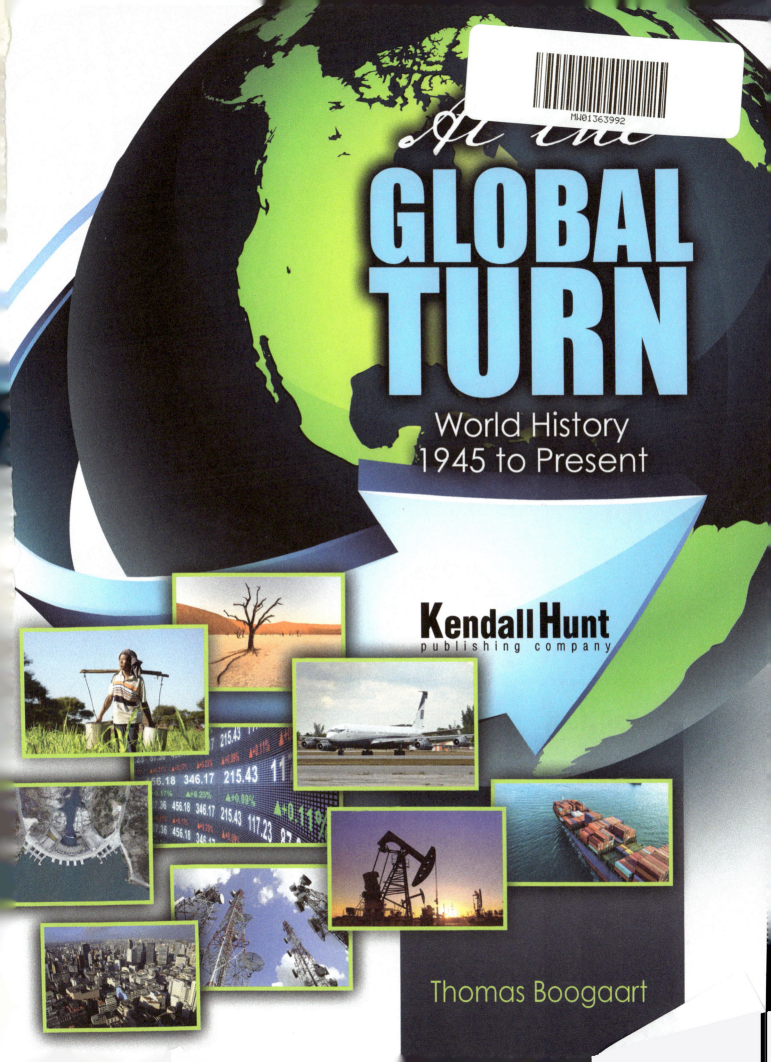

At the GLOBAL TURN

World History 1945 to Present

Kendall Hunt publishing company

Thomas Boogaart

Cover image © Shutterstock.com

www.kendallhunt.com
Send all inquiries to:
4050 Westmark Drive
Dubuque, IA 52004-1840

Copyright © 2019 by Kendall Hunt Publishing Company

ISBN: 978-1-5249-8692-6

All rights reserved. No part of this publication may be reproduced, stored in a retrieval system, or transmitted, in any form or by any means, electronic, mechanical, photocopying, recording, or otherwise, without the prior written permission of the copyright owner.

Published in the United States of America

Contents

Chapter 1: Introduction 1
    Chapter Outline 1
    Dawning of the Global Age 1
    At the Global Turn 4
    Conceptualizing the Postwar Era, 1945 to 2010 6
    Our Shrinking World 15
    Towards a Transnational History 20
    A Canadian Perspective 24
    Echoes of the Past 27
    Conclusion 28
    Questions for Critical Thought 28
    Suggestions for Further Reading 28

Chapter 2: Dreams for a Better World, 1945 to 1949 31
    Chapter Outline 31
    The Atlantic Dream, 1941 to 1949 32
    Postwar Decolonization Wave, 1945 to 1949 36
    West European Social Democracy, 1945 to 1949 43
    Fall of the Iron Curtain, 1945 to 1949 47
    Birth of Israel, 1945 to 1949 49
    Dissolution of the Grand Alliance, 1945 to 1949 52
    Conclusion: Shape of the Postwar World 56
    Questions for Critical Thought 56
    Suggestions for Further Reading 57

Chapter 3: A Revolutionary Wave 59
    Chapter Outline 59
    Decolonization and Development 60
    Clashing Expectations for Decolonization, 1945 to 1955 61
    The Great Unraveling, 1956 to 1966 64

Contents

    Quest for National Development, 1960 to 1975 68
    Postcolonial Challenges, 1973 to 1982 75
    Waning of the Revolutionary Wave 80
    Conclusion 84
    Questions for Critical Thought 84
    Suggestions for Further Reading 85

Chapter 4: The Global Cold War, 1949 to 1991 87
    Chapter Outline 87
    Introduction: A Cold War 88
    Global Spillover, 1949 to 1953 89
    War in Korea 91
    Towards the Nuclear Brink, 1954 to 1963 94
    Third World in the Cross Fire 100
    The Cold War in Popular Culture 106
    Gorbachev's End Game, 1985 to 1991 110
    Conclusion 112
    Questions for Critical Thought 112
    Suggestions for Further Reading 112

Chapter 5: The Postwar West 115
    Chapter Outline 115
    Introduction 116
    Golden Recovery 116
    Society of Affluence, 1950 to 1969 120
    The Anxious 1960s 124
    Stagflation Crisis, 1973 to 1980 133
    Conservative Resurgence, 1980s 135
    Contemporary Western Society 137
    Conclusion: The West in the Twenty-First Century 142
    Questions for Critical Thought 142
    Suggestions for Further Reading 142

Chapter 6: Postwar Latin America 145
    Chapter Outline 145
    Introduction 146
    Postwar Experiment in Populism 147
    Latin America's Cold War 152
    Postwar Culture and Society 160
    Latin America's Debt Crisis, 1982 to 1989 164

	The Democratic Wave	167
	Summary: Latin America at the Crossroads	170
	Questions for Critical Thought	171
	Suggestions for Further Reading	171

Chapter 7: Postwar Middle East 173
- Chapter Outline 173
- Introduction: The Postwar Middle East 174
- Nasser and Revolutionary Nationalism 175
- The Iranian Revolution 182
- The Soviet War in Afghanistan 189
- Postwar Urbanization and Modern Anxieties 193
- Palestinian Intifada and the Oslo Process, 1987 to 2000 196
- Summary: The Postwar Middle East 199
- Questions for Critical Thought 199
- Suggestions for Further Reading 200

Chapter 8: Sub-Saharan Africa 201
- Chapter Outline 201
- Introduction: Postcolonial Africa 202
- Diminishing Hope, 1960 to 1972 202
- Turn towards Kleptocracy, 1973 to 1986 208
- Postcolonial Society and Culture 213
- Democratic Wave, 1987 to 2000 218
- Rwanda's Tragedy 222
- Conclusion 227
- Questions for Critical Thought 228
- Suggestions for Further Reading 228

Chapter 9: Postwar Asia 231
- Chapter Outline 231
- Introduction: Postwar Asia, 1950 to 2000 232
- Asia's Cold War, 1945 to 1975 232
- Japan's Postwar Transformation, 1945 to 1991 239
- Mao and China's Modernization Struggle, 1950 to 1976 244
- The Asian Miracle 249
- The Waking Dragon, 1977 to 2001 253
- Summary: Postwar Asia 257
- Questions for Critical Thought 257
- Suggestions for Further Reading 257

Chapter 10: Life and Death of the Soviet Bloc 259
    Chapter Outline 259
    The Fall of Communism 260
    Mysterious Death of Comrade Stalin 260
    Stagnation under Brezhnev 267
    Destruction of the Aral Sea 269
    Gorbachev Takes the Soviet Helm, 1985 to 1991 272
    The Revolutions of 1989 275
    Trauma of Post-Communist Transition 279
    Conclusion 285
    Questions for Critical Thought 285
    Suggestions for Further Reading 286

Chapter 11: The Globalization of Capitalism 289
    Chapter Outline 289
    Introduction: Globalization 290
    Our Shrinking World 291
    Digitalization of the Economy 300
    Rise of Transnational Corporations 302
    Neoliberalism and the WTO 305
    Globalization's Paradoxes and Discontents 309
    Conclusion: Globalization and Capitalism 317
    Questions for Critical Thought 317
    Suggestions for Further Reading 318

Chapter 12: Bridge to the Twenty-First Century 321
    Chapter Outline 321
    Introduction: New World Order? 322
    Triumphant Liberalism 322
    9-11 and Security in the New Millennium 326
    Kyoto and Tragedy of the Global Commons 333
    Crisis Capitalism and the Great Recession of 2008 340
    The Arab Spring and Digital Populism 343
    Multipolarity and the New Cold War 345
    Conclusion: Bridge to the Twenty-First Century 347
    Questions for Critical Thought 348
    Suggestions for Further Reading 348

    Index 351

Chapter 1

Introduction

Chapter Outline

- Dawning of the Global Age
- At the Global Turn
- Conceptualizing the Postwar Era, 1945 to 2010
- Our Shrinking World
- Towards a Transnational History
- A Canadian Perspective
- Echoes of the Past
- Conclusion

Dawning of the Global Age

Millions watched on television as John Glenn blasted into orbit. For most of human history, our species has closely hugged the terrestrial surface. On February 20, 1962, Astronaut Glenn escaped the cradle of the earth and ascended into the heavens. Many commentators noted the flight's historical significance. In their rush to endorse technological progress, few pundits realized that speeding along at 27,000 km per hour, Glenn was experiencing an epiphany. Gazing through the lonely porthole of his capsule, what sprawled beneath him was not the geopolitical world map dividing people into color-coded states, but a blue ball of life rising against the cold silence of outer space. It struck Glenn that the ties binding humanity ran deeper than the differences setting us apart. Regardless of our creed, skin tone, or nationality, humans stood united as inhabitants of a shared Eden.

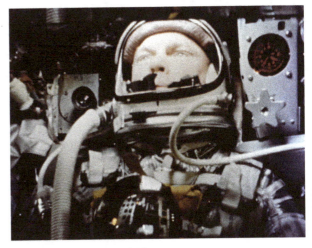

John Glenn aboard Friendship 7.

In 1962, Glenn caught a glimpse of humanity united in a planetary civilization. Since his orbital flight, the process of global integration has intensified. Today, fleets of wide-bodied commercial jets hop over the Rocky Mountains, which only a century and a half ago so frustrated pioneers trekking along the Oregon Trail. Globally, this "death of distance" is mirrored in an increasingly "borderless" economy. Every day, containers full of jeans, vegetables, and electronic components gather on Shenzhen's wharves, Santiago's warehouses, and Tijuana's maquiladoras before moving through global supply chains on their way to big-box store shelves, local souks (markets), or isolated rural homesteads. Few Canadians consider that when settling down for their evening meal, the ingredients sitting upon their dinner plate have already traveled thousands of miles from farm to fork. During the 2010 FIFA tournament, half of humanity used some digital device to tune into the world's most beautiful game.

Globalization is not new. Seven-hundred years ago, the economies of Eurasia and Northern Africa were minimally integrated by the Silk Road that snaked 6,000 km through the mountains, steppes, and parched deserts of Central Asia. Since 1980, however, separate processes of economic, cultural, and technological integration have accelerated and increasingly converged. Over time, incremental changes add up to revolutionary shifts. During the last two decades, we have breezed past several milestones on our road toward planetary civilization. Launch of the World Trade Organization (WTO) in 1995 marked a tipping point toward deeper integration of national economies into a single capitalist system. A decade later, separate fixed, cellular, and broadcast networks merged into a seamless digital mesh wrapping around human society. Fusion of the Internet, social media, and affordable cell phones has culminated in a digital society that changes how we shop, work, and socialize—even how we think.

A paradox defining contemporary integration is that in leveling traditional geographic, state, and cultural barriers, globalization also exposes religious and class differences, while forcing people to adapt to new technologies, practices, and ideas. Rapid integration can stimulate anxiety and a conservative

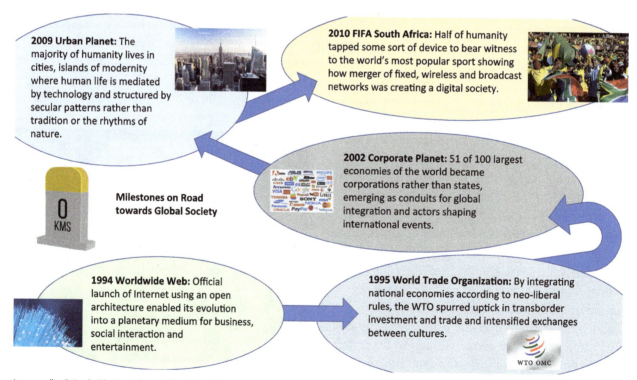

2009 Urban Planet: The majority of humanity lives in cities, islands of modernity where human life is mediated by technology and structured by secular patterns rather than tradition or the rhythms of nature.

2010 FIFA South Africa: Half of humanity tapped some sort of device to bear witness to the world's most popular sport showing how merger of fixed, wireless and broadcast networks was creating a digital society.

2002 Corporate Planet: 51 of 100 largest economies of the world became corporations rather than states, emerging as conduits for global integration and actors shaping international events.

Milestones on Road towards Global Society

1994 Worldwide Web: Official launch of Internet using an open architecture enabled its evolution into a planetary medium for business, social interaction and entertainment.

1995 World Trade Organization: By integrating national economies according to neo-liberal rules, the WTO spurred uptick in transborder investment and trade and intensified exchanges between cultures.

Image credits: © Kusska/Shutterstock.com; © fstockfoto/Shutterstock.com; © Miss Ty/Shutterstock.com; © Turn on/Shutterstock.com; © Pumidol/Shutterstock.com; © Design Prax/Shutterstock.com

reflex towards **glocalization**, where local communities, stakeholders in the mass production model, social conservatives, and religious fundamentalists mobilize to fend off globalization's unwanted effects. In 1999, Shepherd Juan Bové vandalized a local McDonalds that he blamed for contaminating French culture. This elevated Bové into a national hero and icon of the anti-globalization movement.

During the late 1990s, activists, like French Shepherd Jose Bové, promoted resistance to neoliberal globalization as a threat to local culture and traditions.

Symbolic acts of defiance, however, have not dented the scope or pace of global integration. In Asia, hundreds of millions have moved to cities in the last decade seeking jobs, access to consumer goods, and a better way of life. India's middle classes, whether they are Hindu, Sikh, or Muslim, increasingly associate the "good life" with creature comforts ranging from a car to indoor plumbing and electronic gadgets. Similarly, the American model of industrial agriculture has spread around the world, supplanting family farms, local markets, and traditional foods. Asians now are eating more meat and processed foods, while expanding waistlines are leading to higher incidences of obesity-linked diseases.

Across the world stage, militant rejection and enthusiastic assimilation represent poles along a broader spectrum according to which individuals and local cultures are adapting to "modern" life. However, accommodation, rather than resistance, has proven the dominant response to globalization. In Saudi Arabia, the conservative clergy compel women to wear the *chador* to protect their modesty in public. From inside their own homes, however, thousands of highly educated Saudi women waged a successful "Twitter war" against their state's ban on their driving. This represents only the tip of a broader revolution. Across the world, rising female literacy and education is empowering women to enter the workforce, challenge gender disparities, and redefine the patriarchal structure of the family.

> From its origins, Canada has struggled to define itself apart from a neighboring hegemon. Have Hollywood films and US fast food chains "Americanized" Canadian culture, or is our identity too resilient for that?

During the 1990s, some historians rejected globalization as little more than "globaloney." Rather than a fundamental shift, they pointed to deeper continuities, the resilience of cultural identities, and the importance of powerful states in shaping contemporary headlines. All this is true. Revolutions are always partial. Changes happen over time. This does not alter the fact that many contemporary changes are radical and without precedent.

Chapter 1: Introduction

Big Questions

- How is globalization transforming human society?
- How does recent history fit inside the broader tableau of human experience?
- What forces shaped postwar history?
- How is deeper integration impacting local cultures?
- What biases shape the Canadian view of the world?

At the Global Turn

For many Canadians, the twenty-first century arrived with a bang. Three catastrophes; 9-11, severe acute respiratory syndrome (SARS), and the Great Global Recession, ushered in the new century. The 9-11 attack left the World Trade Center towers a smouldering ruin. Al Qaeda revealed the network society's darker side; how in an age of global travel and communications, subnational groups could deliver a devastating blow to the world's hegemonic power on its home soil. Ever since, states have struggled to expand their notion of national defense to address asymmetric threats and to protect their ever-expanding virtual frontier. Although the 2002 to 2003 SARS outbreak was ultimately contained, it served warning that in an age of transcontinental jets and international travel, the vectors for a global epidemic of bubonic proportions are in place. The 2008 **Great Global Recession** highlighted the high-degree integration of global capital markets and the fragility of the world economy. Novel fiscal instruments like derivatives, mortgage-backed securities, and no income, no jobs, or no assets (NINJA) loans in Florida and California easily overwhelmed Canada's otherwise liquid banking sector. Al Qaeda, SARS, and the 2008 meltdown served warning that the physics of human society had changed.

As Dorothy observed in the *Wizard of Oz*, we are not in Kansas anymore. As we push deeper into the twenty-first century, human society is evolving into a more global configuration where geographic distance, cultural differences, and national loyalties matter less than they did a century before. Inside this "shrinking" world, crisscrossed by overlapping planetary networks, events happen faster, their origins are more mysterious and their radius of impact is magnified. Outwardly, Canadian institutions seem mostly unchanged, even comfortingly familiar. But 9-11, SARS, and the 2008 meltdown reveal that Lester Pearson's Canada is no more. The barriers that once insulated Canadians from global forces have steadily eroded. Inside a flatter world, states struggle to meet a range of asymmetric threats, from cyber terrorism to global epidemics, and flash market crashes. The labor market, international politics, and national defense no longer operate according to twentieth-century rules. Increasingly, transnational phenomena like nongovernmental organizations (NGOs), category 5 hurricanes, and black pools of capital—that rarely receive scrutiny inside world history texts—are shaping contemporary headlines. Meanwhile, institutions that we inherited from the previous century are being reconfigured to correspond to the physics of a globalizing society, where relative viscosity is reduced, events happen faster, and distant events can radiate across the planetary surface with sudden and brutal force.

History's New Physics

Transnational corporations (TNCs) represent heralds of a more global age. For multinationals, the WTO's liberal rules represented an emancipation proclamation. From 1960 to 2000, they soared in number from 2000 to 63,000.[1] At the top end, Fortune 500 companies embarked upon a merger wave, buying out foreign competitors, while carving out dominant stake in the extractive industries of the postcolonial world. By 2003, TNCs supplanted states in terms of constituting a majority of the world's hundred largest economies. Twelve years later, corporations trumped states 65 to 35.[2] Critics argue that a country's gross domestic product (GDP) does not correlate to a corporation's market capitalization, but there is no disputing that neoliberal globalization has enabled corporations to grow in size and influence. During the 1990s, just three corporations dominated the banana trade, a cartel that repatriated only 12 percent of net sales back to the countries of production.[3] A 2010 WikiLeaks exposé revealed how Royal Dutch Shell, owner of most of Nigeria's oil fields, kept corporate minders in all of the state's ministries. This leverage enabled them to influence state policy and call upon the national army when rebels attacked their oil installations.[4]

Nigeria's precarious sovereignty offers just one illustration of a seismic shift. Inside developing countries, not only TNCs but also NGOs are as wealthy and influential as the states supposed to regulate them. An increasing segment of international trade is being replaced by transfers inside corporations between separate subsidiaries. States are hardly going extinct; they collect taxes, maintain armies, and set policy inside international bodies like the United Nations (UN) and Organisation for Economic Co-operation and Development (OECD). On the other hand, the world's largest corporations have evolved into truly transnational entities that in important ways transcend the territorial jurisdiction of states. For example, in 2011, the world's wealthiest corporation, Apple, paid only 1.3 percent tax despite an effective corporate tax rate of 19 percent. This highlights how TNCs "offshore" their profits to tax havens. Today, vulture funds of private investors enforce debt payment upon poor states like Tanzania. In 1992, the Bank of England's plans for monetary union were thwarted by private financiers like George Soros that sold the pound sterling short. At rugby matches, fans still boisterously hoist their colors, but what does national rivalry mean in an age where the richest eighty-five families control as much wealth as the bottom half?[5]

Black Pools of Capital: Explosive growth of arcane financial instruments like CDOs, swaps and derivatives have decoupled world economy from state regulation and control.

History's New Physics

Asymmetric Threats: 9-11 attack exemplified how traditional ideas of national defense need to be reconfigured to thwart non-state actors and cyber-terrorists while securing infrastructure.

Transnational Actors: IMF, TNCs and vulture funds serve as primary conduits for investment and enforcement of state debt.

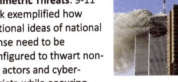

Post-nationalism: Market integration, globalization of media and digital technologies erode identification with state.

Cosmopolitanism: Majority of humans live in cities and connect to nature and others through anonymous market, virtual platforms and global consumer culture.

States as global actors

State-Centric Distortion Field: GDP, national security, international trade, war, sovereignty, development, decolonization

Cultural homogeneity

National Interest

Developed and Third World

International system

Hybrid Conflicts: Wars increasingly intersect ethnic, regional and sectarian fissures, while being driven by foreign arms merchants, ecological degradation and robber rulers, rather than pursuit of grand strategy or the national interest.

Reduced Viscosity: Epidemics, climate change and financial panics rapidly diffuse through integrated system paying little heed to cultural barriers or national jurisdictions.

Image credits: © Who is Danny/Shutterstock.com; © brichuas/Shutterstock.com; © Ken Tannenbaum/Shutterstock.com; © CASTALDOstudio.com/Shutterstock.com; © imtmphoto/Shutterstock.com

Chapter 1: Introduction

In his allegory of the cave, Plato imagined a shackled prisoner. Watching shadows flickering along the cavern wall, how could this prisoner distinguish the hidden figures above from their projection? A similar challenge confronts historians that have long viewed twentieth-century history through the prism of the state. The age of empires, territorially defined jurisdictions, and national identities is waning. To what extent do traditional social science concepts like national interest, international trade, sovereignty, and GDP still correspond to a global society increasingly whipped by transnational networks, global forces, and subnational fractures? Are common expressions like "America" and "Chinese culture" still meaningful? Are traditional tools like maps and timelines rooted in an older metaphysics that exaggerates the importance of states as a container for experience, object for national loyalty, and agents for change? This book explores postwar history from a transnational perspective. It attempts to transcend the black box of the state, analyzing the phenomena that sometimes fall between the analytical cracks, while highlighting how historical events played out divergently across an uneven global landscape.

Conceptualizing the Postwar Era, 1945 to 2010

Imagine an angel in heaven observing human civilization over hundred-year-increments. For millennia, this angel might feel quite bored. For most of our history as a species, humans live short lives of brutish poverty. During the late eighteenth century, this angel might discern a subtle shift in the workshops of the British midlands. There, steam engines and coal were combining to spur a revolutionary transformation in manufacturing. However, not until the late nineteenth century did European cities grow rapidly in size, as international trade and travel accelerated. By the start of the twentieth century, the break from the preindustrial past would be clear as human population and consumption exploded. After World War II, this "modernity" begins to spread out from its core regions, dramatically elevating human population and longevity in the periphery.

Max Roser has created the Our World In Data, a portal that enables us to visualize this great transformation. Taking consumption, literacy, urbanization, and Internet use as indexes, humanity's twentieth-century breakthrough is revealed. Mass inoculations, antibiotics, improved food distribution, and implementation of basic sanitation measures cut deeply into child mortality rates, enabling the life expectancy of Asians and Africans to more than double over the twentieth century.

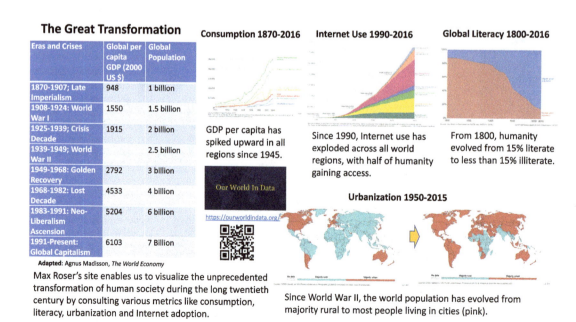

The Great Transformation

Eras and Crises	Global per capita GDP (2000 US $)	Global Population
1870-1907; Late Imperialism	948	1 billion
1908-1924; World War I	1550	1.5 billion
1925-1939; Crisis Decade	1915	2 billion
1939-1949; World War II		2.5 billion
1949-1968; Golden Recovery	2792	3 billion
1968-1982; Lost Decade	4533	4 billion
1983-1991; Neo-Liberalism Ascension	5204	6 billion
1991-Present; Global Capitalism	6103	7 Billion

Adapted: Agnus Madisson, *The World Economy*

Max Roser's site enables us to visualize the unprecedented transformation of human society during the long twentieth century by consulting various metrics like consumption, literacy, urbanization and Internet adoption.

Consumption 1870-2016 — GDP per capita has spiked upward in all regions since 1945.

Internet Use 1990-2016 — Since 1990, Internet use has exploded across all world regions, with half of humanity gaining access.

Global Literacy 1800-2016 — From 1800, humanity evolved from 15% literate to less than 15% illiterate.

Urbanization 1950-2015 — Since World War II, the world population has evolved from majority rural to most people living in cities (pink).

Contemporary Canadians are beneficiaries of industrialization. Today, the average Canadian student, debts and all, is in many respects more affluent than the richest man living in seventeenth-century Europe. Louis the Sun King spent his winters shivering in the damp halls of Versailles. It took armies of servants to feed his fireplaces, but this effort and expense failed to match the efficiency that central heating provides most dorm rooms today. Neither could poor Louis imagine strolling through a modern supermarket and plucking up a fresh plumb out of season. Technology and industrialization have combined to provide Canadians with countless luxuries out of reach of lords living only a century ago.

Technology and industrialization have made the average Canadian more comfortable than the richest man living in seventeenth-century Europe.

> If technology has powered a productivity revolution, why are hundreds of millions still living on less than $1 a day?

Chapter 1: Introduction

Shape of the Long Twentieth Century

To explain the anomaly of contemporary living, we need to dig deeper into the structure of human society by exploring the interplay of technology, investment, and the geographic division of labor with cultural forces like rising literacy, racism, and patriarchy. Ferdinand Braudel named this perspective the **longue durée**. When we examine the twentieth century from a structural perspective, prominent figures like Churchill, Mao Zedong, or Gandhi remain indistinguishable specs, blotted out like the other granular details of national history. At this scale, rising mortality rates would reveal disruptive wake left by events like the 1919 Versailles Conference or the Great Depression. Most events grabbing contemporary headlines, however, would appear only as momentary blips masking a more fundamental trend towards urbanization, industrialization, agricultural intensification, and rising affluence.

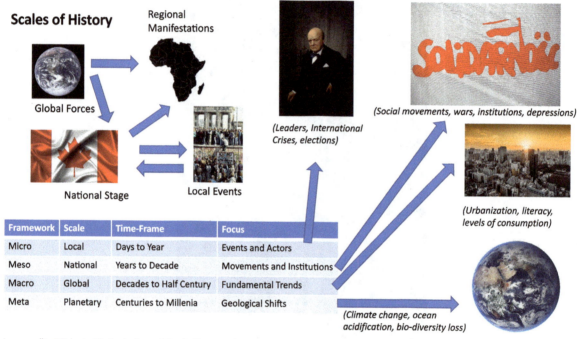

Image credits: © Robert_s/Shutterstock.com; © Armita/Shutterstock.com; © Anton_Ivanov/Shutterstock.com; © Watch The World/Shutterstock.com; © Nessa Gnatoush/Shutterstock.com; © Millenius/Shutterstock.com; Berlin Wall: Source: National Archives Catalog

The structural perspective would reveal a sharp division between the twentieth century's tumultuous first half, punctuated by imperial rivalries, two world wars, a global influenza epidemic, and an economic calamity, with a more tranquil second half where industrialization and urbanization accelerated. Some historians argue that the Cold War maintained the nuclear balance of terror, enforcing a peace among Europe's fractious great powers and transposing conflict to lower intensity proxy wars at the periphery. A more likely explanation is that postwar stability was facilitated by accelerating trade and rising productivity. Economic growth during the postwar era was unprecedentedly robust, interrupted only by a brief slowdown lasting from roughly 1970 to 1982. Subsequently, the economy gradually picked up speed again and prosperity radiated out to the periphery with renewed heft.

Chapter 1: Introduction

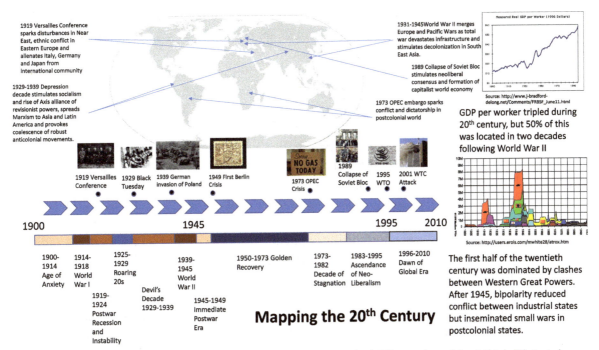

Mapping the 20th Century

Focusing in specifically upon the postwar era, we would notice that although the trend towards urban–industrial civilization began a century before, it left vast areas of the planet untouched. In 1945, a majority of the people living in the non-Western world remained farmers. They lived in rural villages, communities that sculpted local lives according to time-honored values and religious traditions. Only in 2007, did human civilization cross a threshold where most people lived in cities. By the twenty-first century, even in the countryside, technology and industrialization had combined to free most from toil on the land. In the process, local practices and ideas about sexuality, gender, and family are being reconfigured to fit an urban environment and society of mass abundance. This is not to say that across the world stage human experience is becoming homogenous, or human lives better. Significant class, race, and confessional and racial differences continue to separate us. The ecological destructiveness of our economy is not sustainable. The predominant postwar trend, however, is our mutual struggle to reconstitute older identities and reframe our desires to this emerging global society of abundance, possibility, and freedom.

Economic Cycles and Regional Discrepancies

Although rising affluence represents the big story of the postwar era, this trend obscures stark regional lags and sharp local differences. A major disruption in the world economy occurred between 1973 and 1982. Production began to shift to a more decentralized model, services trumped manufacturing inside industrial economies, while the financial and technological sectors of the economy expanded rapidly. The economy also grew more interlinked through containerization, outsourcing component production, the relaxation of capital controls, and the rollout of successive electronic communication platforms. Heavy industries in the West declined rapidly, while new factories and workshops sprouted up, especially in special industrialization zones of the periphery.

Russian theorist Nikolai Kondratieff postulated that economies evolve over roughly fifty-year cycles, correlated to shifts inside a production complex defined by certain core technologies, fabrication methods, and raw material inputs. At least at a superficial level, periods of economic expansion often give rise to optimism, social consensus, and political stability. Conversely, towards the end of the Kondratieff wave, the production complex grows increasingly inefficient. New technologies undermine established economic sectors. Critical resources might have become depleted sparking exhaustion or a peripheral region might carve out a larger market share disrupting global flows of trade. Misalignment shows up in the economic record as high unemployment, deflation, declining investment, agricultural shortages, or sagging productivity. Widespread suffering and disillusionment in turn provides fuel for political radicalism, revolutionary social movements, wars, or a far-reaching realignment of the global economy. Kondratieff's model helps us to relate turbulent events like the 1950 Korean War, 1973 Organization of Petroleum Exporting Countries (OPEC) embargo, and 1982 Debt Crisisto shifts in the production complex. To examine why decolonization largely failed to level the income gap between Western states and former colonies, and why Asia captured a disproportionate share of the world's economy, requires us to dig deeper into how macroeconomic events intersected with regional history.

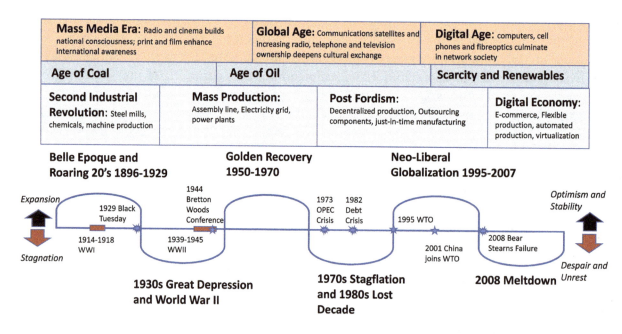

Kondratieff Cycles

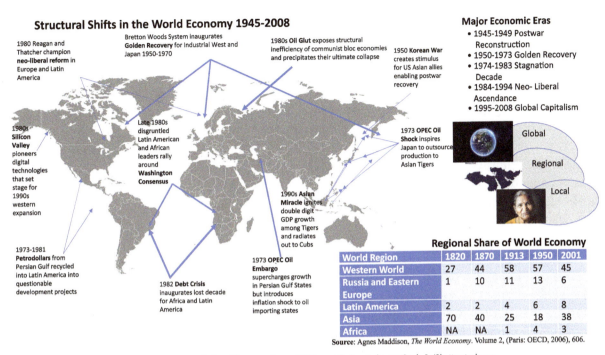

Source: Agnes Maddison, *The World Economy*. Volume 2, (Paris: OECD, 2006), 606.

Image credits: © Andrei Minsk/Shutterstock.com; © Aphelleon/Shutterstock.com; © PSboom/Shutterstock.com; © teja Sv/Shutterstock.com

The Golden Postwar Recovery, 1950 to 1972

For Europe, the robustness of the economic recovery after 1950 was correlated to the depths of destruction by World War II. Cities needed to be rebuilt, industrial machinery retooled, and national economies redirected towards consumer production. The recovery was also abetted by widespread adoption of mass production techniques. Oil replaced coal, factories grew in size to capture economies of scale, consumer credit and redistributive policies expanded demand, and agricultural mechanized powered sustained productivity gains.

International stability also supported Western recovery. The 1944 Bretton Woods agreement established a system for fixed currency exchange backstopped by the United States, its dollar and gold. The 1947 General Agreement on Tariffs and Trade (GATT) mechanism enabled a progressive reduction in national tariffs that fuelled an expansion in trade and deeper integration among Western industrial states. By 1950, high investment, more efficient factories, and expanding international trade combined for economic liftoff. From 1950 to 1970, rising productivity powered fat profits and higher wages, lifting many working-class families into the ranks of the middle class by 1960. Enhanced security deepened the solidarity inside Western societies, curbing prewar radicalism and cementing broad support for welfare states that presided over an expanding economy and ever-widening safety net.

Western prosperity radiated out to the non-Western world, mostly by raising demand for commodities. International loans and higher revenue from exports enabled postcolonial leaders to invest in infrastructure, education, and hospitals, dramatically raising longevity and literacy. Between 1968 and 1973, however, the postwar recovery ran out of steam. Rising inflation led Nixon to devalue the dollar in 1971. This unravelled the Bretton Woods Accord in favor of a floating currency system by 1973. Subsequently, the 1973 OPEC oil embargo injected an inflationary shock to the world economy. Postwar prosperity had hinged upon cheap oil; a critical ingredient in the Fordist model used in transportation, electricity generation, fertilizer, plastics, and chemicals.

OPEC Embargo and the Lost Decade, 1973 to 1985

Throughout the 1950s, Western oil multinationals—the fabled "seven sisters"—monopolized the supply of oil and kept prices low. This established supportive conditions for the Western build-out of the Fordist economic model and high commodity prices benefitting developing countries. Starting in 1960, the Saudi royals began to push for a larger share of petroleum profits. The Saudis and their allies also formed the OPEC. Their leverage increased as European oil consumption rose, and traditional areas of supply petered out. By the early 1970s, OPEC had evolved into a cartel, which by controlling the oil supply, also regulated the price of the world economy's most critical input. The 1973 embargo was rooted in Saudi displeasure with US support for Israel during the Yom Kippur War. However short-lived, the embargo precipitated a fourfold increase in oil prices by 1974, which washed out one of the pillars of the golden recovery. The oil shock's impact, however, was uneven given various levels of oil dependence and gaping differences among states and world regions.

Developed Western economies experienced the 1970s mostly as stagflation; a combination of sluggish growth, high unemployment, and high inflation. Throughout the 1980s, Western statesmen discovered that Keynesian recipes for fiscal stimulus no longer worked because many of their industries had lost their technological lead. Although the oil shock also hurt Japan, the country responded by pioneering new production techniques. In particular, Japanese corporations increasingly outsourced component production to neighboring Tiger economies, where wages were lower. Japan also invested in efficient plants, quality control measures, and research and development. This enabled major Japanese corporations to assume the lead in key sectors. Together, these reforms enabled Japan and its Asian partners to weather stagflation better and carve out increasing market share from the West. From 1973 to 1980, Japan surpassed first France, then Britain, and finally Germany, to become the second leading economy in the world.

Inside the developing world, the oil shock introduced a sharp polarization between petroleum-exporting and petroleum-importing states. Thinly populated Gulf kingdoms were vaulted into the ranks of the world's richest states almost overnight. Non-Arab petroleum exporters like Nigeria, Mexico, and Venezuela also benefitted, but less significantly, given the smaller size of their oil sector relative to their population. Many Gulf sheikhs not only dabbled in a conspicuous consumption, they also channeled their **petrodollars** into infrastructural investments and build-out of welfare measures that dramatically elevated the living standards for their citizens. In contrast, rising oil prices hit most developing countries hard. Slowing Western demand for commodities lowered export earnings just as the costs of imports—tied to the price of oil—rose.

Many Latin American junta responded to adverse headwinds by taking out foreign loans. Petrodollars accumulated by Gulf sheikhs were deposited in Western money center banks and then refunneled as loans to Latin America. Large infrastructure projects, like Brazil's national integration program to develop the Amazon, kept the economy greased and quieted populist unrest, but most development schemes failed to live up to their rosy forecasts. After 1980, when interest rates spiked, and additional sources of capital for Latin America dried up, Latin America fell into a debt trap. In 1982, first Mexico, then Brazil, defaulted on their loans. The former "miracle" economies now headlined an international debt crisis. Financial collapse was averted when Mexico and Brazil's debts were restructured, but most other African and Latin American states languished in a Lost Decade. Debtor states struggled to find credit and were forced to either cut state expenditures and print money. Hyperinflation, economic contraction, and austerity hit the poor the hardest and exacerbated internal fissures, ethnic tensions, and class conflicts.

The oil shock also contributed to the eventual collapse of Eastern communism. Since the 1970s, Eastern Europe's technological deficit and unproductive farms and factories had forced communist regimes to make concessions to their people, while also appeasing foreign lenders. Rising oil prices after 1973 enabled the Soviet Union to provide its allies with a rising subsidy that enabled communist regimes to placate unrest by importing food, tropical products, and technology they could not produce on their own. But Eastern Europe's increasing dependence upon Western loans and the Soviet oil also made their regimes vulnerable when oil markets became oversupplied in the early 1980s. The inability of the Soviet Union to maintain the oil subsidy was an incentive for Gorbachev's liberal reforms that set the stage for the Revolutions of 1989 and collapse of communism in Eastern Europe.

Oil reserves partially insulated the West and the Middle East from macroeconomic headwinds. Oil exporters were the immediate beneficiaries of higher prices. The Saudi royals and other Gulf sheiks also redistributed a share of their windfall among their less oil-rich neighbors. North Sea oil, off-shore drilling, and ownership of the oil majors enabled Western economies to mitigate the worst effects of the oil shock. By the mid-1980s, Western dominance in the rapidly growing high-technology sector also helped to offset losses inside heavy industries. The West also disproportionately benefited from rising interest rates after 1980. As postcolonial states devoted an increasingly larger share of state revenue to repay foreign loans, the Western-dominated financial sector of the world economy boomed. Global financial capitals like London, Berlin, New York, and Tokyo paid out disproportionately high salaries to an expanding army of financial managers, bond investors, and investment bankers.

Pacific Asia ultimately benefitted most from the oil shock because the export industrialization policies converged with a transition in the structure of global manufacturing. Higher oil prices enhanced the competitive edge of Asian factories that relied upon low labor costs. By the 1980s, Asian entrepreneurs expanded their market share inside Western markets where local manufacturers suffered from a combination of outdated equipment, a bloated work force, and lower state subsidies. Simultaneously, improving global logistics incentivized Western multinationals to copy Japan's outsourcing model. By the late 1980s, deindustrialization in established Western manufacturing centers gained momentum as uncompetitive factories, steel plants, and textile mills closed while those in China's special economic zones boomed.

Pathway to Neoliberal Globalization, 1986 to 2007

After nearly two decades of economic headwinds, growth was rekindled by the late 1980s. Shifting manufacturing to the Asia Pacific region was facilitated by conducive international policies. In 1986, postcolonial leaders and dependency theorists joined Western statesmen in the **Uruguay process** to hammer out the rules for a more integrated global economy. Initially, many non-Western leaders resisted pressure to open up their economies to foreign investors, fearful that a resurgent capitalism would usher in a new era of colonial exploitation. Debtor states also complained about the stringent conditions that the International Monetary Fund (IMF) imposed for badly needed capital infusions. Most aid recipients needed to agree to far-reaching **structural reforms** that sliced tariffs, cut state subsidies to indigenous entrepreneurs and social services that struck the poor particularly hard. Initially, postcolonial leaders were wary of liberal reforms that would open their economies to Western investment. The Uruguay Process gained momentum following the dramatic collapse of Eastern European communist regimes in 1989. Simultaneously, improving electronic communications, the container revolution and financial reforms combined to make it affordable to outsource production to suppliers situated in distant low-wage regions. Asia had served as a flashpoint in the Cold War from 1950 to 1970, but Nixon's 1972 visit to China facilitated a gradual Sino-US rapprochement that brought stability over much of Southeast Asia by the 1980s. The region's disciplined workforce, skilled entrepreneurs, and lean firms also received a stimulus from rising Japanese investment. Tiger economies in Taiwan, Hong Kong, and South Korea emulated Japan's export industrialization strategy to carve out a progressively larger share of global manufacturing. By 1990, the divergence between the Asian Pacific and the rest of the world widened. In 2000, leading Tiger economies reached parity with Western industrial states in GDP per capita, and outpaced their postcolonial peers in Latin America, Africa, and the Middle East.

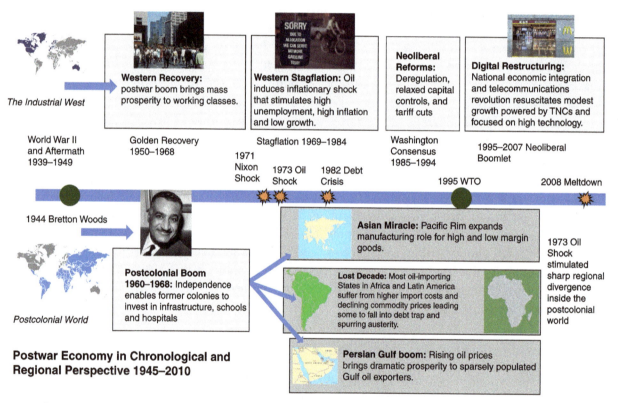

Image credits: © Andrei Minsk/Shutterstock.com; © Everett Historical/Shutterstock.com; © TonyV3112/Shutterstock.com; © Andrei Minsk/Shutterstock.com; Nasser: Everett Collection Historical/ Alamy Stock Photo; © Olga Turkas/Shutterstock.com; © boreala/Shutterstock.com; © PSboom/Shutterstock.com; © Peter Hermes Furian/Shutterstock.com

Relaxed banking rules and lower tariffs powered a massive transfusion of capital from Western states to the Global South. Under the World Trade Organization, capital flows primarily took the form of portfolio and foreign direct investment from TNCs and Western investment bankers, rather than long-term loans. Low interest rates made cheap capital available to local entrepreneurs and stimulated higher growth rates in the developing world. A signification portion of Western investment, however, was directed towards the Pacific Rim, where China particularly emerged as a hub for global manufacturing. Other states, enjoying a comparative advantage or strategic location inside the global economy, also benefitted from the transition to a more decentralized production model. Resumption of world economic growth raised commodity prices, increasing wages inside the developing world, improving state balance sheets, and decreasing global levels of malnutrition. Inside Africa and the Middle East, economic growth barely kept pace with a rising population. In Latin America, and much of Asia, growth was closely tied to extractive industries that benefitted foreign investors and corrupt local elites as much as local workers, while often damaging local ecosystems.

In aggregate, the postwar era represented a period of rising prosperity. At the regional scale, we start to discern significant discrepancies; the Postcolonial World mostly failed to industrialize, Pacific Asia modernized rapidly after 1980, and the communist bloc was reintegrated into the world economy. History never moves according to iron laws, but Kondratieff's theory helps us to appreciate how these broader trends were tied to the critical decade of 1973 to 1982 and the transition to a more integrated global economy.

Our Shrinking World

In addition to affluence, the "death of distance," was a main twentieth-century storyline. After World War II, there was a steady erosion of many of the historic barriers that once separated towns, cultures, and people. The global era began during the 1870s as three distance-leveling technologies, the telegraph, steamship, and railroad, combined to promote international travel, stimulate deeper regional economic integration, and promote a more global consciousness. Since the 1870s, successive new technologies have appeared. Inside the communication field, radio, television, and Internet each played a distinctive role in shaping global integration across multiple scales; the Western core of the economy was coupled more closely to the periphery, colonial subjects were exposed to Western modernity, and improved transportation linked towns to the countryside.

From a global perspective, communication technologies reshaped global society in thirty-year waves as new technologies were invented, improved, acquired mass adoption first in the developed core before being exported out to the periphery. Television can serve as an illustration, as it had a particularly dramatic impact upon rural cultures after 1970. In Iran from 1970 to 1974, television viewership climbed from 2.1 million to 15 million to embrace half the population.[6] As satellite dishes poked up through the roof slats of isolated villages, syndicated episodes of *Dallas* or *Dynasty* beamed into non-Western households and projected a highly distorted image of American culture and Western society. Television shows, and their accompanying advertisements, projected implicit ideas about affluence, gender, and sexuality at odds with local values. In certain corners of the world, television stimulated religious revivalism as local clerics railed against Western materialism and promiscuity. Many rural viewers were not only shocked, but also enamored by the world glittering across their screen. Those watching dubbed episodes of Dallas might have concluded that American women were shameless and that Western culture was decadent, but they also appreciated the luxury of modern life and the convenience afforded by new technologies.

> *Baywatch* was widely syndicated throughout the Middle East during the 1990s. How might Pakistani villagers have gleaned a distorted image of American values and Western culture from watching fictional life guards prancing around Los Angeles beaches?

Chapter 1: Introduction

1866 Trans-Atlantic telegraph cable: enables nearly instant global communication at high cost and low bandwidth.

1896 Wireless telegraphy: Marconi patents blossom into mass market consumer radio by 1920s.

1962 Tel-Star 1: First communications satellite inaugurates era of live trans-oceanic broadcasts.

1983 DynaTAC 8000: provides first commercially viable cellular phone that will evolve into mass market device by late 1990s with advent of G-2 network technology.

1995 World Wide Web Launch: Internet into medium for work, entertainment and social interaction.

2010 FIFA South Africa: Half of human population tunes in to witness soccer tournament.

1870–1920s International Age: International mail, mass circulation newspapers and telegraph enable efficient trans-oceanic correspondence, facilitating planetary consciousness.

1930–1960s Mass Media Age: States use film and radio to build up a national consciousness and cultural orthodoxy overlaying regional and sectarian differences.

1970–1980s Television Age: Communication satellites and diffusion of television sets in non-Western World households intensifies cultural collision.

1990–2000s Digital Age: Linked personal computers and cellphones connect individuals through planetary networks.

Information Revolution 1866–2016
Global Diffusion of Televisions 1950–1980

- 1950s
- 1960s
- 1970s
- 1980s
- Aired in color after first broadcast

Worldwide Internet Users 2005–2016			
	2005	2010	2016
Population	6.5 billion	6.9 billion	7.3 billion
Total users	16%	30%	47%
Developing	8%	21%	40%
Developed	51%	67%	81%

Image credits: © Stocksnapper/Shutterstock.com; © vkilkov/Shutterstock.com; Tel Star: NASA; © Timur Zima/Shutterstock.com; © Oleksiy/Shutterstock.com; © fstockfoto/Shutterstock.com; © Andrei Minsk/Shutterstock.com

Television exemplifies how successive communication technologies leveled distances, reducing cultural frontiers and compressing our sense of time and space. By 2002, the world featured over 21,000 TV stations broadcasting breaking news from around the world stage to over 1.6 billion television sets.[7] But communication technologies were a single conduit shaping global integration. Following World War II, non-Western people gradually threw off European rule. While rejecting racism and colonialism, many first-generation leaders also presented themselves as "modernizers." They promised to bring the wealth and comforts of the Western world to their people.

Inside the postcolonial world, the megacity emerged as an important gateway that acclimated rural immigrant to the modern way of life.

This identification is not surprising when you consider that many "fathers on nations" were educated in Western schools. They shared a belief that postcolonial prosperity hinged upon following the Western path for modernization. Gamal Abdel Nasser embraced "revolution" to undermine Egypt's old elites and to introduce modern science, education, and technology to raise local productivity. Throughout the 1960s, postcolonial investment built out electricity grids, roads, television stations, and international airports. This coupled remote communities more closely to the national capital, world economy, and "modern practices." Non-Western world peasants were also deeply impacted by import-substitution policies that sought to finance industrialization by squeezing small farmers and rural producers. Because most postcolonial states lavished spending on the capital city, sharp gaps emerged between the rural and urban standards of living.

Starting in Latin America during the 1950s, and somewhat later in Asia and the Middle East, urban migration rapidly accelerated. The postcolonial city served as the gateway acclimating rural peasants to modern patterns of life. Immigrants encountered an alien world of foreign products, neon signs, drone of cars, and smog of mopeds. Cities never sleep; electric light dims the glint of the Milky Way. The urban workday is synchronized to the twenty-four-hour production schedule rather than the rhythms of nature. Local spirits are supplanted by alluring adds for consumer products promising a better life. Survival depends on navigating bureaucratic procedures rather than the fickle personality of neighbor and elders. Tanzania's postcolonial development program was very different from Brazil's, but across the developing world, modernization policies were strikingly similar in promoting urbanization. The fact that many peasants had been forced from their land by debt, crop failure, or violence led them to view its "modernity" with suspicion. The city's lack of housing and jobs stimulated populist movements that challenged the state and the local elites, and demanded a larger slice of the pie.

Chapters of Cultural Globalization inside the Postcolonial World 1950-Present

Postcolonial Modernization (Late 1950s-1970s): Postcolonial regimes focus upon economic modernization, infrastructural investment and literacy programs that increase global awareness and bind state closer to international system.

Television Age (1970s-1980s): Increasing diffusion of television sets, communication satellites and syndicated western content disseminates a powerful image of western modernity, wealth and the liberating power of technology to remote areas and isolated non-Western communities.

Digital Revolution (2000s-Present): Proliferation of cell phones and fibre-optic networks enables a deeper cultural exchange and spurs local efforts to appropriate modern technology for local needs and redefine local values in terms of global modernity.

1947-1949 Decolonization in Asia
1960-1968 Global Economic Boom
Lost Decade 1981-1989
1995-Present Neoliberal Globalization

1945 World War II ends | 1947 Indian Independence | 1956 World Bank Loan for Aswan Dam | 1960-1966 Climax of Sub-Saharan Decolonization | 1972 Nixon visits China | 1973 Oil Shock | 1982 Debt Crisis | 1995 WTO | 2010 half of world tunes in FIFA

Struggle for Independence (Late 1940-1950s): Political mobilization creates coalition with nationalist leaders that use radio, print and camera to communicate national vision and identity transcending local traditions, ethnic loyalties and sectarian affiliations.

Import Substitution and Urbanization (1960s-1990s): State focus on urban-based industrialization and mechanization of agriculture disrupts rural economy and sets into motion mass migration to capital cities where immigrants adapt to secular patterns of life.

Neoliberal Globalization (1990s-Present): Expansion of foreign multinationals, global brands and consumer technologies forces people to adapt their traditions, livelihoods and expectations to generic consumer culture.

Image credits: © George Nazmi Bebawi/Shutterstock.com; © favorstyle/Shutterstock.com; © asharkyu/Shutterstock.com; © vkilkov/Shutterstock.com; Nasser: Everett Collection Historical/ Alamy Stock Photo; © dean bertoncelj/Shutterstock.com

The WTO stimulated a particularly raucous chapter of cultural globalization after 1995. Lower trade barriers and richly capitalized American multinational firms flooded local markets with Western products and bought up local firms. Multinationals sought not only to tap "emerging" markets, but to transform local cultures. Corporate advertisements hawked corporate products as staples for a "modern life" that offered unprecedented comfort and new avenues for personal fulfillment, while suggesting that local products were "uncool." Non-Western people sampled, adopted, and sometimes rejected the products offered to them. McDonalds was one of the early corporate pioneers. Corporate executives soon discovered that they needed to adapt their menu, restaurant, and dining experience to fit the local scene and indigenous tastes. Although a rush of foreign imports initially raised anxiety about the loss of local jobs and the erosion of values, over the longer run, many imports, from foreign cars to cell phones, were assimilated by later generations as staples of local life.

To survive, Western franchises like Starbucks needed to assimilate their architecture and menu to fit the local landscapes, tastes, and cultural habits.

> Is the Internet a revolutionary force? Does the free flow of information undermine authoritarian regimes or have states found new strategies for shaping public opinion?

While cultural globalization represented a universal postwar phenomenon, it played out differently across the world stage. Southeast Asia and the Middle East reveal this discrepancy. By theztwenty-first century, China headlined a broader Asian miracle, where local people mostly embraced technology, consumerism, and open market rules. Throughout the 1990s, Asians experienced growing pains ranging from high inflation, rapid urbanization, and long work hours. Many Chinese faced the additional pressure of transitioning from a Maoism– that condemned capitalist "road grading"—to Deng's market socialism, where entrepreneurialism was rebranded as a civic virtue. Despite a collision in the 1989 Tiananmen Massacre, and a deep recession in 1998, by the twenty-first century, the Asian miracle brought prosperity to the Pacific Rim. By 2000, both Oriental and Western observers commented on the emergence of a distinctive "Asian modernity." Enthusiastic Asian leaders claimed that Asian modernity, predicated upon tradition, community, and hard work, supplanted decadent Western "liberalism" that assigned too much freedom to the individual, sparking anomie, social deterioration, and moral decay. Malaysian President Mohamad Mahathir echoed the sentiment of other Asian leaders during the 1990s when he argued that ""the notion that a country must Westernize in order to modernize is ludicrous. Asian modernization occurred as an inevitable stage in our own history, not because we were Europeanized or Americanized."[8]

Inside the Middle East, Islam has long served as a comprehensive framework for culture, social life, and identity. In 1979, the Ayatollah Khomeini overthrew the Shah who had long sought to modernize Iran. Khomeini proclaimed an Islamic Revolution exhorting Iranians not to "listen to those who speak of democracy," but instead "awake" to Islam.⁹ Khomeini's militant condemnation of US imperialism, Western individualism, and consumerism provided the perfect foil for the purer Islamic society he wished to build. But Khomeini's Islamic Republic straddled multiple contradictions. Iran's constitution integrated the clergy into modern departments of state, *Shari'ah* law circumscribed the rights of women while reaffirming their right to vote, and Western notions of sovereignty intermingled with Shia concepts of justice. In short, Khomeini "Islamized" modernity as much as he rejected it.

Iran's Revolution typifies a broader struggle to reconcile national economies, time-honored customs, and cherished values with the technologies and practices shaping a globalizing world. Time does not stand still. The technologies, ideas, and production systems undergirding civilization continually evolve. Throughout the twentieth century, "modernization" has been associated with different institutions, core technologies, and values, but at its core lies a liberal ideology that first crystalized during the Western Enlightenment. Since the eighteenth century, "life, liberty, and the pursuit of happiness" has evolved in tandem with technology and climbing consumer ambitions and rising productivity. By the twenty-first century, many Asians of modest means felt entitled to luxuries that few eighteenth-century English lords could imagine. Consumerism, however, did not extinguish local cultures. Like a vampire, it adapts to —and feeds off—global diversity. Throughout the twentieth century, consumer capitalism has proven flexible and resilient, adapting its wares to new cultural settings, while appealing to diverse groups by stimulating a deeply rooted human instinct for comfort and immediate gratification. Globalization can be seen as polluting local cultures, but it also stimulates them by exposing them to foreign ideas and new technologies.

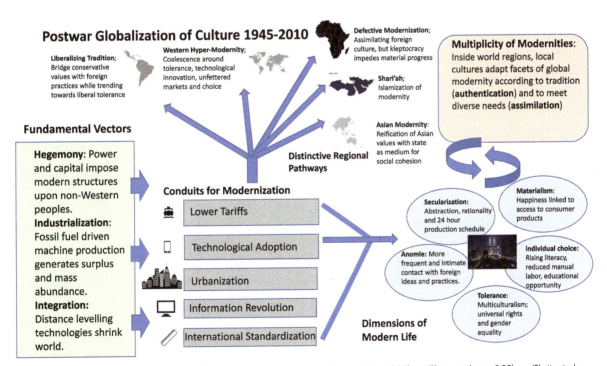

Image credits: © mlopez/Shutterstock.com; © Andrei Minsk/Shutterstock.com; © Armita/Shutterstock.com; © PSboom/Shutterstock.com; © PSboom/Shutterstock.com; © Travel man/Shutterstock.com; © M-O Vector/Shutterstock.com; © Djent/Shutterstock.com; © anthonycz/Shutterstock.com; © T-Kot/Shutterstock.com; © INORTON/Shutterstock.com

The Middle East and Asia illustrate how cultural globalization represents a process of creative assimilation. As local people negotiate their adoption of new technologies, products, and practices, their culture is transformed into a more "modern" form, without losing its local flair or authentic character. Across the world stage, culture is being configured into distinctive "modernities" that correspond to regional traditions, local values, and tastes. In aggregate, humanity is growing more prosperous, individualistic, androgynous, and secular than a century before. On the other hand, rural Peru, Mumbai, and suburban Belgrade remain very different places, while the gap between the rich and very poor is actually increasing.

Towards a Transnational History

According to convention, World War II broke the back of colonialism, while the failure to reach a grand settlement at Potsdam in 1945 ignited a Cold War between Stalin and the West that spilled over into postcolonial world. The orthodox view still holds much appeal. The superpower confrontation spanned most of the postwar era and ideologically partitioned the international system. On the other hand, the Cold War looked very different in the non-Western world than from the Kremlin or White House. The Vietnamese fought thirty years for their independence. At various times, Ho Chi Minh opportunistically turned to Washington, DC, Beijing, and Moscow for support. Land, not ideology, motivated most Latin American peasants. In the Middle East, leaders switched sides for strategic advantage, while European multinationals backed African "strongmen" for loot rather than any moral purpose. Recent research has shifted attention from high-profile international incidents to the shadows where the Cold War was waged mostly by soldiers out of uniform: spies, bankers, publicists, economic hit men, and athletes. The myth of 'bipolarity' not only exaggerates the influence of the superpowers, but puts primarily emphasis on the state's foreign policies, grand strategies, local leaders, and flawed development policies. This perspective obscures the deep ocean of propaganda, economic warfare, sabotage, and assassination that infiltrated the international system, disrupting regional patterns of development and reshaping local history and culture. In particular, the Cold War undermined the Third World project that Sukarno elegantly summarized as "liberation of man from his bonds of fear, his bonds of poverty, the liberation of man from the physical, spiritual and intellectual bonds which have for long stunted the development of humanity's majority."[10] The postcolonial desire for freedom, social justice, racial equality, and economic development was stunted by ensnaring postcolonial states in a wave of military coups, guerrilla insurgencies, debt, embargoes, and dirty wars that ultimately created a stunning divide between "failed" states and miracle economies.

Independence did allow former colonies to take seats in international bodies like the UN, and enabled nationalists to step up investment in schools, infrastructure, and hospitals. A growing body of postcolonial research, however, has shown that decolonization often failed to translate into meaningful sovereignty. Non-Western states acquired independence inside a polarized environment where the superpowers pressured postcolonial leaders to align their development policies with foreign interests. During the 1950s, the Non-Aligned Movement pushed back against the superpowers, but by 1970, its most charismatic leaders like Nasser, Nehru, and Sukarno had been swept from the stage. Modernization proved another challenge. Reformers like Jacobo Arbenz and Patrice Lumumba inherited structurally underdeveloped economies. Their dreams for development clashed with industrialized states that dominated international trade, shipping, insurance, the institutions of global finance, and commodity markets. Multinationals like United Fruit and the Anglo-Iranian Oil Company removed rulers that dared to challenge their control over local resources. Many postcolonial states also bore the scars of colonialism. Internal divisions left them vulnerable to external intrigues. In Asia, postcolonial leaders could often rely upon indigenous civilian service to promote policies for national unification. In Africa, this civil service was less developed, making it challenging for even the ablest leaders to bridge ethnic divisions that colonial states had spent decades fomenting in order to promote white rule.

Revolutionary Waves

Revolutions are a motor of history, providing the raw energy to cut through institutional inertia and cultural conservatism to make lasting changes. From a structural perspective, shock events reverberate across the planetary surface, but as they collide against uneven regional institutions, their impact is blunted and intermixes with local culture. Destructiveness of World War II gave rise to a revolutionary wave. Battered survivors demanded security, social justice, and freedom. The constitution of this reform program inside Europe, Latin America, and the colonial world was modulated by local concerns and conditions. Inside war-torn Europe, revolution manifested in separate programs for socialist reconstruction on opposite sides of the Iron Curtain. In the colonial world, the spirit of revolution manifested in independence movements that challenged white supremacy and colonialism. In Latin America and the West, populists and repressed minorities pushed for social justice and an expansion of the state safety net. In the postcolonial world, new regimes embraced socialism and pursued economic modernization to catch up to Western levels of development.

By the late 1960s, the revolutionary wave that had been gaining momentum since the end of World War II began to ebb. With formal independence largely secured, postcolonial leaders turned to the question of international reform and economic equality. At the 1967 Algiers Conference, the Group of 77 recognized that their pursuit of "economic and social development" was falling short. Attempts to overturn Western property rights through nationalization measures were met with ferocious resistance: embargos, military invasion, or clandestine subversion.[11] By 1970, most of the leaders of the Non-Aligned Movement had been swept from the stage. In 1974, in the midst of sharp economic deterioration sparked by the oil crisis, the proposal of Group of 77 for New International Economic Order, embracing significant development aid as compensation for colonialism, while passing the UN General Assembly, was turned away by Western states. Subsequently, a wave of instability washed over the developing world as the OPEC shock wrecked postcolonial balance sheets. Postcolonial leaders, who had promoted national development and pursued compensation from the West, increasingly saw themselves as elite whose privileges were tied to a global structure of hegemony.

The revolutionary wave succumbed to the forces of reaction. Across the world, ambitious officers and conservative elites fought back against reformers, local insurgents, and ethnic minorities demanding a greater voice inside the state and economy. Such conflicts had a strong local flavor, but often intersected with international currents. Following the Cuban Revolution in 1959, Latin American conservatives opportunistically branded their political opponents "communists" even though most reformers were not Marxists and few local movements had any direct connection to Moscow. This enticed US military support for *junta* regimes bought official silence regarding their brutal tactics of repression. In the Soviet Bloc, Warsaw Pact forces stamped out Czechoslovakia's experiment in socialism with a human face that challenged the hegemony of the communist elite. In the Middle East, frustrations with Arab Socialism to meet popular expectations led nationalist regimes to adopt an increasingly authoritarian character. The army and secret police targeted various forms of dissidence, but their most determined resistance came from Islamists who challenged the deep state's lack of accountability, corruption, and failure to raise dismal living standards.

Across the world stage, the authoritarian wave emerged at different times and in variant regional incarnations, but it was broadly linked to the failure of import-substitution policies to deliver promised results. Inside Africa, postcolonial states were threatened by the absence of any deep sense of national loyalty. Able postcolonial leaders like Nkrumah and Lumumba confronted the daunting task of simultaneously orchestrating economic development and nation building. Declines in local living conditions by the late 1960s facilitated the overthrow of nationalist regimes, particularly by military officers enjoying foreign backing. To maintain their hold on power, putschists relied upon outside help: military hardware, foreign trainers, and loans. Their foreign benefactors were mostly repaid through sweet-heart resource extraction deals. By the early 1970s, "decolonization" had started to coalesce into a neocolonial nexus of illegitimate rulers, corporate bribery, and brutal repression of dissidence. Inside the postcolonial world, superpower intervention became increasingly rare, and in places like Angola lost any sense of strategic objective or moral purpose.

By the 1980s, authoritarianism began to wane. In 1987, Gorbachev cut back Soviet financing for revolutionary movements, which removed oxygen from proxy wars. Subsequent collapse of the Soviet Bloc dried up Western support for brutal despots, especially in a more global age where the global media put a spotlight upon human rights abuses and where more robust NGOs promoted civil society reforms. Initially, the democratic wave was more evident in Africa and Latin America than in the Middle East and Asia. In Sub-Saharan Africa, the damage inflicted by kleptocrats and civil war upon infrastructure and state institutions proved long lasting. Fair elections and removal of despots did not always translate into stable regimes. In Latin America after 1983, the *junta* negotiated the return of national militaries to their barracks. By the late 1980s, constitutional governments launched programs for reconciliation that mostly fell short of holding officers accountable for past abuses. In Asia and the Middle East, reforms were initially focused more on liberalizing the economy than the state. After 1995, the WTO, by lowering trade barriers and integrating capital markets, enabled Western multinationals to stake ownership over the extractive industries inside much of the developing world. Although neoliberal globalization raised wages and living standards after 1995, local development also increasingly reflected the interests of foreign investors rather than the local states and often chased short-term profits rather than being guided by any idea of the public good.

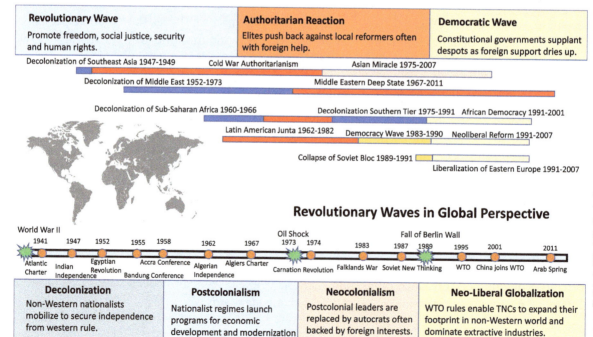

Revolutionary Waves in Global Perspective

Conceptualizing postwar history as a series of waves dispels the illusion of superpower hegemony and casts decolonization in a more critical light. The revolutionary, authoritarian, and democratic waves were loosely tied to geopolitical shock events: World War II, the OPEC embargo, and the fall of communism. However, in washing over an uneven global stage, they also collided with a deeper structure of hegemony embedded in technological patents, entrenched racism, a concession system for resource extraction, and international banking institutions. These institutions were left largely untouched by the waves washing over the turbulent surface of postwar society. As a result, decolonization, postcolonialism, neocolonialism, and neoliberal globalization did not significantly level the wealth gap between core and periphery. The principal exception was the United States' Cold War allies in Asia. Beneficiaries of favorable aid and trade policies, they began to rapidly industrialize after 1970.

A Hybrid Approach

The aspiration to write a universal history is hardly new. Herodotus St. Isidore and Ibn Khaldun each tried to narrate a history of the known world. Despite their compendious knowledge, their chronicles fell short of embracing the entire planetary surface. Even in today's more global age, no history can be comprehensive. Invariably, global history collides with the complexity of a world that embraces 195 states, thousands of biomes, and even more languages and cultures. Twentieth-century historiography is also rich. Historians have explored a broad palette of postwar themes: economic, cultural, military, and international history, while developing countless subfields like gender, business, and ecological history. This scope precludes any exhaustive accounting.

A central thrust of global history is fidelity to scale. Three vectors radiated through human society during the long twentieth century, relentlessly transforming it into a more global form. This book not only explores how integration, urbanization, and technological reliance diffused through the world, but also how these global vectors intersected with deeper regional trends, collided with national institutions and played out divergently inside local cultures. Given the intimate connection between the global, regional, local, and microscales of history, the three units of this book will explore the postwar era simultaneously from "above" and "below." The first unit explores world history from a global perspective. Separate chapters highlight how World War II, decolonization, and the Cold War washed over the world stage and intermingled with local structures. The second unit chronicles world history from a regional perspective during roughly the Cold War era (1949–1991). The third and final unit focuses upon post–Cold War history. These chapters seek to integrate post-1991 events to broader themes that have shaped the twentieth century as a whole and devote particular attention to financial, technological, and environmental history. In exploring postwar era from a transnational perspective, this book will ask important questions about our world:

- How did horrors of World War II invigorate socialist reform?
- How did decolonization become entangled with the Cold War?
- Why the Cold War manifest differently inside Asia, Africa, the Middle East, and Latin America?
- Why did postcolonial programs for modernization often fall short?
- How is increasing urbanization, rising female literacy, and more digitally integrated society challenge traditional ideas about sexuality, gender, and the family?
- How did the oil shocks of the 1970s spur transition towards a more integrated global economy?

- Why did the Asian Pacific surpass other postcolonial regions in terms of economic development by 1990?
- How has the WTO transformed the structure and nature of multinational corporations?
- Why have local cultures responded so differently to global integration?
- How are digital technologies transforming how humans eat, work, live, and think?
- Can a global economy relentlessly focused on mining the earth's living system sustain itself?
- What do recent crises reveal about the changing nature of human civilization?

A Canadian Perspective

What shapes how Canadians view their world? Outlining the "Canadian" perspective proves challenging, considering our nation's increasingly multicultural fabric. According to the popular joke "a Canadian is someone who drinks Brazilian coffee from an English teacup and munches a French pastry while sitting on their Danish furniture having just come home from an Italian movie in their German car."[12] Conservatives have lamented how comfortable many Canadians are with cosmopolitanism, seemingly untroubled by the steady erosion of explicitly defined cultural values or national heroes.[13] Liberals and conservatives alike agree that globalization has transformed "Canada" following the nation's early twentieth-century emergence from the bowels of British Empire and out from the long shadow cast by the United States. Contemporary Canadians increasingly manifest a hybrid identity. Whether one is Jewish or Sikh, romantics argue that what unites Canadians is a shared commitment to liberal values like tolerance, civility, and respect for the law. Identities, however, are notoriously fickle. Our individual viewpoint has multiple roots, not only the values we inherit from our parents and larger cultural community, but also idiosyncratic experiences that define us as unique persons. While every student's perspective is distinct, as citizens, Canadians do share a stake in political institutions, publicly financed schools, and a national media.

> What is the principal bias that Canadian students bring to the study of world history?

From a global perspective, the most defining characteristic of Canadians is wealth. Canadians belong to a privileged global elite that enjoys relative security and aspires for professional fulfillment. In 2010, the median Canadian family after tax income amounted to $69,860.[14] According to the global rich list, this puts the median Canadian household into the top .3 percent of all people living on the earth.[15] In contrast, the global majority is poor. At least six hundred million children go to bed each night fighting pangs of hunger. Those dwelling in the megacities of the developing world confront a future with uncertain prospects. In studying world history, it is important to appreciate this gap. Eighty percent of humanity lives on less than $10 per day, and their horizon is not framed by Canadian hopes, norms, and expectations.

Canadian privilege represents only one ingredient shaping out worldview. Consider the geopolitical map that adorns Canadian classrooms. Maps offer an elegant representation of human civilization. All maps, however, are selective. By highlighting certain features of our world, they obscure others. Many world maps are also **Euro-centric** in featuring the Mercator projection. Flattening the globe onto a two-dimensional surface distorts distance. Western maps address this problem by exaggerating the size of the Northern Hemisphere. This inflates Europe size so that it appears only slightly smaller than Africa. The Peters' projection tries to correct this imbalance by distorting continental borders to keep their areas proportional.

The conventional geopolitical map presents the state as the building block for the international system. Maps graphing global wealth help us to visualize the rift between the developed North (hemisphere) and the poorer "Global South."

This reveals the relatively small size of the Western world. Another hubris embedded in contemporary world maps is the "prime meridian," running through Greenwich, England. This legacy, inherited from imperial days, places Europe at the world's center and pushes Asia and the Americas towards the periphery. During World War II, Imperial Japan commissioned a world map that placed Tokyo at the world's heart. Over the last decade scholars have jostled the geopolitical map by using various data sets to represent global fissures. For example, in the map above, Datawrapper correlates state size to GDP, distorting our traditional way of imaging our world.

Window on World History: Television: Our Window onto the World?

Historically, Canadians defined themselves relative to the wilderness. Today, most of us experience world events sitting on our derriere. During the 1950s, televisions first emerged inside Canadian dens. Originally featuring 9- and 12-inch black-and-white screens, television revolutionized how Canadians understood their wider world. The "tube" made distant events feel close to home and transformed international celebrities into the neighbors next door. Today, geosynchronous satellites and transatlantic fiber optic cables enable news correspondents to transmit "breaking" news. When a rabble pulled down Saddam's statue in Firdos Square in 2003, many Canadians watched "live" on CNN. Television compressed the Canadian sense of time and space. But the picture of the world coming through their screens was also distorted and incomplete. Viewers control the switch. They tune any channel they want. Television, then, allows us to engage the world on our terms, selecting the time, the programming filter while we gawk from the comfort of our Lay-Z-Boy. Many Canada viewers self-censor, shuttering out unsettling images and selecting programming that frames world events according to reassuring narratives. CBC's the "National"

The television emerged after World War II to transmit radio signals into black-and-white audiovisual images.

(Continued)

still bills itself as offering a distinctively Canadian perspective. Its anglophone producers sift through an overwhelming number of stories to select those they deem worthy of knowing. Invariably, "broadcast news" features a heavy dose of domestic politics and hockey news. Those brief snippets featuring the non-Western world often focus on the bizarre or macabre. As private corporations, what drives news coverage today is ratings. Violence and natural disasters sell copy because they hold emotional appeal. Simultaneously, the constraints of the broadcast schedule preclude journalists from delving into the historical context that might explain the mayhem. Television extended our awareness of people we would never personally meet or places we would never corporeally visit. On the other hand, the world glimmering through the neon haze of TV confronts us as simultaneously threatening and incomprehensible. Today, social media and personal devices are replacing television and network news, even if the hours we spend in front of a screen continue to climb. In this more fractured media landscape, Canadian perceptions of the world have grown increasingly distorted as they search out "news" from a market place of ideas that can comfortably confirm preexisting biases. Digital media is building out a vibrant virtual world that exists only inside invisible bits of data. This only seems to amplify the double illusion that while we can engage the world on our terms, Canadians are ultimately powerless to shape it.

Critical Reflection

1. In what ways does the broadcast cast news like CBC's the "National" fall short in terms of covering world events in a balanced way?
2. Has social media expanded our global consciousness or distorted our perception of international events?

Our perceptions about the world have also been shaped by the Canadian school system. National history emerged in the late nineteenth century with Europe in the throes of revolution. Historians were hired as state servants to uncover the deep cultural roots of the newly invented national community and to glorify its language and cultural traditions. Still today, national history serves this propaganda function. The state commissions history textbooks not only to educate young students about their ancestors' past, but to stimulate patriotism. Throughout the late twentieth century, various marginalized groups, Italian immigrants, Franco-Canadians, women, and aboriginal people have challenged the national narrative and pushed to have their story woven into the national memory.

In taking the whole world as its object, global history is subversive. Global history reduces the Canadian story to a thin sliver of the human experience. Giving equal place to the non-Western people marginalizes seminal events in the national memory. Exploring how non-Western people were impacted Western greed and corporate power challenges cherished national myths. At its best, global history, by exposing our biases, can also reveal what makes the Canadian experience truly unique and distinctive.

"Objectivity" requires us to assess our unique position in the world. Internationally, Canada represents a fortunate anomaly. We are a country richly endowed with natural resources, politically stable, and protected by a substantial safety net. Canada is a privileged member of several elite clubs

Settling the Frontier: Traditional Canadian history textbooks depicted the New World as a 'virgin' land that the pioneers transformed. In fact, Canada was inhabited by the first nations peoples, whose populations were ravaged by disease and whose land was conquered.

Canadian Generosity: Many Canadians believe their country plays an important role in terms of humanitarian aid when in fact Canada is a relative dead beat compared to its OECD peers.

What shapes the Canadian view of the world?

Champion for Human Rights: Many Canadians believe their country is a force for good in the world and pivotal players in international peace keeping missions, but during the Cold War the country often embraced unsavory dictators and turned a blind eye to many atrocities they committed.

Proudly Canadian: Many Canadians believe their wealth and privilege is the result of their decency and hard work, rather than a legacy of imperial conquest and exploitation of poor workers who make our consumer products for pittance wages.

Liberal Tolerance: Many Canadian liberals embrace 'multiculturalism,' but historically Anglo-Saxons have sought to suppress French identity and forcefully assimilate indigenous peoples in reservation schools that only closed recently.

Image credits: © Everett Historical/Shutterstock.com; Lester Pearson: Source: National Archives and Records Administration. Office of Presidential Libraries. John F. Kennedy Library.; © Belish/Shutterstock.com; © Gustavo/Shutterstock.com; © capitanoproductions/Shutterstock.com

that set the international agenda: the OECD, North Atlantic Treaty Organization (NATO), and G7. This gives Canadians an outsized role inside the world, and orients our expectations about life. A history written for a Canadian audience will necessarily be different from one written in Cairo, La Paz, or Beijing. Adopting a Canadian lens does not signify formal embrace of any preconceived ideological position. Rather, adopting a "Canadian perspective" acknowledges that the text's author and readers share certain assumptions about the world. This common horizon can be invoked to illuminate past events and appraise their significance.

Echoes of the Past

One gift of the past is self-discovery. As George Santayana colorfully observed in 1903, "those who cannot remember the past are condemned to repeat it."[16] World history has an autobiographical dimension in so far that when we study our world, we encounter the forces, ideas, and events that have shaped us. Sometimes the links between past and present are obvious. It does not take a large leap to see how Cold War politics infused the combat on the ice during the famed Summit Series. Often, however, the echoes of the past are more subtle. Did the postwar collapse of Western Empires provide Canadians a stage to develop an international identity apart from Britain and the United States? Did the suburban home, as Betty Friedan argued, represent a concentration camp for the female soul that stimulated postwar feminism?

At its best, history equals insight. This text is written for students that grew up with digital technologies and inside a global economy where fresh winter vegetables are airfreighted from Chile. To reflect upon how contemporary events and trends have given shape to our world, this text adopts a "Window on World History" feature. Every chapter contains a short vignette that cast a spotlight on how a particular event, institution, or person has a contemporary resonance. Particular emphasis is given to events that shaped the Canadian experience, not only Canadian history in a narrow sense but also hot-button issues and under-the-radar events that illuminate contemporary dilemmas. This *miscellanea moderna* challenges students to consider the complicated ways in which the past lives on in modern patterns of life and thought. It also introduces us to laggard ideas, subtle forces, and distant echoes that have shaped Canadian identity and that will shape our common future on this planet.

Conclusion

Contemporary students were born inside a global world. For many, it is difficult to imagine human existence before cell phones, Facebook, and global supply chains, yet these innovations are recent outgrowths of human history. According to any index, the modern way of life represents a remarkable anomaly. Our degree of freedom, material affluence, and domination over the Biosphere reflects the culmination of multiple twentieth-century processes. Never in history have humans been so abundant, so affluent, or ecologically destructive. One fundamental paradox of modern existence, however, is that while we are increasingly tied to events emanating from distant corners of the globe, the forces shaping our lives and future are also increasingly inscrutable and unmanageable. Recent disasters like SARS, 9-11, and the 2008 Great Global Recession remind us how obscure forces can manifest quite suddenly and with extreme impact. This emerging reality provides a rationale for a new generation of twentieth-century histories that explore the birth and evolution of the global civilization in which we all live.

Questions for Critical Thought

1. How does a photo of the earth taken from outer space render a different view of the world than a geopolitical map coloring in state boundaries?
2. Do you agree with the premise that technological advances, economic integration, and increased interaction have culminated in a global civilization? How do you explain the paradox that globalization spurs convergence but also cultural resistance?
3. In what ways has globalization transformed Canadian society and identity?
4. What are the principal assumptions or biases that shape the "Canadian" viewpoint on world events? How might world history appear different for someone born and bred in Tehran, La Paz, or Beijing?
5. How have new digital technologies, communication satellites, and the Internet reshaped our view of the world?

Suggestions for Further Reading

- Brown, Lester. *World on the Edge: How to Prevent Environmental and Economic Collapse.* New York: Routledge, 2011.
- Giddens, Anthony. *Runaway World.* New York: Routledge, 2002.

- Hobsbawm, Eric. *The Age of Extremes: A History of the World, 1914-1991*. New York: Vintage, 1996.
- Huntington, Samuel. *The Clash of Civilizations and the Remaking of World Order*. New York: Simon & Schuster, 1996.
- Mazlish, Bruce. *The New Global History*. New York: Routledge, 2006.
- McNeil, John R. *Something New Under the Sun: An Environmental History of the Twentieth Century World*. New York: Norton, 2000.
- Prashad, Vijay. *The Darker Nations: A People's History of the Third World*. New York: New Press, 2007.
- Stearns, Peter. *Globalization in World History*. New York: Routledge, 2012.
- Wallerstein, Immanuel. *World-Systems Analysis: An Introduction*. Durham: Duke University Press, 2004.
- Westad, Arne O. *The Cold War: A World History*. New York: Basic, 2017.

Notes

1. Bruce Mazlish, *The New Global History* (New York: Routledge, 2006), 98.
2. Phillip Inman, "Study: Big Corporations Dominate List of World's Top Economic Entities," *The Guardian*, September 12, 2016, accessed July 26, 2019, https://www.theguardian.com/business/2016/sep/12/global-justice-now-study-multinational-businesses-walmart-apple-shell.
3. Mike Mason, *Development and Disorder* (Toronto: Between the Lines, 1997), 443.
4. David Smith, "WikiLeaks Cables: Shell's grip on Nigerian state revealed," *The Guardian*, December 8, 2010, accessed July 26, 2019, https://www.theguardian.com/business/2010/dec/08/wikileaks-cables-shell-nigeria-spying.
5. "Rigged rules mean economic growth increasingly 'winner takes all' for rich elites all over world," OXFAM International national, January, 20, 2014, accessed July 26, 2019, http://www.oxfam.org/en/pressroom/pressrelease/2014-01-20/rigged-rules-mean-economic-growth-increasingly-winner-takes-all-for-rich-elites.
6. Stearns, *Consumerism in World History*, 2nd ed. (New York: Routledge, 2001), 133.
7. Martin Hilbert and Priscila Lopez, "How to Measure the World's Technological Capacity to Communicate, Store, and Compute Information. Part I: Results and Scope," *International Journal of Communication* 6 (April 27, 2012): 956.
8. See Mohamad Mahathir and Ishihara Shintaro, *The Voice of Asia: Two Leaders Discuss the Coming Century*, trans. Frank Baldwin (New York: Kodansha International, 1995), 77.
9. Krista Reinach and Alan Reinach, *Politics and Prophecy* (Nampa, ID: Pacific Press Publishing Association, 2007), 89.
10. Quoted in Vijay Prashad, *The Darker Nations: A People's History of the Third World* (New York: New Press, 2007), xvii.
11. 1967 Algiers Conference
12. Quoted in Johan Norberg, *In Defence of Global Capitalism* (New Delhi: Academic Foundation, 2001), 17.
13. Jack Lawrence Granatstein, *Who Killed Canadian History?* (Toronto: Harper Collins, 1998).
14. Statistics Canada, "Distribution of Total Income by Census Family Type and Age of Older Partner, Parent or Individual, 2014-2016," Statcan, accessed May 1, 2019, http://www.statcan.gc.ca/tables-tableaux/sum-som/l01/cst01/famil108a-eng.htm.
15. See http://www.globalrichlist.com/.
16. George Santayana, *Life of Reason, Reason in Common Sense* (New York: Scribner and Sons, 1905), 284.

Chapter 2
Dreams for a Better World, 1945 to 1949

Chapter Outline

- The Atlantic Dream, 1941 to 1949
- Postwar Decolonization Wave, 1945 to 1949
- West European Social Democracy, 1945 to 1949
- Fall of the Iron Curtain, 1945 to 1949
- Birth of Israel, 1945 to 1949
- Dissolution of the Grand Alliance, 1945 to 1949
- Conclusion: Shape of the Postwar World

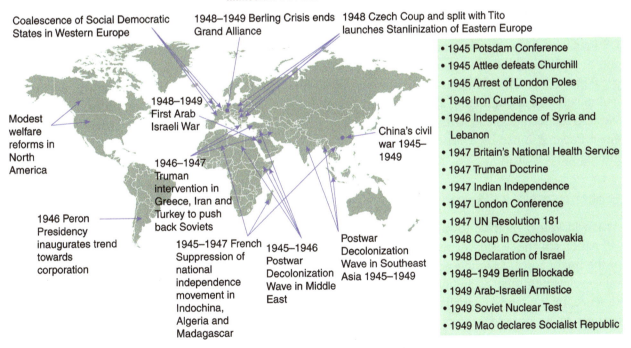

Image credit: © Andrei Minsk/Shutterstock.com

The Atlantic Dream, 1941 to 1949

Following Allied liberation of Buchenwald, inmates affixed a hand-painted sign over their concentration camp. "NEVER AGAIN" blotted out the cynical Nazi lie: *Arbeit macht Frei*. This spontaneous gesture poignantly captured the postwar mind-set of survivors everywhere. After Auschwitz, Hiroshima, and Nanking, how could the war's many horrors be put behind? Following the Great Depression and the flawed 1919 Versailles Conference, how could the victors put the world economy back together again and protect ordinary people from the "scourge of war?"

The dream for postwar redemption was born on August 1941. At a brief meeting off of Newfoundland, Franklin Delano Roosevelt (FDR) and Winston Churchill pledged to rid the world of Nazi tyranny. The Anglo-American agreement stopped far short of bringing the United States into open war against Nazi Germany, but its defiant language led journalists to hail this document the **Atlantic Charter**. The Atlantic dream became concrete several months later during an interallied council in Washington, DC. Twenty-six signatories identified themselves as the "United Nations," engaged in a "common struggle against savage and brutal forces seeking to subjugate the world."[1] The Soviet Union was fighting for survival; not waging some liberal crusade. Stalin mistrusted the West and had started the war as Hitler's ally. Yet, after Hitler's annihilation war ravaged the Soviet Union, no one better appreciated the horrors of Nazism. Stalin's support for Western international initiatives remained half-hearted, but he needed Western aid and feared postwar isolation. This led Stalin's conditional endorsement of the Atlantic vision in the 1943 **Moscow Declaration**. At the October 1944 **Dumbarton Oaks Conference**, the Grand Alliance agreed to reinvigorate the discredited League of Nations. World War II, however, had exposed liberal pacifism as a dangerous illusion. Accordingly, US President Roosevelt championed the "four policemen" concept. China, Britain, the United States, and the USSR would stand guard over the postwar world, quashing any future Hitler before they grew menacing. Churchill preferred more limited and focused regional security organizations. Stalin had misgivings about joining an international body inspired by liberal values and dominated by Western democratic states. Ultimately, the Big Three agreed on the Security Council compromise. The Great Powers, joined by ten rotating members, would contribute soldiers to fend off future threats to international security.

Erecting a New International System

As World War II rumbled towards its devastating climax, it validated the core Atlantic principle that "all nations of the world, for realistic as well as spiritual reasons, must come to the abandonment of the use of force."[2] During wartime conferences, Western diplomats routinely endorsed Atlantic values, elevating them to an unofficial blueprint for postwar reconstruction. In the place of fascist violence, racism, and imperialism, reformers proposed a multilateral international system to unite postwar states in trade, peaceful collaboration, and mutual respect for human rights. In June 1945, the Atlantic dream came to fruition in San Francisco. Representatives from forty-four states founded the **UN** to save "succeeding generations from the scourge of war, which twice in our lifetime has brought untold sorrow to mankind."[3] Behind this lofty rhetoric, sharp debates simmered concerning the UN's structure and mission. New Zealand and Australia protested the undemocratic Security Council structure. Why distinguish between Great Powers and lesser states? Some Western diplomats fretted about the Soviet Union's role. Even before Yalta, Stalin's determined pursuit of Soviet interests struck anti-communist hawks as a threat to postwar reconstruction. Bolshevik dogma, Stalin's past brutality and traditional Russian xenophobia, seemed to make the USSR an unlikely partner inside the postwar international system.

In 1941, Senator Truman expressed the view of many hawks when he commented on the outbreak of Russian–German hostilities: "If we see that Germany is winning we ought to help Russia; and if Russia is winning we ought to help Germany, and that way let them kill as many as possible."[4] But in 1945, Stalin's desire to collaborate with the West was rooted in genuine self-interest. War had devastated the USSR. UN membership would enhance Soviet security by guaranteeing Stalin a predominant place inside the postwar international system. The Soviets did worry that the UN's founding members were mostly liberal democratic states. Ultimately, Soviet participation in the UN was procured by means of a compromise whereby the Soviet Republics of the Ukraine and Byelorussia were granted seats in the General Assembly, while most of the institution's power remained vested in a Security Council. There, the five Great Powers held permanent seats and a veto that prevented the UN from acting contrary to their geopolitical interests.

Nuremberg Tribunals and International Law

At Potsdam, Western leaders insisted that the Nazis be held accountable for their crimes, even if the German people were to be spared the penalties of Versailles. Stalin was unsympathetic to German suffering and less enthusiastic about holding a public trial that might expose his own crimes.

Instead, Stalin proposed summary execution of "fascists." Inside the Soviet zone, German officers and SS members were routinely shot, often arbitrarily without judicial process. When it became clear that the West would push ahead with the **Nuremberg Tribunal**, however, Stalin reluctantly agreed to participate.

In November 1945, twenty-four top Nazi leaders were hauled before an international tribunal. In the spiritual capital of Nazism, they were indicted for "war crimes" and the novel charge "crimes against humanity." As these haggard men shuffled to the microphone to pronounce their innocence, it was difficult to imagine this motley crew had so recently terrorized the world. The defendants claimed that they were merely following orders. They argued that **genocide** was not a crime defined under any international treaty. The Nazi's lawyers also questioned the court's jurisdiction, complaining about victor's justice, while making every effort to expose allied war crimes.

At Nuremberg, top Nazis were held accountable for provoking the twentieth century's worst calamity, but with the exception of Hermann Göring, the most notable Nazis had already escaped justice through suicide.

Source: National Archives Catalog

Did the Western powers mete out victor's justice at Nuremberg in 1946? Were the authors of Dresden, Hiroshima, and unrestricted submarine warfare not equally guilty of war crimes?

There was more than a little irony in having the Soviet Union stand judgment. Soviet aggression and ethnic cleansing policies in Eastern Europe resembled those of the Nazis. At Katyn, in April and May 1940, the Soviet police had secretly executed over 20,000 Polish officers, officials, and intellectuals. German lawyers brought up this affair, which Soviet judges deflected and tried to spin into a Nazi conspiracy. The Democratic West too had committed war crimes; employing saturation bombing, engaging in unrestricted submarine warfare, and detonating nuclear weapons. This complicated the process of establishing the moral high ground and engendered German resentment. More than a few Western jurists protested the tribunal's spurious legal basis. The Western public, however, generally supported the administration of justice to those so clearly guilty of unleashing a war few Westerners had wanted to fight.

Allied lawyers struggled to define genocide or to justify a prosecution that elevated crimes retroactively. An important secondary task of Nuremberg was to erect a framework for human rights to deter future abuses against defenseless civilians. Nuremberg culminated into a framework for what was hailed as international law, laying out universal moral principles that transcended state boundaries, national jurisprudence, or idiosyncratic cultural values. In theory, national leaders could now be sanctioned for violating these principles. International law received a further boost when in January 1948 the UN General Assembly passed the **genocide convention**. This measure explicitly defined genocide and obliged international intervention to prevent such horror. In comparison to Nuremberg, the 1946 to 1947 Pacific War crimes tribunals proved more subdued. Japanese villains were less infamous than their Nazi counterparts, and the prospect of rebuilding now preoccupied most of the Western public.

International law was augmented in 1949 by the Third and Fourth Geneva Conventions that laid out the rules for "just warfare." In the wake of Auschwitz, Hiroshima, and Nanking, postwar reformers were determined to insulate civilians from future dictators or heinous abuse. The conventions' provisions mirrored many of most infamous atrocities of World War II, forbidding belligerents from turning their weapons onto civilians, brutalizing occupied peoples or mistreating prisoners. By far the most ambitious document of this era was the 1948 **Universal Declaration of Human Rights**. The UN Charter had already affirmed the existence of "fundamental human rights, and dignity and worth of the human person."[5] Eleanor Roosevelt headlined an international committee tasked with codifying these values. During the drafting process, however, committee members became locked in a dispute about whether these rights were truly "universal" or reflections of a Western cultural experience? Communists championed the idea of social justice guaranteed by the state, not liberties adhering to the individual. Some Muslim jurists also complained that individual liberties drew from Enlightenment principles at odds with Islamic tradition. The charter's final wording invoked the US declaration of independence, deeming that all individuals possessed *inalienable* rights and *fundamental* freedoms derivative of their *intrinsic humanity*, regardless of their citizenship or cultural mores. This declaration passed unanimously in 1948, although the Soviet Union and eight other states abstained. As a declaration, the charter was not legally binding. Eleanor Roosevelt hoped that as an international *Magna Carta*, it would inspire states to draft laws, institutions, and constitutions consistent with its lofty principles.

Eleanor Roosevelt inspects her handiwork after the Universal Declaration's passage in November 1949.

> Did the Atlantic spirit survive inside postwar international system or did it dissipate when tensions between the superpowers intensified?

Bretton Woods and the Postwar Economy

Economic breakdown during the 1930s had spawned fascist regimes and weakened international resolve to enforce collective security. To create a durable peace, reformers believed that they needed to fix structural problems inside the world economy. In 1944, the United States extended invitations for an international conference convened at the recently refurbished Mount Washington Hotel in New Hampshire. Delegates from forty-three nations ultimately gathered to repair the international economic system and establish institutions to guide postwar recovery. One key objective at **Bretton Woods** was monetary stability. Recalling how predatory devaluations had contributed to a breakdown in international trade during the 1930s, the Bretton architects sought to establish a solid foundation for postwar commerce. A dispute, however, broke out between the British and American delegations concerning the mechanism for currency conversion. The Unites State's Henry Dexter White wanted a system backed by the US dollar. This would guarantee the United States an outsized voice in postwar economic affairs. Britain's John Maynard Keynes pushed for a more multilateral monetary system based on a basket of Western currencies. Through a combination of guile and force, White's vision prevailed and assembled delegates accepted the US dollar as a global reserve currency. The resulting **International Monetary System** enabled member states to convert national currencies into gold or US dollars according to fixed rates, providing a stable foundation for international transactions. The Soviet Union opted against joining Bretton Woods. Stalin feared that closer integration with capitalist economies would undermine the communist party's control over its peoples. This foreshadowed the difficulty Stalin and his Western partners faced in establishing a multilateral system that could accommodate their divergent interests and incompatible systems.

The second institution to come out of Bretton Woods was the International Bank of Reconstruction and Development (IBRD), later called the **World Bank**. Recalling the economic chaos following the Great War, the World Bank would extend loans to rebuild damaged European infrastructure and jumpstart economic recovery. Delegates also agreed to create an International Trade Organization to lower tariffs. The United States ultimately failed to ratify this mechanism, citing fears that it infringed upon their sovereignty. In its place, the 1947 **General Agreement on Trade and Tariffs (GATT)** emerged as a more modest, alternative framework for tariff reduction. After six months of negotiation, a hundred separate agreements were concluded that slashed duties on thousands of manufactured goods. GATT would continue to operate and lower tariffs between Western developed economies during the postwar period. The **most favored nation** principle ensured that any bilateral deal cutting tariffs would immediately apply to all other members.

A Better World?

The Atlantic architects attributed World War II to a breakdown of the Versailles system. To some extent, they sought to rekindle the hopes of Western liberals that had burned brightly during the spring of 1919. In 1945, however, Wilsonian idealism was tempered by a sober realism. The postwar

Chapter 2: Dreams for a Better World, 1945 to 1949

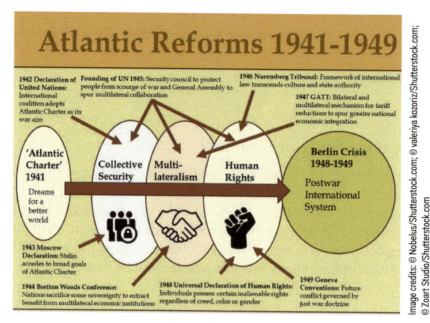

From 1941 to 1949, popular suffering and disgruntlement provided focus and momentum for Atlantic Reforms that culminated in an international system predicated upon multilateralism, collective security, and human rights.

international system was fortified with concrete mechanisms. Survival of the Grand Alliance during the immediate postwar period enabled the Atlantic dream to crystallize into a new international structure fostering multilateral trade, state collaboration, and protection of basic human rights. Ultimately, failure of Stalin and the West to reach a comprehensive peace settlement crimped these institutions' effectiveness. Rather than a forum for international collaboration, the Cold War transformed the UN into a platform for bickering and grandstanding. In a bipolar international environment, the veto system locked the Security Council into a stalemate that prevented the UN from fulfilling its stabilizing role. The Bretton System helped to unite the economies of the Industrial West, but did not incorporate the Soviet Bloc, left out Latin America, and later postcolonial states. International law emerged, but the international community often lacked the will, as well as the means, to enforce its lofty provisions. The UN officially repudiated white supremacy, but Europe's colonial powers insisted that decolonization remained situated in a distant future. Given these shortcomings, the West built up more limited Western organizations like North Atlantic Treaty Organization (NATO) and the Marshall Plan to shore up its international vision, but these forums were more consistent with prewar Great Power arrangements than liberal internationalism.

Postwar Decolonization Wave, 1945 to 1949

The Atlantic Charter had recognized "the right of all peoples to choose the form of government under which they will live; and they wish to see sovereign rights and self government restored to those who have been forcibly deprived of them."[6] During the war, US President Roosevelt put pressure on Churchill and De Gaulle to extend self-determination to their colonial subjects. France and Britain

Chapter 2: Dreams for a Better World, 1945 to 1949

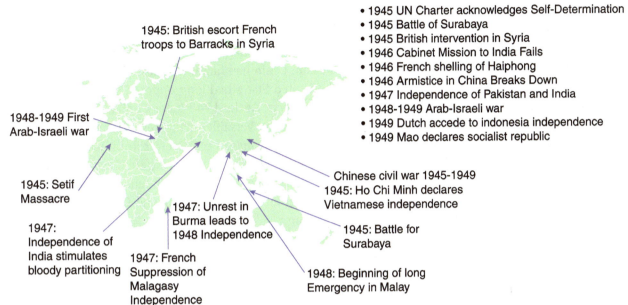

The Atlantic Charter amplified the non-Western desire for freedom that blossomed into robust movements for national independence after 1945.

resisted FDR's pressure to liquidate their colonial empires, but they came under increasing pressure to improve conditions for their nonwhite subjects.

At the war's end, colonial nationalists from Algeria to Vietnam invoked the Atlantic Charter to demand their postwar freedom. Their dream, however, clashed with European desires to harness colonial resources for their own rebuilding. In postwar Syria, when France vacillated on a 1943 pledge for postwar independence, President Shukri al-Quwatli complained: "where now is the Atlantic Charter and the Four Freedoms?"[7] When civil unrest spilled onto the streets of Damascus, Britain intervened. They forcefully escorted French soldiers back to their barracks, paving the way for Syria and Lebanon's formal independence. This humiliation convinced De Gaulle that he needed to crack down upon other nationalist movements in Indochina and Africa. Having been cut out of the Potsdam Conference, restoring France's colonies loomed paramount for confirming the country's continued place among the Great Powers.

> World War represented a global shock wave. In what diverse ways did this conflict undermine Western colonial empires?

Nationalism proved less robust inside Sub-Saharan Africa, where most still lived in rural communities, identified with disparate ethnic groups, balanced conflictual families, and religious and tribal obligations. The nationalist wave, however, did not leave Africa untouched. At the 1945 Manchester Conference, educated and mostly expatriate African delegates invoked "the grim ordeal of the war of liberation against Fascism" to demand freedom for black Africans too.[8] In Kenya, the Gold Coast and Rhodesia mounting discontent with white rule crystallized into the idea of *Uhura*, a multifaceted Swahili notion of freedom that transcended cross-cutting tribal and ethnic loyalties.

After 1945, Europe's colonial powers operated in international environment where both the United States and the USSR were hostile to colonialism. Lenin had famously chastised imperialism as an instrument of capitalist exploitation, while the United States had long opposed colonialism as antidemocratic and crimping American business prospects. At the 1945 Yalta Conference, the United States and Soviet Union pushed for termination of the Versailles mandates. Ultimately, both superpowers bowed to Churchill's intransigence. They managed only to transform former League mandates into UN "Trusts" that tasked colonizing powers with preparing their subjects for independence. The United States also promised their Philippine colony independence on schedule in July 1946. This announcement was subtly timed to undermine British, French, and Dutch efforts to reclaim Pacific colonies following their eviction by Japan.

Europe's campaign for colonial restoration met with particularly ferocious resistance in Southeast Asia. During the war, Japan's occupation regime had ripped out European colonial states, banishing Western languages, renaming streets, and closing European schools. As the war turned against Japan, authorities fostered local nationalism and conferred symbolic "independence" to the Philippines and Burma. Although the "Asia for Asians" slogan had rung hollow to many Chinese, Korean, and Southeast Asian villagers who experienced Japan's brutal occupation, it resonated better with urban dwellers, liberals, and nationalists, especially among Indonesian, Indian, and Burmese elites long exposed to Western racism and colonial discrimination.

The vacuum separating Japan's September 1945 surrender, and the return of Western soldiers to abandoned colonies weeks later, enabled nationalists in Indochina and Indonesia to declare independence and establish provisional governments. In China, the United States ferried in Nationalist troops to secure Eastern and Northern cities before they could be occupied by Mao and his communist army. In Indonesia, the British lost over 600 lives, mostly Indian soldiers, at the 1945 **Battle of Surabaya** when Indonesian militants refused to disarm. This bloody encounter pushed Britain to profess neutrality on the question of Indonesia's future. It also dampened Britain's resolve for tackling nationalism inside its own Asian colonies. The newly installed Attlee regime was focused on building a welfare state in Britain. Their party's rank and file looked upon colonialism as an embarrassment that principally benefitted the capitalist class.

Burma

After recapturing Burma in May 1945, Britain's tone-deaf Governor, Sir Reginald Dorman-Smith, sought to revive a prewar 1935 constitutional arrangement to facilitate Burma's slow transition towards dominion status. This conservative plan was out of step with local desires and shoved aside local hero **Aung San**, whom most Burmese identified as their liberator. Aung San had a colorful past as a communist agent and Japanese collaborator. When British forces advanced upon Rangoon in 1945, however, Aung San pragmatically switched to the allied side. Accordingly, Dorman-Smith did not trust Aung San. Still, Aung San's exclusion from Britain's postwar regime represented a political mistake. After a harrowing Japanese occupation, and two years of nominal independence, the Burmese people had no use for Dorman-Smith or Britain's program for gradual reform. Facing widespread unrest and violence, in 1946 London abruptly reversed course. Their new envoy promptly embraced **Aung San** to broker a deal for swift Burmese independence.

Window on World History: Postwar Asian Nationalism, 1945 to 1949

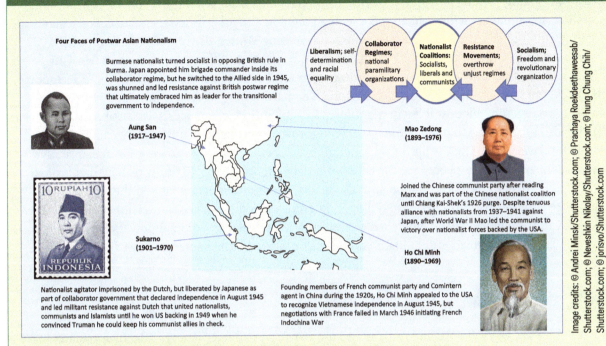

Japan's East Asian War galvanized robust coalitions throughout the Pacific Rim uniting secular liberals, communists, and illiterate peasants into movements for national independence.

Aung San typified the diverse spirits animating Asian nationalism during the summer of 1945. To Asian eyes, the distinction between a freedom fighter, nationalist, socialist, Islamist, or Japanese collaborator often seemed slight and superficial. Whatever their past, or ideological underpinnings, figures like Sukarno, Mao Zedong, Ho Chi Minh, and Aung San symbolized independence from white rule and foreign exploitation. Japan's sudden surrender in August 1945 created a vacuum throughout Southeast Asia that nationalists of all stripes rushed to exploit. From August to October 1945, overstretched British forces rushed in to relieve and disarm Japanese soldiers throughout the Pacific theater. They were often joined by French and Dutch officers eager to restore their prewar administrations. To thwart the European project for colonial restoration, Japan had in the last years of the war established collaborator regimes that gave persecuted Asian nationalists a taste of power and freedom. After their formal surrender, many Japanese officers covertly armed local militants, particularly paramilitary groups they had trained for indigenous collaborator regimes. Communists represented another interest group in Southeast Asia. In fighting Japan, Britain and the United States had crafted a fledgling alliance with communist-linked guerrillas like the Viet Minh, the Philippine Hukbalahap, and the Anti-Japanese Malay People's Army (MPAJA). At an independence ceremony in 1946, Lord Mountbatten personally pinned an Order of the British Empire medal on the chest of Chen Peng, commander of the MPAJA, honoring his contribution to Malaya's liberation. Only three years later, however, Peng would lead the communist insurgency against continued British rule in Malay. In 1945, Britain felt some obligation to help their French and Dutch allies restore their colonial regimes. In Vietnam, British Commander Dick Gracey liberated French troops from Japanese jails so that they could overthrow the newly declared Viet Minh regime. To counteract Indonesian nationalism, the Dutch appealed to ethnic and religious minorities in the outer islands,

(Continued)

fearful of their future marginalization at the hands of Javanese Muslims. Destroyed infrastructure and a devastating famine, however, provided a powerful coagulant that united former collaborators, socialists, and militants with ordinary people in a common struggle for independence. For Asians demonstrating in city squares, taking up arms, or assaulting whites, driving out the Europeans represented a goal that transcended ethnic, religious, or political differences. Aung San, Ho Chi Minh, and Sukarno saw nothing odd in uniting with local communists or appealing for US support to achieve their dream of national independence. The partitioning of Asians into "communists" and "noncommunist" blocs still lay in the future. To achieve independence, Asian nationalists like Mao Zedong adopted a 'big tent' strategy, inviting various groups to join them in a campaign for national rejuvenation. The disruptive war strengthened their hand by weakening European resolve and mobilizing ordinary people for the cause of independence. By 1949, most of Asia had broken free from European rule and common struggle against foreign oppression helped them to congeal into more cohesive nation-states despite lingering ethnic, ideological, and confessional differences. In Malay, Korea, and Vietnam, where nationalism was suppressed by colonial power, the struggle for independence transformed into military conflict that quickly became entangled with the Cold War.

Critical Reflection

1. In what ways did World War II help Europe's Asian colonies emerge into nation-states?
2. Why did most Asians see little contradiction between socialism and nationalism?

Postwar Indonesia

Superpower influence upon postwar decolonization was most evident in Indonesia. In 1945, Dutch administrators returned on British ships to the archipelago they had ruled for centuries. Their return was not welcomed and met with particularly hostile reception on Java where the *pemuda*, a militant nationalist organization, whose core members had been trained and armed by the Japanese, terrorized Dutch settlers and officials. Ethnic, religious, and cultural differences inside Indonesian society, however, enabled the Dutch to seize the upper hand in their colony's reconquest. By 1947, Dutch troops established control over the Eastern Islands and most of Java's cities, but their invasion met with stiff local resistance and growing international condemnation. When a 1948 power-sharing arrangement between the Netherlands and Sukarno's nationalists collapsed, the Dutch were pushed to a breaking point. After Sukarno cracked down on communists inside his coalition, Truman decided that he could be trusted and that the unpopular Dutch regime was an impediment to Asia's postwar stability. Truman threatened to cut off the Netherlands from Marshall Plan funds. This, and uncertain prospects in a bloody colonial war, precipitated the Dutch to cut their ties to their historic colony.

India's Independence

As the crown colony of the world's greatest empire, India's 1947 independence proved highly symbolic. It convinced many observers that a global independence wave was near. Following the failure of the 1942 **Cripps Mission**, momentum had built inside India for postwar independence. After the Labour

Party's victory in 1945, British authorities moved to expedite the process, but the 1946 **Cabinet Mission** failed to get Hindu and Muslim leaders to agree upon the structure for a future independent state. Gandhi lobbied for a united India with a constitution that would recognize equal rights among all citizens, but the rift between Muslims and Hindus had been widening since the 1930s. In August 1946, Muslim–Hindu relations reached a breaking point when a demonstration in Calcutta degenerated into mob violence that left at least 5,000 Hindus dead. Subsequently, a surge of sectarian violence washed over India, especially in the Punjab, the most multiethnic province home to significant Hindu, Muslim, and Sikh communities.

Presiding over a deteriorating security situation, in 1947 Britain rushed Lord **Louis Mountbatten** to India. Mountbatten gathered leading Indian nationalists together, pushing for a federal state that would grant minority-dominated provinces' significant autonomy. **Jawaharlal Nehru** and the Hindu-dominated Indian National Congress, however, insisted upon a centralized state structure, a demand that had become unacceptable to **Muhammad Ali Jinnah's** Muslim League. This impasse rendered partition the only viable option. At the June 3, 1947, press conference, Mountbatten hastily announced that India's independence would transpire in six weeks' time. This ambitious schedule reflected Britain's desire to pull out quickly from a potentially explosive conflict between the country's sectarian groups. The Mountbatten Plan called for referendums in the multiethnic Punjab and Bengal, while hundreds of princely states were given the option to join either the future Hindu-dominated India or Muslim Pakistan. Britain's Parliament ratified the plan as Mountbatten's team raced to draw new borders and apportion the former Raj's resources equitably between the two successor states. When the date for independence arrived on August 14, 1947, however, the future boundaries had not yet been announced. The Mountbatten Plan had envisioned that minorities would remain resident inside their native states, but rising ethnic violence rendered this plan obsolete. In Punjab, millions fled murderous mob violence, abandoning their homes and possessions as they sought shelter among coreligionists across emerging borders. In his speech at India's independence ceremony, Nehru had presented independence as beacon inaugurating a new postcolonial age where nonwhites would take their rightful place as equals inside a democratic international system. Mob violence, mass killings, and gang rapes roiled sullied this historic moment. With security inadequate, seven million Hindus and Sikhs fled the Punjab and Bengal to India, with a like number of Muslims migrated to Pakistan. Aggravating India's crisis was that the assassination of the one transcendental figure in Indian politics. Gandhi had been gunned down by a disgruntled Hindu nationalist, removing the one figure that might have calmed tension. Ultimately, India's bloody birth pangs claimed at least 200,000 lives and rendered 14 million homeless. India served notice that not only were colonialism's days were numbered, but also that the birthing of postcolonial states might prove a messy process, especially inside multiethnic colonies, where animosities between sectarian groups were deeply rooted and had often been amplified by deliberate colonial policies.

In his famous tryst with destiny speech, Nehru envisioned the "soul" of the Indian nation awakening "to life and freedom." Why do you suppose that the transition towards sovereign independence excited ethnic tensions inside some postcolonial states?

China's Civil War, 1945 to 1949

After nearly a century of political instability and war, China desperately needed peace. Japan's surrender dissolved a tense partnership between Chinese Nationalists and Communists. By November 1945, the two rivals came to blows in areas formerly occupied by Japan. Initially, elite nationalist units fared well against their more poorly equipped communist rivals. A January 10, 1946, Armistice brokered by US Secretary of State George Marshall froze China into competing spheres of influence, but neither side desired a negotiated settlement. Both used the ceasefire as a pretext to reorganize their forces. After General Rodion Malinovksy pulled out Soviet soldiers, **Chiang Kai-shek** launched a large-scale assault in June 1946 that initially put communist forces on the defensive. Mao's "people's war" strategy mixed guerrilla tactics with propaganda and popular mobilization of the peasantry. From 1946 to 1947, communist forces wore down the more heavily armed Nationalist Armies, while steadily improving their force structure and logistics. In June 1947, the communists launched three separate counterattacks that destroyed the backbone of Chiang Kai-shek's army. As the tide turned, large numbers of Nationalist soldiers deserted or switched sides, enabling Mao to secure the North quickly. In April 1948, Mao ignored Stalin's urge for caution, instead crossing the Yangtze. The communists quickly captured Nanking, dealing a symbolic blow to the Nationalist coalition already in a state of collapse. On October 1, 1949, Mao Zedong victoriously proclaimed the People's Republic of China at the Heavenly Gate in Tiananmen Square. Chiang Kai-shek and two million supporters fled to the island of Taiwan bringing with them China's gold reserves and all the loot they could carry.

Mao's victory profited from the **Kuomintang's** inability to win public support. The Nationalists were not a coherent party, but a coalition of diverse interests. While Chiang was an able backroom negotiator, he failed to communicate a clear program for China's future. His coalition was also notoriously corrupt. Despite receiving $4.43 billion in aid from the United States, much was diverted from his army into private pockets and many weapons and supplies wound up in the hands of communists. While the Kuomintang had many well-equipped military units, the rank and file's morale was low and Chiang's habit of micromanaging local military commanders undermined their effectiveness. Desertion was a symptom of Kuomintang conscripts suffering from abuse from officers, while forced to fight with inadequate food supplies and ammunition. The rapacious taxes heaped on civilians and persecution of Japanese collaborators turned increasingly large segments of China's population away from the nationalist regime. In contrast, communist soldiers fought with great resolve and determination. They saw themselves fighting for land and a socialist state that promised a better future. While most Chinese were skeptical of Marxism in 1949, and town dwellers remained suspicious of Mao's peasant army, the communists steadily expanded their popular support. Mao's big tent strategy played to a yearning for peace by inviting noncommunist to join his ranks to build a stronger China. There were many reasons for the communist victory, but by 1948, a majority of Chinese had concluded that Mao was their best shot for stability after decades of disorder and suffering.

Dissipation of the Wave

By 1949, the postwar decolonization wave ebbed. Following resolution of the First Berlin Crisis, and Mao's public declaration of "leaning" towards Moscow, the United States shifted course. Rather than seeing European empires as an impediment to US business interests, American hawks increasingly saw them as bulwarks for containing global communism. Outbreak of war in Korea in 1950 led to the US rollout of a global containment strategy that inclined it towards resisting non-Western nationalism. This brought a momentary pause to the more fundamental process of decolonization.

West European Social Democracy, 1945 to 1949

Unlike in 1919, few Europeans could imagine returning to some nostalgic *belle époque*. Depression and the war's many hardships had eroded traditional ideas about justice, sex, property, and gender, incubating a revolutionary mood where returning soldiers, occupation survivors, and demobilized female workers were all open to revisiting accepted conventions. This revolutionary sentiment was apparent as the British headed to the polls in July 1945, only a month after VE Day. In a landslide victory, Britons voted out the bulldog Winston Churchill, in favor of his moustached Labor Party rival, the unassuming **Clement Attlee**. Churchill had not lost an ounce of popularity. Everywhere he ventured vast crowds gathered to greet the feisty war hero that had rallied his people to victory, but Attlee had convinced Britons that he was the better candidate to "win the peace." The Labour Party campaigned openly on the basis of the **Beveridge Report** and promised to build a welfare state. In 1941, William Beveridge had been commissioned to analyze various public insurance schemes. He found uneven benefits for widows, unemployed workers, and orphans. To remedy this, the commission recommended instituting a universal scheme to provide a standard level of benefit across the realm. Despite the war, millions of copies of the 1942 Beveridge Report were printed as Britons digested its contents in neighborhood pubs. This provided the first real indication of how the Blitz had transformed the popular consciousness. In the face of a war with uncertain prospects, the British mobilization strategy had dispensed with traditional class privileges and gender distinctions. Oxford lads were sent to sweat in Welsh mines, government food supplements were given to emaciated working class kids, women were recruited into the workforce in record numbers, and private enterprises were taken over by the state. In 1945, as British soldiers disembarked from troopships, they did not want to return to the class divisions and social barriers of Old England. Recalling the hardships of war and the failures of prewar democracy and capitalism, a majority were determined to build a better society. Many viewed state planning as a key ingredient in Britain's triumph over Nazism and they supported the idea of creating a welfare state to protect citizens from "cradle to grave." When Churchill labeled the Labour Party's proposed reforms "socialism," and likened it to establishment of a "gestapo," he sealed his fate. The Labour Party won an overriding majority and a mandate to build a New Jerusalem, a society free from misery and want.

Throughout 1946, the British Labour government set about nationalizing many large enterprises: coal mines, transportation firms, and utility companies. This dramatically increased the state's economic footprint without supplanting small businesses or abolishing private property. The Labour Party's reinvention of the state and the relationship between society and the economy reflected several precedents. During the 1930s, Sweden had pioneered monetary and fiscal policies that many postwar European governments would borrow to manage the national economy. Wartime administrations that had mobilized private resources for national defense had increased public confidence in the ability of government to manage the economy. Before the Great Depression, few classical economists believed that states could regulate "free" markets, but John Maynard Keynes' 1936 *General Theory of Employment,*

44 Chapter 2: Dreams for a Better World, 1945 to 1949

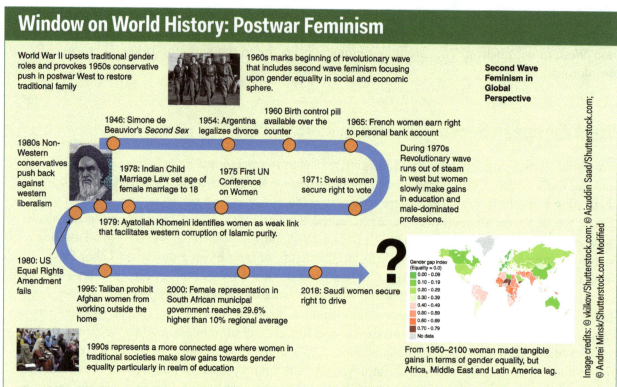

Window on World History: Postwar Feminism

Viewed from a global perspective, postwar feminism emerged in a later, less liberal form inside non-Western societies.

Total war mobilization put multiple stresses upon families. Men shipped overseas found comfort in the arms of strangers, while leaving a vacuum behind that forced wives, fiancés, and girlfriends to assume traditionally male breadwinner and head-of-household roles. In North America and Britain, the state encouraged women to assume their patriotic duty and fill in for male workers conscripted into the armed forces. Women were recruited into the workforce in record numbers, they served in traditionally male professions, and they assumed new responsibilities. Across the world stage, wartime mobilization had cut into traditional ideas about gender differences and women being the "weaker sex." The freedoms and responsibilities heaped upon women led them and men to appreciate new dimensions of femininity and embrace different ideas about sexuality and the family. Western feminists often highlight this wartime experience as a tipping point stimulating second wave feminism. Whereas the suffragettes had focused primarily upon political rights, postwar feminists sought to liberate women from social barriers and cultural expectations. However, women experienced World War II as "liberating" mostly in North America. The Axis powers nurtured a romantic, antimodernist philosophy that pushed women from the workforce into the domestic sphere and traditional roles. Inside occupied Europe and Asia, women were subjected to multiple hardships including rape. During World War II, sexual violence was widespread, if often unpublicized. Infamously, during the battle for Berlin, over 200,000 women are estimated to have been raped, and inside Soviet occupation zones women continued to be molested with such frequency during the postwar period that Hungary legalized abortions in 1946. For Korean comfort women, the nationality of their clientele changed after the war, but often not their degradation and marginalization. From a global perspective, the feminism that emerged after World War II was more subdued than in 1919. The conflict had been destructive and geographically widespread and brought to culmination an earlier decade of depression and hardship. In 1946, Simone Beauvoir's *Second Sex* masterfully trashed conventional gender stereotypes, but many Western women colluded with the postwar era's conservative resurgence that elevated the traditional family into a bastion of stability in a world that had seemingly washed off its moorings. Some historians paint this redomestication in a sinister light. In North America, for example, women were rapidly and systematically pink-slipped to make way for "returning heroes." This conservative backlash represented a broader postwar trend pushing women to resume their traditional roles as nurturing mothers, doting wives, and domestic caretakers whether they wanted to or not. For American women, "settling down" obviously meant something different than for their returning soldier husbands, but to what extent did women themselves embrace the postwar era's nostalgic vision of the family? There is little doubt that World War II stimulated a deeper impulse for security, an urge to bury the past, to escape dark memories of the war, and to enjoy life's simpler pleasures. To what extent did this desire inhibit a robust manifestation of feminism? Ironically, it was in postwar Germany, Japan, and Russia where war widows were most prevalent and where women were forced to assume a wider range of traditionally male roles. For many years after the war, Russian peasant women pulled ploughs having lost draught animals. German women ran their imprisoned husbands' businesses. Japanese widows parented their children and focused on the grim business of survival. It was in North America, largely spared the ravages of war, and where economic recovery arrived earlier and more robustly, that women ultimately rebelled against patriarchy. This feminist movement peaked during the late 1960s in reaction to the domestic paradise Americans had woven around the automobile suburb, Victorian mores, consumerism, and idealized projections of the Ozzie and Harriet family. From this American hearth, second wave of feminism spread around the globe over subsequent decades. In 1965, French women were allowed to open their own bank accounts and Swiss women won the right to vote in 1971. In many non-Western societies, however, the 1970s inaugurated a television age. Already, Hollywood's dominance had stimulated a perception about the promiscuity of Western women. By the 1970s, however, the controversy surrounding silver screen kisses had given way to concerns that television dramas like Dynasty depicted images of liberated women at odds with traditional assumptions about gender and femininity. Increasing television ownership inside the non-Western world precipitated a more forceful collision between the liberalism inside postwar Western societies and traditions inside still rural dominated non-Western societies. Inside the Middle East, conservative Imams in the 1970s responded by embracing the mass media to mount a spirited defense of "Islamic values" relative to an often stereotyped image of the decadent West. In Latin America, the debate concerning gender proved more muted. Most women remained wedded to traditional ideas of courtship, sexuality, and family, even if rising female literacy and levels of nonhousehold employment inaugurated a perceptible shift towards gender equality, particularly inside the urban middle classes. From a global perspective, second wave feminism was slow moving as it washed over islands of tradition, but by the late 1980s, the idea of women as men's social equals had become ascendant and more normalized, even inside conservative societies where it continued to be vociferously rejected.

Critical Reflection

1. While wartime mobilization pushed women into nontraditional roles, the feminist movement gathered steam only a decade later. How do you explain this lag?
2. To what extent did second wave feminism transform Canadian ideas about sexuality, motherhood, and family?

Interest and Money laid out a suite of macroeconomic tools to level out capitalism's boom and bust cycles. Monetary policy, like setting interest rates and controlling the money supply, provided the state one lever over the national economy. Additionally, fiscal stimulus provided a mechanism to offset declining business activity, enabling state managers to pull the economy out of recession and nudge it back towards full employment. To many conservatives, nationalization and planning stunk of Bolshevism, but war had accustomed ordinary people to state intervention. As British voters stared down a future of austerity, they had come to trust the state as a just arbitrator to channel limited resources towards the common good.

In 1947, the British Labour Party implemented the welfare state's capstone program by instituting the **National Health Service**. Following the Beveridge Report's recommendations, the Labour Party merged diverse health and insurance programs that had been instituted over the last half century into one comprehensive national system for "all classes for all purposes." The British example was mirrored across Western Europe from 1945 to 1949 as various social democratic coalitions ushered in mixed economies, which combined state ownership of large industries with welfare measures that offered a limited safety net. Throughout Western Europe, "welfare" revealed many idiosyncrasies reflective of different historical precedents, cultural assumptions, and national priorities. In France, the **Monnet Plan** provided for a far-reaching state takeover of heavy industry, but French postwar governments did not tackle healthcare, contenting themselves with regulating various existing private insurance schemes rather than consolidating them all inside a new universal, state-managed system. German women, as mothers, were expected to stay at home. France developed daycare facilities that enabled greater female participation in the workforce. Scandinavia went the furthest in terms of granting the state power to manage social services. Around the Mediterranean, nationalization programs were less ambitious and left more power at lower levels of government. One universal focus of postwar European governments was housing construction. The combination of depression, total war, and a decade of neglect had created an acute housing shortage. Throughout Europe, the mechanisms to create affordable housing were different, but municipal governments built planned communities and used state funds to rescue young couples from dilapidated tenements.

> World history reveals revolutions to be powerful instruments for reform. How did the welfare state revamp the social contract inside Western societies and restore confidence in state institutions following the crises of the 1930s?

By 1949, the outlines for Western European **social democracy** had emerged, combining parliamentary democracy with state management of the economy, welfare programs that provided citizens opportunity for advancement and a safety net from misery and want. Previously, European quality of life had depended more upon inherited wealth and contacts rather than drive or ability. To achieve a more level playing field, postwar welfare states redistributed income, increased tax revenues, and channeled state investment towards public healthcare, education, and housing. Social democracy marked a conscious response to wartime hardships and the interwar crisis that had stimulated a postwar craving for security. Some traditionalists complained that socialism undermined freedom and represented state overreach, but majorities inside Western Europe consistently voted to continue wartime restrictions on their freedom, wages, and consumption in return for state reforms that promised employment, better housing prospects, and a basic safety net.

Fall of the Iron Curtain, 1945 to 1949

According to the 1945 Yalta Accords, Allied liberation would allow formerly occupied peoples to determine their national future. Stalin did not immediately impose communism in areas liberated by the Red Army. Instead, Stalin returned to his "popular front" strategy where communist parties joined other groups in forming broad-based coalition governments. In 1945, Stalin remained optimistic that he could persuade Eastern Europeans to adopt socialist reforms. To make this sale, Stalin lent considerable support to fledgling communist parties across Eastern Europe. Those joining the party were rewarded with special bread rations, jobs, and housing privileges. In Bulgaria, Stalin restrained indigenous communists from pushing for an immediate purge of their political rivals. Stalin warned them that zealotry for a communist state would alienate the majority. Instead, Stalin instructed regional allies to remain patient, collaborate with more established leftist parties, and build popular support for socialist policies that benefitted the majority. Stalin's pragmatism, however, was rooted in a fundamental expectation that Eastern Europe would remain "Moscow friendly." By early 1946, it was becoming clear that most Eastern Europeans would not freely choose socialism.

Until 1947, most East European heads of state came from the ranks of prominent prewar politicians and most legislatures remained controlled by noncommunist parties. Behind this veneer, however, Stalin kept tight control over Eastern Europe through the Red Army and by assigning communists control over the interior ministry and security establishment. Indigenous communists, especially those with wartime ties to the Soviet Union, were being rapidly promoted to positions of influence inside the local security apparatus, while any individuals suspected of anti-Bolshevist sentiments were systematically purged from the state bureaucracy, universities, and other public institutions. Stalin paid particular attention to recruiting a secret police force throughout Eastern Europe. Its members were screened and provided with Soviet mentors who apprenticed them in Stalin's tactics for purging internal enemies.

Era of Coalition Governments, 1944 to 1947

Few East Europeans protested when Soviet forces punished local fascists and collaborators. The redistribution of "fascist" land property often won the Soviets immediate local support. In those areas brutalized by the Nazis or exploited by German minorities, the Red Army also enjoyed residual prestige as a liberator. Czechoslovakia, betrayed by its Western allies in 1938, saw membership in the communist party rise from 475,000 to 2.6 million from 1945 to 1948, but the Soviets were far from universally welcomed. The Soviets treated Romania, Hungary, Austria, and East Germany as conquered enemies rather than liberated peoples. Not only in former Axis states but also in Poland, Red Army soldiers committed consistent atrocities. Russian commanders mostly tolerated home invasions, pillage, and rape. While this terrorism supposedly targeted "fascists," in practice, rape and robbery were indiscriminate until Soviet soldiers were ordered to their bases in 1947. Soviet technical assistants combed through Eastern Europe identifying any property of value. Whole factories were stripped to the bare walls as iron sheets, grain and industrial equipment was shipped to the Soviet Union as "compensation" for liberation or restitution for war crimes. Soviet confiscations were extensive and often counterproductive. Only a fraction of such spoils could be put to productive use inside the USSR, but these confiscations invariably wrecked local economies and sparked resentment. In 1948, Romania paid 15 percent of its national income in reparations and Hungary 17 percent. In Byelorussia, the Baltic states, Ukraine, and areas of Poland, groups traditionally hostile to Russian influence and Bolshevism engaged in armed resistance that lasted until 1950 in the dense forests of Lithuania.

Stalin's relatively liberal attitude towards Eastern Europe's postwar governments shifted after 1946, when various municipal elections confirmed that despite heavy Soviet sponsorship, communist parties were unlikely to prevail in open elections. Soviet authorities increasingly adopted intimidation tactics to repress and weaken noncommunist parties. In Poland, **Stanislaw Mikołajczyk** had returned from exile hoping to lead the Smallholders Party. Initially, the Soviets welcomed his return because it provided legitimacy to their handpicked Lublin regime. When Mikołajczyk started to draw large crowds and garner national support, however, security forces disrupted his political activities. By 1946, Mikołajczyk fled back to Britain to avoid imminent arrest. He was one of the few to escape a systematic purge of noncommunist politicians throughout Eastern Europe. By late 1947, large socialist parties were forcefully merged into their smaller Soviet-dominated communist counterparts, while leaders of noncommunist organizations were arrested on trumped-up charges of being Western agents.

The Soviet Hammer, 1948 to 1953

The **Iron Curtain** fell in February 1948 when Stalin backed a coup to prevent a noncommunist government from taking power in Czechoslovakia. This marked the beginning of a Stalinist makeover of Eastern Europe. In Western Europe, socialist reforms emerged gradually from populist parties in open elections. Throughout Eastern Europe, **people's democracies** were imposed rapidly from above using deadly force. Local communists leveraged an elaborate police apparatus to attack all forms of dissent, real, and imagined. Joseph Tito's 1948 split with Stalin provided justification for a regionwide crackdown that mostly targeted established communist leaders. For example, Polish communist leader **Władysław Gomułka** was arrested for "right wing reactionary deviation," Soviet code for promoting reforms that were thoroughly socialist but might potentially challenge Soviet domination.

Throughout Eastern Europe from 1949 to 1952, states were forcibly **stalinized**. This meant they adopted five-year plans for crash industrialization modeled upon the Soviet experience of the 1930s. To finance this, the state appropriated houses, factories, and property through forceful seizures, predatory taxes, and repeatedly devaluing currencies. Farmers were pressured into joining collective farms, while police terror systematically targeted clerics, ethnic minorities, bourgeoisie, and "cosmopolitan" Jews for persecution and arrest. No one escaped the Red Terror. Hungarian Cardinal Jozsef Mindszenty's high office did not spare him. Throughout the Eastern Bloc, churches were shuttered and clerics were rounded under the guise of implausible "counter-revolutionary" plots. Religious persecution reflected less the official atheism of communist reformers, than a coordinated attack upon the Church's moral authority and broad-based support. Only in Poland did the Catholic Church officially survive, but even there the communist state confiscated most of its land, transformed clerics into state employees, and gradually closed its schools.

Eastern Europe's radical makeover inspired various forms of resistance, especially among farmers. This was most dramatically illustrated in Hungary where over 200,000 were shipped to gulags from 1949 to 1950 for refusing to surrender their homesteads and livestock to collective farms. In Czechoslovakia, political prisoners were put to work in Uranium mines to provide fissile material for the Soviet nuclear program. Lacking radioactive gear, most quickly died. Throughout Eastern Europe, the structure of people's democracies revealed differences, but Stalinization proved brutal. All the nation's material, capital, and human resources were focused on industrializing as vast as possible. Terror represented the instrument as the secret police employed informers and made large-scale arrests. Arbitrary arrest and brutal punishment deterred resistance from the silent majority, while providing a cadre of slave laborers that could be exploited to build the socialist paradise. Behind the Iron Curtain, the state now monopolized public life, the party took control over all social institutions and systematically undermined alternative forms of identity. Propaganda was used relentlessly to project the promise of a more egalitarian society and to exhort citizens to sacrifice for a better future. Ultimately, people's democracies succeeded in building out an industrial, educational, and medical infrastructure from a primitive base. Living standards improved, and regime allies and the poor were offered unprecedented upward mobility inside education and the workforce. Unlike Western Social Democracy, however, Eastern Communism represented socialism installed from above. "Progress" was defined from the outside and imposed on the backs of hundreds of thousands of victims.

Postwar Crystallization of Distinctive Welfare Systems

Spectrum of Goals: Create Educational Opportunity; Social Justice/Create safety net; Provide Shelter/Build Housing; State Planning/Manage economy for all; Access to Health Care

American Consumerism
- 1944 GI Bill of rights
- 1945 Attlee defeats churchill
- 1945 Arrest of London Poles
- 1947 Britain's National Health Service
- 1948 Communist Coup in Czechoslovakia
- 1948 Stalin-Tito Split
- 1948-1949 Berlin Blockade

Laissez-Faire; Central Bank with some macroeconomic intervention but corporations and consumers set economic agenda

Suburb, television, automobile, advertising

Support; Social security, housing subsidies, mortgage insurance, limited unemployment insurance

House ownership, rising, wages, access to consumer goods, withdrawal from state regulations

Eastern Communism
Solidarity, modern progress, universal healthcare for all, work opportunities for all classes

State seizure, ownership and control over all aspects of the economy and society

Equality and security; shelter, clothing and adequate calories

Stalinscraper, Mega-Industrial complexes, gulag and public parade

Western Social Democracy
- Structure of Economy
- Definition of Happiness
- State's Welfare Mandate
- Symbols

Safety Net; womb to tomb, social housing, subsidized education, public transportation, social security

Mixed Keynesian: nationalization of strategic industries with full employment state goal

Public housing, BBC, British Rail, NHS

Access to housing, higher education, better public schooling, universal healthcare

The suffering of the Great Depression and horrors of World War II broadened popular support for socialist reforms, but across East and West, they were incarnated into divergent configurations.

Birth of Israel, 1945 to 1949

World War II stimulated an outcry for freedom and independence. The birth of Israel represented a special case of postwar decolonization where two peoples' dreams for statehood clashed. **Zionism**, the dream to establish a Jewish state within Biblical Israel, had emerged in late nineteenth-century Europe in reaction to violent pogroms and entrenched anti-Semitism. Although Zionism had enjoyed support from only a minority of Jews before World War II, it gained momentum after 1945. Hitler's death camps impressed even upon Zionist skeptics the importance of having a state where Jews could take refuge. In 1946, however, many Holocaust survivors remained DPs—displaced persons—huddled in overcrowded German refugee camps. Most had lost many of their loved ones. Others were rendered effectively stateless by the redrawing of boundaries and postwar ethnic cleansing. Some Jews ultimately procured visas to immigrate to the Americas, but Britain shut the door to legal migration to Palestine. As the mandatory power, Britain remained sensitive to Jewish immigration following the 1936 to 1939 Arab Revolt. Undeterred, Zionist organizations mobilized an intense public relations campaign that directed international opinion against Britain. Zionists also created an elaborate clandestine network to smuggle Holocaust survivors into Palestine "illegally." Inside Palestine, Jewish terrorist cells applied pressure upon Britain by targeting their soldiers and administrators, most famously in the 1946 **King David Hotel bombing**, which killed ninety-one people, including top British officials. The British responded to terrorism by instituting a more systematic blockade around the Eastern Mediterranean. Apprehended Jews were often deported to concentration camps in Cypress. With Britain's treasury depleted, and its boys returning from Palestine in body bags, in February 1947, Britain's Labour government transferred the question of their mandate's future to the UN.

Jewish terrorists bombed the King David Hotel, killing the British high commissioner and ninety others in 1946. The bombing represented the most dramatic terrorist attack by covert Zionist cells determined to pressure Britain to abandon its strict quotas on Jewish immigration and enable Holocaust survivors to migrate to Palestine.

The Holocaust stimulated Western sympathy for the Jewish plight. Zionist leaders reminded Western leaders how they had refused to take in Jewish refugees before 1939. After Britain passed the Palestine dossier to the UN in February 1947, Truman championed the Zionist cause in part because American Jewish voters represented a key constituency for his reelection prospects. The Western-dominated UN introduced **Resolution 181** that promoted a partition plan that carved the Mandate into two ethnic states. On November 27, 1947, the UN adopted this measure, despite vigorous dissent from Arab members and several neutral states like India and Cuba. Truman and US Congressmen applied heavy pressure upon allies like France and dependent states like Liberia to secure passage. Given patterns of settlement inside Palestine, it proved impossible to partition the Mandate into ethnically homogenous territories. Ultimately, the UN partition plan allotted 56 percent of the territory to Jews even though they constituted less than 30 percent of the population and owned less than 6 percent of the land. Much of the territory designated to Jews was the arid Negev desert, while Palestinians were granted the West Bank that included the Jordan watershed. Still, by any accounting, the partition plan was generous to Jews, because its proposed boundaries would leave only 10,000 Jews resident inside the future Arab state, while 400,000 Arabs were left inside territory designated for the Jewish state. Recognizing the impossibility of partitioning Jerusalem, a holy city for Jews, Muslims, and Christians, it was established as an international city that would remain under UN jurisdiction.

In hindsight, it is difficult to see how Resolution 181 could have produced a peaceful settlement. For partitioning to work, both parties needed to accept the settlement. The Jewish Agency was willing to accept Resolution 181 on the condition that caps on Jewish immigration were lifted. The resolution met with hostility from Palestinian Arabs. Arab states too rejected partitioning as contravening the UN Charter's commitment to self-determination. Britain refused to enforce the settlement that it believed unworkable and which angered its Arab allies. Zionist radicals also were unhappy with Resolution 181, for denying them both banks of the River Jordan.

Passage of Resolution 181 and Arab rejection of it sparked a low-intensity civil war. The British focused upon withdrawal by May 1948. They showed little enthusiasm for containing the escalating sectarian violence. In January 1948, Palestinians established an Arab Liberation Army that launched attacks targeting Jewish settlements and blockading Jerusalem that lay deep inside Arab territory. The Jewish Agency began to establish itself as a state and mobilized Jewish residents for war to secure the territory they had been promised under UN 181. An arms embargo, however, made it difficult to equip the Jewish army, while they faced a complicated strategic map. Jews were threatened by hostile Arab states outside of Palestine and 400,000 Arabs residing inside their zone. To meet this security threat, **Plan Dalet** called for neutralizing hostile Palestinians inside their territory. Even before the formal end of the British Mandate in May 1948, Palestinians began to flee their homes, terrorized in part by the **Deir Yassin massacre** in which Jewish militants slaughtered 250 Palestinian villagers; men, women, and children accused of blocking the road to Jerusalem.

On May 14, as the British Mandate ended, **David Ben-Gurion** proclaimed the state of Israel invoking historical precedent and derelict Resolution 181. The following day the Arab League in Cairo called for armed intervention to restore order in Palestine. Military contingents from Iraq, Egypt, Syria, Lebanon, and Jordan descended upon Palestine to uproot the Jewish state. Diplomacy was dead. Palestine's future would be determined by force of arms. Jordan's vaunted Arab Legion, numbering 10,000 professional soldiers commanded by British officers moved into Jerusalem. Other Arab contingents were initially smaller, but also possessed heavy weapons like tanks and artillery. In the early months of fighting, Jerusalem nearly fell to the Arabs, but the end of the international embargo enabled Jews to bring in foreign reinforcements and arms. By the end of 1948, the Jews had established an air force, navy, and mobile units that operated under a unified command structure. In contrast, Arab armies pursued separate agendas and often worked at cross purposes.

> Could the Arab-Israeli conflict have been averted? Why didn't UN peace keepers impose Resolution 181?

By late 1948, Jewish forces outnumbered Arabs forces two to one and secured West Jerusalem. In 1949, the UN brokered a final ceasefire between Jews and various Arab factions. The Jewish state had become a reality, but the armistice left them controlling 78 percent of the former Mandate's territory. Meanwhile, Jewish authorities forbade hundreds of thousands of Palestinian refugees from returning home citing security. Eighty percent of Arabs that had lived inside the boundaries of the Jewish state were now forced to take up residence in refugee camps in Lebanon, Syria, Jordan, and Egypt. Palestinians on the other side of the armistice line were left with insufficient land to establish a viable state. Palestine's tragedy can be summarized as one land and two peoples. Both Palestinians and Jews had dreams for a state, but once they decided that they could not live together, the small and mostly arid strip of land they shared proved insufficient to support both their national ambitions.

Chapter 2: Dreams for a Better World, 1945 to 1949

Timeline of First Arab-Israeli War
- November 1947: UN 181
- January 1948: Arab Liberation Army
- March 1948: Plan Dalet evicts Arabs from Jewish zone of control
- April 1948: Deir Yassin Massacre stimulates mass exodus of refugees
- May 1948: British Withdrawal
- May 1948: Ben Gurion declares state of Israel
- May 1948: Arab League intervention
- July 1948: Jews secure Jerusalem
- March 1949: Final Armistice

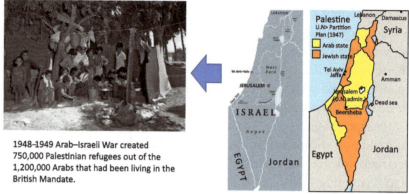

1948–1949 Arab–Israeli War created 750,000 Palestinian refugees out of the 1,200,000 Arabs that had been living in the British Mandate.

On November 27, 1947 the UN voted on Resolution 181. 33 states led by the USA and the western states voted in favor, 11 mostly Arab states rejected the motion, while 10 mostly Soviet Bloc states abstained.

UN Resolution 181 Partition Plan

Territory	Arab and other population	% Arab and other	Jewish population	% Jewish	Total population
Arab State	725,000	99%	10,000	1%	735,000
Jewish State	407,000	45%	498,000	55%	905,000
International	105,000	51%	100,000	49%	205,000
Total	1,237,000	67%	608,000	33%	1,845,000

Jews won the First Arab-Israeli War culminating in the birth of Israel and creating the Palestinian refugee problem that remains unresolved.

Dissolution of the Grand Alliance, 1945 to 1949

Failure to reach a comprehensive settlement at Potsdam set the stage for sniping among the victorious allies. In his 1946 **Iron Curtain** speech, Winston Churchill accused Stalin of violating the Yalta accord. In Fulton, Missouri, Churchill drew popular attention to Soviet actions in Eastern Europe and likened Stalin's behavior to Hitlerism. Returning to his prewar rhetoric, Churchill invoked a sharp contrast between totalitarian tyranny and liberal democracy. Although no longer prime minister, Churchill's speech carried immense weight as the prophet who had warned about the danger of fascist appeasement. Now Churchill roused Americans to confront international communism. Initially, his speech confused the American public focused mostly on domestic issues and accustomed to seeing the Soviet Union as an ally. Ultimately, Churchill's invocation of the "Iron Curtain" as a dark shadow snuffing out the light of Western civilization provided the public a metaphor to conceptualize the communist threat.

Stalin responded to Churchill in the Bolshevik newspaper *Pravda*. Stalin accused Churchill of hypocrisy, noting that he had not complained about the Western Allies' implantation of liberal institutions inside their occupation sphere. Stalin denied Churchill's claims of Soviet interference inside Eastern Europe, claiming that communism was springing up from indigenous roots. Stalin branded Churchill a "warmonger" for inciting hatred against the Russian people who had sacrificed the most to defeat Hitler's armies, while romanticizing world domination by "English-speaking peoples." Stalin's argument captured Soviet perceptions about the Cold War's origins. The West had bled the Russians dry to defeat Hitler. With that task complete, they would deny their beleaguered ally the spoils necessary for its reconstruction.

Stalin and the West had experienced a fundamentally different war. The *Wehrmacht* had destroyed 1,700 Soviet towns and 70,000 villages, while murdering seven million civilians and starving five million prisoners of war to death. Westerners could make a distinction between "Nazis" and the "Good Germans" who had been duped by Hitler. For Soviet citizens, the German people had supported Hitler's annihilation war against their sons, wives, and daughters. The West could afford to invoke the mistakes of Versailles. Although Japan and Germany's devastation ensured Soviet security over the immediate term, their economy lay in shambles and starvation loomed around the corner. In contrast, in 1945, the US economy reached its zenith. Why would the United States refuse to compensate the partner indispensable for collective victory? Already in his February 1946 Bolshoi speech, Stalin returned to his prewar rhetoric warning about how capitalism's monopolization of global resources menaced world peace. In 1946, Churchill and Stalin were trading rhetoric rather than bullets. Both expressly ruled out war as a means to settle their differences, yet both in different ways also emphasized the incompatibility of Soviet socialism and Western democracy. The ideological battle lines for the Cold War had already been drawn.

After the Churchill–Stalin exchange, the breach between East and West only widened as both struggled to work inside the parameters of the Potsdam Agreement. Britain's withdrawal from the Eastern Mediterranean stimulated Truman to deliver a carefully crafted speech before Congress in March 1947 where he asked for $400 million to support the governments of Greece and Turkey, two countries bordering the Soviet Union and confronted by different forms of communist pressure. Truman did not call out the USSR by name, but he did invoke Churchill's rhetoric. He cast the United States as obliged to defend "free peoples" against totalitarian tyranny. By using plain language and a militant rhetoric, Truman tried to shake American public from their isolationist slumber. Unless the United States stepped up against communist aggression, tyranny would spread around the world. Proclamation of the **Truman Doctrine** marked a decisive pivot from trying to reach an accommodation with the Soviet Union to adopting communist containment as the focus of US foreign policy.

Truman's increasing militancy was sourced in deteriorating economic conditions inside Western Europe, violent strikes launched by Soviet supported communist organizations in France and Italy and Soviet obstructionism on the German question. Since late 1945, the Soviets had stymied the Council of Foreign Ministers (CFM), an institution established to hammer out a comprehensive postwar settlement following the impasse at Potsdam. Similarly, the Soviets had tied up the Allied Control Council (ACC), established to administer a jointly occupied Germany. These measures were part of a broader Soviet calculation to pressure the West into fulfilling Stalin's reparation demands. Until May 1946, the United States and British cooperated in shipping some German capital equipment to the Soviet Union from West Germany, but Stalin's refusal to ship East German wheat to feed Germans in the Western zone led US General Lucius Clay to halt this program to a howl of Soviet protest. The United States was forced to import wheat and dispense military rations to feed starving German children, sending the cost of the occupation skyrocketing. Instead of Germany providing reparations, British and American taxpayers now footed the bill for feeding their defeated enemy. In 1946, Britain extracted $40 million in reparations, but dispensed ten times that amount to cover the costs of Germany's occupation. Outraged, the Western public called for a quick settlement of the German Question. In May 1947, Western delegates, led by US Secretary of State George Marshall, flew to Moscow to iron out a deal that would enable the victors to withdraw their troops and enable Germans to support themselves. A haughty Molotov rejected a Four-Power Treaty to guarantee Germany's neutrality and demilitarization, but had difficulty articulating the rationale for his resistance. After six weeks of fruitless negotiations, Marshall confronted Stalin to break the deadlock. Stalin seemed congenial, but offered nothing concrete, counseling Marshall to remain patient. Disgusted, Western delegates left Moscow without a deal. Subsequently, Marshall resolved to impose a unilateral settlement upon the western zones of Germany.

54 Chapter 2: Dreams for a Better World, 1945 to 1949

In June 1947, Marshall announced a bold US initiative for European recovery, popularly known as the **Marshall Plan**. In 1945, the American public refused to play Santa Claus. By 1947, however, a bipartisan coalition recognized Western Europe's crucial significance to the United States' postwar security. The Marshall Plan invited Europe to submit proposals for US aid to accelerate their economic recovery, while trying to wean anxious Europeans from protectionism. Although the Soviet Union did attend initial Marshall Plan meetings, they quickly soured on the scheme. From the Soviet perspective, the Marshall Plan represented a diabolical scheme to undermine the USSR's domination of Eastern Europe. Stalin forbade his satellites from participating and forced Poland and Czechoslovakia to withdraw their delegations. Stalin then upped the ante in September 1947 by relaunching *Cominform*. This international organization connected Moscow to communist parties in Western Europe through covert financing. In 1947, Stalin encouraged them to stage massive strikes in protest of the Marshall Plan. American leaders started to worry that Italian communists might win the 1948 election and that other Europeans disillusioned with slow economic recovery might turn towards communism.

> Was a Cold War between Stalin and the West inevitable or did it germinate from a failure to iron out a comprehensive settlement at Potsdam?

Yalta Division of Germany

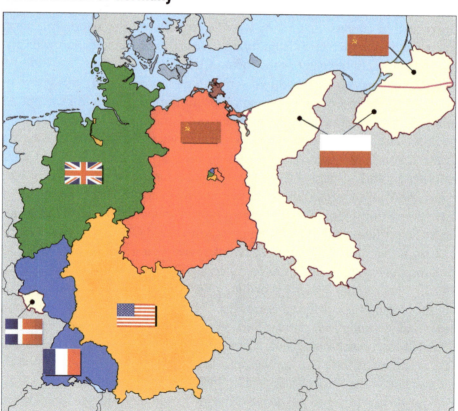

The Yalta Accord had created lines for a temporary military occupation. Following the failure of Potsdam and subsequent conferences to hammer out a permanent settlement, the Yalta lines became the boundary between Europe partitioned into two ideological blocs.

At the December 1947 **London Conference**, Britain and the United States resolved upon a plan to shore up Western Europe's economy by reviving Germany's coal and industrial sectors. Stalin protested this violation of the Potsdam protocols and manifested his displeasure by blocking supply trains to Western Berlin for two weeks. Stalin grew considerably more alarmed in February 1948 when his spies revealed allied plans to introduce a new German currency. This would undermine his ability to print bank notes to finance East Germany's occupation. The move was also a prelude to unifying the Western occupation zones of Germany into a new, Western-dominated state. Having defeated Nazi Germany at tremendous cost, Stalin now faced the prospect of losing the peace. While the Soviets would still retain control over Eastern Germany, Germany's Western zones contained most of Germany's population and industrial base. Even France, the most vocal supporter for dismantling German industries, ultimately agreed to Anglo-American plans for German reunification in return for an American guarantee of West European security. Desperately, Stalin floated an alternative plan for a reunified, neutral, and demilitarized Germany, but it arrived too late.

Berlin Blockade and Airlift

Following introduction of a new German currency in June 1948, Stalin blockaded the western zone Berlin, buried over a 100 km inside Soviet-controlled territory. This not only shut off allied troops, but also held West Berliners hostage by denying them access to food, coal, electricity, and basic consumer goods. Stalin intended to force the Allies back to the bargaining table, or at the very least drive them from Berlin. His plan backfired when the Allies opted to evade his blockade by means of an airlift. At first, it did not seem feasible to supply such a large city through air. Initial flights delivered only 30 of the 110 tons deemed necessary to sustain Berlin at a subsistence level, but as more planes were mobilized and logistics improved, the air lift surpassed its minimum benchmarks.

Children of Berlin simulating the airlift keeping them alive.

To Stalin's surprise and growing embarrassment, the airlift delivered the United States a propaganda bonanza. The efforts of American pilots to feed Berliners contrasted with the image of the Red Army's attempt to starve them. In June 1949, Stalin capitulated and removed the blockade.

The Berlin Crisis marked the informal dissolution of the Grand Alliance. There would be no grand Versailles bargain. Instead, the superpowers informally partitioned Europe between them allowing both blocs to follow their own developmental path. Europe's Cold War division was most visible in the formation of two separate postwar German states, the democratic Federal Republic of Germany (FRG) and the communist German Democratic Republic (DDR). Failure to reach a comprehensive postwar settlement dramatically reshaped the international system, transforming the United States and the USSR from reluctant partners into bitter rivals.

Conclusion: Shape of the Postwar World

World War II represented a catastrophe that motivated survivors to build a better world. The postwar environment, however, proved inauspicious for postwar reconstruction. Throughout Europe and Southeast Asia, infrastructure lay in ruins, national economies were deeply in debt, and survivors grappled with austerity, hunger, and despair. In the weeks following liberation, victims of war, occupation, and genocide retaliated against their tormentors and ethnic minorities. The scale and depth of global suffering brought into being a silent coalition of statesmen, national leaders, and ordinary people. Working in their respective domains, they fought against inherent conservatism, natural cynicism, and institutional inertia. The Atlantic principles of peace and prosperity provided a beacon for postwar rejuvenation. Its principles were directly inscribed into the edifice of a network of international institutions ranging from the UN to the Bretton sisters and international law. At the national level, in both East and West, welfare reforms reinvented the state and reinvigorated the social contract. The Atlantic dream, however, was not fully realized. Europe resisted colonial demands for independence. The failure of Stalin and the West to reach a comprehensive postwar settlement gestated into a Cold War that would polarize the world into competing blocs. For all its imperfections, the international system that crystallized by late 1949 sought to respond to the catastrophe of World War II and gave, shape to postwar history.

Questions for Critical Thought

1. Why did survivors perceive World War II as a catastrophe? How had World War II challenged the previous order predicated upon racism, economic nationalism, and European hegemony?
2. What pressures did survivors face in the war's immediate aftermath?
3. In what ways did the Atlantic Charter renounce the horrors of total war and promise reform? How did dark memories of the Great Depression and fears about postwar recession encourage ordinary people, national reformers, and statesmen to reform the international system and world economy?
4. How did World War II weaken European colonialism? How did the chaos and bloodshed of Indonesian and Indian independence provide global decolonization with momentum while highlighting the challenges for postcolonial leaders?
5. What conditions and concerns precipitated the emergence of the welfare state in Western Europe after World War II? In what ways was Western social democracy distinct from people's democracies that emerged in Eastern Europe?

6. How did the Holocaust improve international conditions for the creation of a Jewish state in British Palestine? How did the UN try to accommodate the interests of Jews and Arabs inside the region? Why did international mediation fail and lead to the First Arab-Israeli War?
7. What stimulated the deterioration of US–Soviet relations? Was a postwar settlement between superpowers possible or was the outbreak of the Cold War inevitable?

Suggestions for Further Reading

- Applebaum, A. *Iron Curtain: The Crushing of Eastern Europe 1944-1956.* New York: Doubleday, 2012.
- Bayly, C., and Harper T. *Forgotten Wars.* Cambridge: Harvard University Press, 2010.
- Betts, L. *Decolonization.* New York: Routledge, 2005.
- Buruma, I. *Year Zero: A History of 1945.* New York: Penguin, 2013.
- Eichengreen, B. J. *Globalizing Capital: A History of the International Monetary System.* Princeton, NJ: Princeton University Press, 1996.
- Lary, D. *China's Civil War.* Cambridge: Cambridge University Press, 2015.
- Morris, B. *One State, Two States: Resolving the Israel-Palestine Conflict.* New Haven, CT: Yale University Press, 2009.
- Smyser, W. R. *From Yalta to Berlin: The Cold Struggle over Germany.* New York: St. Martin's Press, 1999.
- Stafford, D. *Endgame, 1945: The Missing Final Chapter of World War II.* New York: Little Brown and Co., 2007.

Notes

1. Big Four "Declaration of the United Nations," January 1, 1942, accessed July 28, 2019, https://www.un.org/en/sections/history-united-nations-charter/1942-declaration-united-nations/index.html.
2. Anglo-American Joint Declaration, or "Atlantic Charter," August 14, 1941, accessed July 28, 2019, https://avalon.law.yale.edu/wwii/atlantic.asp.
3. Link broken, United Nations, "Preamble of the UN Charter," June 26, 1945, accessed July 28, 2019, https://avalon.law.yale.edu/20th_century/unchart.asp.
4. Quoted in Thomas Patterson, *Meeting the Communist Threat: Truman to Reagan* (New York: Oxford University Press, 1988), 8.
5. See the UN Charter, accessed July 28, 2019, http://www.un.org/en/documents/charter/.
6. See Atlantic Charter, accessed July 28, 2019, http://avalon.law.yale.edu/wwii/atlantic.asp.
7. Quoted in Ian Buruma, *Year Zero: A History of 1945* (New York: Penguin, 2013), 323.
8. Quoted in Minkah Makalani, *In the Cause of Freedom: Radical Black Internationalism from Harlem to London, 1917-1939* (Charlotte: University of North Carolina Press, 2013), 389.

Chapter 3
A Revolutionary Wave

Chapter Outline

- Decolonization and Development
- Clashing Expectations, 1945 to 1955
- The Great Unraveling, 1956 to 1966
- Quest for National Development, 1960 to 1975
- Postcolonial Challenges, 1973 to 1982
- Waning of the Revolutionary Wave

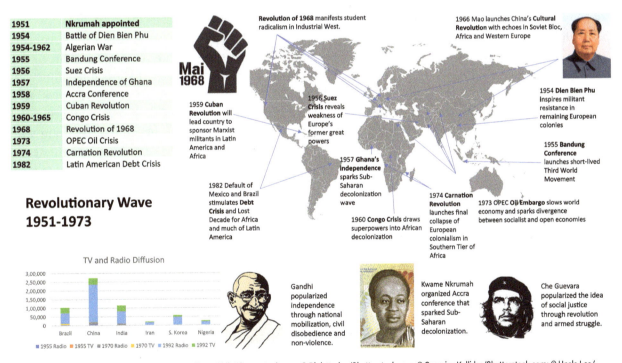

1951	Nkrumah appointed
1954	Battle of Dien Bien Phu
1954-1962	Algerian War
1955	Bandung Conference
1956	Suez Crisis
1957	Independence of Ghana
1958	Accra Conference
1959	Cuban Revolution
1960-1965	Congo Crisis
1968	Revolution of 1968
1973	OPEC Oil Crisis
1974	Carnation Revolution
1982	Latin American Debt Crisis

Revolutionary Wave 1951-1973

Image credits: michaket/Shutterstock.com; © Hung Chung Chih/Shutterstock.com; © Rinlettering/Shutterstock.com; © Georgios Kollidas/Shutterstock.com; © Uncle Leo/Shutterstock.com; © Andrei Minsk/Shutterstock.com

Decolonization and Development

Western empires drove late nineteenth-century world integration. In the four decades following World War II, most disappeared from the global landscape. Resentment among colonial subjects against Western rule and racism had been brewing for decades. The shock of World War II, however, critically weakened Western colonialism. By 1949, much of Southeast Asia and parts of the Near East had escaped from direct European rule if not Western influence. Outbreak of war in Korea in 1950, however, increasingly entangled decolonization with the Cold War. Europe's remaining colonial powers called for US help in fighting "communism," while China promoted socialism as a pathway for Asian independence and Khrushchev embraced non-Western nationalists.

The collapse of European empires was not an isolated event. It intersected a broader revolutionary wave. At the 1955 Bandung Conference, twenty-six African and Asian heads of state cast themselves as the Third World and vowed to recast the international system to reflect the global nonwhite majority. The Afro-Asian Bloc's call for liberation found echo among charismatic guerilla fighters, passionate Western student leaders, and determined agrarian reformers in Latin America. By the early 1960s, leftists around the world had embraced revolution as a pathway for state reform and social justice. The revolutionary 1960s embraced divergent progressive movements. African freedom fighters and American civil rights activists borrowed from the same playbook. Leftist organizers mobilized demonstrations that rocked colonial capitals, Western university campuses, and Chinese cities. Hippies, Eastern communist reformers, Maoists, and hardened peasant guerrillas were fighting very different campaigns, but they were animated by similar beliefs and worked inside a shared international climate.

Revolutions represent one of the driving engines of world history. Social movements can provoke change even where they fail to seize political power by forcing entrenched elites to address their demands. Rising literacy, mounting prosperity, and the internationalization of media inseminated new types of revolutionary movements that transgressed state borders. In a more integrated world, seemingly distant events could cross-fertilize each other even where local activists framed their revolutionary program to fit the indigenous scene. The fervor powering revolutionary 1960s began to fade along with the postwar boom during the 1970s. For Africa and Latin America, the 1982 Debt Crisis inaugurated a "lost decade" of stagnant growth, austerity, and heightened instability. Revolution was also blunted by authoritarian repression. Already by the late 1960s, conservatives mobilized to counterattack revolutionaries and break up progressive coalitions. By the 1980s, the world's remaining revolutionaries grappled with grim realities: police repression, unsustainable postcolonial debt, and slowing global growth. Simultaneously, export-orientated economies in the Persian Gulf and South Asia began to expand spectacularly. Following the 1989 collapse of the Soviet Bloc, the gap between South Asia's newly industrializing countries and rest of the developing world widened. Many former revolutionaries put aside their rifles and socialist texts. Disillusionment left many open to accommodating themselves to a neoliberal order predicated on democracy and free markets. University campuses quieted down, most guerrillas laid down their arms and former dependency theorists braced national economies for incorporation inside the emerging World Trade Organization (WTO).

Big Questions

- How did World War II erode European colonial empires?
- Why did independence often fail to translate into successful modernization?
- How did the slowing global economy during the 1960s ignite political conflict around the world?
- What enabled Southeast Asian Tigers and Gulf states to outstrip postcolonial states in other regions?

Clashing Expectations for Decolonization, 1945 to 1955

The Atlantic Charter's emancipatory rhetoric eroded Western colonialism's last figment of legitimacy. World War II also forced the colonial powers to offer their colonial subjects new concessions. The United Kingdom pulled out many British administrators from India to defend their home islands, replacing them with indigenous officials. In 1941, Free French General Georges Catroux promised sovereignty to Syria and Lebanon while Charles de Gaulle battled the Vichy regime for control over France's overseas possessions. When in 1943 American troops landed in Morocco and disarmed Vichy soldiers, indigenous nationalists arrived with a petition invoking Catroux's concession. In January 1944, the Istiqlal Party declared the end of France's protectorate over Morocco, deeming that "the time has come for France to recognize the blood that Moroccans have shed and will continue to shed if necessary for [France's] ideals and for its own freedom."[1]

The indigenous craving for independence clashed with European designs to leverage colonial resources for Europe's postwar reconstruction. Like in 1919 to 1921, the colonial powers self-righteously insisted that their colonial subjects were unprepared for independence. With European currencies depressed by war debt, colonial "hard" assets seemed indispensable to purchasing foreign machinery necessary for rebuilding a devastated continent. Sensitive to public exhaustion, non-Western nationalism, and superpower pressure, however, Britain and France offered their non-Western subjects a better deal. Britain's 1945 Colonial Development and Welfare Act and the 1946 French Union promised to curb colonialism's worst abuses, confer token representation, and promised significant investment to spur colonial development. As we saw in Chapter 2, however, most colonial elites had moved beyond schemes for gradual reform. The Fifth Pan-African Congress held in Manchester in 1945 expressed this sentiment plainly: "We affirm the right of all colonial peoples to control their own destiny."[2]

Internationalization of the Independence Struggle

After World War II, the struggle for independence increasingly converged with deeper international currents, eroding colonial legitimacy. At San Francisco in 1945, Europe's colonial powers joined the United Nations (UN) whose charter endorsed "the principle of equal rights and self-determination of peoples."[3] This implied rapid postwar decolonization. While Europe's former great powers pretended that independence remained situated in a still distant future, they soon discovered that news travelled more seamlessly in the postwar world. Radio stations, non-Western newspapers, and newsreels spread news about the anti-colonial struggle across the world. These media also enabled non-Western nationalists to broadcast their nationalist message out to distant villages and valleys. International opinion, squarely rooted in liberal values after the horrors of war, also began to influence colonial policy. In a more global news environment, reports of a colonial reform in a neighboring state or distant colonial massacre could now reverberate in unexpected ways.

> How would global communications, particularly radio, have abetted non-Western nationalist movements?

Mahatma Gandhi's rise to prominence during the 1930s foreshadowed the elevation of non-Western nationalists into international celebrities. In 1931, Gandhi had toured Welsh coal towns gouged by the Great Depression. Listening to the British unemployed through kindly eyes as he spun

62 **Chapter 3: A Revolutionary Wave**

Argentine doctor Ernesto Guevara's face was elevated into a global icon during the 1960s as he emerged as the pre-eminent spokesperson for liberation through militant struggle.

wool, Gandhi personified decolonization's moral imperative. Television and moving pictures, however, cast the revolutionary struggle in a more vivid light. Arguably the most telegenic revolutionary of his generation was the flamboyant Argentine doctor, **Ernesto Guevara**. Internationally renowned as "Che," Guevara had played a starring role in Castro's Cuban Revolution. On screen, Che often appeared badly shaven while wearing rough fitting camouflage garb. Guevara's gruff manner augmented his slovenly appearance. They affirmed his revolutionary commitment and manly vigor, but Che's aura came fully alive when he stepped in front of a microphone. Addressing the UN in 1964, Guevara promised that the future would be written by the "hungry Indian masses, peasants without land, exploited workers, and progressive masses."[4] Cameras beamed his poetic invocation of social injustice across the world.

Often Guevara's pleas for social justice combined a penetrating condemnation of Western imperial history with a nonapologetic embrace of violence as a revolutionary tool. Che's embrace of armed struggle inspired many non-Western peasants living in repressive societies. It also riled elites and unnerved sympathetic Western liberals.

Inside a more global media environment, revolutionary figures around the world corresponded, discussed strategy, and copied each other's playbooks. The international press often gave revolutionaries a platform to inveigh against racial injustice or express their dreams for a better future. Television coverage of the US civil rights movement during the 1950s beamed ugly episodes of racial violence into white American living rooms. Television, radio, and film combined to make Canadians feel like previously obscure locales like Ghana, Bandung, and Philippeville seem like next door. Martin Luther King Jr., Jawaharlal Nehru, and Kwame Nkrumah evolved into household names while Latin American guerillas, African leaders, and Marxist intellectuals glamorized revolutionary struggle, inspiring students in the West, China, Latin America, and the Eastern Bloc to fight for a more just society in their towns and campuses.

In the keynote address for the 1955 **Bandung Conference**, Indonesian President Sukarno gave expression to this age's idealism: "Let us remember that the highest purpose of man is the liberation of man from his bonds of fear, his bonds of poverty, the liberation of man from the physical, spiritual, and intellectual bonds which have for long stunted the development of humanity's majority."[5] The Bandung delegates cast themselves as the Third World. Modeled on the idea of the Third Estate during the French Revolution, their goal was to recast the international system to reflect the interests of the world's nonwhite majority.

Following Bandung, a complex dynamic linked the independence struggle with international opinion. For example, French defeat at Dien Bien Phu in Indochina inspired a previously obscure group, the Algerian National Liberation Front (FLN) to demand independence a few months later. British concessions in the Gold Coast during the 1950s brought pressure on France and Belgium to institute similar reforms in neighboring states. In a more interlinked world, anti-colonial victories were celebrated, while inspiring copiers oceans away. To their surprise and horror, Western colonial officials discovered that international events could now catalyze seemingly fragmented opposition groups into robust populist movements that proved difficult to contain or suppress. Better revolutionary organization and more skillful propaganda meant that colonial repression more often intensified rather than stifled popular demonstrations. The arrest of populist leaders usually enhanced their prestige. Martial law and brutal force could still push reformers underground, as it did in French Algeria, Kenya, Malay, and much of South America. But force also became less palatable inside an international arena where domestic liberals, foreign critics, and the international press kept a spotlight fixed upon policies that deviated from the UN's values and mandate. Following French defeat at Dien Bien Phu in 1954, violent repression also grew less effective as revolutionaries grasped the nuances of guerrilla warfare and grew more optimistic about their prospect of prevailing in an armed struggle.

Strategies for Liberation

Mahatma Gandhi inspired others with his tools for mass mobilization, but not all colonial nationalists shared his nonviolent philosophy. **Frantz Fanon** matured intellectually inside French Algeria where colonial authorities used martial law, torture, and terrorism against the Muslim majority. This led Fanon to conclude that "colonialism was violence in its natural state. It will yield only when confronted with greater violence."[6] Fidel Castro and Ho Chi Minh both drew inspiration from Mao's guerrilla tactics. Militant resistance offered an alternative pathway for revolution. Invariably, those copying either Guevara or Gandhi's playbook needed to adapt such tactics to fit their local setting.

Civil disobedience often proved ineffective against colonial regimes willing to impose martial law. In 1945, Ho Chi Minh, despite his earlier proclamation of national independence, acquiesced to the return of French soldiers to Vietnam. Until 1946, Ho Chi Minh tried to negotiate a political settlement, but while in Paris, French soldiers in Vietnam drove the Viet Minh from their Haiphong stronghold. The Viet Minh regrouped in the northern mountains where they resorted to guerilla resistance. At first, small-scale attacks did not dent France's grip over Vietnam. After Mao's victory in China's civil war, however, he sent the Viet Minh heavy weapons. This allowed Vietnamese General **Nguyên Giáp** to establish conventional military units that confronted the French in costly pitched battles, while not abandoning the ambush tactics designed to wear down the more heavily armed French.

Colonial Retrenchment

By 1950, Europe's colonial powers resisted further indigenous calls for independence, especially in their African colonies. This was particularly true in "settler" colonies that contained significant white minority populations. Britain and France introduced ideas like multiracial constitutions and "cosovereignty" to confer the indigenous majority some representation, but also keep whites in charge. After the Suez Crisis in 1956, such schemes were washed out in a rising tide of African nationalism. In both Kenya (1952–1960) and Malaysia (1948–1960), Britain waged costly, lengthy, and brutal counterinsurgency wars. While Britain ultimately prevailed in both struggles, their brass knuckle tactics cost their treasury dear and proved difficult to justify. Subsequently, Britain increasingly opted for negotiation and political settlements that could transfer power to indigenous "moderates." This strategy hoped to marginalize indigenous radicals and prop up a postcolonial regime that would respect Britain's postcolonial economic and strategic interests after independence.

A rising tide of black nationalism stimulated a reaction among white minority communities throughout Africa. In 1948, South Africa's National Party won a narrow victory by playing on the economic insecurity of poor Afrikaners left behind by British development policies and now feeling threatened by black political mobilization. Similarly, in Southern Rhodesia, a 1964 referendum among white voters enabled Ian Smith to declare independence from Britain to forestall London's efforts to enfranchise the black majority. The most violent collision between settler nationalism and decolonization, however, occurred inside French Algeria. There, European immigrants constituted nearly 15 percent of Algeria's population. These **Pieds-Noirs**, named after the cheap black shoes, represented full French citizens and a potent political lobby, even if Algeria remained insignificant in mainland France's economy. Additionally, France had traditionally conceptualized colonialism in terms of a high-minded *mission civilisatrice*. While France's actual record of enfranchising and assimilating nonwhites was modest at best, this ideology led French elites and army officers to construe Algerian nationalism as gratuitous rejection of their culture and benevolence.

Although regarded as "minor powers" by their European peers, both Belgium and Portugal saw their African colonies as key to their global status and national future. Portugal's dictator, António de Oliveira Salazar, promoted colonial migration as a strategy to offset his country's economic difficulties and social woes. Belgian corporations and settlers derived substantial income from colonial investments in the Congo and proved influential advocates for colonialism despite the burdens its administration placed upon the treasury. Throughout the 1950s, Belgian and Portuguese authorities remained confident that they could suppress the nationalism rattling the colonial states of their neighbors. In Rwanda and Burundi, the Belgians had during the 1920s taken loose indigenous notions like "Hutu" and "Tutsi" that referred to historic distinction between more wealthy pastoralists and poorer cultivators and objectified them into separate, distinctive "races." This colonial innovation allotted the "European-like" Tutsi minority–specific rights and privileges over the Hutu majority. Throughout the Congo, Belgium promoted a similar divide-and-conquer strategy by establishing a state structure that promoted regional autonomy, reinforced tribal affiliations, and fostered ethnic competition for Belgian favor. In 1955, after Belgian academic A. J. van Bilsen published a plan for Congolese independence slated thirty years into the future, colonial officials in Léopoldville denounced him as a dangerous radical. Given the absence of an educated indigenous elite, Belgian colonial officers remained confident that they could dominate the Congo for decades to come.

The Great Unraveling, 1956 to 1966

As noted in Chapter 2, with outbreak of the Cold War, Europe's powers rationalized their colonial wars as fighting communism. This argument gained traction after the outbreak of the Korean War in 1950 and roll out of the United States' global containment strategy. Rather than critiquing European colonialism, the United States increasingly sought to rally its Western partners in North Atlantic Treaty Organization (NATO). Through the Marshall Plan, NATO and other means, the United States offered both direct and indirect support for its Western partners fighting colonial wars. In this environment, decolonization slowed to a crawl. French defeat at Dien Bien Phu in 1954, however, tilted the geopolitical landscape back towards anti-colonial forces. At Dien Bien Phu, North Vietnamese troops soundly defeated a French army after inexperienced cavalry commander Henri Navarre unwisely inserted a 16,000 strong force along the Laotian border. The French aim was to construct a fortification to interdict Viet Minh supply lines, and draw Vietnamese forces into an open battle where they could leverage their superior firepower. This "hedgehog" strategy had worked earlier in the war, but Navarre made two fatal miscalculations. First, he failed to appreciate how Mao's victory in the China's civil war enabled him to arm the Viet Minh with heavy artillery. Second, Navarre had insufficient reinforcements to relieve Dien Bien Phu. In March 1954, General Giáp surprised Navarre by disassembling his artillery and mounting his guns onto the high slopes surrounding the French camp. This reversed the trap. Giap's guns pounded France's surrounded soldiers relentlessly. Over two hard months, French soldiers waged a desperate battle for survival as they were slowly overrun. Unable to evacuate or effectively resupply Dien Bien Phu, France's best soldiers in Indochina were forced to surrender in May 1954 after the United States refused to intervene. This debacle coincided with the opening of the previously scheduled Geneva Conference. At Geneva, France agreed to an armistice and a withdrawal from Vietnam. Following the establishment of a demilitarized zone at the 17th parallel, the 1954 **Geneva Accords** called for a general election in July 1956 to determine the country's political future. Throughout the world, French defeat elicited shock. If Vietnamese nationalists could prevail over an elite European force, then colonialism seemed doomed.

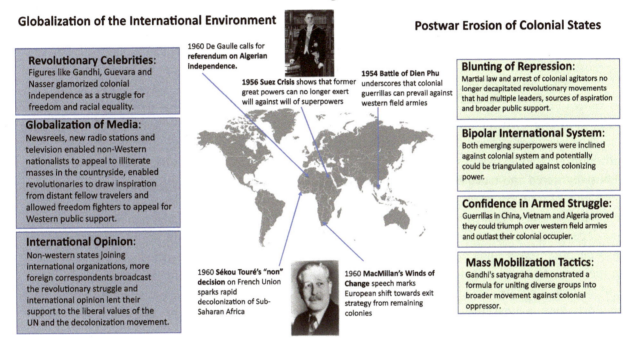

Winds of Change

Britain and France's bungled intervention in the Suez added momentum to decolonization. In 1956, Egyptian President **Gamal Abdel Nasser** abruptly nationalized the Suez Canal. When Britain and France tried to retake the canal by force, they badly misjudged the international mood. The international press condemned their intervention as illegal and unjust, a cynical ploy to maintain colonial prerogatives during an age where the world was moving towards freedom. Under heavy US and Soviet pressure, Britain and France beat an unceremonious retreat from Suez after only ten days. This signaled that they were no longer major powers capable of unilaterally imposing their colonial agenda. In 1960, during a speech delivered in Cape Town, British Foreign Secretary **Harold Macmillan** expressed the shifting European mindset, "The wind of change is blowing through this continent, and whether we like it or not, this growth of national consciousness is a political fact. We must all accept it as a fact, and our national policies must take account of it."[7]

Macmillan's speech met a stony reception from South Africa's Apartheid regime, but it captured Europe's changing mood. Rather than struggling to maintain their colonies through force, Europe's colonial powers increasingly saw their future hinged upon the creation of a common Europe market.

European focus shifted towards an exit strategy in Africa to avoid costly and protracted conflicts. Europe now rushed to transfer power to local "moderates" rather than radicals or socialists. Through this neocolonial strategy, they hoped to safeguard their longer term financial, economic, and strategic interests after independence.

Algerian War of Independence, 1954 to 1962

Algeria represented postwar decolonization's bloody climax, claiming 700,000 lives from 1954 to 1962. This mayhem's root lay in incompatible European immigrant and indigenous Muslim dreams for Algeria's future. France identified Algeria not as a colony, but as a *department du France*. Just under a million *Pieds-Noirs* inhabited Algeria, making independence unthinkable to French politicians of all stripes. However, Algeria's six million Muslims had grown increasingly frustrated with colonial discrimination, the lack of meaningful reform, and deteriorating living conditions. Those living in rural areas were particularly hard pressed given the region's arid ecology and European monopolization of the most fertile land. Several liberal postwar French administrators tried to improve Algerian living conditions, but their reforms were consistently stunted by the *Pieds-Noirs*. By the early 1950s, Algerian discontent intensified, but the colonial opposition remained divided along class and ethnic lines. This changed in 1954 when the FLN issued a radio proclamation calling for the "restoration of the Algerian state."[8] Subsequent attacks on French installations inside Algeria put teeth into their declaration. Although FLN attacks were small in scale at first, during the 1955 **Philippeville Massacre**, the FLN slaughtered and raped scores of French civilians. This event provoked a brutal retaliation that removed any prospect of reconciliation between Muslims and European settlers. It also pushed various Algerian opposition groups to rally around the FLN. After Philippeville, the Algerian War intensified and degenerated into savagery. FLN guerillas specialized in ambushing and slitting the throats of unsuspecting French soldiers. This *sourire rouge* intimidated conscripts and horrified anxious mothers on the home front. The French army responded with systematic torture, summary executions, and reprisal attacks against civilians. French strong-arm tactics represented a desperate attempt to break a stubborn guerilla movement that was meticulously organized into independent cells and supported by an increasingly hostile Algerian population.

France's Unceremonious Exit, 1957 to 1962

At the height of the struggle, over half a million French troops were deployed inside Algeria. This burden precipitated France to concede independence to political moderates in neighboring Morocco and Tunisia. French hardliners hoped that strategic redeployment would enable them to intensify their suppression of the FLN. During the 1956 to 1957 **Battle of Algiers**, French commander Jacques Massu locked down the capital to uproot local FLN cells. The French Army judged the operation a tactical success, but its human toll provoked a political crisis in France. In June 1958, the Fourth Republic collapsed. Charles de Gaulle returned to power once more to set national affairs in order. Although de Gaulle had assured the public he would not surrender Algeria, he quickly concluded the war did not justify its cost. Gaulle nudged the French public towards accepting a political settlement. In 1960, disconcerted *Pieds-Noirs* protested by constructing barricades in Algiers, but Paris roughly broke up their demonstration. Subsequently, a 1961 French referendum revealed overwhelming support for Algerian independence, briefly provoking a French army conspiracy targeting De Gaulle for assassination. By 1962, after six years of heavy fighting, Algeria at last achieved independence. About 800,000 *Pieds-Noirs* fled to Southern France, but over 50,000 off their Algerian collaborators were executed by the FLN after being denied refuge among their former allies.

Nkrumah and Ghana

As the Algerian War intensified, Ghana provided the world a shining model for peaceful postcolonial transition. **Kwame Nkrumah** had spent a decade and a half in Britain and the United States, where he had received an education, briefly taught, and mixed with an eclectic group of radicals, Marxists, and anti-colonial organizers. In 1947, Nkrumah was invited back to the Gold Coast by an elite local political group to lead their campaign for independence. Nkrumah quickly revealed himself an able organizer, mobilizing local cocoa farmers into a potent coalition, challenging women to participate in the electoral process and rapidly building up a national movement opposed to British rule. In 1948, following a riot in the colonial capital of Accra, British authorities arrested Nkrumah on trumped up charges, only to discover that strong-armed tactics had lost their intimidating effect. In 1950, Britain changed tack and reluctantly conceded to national elections to stave off intensifying demonstrations. From his jail cell in 1951, Kwame Nkrumah won an overwhelming majority of the vote, precipitating his release from prison. The following day, Nkrumah was summoned before the British Governor. **Charles Arden-Clarke** tasked Nkrumah with establishing a new government on the basis of the colonial constitution Nkrumah had earlier disparaged. Nkrumah quickly developed a rapport with Arden-Clarke. This culminated in a close partnership that supported the Gold Coast's peaceful transition to full independence. Officially, Nkrumah served as "leader of government business," but after 1952 when Arden-Clarke withdrew from the cabinet, making Nkrumah *de facto* prime minister. Subsequently, Arden-Clarke progressively handed over the reins of state to Nkrumah, while his supporters apprenticed under British bureaucrats. In 1957, Nkrumah declared the Gold Coast's formal independence in a public ceremony where the Union Jack was symbolically lowered. Afterwards, Arden-Clarke warmly congratulated his friend as the new head of state of "Ghana," a name Nkrumah had chosen to memorialize a long-extinct kingdom. This marked a calculated bid to stimulate national pride inside a state where citizens mostly shared the same language, but were also complexly partitioned among diverse ethnic, regional, and tribal groupings.

Ghana's independence proved to be a rolling stone. Its symbolism inspired nationalists throughout the rest of Sub-Saharan Africa still languishing under colonial rule. Britain's peaceful concession of independence put pressure on France, Portugal, and Belgium to adopt more progressive policies. Nkrumah also pushed decolonization along. In December 1958, Nkrumah hosted the **All African People's Conference** in Accra inviting delegates from across Africa to discuss the continent's future. Indigenous nationalists spoke mostly English and French as they discussed colonial injustices and the prospect for independence. Delegates eclectically invoked Marx, the US Declaration of Independence, and Black Power principles. Their final declaration did not mince words. Delegates demanded an immediate "unconditional accession to independence of all the African peoples, and the total evacuation of the foreign forces of aggression and oppression stationed in Africa."[9] The Accra Conference spread nationalist sentiment across the continent. Delegates like **Patrice Lumumba** returned home and immediately launched campaigns of civil disobedience that rocked the unstable moorings of Africa's colonial states. Town dwellers in particular rallied behind national independence movements that united diverse ethnic groups in opposition against a hated external oppressor.

The year 1960 marked decolonization's high tide as sixteen African states secured independence. Over the next half-decade, most of the empires Europeans had built in Africa had disappeared. The collapse of France's Fourth Republic in 1958 had led to De Gaulle to abolish the French Union. The newly proposed "French Community" offered Africans a better deal: they could opt to remain inside the French Empire and enjoy access to French investment, or they could choose independence, in which case France would withdraw all support. De Gaulle was quite confident that Africans would accept this bargain, but Guinea's Sékou Touré opted "non" on the basis of principle. A bitter de Gaulle ordered the removal of all French property from Guinea. Zealous French lieutenants ripped telephones from the walls and ships bound for

Guinea returned to port. Despite French intimidation, Touré's peers soon followed his example. A similar dynamic triggered rapid independence in British East Africa, as designs for biracial constitutions collapsed in a rising tide of indigenous nationalism. By 1966, Sub-Saharan Africa was largely free of colonial rule except for its Southern Tier. There, the Portuguese colonies of Angola and Mozambique, as well as British settler colonies of Rhodesia, Namibia, and South Africa, remained under the rule of white minorities. Within two decades, however, these last colonial outposts also collapsed under the pressure of black guerrilla movement. Decolonization's capstone in Africa arrived with the final dissolution of South Africa's **Apartheid** regime in the free election of 1994 that brought Nelson Mandela to power.

Quest for National Development, 1960 to 1975

Exuberant national celebrations underscored high hopes for an independence dividend. Surely by casting out foreign exploiters, indigenous resources could finally be directed towards uplifting formerly colonized peoples from poverty? Kwame Nkrumah headlined an ambitious group of postcolonial leaders determined to "catch up" to the West as quickly as possible. In 1963, Nkrumah confidently proclaimed: "We have here, in Africa, everything necessary to a become a powerful, modern, industrialized continent."[10] Postcolonial African leaders were encouraged by Western experts to "modernize" in order to improve indigenous living standards. **Modernization theory** maintained that postcolonial states needed to follow the European historical example by shuttling inefficient farmers towards urban factories. This would elevate national productivity and trigger economic takeoff. Decades of high growth would then enable postcolonial states to catch up to the West.

The Modernization Model

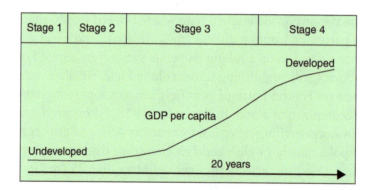

Colonial Economy	Development Plan	Takeoff Stage	Fully Developed
Traditional society, non-entrepreneurial culture, undiversified export economy, primitive technology	Invest in heavy machinery, literacy, and infrastructure to stimulate industrialization	Industrialization stimulates manufacturing, raises wages, attracts rural workers, and stimulates high growth until growth slows as modern society emerges	Urbanized, industrial economy, with large middle class and high standard of living

The idea of modernization anchored development policies pursued by postcolonial leaders around the world. The central premise was to step up state investment in industrialization to ignite economic liftoff.

The big question during the 1960s was not whether modernization worked, but how to catalyze industrialization. In an influential 1949 paper, Argentine economist **Raúl Prebisch** argued that to break the ties of dependency, postcolonial states needed to adopt import substitution polices to protect fragile indigenous economies from more efficient Western competitors. High tariffs on Western manufactured goods, combined with subsidies for indigenous entrepreneurs, would stimulate a virtuous cycle of industrial expansion, economic diversification, and transition the workforce from low-skill agriculture to high-wage factory employment. Many newly independent states adopted a similar modernization strategy. As we shall see in subsequent chapters, Latin American corporatism, African socialism, and Nasserism resembled each other in tasking the state with replacing foreign investors as the principal driver of the national economy. "Socialism" denoted not a program for leveling internal class differences than catching up to the West. Socialism also meant expanding the focus of development from infrastructure to social projects like building schools and hospitals.

Postcolonial Socialism in World Regional Perspective

Middle East	Latin America	Africa	Asia
Arab Socialism	ISI Corporatism	African Socialism	State Socialism
Use radio to mobilize Arabs to drive out imperialists, buy arms to strengthen army and modernize economy by importing western technology, promoting land reform and expanding literacy.	Cut dependency by adopting tariffs to stimulate native industries, diversify economy and raise wages, while expanding state safety net to protect unshirted ones.	Use state to modernize economy, cultivate sense of nation, attract foreign capital to catch up to West and invest in schools, and hospitals to improve indigenous standard of living	Promote land reform, mobilize people through propaganda, use state to enforce harmony and channel capital towards industrialization to catch up to West.

Nkrumah's Development Program

Upon first assuming office in February 1951, **Kwame Nkrumah** alleviated Western concerns about his "radical" past and previous associations with Marxists by declaring his intention to seek dominion status inside the British Commonwealth following independence. Like many of his compatriots, Nkrumah was conflicted about Ghana's path forward. He struggled to accommodate his abhorrence for racism and colonial exploitation with his need for Western investment and projecting the image of respectable head of state during an age of volatile superpower politics. Philosophically, Nkrumah rejected "capitalism" as a colonial mode of development that was fundamentally exploitive and alien to Africa's supposedly egalitarian traditions. Instead, Nkrumah embraced **African Socialism** as an authentic model for development. For many of Nkrumah's peers, "socialism" did not necessarily signify formal allegiance to Moscow. At its core, African "socialism" represented a progressive program for casting off imperialism, catching up to the West and elevating indigenous living standards.

Ideological flexibility was evident in Nkrumah's partnership with Western bankers and foreign corporations to mine gold, process bauxite, and purchase machinery. Initially, Nkrumah benefited from a windfall precipitated by a surge in cocoa prices, Ghana's principal export. This enabled Nkrumah to expand forestry, fishing, and cattle production, while also building schools, roads, and hospitals. By 1958, Ghana's combination of economic growth, expanding social services, and seeming tranquility established Nkrumah as an international role model. The **Volta River Project**, however, represented his dream for a more prosperous future.

> Why were dams so popular at the World Bank and among postcolonial leaders? Why did so many fail to stimulate anticipated industrialization even when meeting their technical benchmarks?

Construction of the Akosombo Dam served as the centerpiece for a national development strategy that would divert irrigation water to expand agriculture and generate electricity to power towns and factories. When Britain declined to fund the project, Nkrumah turned to the United States. With Khrushchev challenging Western support for colonial oppression, the United States was eager to cultivate a charismatic "Third World" client with a record of Western collaboration. Eisenhower connected Nkrumah's government to Kaiser Aluminum. The company sponsored Ghana's loan for the Akosombo Dam after Kaiser agreed to build a smelter in return for buying future electricity at subsidized rates.

Nkrumah's Downfall

Following the **Congo Crisis**, Nkrumah grew disillusioned with the West. Nkrumah resented US implication in the fall of his kindred spirit Patrice Lumumba. As Nkrumah's relations with the West soured, he travelled to Moscow in 1961 and concluded agreements on trade, economic development, and technical cooperation. This irritated Washington, DC, increasingly concerned with expanding Soviet influence in Sub-Saharan Africa. Nkrumah's ultimate undoing, however, was his failure to set Ghana on a sound economic footing. Nkrumah wasted profligate sums on monuments to himself, elaborate national festivals, and expensive foreign machinery that proved ill-suited for Ghana's economy. The resulting debt overhang forced Nkrumah to cut back on social programs. As Ghana's economy faltered, Nkrumah's popularity plummeted. He responded with increasing levels of despotism, curtailing trade union activity, banning rival political parties, and arbitrarily imprisoning opponents.

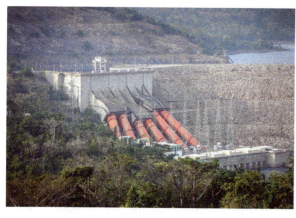 

In 1966, Kwame Nkrumah unveiled the Akosombo Dam as potent symbol of Ghana's coming of age. Big infrastructural projects, even when achieving their technical benchmarks, proved incapable of catalyzing the anticipated industrialization or realizing the promise of uplift the masses from poverty.

By 1964, Nkrumah's palace guard and security apparatus usurped the national police, while Nkrumah proclaimed himself dictator for life and built statues to his honor throughout Ghana. In 1966, Nkrumah celebrated completion of the Volta project in a lavish state ceremony, but during a state visit to Vietnam a month later, an army coup swept the unpopular dictator and former hero of African nationalism from power.

Window on World History: Postwar Decolonization and Canada's Coming of Age

World War II helped Canadians to separate psychologically from the British Empire, while drawing them closer to the United States as bilateral partners in hemispheric defense. As neighbor, ally, and leading trading partner, Canada was deeply impacted by the United States' postwar evolution into a global superpower with a self-defined mission to defend the "free world." Postwar Canadian leaders were united in their belief that their national security depended upon close collaboration with its Atlantic partners and traditional allies. At the same time, more intimate ties with the United States raised concerns about Canada's future independence. The increasingly imperial tack of US foreign policy during the Cold War, and its unsavory embrace of Third World dictators, also discomfited many Canadians. Canada's ambivalent postwar embrace of the United States climaxed during decolonization. As non-Western peoples cast off the imperial yoke, Canadians identified this struggle with their own experience. Some Canadian statesmen exploited decolonization as a golden opportunity to transform their country's international role and image. As a former colony and stable multiethnic democracy, Canada could advocate both for decolonization and the rule of law. During the Vietnam War, Canadian leaders increasingly contrasted their principled foreign policy with that of United States' heavy-handed crusade against communism. Domestic politics encouraged Canadian leaders to make such distinctions, particularly in terms of Canada more collaboratively engagement the non-Western world. This was not purely rhetoric. During the 1950s, Canada rallied former British dominions and European middle powers to champion a more multilateral approach to international security through the UN. Lester Pearson as Secretary of State for Foreign Affairs played an influential role, for example, in carving out a peacekeeping role for the UN during the 1956 Suez Crisis. Peacekeeping enabled the UN to recapture its role as an international facilitator for peace following the Cold War deadlock in the Security Council. Peacekeeping restored the UN's humanitarian purpose, especially after postcolonial states transformed the General Assembly into a rowdy forum for condemning Western imperialism and racism. By the 1970s, Canadian identity became firmly entrenched in a national self-image as a benevolent middle power. Canadian statesmen and diplomats became masters of quiet diplomacy, often subtly criticizing their southern neighbor, while trumpeting Canadian pragmatism and fair play. Canadians also indulged in a national self-image as moderators of US bellicosity. A 1987 national poll revealed that 80 percent of Canadians believed that the best thing about their country was its global generosity, despite the fact that Canadians donated less per capita than most of its Organisation for Economic Co-operation and Development (OECD) allies. Non-Western nationalists like Indonesia's Sukarno rudely dismissed the idea of Canada as some role model for postcolonial states, while the United States grew accustomed to an irritating Canadian tendency to assert independence on symbolic issues before state visits. The myth of the Canadian way, however, played well domestically. For example, Pierre Elliot Trudeau's public embrace of Fidel Castro, and open criticism of the United States,

(Continued)

briefly rattled bilateral relations, but helped him to garnered support from both Anglo-Canadians and Quebeckers increasingly united in their opposition to an unpopular Vietnam War.

Critical Reflection

1. What are some recent examples of Canada's collaborative role in the international arena and the UN?
2. In your view, did the idea of the "Canadian Way" contribute to a more multilateral approach to international relations during the 1970s, or was this primarily a myth to facilitate the development of a unique Canadian identity apart from the Britain and the United States?

Nkrumah blamed his fall on Central Intelligence Agency (CIA) intrigues. This conveniently ignored how most of his former compatriots cheered his ouster. While Nkrumah was a great orator and visionary leader, he proved a less apt politician and a horrible economic manager. Nkrumah's early successes had been predicated on rising cocoa prices and Western loans, but his development policies failed to set Ghana's economy on a path towards sustainable growth. Consequently, Nkrumah left the wealthiest state in West Africa deeply in debt and politically fractured. In exile, Nkrumah penned *Neocolonialism: The Last Stage of Imperialism*, where he lamented how the liberation movement he had championed failed to free Africans from monopoly capitalism. Newly emergent African states were not fully sovereign because they continued to operate inside an international system dominated by Western economies and foreign multinational corporations. Rather than dominating Africa directly, the West imposed a **neocolonial** structure that constrained African states through loans and debt. Many postcolonial leaders would echo these sentiments in later years, but in his final fall from grace Nkrumah also foreshadowed another postcolonial African trend: despotism. The fragility of Africa's postcolonial states and their economic underdevelopment presented a difficult obstacle for even the ablest postcolonial leaders to overcome.

Lumumba and the Congo Crisis, 1960 to 1965

After 1960, the Cold War increasingly impinged upon postcolonial aspirations for development. This dynamic is best illustrated in the Congo. Despite nationalist rumblings in French North Africa and British West Africa, to Belgian officials, independence seemed a long way off. Indigenous graduates of mission schools met informally in Alumni circles or urban clubs, where discussion invariably turned towards the independence question. To Belgian eyes, however, Congolese politics remained local and rooted in ethnically affiliated parties, which ensured Belgium's continued role as an indispensable arbitrator.

The Congo's outward tranquility, however, proved deceptive. The Congolese had not forgotten Belgium's bloody colonial rule, nor were they oblivious to the colonial state's discriminatory policies. The independence of Ghana in 1957 transformed the African mindset from desiring independence towards mobilization to achieve it. In 1958, Lumumba, freshly returned from the Accra Conference, quickly built up a national organization that exposed the fragility of Belgian rule. In January 1959, riots swept through the Congolese capital of Léopoldville. Africans smashed Belgian storefronts, heckled white ladies, and invaded the homes of settlers. Although the scope of violence was relatively modest at first, unrest soon spilled over into neighboring districts, particularly into the Kasai province where long-standing ethnic tensions boiled over into ugly bouts of communal violence. The Belgian authorities tried to crack down on "subversives," but the **Force Publique**, a military force comprised by African soldiers commanded by white Belgian officers, struggled to maintain order.

In 1960, Belgium realized that their colonial regime was disintegrating. Hurriedly, they convened the **Brussels Roundtable** to negotiate a political settlement with a coalition of black nationalists. Belgium agreed to transfer power, wary of becoming embroiled in a bloody civil war. Following Congo-wide elections, Belgium promised to transfer sovereignty to a new African government in June 1960. This rapid transfer left little time for indigenous political organization, or the formation of national parties capable of transcending the Congo's patchwork of regional and ethnic affiliations. National elections confirmed the Congo's sharp polarization. Only Lumumba's *Mouvement National Congolais* claimed something of a national base by winning 23 percent of the vote. Uniting the country would prove a daunting task, but Lumumba's coalition had run on a platform of establishing a strong central state that would channel the country's substantial resources to the benefit of all. The Belgians regarded the charismatic Patrice Lumumba as a dangerous radical. His fiery condemnation of historic injustices and racism, as well as his ambitious schemes for national development, represented a threat to Belgium's postcolonial economic interests inside the Congo. Accordingly, Brussels threw their support behind the more pliable **Joseph Kasa-vubu** of the Bakongo, who had received the third most votes during the recent election. Reluctantly, Lumumba agreed to a power-sharing arrangement where Kasa-vubu served as president, while appointing Lumumba as prime minister tasked with running the independent Congo's government.

No postcolonial African leader better captured the idealistic desire to develop their homeland than the Congo's Patrice Lumumba. Lumumba's dream for a strong, united, and free Congo, however, clashed with the interests of Belgian investors and statesmen, contributing to his sudden downfall.

Postindependence Disintegration

The Democratic Republic of the Congo got off to a rocky start during the June 1960 independence ceremony. After King Baudouin had the temerity to suggest that the "genius" of his illustrious granduncle had dreamed up the Congo as a 'civilizing' project, Lumumba took the stage. Although not slated to speak, Lumumba shredded Baudouin's whitewashing of the Congo's blood-stained colonial past. He reminded the stunned monarch that "no Congolese will ever forget that independence was won in struggle, a persevering and inspired struggle carried on from day to day, a struggle, in which we were undaunted by privation or suffering and stinted neither strength nor blood."[11]

> Was Lumumba wise to challenge the Belgian King's whitewashing of the Congo's brutal colonial history? Would remaining silent equate to accepting some form of neocolonialism?

A visibly shaken Baudouin offered no retort, but Lumumba's harsh criticism sealed Brussels' determination to undermine his regime.

Less than a week after being installed in office, Lumumba faced a crisis when soldiers of the *Force Publique* protested their lack of promotion and rebelled against their white commanders. Mutinous soldiers roved through Léopoldville robbing, raping, and killing several white settlers. As mutiny spread across the Congo, it intersected with intensifying communal violence between ethnic groups. Terrorized white settlers called for Belgian intervention. When Lumumba struggled to restore order, Belgium rushed in paratroopers to protect their citizens despite Lumumba's vociferous protests against this infringement of Congolese sovereignty. The **Congo Crisis** escalated on July 11, when a disgruntled local politician, **Moïse Tshombe**, excluded from Lumumba's unity government, announced the secession of the mineral rich Katanga province that contained 70 percent of the Congo's national wealth. Tshombe's bid for independence enjoyed some local support, but his regime was staffed with Belgian advisors and protected by white mercenaries. Lumumba angrily accused Tshombe, Belgium, and the powerful multinational concern Union Minière with conspiring against his regime.

Using his considerable political skill, Lumumba managed to quell the mutiny in his army, but he lacked the heavy weapons necessary to pacify ethnic violence or to reincorporate the breakaway Katanga province. This led Lumumba to appeal to the United States for assistance. When Lumumba's call for military aid was ignored, Lumumba turned to the UN. Ultimately, the Security Council approved a peacekeeping operation, but Secretary General Dag Hammarskjöld consistently refused Lumumba's pleas to use UN troops to disarm the breakaway Katanga province. In frustration, Lumumba turned to the Soviets for help in August 1960. Khrushchev was only too happy to profit from the Congo Crisis. He rushed in arms and advisors to his new client in the heart of Africa setting off alarm bells in Washington, DC. Never before had the USSR intervened militarily in a conflict beyond their immediate borders. Soviet aid confirmed the assessment of US hardliners that Lumumba's administration was riddled with communists. The Eisenhower administration feared that the Congo Crisis would spill over the entire region. To calm tensions, the CIA was tasked with assassinating Lumumba, while the West

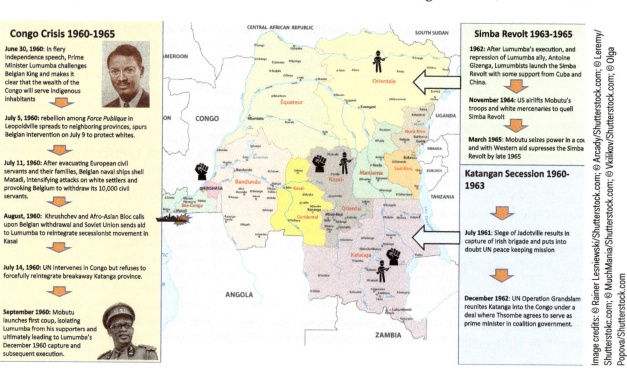

The Congo Crisis featured three distinctive phases: the breakdown of law and order in 1960, the secession of the Katanga that lasted until 1963, and the abortive Simba Revolt that flared among former Lumumba supporters in late 1963.

pressured Kasa-vubu to remove his troublesome prime minister. Kasa-vubu needed little urging. He had grown disillusioned with Lumumba ever since his incendiary speech at the independence ceremony. Kasa-vubu blamed Lumumba for igniting the Congo Crisis, unnecessarily antagonizing the West, and pushing the country into a civil war. On September 5, Kasa-vubu dismissed Lumumba. Lumumba refused to vacate. Instead, he rallied parliament against Kasa-vubu. Paralysis in Léopoldville mirrored the increasing disintegration of Congolese society outside the capital.

Vanished Dream

By late 1960, the Congo had become embroiled in a low-intensity civil war while Lumumba's position in the capital became untenable. Lumumba decided to flee to his supporters in his native Stanleyville, but he was captured by Colonel **Joseph Désiré Mobutu**, a CIA asset and the Congo's emerging strongman. Lumumba had promoted Mobutu, but he now turned his boss over to his archenemy, Katangan separatist Moïse Tshombe and certain death. In January 1961, Tshombe's henchmen relentlessly beat and killed the Congo's first prime minister. Lumumba's death foreclosed on any hope for a strong, united, and prosperous Congo for the immediate future.

> To what extent did the Cold War subvert non-Western dreams for independence? Were postcolonial states really sovereign or were their policy options constrained by the Cold War?

In 1963, the UN managed to reincorporate the Katanga into the Congo by inviting Tshombe into a new unity government. By 1964, order was sufficiently restored that the last UN troops departed the Congo. Subsequently, Mobutu ousted both Kasa-vubu and Tshombe and installed himself as dictator. Mobutu used brutal force to quash dissent while mobilizing state propaganda to glorify his leadership. Resistance to Mobutu simmered for several years in part fueled by a rebellion led by Lumumba's former supporters. Western military aid, economic assistance, and foreign mercenaries, however, helped Mobutu to consolidate his rule.

Postcolonial Challenges, 1973 to 1982

By 1969, the world economy started to slow. This brought into focus that few postcolonial states had realized their dream of catching up to the West. In fact, slumping commodity prices left many postcolonial states straddled with insurmountable debt that forced cutbacks. Overly optimistic expectations about development amplified disappointment. Import substitution represented a common thread uniting most programs for postcolonial development. In different ways they invoked the **modernization model** that laid out a flawed plan for national development. For one thing, many first-generation leaders assumed power in the wake of imperial collapse. They inherited weak state institutions, their infrastructure was underdeveloped and they suffered from a chronic lack of qualified indigenous personnel. Many postcolonial states lacked a deep sense of national feeling and often first-generation leaders struggled to transcend deep-rooted class, ethnic or religious divisions that had been cynically cultivated by the colonial state. Orchestrating development from this context represented a more difficult task that many first-generation leaders and Western experts anticipated. It also called for management skills that many first-generation leaders lacked. Many were charismatic speakers that had matured inside a climate of mobilizing their people against colonial oppression. These skills did not always translate into effective economic management or dealing with international lending institutions. More fundamentally, modernization was flawed in disregarding how historically Western industrialization had benefitted from colonial exploitation. Industries built out in the postcolonial world emerged in an environment where they needed to compete against established and better capitalized Western firms that already had proprietary technology and developed market outlets.

Slowdown in the world economy and postcolonial austerity seeded a backlash during the late 1960s that seeded various types of internal conflict. On a global scale, political violence revealed some broader regional patterns. In Sub-Saharan Africa, military coups, often led by junior officers trained in colonial military academies, and often enjoying some foreign backing, swept away first-generation leaders and parliamentary structures of government. By the 1970s, Sub-Saharan Africa was awash in autocratic regimes that often mobilized the state and the army against internal opponents and rival ethnic groups. Long-serving dictators like Mobutu transformed the army into a bludgeon directed against its own citizens while transforming the state into a vehicle for personal enrichment. **Kleptocracy**, or government by thieves, became a common ailment among regimes, irrespective of whether they were led by revolutionary socialists or anti-communist officers. Corruption, arbitrary rule, and ineffective state power sowed low-intensity civil war, recurrent coups, and rapid decay of national infrastructure.

Latin American states had a longer national history, but the fissures between rich and poor, creoles and indigenous peoples, European immigrants and racial minorities had remained profound. This divide was only superficially bridged by urbanization and industrialization before World War II. Postwar corporative regimes and populist leaders like Juan Peron mobilized the urban working classes, but failed to unite citizens into shared vision of the state or a common dream of the nation. When the global economy slowed during the late 1960s, it disproportionally hit the working poor and amplified older class divisions into a deeper political polarization between the authoritarian right and populist left. By the late 1960s, military junta overthrew constitutional regimes, declared martial law, and often launched **dirty wars** that targeted their leftist opponents as "communists."

Inside the Middle East, the modernizing state proved initially more successful in rallying citizens and ethnic minorities around a common dream of national unity and secular modernization, but when Arab socialist policies failed to raise living standards, and Arab armies were battered and humiliated by Israel after the Six-Day War, popular disgruntlement set in. Islamists increasingly mobilized in opposition against secular nationalists entrenched in a **deep state** where military elites held power by doctoring elections, while offering low-paying public service jobs for the middle classes and food and fuel subsidies for the poor. By the 1970s, secular Arab leaders increasingly mouthed Islamic platitudes and offered some concessions to the poor, while building up a security apparatus to quiet dissidents, minorities, and Islamic activists.

Most of Southeast Asia had reached independence by 1949 in a collective struggle that united people of diverse ethnic groups and sectarian communities against foreign imperialism. This long struggle helped divergent ethnic and religious groups to develop a deeper sense of nation, but postcolonial independence quickly became ensnared in China and the US's battle for hearts and minds. Deadly proxy wars in Korea, Vietnam, and other states inspired the formation of authoritarian states on both sides of the **Bamboo Curtain**. Despite divergent alignment in the Cold War, postcolonial states pursued broadly similar programs of land reform, articulated an ideology of national solidarity, and invested in education and welfare measures. With abatement of the Sino-US rivalry after 1971, a second chapter of nation-building commenced. Freed from the Cold War, many regional states implemented an export industrialization strategy that culminated in robust growth, rising wages, and accelerating urbanization.

A regional survey of the postcolonial world reveals that one obstacle to postcolonial development was the weakness of inherited colonial institutions and an absence of national feeling. Often first-generation leaders articulated nation-building discourses and promised social development policies to benefit all citizens, regardless of their ethnic, religious, and linguistic affiliations. Particularly in Africa, postcolonial leaders struggled because of the relative absence of infrastructure to unite diverse regions and weaker state institutions where white bureaucrats had managed essential department while delegating local authority to indigenous chiefs. This structure, and the rapid process of colonial collapse, resulted in national coalitions with only a superficial sense of collective identity and residual animosities among various ethnic, confessional, and tribal groups. First-generation leaders like Lumumba and Nkrumah had little margin for rallying their people around their progressive programs for national development. One strategy non-Western leaders adopted was framing postcolonial reform as a continuing project for anti-colonial state building. In 1967, Mobutu, for example, introduced the *N'sele* manifesto that combined revolutionary politics with a program for economic modernization. Following Nkrumah's example, Mobutu's "authenticity" program renamed the Congo "Zaire," rechristened cities with African names, and banned Western dress. Most Congolese, however, saw Mobutu's authenticity campaign as a thinly disguised scheme to glorify the "Father of the Nation," who was actually impoverishing them. Mobutu's experiment, however, exemplified a broader struggle to legitimate postcolonial regimes. Most first-generation leaders inherited the prestige of having led their people to freedom. Often their popularity plummeted when modernization programs and promises for a better life fell short. African development policies often straddled a contradiction, affirming African values and traditions, while seeking foreign technology and Western aid to modernize. Given that most first-generation leaders were Western educated liberals, many presumed that Africa needed to follow Europe's pathway to industrialization. Postcolonial states, however, were seeking to catch up inside a two-tiered global economy where Western multinationals already possessed a near monopoly on capital, proprietary technology, highly skilled workers, and established distribution channels. Import substitution policies did stimulate local manufacturing, but indigenous firms were often grossly inefficient. Subsidies gave indigenous entrepreneurs an edge in local markets, but they could not compete in foreign markets against Western corporations already transitioning to more sophisticated products and more efficient mechanized assembly lines. Only in Mexico, Argentina, and Brazil, where a substantial internal market already existed, did import substitution policies enjoy a partial success. More often, postcolonial leaders invested billions in outdated equipment, old technologies, and "white elephant" infrastructure projects that failed stimulate growth, much less generate a return on capital. These modernization policies often promoted by Western experts, international bankers, and foreign multinationals did trap postcolonial states in an unbearable burden of debt once the global economy cooled in the early 1970s and the price for most commodities slackened.

The postcolonial context incentivized the modernization model. Postcolonial leaders sought to legitimate their rule by unveiling signature development projects like dams and airports that symbolized national progress. The global postwar economic boom of the early 1960s seemed to make modernization achievable. Rising commodity prices encouraged postcolonial leaders to borrow money for investments they were assured would pay off. Accordingly, throughout the 1960s, construction teams whirled around postcolonial capitals building highways, bridges, airports, and power plants. Initially, state investment did spur dramatic gains in literacy, public health, and longevity. By the late 1960s, however, it was growing painfully apparent that state-driven industrialization schemes were not sufficiently raising wages. As postcolonial economies stalled, some leaders blamed the Cold War, foreign corporations, or internal enemies. The more painful truth was that modernization was not a viable development strategy and that state investment had often been mismanaged or diverted to private pockets.

By the late 1960s, **nationalization** emerged as an increasingly popular development strategy. Leftist reformers proposed to take over foreign or white-owned factories, plantations, businesses, and mines, and put them to the service of the common good. Over the short term, nationalization rewarded political supporters, but seizure of property without fair market compensation also carried risk. The United States, the former colonial powers, and foreign corporations retaliated against revolutionary regimes with embargoes, capital flight, and clandestine subversion. Often indigenous entrepreneurs or state managers running confiscated enterprises lacked the acumen to manage complex enterprises. In Uganda, Amin's cronies treated the businesses confiscated from Asian citizens in 1972 as their personal booty. They quickly ran them into ground, stimulating a food shortage and public health crisis that victimized Africans.

Nationalization schemes did not always fail. As we shall see in Chapter 7, **Muammar al-Qaddafi** proved quite successful in gradually squeezing out foreign oil companies and channeling windfall profits towards social development programs. Other Persian Gulf states similarly nationalized their oil during the 1970s. For many non-Western leaders, like Salvador Allende in Chile, nationalization resulted in the overthrow of their revolutionary regime and restoration of property to their former owners.

Tyranny of Debt

A principal impediment to postcolonial development was lack of investment capital. During the 1950s, the World Bank (International Bank for Reconstruction and Development [IBRD]) emerged as the principal financier for developing states. The World Bank sold bonds on Western markets at low interest rates and made this capital available to the developing states in the form of long-term loans. Although the Soviet Union nurtured several client states, their assistance often remained limited to barter deals, lending technical assistance and selling military hardware. For capital intensive projects, newly independent states were often forced to turn West, embracing foreign investors, commercial banks, bilateral aid agencies, and the World Bank. Private loans, however, invariably carried higher, often variable, rates of interest that could balloon in cost if international financial conditions shifted. While the World Bank served as an important source for capital, to retain their credit rating, the institution scrupulously avoided investment in "social development" projects like schools and hospitals, in favor of big infrastructure projects that could return the cost of capital. Hydroelectric dams proved particularly popular. Such projects offered a holy grail of cheap electricity, flood control, and irrigation critical ingredients for stimulating modernization. For "social development," postcolonial states needed to turn to foreign donors and their own treasuries. Often this meant reconstituting colonial era marketing boards that forced indigenous farmers and exporters to sell their produce to the state at below market prices. Although such policies provided the state with an influx of capital, over the longer run such policies disincentivized production, increased foreign dependence, and undermined the poor's food security. Although funds provided by bilateral aid and international charities helped to alleviate some of the worst aspects of poverty, and helped to suppress contagious diseases like polio, measles, and tuberculosis, it proved grossly inadequate to overcoming the chronic underdevelopment of postcolonial economies.

Green Revolution

As postcolonial industrialization schemes stalled during the late 1960s, state planners increasingly turned to the countryside, attracted by Western methods for industrial agriculture. After World War II, an evangelical American agronomist, Norman Borlaug, installed himself in Mexico determined to help local farmers escape starvation. Borlaug's mission was to adapt Western farming methods to fit Mexico's more arid climate and marginal soils. Borlaug saw poverty everywhere. The principal culprit was "rust" disease. This weakened the wheat stalk and ate away the germ. The Rockefeller Foundation sponsored Borlaug's research as he poured relentless energy into developing a high-yielding strain adapted to Mexico's Sonoran drylands. Borlaug's critical breakthrough came when he crossbred a Japanese strain of "Dwarf Wheat" to create a hybrid that could resist regional wind gusts. The new wheat strains delivered astonishing results. By 1956, Mexico became self-sufficient in wheat, before evolving into a major exporter.

During the 1960s, the US Department of Agriculture embraced Borlaug's model to launch a **Green Revolution**. With postcolonial industrialization showing modest results, development experts tried to make the deserts bloom. The World Bank helped to expand Borlaug's model to other cereal crops. In absolute terms, the Green Revolution proved an indisputable success. In Pakistan and India, for example, wheat production jumped from five and eight million tons in 1965, to twelve and twenty million tons, respectively, in 1970. After 1970, the Green Revolution was applied to other areas of Latin America and Africa as scientists developed new strains of high-yielding rice, maize, cotton, and other cash crops.

One irony of the Green Revolution is that it often exacerbated rural poverty. Modern agriculture is capital intensive, but most non-Western farmers were small holders lacking the capital to purchase modern machinery, fertilizers, and pesticides necessary to achieving high yields. Even in places where progressive government policies provided small farmers credit to buy "miracle" seeds, the lack of irrigation and pesticides left them vulnerable to debt, draught, and crop diseases. Accordingly, established rural elites proved the Green Revolution's principal beneficiaries, often expanding their holdings at the expense of failing small farms.

Throughout the non-Western world, failed schemes for rural development stimulated a migration wave to regional cities. In slums, like favela Cantagalo depicted here, families often live in one-room shelters lacking running water, sewer, sometimes even electricity service.

Rural Insecurity and Developing World Urbanization

In the non-Western world, state schemes for modernization and commercial agriculture combined to sow rural insecurity. This in turn spurred urban migration. The developing world experienced explosive urbanization from 1950 to 1970, often tightly concentrated in state capitals or the largest cities. Cairo, Mexico City, Istanbul, and Mumbai led the charge of the **megacities**, numbering over five million inhabitants. Most migrants were escaping rural poverty, but the majority did not come from the poorest segment of society. Urban migrants often sought economic opportunities and the amenities offered by bustling capital cities relatively flush with foreign capital and government largesse.

Given that the majority of migrants were poor, however, they often squatted on public land, constructing dwellings from whatever materials they could muster. Throughout the developing world, vast shanty towns formed around older city cores. In the slums of Calcutta, Tehran, or Rio de Janeiro, it often proved difficult to distinguish a bankrupt farmer, environmental refugee, unemployed farm hand, or victim of political violence. Most slums lacked sewage treatment, water service, and at first—electricity. For elites and the middle classes inhabiting carefully landscaped neighborhoods, the slums of Nairobi or the sprawling *favelas* of Rio de Janeiro represented lawless areas that decent folk, even the police, avoided. The image of slums as squalid, crime-ridden warrens of rickety shanties and dark alleys, however, represents a stereotype. Housing in megacities tended to improve as slum dwellers secured better jobs and transformed their domiciles into more comfortable apartments. While most shantytowns had a precarious legal status, many in time evolved into real neighborhoods where residents formed local associations to resolve disputes or manage public health problems. Despite squalor, dense habitation, and poverty, most slum residents had no plans to resettle, showing that they preferred the precariousness of urban life to the grinding poverty—and often the insecurity—of the countryside.

Because postcolonial modernization schemes failed to create sufficient jobs and municipal governments lacked resources for effective urban planning, slum dwellers were imperfectly assimilated either into the city or the nation-state. In Sub-Saharan Africa, slum dwellers often represented persecuted minorities. Officially ignored, and with few available jobs, most were stuck in the informal sector hawking T-shirts, gardening, or looking for menial work in a desperate struggle to earn their daily bread. Throughout the Middle East, private Islamic charities filled some of the void in state services by establishing clinics, schools, and neighborhood associations. In most areas of the postcolonial world, however, uncontrolled urbanization was a symptom of failed programs for state-driven modernization.

Waning of the Revolutionary Wave

The failure of developing states to deliver adequate services, economic opportunity, or land reform triggered a global backlash. Landless workers in South America, Western students, and zealous Chinese factory workers tuned in Che Guevara, Mao, and the discourse of African nationalists. Postcolonial elites that had once channeled popular grievances against white oppression, now mobilized the army and

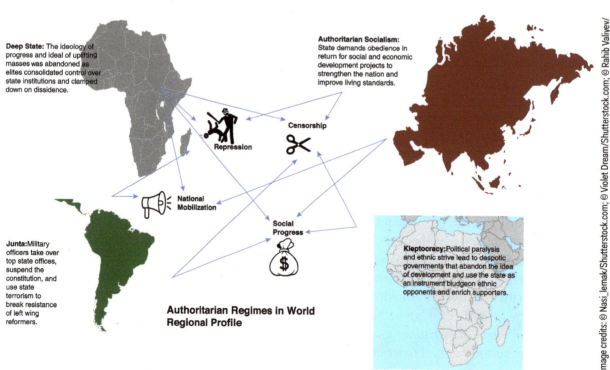

Slowing of the world economy and waning of the dream for postcolonial prosperity spurred a popular backlash and global leftist mobilization that created diverse patterns of political violence and authoritarian states throughout the world during the 1970s.

police to crush dissident movements they labeled as communists, religious radicals, or terrorists. *Juntas* in Latin America, kleptocracies in Africa, military dictatorships in Asia, and the authoritarian **Deep States** of the Middle East were symptomatic of a broader failure among postcolonial regimes to meet popular expectations for development or to integrate sectarian groups inside the fabric of the state.

Across the globe, the revolutionary wave began to fizzle out. During the **Revolution of 1968**, half the French population took to the streets, demanding reform and regime change. A month later, however, the barricades had disappeared after de Gaulle agreed to new elections. By 1969, Mao declared his Cultural Revolution over and used the Red Army to crack down on militants still eager to carry his radical program forward. At the 1972 Munich Olympics, Palestinian terrorists hijacked the world stage in a high-profile attack against Israeli athletes that discredited violence as a political tool.

As noted in chapter 1, another factor dampening the revolutionary wave was shifting economic conditions. By the late 1960s, the postwar boom was losing steam. In 1973, in response to Western support for Israel in the Yom Kippur War, Gulf states declared an oil embargo. Given the importance of oil for transportation, electricity generation, fertilizers, and various synthetic products, the embargo knocked the global economy off its moorings. Nonpetroleum exporting states were hard-hit by rising oil prices, given its indispensability to industry, transportation, electricity, and commercial agriculture. In 1974, petroleum prices quadrupled, inducing an inflationary shock that inaugurated **stagflation**, a decade characterized by high inflation, stagnant growth, and rapidly rising unemployment. Rising prices proved even more devastating to oil-importing states in the developing world, because slowing Western demand drove down prices for exports upon which state budgets depended. By the late 1980s, many postcolonial states were caught with deep deficits and unable to repay their foreign debt. Leftists that had once rallied for a better national future now scurried to safeguard their families as living standards plunged.

In the 1973 Oil Crisis, leaders of Organization of Petroleum Exporting Countries (OPEC) discovered a formula for turning the tables on the industrialized West by imposing an embargo upon petroleum. While the embargo's shock effect quickly wore off, rising oil prices enabled the Persian Gulf states to set the global market and the resulting windfall financed their own rapid economic development.

Organization of Petroleum Exporting Countries and the Persian Gulf States, 1973 to 1982

Persian Gulf states containing the majority of the world's untapped petroleum reserves uniquely benefitted from higher oil prices. By forming a cartel, the **Organization of Oil Exporting Countries (OPEC)** united Persian Gulf states with major non-Western producers like Nigeria, Mexico, and Venezuela. Increasingly under Saudi leadership, OPEC set the global price for the world's most important commodity. From 1973 to 1974, Nixon and other Western states contemplated intervention. In 1953, Britain and the United States had conspired to overthrow **Mohammad Mosaddegh** in Iran after he nationalized the Anglo-Iranian Oil Company (today's BP). In the wake of the Vietnam War, however, Western leaders lacked the stomach for imperial intervention. Their resolve was further undermined by clever OPEC diplomacy that engaged Western oil executives in continual negotiations, which offered them increasingly smaller slices of their national wealth, while steadily raising prices. Western leaders were partially placated by the fact that Arab states recycled their **petrodollars** by placing them in Western commercial banks. This inaugurated a golden era for international finance. While Western consumers were hard-hit by inflation, bankers profited from investing petrodollars, given that Gulf State economies proved incapable of absorbing all this liquidity.

Higher oil prices benefitted many oil-producing states, but Persian Gulf states benefitted disproportionally given their small populations. Windfall profits launched a building spree visible in cities like Jeddah, Kuwait, and Dubai. Seemingly overnight, petrodollars transformed dusty desert towns into oases of modernity, featuring skyscrapers, impeccable blacktop roads, electricity lines, and fleets of luxury cars. Living standards throughout the Persian Gulf spiked upward. By the early 1980s, many had caught up to the West in terms of per capita gross domestic product (GDP), succeeding where import substitution policies had failed. The Gulf states' nationalization strategy, however, was not easily replicated among other postcolonial leaders given oil's unique strategic significance and the Arab World's commanding share of global supply.

1982 Debt Crisis and Lost Decade

Slumping global growth from 1973 to 1981 proved difficult for many postcolonial states, but conditions worsened after Mexico defaulted on their foreign debt in 1982. This ignited a financial panic as investors withdrew capital from developing states around the world. Capital flight, the freezing of additional credit, and inefficient state revenue collection left many Africa and Latin America states saddled with massive deficits and unable to pay interest on their foreign debt. As we shall see in Chapter 8, this distress left many developing states vulnerable to International Monetary Fund (IMF)-imposed structural adjustment mechanisms that encouraged free market reforms and forced deep cuts to social services. Postcolonial states that had mostly failed to industrialize were now forced into austerity measures to cut back state investment in education and healthcare.

Stagflation stimulated a different response from the Tigers of Southeast Asia. For Singapore, Taiwan, Hong Kong, and South Korea, the 1980s represented a period of robust growth where they capitalized on neoliberal reforms to industrialize rapidly despite higher oil prices. In 1950, the living standards of Africans, Asians, and Arabs were roughly equivalent. During the commodity boom of the 1960s, African growth outpaced its peers given abundant resources relative to the continent's sparse population. By 1980, however, a significant disparity emerged inside the postcolonial world that would subsequently widen as the newly industrializing countries in Southeast Asia achieved industrial liftoff. By the 1990s, regional prosperity began to radiate out from the Tigers to their "**Cubs**," including Malaysia, Indonesia, Thailand, and the Philippines, as well as a resurgent China.

One key ingredient powering the **Asian Miracle** was avoidance of debt. Rather than splurging on massive infrastructural projects, Asia's Tiger economies kept a mostly clean balance sheet. They invested in education and subsidized local industrialists who leveraged cheap labor to mass produce mostly unsophisticated products destined for Western markets. Japan during the 1960s had pioneered this **export industrialization** strategy, steadily moving up the value chain to manufacture increasingly sophisticated products like electronics and cars. In response to OPEC-induced inflation, Japan began to outsource their manufacturing to lower wage neighboring states, spurring industrialization in South Korea and Taiwan. By the late 1980s, global capital was increasingly redirected towards Southeast Asian factories, supercharging the region's boom.

In contrast, global investors soured on Latin America where the typical state response to the 1982 **Debt Crisis** was printing money. This short-term fix sparked rampant inflation that often bankrupted the middle-class and unsettled business investors. In 1985, Bolivia's inflation rate reached a staggering

Chapter 3: A Revolutionary Wave 83

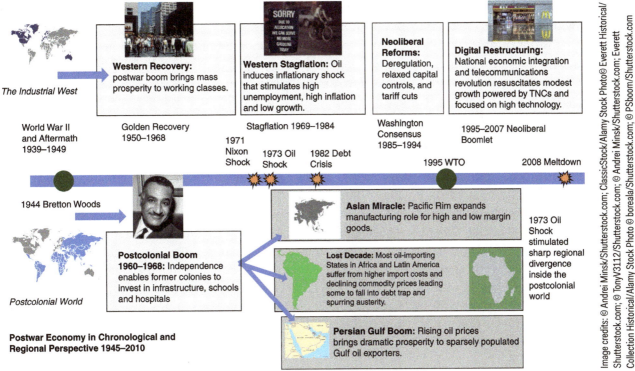

Postwar Economy in Chronological and Regional Perspective 1945–2010

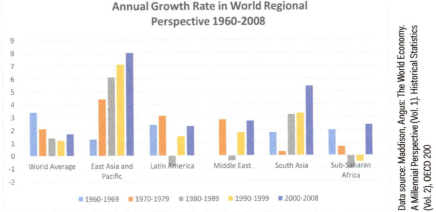

20,000 percent, spurring workers to scramble to stores with their paychecks before their earnings dwindled below the cost of the paper they were printed on. Unable to meet their debt obligations, many debtor states turned to the IMF that demanded the imposition of austerity measures in return for short-term liquidity. For ordinary people facing job insecurity and lower wages, disillusionment turned to despair. State austerity inaugurated a lost decade where economies stagnated, safety nets were cut, and living standards plummeted.

In Africa, structural economic problems exacerbated political instability. Despotic rule, waves of military coups and endemic corruption were symptomatic of a larger regional breakdown of state legitimacy. State "failure" in Africa struck a sharp contrast with the relative success of Southeast Asian states in incorporating diverse ethnic, linguistic, and religious groups. One key variable setting Asian states apart was their policies for comprehensive land reform. During the 1950s and 1960s, Southeast Asia had served as the principal theater of the Cold War. The bloodletting stimulated the formation of authoritarian states with institutions designed to enforce harmony and economic collaboration, combined with largely effective instruments for tax collection and income redistribution despite residual corruption. During the 1950s, both Taiwan and South Korea were poor and war ravaged, but they embarked upon substantial land reform measures. In contrast, Middle East and Latin American elites resisted land reform, while state modernization policies often exacerbated rural poverty. Throughout the developing world, repression of dissidence undermined the legitimacy of revolutionary regimes, particularly in Sub-Saharan Africa, where revolutionary states were captured by predatory elites that transformed the state from a vehicle for collective development into an instrument for capturing personal wealth.

The Cold War exacerbated postcolonial divergence. In Latin America and Sub-Saharan Africa, the United States supported right wing regimes against populist reform movements, while proxy wars ravaged states like Vietnam, Cuba, and Somalia. In contrast, Singapore, South Korea, Hong Kong, and Taiwan profited from the United States' liberal trade policies. Export industrialization could not have worked if the United States had barred its Asian allies from its markets. The record of postcolonial regimes across the world stage varied, but by the 1970s many had failed to either catch up to the West or to create more egalitarian societies. During the **Lost Decade** of the 1980s, disillusionment ripened into despair as living standards for many people living in the non-West dropped.

Conclusion

At Bandung in 1955, the most flamboyant leaders of the non-Western world expressed their determination to end colonialism, to sit out the Cold War and catch up to the industrialized West. Two decades later, the Non-Aligned Movement had faded into near insignificance, while the "Third World" became synonymous with political instability and failed modernization. Decolonization transformed the UN General Assembly into a rowdy forum where the postcolonial majority condemned racism and imperialism, but their calls for restructuring the global economy were ignored. Inside postcolonial states, programs for modernization failed to keep pace with popular expectations. Growing inequality and the failure of development programs to raise living standards precipitated a global backlash. Guerrillas, student organizations, labor unions, and rural associations challenged national elites, demanding a bigger slice of the economic pie and stimulating authoritarian reaction. With onset of the 1982 Debt Crisis, the revolutionary wave began to dissipate. Africa and Latin America became mired in a Lost Decade where economic growth and social progress screeched to a halt. Hope soured into despair as leftists abandoned socialism and warmed to the idea of free market reforms. The emerging **Washington Consensus** proposed to reunite former colonies with Western economies inside a neoliberal World Trade Organization. After the failure of import substitution, the disappointments with rural development and the turmoil of 1973 to 1989 seemed to many non-Western leaders the best path forward.

Questions for Critical Thought

1. How did the shock of World War II destabilize the international system of Western colonialism?
2. How did events in India, Indochina, and Ghana set the stage for the rapid unraveling of the colonial system in Sub-Saharan Africa?
3. Why did the European powers respond differently to colonial demands for independence?
4. How did the Algerian War, Ghana's independence, and Congo Crisis highlight different dimensions of the independence struggle?

5. In what ways were newly emergent states in Africa "underdeveloped"?
6. Why did so many newly independent countries adopt "socialism" as a development strategy? What did the modernization model proscribe in terms of catching up to the West? Why did this strategy often lead to state investment in dams and why did such projects so often disappoint?
7. How did the increasing gap between the dream for independence and postcolonial development exacerbate conflict and political instability?
8. Why did the newly industrializing countries in Asia outstrip its counterparts in Africa and Latin America? What was the secret to their success?

Suggestions for Further Reading

- Armstrong, P., Andrew G., and John H. *Capitalism since World War II: The Making and Breakup of the Great Boom.* London: Fontana, 1991.
- Betts, M. *Decolonization.* 2nd ed. New York: Routledge, 2004.
- Brendon, P. *The Decline and Fall of the British Empire, 1781-1997.* New York: Vintage, 2001.
- Fieldhouse, D. K. *Black Africa, 1945-1990: Economic Decolonization and Arrested Development.* New York: Routledge, 2010.
- Halperin, S. *Re-Envisioning Global Development: A Horizontal Perspective.* New York: Routledge, 2013.
- Horne, A. *A Savage War of Peace: Algeria 1954-1962.* New York: NYRB Classics, 2006.
- Prashad, V. *The Darker Nations: A People's History of the Third World.* New York: New Press, 2007.
- Rist, G. *The History of Development: From Western Origins to Global Faith.* London: Zed, 2008.
- Young, R. J. C. *Postcolonialism: An Historical Introduction.* New York: Wiley-Blackwell, 2001.

Notes

1. Quoted in Malcolm Betts, *France and Decolonization* (New York: MacMillan, 1991), 63.
2. Toyin Falola, *Nationalism and African Intellectuals* (New York: University of Rochester Press, 2004), 155.
3. United Nations Charter was signed on June 26, 1945, in San Francisco, accessed July 28, 2019, http://www.un.org/en/sections/un-charter/un-charter-full-text/.
4. Quoted in Richard Harris, *Che Guevara: A Biography* (New York: Greenwood, 2010), 99.
5. Quoted in Vijay Prashad, *Darker Nations: A Biography of the Shortlived Third World* (New York: Left World Books, 2007), 14.
6. Quoted in Betts, *France and Decolonization*, 106.
7. Harrold MacMillan, "Winds of Change," delivered in Cape Town, February 3, 1960, accessed July 30, 2019, transcript, http://africanhistory.about.com/od/eraindependence/p/wind_of_change2.htm.
8. Tracey J. Kinney, *Conflict and Cooperation* (Don Mills, ON: Oxford University Press, 2014), 270–71.
9. All African Peoples Conference, "Resolution on Colonialism and Imperialism." Adopted in Accra, Ghana February, 5–13, 1958, Modern History Sourcebook, accessed July 30, 2019, https://sourcebooks.fordham.edu/mod/1958-aapc-res1.asp.
10. Kwame Nkrumah, *Africa Must Unite* (New York: Praeger, 1963), 23–24.
11. Patrice Lumumba, "Independence Address," delivered in Leopoldville, June 30, 1960. Patrice Lumumba, *The Truth about a Monstrous Crime of the Colonialists* (Moscow: Foreign Languages Publishing House, 1961), 44–47.

Chapter 4
The Global Cold War, 1949 to 1991

Chapter Outline

- Introduction: A Cold War
- Global Spillover, 1949 to 1953
- War in Korea
- Towards the Nuclear Brink, 1954 to 1963
- Third World in the Cross Fire
- The Cold War in Popular Culture
- Gorbachev's End Game, 1985 to 1991
- Conclusion

Global Cold War 1949–1991

1948–1949 Berlin Crisis results in Partitioning of Europe into competing idelogical blocs

Revolutions of 1989 wash out unpopular communist regimes in Eastern Europe and spill over into USSR.

1969 Ussuri River incident breaks Sino-Soviet wide open

Implication of US, USSR and China in Korea's civil war 1950–1953 escalates Cold War into global struggle.

1962 Cuban Missile Crisis Nearly ignites nuclear war

Nixon's 1971 visit to beijing abates US–Chinese proxy War in Asia and sets stage for more liberal reform

Khomeini articulated a Vision for Islamic monderntiy apart from both East and West.

1979 Iranian Revolution and Soviet–Afghan War entangle superpowers with islaamic fundamentalism

1973 OPEC oil embargo shows global economy, destabilizes postcolonial states in Africa and Latin America and ignites proxy wars and military dictatorships during era of détente.

Gorbachev's new thinking ultimately opened the possibility for normalized US–Soviet relations.

In October 1962 JFK restrained American 'Hawks' enabling diplomatic Resolution of Cuban Crisis.

Khrushchev's embrace of Afro–Asian bloc entangled decolonization with the Cold War.

Nasser tried to play the superpowers off against each other, but ultimately failed to modernize Egypt.

Main Cold War Eras
1948–1949 Berlin Crisis
- 'Fall' of China 1949
- Korean War 1950–1953

1950–1956 Globalization of Conflict
1957–1962 Crisis Years
- 1962 Cuban Missile Crisis

1963–1980 Age of Détente
- 1969 Ussuri River Incident
- 1972 Nixon Visitng Beijing
- 1972–1980 Proxy Wars in Africa and Latin America

1980–1984 Reagan's Hot Phase
1985–1989 Gorbachev's End Game
- 1989 Fall of the Berlin Wall
- 1991 Collapse of the Soviet Union

Image credits: © Andrei Minsk/Shutterstock.com; © spatuletail/Shutterstock.com; Cecil Stoughton. White House Photographs; National Archives Catalog; Everett Collection Historical/Alamy Stock Photo

Chapter 4: The Global Cold War, 1949 to 1991

Introduction: A Cold War

At Potsdam in 1945, the victorious allies failed to hammer out a comprehensive settlement. This created a gap between Stalin and the West that was never bridged. By 1947, Western journalists began to apply "Cold War" to describe mounting US–Soviet hostility. Slowly, the "peace that was not peace," brewed into open hostility even if neither party desired war.

The Cold War blossomed inside an older rivalry. Already in the nineteenth century, the United States and the USSR had identified themselves as torch bearers for rival civilizations. When Truman cast the United States as defender of the "free world" in 1947, he was invoking American exceptionalism; a belief that the United States had been born in a revolution with a sacred mission to liberate humanity from tyranny. After the Bolsheviks seized power in 1917, they promised to liberate the oppressed masses. Defining "justice" and "freedom" in variant ways infused the US–Soviet rivalry with ideological intensity. Following the 1948 to 1949 Berlin Crisis, both sides embraced the idea of "Cold War." They saw their rivalry as a clash of civilizations; a zero-sum game where their respective ways of life were at stake and only one side could emerge victorious.

Armageddon haunted postwar society. Hiroshima has inaugurated the nuclear age. Atomic weapons represented a class apart. They could level cities and poison ecosystems for generations. By the late 1960s, the superpower arsenals had grown sufficiently large to snuff out all planetary life. This horrific reality produced the Cold War's paradoxical mix of paranoia and restraint. While both superpowers struggled to expand their global influence, they also modified their strategic doctrines to prevent inevitable disputes from escalating into catastrophe. Both sides adopted informal rules for limited warfare that led both to explore various forms of asymmetric warfare. In terms of intensity, however, Cold War resembled a "total war." Citizens lived in the shadow of the bomb and both sides mobilized their citizens, economies, and allies in a battle for the "soul of mankind."

The Cold War matured inside a unique international environment. World War II had devastated Europe and Asia, weakening Japan and Germany, while loosening Europe's grip over its colonies. As European empires collapsed in the decades following World War II, the superpowers filled this vacuum. In the postcolonial world, they fought deadly proxy wars that devastated some states while forcing postcolonial elites to subordinate their development priorities to outside interests. After the 1962 Cuban Missile Crisis, the experience of the Cold War sharply diverged. East and West enjoyed an age of détente, where the battle between democracy and communism shifted to the cultural sphere: United Nations (UN) forums, international conferences, and the Olympic stage. Inside the "Third World," the Cold turned "Hot." Adverse economic conditions triggered a popular backlash against postcolonial regimes as their modernization programs fell short. A series of proxy wars and military coups wrecked local infrastructure, eroded state authority, and left many postcolonial states saddled with unmanageable debts.

Big Questions

- Why did the US–Soviet rivalry turn global after 1949?
- How did the Korean War shape subsequent Cold War battlefields?
- What allowed the superpowers to step back from the Cuban brink?
- How did the Cold War sabotage non-Western dreams for postcolonial independence?
- How did nuclear weapons contaminate postwar culture?

Global Spillover, 1949 to 1953

At Potsdam in 1945, Truman informed Stalin that the United States had developed a nuclear bomb. Stalin told Truman to make good use of his "secret" new weapon, careful to conceal any trace of concern. Subsequently, developing a nuclear bomb became the Soviet Union's highest priority. From 1946 to 1947, Stalin retreated from crises he provoked in Iran and Turkey in part because of the United States' "atomic diplomacy." Stalin, however, refused to be cowed by nuclear blackmail, so he put **Lavrentiy Beria** in charge of the Soviet nuclear program. The head of the Soviet secret police spared no effort, working prisoners to death and threatening top scientists with execution should their experiments fail. In August 1949, the Soviet Union shocked the West by achieving nuclear fission. A Soviet bomb tipped the strategic balance in Europe. The United States had mostly demobilized and nuclear parity would mean the absence of an effective deterrent to offset the Red Army's massive superiority in tanks and artillery in Europe. To restore the balance of power, the United States gradually built up its conventional forces by establishing North Atlantic Treaty Organization (NATO) into formal organization, ultimately backstopped by a remilitarized West Germany.

Decline of the British Empire

The British Empire's unanticipated decline contributed to a global vacuum that helped to push the Cold War outside of Europe. Following Clement Attlee's July 1945 victory, the British Labour Party prioritized building a welfare state at home. Also, many Labour MPs viewed the British Empire with skepticism. Confronted with simultaneous crises in Palestine, Greece, and India, Britain's depleted treasury reached a breaking point. From 1947 to 1949, the fate of the vast territories constituting the British Empire suddenly appeared very uncertain. This international context animated Truman's 1947 address to Congress where outlined **containment** as the United States' new grand strategy. Having artfully written the speech himself, Truman aimed to rally Americans around defense of the "Free World." Truman identified "tyranny" as a global threat. The American public easily read "Russia" and "communism" into these code words, even though Truman avoided calling out the USSR by name.

Fall of China and the Red Scare

Close observers had anticipated Mao's triumph in China's civil war since the summer of 1948. Mao's 1949 announcement that he would "lean" towards Moscow, however, alarmed Washington, DC. It suggested the existence of a monolithic Communist Bloc. The US media painted China's "fall" in sinister terms. Communism was "on the march" and American freedoms were imperiled. That autumn, the **Red Scare** reached fever pitch inside Middle America. Paranoia about communist infiltration built upon highly publicized cases of Soviet espionage. Unscrupulous politicians like Senator Joseph McCarthy fed irrational fears. Not only did state officials came under scrutiny, but the public worried about the loyalty of Hollywood actors, even local milkmen. In Peekskill, New York, a riot ensued in 1949 when news broke that popular singer, and well-known communist sympathizer, Paul Robeson would hold an outdoor concert. Demonstrators held up placards, hurled racial epithets, and clubbed prospective concert goers with baseball bats as the police mostly looked on.

Peekskill Riot

Angry mob berates concert goers in Peekskill, New York, after news breaks that African American singer and communist sympathizer Paul Robeson would perform.

Emergence of the US Empire

Truman came away from 1949, battered and embittered. The public blamed him for China's "fall." During the **Admiral's Revolt**, military hardliners attacked Truman for being weak on communism. The National Security Council produced a secret directive, **NSC-68**, calling for a peacetime buildup of a standing army. Initially, Truman and fiscal conservatives pushed back. A month into the Korean War, however, Truman affixed his signature to NSC-68. US defense expenditures quickly tripled.

The official response to communism's threat was shaped by US diplomat George Kennan's 1946 "long telegram." Stationed in Moscow, Kennan had argued that internal dynamics inclined the USSR towards expansion. A central problem facing US planners was developing a coherent containment strategy. NSC-68 deemed that the Soviet Union was "animated by a new fantastic faith, antithetical to our own, and seeks to impose its absolute authority over the rest of the world." Moscow had two levers: a massive Red Army, which could apply military force across Soviet borders, and a global network of spies, which often worked clandestinely through subversive communist organizations.[1] NSC-68 depicted communism as a monolithic movement incubated and directed from Moscow. Monolithic communism distorted the complicated relationship between Stalin, Marxist-Leninist dogma, and Soviet allies. While Stalin financially supported communist parties throughout the world, and often used them as tools for promoting Soviet interests, he prioritized the security of the USSR first and foremost. Communist allies abroad routinely complained about the insufficiency of Soviet support and how their activities were rigidly subordinated to Russian interests, often at expense of their own. Stalin's strained relationship with his allies came into full view in 1948 when Tito broke from the Soviet Bloc. Stalin had a history of using intimidation or force to get his way, but crop failures and food shortages from 1946 to 1947 had weakened his regime. Even with partial economic recovery after 1950, Soviet industrial capacity stood at only a fifth of the United States total. Stalin's principal strategic goal after 1947 was to assimilate Eastern Europe into the Soviet Empire and secure his immediate borderlands. Stalin's caution intersected with Bolshevik dogma that predicted postwar economic instability would culminate in capitalism's collapse. At best, US theories about global communism in the late 1940s exaggerated the scope and nature of the Soviet threat. Straddling Northern Eurasia, the Soviet Union was a military juggernaut that could project conventional forces into Europe, the Middle East, and Asia. But the USSR was economically weak and lacked a significant navy, a network of global bases or embassies, and a long-range transport aircraft to project global power. These weaknesses limited the USSR's global reach and the scope of its international influence. They were only partially offset by a first-rate clandestine service.

War in Korea

Neither Stalin nor Truman anticipated that Korea would emerge as the Cold War's first major battlefield. The Peninsula had been divided along the 38th parallel at the Potsdam Conference. Both the Soviet Union and the United States had built up client states within their respective zones, but both had also by 1950 evacuated the Peninsula. The leader of the communist North, **Kim Il Sung**, and his southern counterpart, Western expatriate dictator **Syngman Rhee**, were both dissatisfied with Korea's artificial partitioning. In 1948, Rhee rejected an international accord to hold a Peninsula-wide election he would have lost. Instead, the United States backed Rhee's "election" as South Korea's leader, a contest he won following a brutal crackdown on dissidents. Subsequently, Rhee and Kim Il Sung ratcheted up tensions on the Peninsula, trading public insults while engaging in sabotage missions on each other's territory.

Kim Il Sung's trump card was a disciplined army, augmented by Soviet trainers and materiel. In April 1949, Kim traveled to Moscow seeking Stalin's consent for an invasion to reunite Korea. Stalin was not interested: "The Americans will never agree to be thrown out of there and because of that, to lose their reputation as a great power. The Soviet people would not understand the necessity of war in Korea, which is a remote place outside the sphere of the USSR's vital interests."[2] When US Secretary of State Dean Acheson announced that Korea lay outside of its Asian defense perimeter in January 1950, however, Stalin changed his mind. Soviet generals planned the invasion while Moscow shipped in additional supplies, now convinced the United States would not intervene. Mao also chipped in 30,000 People's Liberation Army (PLA) veterans of Korean descent, who were integrated into Kim's forces.

On June 25, 1950, Kim Il Sung launched his "fatherland liberation" war. The South Korean army lacked heavy weapons to counteract North Korea's tanks, artillery, and aircraft. Outgunned, South Korea's army quickly grew demoralized. Most conscripts resented Rhee's authoritarian regime. Rhee's resistance to land reform and brutal crackdowns in 1948 had left tens of thousands dead and sent over 300,000 to harsh reeducation camps.[3]

Facing imminent defeat, Rhee called out for international help. Kim Il Sung's attack had caught the United States off guard. Fearing Rhee's peninsular ambitions, the United States had refused to provision him with heavy weapons or to adequately train his army. While not obliged to intervene by treaty, domestic fears called for a firm American response against a clear case of "communist" aggression. US planners also grappled with how a communist-dominated Korea would isolate Japan, seemingly their last bastion in the Pacific.

UN Intervention

To provide international legitimacy for military intervention, the United States convened an emergency UN meeting to condemn North Korea's unprovoked attack. This paved the way for Resolution 83 on June 28, 1950, authorizing UN intervention just as Seoul fell into North Korean hands. UN 83 provided a cloak of international legitimacy, even if US soldiers would constitute the bulk of the UN's fighting forces. Resolution 83 was also of dubious legality because the UN Charter forbade intervention in civil wars. The resolution bypassed a certain Soviet veto because Stalin had withdrawn from the Security Council to protest Western refusal to seat Mao on China's permanent seat.

> Was Korea a coordinated communist attack against a peaceful democratic state or better seen as a civil war outside the scope of UN intervention?

Korea marked the first test of the United States' containment strategy. In deeming Kim Il Sung's attack "communist aggression," the USA invoked the memory of Munich. According to the domino theory, failure to show strength would incentivize future communist attacks and disillusion allies. Intervention gave official endorsement to an expansive definition of containment that created open-ended commitment to deploy Western ground forces in other postcolonial settings.

Inchon Landing

Following the fall of Seoul, South Korea's remaining military forces retreated in panic. Truman rushed in two American divisions from nearby Japan, but these (green) troops lacked discipline or the heavy weapons necessary to blunt North Korea's advance. By September, American forces were pushed back to a tiny toehold around the Port of Pusan. On September 15, US General **Douglass MacArthur**—appointed commander of the UN forces—turned the tables by launching a risky amphibious invasion behind enemy lines at **Inchon**. The landing succeeded, however, and within days, the UN forces had cut North Korea's supply lines. This forced them into a confusing retreat. North Korean forces had all but disintegrated as UN forces approached the 38th parallel in early October. The question of whether to pursue North Korea's army gained urgency when **Zhou Enlai** publicly threatened Chinese intervention should UN forces cross into North Korea.
At Guam, on October 15, MacArthur and Truman deliberated. MacArthur brushed aside the Chinese threat, reasoning it a bluff. In any case, Chinese forces lacked air power. Even if China mobilized, MacArthur reckoned they would arrive too late to make much difference. Truman worried about escalation, but ultimately endorsed MacArthur's plan to advance north and mop up Kim Il Sung's remaining forces. Neither man knew that China had already secretly authorized intervention. Given US support for Chiang Kai-shek and his runaway Republic in Taiwan, Mao already saw himself in a state of war with the United States. He would not tolerate creation of a puppet state on his southern border, mindful of how Japan had used Korea as a springboard for attacking Manchuria. When Mao's adjutants urged caution and fretted about US nuclear response, Mao responded defiantly: "the death of ten or twenty million people is nothing to be afraid of."[4] Stalin supported China's intervention and provided material assistance, but Stalin also refused to be dragged into the conflict openly. Particularly, he refused to allow the Soviet air force to operate outside of Chinese controlled air space. In consequence, Chinese units dug in along the frontlines suffered mounting casualties from mostly unmolested UN air attacks.

Chapter 4: The Global Cold War, 1949 to 1991

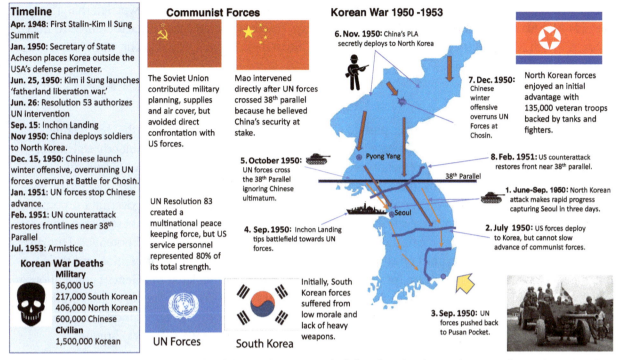

China's Offensive

In late October 1950, UN forces approached the Yalu Mountains demarcating the Korean-Chinese border. They were unaware that Chinese soldiers had used the cover of darkness to move into position deep inside North Korea. On November 25, the Chinese launched an offensive against the badly outnumbered UN forces. Using infiltration tactics, night attacks, and gongs to confuse their enemy, veteran Chinese soldiers overran UN forces, pushing them well behind the 38th parallel. Around Chosin, US marines only narrowly escaped Chinese encirclement, but the Eighth Army's morale was shattered. By March 1951, air power and napalm, a fuel air explosive that indiscriminately burned everything in a wide radius, slowed the Chinese advance that had outrun its supplies. This breathing space enabled General **Matthew Ridgeway** to rally UN forces and stabilize the Korean front just below the 38th parallel.

General Matthew Ridgeway earned the title "iron tits" for his habit of walking around with a grenade and med kit strapped to each shoulder.

China's winter offensive set the stage for the famous battle of wills between Truman and MacArthur. MacArthur threatened China and publicly advocated bombing their staging bases north of the Yalu River. From MacArthur's perspective, a sustained bombing campaign, or a nuclear strike, would cut the communist supply line and ensure rapid victory. Truman forbade any attack on the Chinese mainland, fearing escalation and Russian intervention. Truman took charge of the US nuclear arsenal, worried that a renegade MacArthur might trigger a global war. Publicly, Truman ordered MacArthur to adhere to his UN mandate. When MacArthur complained in private and disparaged Truman in public, he was dismissed for insubordination in April 1951.

Broader Legacy

During the summer of 1951, UN forces pushed Chinese forces back mostly behind the 38th parallel. When negotiations for peace went nowhere, the Korean War settled into a long and bloody stalemate. Armistice talks lingered, but no agreement was signed until 1953 after Stalin died and Eisenhower threatened to use nuclear weapons to resolve the stalemate. By that time, both sides had tired of the war. As the first battle of the Cold War, the Korean War established informal precedents governing superpower confrontation during the postnuclear age. Both Truman and Stalin had worried about escalation. In this way, the Korea War gave shape to the idea of **limited war**. Despite their tactical potential, Truman forbade the use of nuclear weapons on strategic grounds. Despite this restraint, both China and the United States saw Korea as a test case for their ideological battle. Both violated the Geneva conventions in pursuit of victory. UN soldiers, for example, shot thousands of Korean civilians fleeing south because they worried that they harbored North Korean insurgents in their midst. North Koreans conducted assassination missions behind enemy lines, while the Chinese treated allied prisoner of wars (POWs) brutally.

> Newly released documents show that Canadian forces were ordered to fire upon civilian crowds fearing that communist agents had infiltrated the ranks of refugees. Was the public manipulated into intervening in a civil war peripheral to national security?

The *end justifies the means* rationale informed subsequent Cold War conflicts. It cast aside the grand principles of human rights and just war that had been idealistically inscribed into the UN Charter. The Korean War also signaled the dangers lurking within an emerging postcolonial landscape. In Korea, two dictators had drawn outside powers to intervene on their behalf, embroiling both in a costly struggle peripheral to their own security. By the mid-1950s, the process of decolonization was accelerating. Dozens of potential Koreas were emerging, creating a playing field of ostensibly neutral and often weak states that could be persuaded to join either Bloc.

Towards the Nuclear Brink, 1954 to 1963

The years from 1954 to 1963 represented the climax of the Cold War, as both superpowers expanded their militaries and nuclear arsenals, while confronting each other more aggressively in the postcolonial world. By 1956, Nikita Khrushchev emerged as Stalin's clear-cut successor, determined to set the USSR upon a "new course." This included promoting **peaceful coexistence**, a concept that both superpowers could cohabit the planet without engaging in a costly struggle for global dominance. While coexistence had the potential for détente, Khrushchev served as a flawed messenger. To many Soviet citizens, Khrushchev wielded a folksy charm. Westerners, on the other hand, mostly saw Khrushchev as a tiresome and unpredictable bore. Khrushchev was convinced that his empty threat to lob Soviet intercontinental ballistic missiles (ICBMs) at London and Paris during the 1956 Suez Crisis had led Britain and France to withdraw from Egypt. This mistaken belief fueled recurrent threats of nuclear blackmail from 1957 to 1962. Western leaders mostly ignored Khrushchev's bluffs, but the threats intensified popular fears about Armageddon. Comrade Khrushchev's US visit in 1959 revealed his petulance, sowing American mistrust about the man with his finger on the Soviet nuclear trigger. Subsequently during a rowdy 1960 UN session, Khrushchev led the Soviet delegation in pounding their fists on the table in a clownish attempt to oust Secretary General **Dag Hammarskjöld**.

Irritated that the West spurned his invitations for détente, Khrushchev launched a diplomatic offensive to reveal the futility of the Cold War. Decolonization presented Khrushchev with a golden opportunity to expand Soviet influence beyond traditional border regions. During 1960, the Soviet Union reached the peak of its international influence by allying informally with the Non-Aligned Movement (NAM). Despite the USSR's limited resources, Khrushchev offered public support for postcolonial leaders and cultivated client states in Africa, the Middle East, and Cuba. Soviet diplomats, technical experts, and spies ventured far wider than ever before as they tangled with their "Main Adversary" to spread disinformation, build dams and steel mills, bribe and blackmail foreign bureaucrats, and foster insurgent movements. In all these ways, Khrushchev broadened the scope of the Cold War and elevated its intensity. During Khrushchev's tenure, the superpower rivalry most exemplified a global struggle between socialism and capitalism.

After Khrushchev sent advisors and military aid to the Congo in 1960, the United States grew increasingly alarmed about the Soviet Union's ability to win new allies inside the postcolonial world. As noted in Chapter 3, during the **Congo Crisis**, the United States colluded with their European allies to oust Prime Minister Patrice Lumumba in favor of Joseph Mobutu. Subsequently, the US policy increasingly veered towards supporting "strong men" in Africa, particularly officers trained in Western military academies. They could be counted upon to maintain order inside fragile political states, to deal harshly with communist insurgents and respect Western property rights. By the mid-1960s, US policy crystallized into a Machiavellian logic that brutish dictators that terrorized their own peoples were preferable to disorder or communist "tyranny." In 1965, Senator Fulbright noted the contradiction embedded in US policy towards Latin America. Publicly, the United States continued to champion human rights, but its foreign policy increasingly veered towards providing military aid to right-wing governments. "We cannot successfully advance the cause of popular democracy and at the same time align ourselves with corrupt and reactionary oligarchies; yet that is what we seem to be trying to do."[5]

Already in the late 1950s, anti-communism and support for US corporations and Western property rights had merged inside a foreign policy that routinely undermined democratically elected socialist regimes in Latin America. Most regimes subverted clandestinely were not formally communist, nor did they enjoy formal Soviet backing. Anti-communism became a pretense that could justify removal of any regime challenging the United States' informal hegemony. A similar logic prevailed inside the Soviet Bloc when Russian tanks rolled into Budapest in 1956 after an experiment in "national communism" threatened to break up the Warsaw Pact and undermine Soviet control over Eastern Europe.

Khrushchev's Escalation

Khrushchev's prickly personality incubated a vicious cycle of misinterpretation and escalation that led to deteriorating East–West relations from 1957 to 1962. During the 1957 *Sputnik* launch, Khrushchev unveiled the first man-made satellite at a surprise news conference. Khrushchev instructed Western reporters and HAM operators to tune their crystal sets to record the "beep" of Sputnik as it passed overhead. Khrushchev's demonstration of the prowess of Soviet engineering was meant to show the futility of an arms race. Instead, Khrushchev set off a panic in the West about a nonexistent "missile gap." A third Red Scare rolled through Middle America. Primary schools organized "tuck and duck" drills, where young children were terrorized by dubious strategies for dodging nuclear explosions. Ordinary families began to build fallout shelters stocked with tin cans, kerosene lamps, and wool blankets. Eisenhower knew that the Soviet edge in rocketry was minimal at best. The Soviets were quickly overtaken in the race to the moon. A slight Soviet edge in ICBMs during the late 1950s obscured that they carried fewer warheads and that their guidance systems were unreliable. While US rollout of nuclear submarines also neutralized the threat of any theorized Soviet first strike.

From 1958 to 1962, a series of international crises seemed to push the world closer to nuclear war. During the 1958 Taiwan Straights Crisis, Mao—without Khrushchev's knowledge or blessing—shelled the island of Quemoy and threatened to invade Taiwan. In 1960, Khrushchev was pressured by East German leader Walter Ulbricht to stop the exodus of hundreds of thousands of East Germans. The regimes best and brightest were fleeing the socialist paradise for greener pastures in the West, using West Berlin as their exit. This was not only an embarrassment for international socialism, but represented a brain drain, threatening East Germany's survival. Khrushchev responded by issuing an ultimatum: The Great Powers needed to normalize Berlin or he would unilaterally hand over its control to East Germany. The West ignored Khrushchev. Tensions mounted as Russian and American tanks shadowboxed through the streets of Berlin, while Khrushchev angrily alluded to nuclear war. Ultimately, the matter was resolved through construction of a concrete wall separating Eastern and Western sectors of Berlin in 1961, but US–Soviet relations seemed to have reached the breaking point. Public bluffs about willingness to use military weapons, officially dubbed the art of "brinkmanship," had the effect of terrorizing the public.

Tensions in Berlin 1961

When the West failed to oblige Khrushchev's demand for normalization of Berlin's status, the East Germans constructed the Berlin Wall to close the last hole in the Iron Curtain and lock their citizens into the Socialist Bloc.

Cuban Revolution

The immediate roots of the Cuban Missile Crisis lay in the 1959 **Cuban Revolution**. In December 1956, the *Granma*, a refitted yacht cast anchor from Mexico with Fidel Castro and eighty comrades aboard. Flush with enthusiasm, they were determined to overthrow Cuban despot **Fulgencio Batista**. But Castro's motley band was intercepted by Cuban soldiers shortly after landfall. Most were captured or killed. Castro, however, escaped and continued his insurgency in the rugged Sierra Maestra mountains.

Primary resistance to Batista remained centered in the cities, where in 1957 a coalition of liberals, communists, and students orchestrated a coup that reached all the way to the presidential palace before being turned back. Batista responded with repression that destroyed the urban resistance movement. Many survivors of the ill-fated coup fled into the mountains to join Castro's guerillas. Following a disastrous Battle for Santa Clara in 1958, where many conscripts deserted despite outnumbering Castro's rebels, Batista fled Cuba on New Year's Eve. Castro drove down into Havana in triumph. Washington, DC, wary of Batista's corruption and unpopularity, hoped Castro would bring stability to Cuba. Some in Moscow wondered whether Castro was a Central Intelligence Agency (CIA) agent.

Castro was a nationalist who believed that Cuba needed a revolution to restore the country's wealth to its people. To cement its authority, Castro's regime rounded up Batista collaborators and executed some in revolutionary tribunals that fell well short of due process. In Cuba, a silent majority worried about the increasingly radical drift of Castro's regime, but his 1959 land reform act, which purchased land from plantation owners and redistributed it among the poor, met with enthusiasm. The United States protested Castro's reform measure as an infringement of property rights. Castro insisted he was a nationalist and "not a communist."[6] Castro's nationalization of foreign corporations in 1960 represented the last straw for Washington, The United States cut off diplomatic relations and gradually imposed an embargo that delivered a sharp blow to a fragile economy dependent upon US markets. The United States hoped that economic pressure would encourage the Cuban people to oust Castro especially as his regime spoke openly about exporting the Cuban Revolution to Latin America. During the 1961 **Bay of Pigs** invasion, the United States financed a small band of Cuban exiles with the hope that their landing would instigate a popular insurrection. When no such uprising occurred, the Cuban exiles were caught on the beach and gunned down by Castro's army. The Bay of Pigs embarrassed President Kennedy. No one believed his denial of US involvement. The operation also revealed that whatever reservations Cubans had about Castro, a majority preferred his regime to a return of Batista's cronies. Following the Bay of Pigs, the United States resorted to regime change through assassination. The CIA dreamed up hundreds of plots, from poisoning cigars to mining seashells around a beach Castro was believed to snorkel. When multiple plots failed, the United States prepared for military invasion. Faced with intense US pressure, Castro declared himself a Marxist and reached out for Soviet protection. For Khrushchev, Cuba represented a propaganda coup and strategic bonanza. The United States had recently deployed Jupiter nuclear missiles in Italy and across the Soviet border in Turkey. Soviet ICBMs were very inaccurate. Cuba provided an ideal launching pad for the medium and short-range nuclear rockets that the Soviets possessed in abundance.

Thirteen Days in October

Khrushchev had publicly announced to the world that he would provide Cuba only with defensive weapons, but in 1962, thousands of Soviet personnel, under the cover of an agricultural mission, arrived in Cuba to prepare missile sites. In early October 1962, U-2 planes spotted these launch sites, sparking the **Cuban Missile Crisis**. The United States identified the missile sites as belonging to the medium-range SS-4 that could reach targets from Washington, DC, to Texas in as little as five minutes. Suddenly, Cuba was no longer an annoying communist beachhead, but a Soviet missile base that brought 60 percent of the US population in reach of nuclear attack. Members of the Executive Committee of the National Security Council (EXCOMM) chose to interpret the Soviet missiles as an offensive threat to the United States rather than deterrent to their invasion of Cuba. This assessment, however sincere, blissfully ignored US aggression against Cuba, active subversion of Castro's regime, and US deployment of nuclear missiles to Turkey. US policy-makers, however, quickly agreed that the Soviet missiles could not be allowed to become operational. What they debated was how to neutralize them. Some advocated bombing the missile sites, while others proposed invasion. Unless the United States got rid of Castro, the Soviets would eventually find a way to sneak nuclear weapons to Cuba. President Kennedy balked at taking immediate

Chapter 4: The Global Cold War, 1949 to 1991

action fearing that if the United States struck Soviet personnel, it risked escalating the Cuban Crisis into world war. This turned out to be a prudent instinct, because Kennedy did not know that the Soviets had already mobilized 40,000 personnel in Cuba armed with short-range nuclear weapons.

The Cuban Missile Crisis

13 Days in October 1962

October 15: U-2 mission spots Soviet missiles.
October 16: President Kennedy assembles EXCOMM to hash out policy options.
October 21: After weighing various options, President Kennedy opts for 'quarantine' of Cuba to interdict transport of Soviet warheads to Cuba.
October 22: President Kennedy addresses the American public and need to remove Soviet missiles.
October 23: Organization of American States votes in favor of US blockade.
October 24: Soviet ships stop short of US naval blockade.
October 25: Adlai Stevenson confronts Soviet Union inside the U.N.
October 26: Khrushchev offers diplomatic settlement, while RFK meets secretly with Soviet Ambassador.
October 27: Soviet SAM battery shoots down U-2 plane over Cuba while US destroyers drop depth charges on Soviet submarine B-59.
October 28: On Radio Moscow, Khrushchev publicly announces acceptance of settlement terms, ending the Cuban Missile Crisis.

1962 Resolution: Defusing of the crisis contributes to Nuclear Test Ban Treaty in 1963 and international climate of détente.

1962 US Blockade: US refuses to accept Soviet deployment and implements blockade.

1959 Cuban Revolution: Batista flees enabling Castro to implement his Cuban Revolution. US is apprehensive, but encouraged that Castro casts himself as nationalist rather than communist.

1961 US Policy of Regime Change: Following nationalization of US corporations, Kennedy implements an embargo and authorizes the clandestine overthrow of Castro

1961 Bay of Pigs: US covert mission to overthrow Castro through Cuban exiles backfires as anticipated revolt never materializes.

1961 Havana Declaration: Castro identifies himself as Marxist and casts the USA as an imperial power that has consistently attacked Latin American freedom fighters.

1962 Operation Anadyr: In the wake of the 1961 Bay of Pigs invasion, Khrushchev opts to secure the Cuban Revolution by covertly introducing nuclear missiles into Cuba.

Image credits: © Universal History Archive/Contributor/gettyimages.com: © Everett Historical/Shutterstock.com: © Rainer Lesniewski/Shutterstock.com

Window on World History: Two Men Who Saved the World

In a horrifyingly close encounter, the US dropped depth charges upon B-59 nearly provoking war.

Famed astronomer Carl Sagan noted that advanced civilizations are defined by their capacity to destroy themselves. Robert Oppenheimer, the "father of the bomb," in witnessing the Trinity explosion on July 16, 1945, invoked a Hindi saying "Now I am become Death, the destroyer of worlds." Nuclear fission signified a tipping point in human history where we developed the technological capacity to destroy planetary life. Recently, new evidence has revealed how tantalizingly close humanity stepped to nuclear war during the Cuban Missile Crisis. On October 27, 1962, Soviet missiles shot down an American U-2 spy plane killing its pilot Major Rudolf Anderson. US hardliners ordered immediate retaliation, but Kennedy held them back, calculating that the Russians had made a mistake. Simultaneously, a more harrowing incident unfolded in the waters off Cuba. US destroyers discovered a Soviet submarine and dropped "practice" depth charges to induce it to surface. What they did not know was that the air conditioning had broken down on B-59. Inside the submerged submarine, temperatures flared and tempers frayed. Believing himself under attack, and having lost all contact with Moscow, Captain Savitsky imagined the worst and ordered the arming of his nuclear torpedo. When Flotilla Commander Vasili Arkhipov countermanded Savitsky's order, a tense debate ensued. Eventually, the nuclear torpedo was safely stowed away. B-59, running critically short of battery power, surfaced in front of American destroyers before limping back to port. Both President Kennedy and Commander Arkhipov had stared into abyss and each had taken a step back. This gave the world a reprieve, making us all the children of October. For thirteen days, humanity flirted with Armageddon. Thankfully, humanity escaped, but the story of B-59 reminds us that nuclear arms are a dangerous tool in the hands of flawed and emotional human beings.

Critical Reflection

1. Did the balance of nuclear terror keep the peace during the Cold War, or did doctrines like mutually assured destruction highlight the irrationality of this era?
2. The end of the Cold War abated public fears about nuclear war. Is the era of the "bomb" really over, or are we entering a more dangerous era of nuclear proliferation?

Ultimately, JFK steered a middle course, ordering a blockade of Cuba, which he termed a "quarantine" to mask that it violated international law. Kennedy's objective was to prevent Soviet ships from bringing nuclear warheads to Cuba. In a long October 22 radio address, he explained the nature of the Soviet threat to the American public and prepared them for war. To the Soviets, Kennedy's militant speech signaled his resolve. Kennedy's address was followed with a diplomatic blitz to pressure Khrushchev to back down. On October 26, UN Ambassador Adlai Stephenson confronted his Soviet counterpart with spy photo evidence. When Valeri Zorin denied knowledge of the missiles, he was widely seen as stonewalling. International opinion turned against Khrushchev.

On October 27, the world held its collective breath as Soviet vessels approached the US blockade. Then, Soviet ships stopped dead in the water and Khrushchev cabled the White House. The USSR would remove its missiles in return for a noninvasion pledge. Before the United States could accept, however, an ultimatum arrived. It threatened massive retaliation if the United States invaded Cuba. This communiqué proposed removal of the Cuban missiles in exchange for a simultaneous withdrawal of US missiles from Turkey. The two cables were divergent in tone and raised concerns about whether Khrushchev was in charge. Llewelyn Thompson, former ambassador to the USSR, urged Kennedy to look at the Cuban Crisis from Russian eyes. Khrushchev needed a diplomatic solution that would enable him to retreat while saving face. Independently, Kennedy had already started to question the US strategic doctrine. Now Kennedy started to appraise Khrushchev not as some fanatic but as a rational being, with concrete interests that could be identified, studied, and countered. President Kennedy dispatched his brother Bobby Kennedy to secretly negotiate a deal with the Soviet Ambassador Gromyko to resolve the standoff. In return for a Soviet withdrawal of nuclear missiles, the United States pledged not to invade Cuba. The deal was sealed by a secret codex in which the United States agreed to remove its missiles from Turkey. On October 28, Khrushchev publicly accepted the US offer. This averted an US invasion, but humanity had stepped perilously close to the brink.

Crisis Aftermath

The Cuban Missile Crisis laid the foundation for improved US–Soviet relations, later referred to as détente. The superpower rivalry did not end, but the Cold War changed as both sides took concrete steps to prevent local conflicts from escalating into catastrophe. The famous hotline connecting the White House and Kremlin was established to ensure better communication during crises. Resolution of the Cuban Crisis also laid the foundation for various arms control measures, including the 1963 **Limited Test Ban Treaty** for nuclear weapons. In certain crises, like the 1973 Yom Kippur War, the superpower rivals even colluded to settle conflicts among their allies. After Cuba, the Cold War entered a new era. Public fears about nuclear war waned. Before his premature death, President Kennedy could imagine the possibility of a world free from the Cold War and its nuclear terror. In 1963, Kennedy spoke publicly of a "genuine peace, the kind of peace that makes life on Earth worth living, the kind that enables men and nations to grow and to hope and to build a better life for their children-not merely peace for Americans but peace for all men and women-not merely peace in our time, but peace for all time."[7]

Third World in the Cross Fire

While détente represented a tangible phenomenon, for people living in the developing world, the 1960s and 1970s represented the climax of their suffering. Of the twenty million people who died in wars fought between 1945 and 1990, 99 percent were located in the Third World.[8] As we shall see in Chapters 6 to 9, the Cold War rivalry manifested into distinctive regional configurations. At a global scale, superpower conflict tended to exacerbate internal rivalries while disrupting the trajectory of postcolonial development. One superpower lever over postcolonial states came from crafting alliances with local elites. While the superpowers sought to rally surrogates against their main adversary, local elites also exploited the bipolar international system to win support for their national agenda or to secure external aid for their fight against internal opponents. From a global perspective, however, there were important regional differences in terms of how the Cold War intersected with local politics and the ways that local elites aligned with outside forces. In Latin America, *junta* overthrew civilian governments starting in the late 1960s, launching dirty wars against leftist reformers demanding land reform and socialist reforms. A similar pattern was evident in the Middle East where secular elites first rallied the people against Western influence, but after 1970 increasingly allied with outsiders to squelch internal dissenters. In Sub-Saharan Africa, the process of colonialism had created the most fragile states. This left them vulnerable to recurrent coups that often failed to produce decisive outcomes. Foreign intervention in African politics reignited ethnic fissures inherited from the colonial era. Inside Asia, local elites initially split along ideological lines, but after a fractious experience with the Cold War, by the late 1970s, national elites mostly united their peoples around state programs for industrial development on both sides of the Bamboo Curtain.

The ability of states and national leaders to deflect superpower pressure and channel it towards their own national interest varied wildly. Generally, the "Third World" was caught in the cross fire. The economic, financial, and military preponderance of the superpowers relative to their "client" states meant that foreign interests often trumped indigenous desires in shaping national policies. In cases like Vietnam, Korea, and Angola, where outside powers matched each other in pouring arms into a conflict zone, civilians paid the price. In both ways, the Cold War often corrupted the dream among non-Western peoples for an independence that would deliver true freedom and material progress. The Cold War rendered postcolonial politics toxic. Proxy wars and coups weakened postcolonial states, inhibited national leaders from exercising real sovereignty, and prompted the rise of "strong men" whose power often depended upon outside aid. By the 1970s, authoritarian repression, despotism, and civil wars resulted in broader neocolonial settlement, where local despots crafted deals that diverted local mineral wealth towards foreign investors rather than projects to improve indigenous living standards.

Non-Aligned Movement

As European colonialism began to collapse, non-Western leaders were conscious of the danger posed by the Cold War. At the 1955 **Bandung Conference**, Indonesian President **Sukarno** opened the conference by noting "this is the first international conference of colored peoples in the history of Mankind."[9] Sukarno and his colleagues took turns condemning the Cold War as an infringement upon national sovereignty. Rejecting bipolarity, the world's most dynamic postcolonial leaders advocated for neutralism and non-Western solidarity. Their ambition was to craft a "Third World" bloc that could promote peace and racial equality, and realign the world economy towards colored peoples.

Kwame Nkrumah defined nonalignment as favoring neither East nor West, but as embracing a fundamental freedom "to judge issues on their merits and to look for solutions that are just and peaceful, irrespective of the powers involved."[10] At the 1961 Belgrade Conference, the **NAM** was formally established with the ambition to recast the international system to reflect the interests of the nonwhite majority. Although the NAM did convene periodic summits, and operated unofficially inside the UN General Assembly throughout the 1970s, the bloc struggled to substantially influence superpower policy or redirect established patterns of trade and finance. Despite public expressions of solidarity, members of NAM were often regional rivals. Occasionally, they fought wars against each other. More fundamentally, postcolonial leaders dealt with immediate concerns that made it difficult to subordinate concrete national interests to an idealistic international agenda.

One strategy pursued by some adventuresome postcolonial leaders was to leverage the superpower rivalry to their advantage. As we shall see in Chapter 7, Egyptian President Gamal Abdel Nasser proved the most adept at pivoting between superpower patrons. His audacious approach represented a delicate balancing act, but Nasser's dance was mimicked to a lesser extent by Indonesia's Sukarno, India's Jawaharlal Nehru, and Yugoslavia's Josip Broz Tito during the late 1950s and early 1960s. Each of these leaders leveraged their country's strategic importance to enlist superpower support from either or both sides, without formally aligning in the Cold War or compromising their own national objectives. For most new states, neutrality proved a less viable option. Ho Chi Minh tried to broker a negotiated settlement with France, but was rebuffed in 1946, triggering a devastating thirty-year war for independence. Patrice Lumumba was assassinated in part because his plans for national development clashed with the financial interests of Belgium and Union Minière. When Salvador Allende tried to institute socialist reforms in Chile, he was overthrown by coup supported by ITT and the CIA. By the time of Nasser's death from a heart attack in 1970, the NAM had faded into virtual insignificance. The Cold War had already swept away most of the Bandung delegates from the international stage.

War in the Shadows

The Korean War exposed the potential cost of Cold War confrontations. In 1955, President Dwight Eisenhower developed the **New Look Doctrine** to reconceptualize the United States' containment strategy. Eisenhower advocated expansion of the United States' nuclear arsenal, while reclassifying the "bomb" as a strategic weapon reserved only for when national security was directly threatened. In "Third World" settings, Eisenhower privileged the use of "soft" power. The United States had significant diplomatic and economic leverage that it could bring to bear upon smaller states. If such pressure failed, successful CIA coups in Iran and Guatemala from 1953 to 1954 demonstrated that clandestine subversion could remove leaders that dared to buck US interests. Covert regime change presented a cost-effective and more politically palatable alternative to sending in US Marines. The New Look doctrine transformed the United States' approach to fighting the Cold War inside the postcolonial world without revising the US security establishment's core beliefs about global communism. Notably, Eisenhower spurned multiple Soviet attempts to normalize relations after Stalin's death in 1953.

The transition from conventional wars and nuclear brinkmanship to asymmetric warfare during the late 1950s coincided with a major geopolitical shift. Decolonization brought the Third World into a polarized international environment. The often turbulent process of postcolonial transition intensified internal fissures along ethnic, racial, and ideological lines. Conflicts inside postcolonial states attracted external involvement. The superpowers, China, France, and foreign multinationals participated in **proxy wars** that cost relatively little in comparison to conventional wars. Backing different internal factions often carried little risk of escalation, while promising potentially lucrative awards: basing rights, mineral concessions if their party emerged victorious. Although the Cold War contorted the postwar international system around two ideological poles, Western influence remained preponderant. The US economy outclassed the USSR's by a significant margin, and many of its European allies were major industrial states that retained colonies, global bases, multinational corporations, and treaty networks of their own. Western industrial predominance gave them leverage over the prices of commodities that developing states exported. Western capital held the key for postcolonial investment and the West used their predominance over international financial institutions like the World Bank and International Monetary Fund (IMF) to steer postcolonial leaders to their camp. Even socialists and dependency theorists inclined to use sharp rhetoric proved wary of overtly bucking Western strategic interests. Western economic hegemony also dimmed the attractiveness of any potential Soviet alliance, despite the ideological appeal of its development program, which linked class struggle, rapid industrialization, and anti-imperialism. Some strategically significant countries like Egypt and Cuba did appeal for Soviet patronage, but the USSR had limited resources, and their assistance came with strings of its own. Nationalization of Western businesses represented another development strategy. Crossing this red line, however, risked retaliation. As we will see in Chapter 6, Guatemala's Jacobo Arbenz was branded a "communist" after embarking upon a relatively modest land reform program that appropriated uncultivated lands belonging to the United Fruit Company. A covert CIA plot ousted this democratically elected leader for a measly $3 million, while his handpicked successor immediately set about slicing the voter rolls by 75 percent to ensure elite interests would dominate inside "democratic" Guatemala.

The following multi-graphic highlights Sub-Saharan Africa's particular vulnerability to asymmetric warfare. As noted in Chapter 3, the African process of decolonization left many postcolonial states weak and divided, which amplified their vulnerability to covert subversion. The KGB, foreign multinationals, and the White House used various clandestine tools ranging from disinformation, bribery, predatory treaties, economic sabotage, and assassination to influence local politics, gain mineral concessions, acquire rights, or weaken their geopolitical rivals.

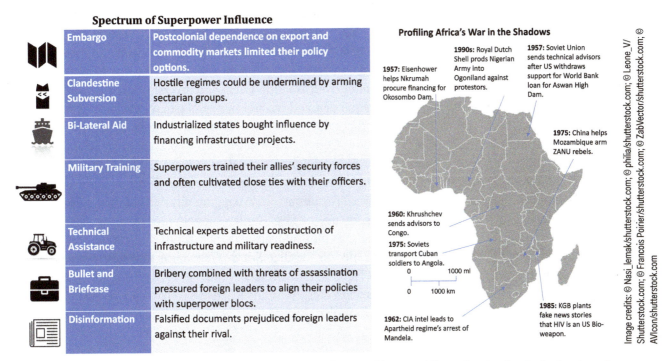

The Cold War was waged clandestinely using spies, diplomats, engineers, athletes, and film makers battling for the hearts and minds of people in the Third World. Superpowers, China, the European colonial powers, and multinational corporations offered loans, technical assistance, and military aid to allies, while sabotaging and subverting clients of their rivals.

Starved for capital, and often dependent on Western markets, many postcolonial leaders were forced to align their development agenda with the priorities of foreign investors, international bankers, or the policies of their sponsors. On this basis, Kwame Nkrumah denounced the Cold War for inducing "neocolonialism," a condition where a state "is, in theory, independent and has all the outward trappings of international sovereignty. In reality, its economic system, and thus its political policy, is directed from outside."[11] A principle lever for superpower influence was cultivating local surrogates. Corporate bribes of local ministers, predatory foreign loans, and covert arms shipments to regime opponents corrupted postcolonial states by creating a divide between a class of local elites at the expense of the indigenous majority. As will be noted in Chapter 10, in Eastern Europe, nationalist reform movements were similarly stymied by Soviet tanks. A pillar of Moscow's system for informal imperialism was an indigenous security elite originally trained by the KGB, deeply integrated with the Soviet security apparatus and backstopped by Russian tanks. This structure of influence left local communists in charge, while mitigating the irritant of direct Russian rule. It also restrained communist leaders from imposing policies deemed inconsistent with Soviet security interests.

The Vietnam War

The United States' relative success in exerting "soft power" during the 1950s and 1960s left them ill-prepared for Vietnam. US involvement dated back to 1950 when Truman agreed to bankroll France's struggle against the communist Viet Minh. Following French withdrawal in 1954, the United States emerged as South Vietnam's principal patron. Enamored with newly elected **Ngo Dinh Diem's** fierce anti-communism, the United States trained and equipped his army. Diem's regime, however, was unpopular. He was not only a Catholic in a predominantly Buddhist country, but also an outspoken Evangelical and authoritarian leader. Diem was also aloof and out of touch with his ordinary people. He consistently resisted calls for land reform, while ruthlessly crushing any form of dissent. Locals saw Diem's anti-communism as mere authoritarianism, while they resented his regime's appalling nepotism and corruption. Diem's unpopularity provided an opening for communists. In 1957, the National Liberation Front (NLF) emerged with the goal of overthrowing Diem and reversing their country's illegal partitioning. Their guerilla force was equipped and trained by the North Vietnamese government. In 1958, they launched a terrorist campaign that targeted South Vietnamese military installations and government officials. Derisively Named the "Viet Cong" by Diem the NLF represented an eclectic force. They included refugees from South Vietnam, opponents of Diem, as well as Viet Minh veterans who were infiltrated into the South. After 1960, Viet Cong attacks intensified. They sowed insecurity and highlighted the weakness of Diem's regime. To support their flagging ally, US military stepped up their assistance, but this failed to curb the insurgency or to galvanize support for Diem. In 1963, the United States reluctantly sanctioned an indigenous plot to overthrow Diem. Diem's brutal assassination, however, embarrassed the United States and failed to stabilize South Vietnam. A series of new regimes came and went. By 1964, President Johnson faced a stark choice: South Vietnam would collapse unless the United States deployed its own combat troops. Despite Johnson's hope to launch a domestic war on poverty, he saw South Vietnam as a test of US resolve: "if we are driven from Vietnam, then no nations can ever again have the same confidence in . . . . American protection."[12]

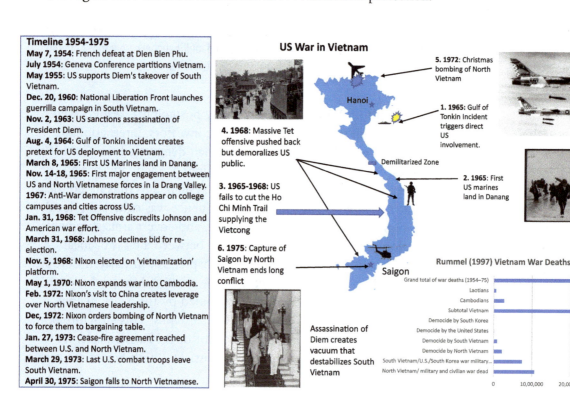

Timeline 1954-1975
May 7, 1954: French defeat at Dien Bien Phu.
July 1954: Geneva Conference partitions Vietnam.
May 1955: US supports Diem's takeover of South Vietnam.
Dec. 20, 1960: National Liberation Front launches guerrilla campaign in South Vietnam.
Nov. 2, 1963: US sanctions assassination of President Diem.
Aug. 4, 1964: Gulf of Tonkin incident creates pretext for US deployment to Vietnam.
March 8, 1965: First US Marines land in Danang.
Nov. 14-18, 1965: First major engagement between US and North Vietnamese forces in Ia Drang Valley.
1967: Anti-War demonstrations appear on college campuses and cities across US.
Jan. 31, 1968: Tet Offensive discredits Johnson and American war effort.
March 31, 1968: Johnson declines bid for re-election.
Nov. 5, 1968: Nixon elected on 'vietnamization' platform.
May 1, 1970: Nixon expands war into Cambodia.
Feb. 1972: Nixon's visit to China creates leverage over North Vietnamese leadership.
Dec, 1972: Nixon orders bombing of North Vietnam to force them to bargaining table.
Jan. 27, 1973: Cease-fire agreement reached between U.S. and North Vietnam.
March 29, 1973: Last U.S. combat troops leave South Vietnam.
April 30, 1975: Saigon falls to North Vietnamese.

Mass deployment of US combat troops to Vietnam followed the 1964 **Gulf of Tonkin Incident**. The United States claimed that North Vietnamese patrol boats had fired on the *USS Maddox* in international waters. In fact, its deck had been sprayed by bullets several days before while supporting a covert mission inside North Vietnamese waters. This false flag "incident" led Congress to authorize Johnson to send US troops to Vietnam absent a declaration of war. General William Westmoreland promised a quick and decisive victory. From 1965 to 1968, the number of US troops deployed in Vietnam steadily climbed to over half a million. Despite bloody battles, followed by news conferences where Westmoreland strutted out gaudy enemy casualty figures, the conflict showed few signs of abating. With mounting US casualties and little discernible progress, public support for the Vietnam War waned. The 1968 **Tet Offensive** pushed the United States to a breaking point. Under the cover of a New Year's truce, Vietnamese forces launched an all-out assault on South Vietnam. During a chaotic night in Saigon, the Viet Cong even managed to infiltrate the US Embassy. By coming out into the open, however, the Viet Cong exposed themselves to US firepower. Suffering nearly 50,000 casualties, Tet destroyed the Viet Cong as an effective fighting force. However, the frustrated American public had seen enough. President Johnson, who weeks before had promised victory, was discredited. The American public saw Vietnam as a quagmire: no amount of US troops could win a war where the Vietnamese refused to give up. Johnson opted not to run for reelection. Richard Nixon won the presidency in 1968, promising "vietnamization" of the war. Under Nixon's leadership, the United States invaded Cambodia, bombed Hanoi, and engaged the Chinese diplomatically. Ultimately, these initiatives facilitated a delicate deal that enabled the withdrawal of the last US combat troops by 1973. In 1975, the North Vietnamese attacked again. South Vietnam's army, abandoned by its American allies, disintegrated in a wave of desertions. In Saigon, helicopters frantically circled to evacuate the last US personnel from the embassy roof. Thousands of the United States' South Vietnamese allies were left behind facing reprisals from advancing communist forces.

Emerging Détente

US defeat in Vietnam stimulated considerable American soul searching. Military assessments focused on errors in a US counterinsurgency strategy that failed to win "hearts and minds." Many leftists used Vietnam to ridicule the containment strategy. They argued that the Vietnam quagmire resulted from outdated ideas about monolithic communism. Mistaken presumptions about the communist threat entangled US troops in a civil war they could not win. While Ho Chi Minh was communist, his grand ambition was national unification, not exporting communism. This assessment gained credence following the 1979 Chinese-Vietnam War, when China temporarily invaded North Vietnam as punishment for their ousting ally Pol Pot in Cambodia. By the mid-1970s, the United States and China were often informally aligned against the "Socialist Hegemon" the USSR and its regional communist allies.

Vietnam sharply divided the American public and alienated the United States' Western allies. After the Fall of Saigon, the United States also suffered from "Vietnam syndrome." The public proved reluctant to support military intervention abroad. The 1973 War Powers Act sharply limited the US president's ability to send troops abroad without Congressional approval. The 1975 **Church Committee** revealed a host of illegal and immoral CIA activities from bribery to assassination. Public outrage now constrained US foreign policy, while a liberal discourse of human rights prevented Hawks from employing many of the dark arts they had exercised during previous decades.

Internationally, Vietnam showed that even lightly armed guerilla forces could prevail against the world's foremost military power. This lesson was further driven home when the Soviet Union suffered its own Vietnam after being sucked into Afghanistan from 1979 to 1989. Both quagmires highlighted limits to superpower hegemony and gave hope and confidence to insurgents in the Horn of Africa and

Central America. Following Vietnam, there was an increasing trend towards US-Soviet collaboration on international security issues, particularly with respect to arms control measures. The Strategic Arms Limitations Talks (SALT) resulted in the 1972 Moscow Summit and a treaty that put a brake to the nuclear arms race. The 1975 **Helsinki Accords** represented the most tangible manifestation of détente. While its terms were nonbinding, the Soviet Union agreed to adhere to fundamental human rights principles. While Brezhnev thought he had traded empty words for concrete Western security guarantees, he quickly discovered that Helsinki provided discontented Eastern intellectuals, artists, and dissidents inside the Communist Bloc more freedom of expression. On the international level, détente established a climate of peaceful coexistence. By the late 1970s, European observers began to speak about a convergence between socialist democracy and a more humanitarian form of state socialism.

Cold War's Distortive Effects

As noted in Chapter 3, through financing allies and subverting enemy regimes, the Cold War distorted the trajectory of postwar development. Japan, Germany, and the Asian Tigers' postwar miracle economies benefitted immensely from the United States' containment policy that provided close allies' favorable entry into the US market. The seeds for the Asian Miracle of the 1980s were laid with US implication in wars in Korean and Vietnam that funneled money towards allies and stimulated demand for local goods. The Soviet Union similarly—but less successfully—subsidized its client states in Eastern Europe, Africa, and Cuba. Their principal conduit for aid was offering fossil fuels and other natural resources at a discount to market prices. Socialist allies were allowed to purchase such hard assets with local "soft" currencies that were subsequently returned by purchasing the Soviet Union's allies' exports at favorable rates. The Soviet Union's structural problems, however, made subsidies increasingly difficult to sustain by the late 1970s. As we shall see in Chapter 10, collapsing oil prices and the accelerating economic gap between the Communist and Western Bloc would play an instrumental role in the collapse of the Soviet Union's informal empire by 1989.

The Cold War in Popular Culture

Fears of Armageddon intensified during the late 1950s as nuclear arsenals expanded and became capable of destroying planetary life. Policy-makers justified the buildup by invoking macabre security concepts like **mutually assured destruction**. Bracketing security policy with the prospect of planetary annihilation amplified popular anxiety. A robust nuclear disarmament movement emerged, particularly in Britain and Germany, which would serve as the frontline in any future war. Fears about the bomb percolated inside popular culture; manifesting in films, novels, and comic books. Fiction provided a medium for gaming out doomsday scenarios, perhaps vicariously alleviating some of the crippling anxiety that drove some Western families to construct backyard nuclear shelters. Inside the United States, school children were trained in pathetically inadequate "tuck and duck" drills that convinced adolescent brains that their world might disintegrate at any moment. Some families, like the Marsh of Blackpool, found this too much to bear. In 1957, Elsie and Andrew Marshall gassed their children, bound themselves together with a cord, and drowned themselves in the North Sea. Their suicide note recorded a deeper anxiety percolating in Western culture: "in view of all the things that are happening in the world and the talk of new wars which will mean extermination of masses of people and especially children we decided we could not allow this to happen to our children."[13]

Western artists rebelled against the absurdity of nuclear war. Satire emerged as one medium for mocking the irrationality of leaders. Stanley Kubrick's 1963 *Dr. Strangelove* illustrated the irrationality of Western strategic doctrines to expose the brute reality that nuclear wars weren't winnable. Public anxiety about the bomb created pressure on political elites on both sides of the Iron Curtain to agree to nuclear arms limitations. Over the longer run, it also bred skepticism not only about nuclear armaments, but their promoters. States fought back through various forms of propaganda. In the United States, the CIA and defense establishment both overtly and covertly promoted films and novels that dramatized the threat of communist subversion, but they found willing allies among evangelicals, social conservatives, and white supremacists that appropriated state's Red Menace narrative to fit their own agenda. The Red Scare provided a structure where popular fears about Soviet subversion and nuclear war intermingled with more general anxieties rooted in postwar suburbanization, racial integration, and secularization.

Both blocs experienced witch hunts where modest enemy campaigns of espionage were inflated into vast programs for subversion. The unscrupulous **Joseph McCarthy** hunted for Soviet agents inside the State Department during the 1950s, while the House Un-American Activities Committee used questionable tactics to expose communists inside Hollywood. McCarthyism ended a few careers, but it proved mild in comparison to Soviet campaigns to uproot "enemies of state" or Mao's hunt for capitalist "road graders." Stalin's Red Terror in 1949 to 1953 snuffed out hundreds of thousands of lives and sent millions to Gulags. Under Mao, during various state campaigns from 1951 to 1969, millions of political prisoners were rounded up on trumped up charges and placed in reeducation camps that often represented a death sentence. The principal source for the Cold War's psychological intensity, however, remained the ever-present threat of Armageddon. Although the danger of nuclear war diminished after the Cuban Missile Crisis, anxiety continued to flare up during periods of international crisis. During NATO's 1983 *Able Archer* training exercise, the Kremlin became convinced the operation was a pretext for invasion. Television dramas like *The Day After*, which depicted ordinary people struggling to survive in a post-Armageddon Kansas, drew a record hundred million viewing audience in 1983. Hollywood exploited Soviet troops and communist agents as stock villains inside popular films. In his 1985 song *Russians*, British musician Sting took such caricatures to task in his sarcastic refrain, "I hope the Russians love their children too."

Fear of Armageddon promoted an escapist culture where citizens tuned out state propaganda and withdrew from public life. In the West, this survivor's instinct fueled the rise of a consumer culture. People sought out simple pleasures and diversion through spectator sports and other forms of "popular" entertainment like the cinema. Consumer products ranging from cars to new appliances and electronic gadgets focused attention away from international scene. In automobile suburbs, GIs "settled down" around backyard barbeques that represented an oasis from the noise of the city, the racial integration of society, and pressure from the workplace. Inside the police states of Eastern Europe, citizens robotically participated in state-supervised celebrations, while resisting party designs to colonize their minds. Those living under communism particularly relished sarcastic jokes. Exposing party lies or corruption among intimate friends felt therapeutic, because it was officially "subversive" yet difficult to police. Humor represented a form of resistance, and helped to carve out a private sphere immune from the communist party's totalitarian ambitions. After Khrushchev's Thaw, the threat of summary arrest inside communist societies diminished. The police state mostly limited itself to harassing public dissenters. The East German Stasi excelled at curbing dissidence in this new climate. They recruited a vast army of informers and used elaborate tactics of psychological warfare against dissidents including breaking into their homes and displacing common household items.

108 Chapter 4: The Global Cold War, 1949 to 1991

The Cultural Arena

The seeming impossibility of open war in the nuclear age tended to push the US–Soviet rivalry into the cultural arena. When the mercurial Bobby Fischer squared off against Soviet champ Boris Spassky for a chess match in neutral Iceland in 1972, both sides hailed it the "match of the century." As the world watched, Fisher and Spassky's contrasting playing styles were elevated into archetypes not of their individual genius, but as exemplifying the virtues of their nurturing social systems. Sports, particularly the Olympic stage, served as Cold War battlefields. In a life and death struggle devoid of direct military confrontation, the ice rink provided a medium for measuring both civilizations' prowess. Inside the Soviet Bloc, sport science and sophisticated amateur youth programs were promoted by the state to develop elite athletes. Those gaining success on the international stage were given special privileges and lauded as heroes, signaling socialism's imminent triumph.

Window on World History: Canada's War on the Ice

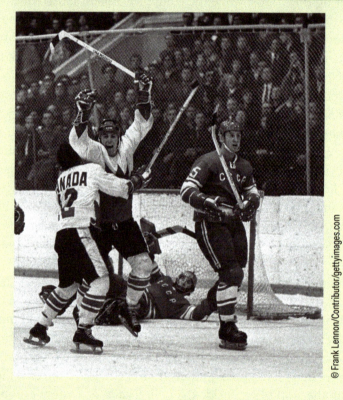

© Frank Lennon/Contributor/gettyimages.com

Canada was deeply implicated in the Cold War as a founding member of NATO. The intensity experienced by Canadians during the Cold War is best illustrated in the famous 1972 Summit Series. Canadians still consider hockey to be "their" game. During the 1950s and 1960s, however, the Soviet Union dominated international hockey. Canadians attributed this to the fact that their best players were barred from participating in amateur tournaments as National Hockey League professionals. In 1972, during the height of *détente*, an arrangement was made to pit Canada's best players against their Soviet counterparts. For the first time, Canada's heroes—legends such as Esposito, Orr, and Dryden—were set to square off against the socialist hockey automatons. Before the puck dropped, most Canadians were already celebrating their well-deserved revenge for the drubbing their amateur teams had suffered during previous years. Ken Dryden expressed public sympathy for his Soviet counterpart, the famed Vladislav Tretiak. Although a few North American sportswriters predicted that the Soviets might win a game, Canada's victory was assured. In game one, Canada staked an early two goal lead. Subsequently, they grew frustrated with a Soviet style of play predicated on athletic skill, precision passing, and teamwork. By game four, fans in Vancouver's Pacific Coliseum rained down boos on Team Canada. A loss had left them behind in the series 1-2-1. A sweaty and disheartened Phil Esposito stared up at the rafters as he took the microphone to remind fans that they were "trying." Canadian pride had been bruised by the marvelous Valeri Kharlamov. An acrobat on skates, he sliced through Canada's lumbering defense with the finesse of a ballet dancer. After the series moved to Moscow, the Canadian team promptly dropped another game. Now at the brink of defeat, assistant coach Ferguson reportedly ordered his most physical player, Bobby Clarke, to "take care" of Kharlamov. Early in game six, Clarke complied by delivering a wicked two-handed slash to the Soviet center's already injured ankle. While Kharlamov tried to return to the ice, he was no longer the same player. Canada's prospects suddenly brightened. The Summit Series, inaugurated as a gesture of goodwill, had degenerated into a brawl. The Cold War had also descended onto the ice. Players were no longer athletes, but elevated to symbols of their respective social systems. Soviet media criticized Canada's physical style of play as criminal. Canadians denigrated the Russian propensity for "diving." Canada ultimately prevailed by taking the last three games of the series in dramatic fashion. During the climatic game eight, Canadian stores and factories shut down. TVs were rolled into classrooms. In the first period, a Soviet referee called two early penalties on Team Canada, sparking a bitter confrontation in the stands between Canadian team boss Alan Eagleson and Soviet militia. Canadian players jumped to the rescue, freeing Eagleson and escorting his across the ice to the safety of their bench. No Canadians can forget that final minute of regulation. In a desperate scramble before the goal mouth, Henderson tucked the puck just under Tretiak's left elbow. For many Canadians, this image crystallized the heart of Canadian team that never quit. Most Russians, naturally attribute Canada's victory in the "match of the century" to cheating and Clarke's wicked slash.

Critical Reflection

1. Why did international sporting events assume particular significance during the Cold War?
2. After World War II, Canada cultivated its image as an ambassador for international peace. In what ways did Canada's physical style of hockey counteract its international image?

Military Industrial Complex

The Cold War placed a heavy burden on both superpower economies. Upon leaving office, Eisenhower warned about the rise of what he termed a "military–industrial complex," but he also rebuffed Soviet offers of peaceful coexistence after Stalin's 1953 death. This stimulated another three decades of intensive military investment. The cost of developing weapon platforms skyrocketed as they grew increasingly sophisticated. Maintaining vast standing armies and deploying forces across the globe placed a heavy burden on both superpower economies. Military spending did have commercial spin-offs, helping to launch the electronic, telecommunications, and computer industries in the West. It also generated jobs, but the Cold War also siphoned away capital that could have been channeled towards infrastructure, commercial research, and social services. In throwing their weight around the world stage, both superpowers overstretched their resources. The Soviet Union collapsed in part because its economy failed to keep up with US military investments or maintain its commitments to socialist allies. Although the United States is commonly viewed as winning the Cold War, following the Vietnam War, Nixon was forced off the gold standard in 1971. This established a trend towards rising budget deficits, which steadily eroded US power.

Gorbachev's End Game, 1985 to 1991

The end of the Cold War was closely tied to Mikhail Gorbachev's unlikely partnership with US President Ronald Reagan. Reagan stormed into office in 1981 with a telegenic smile and a fistful of aphorisms about the American way of life. Anti-communism represented a central ingredient of Reagan's identity and worldview. During his inaugural address, Reagan shrugged off Vietnam and championed American exceptionalism. The United States had a global destiny to "be the exemplar of freedom and a beacon of hope."[14] For a public that had suffered from a slowing economy, internal divisions, and an erosion of global influence, Reagan's confidence helped Americans to "feel good again." The celebration of American virtues was cast against the dark foil of Soviet power. Reagan depicted the Soviet Union as an "evil empire" that reserved "unto themselves the right to commit any crime, to lie, to cheat."[15] Reagan's frequent denunciations of "godless" communism reflected a naive but sincere belief that socialism sowed moral degeneracy. Reagan also viewed Soviet power as the principal obstacle to making international progress on human rights. Although usually casting the Cold War in moral terms, Reagan also believed that peace could only be won through strength. Accordingly, his first initiative was to launch a massive program for US military modernization. If the Soviet invasion of Afghanistan in 1979 had interrupted *détente*, Reagan's militancy proved decisive in pushing the Cold War into a "hot" phase.

Gorbachev came to power after two sickly Brezhnev era cronies died in rapid succession from 1984 to 1985. Gorbachev offered the Kremlin a fresh face. Western leaders like Margaret Thatcher were struck by Gorbachev's vigor, charm, and intelligence. Gorbachev was a proponent of "new thinking," which meant questioning traditional Bolshevik premises, particularly the fundamental hostility between capitalism and socialism. Gorbachev and his new guard were certain that socialism was morally superior to the inequities generated by capitalism. However, they also recognized the urgent necessity for internal reform. The Soviet system badly lagged the West in terms of consumer goods, technology, food, and housing. Like Khrushchev, Gorbachev believed that reviving the Soviet economy was diminishing the drain of military spending.

Despite his hostility to communism, Reagan was also deathly afraid of nuclear war. Already in 1981, Reagan had proposed destroying all nuclear arms, but failed to find a negotiating partner. In 1983, Reagan instead unveiled the **Strategic Defense Initiative (SDI)**, a research program dedicated to developing antiballistic missile technology that would shield Americans from Armageddon. For the Soviet Union, SDI represented unwelcome news—not because they believed the United States capable of constructing an impenetrable shield, but because "Star Wars" risked triggering a new arms race in space.

Disappointment at not reaching a historic deal can be read into the faces of Reagan and Gorbachev. Despite failure to agree on Strategic Defense Initiative (SDI), ultimately Reykjavik set the stage for a partnership that would bring the Cold War to an end.

At Geneva in 1985, Reagan and Gorbachev struck an immediate rapport, which built hope that the 1986 **Reykjavik Summit** might culminate in a landmark nuclear arms pact. In order to get Reagan to drop SDI, Gorbachev offered total elimination of nuclear weapons. This was not on the official agenda. It caught Reagan's team flat-footed. After Reagan confirmed Gorbachev's offer with his translator, however, he agreed. In light of their historic accord, Gorbachev now demanded that Reagan give up SDI. To his frustration, Reagan refused. Instead, Reagan tried to convince Gorbachev that he would share his ABM technology with the Soviets. Many speculate that Reagan's faith in SDI originated in his casting as a secret agent in the 1940 film *Murder in the Air*, which featured an "inertia projector" that hurled electrical currents at enemy planes. Critics dubbed Reagan's dream of a nuclear shield "Star Wars," because experts deemed it infeasible with current technology. Gorbachev could not grasp that Reagan's refusal to scuttle SDI was rooted in an irrational fanaticism that could not be trumped through logical argument. Accordingly, both men left Iceland dejected. A landmark deal to destroy nuclear weapons had fallen from their grasp. Returning to Moscow, Gorbachev became increasingly hemmed in by Soviet hardliners. They took Reykjavik as clear evidence that the United States intended to leverage its economic and technological advantages to destroy socialism. US Hawks, in contrast, were relieved that a simplistic Reagan's fear of nuclear weapons had not resulted in a rash deal. Now they pushed Reagan to press Gorbachev harder on human rights and the war in Afghanistan.

Following Reykjavik, US–Soviet relations reached low ebb as proxy wars in Nicaragua, Angola, and Afghanistan allowed hardliners on both sides to sabotage momentum towards further arms control measure. The critical breakthrough in East–West relations came in 1988 when Gorbachev carried his "new thinking" towards its logical conclusion. To the surprise of the West, Gorbachev announced that the Soviet Union would unilaterally cut its conventional forces in half. Gorbachev had come to realize that a massive Red Army was not required for the defense of the Soviet Union. Gorbachev also appreciated that the principal stumbling block in negotiations was the persistence of irrational US myths about Soviet intentions. By disarming unilaterally, while speaking about the humanist goals of socialism, Gorbachev won international prestige and undercut the American Hawks' argument. Embarking initially on peace alone, Gorbachev would ultimately force the United States to respond as the American people would no longer support massive weapons expenditures to deter a nonexistent enemy.

Gorbachev and Eastern Europe

Many of Gorbachev's calculations were confirmed during subsequent events, but he did not anticipate how his policies would rapidly destabilize the Soviet system. As will be noted in Chapter 10, Gorbachev's push for reform among his allies and his decision to renounce the Brezhnev Doctrine unleashed a chain reaction that precipitated the rapid collapse of communism in Eastern Europe. Soviet hardliners were alarmed. Not only were they losing their empire, but the integrity of the Soviet Union was at stake. Already the Baltic states were agitating for secession. Ethnic nationalism, long suppressed by the repressive socialist federal system, reasserted itself forcefully by 1990. In 1991, Soviet hardliners launched a desperate coup to preserve communism. The plotters half-hearted attempt quickly fizzled out after Boris Yeltsin confronted the tanks before a burning Russian parliament. When Gorbachev returned to office, the Soviet Union had already died. In 1991, its constituent republics split apart. Some reformed themselves inside a loose federation, while others broke away as sovereign states. With dissolution of the Soviet Union, the communist system and the socialist ideal died. The Cold War, a defining feature of the postwar system, had ended.

Conclusion

Following their inability to reach a postwar settlement, the animosity between the United States and Soviet Union escalated into a global struggle. One casualty of the Cold War was the idealistic ambitions that had shaped the formation of the UN and other international institutions in the aftermath of World War II. Rather than an international system founded upon moral principles to check national aggression and facilitate cooperation among civilized nations, the postwar world became increasingly polarized and dominated by cynical superpower calculations. The terrifying prospect of nuclear catastrophe pushed the rivalry between communism and capitalism into the realm of culture and out along the global periphery, where the superpowers often fought through proxies. During the Cold War era, people lived in fear, some states were devastated and few escaped the conflict's influence. On a global scale, the Cold War was not as destructive as the crises that racked the preceding half-century. Some even credit bipolarity with stabilizing the international system. Certainly, the three decades following World War II were a period of economic recovery and robust growth, but one can hardly attribute this to the superpower struggle. The Cold War inflicted massive collateral damage on developing nations, it diverted their sociopolitical development and placed a heavy strain on superpower economies. The Cold War was as illogical as it was unnecessary, but it was a unique ingredient that pervaded the postwar international system, shaped its economic development, and spiced its culture.

Questions for Critical Thought

1. What made the Cold War unique in world history? Was it a "war" even if it lacked some of war's most defining characteristics?
2. Why was the Cold War principally waged in the realm of culture and on the "Third World" stage?
3. What assumptions and fears shaped the American public's view of the "Fall of China"? How were their perceptions of the dangers of communism irrational?
4. Why did Korea's Civil War become the first battlefield of the Cold War? How was this conflict significant in setting the informal rules of the Cold War?
5. What lessons did Eisenhower draw from the Korean War and enshrine into his New Look doctrine?
6. What events preceded the Cuban Missile Crisis and contributed to the high state of tension between East and West? What was the turning point of the Cuban Crisis that enabled Khrushchev and Kennedy to step back from the brink?
7. Why did détente set in after the Cuban Missile Crisis and what did this mean in terms of the rivalry and relationship between the United States and Soviet Union?
8. Why did Vietnam represent a strategic defeat for the United States despite never losing a battle? How did Vietnam and Afghanistan expose superpower limits that heralded the emergence of a more complicated international reality?
9. In what ways did the Cold War impact the realm of culture?
10. Which world regions were the most affected by the Cold War from 1949 to 1991? Why were the Cold War's impacts not evenly distributed among diverse world regions?

Suggestions for Further Reading

- Gaddis, J. L. *The Cold War*. London: Allen Lane, 2006.
- Grachev, G. *Gorbachev's Gamble: Soviet Foreign Policy and the End of the Cold War*. Cambridge, MA: Polity, 2008.

- Kolko, G. *The Age of War: The United States Confronts the World*. Boulder, CO: Lynne Rienner, 2006.
- Leffler, M. P. *For the Soul of Mankind: The United States and the Soviet Union, and the Cold War*. New York: Hill and Wang, 2007.
- Leffler, M. P., and Odd A. W. *Cambridge History of the Cold War*. 3 vols. Cambridge, UK: Cambridge University Press, 2010.
- McMahon, R. J., ed. *The Cold War and the Third World*. New York: Oxford University Press, 2013.
- Statler, K. *The Eisenhower Administration, the Third World, and the Globalization of the Cold War*. Lanham, MA: Rowman and Littlefield, 2005.
- Stern, S. J. *The Cuban Missile Crisis in American Memory: Myths versus Reality*. Stanford, CA: Stanford University Press, 2012.
- Westad, O. A. *The Global Cold War*. Cambridge, UK: Cambridge University Press, 2005.
- Whitfield, S. J. *The Culture of the Cold War*. Baltimore: John's Hopkins, 1996.
- Zubok, V. M., and Konstantin P. *Inside the Kremlin's Cold War: From Stalin to Khrushchev*. Cambridge, MA: Harvard University Press, 1996.

Notes

1. National Security Council Report 68, "United States Objectives and Programs for National Security," presented to Harry Truman, April 14, 1950, accessed July 30, 2019, http://digitalarchive.wilsoncenter.org/document/116191.
2. Quoted in Sergei Goncharov, John Lewis, and Xue Litai, *Uncertain Partners* (Stanford, CA: Stanford University Press, 1993), 138.
3. Jerry Carter, *Hard Right Turn: The History and the Assassination of the American Left* (New York: Algora, 2015), 140.
4. Quoted in David Curtis Wright, *The History of China*, 2nd ed. (Oxford: Greenwood Press, 2011), 160.
5. United States Government Printing Office, *Congressional Record: Proceedings and Debates of the 89th Congress, 1st Session*, vol. III, No. 170, Daily Edition (September 15, 1965), 22998–3005.
6. Quoted in Jim Rasenberger, *The Brilliant Disaster* (New York: Scribner, 2011), 27.
7. Quoted in John Lewis Gaddis, *For the Soul of Mankind: The United States and the Soviet Union, and the Cold War* (New York: Hill and Wang, 2007), 182.
8. Robert McMahon, *The Cold War in the Third World* (New York: Oxford University Press, 2013), 7.
9. Quoted in McMahon, *The Cold War in the Third World*, 5.
10. Quoted in Jussi Hanhimäki and Odd Arne Wested, *The Cold War: A History in Documents and Eyewitness Accounts* (Oxford: Oxford University Press, 2003), 355.
11. Quoted in Opoku Agyeman, *The Failure of Grassroots Pan-Africanism; The Case of the All-African Trade Union Federation* (New York: Lexington Books, 2004), 5.
12. Quoted in John Lewis Gaddis, *The Cold War* (London: Penguin, 2005), 133.
13. Jonathan Hogg, The Family that Feared Tomorrow: British Nuclear Culture and Individual Experience in the late 1950s," *The British Journal for the History of Science* 45, no. 4 (2012): 536.
14. Ronald Reagan: "Inaugural Address," January 20, 1981. Online by Gerhard Peters and John T. Woolley, *The American Presidency Project*. Accessed July 29, 2019, https://avalon.law.yale.edu/20th_century/reagan1.asp.
15. Quoted in Leffler, *Soul of Mankind*, 339.

Chapter 5
The Postwar West

Chapter Outline

- Introduction
- Golden Recovery
- Society of Affluence, 1950 to 1969
- The Anxious 1960s
- Stagflation Crisis, 1973 to 1980
- Conservative Resurgence, 1980s
- Contemporary Western Society
- Conclusion: The West in the Twenty-First Century

1947 Founding of Levittown
1949 NATO formed
1954 Brown vs. Board of Education
1955 West Germany joins NATO
1957 Treaty of Rome establishes EEC
1967 San Francisco's 'Summer of Love'
1969 Willy Brandt Chancellor of Germany
1971 Justice Powell Memo
1973 OPEC Oil Embargo
1979 Thatcher elected PM
1980 Reagan's Election
1982-83 Mitterrand abandons socialism
1989 Fall of Berlin Wall
1993 European Union
1994 NAFTA
2001-9-11 Attack

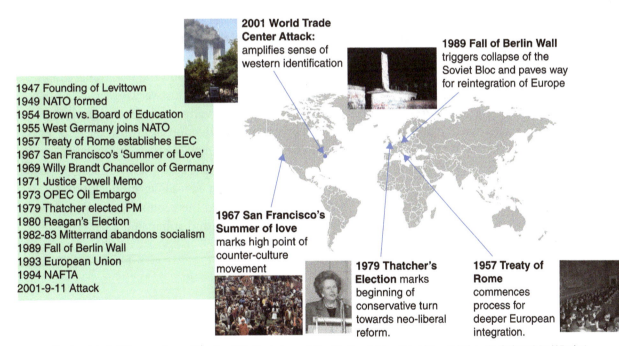

2001 World Trade Center Attack: amplifies sense of western identification

1989 Fall of Berlin Wall triggers collapse of the Soviet Bloc and paves way for reintegration of Europe

1967 San Francisco's Summer of love marks high point of counter-culture movement

1979 Thatcher's Election marks beginning of conservative turn towards neo-liberal reform.

1957 Treaty of Rome commences process for deeper European integration.

Image credits: © Andrei Minsk/Shutterstock.com; © Dan Howell/Shutterstock.com; National Archives Catalog; Pictorial Press Ltd/Alamy Stock Photo; © David Fowler/Shutterstock.com; © Umberto Cicconi/Contributor/gettyimages.com

Introduction

The "West" is more of an identity than a place. Geographically, the "Western World" encompasses the European peninsula where the Judeo-Christian traditions first crystalized into a distinctive culture. By the twentieth century, the "West" also incorporated those subtropical frontiers where European settlers had overwhelmed the indigenous population and founded societies based predominantly upon Anglo-Saxon traditions. North America, Australasia, and Western Europe share a common heritage, a high level of economic development and relatively liberal social and political systems.

Postwar forces brought Western states closer together and eroded cultural difference. World War II had discredited militant nationalism and encouraged deeper postwar collaboration. Fear of communism inspired Western Europeans to rally around an Atlantic Bloc united in the collective defense of Western Europe and democracy. Technological advances and structural shifts inside the world economy accelerated postwar convergence towards a postindustrial society defined by urban living, expanding service sector employment, and higher female participation inside the labor force. By the 1990s, digital technologies, neoliberal reforms, and the easing of border controls further diminished national differences and stimulated a liberal reformulation of traditional ideas about family, sexuality, and leisure.

The history of the postwar West falls into three main eras. Starting around 1950, a golden economic recovery restored Western optimism. Postwar welfare states combined state planning with an expanding safety net, while growing affluence pushed World War II into the rearview mirror while easing class tensions. Western society grew more urban and secular, while citizens adopted increasingly liberal attitudes towards sex, divorce, and family life. Mass prosperity, however, also bred discontent. Affluence did not trickle down to ethnic minorities, liberal reforms unsettled conservatives, and consumerism left many adolescents unsatisfied. As the postwar economy slowed during the mid-1960s, discontent fed a counterculture movement that challenged both the postwar establishment and the traditional mores. When stagflation hit Western economies during the 1970s, it fractured the postwar consensus. British Prime Minister Thatcher and US President Ronald Reagan led a conservative resurgence during the early 1980s. Both called for a return to traditional values and the introduction of promarket reforms to reinvigorate Western society. Collapse of the Soviet Bloc in 1989 rekindled Western optimism. Western states working through the World Trade Organization (WTO), European Union (EU), and Organization for Economic Cooperation and Development (OECD) brought Western economies more closely together and sought to promote liberal reform abroad. Rapid changes in the economy, the workplace, and the family, however, also spurred increasing economic polarization and stimulated a backlash against globalization and multiculturalism.

Big Questions

- How did postwar economic recovery transform Western society and promote cultural convergence?
- What concerns and goals inspired the counterculture movement?
- How has cultural liberalism sowed anxiety and conflict inside Western society?

Golden Recovery

In 1945, Western leaders confronted a world in ruin and a society afflicted by doubt. Rebuilding damaged infrastructure and tackling a mountain of debt ensured shortages and a long period of belt tightening. For returning veterans "settling down" captured diverse aspirations: finding a job, starting a family, and finding affordable housing. In North America, GI Bills provided public funds for university education, vocational training, and mortgage insurance. A decade later, millions had taken advantage. By 1950, most GIs had found work and many began to settle inside rapidly expanding suburbs. British soldiers returned to a bankrupt country and an empire facing multiple challenges to its authority. The Labour Party had promised to build a "New Jerusalem" by continuing the wartime scheme of "fair share." The state bought out railroads, utility companies, and mines from their private owners, creating a public sector that would work towards the "common good" rather than "private profit." Across Western Europe, many postwar governments copied Britain's welfare reforms, adapting them to fit local needs and precedents. By 1949, the outlines for European **social democracy** had emerged. State planning and private enterprise collaborated inside mixed economies. A welfare system established a universal safety net from "womb to tomb." The state also assumed responsibility for an equitable distribution of scarce national resources, while expanding avenues for social advancement. In North America and Australasia, the state focused more economic stimulus than social reform. State-managed industries were returned to their private owners. Factory bosses often "pink slipped" female and ethnic minority employees they had hired during the war to make room for returning "heroes." From 1946 to 1949, many North American women got "hitched" to wartime sweethearts, starting a "baby boom." For many African Americans, racism clouded the postwar recovery. Across the Western world, minorities suffered from housing and workplace discrimination.

The Atlantic Settlement, 1947 to 1955

International tensions haunted postwar Europe's recovery. As noted in Chapter 2, Stalin threatened states bordering the USSR and increasingly hijacked international organizations established to foster postwar collaboration. In 1947, Stalin instructed West European communists to launch strikes against the US Marshall Plan. Upheaval in France and Italy raised concern that Western Europe too could fall under communist influence. The 1948 to 1949 Berlin Crisis alarmed European elites and motivated their pursuit of a security alliance with the United States. April 1949 deliberations culminated in the North Atlantic Treaty Organization (NATO), which committed the United States and Canada to Western Europe's defense. A successful Soviet nuclear test in August 1949 underscored NATO's need to develop a conventional deterrent to offset the Red Army's advantage in tanks and artillery. Bogged down in the Korean War during the early 1950s, the United States pushed its wary European partners to rehabilitate West Germany. In May 1955, France agreed to restore the Federal Republic of Germany's full sovereignty. Subsequently, Germany's ***Bundeswehr*** became the backbone for NATO forces defending Europe from Soviet attack, albeit under permanent US command.

US implication inside postwar Europe marked a sharp reversal from its historic isolationism and traditional focus upon the Western Hemisphere. The Soviets viewed the Marshall Plan and NATO as conduits for US imperialism. The Atlantic System, however, represented an "empire by invitation." European elites recognized the need for US soldiers, capital, and products for their security and economic recovery. They persuaded the United States to invest in Europe's defense inside a multilateral structure that theoretically put the United States on an equal footing with its Western partners. *De facto* US hegemony and episodes of imperial hubris did spark moments of friction, including De Gaulle's noisy withdrawal from NATO in 1963. A convergence of interest, however, provided the cement for an enduring partnership. At times, American economic strength, or Europe's declining geopolitical influence, raised nativist concerns. US businessmen were not shy in expressing their belief that what "old" Europe most needed was more American-style modernization. Alarmed by the socialist turn inside many postwar European states from 1945 to 1946, the United States had founded libraries and financed academic exchanges to promote European adoption of America's laissez-faire policies.

Such ventures did not meaningfully shape either European identity or regional policy. By the 1960s, however, many European firms had adapted US business practices. European consumers adopted American products from cars to blue jeans and Hollywood films. Europeans, however, always assimilated American culture on their own terms. They rejected laissez-faire capitalism by recognizing the state as an indispensable medium to ensure fairness and deliver social services. European states also retained tight control over national broadcasting. Public funds subsidized local artists and created indigenous content for television and radio and insulated national cultures from excessive Americanization and commercialization. Throughout the postwar era, American cultural influences remained pervasive, but its influence was never one sided. Europe's new wave filmmakers pioneered a cinematic tradition probing the assumptions of everyday life. In 1964, the Beatles appearance on the Ed Sullivan Show stirred a mania inside the United States that marked the beginning of the British invasion. *Skippy the Bush Kangaroo* won Western hearts by glamorizing the Australian Outback. In short, postwar Western culture represented a collaborative enterprise and fusional affair. Indigenous cultural products catered to unique national tastes, while Western culture grew increasingly international. Novels, musicians, and films flowed across national borders. Wide-bodied commercial jets, communication satellites, and transatlantic phone cables facilitated deeper exchanges across the Atlantic "pond" and stimulated the coalescence of shared popular culture.

Deeper West European Integration, 1951 to 1967

Nationalism had plunged Europe into two devastating world wars. Wartime suffering planted the seeds for a more postnational future. In a 1946 speech in Zurich, Churchill proposed the founding of a United States of Europe, "a structure under which it can dwell in peace, in safety and in freedom."[1] The first tangible manifestation of this collectivist impulse came in 1947 when the Low Countries ratified **Benelux**, a customs union negotiated during the war. The US Marshall Plan gave further momentum to European integration by creating the Organization for European Economic Cooperation (OEEC) to coordinate the disbursement of aid money. Subsequently, the 1951 the **European Coal and Steel Community (ECSC)** united the Benelux countries with France, West Germany, and Italy into an international consortium that eliminated tariffs for the principal commodities powering heavy industry. First proposed by French Foreign Minister Robert Schuman in 1950, the ECSC had only a minimal economic impact. It did, however, cultivate trust between France and Germany. This laid the foundation for more ambitious future integration initiatives. Robust recovery after 1949 precipitated a shift from more rigid forms of state planning towards loser forms of national economic "guidance," especially as conservative governments won elections across Europe. Christian Democratic coalitions were fiercely anti-communist and more apprehensive about state planning, but not opposed to offering state support for families. Throughout the Golden Recovery from 1950 to 1968, political power shifted back and forth between centrist parties. Europe's Right and Left leaning coalitions, however, both embraced the welfare state and a collaborative model of capitalism that balanced the interests of industrialists and trade unionists.

The 1957 **Treaty of Rome** represented a milestone for deeper integration of European markets as France, Germany, and Italy joined the Benelux countries inside a single customs union. The **European Economic Community** (EEC) set a precedent where member states surrendered a degree of sovereignty in return for tapping the mutual benefits of greater economic efficiency. The EEC's emergence came at a critical moment when colonial states were withdrawing from their empires and losing access to these markets. Throughout the 1960s, European trade was redirected inward. Initially skeptical of the EEC project, Britain had formed a less formal Nordic free trade bloc. By 1961, however, Britain petitioned for EEC membership, although De Gaulle delayed their admittance until 1973.

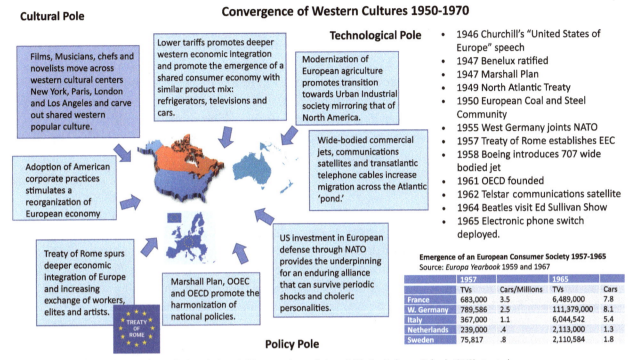

Image credits: © mark stay/Shutterstock.com; © Alexander Lysenko/Shutterstock.com; © charnsitr/Shutterstock.com; © ricochet64/Shutterstock.com

Robust postwar economic growth supported the welfare consensus. Workers benefitted from rising wages and an expanding social safety net. Industrialists enjoyed fat profits while labor conflict eased. Socialist parties joined the establishment and embraced growth over revolution. By 1964, the United States, Canada, and Japan had joined the OECC. Now renamed the **Organization for Economic Cooperation and Development (OECD)**, this body helped to forge consensus on economic policy and paved the way for deeper integration among advanced industrial economies.

Window on World History: From Dominions to Nations

Western Europe compensated for the loss of global empires by erecting institutions to facilitate interregional trade. Postwar disintegration of the British Empire proved traumatic for the former white dominions like Canada, Australia, and New Zealand. While politically independent for decades, their citizens continued to identify with Britain the Empire, and their common Anglo-Saxon heritage. World War II and the ensuing Cold War, however, brought white dominions into a closer alliance with the United States. Canada's postwar incorporation inside NATO and North American Aerospace Defense Command (NORAD) eased many of its postwar security concerns. Australia and New Zealand, however, felt exposed after the 1953 ANZUS pact failed to confer an ironclad US security guarantee. A second blow came after the 1956 Suez Crisis precipitated British Prime Minister Harold MacMillan to push for Britain's entry into the EEC. Australasians now faced the prospect of losing their leading trade partner. Involuntary cleavage from their historic motherland stimulated all the dominions to reexamine their imperial past and reorient their economy towards regional neighbors. It also stimulated efforts to redefine a national identity apart

(Continued)

from loyalism and Britishness. The dominions shared a frontier past. They identified with liberal democracy and a postwar experience of assimilating mostly European immigrants. This history emerged as an alternative source for redefining the nation during the 1970s. In Australia, "loyalism" became tainted as liberal historians exposed the sins of Empire and dispossession of the aboriginals. Australian Prime Minister Gareth Evans speaking in Kuala Lumpur in 1991 laid out a new course for Australia: "are we to be forever seen as a European outpost, a kind of cultural misfit, trapped by geography in an alien environment, or are we to recognize that Australia's future lies in the Asia-Pacific region. This is where we live."[2] Canada's postwar integration into the US economy insulated it from British policies and enabled loyalism to survive as a counterweight to America's hegemonic popular culture. This strategy, however, grew less appealing in the face of Quebec's growing sovereignty movement that threatened to split Canada along older ethnic fault lines. Prime Minister Pierre Trudeau embraced immigration history as means to reinvent Canada as a multicultural society, where citizens retained their distinctive ethnic identity, while collectively endorsing historic Western democratic values and Canadian institutions. In all former dominions, television emerged as an important medium to cultivate a national identity and assimilate various immigrants into a shared culture. Some critics, however, complained that the rush towards national "invention" felt coerced and inauthentic. Many conservatives in the former dominions lamented the erosion of the ideals and values that had once defined their nation.

Critical Reflection

1. How did the idea of the Crown and loyalism evolve in Canada after World War II?
2. In what ways has Canadian identity been shaped by closer postwar integration with the United States?

Society of Affluence, 1950 to 1969

After 1950, Western states enjoyed an economic boom characterized by sustained high levels of growth without any major recession. By the 1960s, family incomes had risen spectacularly and Europe's working classes began to enjoy the fruits of middle-class life, buying televisions, refrigerators, and washing machines. Affluence stimulated new patterns of living and the reimagining of traditional ideas about the family, gender, and sexuality.

The foundation for US postwar recovery was laid during the war. US President Roosevelt commissioned the **Ad Council** to mobilize public support for war bonds, recycling, and other state mobilization campaigns. Before the fighting stopped, the Ad Council turned its attention towards staving off a postwar recession. Unlike European socialists, American liberals viewed the state's role was to promote economic growth rather than social justice. While **Edward Bernays** invented modern advertising during the 1920s, only after the war did marketing mature into a pillar of US consumer capitalism. Rather than touting the quality of their wares, US corporations increasingly turned towards psychology to stimulate their customers' subliminal desires. For state planners, the key to US recovery was to tap pent-up consumer demand following a decade of depression and four years of wartime shortages. Corporations responded by bringing an array of "modern" products to the market that promised a "better life." The United States' postwar recovery also relied upon Federal subsidies, particularly for the housing, automobile, and defense sectors. The 1934 US National Housing Act had already established insurance to enable families of modest means to contract a mortgage from a bank. After World War II, however, the Veteran's Administration provided low-interest loans that made home ownership more affordable than renting. In war-ravaged Europe, reconstruction initially focused upon public investment to repair infrastructure, retool factories, and build public housing. After 1950, however, Europe increasingly followed the more liberal US economic model. New forms of consumer credit emerged that enabled working-class families to purchase durable goods through installment plans. By the 1960s, banks rapidly replaced pawn shops and loan sharks to provide consumers with credit.

> Credit represents a precondition for consumer societies. Does the extension of credit cards to students and ethnic minorities provide them with access to consumer goods or entrap them in debt?

One symbol of postwar recovery was housing construction. Britain's council housing system cleared rubble from the Blitz and disbursed public funds for constructing new apartment complexes. In North America, construction was mostly left to the private sector. The **bungalow** emerged as the epitome of the American Dream: a single-story detached dwelling ideally situated in a quiet, tree-shaded corner, with a tire swing swaying in the backyard. From 1950 to 1970, the US suburban population grew from 36 to 74 million.[3] In Europe, the idea of garden cities and escaping to the countryside also emerged, but less land, fewer cars, lower incomes, and restrictive zoning regulations inhibited suburbanization.

Across the Western world, advertisers glamorized a "modern" lifestyle characterized by an ever-changing set of consumer goods. Vacuum cleaners, refrigerators, electric ovens, and washing machines had been introduced before World War II. Rising incomes and consumer credit, however, transformed former luxuries into household staples. US corporations pioneered television advertising where they sponsored situational comedies, periodically interrupted by ads that sold everything from Campbell's soup to the latest "conveniences" from electric mixers to Tupperware. Europe's state-controlled media limited commercial advertising, but there too postwar gadgets promised convenience, modern living, and social advancement. From 1957 to 1965, the number of televisions inside European households exploded, while car ownership more than doubled.

Europe's Golden Age, 1950 to 1973

The **German Miracle** headlined Europe's postwar recovery. By 1955, West Germany—less than a decade removed from total war devastation—had regained its footing as the industrial dynamo powering Europe's economy. The timing, pace, and strength of Europe's postwar recovery varied. Generally, the regions bordering the Mediterranean lagged Northern Europe. Much of Europe's productivity growth derived from agricultural modernization. Introduction of tractors, fertilizers, and hybrid seeds, as well as the consolidation of unprofitable small farms, released rural workers for employment inside more efficient urban factories. After 1960, increasing levels of international trade inside the EEC unlocked competitive advantages that spurred additional productivity gains. Discovery of North Sea petroleum provided a windfall for neighboring states that abetted a doubling in welfare expenditures from 1950 to 1970.

Many religious conservatives and cultural elites found rapid postwar changes unsettling. They worried that rising consumerism eroded the moral fabric of society: its piety and historic character. French intellectuals lamented the "American invasion" of "bathtubs and frigidaires," as well as the rising tide of Anglicisms-like jukebox inside the "language of culture."[4] Intellectual polemics against Coca-colonization, however, failed to slow the pace of consumerism. The working classes of Nantes, no less than those of Leeds or Dusseldorf, enthusiastically embraced electronic gadgets and modern conveniences that they associated with a better, "modern" life.

Window on World History: Levittown and the Suburban Way of Life

Using prefabrication techniques and exploiting abundant land, William Levitt pioneered automobile suburb model. This model was scalable and popular because it met diverse aspirations contained inside the "American Dream."

After World War II, returning American servicemen wanted to "settle down," but the Great Depression and wartime shortages had crippled housing construction. William Levitt devised a plan to meet the postwar crush for affordable housing. In 1947, Levitt and Sons purchased 1,000 acres of potato fields on Long Island New York. Likening housing construction to "a stationary outdoor assembly line," Levitt pioneered mass production techniques. Using precut lumber, specialized assembly teams, uniform design, and timber frame construction on concrete slabs, Levitt raised forty houses a day. Levitt also contributed key elements of contemporary suburban design. To make Levittown feel like a neighborhood, he laid it out according to rolling country lanes, while giving streets suggestive names to dispel the bustle and anonymity of urban life. Among the initial batch of 17,000 "Levitt houses," all were single-story, 750-square feet Cape Cod cottages. Industrial standardization meant that everything, from their paint to interior layout and location of the toilet paper roll, was identical. This led to inadvertent home invasions as tipsy men staggered home after 'Happy Hour' only to discover another family supping at "their" dinner table. Despite stifling conformity, for millions of mailmen, boilermakers, and electricians, Levittown-like communities represented a dream come true. Automobile suburbs provided GIs, often still suffering from undiagnosed posttraumatic stress syndrome, an escape from dark memories of the war, urban congestion, and the growing diversity of North America's inner cities. Levitt sold out his initial lot in two days, a success that sparked widespread copying. Consumer credit, abundant land, and subsidized infrastructure elevated the automobile suburb into the symbol of the American Dream. While contemporary visitors are struck by these houses' small size and cookie cutter quality, Levittown pioneered a materialistic lifestyle that remains at the core of today's more luxurious version of mass consumerism.

Critical Reflection

1. What innovations did William Levitt pioneer that facilitated North American suburbanization?
2. In what ways was historical Levittown different from today's suburbs?

Transformation of Western Society, 1955 to 1979

In the immediate aftermath of World War II, many Europeans fled for greener pastures in Australia, New Zealand, Latin America, and Canada. When Europe's economy started to recover, a labor shortage developed inside the lowly paid service sector. Europe's booming industrial economies instituted various measures to attract foreign workers from Italy, Turkey, North Africa, Greece, and the Iberian Peninsula. Germany, lacking colonial affiliations, instituted a **Gastarbeiter** system in 1955 to recruit temporary workers from Spain, and later Italy and Turkey. Until 1970, most migrants remained white Europeans resettling from the Mediterranean periphery. In the wake of imperial collapse, more visible minorities moved to Europe. Algerians fled to France, West Indians moved to Britain, and Moluccans trekked to the Netherlands. As a result, Western Europe grew more multicultural. Between 1955 and 1974, France assimilated over 4 million immigrants, while 1.3 million Turks resided inside Germany by 1961. Occasional race riots foreshadowed a growing nativist anxiety about rising ethnic diversity.

Urbanization represented the most powerful force shaping European society before 1970. Agricultural modernization transformed Europe's historic cities into burgeoning centers of modernity. They acclimated rural workers to factory work, urban life, technological conveniences, and modern fashions. Throughout Europe, emerging mass media promoted the attitudes, products, and practices of modern life. Television, corporate advertising, and school projected national norms over a patchwork of regional affiliations, local dialects, and rural traditions. Inside European cities, a new generation benefited from robust state investment in education. Literacy rates spiked towards 100 percent, while rapid expansion of universities and the founding of various technical schools provided multiple pathways for social advancement. For those growing up during this golden age, war and depression seemed a distant memory. Robust economic growth and unlimited social advancement were reconceptualized as a birthright and permanent feature of modernization.

President Lyndon Johnson's 1964 **Great Society** program marked the high tide for Western liberalism. Sitting on a porch in rural Kentucky, Johnson articulated his vision of uplifting those left out of the postwar boom to a television audience. The Great Society launched ambitious programs to end rural poverty, improve preschools, and offer health assistance for the elderly. These programs went a long way towards bringing the United States into closer alignment with the safety net provided by European social democracies.

President Johnson used television to introduce his Great Society program and convey his aspiration to expand the welfare state to extend the American Dream to the poor.

Another dramatic experiment in Western liberalism occurred in Quebec, where the Catholic Church and Anglophone businessmen dominated separate dimensions of provincial life. During the **Quiet Revolution** of the 1960s, francophones mobilized to take control over their provincial government. The government expanded in size as francophones used it as vehicle to promote their social and economic advancement. Over the next decade, the state took control over education and healthcare from the Catholic Church, nationalized utility companies, invested in public works, and established a uniform school curriculum. The Quiet Revolution epitomized a wider liberal wave washing over Western society and transforming it into a more urban, liberal, and secular form. Liberalism was manifested in legal reforms that decriminalized sodomy, relaxed state censorship, and simplified divorce procedures. Western artists harvested their newly won freedom to explore formerly taboo subjects like incest and homosexuality, while academics asked critical questions about aboriginal populations, racial prejudice, and Church corruption. Throughout the West, but particularly in Europe, religious identification and church attendance waned following a brief resurgence in Christian piety in the aftermath of World War II. In Europe, the liberal state increasingly supplanted the Church as the basis for civic life. Mass affluence enhanced the interventionist state's prestige and inspired faith in its promise to improve material living conditions and remove social barriers. Quebec's Quiet Revolution was unique in its nationalist bent. The provincial government attacked both tradition and discrimination with the goal of creating not only a better society, but also one reflecting francophone traditions and cultural values. Quebec's liberal program received implicit validation as French-Canadian incomes and educational levels soared during the late 1960s and early 1970s. Ultimately, it would birth a sovereignty movement as some francophones pushed the liberal experiment towards the development of their own *pays*.

The Anxious 1960s

Despite rising prosperity, various anxieties haunted postwar society. This was most visible in a string of ugly racial incidents that plagued metropolitan centers in Europe and America where immigrants and ethnic minorities clustered. North American suburbanization was powered by "white flight" from racially integrating neighborhoods. Suburbanization brought new communities into being, but also eroded traditional ethnic neighborhoods. Jews, Poles, and Germans, and especially their suburban children, became less rooted in church activities and ethnic traditions as postwar families gravitated towards multiethnic suburban schools. Friday Night Football supplanted Church League softball, while the new generation acclimated to more universal American norms propagated through television and advertising. "Leave it to Beaver" and other situational comedies glorified the Ozzie and Harriet family, with a stern, yet genteel patriarch ruled over a happy household. A common theme projected by sitcoms was a sharp gender division of labor, the nuclear family as the basis for social life and an optimism sourced in a booming consumer economy. TV land presented the suburb as a paradise where citizens faced no greater stress than an errant baseball smashing through the neighbor lady's basement window.

Idealized projections of modern family life on "television land" papered over multiple tensions brewing inside postwar households, while reinforcing the postwar cult of domesticity and gender differentiation. Mothers were pressured to serve as "homemakers," sacrificing their own careers and pleasures to tend to the needs of other family members. Betty Friedan's 1963 the *Feminine Mystique* likened suburbs to concentration camps for the female soul. Given that suburban communities often lacked public transportation, neighborhood shops, or libraries, they left many women feeling isolated, tending to young infants without community support.

> Do you agree with Friedan that the automobile suburb incubated contemporary Feminism? In what ways did automobile suburbs marginalize women?

World War II had created many hastily consummated weddings. Some united couples with incompatible personalities or different ethnic backgrounds. During the 1950s, however, divorce remained stigmatized. Women did not have an easy exit from unhappy marriages given a labor market that tilted towards male breadwinners and provided only limited opportunities for female advancement. Many postwar couples accordingly suffered in silence, but conjugal violence, physical discipline, and incest could translate into traumatic family experiences. Many children growing up in postwar suburbs felt the outward prosperity and security to be empty, restrictive, and unsatisfying.

The US Civil Rights Movement, 1954 to 1965

African Americans most sharply felt the disjunction between the promise of the American Dream and the reality of postwar living. The **civil rights movement** manifested multiple frustrations. In Northern cities, discrimination put African Americans at a disadvantage for housing and jobs. In the Deep South, late nineteenth-century Jim Crow laws continued to deny most African Americans' basic civil rights, while legalizing separate "white" and "black" theaters, schools, restaurants, and drinking fountains.

After World War II, lawyers from the National Association for the Advancement of Colored Peoples (NAACP) designed an attack upon segregation by appealing to US Federal Courts to enforce the Constitution's "equal protections" clause. The most tangible outcome of this legal strategy was the 1954 Brown versus Board of Education decision, where the US Supreme Court unanimously struck down the "separate but equal" doctrine that had legitimated segregation since 1896. Many white Southerners resisted racial integration as a federal attack upon their way of life. Reviving bitter memories of the Civil War, local politicians complained about being "crucified on the cross of civil rights." A sense of victimization fueled racial violence against African Americans in the South. White policemen harassed NAACP activists while angry lynch mobs terrorized African American share croppers in rural areas. In the autumn of 1957, Little Rock, Arkansas emerged as a flashpoint when nine African American students sought to attend a formerly all-white high school. Confronted by a ring of angry segregationists hurling threats, phlegm, and insults, the students were forced to retreat as the National Guard passively looked on. Initially reluctant to intervene, President Dwight Eisenhower was forced to send in federal troops to uphold the rule of law.

School integration marked only the opening chapter in a decade long struggle to tear down institutionalized racism. After Little Rock, leadership of the civil rights movement shifted away from NAACP lawyers to young activists working inside local communities. Many found inspiration in Gandhi's philosophy of nonviolent resistance. Activist organizations strategically targeted segregated stores, restaurants, and public transportation by staging boycotts or **sit-ins**. Such actions invariably triggered violent retribution. By refusing to retaliate, activists steadily undermined the legitimacy of segregation. For example, in 1961 the **Freedom Riders** rolled into Montgomery, Alabama, determined to challenge bus segregation. Sheriff "Bull" Conner welcomed them by mobilizing the local chapter of Ku Klux Klan. When the Freedom Riders arrived in Montgomery, their bus came under immediate attack. The bus driver tried to roll out despite slashed tires, but firebombs brought the stricken Greyhound to a halt. Passengers escaped the blaze only to be severely beaten by a white mob. While racism remained deeply rooted in the American psyche, such episodes of wanton cruelty also discredited Southern racism in the eyes of a silent majority.

Martin Luther King Jr. Leads a Demonstration

Televisions beamed ugly episodes of racial violence into American living rooms, discrediting racism in the eyes of the silent majority and broadening support for civil rights reform.

March on Washington, DC

In 1963, Baptist Minister **Martin Luther King Jr.** led a march on Washington, DC, to demand jobs and freedom. Moving on from segregation, the civil rights movement now turned towards challenging subtler forms of discrimination. On the crowded lawn of the Washington Mall, King delivered his now famous "I have a Dream" speech where he painted a vivid image of a racially integrated America where everyone could realize their potential regardless of creed or skin tone. In many respects, King's speech marked the high tide for the civil rights movement. Subsequently, a new generation of African American leaders emerged and promoted a more militant approach for fighting racism. Both the **Nation of Islam** and the **Black Panthers** connected racial discrimination inside American society to US imperialism abroad. In a highly charged 1964 speech, **Malcolm X** warned that "there's new strategy coming in. . . It'll be ballots, or it'll be bullets."[5]

Fissures inside the civil right movement in part reflected the movement's growing success, particularly the 1965 **Voting Rights Act** that quickly doubled African American voter registration. Increased suffrage spurred the eviction of racist white sheriffs across the American South, while producing a record number of African American officials. Federal legislation tackled the most visible aspects of discrimination, but also failed to eradicate the latent racism entrenched in local institutions and popular attitudes. Following a seemingly routine drunk driving arrest in Los Angeles in 1965, African American frustrations with abuse from the white-dominated police force escalated into six days of rioting that left thirty-six dead and put streets ablaze. The **Watts Riot** would foreshadow similar riots that swept across US industrial cities from 1966 to 1967.

Watts commenced a series of race riots that ripped through American cities that had failed to remove the social and economic barriers to enable minority advancement.

> In 2008, many Americans hailed Barack Obama as a postracial president. The August 2014 shooting of Michael Brown, an unarmed black teenager, by a white police officer in Ferguson, Missouri, however, stimulated a month-long protest and the Black Lives Matter movement. How has the question of race evolved inside the United States since the 1960s?

These incidents highlighted mounting African American frustration with the inability of reform to keep pace with their rising expectations for justice, equality, and access to the American Dream.

Rachel Carson and Environmentalism

The idea that scientific inventions could improve society was beautifully captured in DuPont's postwar slogan "better living, through chemistry!" World War II had stimulated the development of synthetic chemicals, including **DDT**, which was used to combat cholera, malaria, and pests that consumed crops. DDT's power to kill bugs "safely" led to a dramatic upsurge in its use. During the 1950s, chemical companies invented a range of new products from pesticides to fertilizers, plastics, and pharmaceuticals that promised modern convenience and a better life. Few chemicals introduced into American homes and neighborhoods, however, were rigorously tested. During the 1950s, children in suburban America eagerly anticipated the arrival of the "fog man," who would dust their neighborhood with DDT. Despite official warnings that it was best to stay inside, children often frolicked through the dense haze. This casual attitude towards household chemicals resulted from their invisibility and from repeated government assurances that they were not toxic. By the late 1950s, DDT use had grown so pervasive that in some towns it evolved into a ritual feature of successful church BBQs. DDT, however, represented just the tip of a poisonous iceberg as families kept arsenic in sheds, leaded gasoline–filled city skylines in an acrid smoke, and asbestos-lined ducts in schools and factories.

Carson's *Silent Spring* brought the poisonous effects of pesticides into the consciousness of Americans.

When Rachel Carson warned about "bioaccumulation"—that untested toxins were accumulating in higher doses up the food chain—it caught most Americans off guard. Officially released in the *New Yorker* during 1962, *Silent Spring* struck a chord, not only because of Carson's ability to establish a scientific link between pesticides and human health, but because she was a gifted storyteller. The image of songbirds falling silent left an indelible image in Americans minds already tuned to evangelical ideas about Armageddon and polluting Eden. DuPont pushed back vigorously, attacking Rachel Carson's credentials and her "hysterical" character. Male scientists lent their impressive credentials to DuPont in castigating Carson as a "communist" and a "spinster," sly allusions to her sexual orientation. In a nationally televised interview on CBS, however, a cancer-stricken Carson handled the furor with aplomb. Carson's calm rebuttal of DuPont's hatchet man sealed the debate in the public's mind. *Silent Spring* pushed President Kennedy to regulate the chemical industry, while shifting the American mindset. Rather than a trail blazer for modern progress, the public identified the chemical industry with corporate greed and government corruption. Since the Enlightenment, a central myth of Western society revolved around a faith in technology and science to improve human life. The environmental movement coalesced in the 1960s around the radical idea of limits to growth. Nature was not an infinite resource for exploitation, but a fragile system needing human protection. Ecocentrism crystallized in the inaugural **Earth Day** in 1970 when ordinary people rallied to preserve the environment for future generations.

North American Counterculture Movement, 1965 to 1975

The United States tiptoed into Vietnam after 1954, but by 1963 President Lyndon Johnson faced the monumental choice of letting South Vietnam collapse or sending in American ground forces.

Although popular opposition to the Vietnam War did not directly stimulate the counterculture movement, it evolved into its most powerful catalyst. Television coverage of Vietnam made it difficult to reconcile the war's brutality with the high-minded ideal of fighting communism. Well-publicized atrocities by American troops raised troubling questions about the military mission and the political establishment that kept pushing for further escalation. By 1965, demonstrations had become regular features on college campuses. Some students defiantly burned their draft cards, while others dodged conscription by moving to Canada. The 1968 **Tet Offensive** discredited Johnson by exposing the lie of imminent victory. A visibly weary Johnson declined the opportunity to run for the presidency, while the subsequent 1968 Democratic National Convention splintered the party into pro- and antiwar factions. At Kent State in May 1970, anxious National Guardsmen fired indiscriminately into a crowd of protestors, killing four and wounding nine others. This intensified popular opposition to Vietnam and contributed to Nixon's decision to pull out ground forces.

Many university students had grown up with images of racial violence on television. Their struggle on college campuses copied from the civil rights movement's mass mobilization tactics. They also drew energy from a deeper generational divide. By the mid-1960s, it became "hip" to reject antiquated

By 1965, antiwar protests emerged as a regular feature of college campuses.

Victorian sexual mores, industrial practices that poisoned the environment, and a political establishment that propagated inhumane colonial wars. The *Beatles* catchy "Can't Buy Me Love" captured the rebellious spirit percolating among **baby boomers**. Playful rejection of the superficial materialism in Western society reflected a deeper search for authenticity. The Hippie "uniform" consisted of blue jeans and T-shirts, while "flower girls" adopted loose fitting and flashy patterned clothes that challenged prevailing conventions of feminine modesty. By the mid-1960s, affordable and accessible contraceptives permitted not only women, but also men to explore sex outside the confines of traditional marriage. The "pill" divorced sexual pleasure from the risk of unwanted pregnancies and the weighty responsibilities of child-rearing. "Free Love," on open display at **Woodstock** in 1969, however, horrified traditionalists and stimulated a conservative backlash.

Rock and roll emerged as one medium for adolescent protest. Musically, it fused African American blues with white country music. Popular artists like Jimmy Hendrix and Janis Joplin often performed in open-air festivals, placing love, relationships, and developing a higher conscious through psychedelics at the center of their lyrics. In its most evolved form, the Hippie movement sought to transcend the psychological repression and empty consumerism of postwar society. Rather than launching into a career, Hippies glorified the "experiment" of "dropping out" and trying to live free from sexism, racism, and repression. The Volkswagen camper, painted with flashy colors, became a symbol for the Hippie adventure to find their authentic selves.

Western Feminism

During the 1960s, **second wave feminism** emerged as an offshoot of the counterculture movement, concerned less with political rights, than tackling the latent sexism inside society and the workplace. In the United States, the Equal Rights Amendment passed Congress easily in 1971, even if it ultimately failed to achieve ratification. Feminism emerged later and in a less concentrated form inside Western Europe. Until 1971, Swiss women were denied the right to vote. In Southern Europe, "women's work" remained mostly confined to the "caring" professions, lowly remunerated posts in nursing, teaching, and secretarial work well into the 1980s. Hannah Gavron's *The Captive Wife* captured many of the frustrations European women felt relative to misogynistic attitudes and informal barriers that inhibited them from reaching their full potential during the 1960s.

> Western liberals often complain about Islamic discrimination against women, but is feminism a distinctive outgrowth of Western liberalism? To what extent was gender equality a hard-won—and still incomplete—victory against conservative resistance?

Scandinavia represented Europe's most liberal corner. In 1961, already 45 percent of Swedish women worked outside the home, even if they fell short in terms of pay equity. Only during the 1980s, did European women start to close the gender pay gap, mostly by increasing their representation inside universities, male-dominated prestige professions like medicine and law, the state bureaucracy, and ascending into the middle rungs of corporate management.

Europe's Counterculture Movement

Vietnam also inspired European dissidence. Not facing conscription, many European students took their cue from leftist critics of bourgeois capitalism. Herbert Marcuse's *One-Dimensional Man* offered a spirited critique of the mind-numbing conformity of Europe's emerging consumer society. Student groups at the movement's heart were "radical" in embracing revolution as a tool for institutional change and social improvement. The sixties generation identified themselves as untainted by commercialization. They believed themselves a vanguard engaging in a moral campaign to wrest power from corporations, racists, and cynical elites. Officially, the European dissident movement commenced in the November 1967 student occupation of the *Palazzo Campana* at the University of Turin's law faculty. Following their forceful eviction, angry students engaged local police in bloody street battles. From Turin, student radicalism spread to Milan and Rome, before heading north to Paris, Amsterdam, Germany, and Scandinavia in 1968.

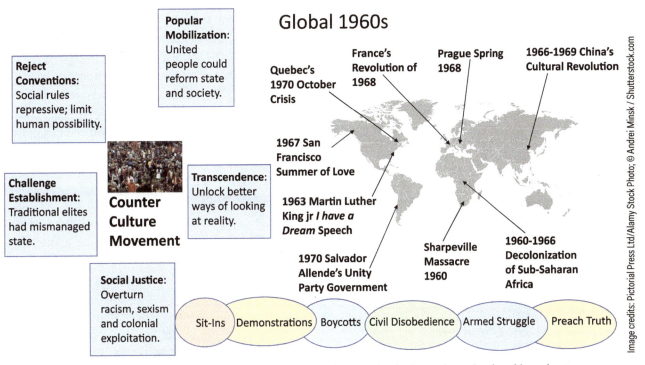

The Western counterculture movement was rooted in a deeper revolutionary *zeitgeist* that embraced various ideas about revolution, social justice, and state reform. Throughout the 1960s, leftist populist movements challenged entrenched elites, although the spirit of reform manifested in unique local environments.

In France, student radicalism exploded into a political crisis that toppled the government. French students, originally from the University of Nanterre, occupied university buildings and transformed Paris' Odéon Theatre into their unofficial revolutionary headquarters. In May 1968, French authorities had tired of this radicalism and decided to evict students by force. Student activists responded by erecting barricades in the Latin Quarter, recalling revolutions past. Conservative critics complained that the student revolution lacked focus. "Rêve + evolution = revolution" was a slogan frequently splashed onto Parisian buildings. It captured the movement's ephemeral quality, an intense enthusiasm for revolution, without any central cause or clear direction. But the movement turned serious after student activists persuaded workers from a nearby Renault factory to join their protest. Ultimately, sympathetic workers from throughout France joined in a national strike that mobilized seven million people. The French economy grounded to a halt. President de Gaulle inexplicably disappeared. Rumors swirled that de Gaulle had fled into exile. The movement's climax came on May 11. A nervous Prime Minister Georges Pompidou took to the television in an attempt to placate the restless masses. Pompidou's obvious unease, and offer of concessions, seemed to spur the protestors on. With the government tottering at the brink, De Gaulle hastily returned to Paris. In a brief four-minute televised speech, he announced that he would dissolve parliament and call for new elections. Slowly, workers returned to work. Subsequent parliamentary elections provided De Gaulle a mandate to forcefully eject students from the university buildings they occupied. As quickly as it had appeared, France's Revolution of 1968 had fizzled out.

The Radical Fringe

Urban guerrillas represented the most radical fringe of the counterculture movement, forming terrorist cells in an attempt to overthrow the monied elites that dominated the state. In Italy, Germany, the United States, and Canada, terrorist cells targeted bankers, diplomats, and politicians, with bombs, kidnappings, and assassinations. During the **October Crisis** in Quebec in 1970, the *Front de Libérationdu Québec* kidnapped and assassinated Labor Minister Pierre Laporte in a short-lived campaign for independence. In Italy, the *Brigate Rosse* murdered former Premier Aldo Moro in 1978. These shocking acts, however, deprived left wing terrorists of public sympathy and support. By the early 1980s, most members of the urban guerrilla movement had been arrested, pushed into exile, or had abandoned their violent campaign.

Brandt's *Ostpolitik*

Challenging convention was not reserved to populist movements. Western political leaders also tried to channel discord and popular unease into programs for state reform. In 1969, **Willy Brandt** became the first Social Democratic prime minister in West Germany. Despite a narrow election victory, Brandt pursued a bold policy of reconciliation with Germany's communist neighbors. Reversing precedent, Brandt boldly articulated a vocabulary of East–West reconciliation, captured in his phrase "two German states in one nation." In a bid for détente, Brandt's *Ostpolitik* offered to renounce Germany's claim to former Reich territories. The sincerity of his reconciliation offer was captured when Brandt kneeled before the Warsaw Ghetto memorial. This expressed atonement for the brutal suppression of a Polish uprising twenty-five years before. Brandt's diplomacy bore fruit in the 1970 **Moscow Treaty**, where West Germany formally recognized the postwar partitioning of Europe. Brandt had bucked the eight million strong German refugee community that had fled the Red Army. His diplomacy also elicited concern from US Secretary of State Henry Kissinger, but his East Policy also normalized relations with East Germany, relaxed Berlin's border controls, and paved the way for greater trade and cultural exchanges with the Soviet Bloc. Despite the controversy surround Brandt's policies, his November 1972 reelection marked public endorsement for détente. At a deeper level, it reflected an increasing public willingness to revisit the iron logic of the Cold War. Groups like Britain's Coalition for Nuclear Disarmament challenged the stationing of US nuclear weapons on their soil. The unpopular Vietnam War enabled European politicians to challenge American leadership of the Western Bloc, while a climate of

Willy Brandt

détente gave credence to the idea of a structural convergence between Eastern socialism and Western social democracy. During the late 1970s, green parties emerged to promote environmental concerns, foreshadowing single issue groups that would splinter the Western electorate and undermine support for establishment parties in later decades.

Waning Liberalism

The counterculture movement unsettled Western elites. They resented their children for spurning traditional values and rejecting the material comforts and security the "Greatest Generation" had sacrificed so much for. Conservatives were also skeptical that biological, class, and racial differences could be transcended simply by reshaping cultural attitudes. Exasperated mothers urged their daughters heading out to outdoor concerts to be sensible, while frustrated fathers ordered their sons to shave. In the United States, future Chief Justice Lewis Powell in a confidential 1971 memorandum to the Chamber of Commerce advocated for corporate America's mobilization to defend the "American Free Enterprise system."[6] Powell's memo found support among industrialists who financed "think tanks" such as the CATO institute and Heritage Foundation with the aim to challenge "liberal" research universities and transform the public debate by producing "research" that promotes the adoption of economic policies more conducive to business interests.

At its deepest level, the counterculture movement tried to liberate society from sexism, racism, and consumerism. Some Hippies sought to put their values into practice, but few of their communitarian experiments endured.

> Were the Hippies authentic revolutionaries seeking to create a more just and equitable society or was the counterculture movement superficial and hedonistic?

After Nixon announced his intention to withdraw from Vietnam, the counterculture movement lost its strongest catalyst. Also, during the 1970s, mainstream parties adopted many of the counterculture movement's liberal reforms. The stagflation crisis also sapped liberal momentum by threatening the material security many sixties "rebels" had taken for granted. Some hippies persisted in their alternative lifestyle, but most often this denigrated into a superficial nihilism wrapped in marijuana. By the late 1970s, most hippies had shaved their beards and traded in their tie-dye shirts for Gucci shoes and careers inside the establishment.

Stagflation Crisis, 1973 to 1980

From 1973 to 1979, dramatically rising oil prices spurred a combination of high inflation and unemployment that Western economists quickly dubbed **stagflation**. The 1973 Organization of Petroleum Exporting Countries (OPEC) oil embargo exposed Western oil dependence and exacerbated deeper structural problems inside industrial economies. Decades of prosperity had bred complacency. Inside the West, wages among Western workers had climbed steadily since 1950, along with social benefits like free healthcare, subsidized housing, and paid vacations. By 1970, the living standards among workers had more than doubled, but many traditional industries suffered from high overhead costs. Brazilian and Indian steel producers supplanted their Western counterparts during the 1970s, while American electronics and car manufacturers lost their technological lead to their Japanese competitors. For years, European state-owned industries had underinvested in new machinery. Loss of global competitiveness meant that fiscal stimulus could not lower unemployment and only accelerated inflation. By the early 1980s, Europeans were forced to acknowledge that the Keynesian policies that had powered the postwar recovery no longer worked. Western leaders and their electorates slowly grappled with the emerging reality that high growth was not perpetual. In fact, earlier gains in the standard of living could be sustained through foreign borrowing.

The oil shock accelerated Western transition towards a **postindustrial** economy. The manufacturing sector of Western economies shrunk, female participation in the workforce jumped, and "white-collar" jobs inside the service sector grew. Deindustrialization accelerated a decline in union membership. The introduction of neoliberal reforms during the 1980s amplified deindustrialization by incentivizing Western corporations to outsource production. The decline in traditional industries was partially offset by growth inside the service sector. Inside the emerging economy, unemployed blue-collar workers often struggled to find work or earn the same benefits or wages. Economic recovery by the mid-1980s lowered unemployment rates, but the boom never returned while the labor market grew increasingly polarized. The service sector provided well-paying jobs for those with university degrees, but many were poorly paid and offered little security. In the United States, Tax "reforms" under President Reagan exacerbated social inequality. The top 10 percent saw their net worth spike, while the bottom 30 percent saw their real incomes drop because of cuts in the welfare system and structural underemployment. During the 1980s, armies of homeless men—often Vietnam veterans expelled from psychiatric institutions shuttered to close state deficits—washed up on the streets of metropolitan United States. They represented the vanguard for a new impoverished class that particularly afflicted the less educated, racial minorities, and single-parent households. In Europe too, poverty climbed to over 14 percent of the population. By 1990, the unemployment rate among young black men in Britain rose to 50 percent, reaching similar levels for young men of Arab descent in Southern France. Structural unemployment in the 1980s translated into high incidences of truancy, violent crime, and drug abuse, particularly inside minority communities, impoverished rural areas, and urban ghettos.

Changing Western Family

By 1970, the postwar baby boom had ebbed. A decade earlier, divorce rates shot up as Western states moved towards "no-fault" divorce policies. In 1980, one in six French marriages ended in divorce, a dramatic increase from twenty years before, but lagging far behind the 50 percent rate prevailing inside Britain and North America. The fading of traditional mores is well captured by children born outside of wedlock. In Western Europe during the 1980s young European couples increasingly opted for partnerships outside the framework of traditional marriages. In the more conservative Catholic Mediterranean region, couples began to cohabit before marriage. In the United States, the number of children born out of wedlock rose from 5 percent to 25 percent for Caucasians, and a staggering 66 percent among African Americans. Changing attitudes about sex and divorce, combined with a sluggish and evolving labor market, delayed the age of motherhood, spurred lower fertility rates, and increased the number of single-parent households. The 2011 Canadian census, for example, revealed that one-person households outnumbered those of couples with children for the first time.[7]

Conservatives lamented the breakdown of the family, attributing poverty, crime, and drug abuse to single-parent households; promiscuity; and an eroding work ethic. In the United States during the late 1970s, establishment backlash against liberalism began to coalesce with the **Born Again** movement. Televangelist Jerry Falwell credited his Moral Majority with securing the conservative Ronald Reagan's 1980 presidential victory. The Southern Baptist Convention emerged as the most prominent evangelical coalition, organizing a grassroots right-to-life movement to overturn *Roe v. Wade*, a 1973 US Supreme Court ruling legalizing abortion. By the 1990s, Ralph Reed's Christian Coalition mobilized "values voters" into a powerful political force. Declining voter participation enabled single issue coalitions to propel Republican electoral gains in Congress. In Europe, conservative backlash against untraditional partnerships, birth control, and sexual orientation proved more muted. Polls revealed a steady decline in both religious identification and church attendance, which contributed to eroding support for Christian democratic parties.

Conservative Resurgence, 1980s

In May 1979, **Margaret Thatcher** led the British Conservative party back to power defeating Labor by a narrow 43.9 to 36.9 percent margin. Thatcher had appealed to Britain's middle classes worried that sluggish growth threatened their advancement. Thatcher promised to reinvigorate the economy by curbing trade union power, tackling crime, and restoring British self-confidence. Thatcherism reflected a belief that socialism slowed business investment and sapped the drive for hard work. The success of Thatcher's message illustrates how by 1979, after years of stagnation, a majority of British voters had come to question the efficacy of Keynesian policies. Thatcher critiqued the socialist "nanny state," depicting stagnation not as a symptom of higher oil prices and rising Asian competition, but as a cultural problem that could be solved by cutting an overly generous safety net.

In 1979, however, most Britons continued to support welfare measures. Thatcher's popularity dropped when her policies sparked a rapid decline in the United Kingdom's uncompetitive manufacturing sector, rendering three million unemployed by 1982. Thatcher, however, won reelection in a 1983 landslide victory largely because of the disintegration of the Labour Party. Thatcher used her newfound mandate to implement more far reaching neoliberal reforms, cutting state spending and breaking the powerful mining union from 1984 to 1985. British conservatives balanced the state budget primarily by privatizing state assets, especially those industries nationalized after World War II. Tories argued that they would operate more efficiently under private management. In the case of British Rail, however, privatization resulted in drastic cuts in service, as well as a decline in quality. By the late 1980s, Thatcherism had produced higher incomes for the urban middle classes in urban South West England, but her policies also undermined the security of workers, spurring a growing polarization among rich and poor.

Thatcherism began to exercise influence over continental Europe after 1983, where various coalition governments lacked the will to cut back popular welfare programs, but also lacked a formula for tackling persistent economic difficulties and mounting deficits. Thatcher's union busting and deregulatory policies were prominent features in the 1986 **Single European Act** that paved the way for closer European economic integration on the basis of neoliberal principles. Perhaps more significant in Europe's rightward

Thatcher's animated championing of neoliberal reform gained momentum when Keynesian policies failed to simulate growth throughout Europe.

pivot was French President **François Mitterand's** failed experiment in socialism. Mitterand ascended to power in 1981 with a mandate to launch a broad stimulus program. Keynesian policies, however, once more failed spectacularly. By March 1983, French voters punished the Socialist Party in various municipal elections, provoking Mitterrand to embrace deflationary policies geared towards modernizing the French economy and trimming inefficient state-owned industries. From 1984 to 1986, the economic tide turned and France entered into a tepid recovery, even if unemployment remained stubbornly high. Economic stability enabled Mitterrand to win reelection, while cementing a broader European perception that the Keynesian policies that had powered Europe's golden recovery were now dead.

Reagan and Conservative Resurgence in the United States

In the United States, the reforming spirit powering the sixties generation drew to a symbolic close following President Jimmy Carter's disastrous 1979 "malaise speech" that the public perceived as proclaiming the death of the American Dream. "Our people are losing that faith, not only in government itself but in the ability as citizens to serve as the ultimate rulers and shapers of our democracy."[8]

In 1980, American voters rejected Jimmy Carter's vision of austerity and declining influence by embracing Reagan promise to "feel good again."

Carter's challenger during the 1980 presidential election, former Hollywood actor Ronald Reagan, promised to make Americans "feel good again." By a narrow margin, Americans voted in Reagan, implicitly turning the page on the liberal experiment. Reagan's first term as president, however, got off to a rocky start. His policies lowered taxes, while raising military expenditures, producing a whopping budget deficit that fueled a dramatic uptick in interest rates and pushed the US economy into a deep recession.

> How do you explain that the American public that broadly supported environmental policies during the 1970s rejected Carter's austerity message only a few years later?

Reagan tasked Treasury Secretary Paul Volcker with taming inflation, a feat he accomplished in 1982 by aggressively raising interest rates. Interest rates briefly spiked to 20 percent, but by late 1983 inflation dropped and the United States entered into a robust economic recovery that precipitated Reagan's landslide reelection over liberal Minnesota senator Walter Mondale. Reagan's reelection marked the symbolic death of old liberalism, and tilted the United States into an increasingly conservative direction. The United States' conservative tilt was mirrored throughout the Anglo-Saxon world as center-right regimes in Britain, Canada, and Australia held power during much of the 1980s. The political renaissance of conservatism facilitated the promotion of unsubstantiated free market theories. Conservative think tanks established during the 1970s, for instance, promoted Arthur Laffer's fantastic supply-side theory that lowering tax rates increased state revenues. While Western economic recovery during the 1980s did tame inflation and lower unemployment, growth was fueled mostly by selling crown corporations and public borrowing rather than substantial gains in productivity. During the 1980s, the US computer industry did grow robustly, but jobs inside the technology sector were insufficient to offset the loss of high-paying manufacturing jobs. Under conservative regimes, state deficits soared and economic growth was inflated by questionable financial reforms that fueled consumer debt while spurring Asia's industrial expansion.

Contemporary Western Society

During the 1960s, Europeans had viewed "guest workers" as temporary migrants to address a crushing labor shortage. As economic conditions worsened after 1970, right-wing parties blamed visible minorities for "stealing" jobs or "refusing" to assimilate. Relatively liberal regional immigration laws enabled "guest workers" to claim citizenship and sponsor multiple relatives, rapidly transforming Europe's cultural fabric. By 1970, three million people inside France and Germany had been born abroad. Many Turks in Germany, and Muslims in Southern France, increasingly lived in quasi-ethnic ghettos concentrated in large cities. As visible minorities, they confronted employment and housing discrimination that translated into mounting levels of youth truancy and crime.

An immigrant backlash also surfaced inside the United States as unemployment hit the auto, textile, and steel industries during the late 1970s and early 1980s. Many Hispanic immigrants had settled in the American Southwest after fleeing political violence in Central America. While nativists complained about this influx of illegal aliens, the federal government initially showed little interest in clamping down on migrant labor that mostly took up low-wage labor inside corporate farms, meat packing plants, and canning factories. A 1986 amnesty deal tried to regularize the status of illegal immigrants that in some cases had lived inside the United States for decades and who remained indispensable for keeping corporate farms profitable.

Return to the Political Center, 1990s

In 1992, battling a popular incumbent following twelve years of uninterrupted Republican control over the White House, **William Clinton** cast himself as a "new" Democrat, a pragmatic centrist untainted by the discredited liberal ideals of his predecessors. This pragmatism was manifested in Clinton's willingness to cut social programs and embrace market-based solutions, exemplified in his willingness to sign the 1994 North American Free Trade Agreement (NAFTA), removing many tariff barriers between Mexico, the United States, and Canada. Clinton also later partnered with Republicans against his own party to institute welfare "reform" that aimed to transition recipients from "permanent dependency" into "gainful employment." Clinton's willingness to compromise between the old ideologies of "right" and "left" was matched by Tony Blair's New Labor coalition that took the reins of power in 1997 following a decade and a half of uninterrupted Conservative rule. Blair highlighted the pragmatism emerging throughout Western Europe. New center parties on both right and left preached the value of fiscal responsibility, effective management, while endorsing free market policies as pathway for spurring growth. Left center governments often advocated for responsible cutbacks to welfare programs in order to spur national competitiveness and preserve state benefits for future generations.

Free Trade Blocs

To rekindle growth, centrist regimes put faith in free trade arrangements they calculated would increase economic efficiency. This trend was exemplified in the deepening and widening of the European Community after the fall of communism. The EEC's initial economic success had spurred its steady expansion from its original six members to twenty-seven by 1989. This included a Nordic Bloc headlined by Britain that joined in 1973, followed by the fledgling democracies that supplanted the former dictatorships of Spain, Portugal, and Greece.

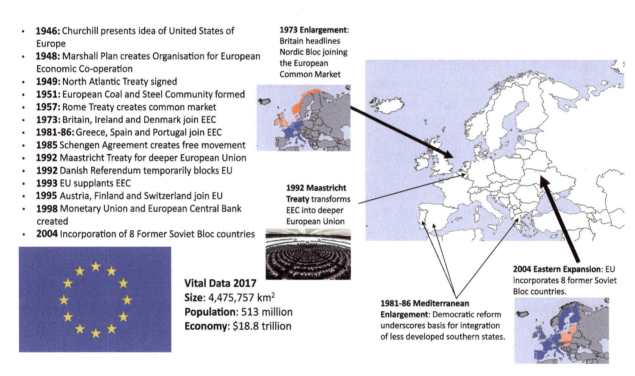

- **1946:** Churchill presents idea of United States of Europe
- **1948:** Marshall Plan creates Organisation for European Economic Co-operation
- **1949:** North Atlantic Treaty signed
- **1951:** European Coal and Steel Community formed
- **1957:** Rome Treaty creates common market
- **1973:** Britain, Ireland and Denmark join EEC
- **1981-86:** Greece, Spain and Portugal join EEC
- **1985** Schengen Agreement creates free movement
- **1992** Maastricht Treaty for deeper European Union
- **1992** Danish Referendum temporarily blocks EU
- **1993** EU supplants EEC
- **1995** Austria, Finland and Switzerland join EU
- **1998** Monetary Union and European Central Bank created
- **2004** Incorporation of 8 Former Soviet Bloc countries

1973 Enlargement: Britain headlines Nordic Bloc joining the European Common Market

1992 Maastricht Treaty transforms EEC into deeper European Union

1981-86 Mediterranean Enlargement: Democratic reform underscores basis for integration of less developed southern states.

2004 Eastern Expansion: EU incorporates 8 former Soviet Bloc countries.

Vital Data 2017
Size: 4,475,757 km²
Population: 513 million
Economy: $18.8 trillion

Image credits: © Spacedromedary / Shutterstock.com; © Ikars/Shutterstock.com; © Volina / Shutterstock.com

In 1991, European representatives agreed to deepen their partnership. The 1992 Maastricht Treaty brought into being the EU by 1993. Ultimately, this federation established European citizenship, a Central Bank, a European Parliament, and common currency, the Euro. Arguably, the most visible change inside Europe was the closing of internal border stations. The 1985 Schengen Convention produced a common visa policy that led to dropping border controls by 1995 and free movement inside much of the EU zone. By facilitating transnational immigration, particularly among students, entrepreneurs, and pensioners retiring to the warmer south, European states grow more diverse, while Europe as a whole grew at once more multicultural and homogenous in terms of the patterns of modern life. While progressive reforms during the late 1990s have transformed the EU from a customs union into a federation, its political future remains unresolved. The mechanisms binding sovereign states to Brussels remain convoluted, contested, and open to revision. In 2005, French voters rejected a measure to pave the way for a European Constitution, mirroring nationalist concerns in other states that a deeper partnership would undermine sovereignty and erode cultural uniqueness. British-Euro skeptics have proven particularly vocal in challenging "Brussel-crats" for imposing unwanted immigration standards. In 2016, a majority of Briton opted to leave the EU in a national referendum. The 2008 **Sovereign Debt Crisis** also exposed fissures, not only between German bankers and Greek voters, but deeper philosophical differences between Nordic and Mediterranean states concerning fiscal policy. All this leaves the EU's future form and configuration in doubt.

In North America, the Canada–US free trade pact of 1987 was expanded into the NAFTA by incorporating the much less industrialized Mexico in 1994. Similarly, following intense discussions from 2003 to 2013, the EU incorporated many of the states of the former Communist Bloc, despite their lower level of industrialization. Together these agreements spurred the relocation of many Western factories to China, Hungary, and Mexico.

Rise of the Militant Right

During the 1990s, Right Wing parties increasingly exploited economic insecurity to expand their political support, particularly inside municipalities and provinces featuring a high index of visible minorities. In France, the 1989 *l'affaire du foulard* encapsulated the mounting tensions between native-born citizens and a growing Muslim minority after school officials suspended three female secondary students for refusing to remove their *hijab* in class. Subsequently, the state ruled that the *hijab* represented a quasi-religious symbol that contradicted the French tradition of *laïcité* in public schools.

Deindustrialization, and relocation of Western factories to Asia during the 1990s, led many blue-collar workers to shift support from established labor parties that lobbied for worker protections to anti-immigration parties that blamed minorities for crime, social breakdown, and national decline. **Jörg Haider** represented the most charismatic and successful politician of the militant right. Haider attracted international attention for his harsh anti-immigrant rhetoric and ambivalent statements concerning Austria's Nazi past. From its stronghold in Carinthia, however, Haider's Austrian Freedom Party steadily expanded its popular base from 5 percent of the electorate in 1983 to 27 percent in 1999, when Haider's party won a majority share in parliamentary elections. Haider's success was mirrored across Western Europe. Before his assassination, Dutch politician Pim Fortuyn harshly criticized Islamic immigrants and their "backward culture," casting multiculturalism as a threat to Western civilization. In Southern France, **Jean-Marie le Pen** built up his *Front Nationale* during the 1970s by opposing Islamic immigrants. Le Pen's high tide came in 2002 when he defeated the mainstream socialist candidate before losing a runoff election for the French presidency against Jacques Chirac.

The Culture Wars

In the United States, Clinton's presidency spurred political polarization, with gender equity emerging as a flashpoint. By the century's turn, Western women were breaking through the glass ceiling and procuring more posts inside upper management, outstripping men in terms of university enrollment, while enhancing their presence inside the legal and medical professions. As women evolved into "breadwinners" or outearned their spouses, it sparked a reordering of the family and household tasks. By the twenty-first century, husbands started to take paternity leave and assumed a greater role in child-rearing. Dual-earner couples also start to split household chores in nongendered ways. Concurrently, reconstituted or "blended" families juggled custody obligations, while same-sex couples and lesbian adoption spurred increasing diversity among Western families. For traditionalists, and marginalized blue-collar workers, late twentieth-century liberalism represented an existential threat. American evangelicals mobilized their flock to defend holy matrimony, particularly against gay marriage, an issue that they elevated into culture war to save soul of the nation. In select US states, Christian fundamentalists went on the offensive, seizing control over school boards in order to rewrite high school textbooks to preach creationism. Declining union membership led some blue-collar workers and the rural poor to form "patriot" militias to defend the constitution, their second amendment right to bear arms and traditional "American" values. The culture wars, instigated and financed in part by Libertarian industrialists, mostly distracted "value voters" from the structural forces transforming the world economy. The bitter 1996 US midterm elections inaugurated legislative paralysis, as Republicans abandoned bilateral compromise in favor of a combative strategy built upon maintaining ideological purity, promoting libertarian reforms, and voicing nationalistic appeals to mobilize white voters, evangelicals, and blue-collar workers dislocated by deindustrialization and anxious about multiculturalism and the liberalization of social attitudes.

The emergence of new and more complex family structures reflected not only shifting social attitudes but changing economic conditions. Lifetime employment positions and guaranteed pensions largely disappeared from the postindustrial economy. Corporate "downsizing" during the 1990s resulted in more contract work and part-time positions that lacked medical insurance or defined benefits. This left workers less secure and forced to juggle competing family and employer obligations. Technology also disrupted the workplace rendering many well-compensated manual jobs obsolete, and creating barriers in the labor market for older workers with less sophisticated computer skills. While digital technology helped some modern families maintain a work–life balance by facilitating telecommuting, rising stress was evident in rising medical diagnoses for depression, burnout, anxiety, drug addiction, and other psychiatric illnesses. From 1996 to 2005, the number of antidepressants prescribed doubled inside the United States, incorporating over 10 percent of the population.

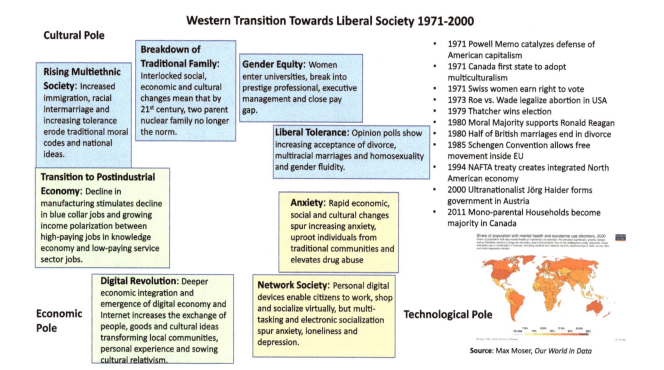

Source: Max Moser, *Our World in Data*

> Has late liberalism promoted a healthier and more inclusive society or is "breakdown" of the traditional family sowing anxiety as conservatives maintain?

Global March towards Hypermodernity

Collapse of communism infused Western liberals with confidence that their society offered a model for the rest of the world to follow towards greater prosperity and happiness. Contemporary progressives embraced information technology as an instrument that could break down old social barriers, spread economic opportunity, and diffuse freedom inside repressive societies. Cellphones would enable small farmers to fetch better prices. Computers could promote rural literacy. Global media could inspire reform inside despotic regimes. Social media would enable repressed groups to mobilize for their rights

By the twenty-first century, liberal optimism had grown more tempered. Rapid advances in global communication technologies did intensify cultural dialogue and stimulate the reinvention of older identities and traditions. Following passage of the WTO, levels of poverty and malnutrition began to drop, while rates for female literacy began rising. Increasing availability of affordable cellphones and Internet access began to connect formerly remote regions to an emerging global culture defined by core technologies, consumer gadgets, and signature brands. However, conservatives around the globe perceived the individualism, secularism, and consumerism at the heart of Western society as a dangerous dystopia. As transnational corporations (TNCs) have spread their influence across the world stage, American franchises and global brands projected a highly materialistic notion of happiness that many traditionalists saw as sterile and corrosive. In the place of nurturing ethnic communities, neighborhood churches, and state institutions that once anchored individuals firmly in place, modern workers now drift through a liquid world of technology and sterile high rises, interacting increasingly with superficial online acquaintances. To Western conservatives, Islamists and Asian conservatives alike, multiculturalism and liberal tolerance threaten the social order. Individuals once firmly planted in traditional ideas of gender, loyalty to the nation-state, and cultural mores are now anxious souls that struggle to reconcile conflicting identities, juggle multiple roles, and lead highly compartmentalized lives. Hypermodernity breeds a profound alienation that manifests in a rising index of social dysfunction: childhood obesity, gaming addiction, clinical depression, alcohol and drug abuse, and random gun violence.

> Millennials represent the first generation to come of age inside a digital society. Do social media platforms like Facebook help to connect your generation to world events or do they promote primarily superficial relationships?

During the 1990s, several Asian politicians boisterously denounced Western liberal society as corrosive. Malaysian President Mahathir argued that "the notion that a country must Westernize in order to modernize is ludicrous," joining a chorus of regional leaders endorsing "Asian values" as offering a more solid foundation for twenty-first century modernity.[9] The preponderance of US corporations among global TNCs, particularly global media companies, helped to diffuse Western ideas, products, and values during the early stages of neoliberal globalization. This led early critics of the emerging culture of global modernity to associate it with Western values. As we move into the twenty first century, however, non-Western cultural groups have increasingly assimilated Western products, ideas, and practices selectively on their own terms. In the process, they have also inscribed global culture with their own traditions and innovations. Western cities have grown more cosmopolitan with Chinese restaurants, Korean electronics, and Jap-animation evolving into staples of modern life. They highlight the coalescence of global society that is reconciling technology, multiple cultural traditions, and consumerism in diverse configurations around the world.

Conclusion: The West in the Twenty-First Century

The end of the Cold War instilled among Western liberals a sense of triumph that spurred multiple initiatives to integrate diverse countries, economies, and cultures into a global village. The EU, NAFTA, and the WTO worked in tandem to accelerate the diminishing frictions between national economies and to increase the flow of goods and capital across state borders. Deeper integration also increased immigration and cultural exchange, spurring increasing convergence among local patterns of life as well as a defensive conservative backlash against "modernity." During the 1990s, the West self-confidently extended liberal institutions into Eastern Europe and Mexico, while TNCs promoted a generic consumerism that many non-Western peoples embraced as modern progress. The 2001 World Trade Center attack marked a high-profile rejection of Western modernity, but also spurred Western states to rally together in common defense of liberal democracy, gender equality, human rights, and open markets. Western traditionalists, however, continue to fret about multiculturalism, urban crime, and the breakdown of traditional family structures. For many non-Western peoples, Western society symbolizes at once modern progress to be emulated and an extreme liberal experiment to be avoided.

Questions for Critical Thought

1. What fears and concerns shaped the structure of Europe's postwar settlement?
2. Why did Levittown prove so significant in spurring and shaping North American suburbanization?
3. How did Europe's golden recovery help to diminish national rivalries and class tensions?
4. Through what tactics did the civil rights movement challenge institutional racism?
5. What were the origins of the 1960s counterculture movement? In what ways did the Hippies seek to transform society?
6. How did stagflation set the table for the neoliberal reform during the 1980s? How did this crisis stimulate extreme right-wing parties and immigration reform?
7. In what ways has globalization stimulated a stronger sense of Western identity while simultaneously undermining traditional values?

Suggestions for Further Reading

- Berend, I. T. *Europe Since 1980*. Cambridge: Cambridge University Press, 2010.
- Branch, T. *Parting the Waters: Martin Luther King and the Civil Rights Movement 1954–63*. New York: Papermac, 1990.
- Gillingham, J. *European Integration, 1950–2003: Super-State or New Market Economy?* Cambridge: Cambridge University Press, 2003.

- Judt, T. *Postwar: A History of Europe Since 1945*. New York: Penguin, 2006. Marwick, A. *The Sixties: Cultural Revolution in Britain, France, Italy and the United States, 1958–1974*. New York: Bloomsbury, 1999.
- Patterson, J. T. *Grand Expectations: The United States, 1945–1974*. New York: Oxford University Press, 1996.
- Zinn, H. *A People's History of the United States*. New York: Harper, 2005.

Notes

1. Winston Churchill, "United States of Europe, Zurich," September 19, 1946, accessed July 30, 1930, https://winstonchurchill.org/resources/speeches/1946-1963-elder-statesman/united-states-of-europe/.
2. Bruce Daniels, "Learning to Live with Britain's Eldest Daughter: Anti-Americanism in Canada and Australia," *Journal of American & Comparative Cultures* 25 (Spring-Summer 2002): 173.
3. Quoted in David Reynolds, *One World Divisible* (New York: Norton, 2001), 154.
4. Quoted in Wasserstein, *Barbarism and Civilization* (New York: Oxford University Press, 2007), 778.
5. Christopher Strain, *Pure Fire: Self-Defense as Activism in the Civil Rights Era* (Athens, Ga: University of Georgia Press, 2005), 92–93.
6. Lewis Powell, "Confidential Memorandum: Attack on the Free Enterprise System," August 23, 1971, quoted in Kim Phelps-Fein, *Invisible Hands: The Making of the Conservative Movement from the New Deal to Reagan* (New York: Norton, 2009), 158, 160.
7. Statcan, "Canadian Households in 2011: Type and Growth," accessed July 30, 2019, https://www12.statcan.gc.ca/census-recensement/2011/as-sa/98-312-x/98-312-x2011003_2-eng.cfm.
8. "Jimmy Carter Televised Address," July 15, 1979, http://www.pbs.org/wgbh/americanexperience/features/primary-resources/carter-crisis/.
9. Quoted in Mohamad Mahathir and Ishihara Shintaro, *The Voice of Asia: Two Leaders Discuss the Coming Century*, trans. Frank Baldwin (New York: Kodansha International, 1995), 77.

Chapter 6
Postwar Latin America

Chapter Outline

- Introduction
- Postwar Experiment in Populism
- Latin America's Cold War
- Postwar Culture and Society
- Latin America's Debt Crisis, 1982 to 1989
- The Democratic Wave
- Summary: Latin America at the Crossroads

Timeline of Postwar Latin American History: 1946-1999

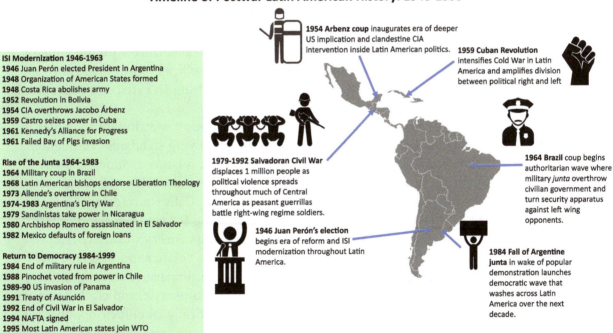

ISI Modernization 1946-1963
1946 Juan Perón elected President in Argentina
1948 Organization of American States formed
1948 Costa Rica abolishes army
1952 Revolution in Bolivia
1954 CIA overthrows Jacobo Árbenz
1959 Castro seizes power in Cuba
1961 Kennedy's Alliance for Progress
1961 Failed Bay of Pigs invasion

Rise of the Junta 1964-1983
1964 Military coup in Brazil
1968 Latin American bishops endorse Liberation Theology
1973 Allende's overthrow in Chile
1974-1983 Argentina's Dirty War
1979 Sandinistas take power in Nicaragua
1980 Archbishop Romero assassinated in El Salvador
1982 Mexico defaults of foreign loans

Return to Democracy 1984-1999
1984 End of military rule in Argentina
1988 Pinochet voted from power in Chile
1989-90 US invasion of Panama
1991 Treaty of Asunción
1992 End of Civil War in El Salvador
1994 NAFTA signed
1995 Most Latin American states join WTO
1997 Mexico PRI loses first election in 71 years

1954 Arbenz coup inaugurates era of deeper US implication and clandestine CIA intervention inside Latin American politics.

1959 Cuban Revolution intensifies Cold War in Latin America and amplifies division between political right and left

1979-1992 Salvadoran Civil War displaces 1 million people as political violence spreads throughout much of Central America as peasant guerrillas battle right-wing regime soldiers.

1946 Juan Perón's election begins era of reform and ISI modernization throughout Latin America.

1964 Brazil coup begins authoritarian wave where military *junta* overthrow civilian government and turn security apparatus against left wing opponents.

1984 Fall of Argentine junta in wake of popular demonstration launches democratic wave that washes across Latin America over the next decade.

Image credits: © mlopez/Shutterstock.com; © cube29/Shutterstock.com; © Leremy/Shutterstock.com; © Leremy/Shutterstock.com; © Zoart Studio/Shutterstock.com; © puruan/Shutterstock.com; © Leremy/Shutterstock.com

Introduction

From the isolated hamlets of Argentina's Pampas to the sprawling *barrios* of Mexico City and the tourist bedecked beaches of the Caribbean, Latin America remains a region defined by sharp contrasts and contradictions. "Latin America" invokes a nineteenth-century distinction between North America and its southern neighbors whose culture, economy, and politics were imprinted by Iberian colonialism. Despite regional and national differences, most residents of Latin America still speak Portuguese or Spanish, and a reactionary Counter-Reformation Catholicism continues to saturate local cultures with conservative values, many shared customs, and a collective ethos. Historians often label the region's society and politics as "corporate," a legacy of nineteenth-century state-building that asserted collective identity, but failed to penetrate deeply into the rural periphery or fully assimilate non-European groups. After World War II, populist politicians embarked upon ambitious modernizing projects to industrialize the economy, to expand the role of the state, and to assimilate marginalized groups inside an enlarged political community. Progressive postwar reforms, however, mostly failed to catalyze industrialization or to level entrenched class, ethnic, and gender differences. Brazil and Mexico were hailed as miracle economies, but many of the small states of Central America and Caribbean urbanized rapidly without developing an advanced manufacturing base or liberating the economy from fickle commodity markets. Throughout Latin America, poverty remains pervasive, clustered in shantytowns ringing large capital cities, as well as rural areas and remote regions like the Amazon, Central American jungles, and the Andean highlands that house remnants of aboriginal civilizations. Latin America's urban middle classes aspire for economic progress and deeper global integration, but their dreams are tied to that of a narrow elite, whose wealth rests in ownership of land and industry, and whose power is maintained through an informal alliance with top military officers. In many Latin American states, the military represents an unofficial fourth branch of government, seeing itself as sacred guardian of the nation and exercising an extraconstitutional role to step in whenever disorder threatens the republic.

Following World War II, Latin American states implemented import substitution strategies to stimulate industrialization, accelerate growth, and elevate regional living standards. Throughout most of the 1950s, Latin America experienced robust growth inside a larger economic boom that raised commodity prices. By the late 1950s, however, the poor and working classes grew increasingly frustrated with a prosperity that failed to trickle down. Calls for reform took many shapes: union organizers demanding higher wages, peasants pushing for land reform, priests advocating for social justice, and guerrillas espousing Marxism. Latin American society has a long history of political violence. During the late 1960s, increasing polarization triggered an authoritarian reaction. Many states fell victim to *junta*, an oligarchical system where top military officers suspend the constitution, replace civilians at the departments of state, and crack down on left-wing reformers. The Cold War enabled the *junta* to opportunistically label their opponents as "communists" and call upon US support. Through systematic terror, the *junta* imposed a superficial stability over Latin American society, but they had few solutions for the economy's deeper structural problems. Heavy borrowing after 1973 inaugurated a short-lived economic boom until rising interest rates pushed Mexico and Brazil into default in 1982. The subsequent Debt Crisis inaugurated a Lost Decade of state austerity, hyperinflation, and high unemployment that wiped out many of Latin America's earlier developmental gains. By the decade's end, disillusionment swelled into a democratic wave that slowly pushed out regional *junta* in favor of left-of-center governments. Abandoning import substitution, many reformers opted to join the World Trade Organization (WTO) and introduced neoliberal reform measures at home. By the 1990s, stepped-up foreign investment enabled Latin America's extractive industries to boom. This restored economic growth and contributed to political stability, but the resulting prosperity remains fragile and unequally distributed. Various interest groups are not fully reconciled to their bloody past or committed to the same ideals of political community.

Big Questions

- How did postwar populists try to reform Latin American states?
- Why did the import-substitution strategy fall short?
- How did Latin American politics increasingly converge with US foreign policy after 1959?
- How is globalization transforming Latin American culture?

Postwar Experiment in Populism

World War II raised demand for commodities and lifted Latin America's export economies from the depths of global depression. Latin American leaders, however, never forgot the collapse in world trade during the 1930s. After the war, a consensus united workers, landowners, and politicians around a state program for modernization. Argentine politician **Juan Perón** exemplified Latin America's drift towards populism. Addressing the *descamisados*, or "unshirted ones," Perón proposed to redirect the national economy from lining the pockets of foreign investors towards serving the common good. The state would buy out foreign businesses, spur industrialization, diversify the economy, and build out a basic safety net. Perón's program was echoed by other regional leaders, including Mexico's Lázaro Cárdenas, Brazil's Getúlio Vargas, the Dominican Republic's Rafael L. Trujillo, and Cuba's Fulgencio Batista. Although Perónism would impassion Argentina's marginalized for generations, the country's

Juan Perón blazed a trail for postwar reform in Latin America by tapping the desires of the urban lower class for fuller incorporation inside the state and a stronger footing inside the national economy.

conservative elites denounced him as a demagogue. Perón's greatest failing was a lack of policy focus. As president, Perón's measures cut unemployment, raised incomes, and increased the security of the urban poor; however, he soon exhausted Argentina's financial reserves. By 1952, mounting deficits crippled the economy and forced Perón to reverse course and entice back foreign investors. Instead of cutting benefits for his supporters, Perón decided to manipulate exchange rate mechanisms and force the country's powerful cattle barons and wheat merchants to sell their produce at below market prices. When this measure failed to stabilize the economy, Perón opted to print money to pay the state's bills. As inflation spiked, Argentina's economy slipped off the rails. Facing mounting criticism, Perón clamped down on political opponents; censoring radio broadcasts, newspapers, even the film industry. Peron's downfall came in 1955 as he sought to liberalize divorce laws and legalize prostitution. The Church galvanized opposition to his regime and set the stage for a military coup that chased Perón into exile for over a decade.

Dependency Theory and Import Substitution

Arguably, the figure that most influenced Latin America during the postwar era was Argentine economist **Raúl Prebisch**. In a 1950 article, Prebisch argued that while Latin Americans seized their political independence during the early nineteenth century, they had remained locked inside a Western-dominated world economy. This forced Latin America to trade on disadvantageous terms, exchanging primary commodities for value-added Western manufacturing goods. To escape poverty and economic dependence, Latin American states needed to catch up to the West by promoting manufacturing. **Import substitution industrialization** (ISI) represented a comprehensive strategy for cutting Western imports by establishing high tariffs, while investing in infrastructure and providing incentives to indigenous entrepreneurs. ISI was designed to spark industrial takeoff, raising productivity to spur a decade of high growth. **Dependency theorists** argued that rising wages would lift the poor into ranks of the working classes and enable Latin America to catch up to Western levels of prosperity. From within the Economic Commission for Latin America and the Caribbean (ECLAC) in Santiago, Chile, Prebisch trained a generation of Latin American economists. During the late 1940s and early 1950s, most returned home and tailored the ISI program to fit their local economy.

From 1950 to 1960, Latin American economies grew quite robustly. Local exporters benefitted from high commodity prices, while workers and capitalists profited from an expanding manufacturing sector. ISI policies accelerated industrialization in Mexico and Brazil, but ISI had less impact upon the High Andes and Central America. There, extractive industries and export agriculture remained predominant. ISI also created fewer jobs than dependency theorists anticipated. Indigenous entrepreneurs often invested in outdated equipment that resulted in inefficient factories. Protectionism provided a captive domestic market in large states like Mexico and Brazil, but Latin American–manufactured goods were uncompetitive abroad. This meant that once the national market was saturated, local industries stagnated. Expansion of the state bureaucracy did provide employment for a growing middle class,

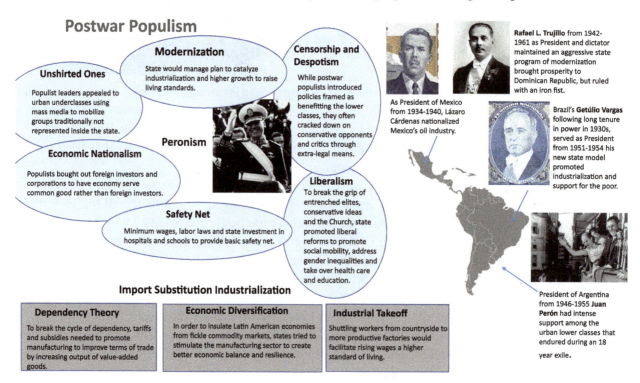

Image credits: World History Archive/Alamy Stock Photo; © Janusz Pienkowski/Shutterstock.com; Album/Alamy Stock Photo © Janusz Pienkowski/Shutterstock.com; © mlopez/Shutterstock.com; Keystone Press/Alamy Stock Photo

but the fledgling manufacturing sector proved unable to absorb rural workers fleeing low wages and political violence in the countryside.

By the early 1960s, it was becoming clear that despite robust growth, regional states were not industrializing and profits were not trickling down to the poor. Growth remained concentrated inside the export sector where profits depended on cheap manual labor. Local frustrations with stagnant incomes worked their way through a Latin American culture rich in political violence. In Guatemala, and some other Central American states, rising commodity prices destabilized rural society as commercial planters, backed by the state, army, and local thugs confiscated land, broke up indigenous communities, and transformed many peasants into landless migrants. During the 1950s, hundreds of thousands of rural workers fled mines, plantations, and failing subsistence farms for a better life in cities. With inadequate housing and jobs available, however, most migrants squatted on land sitting at the periphery of Latin American capitals. Under ISI, regional states had redirected national revenue towards cities to build infrastructure, schools, and clinics. This accentuated an already sharp disparity between the urban and rural standard of living. Rural migrants, however, were often illiterate and many struggled to find work and housing. Over subsequent decades, many shantytowns evolved into neighborhoods as squatters improved their dwellings and sent their kids to school. Many *barrio* and *campamentos* families, however, resisted acquiring land titles that would trigger a formal tax obligation. This left residents in a legal limbo with limited urban services. Residents responded to such shortfalls through ingenious strategies, establishing communal centers to mediate disputes, tapping the electric grid illegally and contracting out for drinking water delivery.

A Revolutionary Wave

Latin American Populist regimes had promised economic progress and increased social security and greater political inclusion. By the early 1960s, however, ISI had mostly failed to radiate out. The traditional elite had profited from ISI policies by redirecting capital from rural estates towards urban industries to capture state subsidies, but this growth had only modestly expanded the ranks of the urban middle classes in Brazil, Chile, Mexico, and Argentina. ISI brought fewer jobs to the rapidly expanding shantytowns surrounding regional capitals. By the 1960s, university students, highly educated, but with limited job prospects, helped to give popular discontent a revolutionary focus. Many students had studied dependency theory. This hardened their attitude towards the conservative indigenous elites, exploitive foreign businesses, and heavy-handed *Yanqui* (US) imperialism. Latin America's small communist parties mostly faded into irrelevance as a new generation of leftists often took their cue from Ernesto "Che" Guevara and his "foco" theory of revolutionary change. Idealistic students were appalled by inequality, while their desire for reform found inspiration in the independence movements sweeping across Asia and Africa. Many believed that Latin America too was ripe for revolution. Economic frustrations seeded increasingly robust reform coalitions, uniting mining associations, peasant leagues, and urban-based student groups and labor unions. Mining syndicates, industrialists, and land owners that traditionally responded to calls for higher wages or land reform by arming local thugs discovered that intimidation proved less effective in the face of national movements. By the mid-1960s, tensions mounted inside national communities only superficially united under the ideology of the modernizing state. A much older divide between rich and poor, governing elites and the masses, patron and peon increasingly involved into a growing polarization into "left-" and "right-wing" camps. The timing and dynamic of this process varied across Latin America. Generally, the "left" demanded higher wages, land reform, political inclusion, and better living conditions. Conservative elites on the "right" increasingly responded to local agitation with political violence. The police and army arrested squatters, while elites called for support from the Church, the middle classes, and the United States to protect tradition, smash "godless communism," and restore law and order.

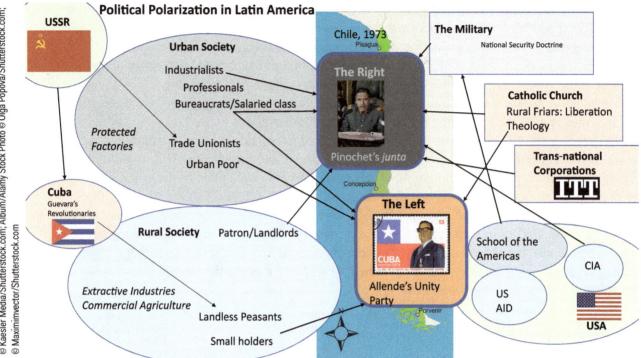

The polarization of Latin American society is well illustrated by Chile from 1970 to 1973. External actors from multinational corporations, the Church, Cuba, and the Central Intelligence Agency (CIA) at once exploited and amplified the conflict between Allende's Unity Party and Chile's conservative elite.

There were variations and exceptions to this regional pattern. Mexico had experienced its revolution during the early twentieth century. This culminated in a state where the broad-based **Institutional Revolutionary Party** (PRI) held power for seventy-one uninterrupted years. Mexico's political system sublimated tension by incorporating peasants and the urban working classes into a single party that dominated the state and distributed economic benefits to its supporters. Following a 1948 Civil War, Costa Rica established a new constitution and abolished its army. This set the stage for a string of thirteen straight free and fair presidential elections. Venezuela mostly escaped the turmoil during the 1960s and 1970s, in part because petroleum exports provided a revenue stream that enabled the state to finance social programs that could release pent-up pressures.

Rise of the Junta, 1964 to 1973

During the 1960s, thirteen constitutional governments fell to military *junta*. Latin America had a *caudillo* tradition dating back to the nineteenth century when military strong men presented their takeover of the state as a nationalist project to safeguard the republic. Regional military academies like Brazil's *Escola Superior de Guerra* preached the **national security doctrine** that encouraged young officers to view the military as progressive force for modernization and ultimate protector of the state. As guardians of the nation, an officer's primary allegiance lay with his commanders rather than civilian authorities that could be put into power by the mob.

Across Latin America, officers were hardly a uniform bloc. Top officers in Chile had different political inclinations, but in the aftermath of the 1973 coup junior officers with a more liberal orientation were purged from the ranks. Also, some Latin American officers, like Roberto d'Aubuisson and Augusto Pinochet, had as young officers graduated from the United States' School of the Americas. Throughout their careers, they maintained contacts with the US security establishment. The relationship between *junta*, social and religious conservatives, the landed elite, foreign corporations, and US officials was often complex, but a staple feature of the Latin American right. Although the Latin American "left" was larger, it was also more divided and counted upon less substantial external support from Cuba, liberal international opinion, and sometimes the USSR.

By the late 1970s, a wave of authoritarian reaction had left only Costa Rica and Venezuela standing as liberal democracies holding fair and open elections with constitutional governments that operated according to the rule of law. The crisis triggering the military takeover of the state and the composition of the ruling *junta* varied. Typically, officers blamed the "left" for destabilizing the state. Martial law provided a mechanism for suspending civil liberties guaranteed under the constitution and launching a brutal crackdown on opponents. The 1959 Cuban Revolution provided another stimulus for repression. Until his death in 1967, Che Guevara called upon regional leftists to follow Cuba's example and form revolutionary cells to overthrow the state. While despotic, most *junta* took power promising an eventual return to civilian rule once order was restored. Most *junta* also counted upon at least tacit support from the Catholic Church that viewed communism as an existential threat to the Christian faith and their traditional role inside education and healthcare. Significant portions of Latin America's middle classes also initially supported authoritarian regimes because they worried that radicals would erode their precarious privileges.

Chile's junta seized power in a September 11, 1973 coup, emblematic of broader authoritarian wave where the conservative elites backed the military's takeover of government and the imposition of martial law to crack down upon their opponents.

Latin America's Cold War

During the Cold War, Latin America's domestic politics grew increasingly intertwined with US foreign policy. Since the 1823 Monroe Doctrine, the United States had asserted hegemony over the Western Hemisphere. In the early twentieth century, the United States adopted a more muscular **dollar diplomacy**, where US presidents regularly dispatched American marines to Central America to quash rebels that challenged US business interests. Before President Roosevelt proclaimed a "good neighbor policy" in 1932, over thirty US military interventions took place inside Latin America. In Nicaragua during the 1930s, the United States pioneered the constabulary option. Training the local police cultivated surrogates that could prop up the local dictator who could defend American business interests. Ties with local security forces gave the United States subtle leverage inside Central America's "banana republics." Politics remained local, but state policies were constrained by foreign business interests with ultimate sovereignty resting in Washington. This convention is well established in historiography.

During World War II, Latin American states had mostly rallied behind the United States. By 1945, most offered enthusiastic support for the American vision of building a multilateral postwar international system, which they hoped to join as equal members. During the War, Latin American export industries had become more closely integrated with the United States' "arsenal for democracy." As tensions with Stalin mounted, Truman in 1947 recast the United States' international mission as defender of the "free world." In subsequent months, the United States pressured its Latin American allies to sign the 1947 **Rio Pact**. The US objective was to update the older notion of "hemispheric defense" to meet the threat now posed by communism. The United States saw this treaty as formalizing the Monroe Doctrine and authorizing their intervention against any Soviet incursion into their "backyard." Although Latin American elites abstractly shared US fears about communism, they felt insulted by this treaty's unilateral tone. Conscious of the United States' long history of intervention in their states, Latin American delegates insisted upon a more multilateral structure and language that respected their sovereignty. They anticipated, however, that their informal acquiescence to US hegemony would be reciprocated in the newly announced Marshall Plan. At the 1948 Pan-American Conference in Bogota, Latin American leaders were bitterly disappointed when Secretary of State George Marshall announced that US aid would be reserved for Europe. Instead, Marshall urged his Latin American "friends" to open up their markets to make them more attractive to US investors. Disillusioned, Latin American states agreed to join the US-dominated **Organization of American States (OAS)**. It supplemented the Rio Pact's focus on military collaboration with a forum for hemispheric cooperation. Latin American hopes that the OAS would evolve into a conduit for investment capital, however, were never met. Following the 1948 to 1949 Berlin Crisis, the United States' strategic focus shifted towards the Atlantic. Subsequently, the Korean War amplified international polarization, eroding some of the prestige of the United Nations (UN) and undermining the multilateral structure of the international system in which Latin American states had played a prominent founding role.

The 1959 Cuban Revolution rekindled US interest in Pan-American affairs. Washington, DC, realized that Central America featured many unpopular dictatorships that had tacitly acquiesced to US hegemony, but failed to meet their own citizens' aspirations for a better life. Suddenly, solidly anti-communist regimes in Latin American appeared vulnerable to revolution. President Kennedy worked to isolate Cuba by tightening the embargo on its economy and kicking it out of the OAS by 1962. Kennedy also introduced the **Alliance for Progress** in 1961, offering US investment in Latin America with the idea of accelerating economic development and democratization to immunize regional governments from communist subversion. From 1962 to 1967, the United States funneled roughly $22 billion to Latin America, but little aid distributed to Latin American partners reached rural communities where poverty was clustered. Under President Johnson, and especially Nixon, any pretense of building up civil society in Latin America was abandoned in favor of a **Real Politik** strategy that disbursed military aid directly to *juntas* waging war upon their left-wing political opponents.

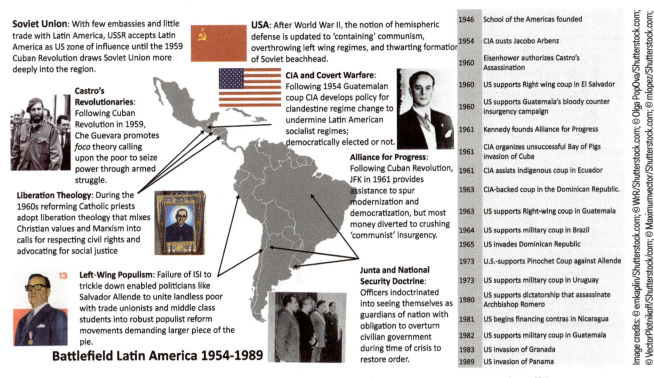

Battlefield Latin America 1954-1989

After the Cuban Revolution, a militant US policy for communist containment intersected with a Latin American rift between conservative elites and leftist populists agitating for socialist reforms.

Coup in Guatemala

The US policy towards Latin America remained fluid from 1948 to 1954, but the Eisenhower administration's **New Look** doctrine marked a shift in US strategic thinking from sympathizing with "Third World" nationalist movements to worrying that political instability could facilitate communist expansion. In Latin America, this shift was evident in the diverse US reaction to socialist movements springing up in Bolivia and Guatemala. In 1952, the **Revolutionary Nationalist Movement** (MNR) uniting tin miners, peasants, and urban liberals assumed power in Bolivia after defeating the national army. The revolutionary regime introduced a wide range of reforms, including nationalization of tin mines, universal suffrage, literacy campaign, and land redistribution. The United States elected to recognize the revolutionary Bolivian regime because it enjoyed broad support, had no links to the Soviet Union, and state confiscation targeted a local family rather than US businessmen. US reaction to Guatemalan reforms proved starkly different. Guatemala represented Latin America's quintessential banana republic. The US conglomerate **United Fruit Company** (UFCO) represented a state within a state. It owned Guatemala's port, its best arable land, most of the railroad, and employed its own police force to discipline its 10,000 strong workforce. While profitable for US investors, the company was intensely disliked by Guatemalans because UFCO paid few taxes and conferred only pittance wages.

In 1950, Colonel **Jacobo Árbenz** won the presidency in Guatemala by a sweeping 50 percent margin. The key to Árbenz's campaign was a program for land reform, a popular measure inside a state where 2 percent of the population owned 72 percent of the agricultural land. Land reform, however, threatened Guatemala's elites. Church officials protested Árbenz's incorporation of communists inside his cabinet. In June 1952, Árbenz began to purchase uncultivated land from large estates. As Guatemala's largest landowner and employer, UFCO was disproportionately impacted. Árbenz offered landowners compensation, based on the supressed values they themselves had declared to Guatemalan tax authorities. When UFCO protested that the land they had assessed at $600 million was actually worth $16 billion, Árbenz refused to pay out that higher amount. Boston-based UFCO, however, could call upon powerful allies, including Allen and John Foster Dulles, US director of Central Intelligence Agency (CIA) and its former secretary of state. In November 1953, the United States dispatched Ambassador John Peurifoy to talk sense into Árbenz. Peurifoy insisted that the United States would not tolerate communism in its backyard. Árbenz tried to explain that he was a Christian socialist and not a Marxist. He denied having ties to the Soviet Union. UFCO publicists in the United States raised alarm about communists in Árbenz's cabinet and spread fear about a Soviet "beachhead."

> Why would the United States overthrow a democratically elected leader like Arbenz? Was US foreign policy motivated by an exaggerated fear of communism or did anti-communism provide cover for protecting American business elites?

Washington, DC, hauled Guatemala before the OAS and urged regional allies to cast Árbenz out. Latin American delegates rejected US heavy-handedness. Thwarted at the OAS, Eisenhower turned to clandestine warfare. The CIA recruited Colonel **Carlos Castillo Armas** and trained a militia for him in neighboring Honduras. In November 1954, the CIA launched Operation WASHTUB, an intense propaganda campaign designed to destabilize Árbenz's regime. Caches of weapons and Marxist literature were planted to assert a mostly fictitious Árbenz–Soviet connection. The CIA also financed the political opposition, winning support from Guatemala's principal cleric, Archbishop Mariano Rossell Arellano, who saw Árbenz's regime as a threat to the Church's traditional influence in society. Judging conditions for a coup ripe, in June 1954, the CIA ordered Armas to invade Guatemala. When his fledgling force became bogged down, the CIA brought in its covert air force to strafe Guatemala City and sow panic. Conservative officers in Guatemala's army, some of them bribed by the CIA, now turned against Árbenz and forced him to resign. Armas marched into Guatemala City and turned his henchmen loose upon Árbenz's supporters using CIA hit lists. Armas also quickly returned the UFCO's property.

For the US security establishment, the Guatemalan coup provided a blueprint for subsequent clandestine interventions inside Latin America. Guatemala also established a model for cooperation between the US businesses, the CIA, and the Oval Office. For Latin American leftists, Guatemala sent clear warning about the limits of US toleration for "socialist" regimes, regardless of whether they were democratically elected or not.

Allende's Chilean Way

Following the Cuban Revolution, the United States grew less discriminate in its use of force to "contain" Latin American "communism." This hardline stance became apparent in the Nixon administration's deep involvement in Chile. In 1970, **Salvador Allende** came to power as leader of the **Popular Unity** (UP) movement uniting communist, socialist, and left-wing parties. Articulate, polished, and immaculately dressed, Allende had sought the presidency since 1952. He secured it in 1970 following parliamentary endorsement after a hard-fought three-way election failed to culminate in an absolute majority for any party. Allende had campaigned on a promise to nationalize foreign corporations, redistribute land,

and build a socialist state to benefit the downtrodden. Following his election, Allende raised wages and nationalized Chile's two large, American-owned mining corporations. Allende's measures raised living standards for the poor and spurred a brief boom in consumer spending. In a 1971 speech before jubilant supporters, Allende triumphantly proclaimed "our copper, our coal, our iron, our nitrates, our steel, the fundamental bases of heavy industry today belong to Chile and Chileans."[1] Allende brushed off radicals inside his coalition calling for armed revolution. Instead, he sketched out a peaceful middle course. The *via Chilena*, or Chilean Way, sought to build a socialist society through constitutional means and nonviolence. This commitment, however, won Allende few favors from the Nixon administration. Richard Nixon fumed at news of Allende's election. He disbursed $8 million to the CIA as "meddling money" to destabilize his government.

By late 1971, Chile's economy started to sputter, in part because of US subversion and economic warfare. Freezing credit to Chile sent its stock market reeling in a fury of panic selling. Subsequently, food shortages, hoarding, and closed shops contributed to public anxiety. Allende's consensus building approach made sense inside a polarized society, but it also resulted in a slow pace of reform. His admirable commitment to nonviolence translated into passive reaction towards his increasingly militant opponents. An October 1972 trucker strike paralyzed Chile's economy. This emboldened right-wing paramilitary groups to attack Allende's supporters with clubs and guns. Mounting political violence began to discredit Allende's government and led the anxious middle classes to call for law and order. As civil society began to disintegrate, Chile's security forces increasingly broke free from civilian oversight. On their own initiative, right-wing officers ordered their troops to crack down on Allende supporters, which were occupying farms and factories throughout the country. Nixon's covert destabilization program had by 1973, created ripe conditions for a military coup.

Pinochet's Coup

On September 11, 1973, **Augusto Pinochet**, along with heads of the other branches of the armed forces and the national police launched a *coup d'etat*. In the barracks the night before, soldiers and sailors deemed unreliable were arrested. The next morning, an armored regiment moved in on *La Moneda*, the presidential palace defended by lightly armed Allende supporters. Pinochet offered Allende exile, but in his final radio address Allende announced his intention to "pay with my life for the loyalty of the people."[2] After strafing *La Moneda* with rockets, Chilean troops stormed the palace. Details of Allende's death remain obscure. Coup plotters claimed that Allende took his own life with a pistol given to him by Fidel Castro.

The *junta* declared a seventy-two-hour curfew as Chilean security forces swarmed Santiago and fanned out through the countryside to assassinate "enemies" that had been placed on a hit list. Subsequently, repression turned towards the factories, shantytowns, and university

The most memorable image of the September 11 coup was the burning of La Moneda after being assaulted by Chilean tanks, planes, and soldiers.

campuses that had served as the bastions for the UP's support. Suspected leftists were rounded up and temporarily herded into the *Estadio Chile* soccer stadium. There, many faced interrogation, torture, and sometimes summary execution. Victor Jara, a playwright and leader of Chile's new song movement, was killed after Chilean officers played a game of Russian roulette. For months, the junta's victims washed up on the *Río Mapocho* with their hands tied behind their backs with barbed wire.

The level of violence shocked many in Chile, even opponents of Allende's regime. State-owned media mollified the public by bombarding them with coverage of "Plan Z." This disinformation campaign presented the regime's pacification measures as a defensive measure to preempt an imminent Marxist coup planned by Allende using Cuban troops. Despite the implausibility of this claim, relentless coverage of planted evidence cemented public perception that the *junta's* coup had been provoked. Although the numbers remain approximations, Chile's *junta* killed 2,279 opponents, tortured 31,947, and exiled 1,312 more. With **Operation Condor**, Chile's *junta* extended its terror campaign abroad, collaborating with neighboring intelligence agencies to assassinate prominent regime enemies that had fled into exile.

Although Pinochet's coup was indigenously plotted and executed, it benefitted enormously from US support. US implication commenced in October 1970 when the CIA trained, hired assassins to murder General Rene Schneider, Army Chief of Staff and one of Allende's most ardent supporters. Subsequently, Nixon authorized an "invisible blockade" to "make the economy scream."[3] These policies undermined the success of Allende's economic reforms, while CIA 'meddling' money helped to mobilize the political opposition. Before his coup, Pinochet sought and received US Secretary of State's Henry Kissinger's personal assurance of US support.

Argentina's Dirty War

Across South America, *junta* used similar tactics, but Argentina's *guerra sucia*, or **dirty war**, ranked among the bloodiest. Since forcing Perón into exile in 1955, Argentina had suffered from chronic instability. A series of unpopular governments had fallen in rapid secession unable to bridge the deep fissure between Perónists that included the working classes and Marxists versus the middle classes and elites that enjoyed the backing of the military. Radicalization of the left and right led to escalating political violence, bombings, and assassinations on both sides. In 1973, in a bid to placate the Left, the Right invited outlawed *Perónistas* to participate in an open election that the Left subsequently won. This set the stage for Juan Perón's triumphant return to Buenos Aires in 1974. Perón's short-lived bid to unite his deeply fractured country, however, floundered even before his death in 1975. His overmatched wife and successor, **Isabel Perón**, increasingly turned to the military to supress a mounting leftist insurgency. In 1976, the *junta* shunted Isabel aside and launched the **Process of National Reorganization**, a euphemism for a gruesome campaign of terror that endured until 1983. Argentine security forces operated in close conjunction with death squads (often security personnel working out of uniform) that systematically hunted down, tortured, and assassinated their political enemies. Security forces also battled the resilient Montoneros guerrillas ensconced in the Western mountains, while targeting a liberal opposition in cities composed of union activists, student leaders, and liberal journalists. The *junta's* most infamous tactic was making its enemies "disappear." Of the 30,000 arrested, 13,000 are estimated to have been killed without a trace. Often victims were tossed from helicopters alive to plummet to their death over the Atlantic. One psychologically crippling aspect of the dirty war was not knowing what happened to loved ones. Since the ***desaparecidos***, or disappeared, were rounded up without a warrant, local police could not verify arrests, and there was no possibility of juridical appeal. Relatives suffered intensely from the uncertainty of not knowing whether their loved ones were alive.

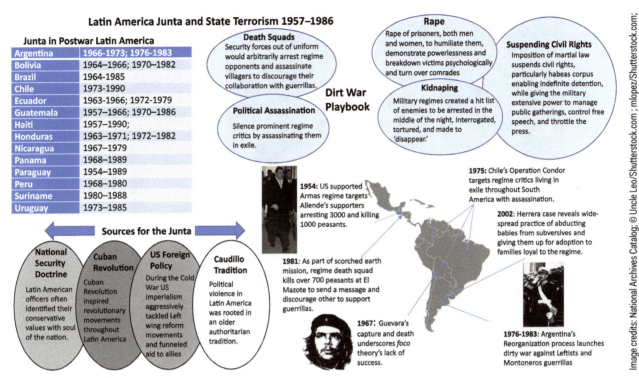

From 1957 to 1983, political violence swept through Latin America after import substitution industrialization (ISI) failed to promote growth and those left behind increasingly mobilized inside Left-wing coalitions demanding land reform, higher wages, and expansion of the safety net. Opportunistic elites lobbied the United States to support their suppression of local "communists" that often lacked any close ties to the Soviet Union.

The Sandinistas in Nicaragua

During the 1970s, polarization shifted from South to Central America, where battle lines formed between landed elites that monopolized the plantation complex and the state versus an impoverished peasantry. During the late 1970s, disgruntled Nicaraguan peasants organized a militant resistance movement targeting the country's powerful coffee barons. Armed rebels took control over part of the countryside, confiscating large estates, raising taxes, and redistributing land among their supporters. **Anastasio Somoza** called upon the United States for support against this "communist" threat, but his brutality quickly alienated Nicaragua's middle classes and US President Jimmy Carter alike.

After a brutal war that left over 30,000 dead, on July 19, 1979, the **Sandinistas**, named after nationalist hero Augusto Cesar Sandino, marched into Managua and drove out the unpopular Somoza dynasty that had ruled Nicaragua since 1950. The Sandinista coalition embraced multiple groups, but **Daniel Ortega's** leftist revolutionaries monopolized power. Upon assuming office, US President Ronald Reagan condemned the Sandinistas as a "Marxist" regime in league with Cuba. Reagan authorized the CIA to support the **Contras**, a group patched together from the remnants of Somoza's national guard. Operating from camps in Honduras and Costa Rica, the Contras quickly earned a reputation for rape and murder. Reagan's proxy war backfired by rallying Nicaraguan peasants to the Sandinista regime.

Public opinion and the international press had offered only muted criticism of US support for Latin American *junta* in the past, but during the 1980s Reagan found it increasingly difficult to deploy traditional counter insurgency tools during an age of détente and global media coverage. Reagan's mining of Nicaragua's Managua harbor earned condemnation from the World Court.

Daniel Ortega.

The international press, human rights groups, and American liberals criticized Contra terrorism, stimulating Congress to cut their funding in 1985. Reduced pressure enabled Daniel Ortega to launch a popular program for mass literacy, land redistribution, healthcare investment, and gender equality. His regime, however, lost a close election in 1990 as a majority of Nicaraguans embraced the possibility of reconciliation with the United States. Ortega conceded power peacefully, even supporting the subsequent Ingrid Betancourt regime, before successfully returning to power during the 1996 election.

Civil War in El Salvador

Latin America's most deadly civil war took place in tiny El Salvador. On October 15, 1979, a military coup and a subsequent crackdown against left-wing protesters stimulated the merger of various left-wing groups under the *Farabundo Marti National Liberation Front* (FMLN) (banner, sparking a civil war that would endure until 1992. The United States contributed to the conflict by providing large amounts of military aid to El Salvador's right-wing government. The civil war gained international notoriety in February 1980 when **Archbishop Oscar Romero** implored the government "in the name of God and this suffering population, whose cries reach to the heavens more tumultuous each day, I beg you, I beseech you, I order you, in the name of God, cease the repression."4 Romero's rhetoric embarrassed El Salvador's government and angered the Salvadoran oligarchy. On March 24, 1980, Romero was shot through the head while celebrating mass. **Roberto D'Aubuisson**, head of El Salvador's death squads, was ultimately apprehended for Romero's assassination, but soon released.

To break a well-organized insurgency, the Salvadoran armed forces carried out a "scorched earth" strategy designed to drive a "wedge" between guerrillas and their rural supporters. In December 1981,

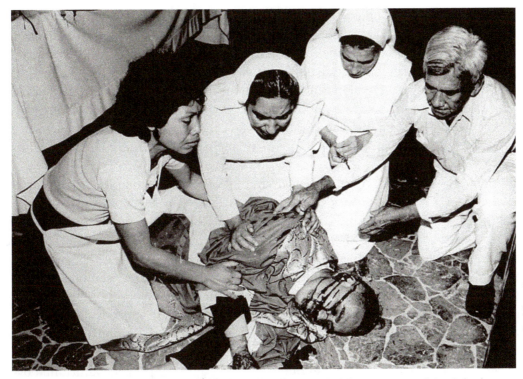
Archbishop Romero shot in Church while administrating mass. Leaked documents reveal that Salvadoran security officers drew lots in the US ambassador's office for the privilege of assassinating him.

the Atlacatl Battalion infamously massacred over seven hundred civilians in a remote village of El Mozote. This indiscriminate slaughter highlighted the depth of the US commitment to the regime's fight against communism, but "saving" El Salvador came at a fearful price. After ten years of civil war, 75,000 were killed and a fifth of the country's population had been displaced.

> How did US implication in the dirty wars in the 1980s destabilize Central American states and contribute to contemporary migration?

Junta and State Terrorism

Throughout Latin America, political violence was not accidental or gratuitous. Argentina's General Iberico Saint-Jean summarized the *junta's* logic well: "First we will kill all the subversives; then we will kill their collaborators; then their sympathizers; then all those who remain indifferent; and then finally we will kill the undecided."[5] Restoring order represented a euphemism for a campaign of systematic terror designed to break the will of their political opponents. Although the scale and scope of the violence during the authoritarian wave varied, the *junta* used similar tactics throughout Latin America in part because they relied on Western counterinsurgency experts: former Green Berets, Nazis, and French veterans of Algeria's civil war.

Latin America's *junta* tradition predated the Cold War and their postwar emergence invariably reflected local dynamics, but the United States played a key role in supporting right-wing regimes. Leading figures in the *junta* often had close ties to the US security establishment. Brazil's General Branco served with General Mark Clark during World War II. Pinochet and D'Aubuisson headlined a prestigious list of graduates from the **School of the Americas**. Founded in 1946 to provide "anti-communist counterinsurgency training," the school featured a "wall of fame" that numbered dozens of Latin American generals, colonels, and heads of state. These "graduates" also received prominent mention in Amnesty International's lists of worst human rights abusers.[6] Inside United States Agency for International Development (US AID), the Office of Public Safety (OPS) hired CIA and defense department contractors to train Latin American police forces in enhanced interrogation methods. While much of this aid was clandestine, and most records remain sealed, the United States was deeply implicated not just in "training," but also in "advising" their Latin American counterparts conducting dirty wars.

At the height of the counter culture movement in the 1960s, liberals like US Senator **William Fulbright** discerned "a general tendency on the part of our policy makers not to look beyond a Latin American politician's anti-communism."[7] US interventionism inside Latin America reflected a broader strategy of communist containment where all socialist movements were indiscriminately branded "communist" and any guerrilla movements were targeted as threats to the US. Although some Latin American reformers, particularly intellectuals and students living in the cities, embraced Marxism, their organizations were mostly focused on domestic issues and rarely drew support or direction from abroad. Cuba, rather than the USSR, emerged as the principal sponsor for Latin American guerrillas, but its resources were paltry and local peasants often mistrusted middle-class revolutionaries that often did not speak the local language and forcefully advocated for Marxist principles out of tune with communal concerns. Che Guevara was gunned down in Bolivia in 1967 after the peasants turned him over to the authorities. The fledgling Sandinista regime in Nicaragua received assistance from the communist bloc only after open US hostility. The principal catalysts for left-wing populism in Latin America were trenchant inequalities, the brutal repression exercised by military *juntas*, and exploitation by landed elites and foreign investors.

Postwar Culture and Society

Latin America remains a region defined by sharp contrasts. Economically, the geographically large and industrialized states of South America and Mexico hardly compare with the small and often poor republics of Latin America or the Caribbean. One larger postwar trend, however, was rapid urbanization in the context of limited state resources. In 1950, 40 percent of Latin America's population was urban. By 1990, this had risen to 70 percent, before leveling off at 80 percent by 2015. Today, Latin America constitutes the world's most urbanized region, featuring many megacities that present a complex array of challenges from gridlock to air pollution and crime. In 1992, Mexico City won UN notoriety as the most polluted city on the planet, situated inside a high basin inhibiting air filtration, ozone, carbon monoxide, and other particulates buildup, contributing to cardiovascular problems, lung diseases, and shortened life spans. In 2013, Honduras won infamy as the murder capital of world, counting thirteen homicides a day, the tragic confluence of poverty, drug trafficking, and corruption.

Nowhere is the income polarization sowed by neoliberal globalization more evident than in Latin America's capital cities. After 1990, an infusion of foreign capital transformed the central business districts of cities with sleek skyscrapers, multinational logos, and cybercafes, but street level crime and violence continue to haunt regional cities. Inside the grinding poverty of Brazil's *favelas* drug traffickers' rule, the police rarely intervene except in military-style incursions. Today, some 111 million Latin Americans live in shantytowns that often lack sewer, garbage, and water service. Between these urban

Latin America in Profile

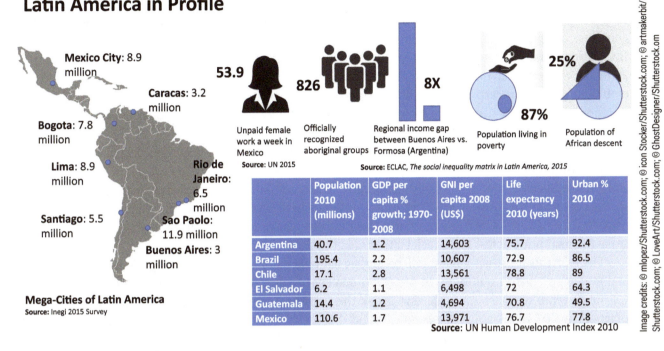

Mega-Cities of Latin America
Source: Inegi 2015 Survey

	Population 2010 (millions)	GDP per capita % growth; 1970-2008	GNI per capita 2008 (US$)	Life expectancy 2010 (years)	Urban % 2010
Argentina	40.7	1.2	14,603	75.7	92.4
Brazil	195.4	2.2	10,607	72.9	86.5
Chile	17.1	2.8	13,561	78.8	89
El Salvador	6.2	1.1	6,498	72	64.3
Guatemala	14.4	1.2	4,694	70.8	49.5
Mexico	110.6	1.7	13,971	76.7	77.8

Source: UN Human Development Index 2010

poles lie the tree-shaded lanes of middle-class suburbs, where fences and armed guards protect elites from abduction, while city police chase away street kids orphaned by misfortune. In the apartment blocks of working-class neighborhoods, sweatshops and domestic service provide a steady paycheck, but little hope for upward mobility.

After World War II, Latin America transformed into an increasingly urban society as modernizing states launched ambitious programs for town planning. The modern architecture, geometric order, and parks of inner cities contrast with the shacks and serpentine streets of Brazil's *favelas*.

Contemporary Latin America's polarization reflects the failure of postwar populists like Perón to ignite growth that could uplift the masses from poverty. Postwar leaders did embark upon self-conscious campaigns of nation building, which included heavy investments in urban infrastructure. International competitions attracted top architectural talent to transform capital cities and project out an image of national dynamism, both internally and abroad. Brasilia represented Latin America's most ambitious postwar undertaking, a planned capital city built in the Amazon around a conscious program to reposition a society historically rooted on the coast, but city planning and modernist architecture represented regionwide trends.

State-financed radio and spectator sports provided mediums for counteracting deep class, race, and gender fissures. Television broadcasts of soccer matches attract audiences from across the realm and stoke frenzied celebrations, especially when Latin America's skilled teams triumph over the Western soccer powers in the World Cup. Latin American states have invested heavily in national stadiums, like Mexico City's *Estadio Azteca*, transforming them into secular cathedrals. During matches, ritual chants stoke national pride across class, racial and ethnic lines.

The effort to construct a more self-conscious national culture cut against the grain of older identities and more conservative traditions. In 1960, 90 percent of Latin America's population identified as Catholic even if in the countryside, and inside the Caribbean, it never fully supplanted older religious practices. A 2013 Pew poll, for example, found that more than 60 percent of Mexicans made offerings of food, drinks, candles, or flowers to spirits.[8] The force of Catholic identity waned during the 1960s in part because the Church opposed state modernizing efforts. Often the Church resisted literacy campaigns that undermined its traditional influence inside education, while consistently siding with conservatives, even implicitly supporting repressive regimes. This contributed to a backlash, although secularism represented a broader postwar phenomenon that particularly impacted urbanites who grew steadily more liberal and less religiously devout. Inside a climate of growing secularism, protestant *evangélicos* started to make major inroads during the 1970s, appealing particularly to Latin America's urban middle classes who desired a more personal connection to God.

The Catholic Church responded to both rising liberalism and secularism in diverse ways. During the Cold War, the institutional Church saw communism as an existential threat. Church leaders instinctively opposed progressive state initiatives that they saw as undermining their traditional influence inside the education and healthcare sphere. By the 1960s, however, many liberal priests increasingly identified with the hardships of their flock. During a regional 1968 conference in Medellin, Colombia, liberals lobbied the Church to refocus its mission on the poor. For liberal clergymen, Marxist ideas about injustice echoed Christ's teachings. **Liberation theology** had various tenets, but invariably it invoked the Bible to criticize social injustice and state repression. Religious conservatives worried that liberation theology would pull the Church into politics. Polish Pope John Paul II's 1978 ascension settled this debate by condemning Marxism and defrocking dissident priests who continued to insist on "this conception of Christ, as a political figure, a revolutionary, as the subversive of Nazareth."[9]

Women Inside Latin American Society

The postwar experience of Latin American women has been caught inside the confluence of traditional mores, Catholic doctrines, and the multidimensional forces of modernization that spur people to reinvent traditional ideas about love, marriage, and sexuality. For much of its history, Latin American femininity has been defined in terms of a predominant machismo identity that relates maleness to ruggedness, virility, and patriarchy. These values reinforce the traditional identification of women in terms of their modesty, submissiveness, and respectability. In practice, however, Latin American ideas about gender reveal many nuances. In elite families, matriarchs are notorious for ruling the household.

Middle-class girls avoid socializing in public with male compatriots to avoid damaging their reputation, but they also reject any pretension on the part of fathers or husbands to influence how to vote. In the countryside, lower class men and women often work together in tight quarters. This proletarian gender leveling can promote solidarity, but it also exposes women to the risk of abuse and sexual assault.

The conflictual impulses defining Latin American femininity are captured in the strong emotions Evita Perón evoked in postwar Argentina. For working-class women, Evita represented a hero who had escaped obscurity and rural poverty through wit and passion. Upper-class women curled their lips at Evita's flamboyant clothes and uncultivated manners. Her dress, hairstyle, and modest talent became a matter of intense ridicule because Evita audaciously subverted traditional gender mores upon which elite women had staked their identity. Spiteful attacks, however, only bolstered Evita's popularity among working women subjected to these same-sexist prejudices.

After World War II, dubbed Hollywood pictures and Western magazines began to wash over Latin American society. They presented the leading edge of a modernist culture rooted in Western liberal norms of love, sexuality, and romance. Such images angered some conservatives, but over time also chipped away at more traditional Latin American notions about courtship, love, and marriage. In working-class neighborhoods, class, and race identities that earlier barred intermarriage started to break down. By the late 1950s, farming ceased to be viable for many *campesinos*. To supplement family incomes, fathers and unmarried males engaged in wage labor. This survival strategy often required migration to cities or between plantations. Often male head of households returned for the harvest, but other times they remitted their pay back home. New work patterns forced mothers to take charge over their family's farm and rear children alone. Low literacy rates among rural women impeded their economic advancement. Inside cities, working-class women often took jobs as servants or sweatshop laborers, enduring low wages while working long hours in conditions that prematurely aged their bodies. Postwar state investment in education did provide middle-class girls access to professional careers, but there too entrenched gender stereotypes curbed their freedom. Men continued to define cleaning, shopping, cooking, and child-rearing as women's work. The *junta* tried, mostly unsuccessfully, to reinforce conservative gender roles. Latin American revolutionary movements, despite challenging various dimensions of social injustice, often remained conspicuously silent about the double burden working mothers faced as both laborers and homemakers.

Latin American feminists like Paulina Luisi of Uruguay and Bertha Lutz of Brazil had championed the global fight for suffrage from 1932 to 1945. This legacy resulted in eight Latin American states granting universal suffrage several decades later, following the Western example. Throughout the postwar era, women played a prominent role inside regional political life. Argentina's **Mothers of the Plaza de Mayo** subverted their identity as bastions of the nation to defy the *junta* by holding up placards of their abducted children. Similarly, in Chile, the *protestas* contributed to the 1983 to 1986 demonstrations and the 1988 "Non" referendum that ultimately brought down Pinochet's regime. Since 2005, five women have won presidential elections in Latin America, while their representation inside regional parliaments outstrips every world region except Scandinavia. Despite civic inclusion, gender equity still lags inside the social and legal spheres. Most Latin American women remain confined to low-paying service jobs, while men are overrepresented in the high-tech sector, construction trades, skilled industries, and corporate boardrooms. Only during the 1970s did most Latin American states begin to legalize divorce. Alimony and property rights, however, often remain poorly defined in conservative societies where clear majorities frown upon abortion, premarital sex, gay marriage, and even alcohol consumption. Traditional mores particularly prevail in the countryside, while the urban educated classes have moral views that correspond more closely to those of the West. Still, Latin America suffers from a high incidence of domestic violence and rape in part because of engrained beliefs that men cannot control their impulses and that women must accordingly, avoid compromising situations.

In contrast to Western feminists, many Latin American women more readily accept gender differentiation, including highly commercialized ideas about feminine beauty. Throughout Latin America, pageants and bikini contests are popular, projecting unrealistic body images. To help women achieve artificial standards of beauty, many states subsidize plastic surgery. Brazil and Colombia represent world leaders in cosmetic procedures. Polls reveal wide public acceptance of this practice despite the fact that "fashion model syndrome" causes high incidences of depression and eating disorders.

Emerging Cultural Trends

Latin American conservatism is counterbalanced by a long-standing desire to emulate the West and escape international obscurity and economic marginalization. In 1968, Mexico hosted the summer Olympics, wresting the international stage from the West to celebrate its economic miracle. Latin America's coming of age was echoed inside the cultural realm. Regional *junta* drove many writers, professors, and journalists into exile. This increased international exposure to regional poets, novelists, and musicians who brought a spotlight upon Latin American politics. The most recognizable Latin American celebrity, however, was **Pele**. His irrepressible charisma was matched to graceful feet that produced 1,281 goals during a long professional career. Latin American players also broke into the ranks of major league baseball during the 1950s, headlined by all-stars Roberto Clemente and Juan Marichal who shared the all-star stage with Northern born legends like Mickey Mantle. By the 1970s, a Latin invasion had remade baseball, while Brazil and Argentina dominated international soccer, stocking the Premier Leagues with its most notable stars.

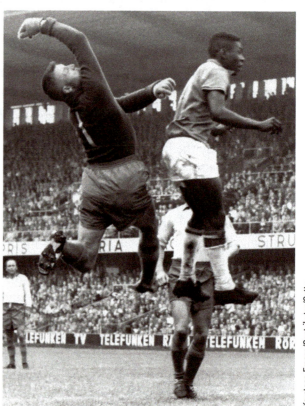

Pelé faces Sweden at the 1958 World Cup.

The fall of the *junta* during the 1980s ended censorship, while subsequent deregulation of the telecommunications industry flooded Latin American markets with Western content. While Hollywood blockbusters with multimillion-dollar budgets drew wide audiences across Latin America, Argentina's new cinema also won international acclaim and multiple cinematic awards for bringing the grit of everyday life onto the silver screen. Mexican soap operas swept across the US border in the 1990s, while Salsa and "Latin" rhythms, powered by international celebrities, like Gloria Estefan, Enrique Iglesias, and Shakira, became staples inside a global pop culture.

Latin America's Debt Crisis, 1982 to 1989

The Debt Crisis commenced following a fateful August 1982 meeting between Mexico's finance minister and US bankers, where Jesus Silva-Herzog surprised his counterparts by announcing that his country could not pay. The crisis' roots, however, lay in the 1973 Organization of Petroleum

Exporting Countries (OPEC) embargo. This raised the cost of development for oil importers inside Latin America, while sending commodity prices lower as inflation jarred their traditional export markets. Many *junta* responded to adverse economic conditions by borrowing. Easy credit and low-interest loans kept most Latin American economies afloat during the late 1970s, but the region's foreign debt increased over 1,000 percent to $200 billion by 1980. Unlike World Bank loans, private loans carried variable interest rates over shorter terms. When interest rates edged higher after 1979, it dramatically raised Latin America's cost of capital. Disaster struck in 1981 when Reagan instructed Fed Chairman Paul Volcker to "kill" inflation. As US interest rates spiked towards 15 percent, Latin America became caught in a **liquidity trap**. Following Mexico's default, Western lenders shut off further loans to the rest of Latin America. Unable to attract new capital, or effectively raise taxes, many regional states resorted to printing money. Inflation averaged 150 percent in the region, exploding into hyperinflation in Bolivia, Argentina, and Brazil that eviscerated the savings of the middle class.

As the financial crisis intensified during 1983, Latin America turned to the International Monetary Fund (IMF) for relief. In return for emergency funds to forestall financial collapse, the IMF insisted on **structural adjustment** mechanisms that included removing foreign trade barriers, currency devaluation, and cuts to social spending. Throughout Latin America, subsidies for gasoline, housing, education, medical care, and infrastructure were cut, striking the poor hard. Nowhere did austerity spark economic recovery. Indeed, critics charged that lowering state spending could only intensify the economic downturn. Currency devaluations did balance budget deficits, but at the price of raising the load of debts denominated in dollars. From 1983 to 1990, capital fled Latin America for Western and Asian markets, inaugurating a deep recession known as the **Lost Decade**. Misery manifested across the region. Living standards plunged, the ranks of the poor swelled as millions of miners and peasants flooded shantytowns, while many urban professionals sought better opportunities abroad.

El Norte

Political repression and the Debt Crisis stimulated a migration wave. Central American peasants followed a migration chain, ominously described as the *tren de la muerte*, or "the train of death," huddling on top of train cars controlled by Mexican gangs, subjected to constant robbery and rape. Dirty wars and repression had made life unbearable in certain areas of Central America, while global diffusion of teledramas like *Dallas* had cemented into the minds of isolated Guatemalan villagers the unimaginable wealth lying north. Northern migration has boosted Latin America's economy. One in four families in Central America receives remittances from relatives working abroad, contributing over 10 percent of GDP to Honduras, El Salvador, Haiti, Nicaragua, and Guatemala.[10]

Chile's Shock Therapy

Following Pinochet's coup, Chile's economy fell into a deadly tailspin. Inflation approached 1,000 percent, the national treasury lay bankrupt, and the economy was contracting rapidly. Pinochet reversed the previous regime's appropriations and sold off state businesses, but the economy remained stuck in a slump. Pinochet turned to the **Chicago Boys**, Chilean economists who had studied free market economics at the University of Chicago. The Chicago Boys presented Pinochet with *El Ladrillo*, or the brick, an economic plan to "shock" the Chilean economy back to health. Pinochet not only agreed to this policy, but stuck to it despite modest results. For the urban middle classes, economic conditions improved, but real wages fell 8 percent and unemployment rose sharply. Steep cuts in family allowances and social services ripped out Chile's safety net upon which the most vulnerable depended. Shock therapy did drop inflation from 1,000 percent in 1975 to a manageable 10 percent in 1980. By 1977, Chile's economy finally lifted up from recession, in large part by borrowing as the level of foreign debt rose 300 percent from 1974 to 1988. During the **Lost Decade**, however, many dependency theorists began to look at Chile's growing economy with envy. In 1985, the newly elected Gonazlo de Lazada regime in Bolivia decided to copy Chile's shock therapy program. After shock therapy there too tamed inflation, it gave momentum to the neoliberal reform program.

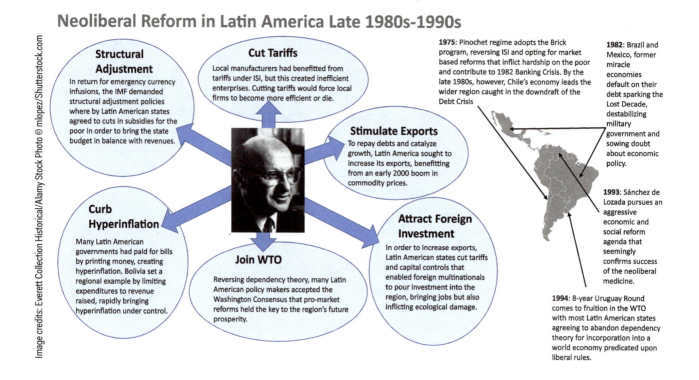

Neoliberal Reform in Latin America Late 1980s-1990s

Structural Adjustment: In return for emergency currency infusions, the IMF demanded structural adjustment policies where by Latin American states agreed to cuts in subsidies for the poor in order to bring the state budget in balance with revenues.

Cut Tariffs: Local manufacturers had benefitted from tariffs under ISI, but this created inefficient enterprises. Cutting tariffs would force local firms to become more efficient or die.

Stimulate Exports: To repay debts and catalyze growth, Latin America sought to increase its exports, benefitting from an early 2000 boom in commodity prices.

Curb Hyperinflation: Many Latin American governments had paid for bills by printing money, creating hyperinflation. Bolivia set a regional example by limiting expenditures to revenue raised, rapidly bringing hyperinflation under control.

Join WTO: Reversing dependency theory, many Latin American policy makers accepted the Washington Consensus that pro-market reforms held the key to the region's future prosperity.

Attract Foreign Investment: In order to increase exports, Latin American states cut tariffs and capital controls that enabled foreign multinationals to pour investment into the region, bringing jobs but also inflicting ecological damage.

1975: Pinochet regime adopts the Brick program, reversing ISI and opting for market based reforms that inflict hardship on the poor and contribute to 1982 Banking Crisis. By the late 1980s, however, Chile's economy leads the wider region caught in the downdraft of the Debt Crisis

1982: Brazil and Mexico, former miracle economies default on their debt sparking the Lost Decade, destabilizing military government and sowing doubt about economic policy.

1993: Sánchez de Lozada pursues an aggressive economic and social reform agenda that seemingly confirms success of the neoliberal medicine.

1994: 8-year Uruguay Round comes to fruition in the WTO with most Latin American states agreeing to abandon dependency theory for incorporation into a world economy predicated upon liberal rules.

Image credits: Everett Collection Historical/Alamy Stock Photo © mlopez/Shutterstock.com

Fall of the *Junta*

Throughout Latin America, the Debt Crisis brought pressure on military-dominated regimes, provoking diverse strategies to coopt the public and quash dissent. On April 2, 1982, Argentina occupied the British Falklands. Argentina had long claimed sovereignty over these islands, but the *junta* sought to distract public attention away from the country's failing economy. The *junta* believed that Britain would acquiesce to this *fait accompli*. After all, the British Navy was a shadow of its former self, and the Falklands were not particularly valuable and a world away. Argentina had advanced fighters, and a few modern ships, but the *junta* miscalculated Prime Minister Margaret Thatcher's resolve. Initially caught off guard, the "Iron Lady" marshalled a fleet to retake the Falklands. Argentina scored several early successes when its *Exocet* anti-ship missiles sunk four British vessels. By June 14, 1982, however, British forces had recaptured the Falklands' capital and the remaining Argentine soldiers laid down their arms. The flagging *junta*, having staked their prestige on the Falklands campaign, collapsed. In 1983, Argentina returned to civilian government, foreshadowing a broader democratic wave.

The Democratic Wave

The Debt Crisis discredited the economic stewardship of Latin America's military regimes and spurred a gradual return to civilian governments from 1982 to 1992. Austerity measures inspired demonstrations that steadily grew in size and more audacious in their demands.

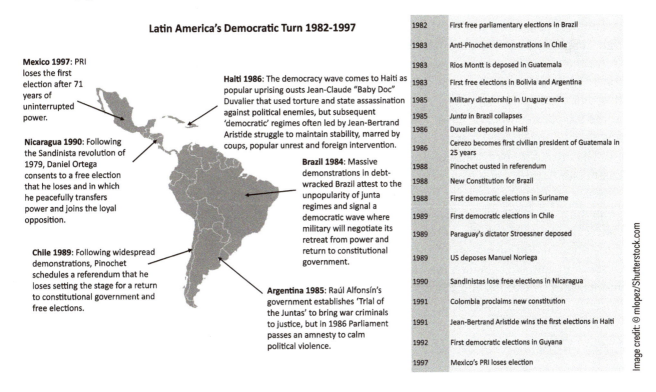

Latin America's Democratic Turn 1982-1997

Mexico 1997: PRI loses the first election after 71 years of uninterrupted power.

Nicaragua 1990: Following the Sandinista revolution of 1979, Daniel Ortega consents to a free election that he loses and in which he peacefully transfers power and joins the loyal opposition.

Chile 1989: Following widespread demonstrations, Pinochet schedules a referendum that he loses setting the stage for a return to constitutional government and free elections.

Haiti 1986: The democracy wave comes to Haiti as popular uprising ousts Jean-Claude "Baby Doc" Duvalier that used torture and state assassination against political enemies, but subsequent 'democratic' regimes often led by Jean-Bertrand Aristide struggle to maintain stability, marred by coups, popular unrest and foreign intervention.

Brazil 1984: Massive demonstrations in debt-wracked Brazil attest to the unpopularity of junta regimes and signal a democratic wave where military will negotiate its retreat from power and return to constitutional government.

Argentina 1985: Raúl Alfonsín's government establishes 'Trial of the Juntas' to bring war criminals to justice, but in 1986 Parliament passes an amnesty to calm political violence.

1982	First free parliamentary elections in Brazil
1983	Anti-Pinochet demonstrations in Chile
1983	Rios Montt is deposed in Guatemala
1983	First free elections in Bolivia and Argentina
1985	Military dictatorship in Uruguay ends
1985	*Junta* in Brazil collapses
1986	Duvalier deposed in Haiti
1986	Cerezo becomes first civilian president of Guatemala in 25 years
1988	Pinochet ousted in referendum
1988	New Constitution for Brazil
1988	First democratic elections in Suriname
1989	First democratic elections in Chile
1989	Paraguay's dictator Stroessner deposed
1989	US deposes Manuel Noriega
1990	Sandinistas lose free elections in Nicaragua
1991	Colombia proclaims new constitution
1991	Jean-Bertrand Aristide wins the first elections in Haiti
1992	First democratic elections in Guyana
1997	Mexico's PRI loses election

Image credit: © mlopez/Shutterstock.com

The collapse of the Soviet Bloc in 1989 added momentum to Latin American democracy movements. Dramatic images of massive crowds defying despotic governments demoralized Latin American elites. Simultaneously, Southeast Asia's rapid industrialization brought into question the fundamental assumptions of dependency theory. A broader Latin American coalition warmed to liberalism and the virtuous link between free markets and democratic institutions. With the lapsing of the Cold War, the United States had less incentive to support regional *junta* or to overlook human rights violations. The combination of these pressures stimulated a gradual return to civilian government. While Latin American elites and military officers relinquished power voluntarily, they remained influential inside new governments, often exercising an extraconstitutional veto power over state policies through coup threats. Cautious civilian governments often chose to placate officers with handsome defense spending measures and informal promises to respect handover bargains.

Justice and Reconciliation

Before vacating power, Latin American *junta* passed amnesty measures to insulate their members from prosecution for acts carried out during dirty wars. A decade into civilian government, some regimes felt sufficiently secure to launch public inquiries into the past. In 1998, an ailing Pinochet was arrested after receiving back surgery in Britain. Officially indicted in 2000 for personal involvement in the torture of seventy-five dissidents, legal wrangling prevented Pinochet from standing trial, but his reputation suffered from a string of investigations that revealed not only his direct implication in torture and murder, but also graft and corruption. In 2005, the Chilean army publicly accepted responsibility for Pinochet era abuses, while foreclosing upon any effort to try its officers for war crimes. Pinochet's death from a heart attack in 2006 prevented him from standing trial, but brought a welcome respite for a Chilean society still divided and haunted by his legacy.

Argentina went the furthest in terms of confronting a painful past. In 1985, **Raúl Ricardo Alfonsín's** government established the "Trial of the Juntas" aiming to bring top military brass to justice. The extreme right fought back, threatening, kidnapping, and torturing lawyers, human rights activists, and witnesses. In Argentina, public pressure enabled three hundred regime operatives to be indicted, but threats of a coup forced the government to retreat. Parliament ultimately passed a 1986 amnesty measure for those doing their "jobs," but genetic testing soon rekindled interest in Argentina's dirty war by enabling grandmothers of the disappeared to track down their offspring. Over sixty middle-aged people have already discovered that their adoptive parents were linked to the military regime that murdered their mothers.

The most popular Latin American mechanism for atonement represented truth and reconciliation commissions. Borrowing from South Africa's post-Apartheid model, rather than seeking legal prosecution, such commissions sought to spur healing by documenting history, exposing the truth, and promoting moral accountability. In El Salvador an inquest registered more than 22,000 complaints concerning murder, torture, and kidnapping. Subsequent investigation revealed that the Civil War killed more than 70,000 people and displaced a quarter of the population before the UN-brokered peace treaty came into effect. While the inquest produced no prosecutions, it did discredit the military regime and its allies by establishing that 95 percent of the atrocities traced back to the Salvadoran security forces and their associated death squads.

Latin America's Neoliberal Turn

As democracies, Latin American states participated in the Uruguay Round of General Agreement on Tariffs and Trade (GATT) that culminated in the WTO in 1995. In the years before, left-of-center coalitions pushed through neoliberal reform packages. In 1985, Argentina's Raúl Alfronsin and Brazil's José Sarney signed an economic cooperation pact that would inspire neoliberal reform across the region. The 1991 **Treaty of Asunción** united Brazil and many of its smaller neighbors into the *Mercado Común del Sur* (Mercosur), a common market in which trade rapidly accelerated from US$10 billion in 1991 to US$88 billion in 2010. Neoliberal reforms often enjoyed popular support because they coincided with a broader regional economic recovery after 1990, powered by foreign investment that rose from US$14 to US$86 billion from 1990 to 1997. By the late 1990s, however, skepticism about free trade returned. While Latin America's per capita gross domestic product (GDP) increased 12 percent from 1990 to 2000, the poverty rate slipped only modestly, while a 2001 to 2003 recession raised doubts about whether the neoliberal model provided a platform for sustainable growth. Subsequently, a **Pink Tide** returned more leftist governments, headlined by Hugo Chávez's regime in Venezuela that rekindled the populist rhetoric of Perón. Throughout Latin America, economic growth and lower interest rates have diminished the weight of debt, but the future reads much like the past. Latin politics and its people's dreams for economic advancement still remain disproportionately tied to fluctuating global market forces.

Amazon Apocalypse

Brazil's political establishment long conceived the Amazon as a "vast hinterland waiting and hoping to be aroused to life."[11] Covered by a thick, nearly impenetrable rain forest, however, developing this frontier required substantial state investment. By the late 1960s, agricultural mechanization increased rural unemployment, stirring calls for land reform and pushing impoverished peasants into the *favela* of

Rio de Janeiro and Sao Paolo. For Brazil's *junta*, developing the Amazon represented a safety valve. It would provide land for resettlement, resources for industrialization, and an opportunity to integrate a country whose population was concentrated along the coasts.

In 1966 General Humberto Castelo Branco unveiled **Operation Amazonia**, an ambitious development plan for Brazil's vast interior by providing tax breaks, land concessions, and fixed rate loans. The key to unlocking the Amazon, however, was roads. In 1972, Brazil's National Integration Plan (PIN) introduced the **Trans-Amazonian Highway**, a plan to construct a 5,200-km paved highway from the Atlantic to the Pacific. Despite handsome financing, various schemes to develop the Amazon failed. A colonization plan to resettle 100,000 landless peasants attracted only 8,000, most of whom soon abandoned their farms. The rain forest was mostly unsuitable for cultivation. Burning the forest cleared the land and provided a layer of ash for fertilizer, but high rainfall quickly eroded away the thin layer of topsoil, leaving the land barren. The primary beneficiaries of Amazonian development were land speculators and cattle barons. Ranchers often used violence and bribes to consolidate vast holdings, but generated profits mostly by harvesting state subsidies. In its final incarnation, Brazil's generals unveiled the Program for Amazon Development (PDAM), encouraging foreign corporations to invest in the region's mining and timber resources. Like the ranchers and colonists before them, most of these ventures failed to catalyze growth, but they did spur deforestation. Throughout the Amazon, illegal timber harvesters, gold miners, and colonists cut down trees, drive out rubber tappers and forest people, and poison waterways. Amazonian deforestation represents a peculiar tragedy, but it is not particularly exceptional. WTO membership opened up Latin American resources to development and transnational corporations rushed in to purchase concessions and expand their resource reserves. Extractive industries powered Latin American growth from 1990 to 2001, but much of this development is not sustainable. Costa Rica has served as regional leader in terms of ecotourism, but throughout Latin America parks are fragile because profits are funneled towards large tour operators at the expense of local resource users.

Window on World History: Mexico and North American Free Trade Agreement (NAFTA)

Mexican drug lord El Chapo Guzman extradited to the United States after running Sinaloa Drug Cartel, which bathed Northern Mexico in violence.

(Continued)

North American Free Trade Agreement (NAFTA) seemed to promise Mexico prosperity. Trade between Mexico and North America trebled within a decade after 1994, and border towns like Tijuana and Ciudad Juárez boomed as Western manufacturers relocated to profit from lower taxes and labor costs, as well as less stringent environmental regulations. Between 1996 and 2000, 1,460 new *maquiladora* opened, bringing over one million jobs. Plant owners, however, hired primarily young women, valuing their endurance, dexterity, and docility. While *maquiladora* provided a steady paycheck, employees suffered from unsafe and unsanitary working conditions, while many complained their wages could not support a family. Globalization's boosters promise a ladder of rising prosperity, but after 2000, manufacturing in Northern Mexico declined as China joined the WTO and many textile manufacturers relocated to less expensive areas of Central America. From 2006 to 2010, the proportion of the Mexican population living in extreme or moderate poverty increased from 35 to 46 percent. Some unemployed men found work in the lucrative drug economy. Mexico's cartels grew more powerful as US interdiction efforts disrupted the Colombia–Florida route. This elevated the porous 2,000-mile US–Mexico border as the principal transit route for narcotics into North America. As drug money funneled into Mexico, cartels redirected profits into the real economy, corrupting local police while waging brutal turf wars. US legalization of assault rifles in 2004 exacerbated violence as military grade weapons flooded into North Mexico and left local police overmatched. In 2006, break down in law and order inside Northern Mexico led President **Felipe Calderón** to launch Operation Michoacán, dispatching 45,000 federal troops in a military-style offense to break the cartels. The war on drugs culminated in thousands of arrests, but ultimately few prosecutions. It also left over 60,000 dead as locals complained that the campaign failed to bring security. In Northern Mexico, battles between cartels, vigilante groups, and Mexican security forces continue to rage. With profits ranging from $18 to $39 billion annually, the drug industry will not soon disappear. In comparison to Mexico, the Carribbean has more successfully navigated the tides of globalization. While the WTO wreaked havoc on local subsistence farmers, Bermuda, Cayman Islands, and St. Maarten have flourished as banking centers for drug cartels, while also providing tax havens for the profits of transnational corporations.

Critical Reflection

1. To what extent has Mexico benefitted from NAFTA and to what degree is their experience with neoliberalism similar to that of Canada?
2. How does the American appetite for narcotics threaten civil society in Mexico?

Summary: Latin America at the Crossroads

After World War II, corporatism provided an ideology for a regional modernization, social inclusion, and economic diversification. Reconstruction stumbled during the 1960s when import substitution schemes failed to improve living standards for the majority, while the 1959 Cuban Revolution raised concerns about communist subversion. From 1964 to 1983, military regimes seized power in much of Latin America using terror to silence leftist opponents. The *junta*, however, had no effective strategy for reviving regional economies. The 1982 Latin American Debt Crisis inaugurated a Lost Decade that ushered in a gradual return to civilian governments and wave of

Brazil's Lula embodied the hope of left-of-center postjunta governments to stabilize the political system, maintain civil peace, and successfully transition the economy towards the global economy while reinforcing the safety net.

neoliberal reforms that more closely integrated Latin America to the global economy. Economic growth after 1990 rekindled social progress, but extractive industries do not offer a sustainable path for development.

Questions for Critical Thought

1. How did Perón's political success reflect fundamental changes inside Latin American society?
2. How did ISI propose to overcome economic dependency? For what reasons did ISI fail to achieve its benchmarks?
3. Through what instruments did the United States try to integrate Latin American states into its sphere of influence? How did the Cuban Revolution reshape the United States' foreign policy in Latin America?
4. What motivated the United States to overthrow the Árbenz government in Guatemala?
5. Why did civilian governments throughout Latin America fall to military dictatorship during the 1960s?
6. Through what tactics did Latin American *juntas* clamp down on popular dissidence? How did the United States abet military dictatorships in Latin America?
7. What events precipitated the Latin American Debt Crisis? How did the Debt Crisis spur political and economic reform?
8. How does Mexico reveal the promise and perils of neoliberal globalization?

Suggestions for Further Reading

- Chavkin, S. *Storm Over Chile: The Junta under Siege.* New York: Lawrence Hill & Co, 1989.
- Cortes, C. R., J. H. Coatsworth, and V. Bulmer-Thomas. *The Cambridge Economic History of Latin America*, vol. 2 of *The Long Twentieth Century*. Cambridge: Cambridge University Press, 2006.

- Grandin, G., and J. Gilbert, eds. *A Century of Revolution: Insurgent and Counterinsurgent Violence during Latin America's Long Cold War.* Durham, NC: Duke University Press, 2010.
- Hecht, S., and Cockburn, A. *The Fate of the Forest: Developers, Destroyers and Defenders of the Amazon.* Chicago: University of Chicago Press, 2010.
- Holden, R. H., and R. Villars. *Contemporary Latin America.* Malden, MA: Wiley-Blackwell, 2013.
- Hartlyn, J., L. Schoultz, and A. Varas. *The United States and Latin America in the 1990s: Beyond the Cold War.* Chapel Hill: University of North Carolina Press, 1992.
- Sieder, R., ed. *Multiculturalism in Latin America: Indigenous Rights, Diversity and Democracy.* New York: Palgrave Macmillan, 2002.
- Skidmore, T., P. Smith, and J. Green. *Modern Latin America.* 7th ed. New York: Oxford University Press, 2010.
- Wright, T. *State Terrorism in Latin America.* New York: Rowman & Littlefield Publishers, 2006.

Notes

1. Peter Winn, "The Furies of the Andes." In *A Century of Revolution*, edited by G. Grandin and Gilbert Joseph, 241. Raleigh, NC: Duke University Press, 2010.
2. Ibid, 243.
3. Richard Helms, "Notes," September 15, 1970., accessed July 31, 2019, https://www.theguardian.com/world/2015/may/22/hundreds-of-thousands-to-attend-oscar-romero-beatification-in-el-salvador.
4. Roberto Lovato and Jonathan Watts, "Civil war Still a Bitter Memory as El Salvador Prepares to Beatify Romero," *Guardian*, May 22, 2015, accessed July 31, 2019 https://www.theguardian.com/world/2015/may/22/hundreds-of-thousands-to-attend-oscar-romero-beatification-in-el-salvador.
5. Quoted in Piera Paola Oria, *De la casa a la plaza* (Buenos Aires: Editorial Nueva America, 1987), 61.
6. Steven Metz, *Counterinsurgency and the Phoenix of American Capability* (Carlisle Barracks, PA: Strategic Studies Institute, 1995).
7. William Fulbright, "Appraisal of US Policy in the Dominican Crisis," September 15, 1965, accessed July 31, 2019 http://www.fordham.edu/halsall/mod/1965Fullbright-US-DomRep1.html.
8. Pew Research Center, *Religion in Latin America,* November 13, 2014, 58, accessed July 31, 2019 http://www.pewresearch.org/wp-content/uploads/sites/7/2014/11/Religion-in-Latin-America-11-12-PM-full-PDF.pdf.
9. John Paul II, "Address to the Third General CONFERENCE OF THE Latin American Episcopate," Puebla, Mexico, Sunday, January 28, 1979, accessed July 31, 2019, http://w2.vatican.va/content/john-paul-ii/en/speeches/1979/january/documents/hf_jp-ii_spe_19790128_messico-puebla-episc-latam.html.
10. Roberto Suro, *Remittance Senders and Receivers: Tracking the Transnational Channels* (Washington, DC: Pew Hispanic Center, November 23, 2003) and World Bank, *Migration and Remittances Unit, Migration and Remittances Factbook,* 2011, accessed July 25, 2011, www.worldbank.org.prospects/imigrantandremittances.
11. Susan Hecht and Alexander Cockburn, *Fate of the Forest* (Chicago: University of Chicago Press, 2011), 114.

Chapter 7
Postwar Middle East

Chapter Outline

- Introduction The Postwar Middle East
- Nasser and Revolutionary Nationalism
- Six-Day War
- The Iranian Revolution
- The Soviet War in Afghanistan, 1979 to 1989
- Postwar Urbanization and Modern Anxieties
- Palestinian Intifada and the Oslo Process, 1987 to 2000
- Summary: The Postwar Middle East

The Last Days of Colonialism 1946–1956
1946 Independence of Syria and Lebanon
1947 UN Resolution 181
1948 Declaration of Israel
1948–1949 First Arab–Israeli War
1952 Free Officer's Coup in Egypt
1955 Baghdad Pact
1956 Suez Crisis

Struggle for Modernization 1957–1978
1957 Ba'ath Party comes to Power in Syria
1958 Nationalists seize power in Iraq
1958 Establishment of United Arab Republic
1962 Algerian independence from France
1964 PLO Founded
1967 Six Days War
1969 Qaddafi Coup in Libya
1973 OPEC Oil Embargo
1978 First Camp David Accords

Islamic Awakening 1979–2000
1979 Khomeini founds Islamic Republic
1979–1989 Soviet Afghan War
1987–1991 Palestinian Intifada
1990–1991 First Gulf War
1991 Algerian Civil War begins
1993 Oslo Accords
1995 Rabin Assassinated
1996 Taliban conquer Kabul

1956 Egypt: Nasser defiance of British and French power in Suez inaugurates era where secular nationalism inspires Arab world

1948–1949 Palestine: Jewish victory over Arab armies secures birth of Israel and animates revolutionary nationalism against western colonial influences.

1973 Saudi Arabia: Faysal lead oil embargo spurs economic boom in Persian Gulf and centralizes region in global geopolitics.

Algeria 1962: Algerian independence after bloody war of liberation marks symbolic end of colonialism in Middle East

1978 Iran: Khomeini introduces an Islamic Republic; a novel experiment that harmonizes Islamic tradition with infrastructure of modern state

1979 Afghanistan: Soviet invasion of Afghanistan creates a cauldron for jihadism that provides a model for revolutionary change through militant resistance.

Image credits: © PSboom/Shutterstock.com; © Leremy/Shutterstock.com; © MuchMania/Shutterstock.com; © MuchMania/Shutterstock.com; © Muchania/Shutterstock.com; © galaira/Shutterstock.com; © andromina/Shutterstock.com; © Leremy/Shutterstock.com; © MuchMania/Shutterstock.com

Introduction: The Postwar Middle East

The "Middle East" invokes a colonial legacy, referencing those territories separating Europe from the Far East. Geographically, this arid region is roughly bounded by the Mediterranean Sea, the Saharan Desert, the Indian Ocean, and the Caucus and Himalayan Mountains. Historically, the Middle East encompasses those territories enveloped by the Arab conquest before the tenth century. This infused regional institutions and culture with Islamic influences. Today, *Dar al Islam*, or the House of Islam, embraces the Near East, Maghreb, Central Asia, and Arabia. Inside these distinctive geographic subregions, 90 percent identify as Muslim, but they are divided among the major Sunni and Shia branches and multiple smaller sects. Although most Muslims see themselves as belong to the *ummah*, or broader community of the faithful, this abstract identification belies considerable diversity in Islamic faith and practice. Historically, Middle Eastern kingdoms and Muslim empires incorporated divergent ethnic groups and accommodated many religious minorities. Geographical cleavages often accentuated a local desire to live in supportive communities defined by local kin, tribal, and confessional ties and only loosely integrated into regional states.

After World War II, the Middle East gradually shook free from Western rule and influence. Postcolonial leaders expanded the scope of the state to pursue modernization and exploited mass media to cultivate a new sense of national identity to project over an older patchwork of clan, tribal, and ethnic affiliations. The devastating 1967 defeat of Arab armies by Israel bred skepticism about the secular nationalism. At the same time, Arab society underwent traumatic changes as an oil boom inaugurated a period of rapid urbanization and deeper integration with the non-Muslim world that created pressure to reconcile local traditions and Islamic values with Western ideas and practices. Ultimately, this dialogue stimulated an Islamic revival movement that embraced both conservative and reformist impulses. Islamists sought to reinvigorate society by harmonizing it more with the state and conservative version of Islam.

This chapter surveys the contradictory currents driving Middle Eastern history until roughly 1990. The first section explores revolutionary nationalism. Until 1967, Egyptian President Gamal Abdel Nasser spearheaded the Arab challenge to Western hegemony. Nasser's nationalist message enjoyed broad appeal, while his socialist program inspired many copiers. Following a lop-sided Arab defeat during the 1967 Six-Day War, however, support for secular nationalism waned. The second section explores how the *Sahwa* gave rise to a broader movement to Islamize modernity. The 1979 Iranian Revolution, the Soviet War in Afghanistan, and the 1987 Palestinian *intifada* represented distinct challenges to the region's repressive, secular regimes. The final section explores how intensive urbanization and modernization has transformed regional patterns of life while provoking sharp debates concerning gender, state, and religion.

Big Questions

- What goals inspired Nasser's Arab socialism?
- How did the post-1973 oil boom transform Middle Eastern society?
- How did Islamism reshape Middle Eastern politics after 1979?
- How do contemporary Muslims reconcile their faith with modern patterns of life?

Nasser and Revolutionary Nationalism

Popular revolts rocked the Middle East from 1919 to 1923 as Arabs resisted British and French efforts to impose colonial mandates upon lands formerly ruled by the defeated Ottomans. France and Britain quelled these uprisings through brutal force, but responded to local sentiments by installing Arab proxy rulers throughout the Near East and along the Persian Gulf. This neocolonial settlement gave Arabs the semblance of independence, while keeping state authority firmly in European hands. Between the Great Wars, Arab nationalism expanded, particularly in Near Eastern cities where literacy rates steadily rose. Most Arab nationalists were secular elites. They defined Arab identity in contrast to both the West and Islam. Regional writers celebrated Arab literature and past scientific achievements, and invoked multiple Western grievances. World War II sapped the strength and eroded the legitimacy of Europe's colonial states. It also transformed Arab nationalism into a more powerful, broad-based movement. In 1946, France abandoned the restive Levant (Syria and Lebanon), while Libya and Jordan also secured independence. Following tense wartime occupations, Britain also entered into negotiations with nationalists in Iraq, Iran, and Egypt about their future.

Western postwar support for Zionism radicalized Arab nationalism. Arab states unilaterally rejected United Nations (UN) Resolution 181. Their 1949 defeat left Arab nationalists disgruntled with both the West and their own puppet rulers. **Al Nakbah**, or "disaster," fuelled a more radical strain of nationalism, exemplified in Egypt's 1952 Revolution. Frustrated with Britain's refusal to vacate the Suez, demonstrations erupted throughout Egypt. A group of junior officers seized this opportunity to drive Egypt's unpopular "playboy" king Furuq into exile. In the streets of Cairo and Alexandria, Egyptians celebrated their liberation from British rule.

In 1954, **Gamal Abdel Nasser**, a lieutenant colonel and unofficial leader of the Free Officers, emerged as Egypt's formal head of state. Nasser brought a fresh style to Egyptian politics. For centuries, Arabs had endured distant rulers disconnected from their subjects. Nasser exploited emerging mass media, particularly radio, to communicate his dreams for Arab rejuvenation directly to his people. Handsome and charismatic, Nasser could spend hours in front of a microphone ruminating about his dreams for the "Arab nation" or elaborating upon schemes for uplifting the "forgotten ones." His appeal to ordinary Egyptians, and promises to restore Arab dignity, stirred tremendous excitement.

At first, Islamic conservatives also hailed Nasser, but they soon turned against his regime. A secular nationalist, Nasser saw local mullahs as vestiges of Egypt's past, and obstacles to Arab modernization. Although Nasser often invoked Islam to justify his policies, to build a strong state and army, Egypt needed to adopt modern technology and Western institutions. Initially friendly with influential members of the Muslim Brotherhood, their dreams proved incompatible. After a failed 1954 assassination attempt, Nasser cracked down on the Muslim Brotherhood and locked up many religious conservatives with communists and other dissidents. Populist politics did not prevent Nasser from ruling as a despot.

Pan-Arabism and Arab Socialism

The British did not oppose the 1952 Free Officer's coup. Their attitude towards Nasser soured after he began to challenge their regional influence. At the heart of Nasser's revolutionary nationalism lay two interwoven ideas: Pan-Arabism and Arab Socialism. **Pan-Arabism** drew upon an older dream of overturning the artificial borders the West had forcefully imposed upon Ottoman lands after 1920. It resonated with a deeper nationalist desire that Arabs sharing the same language and cultural heritage should be united inside a singular state. From Cairo-based "Voice of the Arabs" radio station, Nasser encouraged patriots in neighboring states to overthrow their conservative monarchs and Western-imposed proxy rulers. This revolutionary summons excited young officers that had tasted bitter defeat against Israel in 1949. At the 1955 Bandung Conference, the telegenic Nasser cemented his image as leader of the Arab world. Nasser's growing popularity, regional influence, and revolutionary program threatened Britain's alliances with the Middle East's conservative monarchs.

In writings and speeches, Nasser also laid out a program for modernization. **Arab Socialism** was a modernization strategy that invoked various progressive goals like social justice, land reform, mass literacy, and economic development. In Egypt, Nasser launched a land reform initiative, nationalized foreign businesses, and invested in heavy industry. Nasser's socialism closely intersected with his nationalism in targeting foreigners and the traditional elite that had often collaborated with foreigners to siphon off Egypt's wealth. Smashing this old guard would help liberate Egypt from its past. Nasser's revolutionary program was more statist than Marxist. Strengthening Egypt took precedence over its calls for social justice. Nasser's most progressive impulses revolved around land reform and literacy, but socially conservative, he did not focus on leveling gender and class differences. State-driven modernization ultimately achieved little for the poor. Military officers took over state departments and expanded their control over the economy, but a bloated bureaucracy stifled economic efficiency, while military spending siphoned off badly needed investment capital.

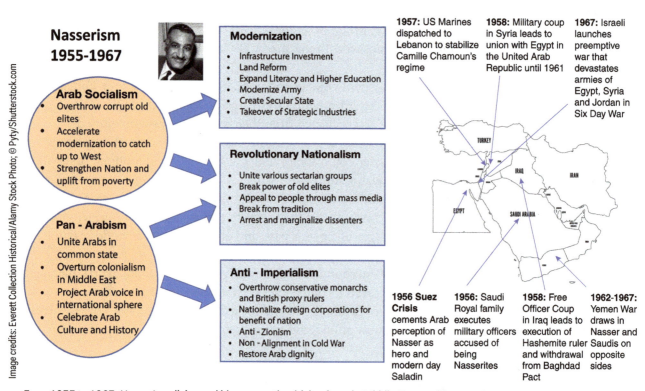

From 1955 to 1967, Nasser's policies and ideas were the driving force in Middle Eastern history.

At first, Washington, DC, sympathized with Nasser's nationalist agenda. American leaders presumed that pushing Britain out of the Middle East would temper Arab nationalism. Accordingly, the United States pressured Britain to evacuate their Sinai base. To moderate Nasser's revolutionary aspirations, Washington, DC, backstopped a World Bank loan in 1955 to help him construct the Aswan High Dam.

Nasser's Break from the West, 1955 to 1966

The British had first envisioned constructing a dam on the High Nile. They abandoned the project because of significant technical barriers and the project's astronomical cost. Upon assuming power, Nasser, however, quickly embraced the Aswan High Dam as the key ingredient for Egypt's modernization. The dam would harness Egypt's historic asset, double the arable land, produce cheap electricity for industry, and protect Egyptians from recurring floods.

Nasser's ambitions, however, stretched beyond Egypt. Since boyhood, he had dreamed of liberating Arabs from foreign oppression. This required Egypt to develop a stronger military, but Nasser's efforts to purchase modern arms from the West were continually rebuffed. In 1955, Nasser turned towards the Communist Bloc for help. Although Nasser's jails were filled with communists, Khrushchev welcomed the opportunity to expand Soviet influence inside a traditionally Western-dominated region. The alliance also lent credibility to Khrushchev's claim that the Socialist Bloc stood shoulder to shoulder with Third World nationalists fighting Western imperialism. Britain and the United States retaliated by slowing funding for Aswan. When Nasser recognized Mao's communists as China's legitimate government, Washington, scraped all funding for Nasser's signature development project.

Nasser responded by seizing the British- and French-owned Suez Canal Company. The Suez represented a strategic artery that provisioned Western Europe with Persian Gulf oil. Nationalizing the canal risked foreign intervention. Britain quickly challenged Nasser by withdrawing their tugboat captains that guided petrol tankers through the narrow Suez. Egyptians, with Soviet help, however, replaced their Western counterparts without mishap. Soviet engineers came to replace Western dam experts, while higher tariffs on Suez traffic raised the capital necessary for Aswan. Nasser's gamble seemed to have paid off.

Eden and the Suez Crisis, 1956

British Prime Minister Anthony Eden often likened Nasser to Hitler, citing his anti-Semitism and ambitions to overthrow regional monarchs supported by Britain. The French too despised Nasser for supporting Algeria's guerrillas. Eden secretly ordered MI5 to assassinate Egypt's head of state. When these plots failed, and economic pressure proved unsuccessful, Eden opted for direct intervention. In a secret meeting, France and Britain conspired with Israel to undermine Nasser. They all feared Nasser's growing influence, his ties to the Soviet Bloc, and his support for regional revolutionaries. Under terms of their secret bargain, Israel agreed to invade the Sinai. This would provide Britain and France a pretext for intervening as "peacekeepers" to protect international shipping.

> ### Window on World History: Pearson and the Suez Crisis
>
> While Lester Pearson would serve as Canadian prime minister from 1963 to 1968, his most memorable performance came while serving as Foreign Minister during the 1956 Suez Crisis. Internationally, the French and British military invasion of Suez stirred nearly universal reproach. The bombing of Cairo, Alexandria, and Port Said provoked indignation among Arabs and outrage among nonaligned nations. The Suez Crisis also split the Commonwealth along racial lines and brought pressure upon North Atlantic Treaty Organization (NATO) after US President Eisenhower complained that he had not been consulted. After striking Egypt, British Prime Minister Eden dispatched an urgent cable to Canada asking for their public approval: "I

(Continued)

know we can look for your understanding and much hope for your support."[1] Prime Minister St. Laurent was incensed at Eden's gall, but Pearson encouraged Canada to pursue a diplomatic resolution. This caution proved warranted as the Canadian public split on Suez. Polls revealed that 43 percent supported British and French military action, while 40 percent criticized it. Canada also found itself wedged between the United States, its superpower ally and leading trading partner, and a sense of loyalty towards their country's historic motherlands. While the Suez invasion betrayed Canada's sense of justice, local patriotic organizations, like the Sons of Scotland, pushed St. Laurent to publicly endorse Eden. Initially, diplomatic efforts failed because of the French and British veto in the UN Security Council. Once the Suez dossier was moved to the General Assembly, Pearson tapped contacts accumulated during decades of foreign service. Addressing the UN General Assembly, Pearson called for a "peace and police force" to diffuse the crisis. After four days of intense deliberations, Pearson helped to stitch together a coalition of fifty-seven states that voted in favor of establishing a robust United Nations Emergency Force (UNEF) led by a Canadian commander to oversee a ceasefire. Initially, British and French forces continued to storm the Canal Zone. As international pressure mounted, Eden gave way to UN peacekeepers. For his efforts, Pearson won the Nobel Prize in 1957, graciously crediting his country's "devotion to peace." However, the Liberal Party lost its parliamentary majority during the subsequent election. Blowback from Suez, particularly from loyalists, played a role in St. Laurent's defeat. The UNEF's role in defusing the Suez Crisis, however, set an important international precedent. Subsequently, UN peacekeepers would deploy to crisis zones not just as observers, but with heavy equipment that could deter aggression. Pearson helped to carve out an important role for the UN paralyzed since 1949 by Cold War rivalries. The Suez Crisis also led to closer Canadian identification with the UN, while eroding the significance Britain had attached to the Commonwealth.

Critical Reflection

1. To what extent have UN peacekeepers played a constructive role in maintaining international security since the Suez Crisis?
2. Did Pearson's election as prime minister signal implicit endorsement of a new Canadian identity less rooted in loyalism and more grounded in the UN's humanistic values?

Nasser did not have a navy or antiair defenses to prevent British and French capture of Egyptian ports. However, citizens took up arms and offered unexpectedly fierce resistance against the European occupation.

In October 1956, Israel launched an attack that captured thousands of Egyptian troops in the Sinai. When Nasser refused calls for a ceasefire, British and French planes bombed Cairo and Alexandria. Subsequently, Western paratroopers secured Suez, while an amphibious assault targeted Port Said. Eden assumed that a show of force would turn Egyptians against Nasser. Instead, they rallied to the barricades. Eden had also misjudged the international mood. Nasser attracted support not only from Arabs, but also from the international community that saw through the flimsy subterfuge of "peacekeeping." Khrushchev boisterously threatened to lob missiles at Paris and London. Antiwar protests erupted throughout Britain. The biggest blow came from US President Eisenhower. He ordered the US Treasury to sell the Pound Sterling. As speculators relentlessly attacked the British pound, Eden reached a breaking point and announced Britain's withdrawal. France had no choice but to follow suit. Around the world, non-Western nationalists cheered this blow to imperialism. Arabs celebrated Nasser as a modern-day Saladin.

Arab Nationalism after Suez

The Suez Crisis accelerated Westerns efforts to contain Nasser and the Soviet Union's expanding regional presence. In 1955, Eden had pushed local allies to form a regional security organization modeled upon NATO. Britain joined its allies Iran, Iraq, Pakistan, and Turkey in the **Baghdad Pact** to "co-operate for their security and defence."[2] The Soviets protested that they had no troops based inside the Middle East and condemned the pact as a Western subterfuge for "exploiting the people of the countries of the Near and Middle East so as to enrich their big monopolies."[3] From Cairo, Nasser similarly denounced the Baghdad Pact. Lacking a formal military establishment or unified command, the Baghdad Pact never got off the ground before it suffered a fatal blow in 1958 when a coalition of "Free Officers" seized power in Iraq. They unceremoniously executed the Hashemite monarch Britain had placed on their throne. Subsequently, Iraq's revolutionary regime withdrew from the Baghdad Pact, opened diplomatic relations with Soviet Union, and demanded the return of Kuwait.

After Suez, President Eisenhower tried to contain Soviet influence by offering US support to regional allies. This commitment led him to dispatch US Marines to Lebanon in 1958. Britain lent military aid to its Gulf allies and King Abdullah in Jordan. Saudi Arabia, however, emerged as the Nasser's principal nemesis. Nasser's revolutionary nationalism threatened the Arabian peninsula's conservative monarchs. The Saudis executed dozens of their own military officers, accusing them of being closet Nasserites conspiring against the royal family. In 1958, the Syrian chief of security revealed a Saudi plot for Nasser's assassination. Instead, Syria's Ba'ath party invited Nasser to become their head of state. In 1958, Nasser stood at the height of his power. Arab unification seemed within reach. But three years later, Nasser's **United Arab Republic** (UAR) spectacularly collapsed. Syrian officers threw out their Egyptian supervisors, frustrated with Nasser's policies and their marginalization inside the combined state. When a Nasserite faction seized power in North Yemen in 1962, Egypt immediately sent support, motivating Saudi Arabia to back the deposed Sultan. The brutality and expense of the Yemen War, however, crippled Nasser's prestige and placed a heavy burden upon Egypt's economy. Until 1967 the dream of Arab union remained alive, but support for Nasserism was eroding.

The Six Day-War, 1967

Since the Suez Crisis, Israeli troops had continued to strike against Palestinian militants operating from inside Egyptian refugee camps. To counter Israeli incursions into his territory, Nasser had brought in Soviet military advisors and heavy weapons. Nasser also built up a network of alliances with the Arab states bordering Israel. In May 1967, Nasser closed the Gulf of Aqaba to Israeli ships. Although Nasser did not intend to invade, he threatened Israel's "total destruction." Alarmed about Nasser's threats and military buildup, on June 5, 1967, Israel launched a preemptive strike. French made Mirage jets thundered low over the Mediterranean to elude Egyptian radar. When the alarm sounded, Israel jets had already arrived over Egyptian air fields. Within minutes, most of the Egyptian air force lay burning on the tarmac.

Destruction of Egypt's air force enabled Israeli motorized units to overwhelm Nasser's border forces and charge across the Sinai. Other Israeli units pushed into Syria and Jordan. In six days, Israeli forces secured a lop-sided victory. They seized Jerusalem and the West Bank from Jordan, the strategic Golan Heights from Syria, and reached the Suez Canal when an internationally brokered armistice ended the fighting. Despite modern arms and Soviet training, many of Egypt's desperate conscripts had fled the battlefield. Nasser was exposed as a paper tiger whose rhetoric fell short of his prowess. Any Arab hope of destroying the Zionist state seemed to have vanished. Nasser took to the radio to announce his resignation. A popular outcry led him to withdraw this offer, but Nasser never recovered his former prestige. At the Arab summit in Khartoum in 1967, Nasser mended fences with the Saudis. Unofficially, he renounced his project for Arab Union and humbly accepted a lifeline of Gulf State oil money. Diabetes and heart trouble sapped Nasser's energy and he died three years later a broken man.

Aftermath of the Six-Day War

International observers anticipated that Israel's decisive victory would resolve the Palestinian question, but a land for peace deal never materialized. In Khartoum in 1967, defiant Arab League delegates refused to negotiate fearing their weak bargaining position. Simultaneously, Israeli leaders grew reluctant to relinquish the Arab territory they had seized. The Israeli parliament hired Theodor Meron, a famed Nuremberg lawyer, to consult his opinion on whether Jews could settle the occupied territories. Meron argued that settlement contravened the Geneva Conventions, but his legal brief was buried in the Knesset archives for forty years. Within months of the armistice, Jews began to resettle areas they had abandoned in 1948. Israeli military officers argued that conquered Arab territory provided a strategic buffer against hostile neighbors, while state planners recognized the significance of the Jordanian watershed to Israel's development.

Demise of Nasserism

The Six–Day War dealt a fatal blow to Nasserism. Despite Nasser's earlier popularity and influence, his revolution had stalled. Regional Ba'ath parties had adapted significant elements of Nasser's program. In Syria and Iraq, like in Egypt, Nasserism resulted in a bloated state bureaucracy and a stagnant economy that provided mostly menial and low-paying jobs for university graduates, but did not stimulate sufficient growth to accommodate a rapidly growing population.

Nasserism's decline is exemplified in the careers of his most prominent successors. In Egypt, Anwar al Sadat kicked out Soviet advisors in 1972 in a bid to reestablish relations with the United States. Sadat tried to erase the humiliation of the Six Days War by launching a surprise attack on Israel in 1973 with Syrian support. Despite initial success, ultimately this campaign bogged down and reconfirmed Israel's military dominance. Sadat, however, presented the **Yom Kippur War** as a moral victory that restored Arab honor. Subsequently, Sadat tried to revive Egypt's economy by adopting an "open door" policy that privatized many state corporations and opened up Egypt to foreign investors. Although Sadat's liberalization measure failed to stimulate growth, it did secure a generous US aid package that continued to grow over subsequent decades.

Nasser's most resilient disciple proved to be Libya's **Myanmar Qaddafi**. Born into a family of Berber goat herders in the Sahara, the flamboyant Gaddafi enjoyed the privilege of a Western education after his father settled in Sirte. As a young man, Qaddafi proved quick to strike up friendships, and even quicker to rebuff perceived insults. Despite modest academic success, Qaddafi's charm and passion helped him to rise up the ranks in Libya's armed forces. Organizing his own Free Officer cell, Qaddafi launched a successful coup in 1969. To remove imperial influences from Libya, Qaddafi focused on nationalizing foreign oil companies. State oil revenues tripled from 1969 to 1974, enabling Qaddafi to raise Libyan living standards on par with that of Italy. After Nasser's death, Qaddafi tried to carry his revolutionary torch by becoming a financier for diverse terrorist organizations, from Palestinian militants to the American Black Panthers. But Qaddafi's lavish funding for revolutionaries delivered few tangible results. Internally, Qaddafi's "Islamic Socialism" struggled to unite a people partitioned along tribal, ethnic, and regional lines. After 1977, Qaddafi published a "green book" that

Through use of radio to address the broader Arab public, his championing of anti-Zionism and in his embrace of other secular nationalists, Nasser established himself as unofficial leader of the Arab world during the 1950s.

developed the "Third International Theory." Qaddafi proclaimed it an intellectual breakthrough. Most Libyans ignored their increasingly eccentric "Brotherly Leader," joining international observers in ridiculing Qaddafi's "Great Socialist People's Jamahiriya" as thinly disguised megalomania. Qaddafi's increasingly radical revolutionary program masked his growing despotism and unpopularity. Like Nasser, Qaddafi had failed to craft a coherent national polity despite Libya's oil wealth. Other Ba'athist leaders, like Syria's **Hafiz al Assad**, continued to endorse the platitudes of revolutionary nationalism, but Pan-Arabism was losing appeal. Arab armies had failed to destroy Israel, while Ba'athist regimes had mostly failed to deliver prosperity. Beneath the veneer of modern government departments and faux legislatures elected through doctored ballot boxes, Nasserism steadily evolved into a "**deep state**" of connected elites that monopolized state power. They used the army and security forces to crush dissidents, while buying off the middle class with lowly paid public service jobs and placating the masses through fuel and food subsidies.

Nasserism had invested in a modern state to supplant traditional Arab institutions: the tribe, mosque, and extended family. By the 1970s, the failure of secular nationalism was apparent in the expanding slums ringing Cairo, Istanbul, Amman, and other regional cities. Far from uplifting the poor, state modernization strategies had often disrupted the rural economy, while an inefficient manufacturing sector proved incapable of absorbing migrants fleeing rural poverty. Inside bulging capital cities and provincial centers, tensions mounted. Local mosques, Islamic charities, and neighborhood societies met some of the poor's needs by establishing food banks, schools, clinics, and other facilities to help their impoverished brethren. As a result, immigrants from the conservative countryside came to more closely identify with the Islamist reform program that preached tradition, piety, and social welfare. Regional states responded to Islamist groups like Egypt's Muslim Brotherhood by outlawing them and using the state security apparatus to disrupt their activities. At the municipal level, however, Islamist groups continued to secure increasing grassroots support. The twin planks of Islamism were social justice and *shari'ah*, a belief that Arab states, their laws, and institutions needed to better conform to Islamic tradition and practice.

> Is Islamism best described as religious fundamentalism or as a progressive movement for social justice?

The Iranian Revolution

The clearest illustration of Islamism's growing influence during the 1970s was the Iranian Revolution. Occupation by the allied powers during World War II had stimulated Iranian nationalism. From 1945 to 1947, Mohammad Reza Shah tried to reassert the crown's authority by securing the withdrawal of foreign troops and marginalizing the Marxist Tudeh Party. After 1947, however, Iranian elites grew increasingly disenchanted with their Shah. They resented his ties to the West and his ambitious plans for state centralization and modernization that threatened their interests and influence. In 1951, Iran's legislature defied their monarch by opposing the renewal of the unpopular concession that enabled Anglo-Iranian Oil Corporation (AIOC, or today's BP) to walk off with most of the country's oil wealth. A National Front led by Prime Minister Mohammad Mossadegh pushed for nationalization of the AIOC and reintroduction of the liberal 1906 constitution to curtail the Shah's powers. The National Front was a loose coalition that drew energy from widespread resentment with the country's foreign domination. Following a 1953 showdown with Mossadegh, the Shah fled Iran for Italy. Britain, however, refused to relinquish its most valuable corporation. Britain first blockaded Iran to weaken Mossadegh's regime. Subsequently, MI5 and the Central Intelligence Agency (CIA) hatched a plan for covert subversion. After bribing high-ranking Iranian officials, and paying a mob, a military coup ousted Mossadegh, brought back the Shah and returned the AIOC to its foreign owners.

Restoration of the Pahlavi dynasty ushered in a period of "guided democracy." Despite a legislature, the Shah unilaterally dictated his country's modernization program. In 1963, to broaden his support, and undermine the communist-linked Tudeh Party, the Shah's **White Revolution** focused on land reform and improving rural literacy. Land redistribution, however, failed to raise peasant living standards mostly because mechanization rendered subsistence agriculture obsolete. Instead, thousands of peasants washed up in Iran's cities. In Tehran, migrants struggled to find housing and jobs in a city flush with cash, foreigners, and Western consumer goods. Rising oil revenue during the 1970s had enabled the Shah to finance industrialization, military modernization, and infrastructure. Foreigners and a connected few profited handsomely, but high inflation also ate into the earnings and savings of the middle classes, while oil prosperity mostly failed to trickle down to the urban poor.

Lacking charisma or popular support, throughout the 1970s, Iran's Shah relied on oil wealth to expand the welfare state. The United States also helped him to build up the region's largest army and most formidable secret police force. The CIA trained **SAVAK** relentlessly rounded up tortured and murdered dissidents. By the late 1970s, however, liberal professionals, bazaar merchants, and the urban middle classes had grown frustrated with their lack of voice inside government. The spark igniting the Iranian Revolution came in January 1978. A government newspaper accused the exiled Ayatollah Khomeini of being a British spy. In Qum, state suppression of a demonstration turned violent. This ignited a cycle of protest and police repression that rumbled through Iranian cities for months. An increasingly broad coalition was drawn into Iran's streets, increasingly with the aim of overthrowing the Shah.

Iranian Revolution 1978-1989

Shah's decision to pull back SAVAK repression encouraged the disaffected to join demonstrations for regime change.

Upon his return to Iran, Khomeini called for continuation of demonstrations to overthrow regime and create Islamic State.

Bani-Sadr's impeachment marks final triumph of radical Islamist over moderate reformers desiring a more secular state.

Worried that Khomeini's call for Islamic Revolution will whip Iraq's Shias into revolt, Saddam invades Iran.

Iran Hostage Crisis cements Western perception that Islamism, rather than a populist movement for justice and reform is a fundamentalist movement hostile to Western liberalism.

Time Line
June 1963: Shah's Arrest of Khomeini leads to his 13 year exile.
January 1978: Popular Demonstrations against Shah after government newspaper accuses Khomeini of being a British spy.
November 1978: Black Friday Massacre galvanizes public opinion around ouster of Shah.
January 1979: Shah flees into exile.
February 1: Ayatollah Khomeini returns to Tehran.
February 11: Iranian Military declares itself 'neutral' enabling Khomeini to consolidate leadership of the Revolution
March:: During referendum 98% vote in favor of Islamic Republic.
November 1979: Iranian Hostage crisis lasts 444 days and creates tension with USA and Western states.
December 1979: Constitution for Islamic Republic ratified.
1980-1988: Iran-Iraq War leaves 260,000 Iranians dead, devastates economy, stimulates patriotism and strengthens Islamic radicals.
1981: Impeachment of President Bani-Sadr solidifies control of clerics over state.
1987: Abolition of Islamic Republic Party brings revolution to symbolic end.
1989: Death of Khomeini dies.

Image credits: © Schwabenbitz/Shutterstock.com, World History Archive/Alamy Stock Photo; © vkillkov/Shutterstock.com; Historic Collection/Alamy Stock Photo © vkilkov/Shutterstock.com; Historic Collection/Alamy Stock Photo

Iran's Shah lived with his family in a world of luxurious splendor far removed from the struggles of ordinary Iranians. Throughout the 1970s, his authority depended not on popular support, but his army and the SAVAK's deadly efficiency. By 1977, however, the Shah's health had declined and his spirit faltered. When Iran's military hardliners urged crackdown, the Shah tilted towards pressure from Jimmy Carter's White House to respect human rights. The Shah embraced the revolution brewing in Iran's streets by appointing a moderate reformer as prime minister. He also retracted many of the hated SAVAK's powers. Appeasement backfired. From exile, France **Ayatollah Khomeini's** secretaries diligently transcribed his speeches and transmitted them back to Iran via tape cassettes and telephone. Khomeini egged demonstrators to step up their protests and overthrow the Shah's corrupt regime.

Black Friday Massacre

The turning point in the Iranian Revolution came on September 8, 1978. During **Black Friday** a large crowd chanting "Death to the Shah!" approached a terrified corps of inexperienced conscripts in Jaleh Square. They fired indiscriminately into the angry crowd, killing at least eighty-eight, but leaving scores more wounded. From Paris, an indignant Khomeini exaggerated the body count and promoted wild rumors about the Shah directing fire upon peaceful demonstrators from a circling helicopter. Black Friday broke all possibility for reconciliation. Liberal opposition groups lost hope in political reform. The sickly Shah lost his nerve. At news conferences, the Shah's haggard face stared out at the world through thick lenses like a mole staggering through the dark. Over a four-month span between October 1978 and January 1979, the Shah's legitimacy s eroded in a rising tide of public demonstrations. On January 16, 1979, the Shah flew to Cairo. Everyone realized that this "state visit" represented an abdication. Fatally stricken by cancer, the ailing Shah would soon die.

The Shah and his wife in US exile. Acceptance of the Shah for cancer treatment was a catalyst for the Iran Hostage Crisis.

With the Shah gone, the Iranian regime invited Ayatollah Khomeini back to Tehran in a bid to mollify demonstrators. On February 1, 1979, Khomeini stepped onto the tarmac of Tehran's airport before a roaring crowd of several million. Back in Iran, Khomeini quickly asserted leadership over the revolution. He surprised the regime that welcomed him back by directing demonstrators to ramp up pressure against the state. Iranian conscripts increasingly cast aside their uniforms and "defected to the Revolution."

The Shah's regime officially collapsed a month following Khomeini's return. Top officers gathered on February 11 and decided to sign a public memorandum renouncing the use of force. Over ensuing months, Iran twirled in the vortex of revolutionary forces, including the taking of hostages from the US embassy. Iran's economy fell into a tailspin. State institutions all but ceased to function. A March 1979 referendum revealed broad support for an "Islamic Republic," an idea that was not explicitly defined. Iranians, however, were roughly divided between liberal reformers that wanted a secular state informed by Islamic cultural values versus radicals who desired the Islamization of all aspects of Iranian life. The November 1979 constitution marked a triumph for Islamists. The constitution's preamble pledged to extend "God's law throughout the world." Iran's constitution was a synthesis that married modern institutions and Western concepts and with Islamic tradition and Iranian precedents. The constitution created a popularly elected parliament and preserved the machinery of the Iranian state with a prime minister, cabinet, and professional bureaucracy. These institutions conformed broadly to liberal orthodoxy and resonated with Enlightenment principles like representation, sovereignty, and separation of powers. Iran's constitution proved innovative in how it translated the idea of divine sovereignty into the executive and judiciary branches of government. Unlike the Middle East's repressive regimes, Iran created a system with open elections, but where popular sovereignty was simultaneously constrained by an appointed Revolutionary Council and a novel institution: the *vilayat-i faqih*, or "supreme jurist" who exercised authority in the name of the hidden Iman. It was not immediately clear how a spiritual guide and scholar of Islamic law would operate inside the state. In his early years as supreme jurist, Khomeini established an informal precedent by setting the broad agenda for the state, but also delegating its everyday operation to subordinates. This suggested a consultative role, but in practice, the supreme jurist was appointed for life and had nearly unchecked authority over the state, supreme command over the military, and a unilateral prerogative to declare war or negotiate peace. The Islamization of the state was mirrored in the clergy's domination over the legislature and the judiciary. Western critics derisively labeled Iran's constitution a "theocracy," although it was not in principle inconsistent with the idea of creating an Islamic Republic. The Council of Experts, for example, plays an important role as final arbitrators of Islamic law, ensuring that officials, state institutions, and laws conform to Islamic tradition.

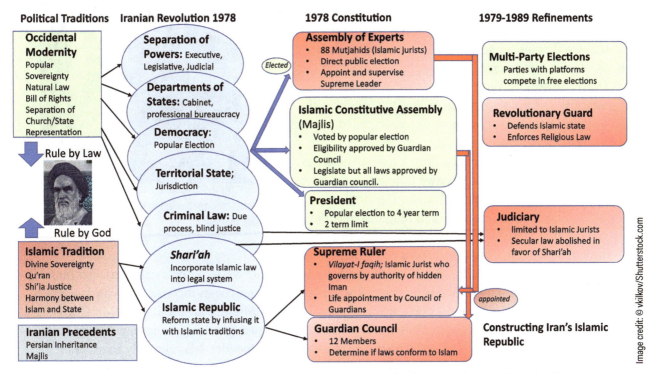

Khomeini's constitution mixed Western political concepts with traditional Iranian institutions with novel Islamic institutions.

Adoption of the 1978 constitution did not mark the endpoint for Iran's revolution. Over the next three years, Iran's political experiment continued as secularists and Islamists debated, tested out the new machinery of government, and battled to hammer out the constitution's words into a viable political system. Saddam Hussein's 1980 invasion of Iran created great hardships and strengthened the hands of Islamists. Impeachment of moderate Prime Minister Bani-Sadr in 1981 marked their final triumph and culminated into a political system where clerics dominated all branches of government. In 1982, Khomeini declared the revolution over, galvanizing Iran's Revolution into a stable system of government. By then, Iranian society had been systematically Islamized. Secular courts were abolished, women were mandated to wear the veil, and a revolutionary guard functioned as an unofficial police force cracking down against violators of Islamic law, including offenses like drinking alcohol or applying lipstick. This was not the revolution that Iran's liberals and most of Tehran's middle classes had fought for.

Window on World: Women in the Contemporary Islamic World

During the Iranian Revolution, the Ayatollah Khomeini depicted women as the weaker sex through which the West sought to corrupt Islamic society. *Gharbzadegi* represented an Iranian concept of West-toxification. The idea that women served as a conduit for corruption elevated the *hijab* that many Iranian women had chosen to wear as a symbol of protest during the Iranian Revolution into a barometer for Islamic purity after 1979. After Iran's Revolution, the veil became mandatory in public. This law was enforced by revolutionary guards and local police. Iran's veil mandate mirrored a broader regional trend as Islamist movements gained prominence during the 1980s. In secular Turkey, women were allowed to wear the veil inside universities in 2008, while in the Taliban's Afghanistan, women were compelled to don the restrictive *burqa* to protect their modesty.

Veil politics intersected a deeper dispute between Western liberals and conservative Islamists concerning fundamental rights. The 1990 Cairo Declaration rejected both gender equality and religious freedom, arguing that these were not universal rights, but liberal notions sourced in a Western experience. The Islamic

Women played an active role in the demonstrations that led to the collapse of the Shah's regime.

world did not have a tradition of Church and State separation. Western liberalism translated into a conceptualization of individual rights that some Islamic jurists saw as inconsistent with Islam's more collectivist assumptions. The Cairo Declaration echoed Muslims critics of the 1948 Universal Declaration of Human Rights. While Muslim jurists condemned discrimination, they also asserted that equality should be based on "human dignity" rather than gender. Islam literally translates into submission before God. Many Muslims—not just fundamentalists—support the idea of *shari'ah* that the Qur'an and Islamic traditions should anchor their social and cultural lives. While the Qur'an says little about gender, it does affirm dissymmetry. While establishing women equals before God, the Qur'an also gives their testimony half the weight of a man. Such passages can justify contemporary traditionalists who argue that women must submit to their husbands, fathers, and brothers. Muslim liberals counter that most customary restrictions on women are rooted in Arab culture rather than scripture. The *purdah*, or curtain, that traditionally separates the worlds of men and women became increasingly politicized during the 1970s in an environment where many Muslims came into deeper contact with Western culture and its more liberal attitudes towards gender, family, and sexuality. Urbanization and television exposed rural people and Muslim conservatives to foreign ideas and practices. Satellites broadcasted shows like Dallas and Baywatch, which offered a distorted picture of American society as materialistic and promiscuous. Decades earlier, Salafists like Sayyid Qutb had placed male guardianship over women as central to his program for Islamic purification. Later Islamist movements followed his example in trying to inscribe gender inequality into law. Several contemporary events have demonstrated that this can lead to abuse. Pakistan's Hudud law, for example, requires a woman to provide three male witnesses to substantiate a charge of rape. Failing that high bar, an accused rapist would run free, while her accuser would be flogged for confessing adultery. When the Taliban seized power in Afghanistan, war widows were barred from working, forcing many to beg or prostitute to feed starving children. Even in more liberal Arab states, a woman's secondary status in the law can impose severe restrictions on their effective civil rights. This was illustrated in Morocco in 2011 when 16-year-old Amina Filali imbibed rat poison rather than obey a court order to marry her accused rapist. This tragedy provoked sharp debate inside the Islamic world concerning gender conventions that often have only a sketchy basis in scripture. Globally, Middle Eastern states rank last in terms of women's participation in the labor force, education, and civil society. This gender gap is most acute in the conservative Persian Gulf states. The Philippines, Malaysia, and Indonesia have elected female heads of state and South Asian states generally provide more educational opportunities for women. Western stereotypes about female repression in the Islamic World, however, obscure the diversity of feminine experience. Some women welcome the veil as liberating or enabling them to affirm their identity. Others have used Islam as a framework to subvert misogyny. The *Sahwa* was a broad-based movement that is often mislabeled as "fundamentalist." Reform represented its dominant impulse, with Islamic tradition serving as its template. Over the last two decades, *shari'ah* has proven malleable in terms of fusing civil law and Islamic practice into diverse configurations inside regional states. The question of gender remains contested, but even in conservative Gulf States progress towards gender equality can be noted, including Saudi Arabia's recent lifting of the ban on female driving.

Critical Reflection

1. Do you agree with the Cairo Declaration's assessment that universal rights represent a Western idea not applicable to non-Western societies?
2. Can you reconcile the claim of conservative Imams that gender distinctions honor women with the feminist charge that civil discrimination produces misogyny?

Rise of Islamism

Khomeini's call for "Islamic Revolution" coincided with the television age. Images of massive street demonstrations in Tehran inspired Islamists in neighboring states to follow his example. Mass media also provided other clerics a platform for articulating their vision for a purer form of Islamic society. Most Islamists bought into Khomeini's sharp distinction between Western materialism and Islamic spiritualism, even if most Iranians also saw their revolution as a progressive movement to reform government and create a more just society.

The *Sahwa* (Islamic Awakening)

Spectrum of Values

- **Salafism**: Purify society; insulate from corruption
- **Jihadism**: Resist invaders oppressing Muslims
- **Shari'a**: Harmonize state institutions with Islamic law
- **Islamic Revolution**: Islamize modernity
- **Social Justice**: Care for poor and feeble

Timeline 1979-1989
- **1979**: Overthrow of Iran's Shah
- **1979**: Islamic radicals seize Mecca Grand Mosque
- **1979**: Soviet troops move into Afghanistan
- **1980**: Saddam Hussein invades Iran
- **1981**: Islamists assassinate Egypt's Anwar Sadat
- **1982**: Israel invades South Lebanon
- **1980s**: Lebanon's Shi'ites form Hezbollah, the party of God
- **1987**: Palestinian *Intifada* challenges Israeli occupation
- **1988**: End of Iran-Iraq War
- **1989**: Last Soviet Troops leave Afghanistan
- **1989**: Death of Khomeini

1980s Lebanon: Israeli invasion and Khomeini's call for Islamic Revolution lead Lebanese Shi'ites to form *Hizbullah*, a militant nationalist movement with Islamist message.

Egypt 1980s: Following Sadat's 1981 assassination, Muslim Brotherhood switches tactics to build support for its Islamist program at the grass roots level.

1987 Palestinian *Intifada*: Islamists play critical role in organizing Palestinian protest, while international media coverage stimulates sense of Islamic solidarity across state and ethnic boundaries.

Afghanistan 1979-1989: Soviet military intervention spurs Afghanis to cast themselves as *mujahedeen* and call upon fellow Muslims to join their jihad against the godless Soviets.

1980-1988 Iran-Iraq War: Devastating war strengthens hands of Islamists in Iran and forces secular leaders everywhere to frame their policies in more Islamic terms.

1979 Saudi Arabia: Islamic radicals seize the Grand Mosque in Mecca and call for ouster of corrupt House of Saud. During 1980s tensions mount as the country rapidly modernizes, while Saud family promotes Wahhabi clerics that advocate for more puritanical form of Islam in conflict with liberal western modernity.

After American diplomats were imprisoned during the hostage crisis, many Westerners saw the Iranian Revolution as an expression of Islamic fundamentalism. Pundits labeled "political Islam" as an intolerant revolutionary force directed against Western interests, liberal values, democracy, and modern progress. Khomeini's idea of Islamic Revolution threatened neighboring regimes. Initially, Khomeini tried to export Iran's revolution by lending material and ideological support to Shi'ite minorities repressed inside neighboring states. In Lebanon, **Hizbullah**, the Party of God, united Shi'ites in challenging their traditional marginalization by Sunni elites and Maronite Christians. In part, because he feared that Khomeini might inspire Iraq's Shi'ite majority against him, Saddam Hussein invaded Iran in 1980, with the backing of conservative Gulf States. The **Iran–Iraq War** would embroil both countries in a costly stalemate that endured until 1988 at the cost of over a million lives.

Ultimately, Khomeini's influence stretched far outside the Shi'a Crescent because Iran's Revolution coincided with the broader *Sahwa*, or Islamic awakening that rejected the "Westernization" approach adopted by secular Nasserites. By the 1980s, "Islamism" evolved into a grassroots movement that embraced different coalitions in various countries. One common strand was support for *shari' ah*, the idea that Islamic traditions should serve as a template for state and social reform. Most Islamists believed themselves progressive, rather than fundamentalist. They did not want to retreat into the past, but create a better future. However, they also identified rejuvenation with overturning a secular program of reform and aligning their state and law more closely to Islamic tradition. Turning Nasser on his head, Islamists sought to *Islamize modernity* rather than *modernize Islam*.

One fuel for the *Sahwa* was the rapid social and economic transformation of the Middle East after 1960. Secular modernization schemes had intensified urban migration, while the state did little to accommodate poor migrants. Their struggles to find work and adequate housing intensified their dissatisfaction with the state. The Gulf region, however, experienced the most rapid transition as rising oil prices transformed dusty towns into shining oases of modernity in less than a decade. For nomadic peoples traditionally isolated from foreign cultures, urban settlement exposed them to an alien world of foreign workers, Western products, and modern infrastructure. Nonoil producing states also benefitted from this windfall. The Saudi royal family generously dispensed aid to Arab allies, while offering work to Palestinians and other Muslims inside the Persian Gulf's booming oil and construction sectors. Throughout the Middle East, the timing and intensity of urbanization varied. Everywhere rapid change rankled conservatives. To maintain the social order, many Persian Gulf sheikhs followed the Saudi royal family's paradoxical policy of both promoting modernization and defending tradition. Oil money facilitated the investment of billions in infrastructure, housing, schools, and hospitals to make their citizens' lives more comfortable, while simultaneously, Gulf sheikhs funneled billions towards conservative clerics to finance religious schools, radio stations, and mosques to maintain traditional values. This strategy secured the clergy's political support, but over the longer run it amplified the divide between their society's ideology and the structure of contemporary life.

Islamization of Society

By the 1980s, television ownership inside the Middle East had increased dramatically, while communications satellites facilitated regional programming. Religious conservatives in the Gulf region used these platforms to propagate the awakening and advocate viewers to adopt their puritanical brand of Islam. Increasing adoption of the veil was one reflection of a conservative drift inside a religion traditionally characterized by considerable diversity in belief and practice. Television coverage of the Afghan War and Palestinian *Intifada* also contributed a sense of victimization to Islamist movements. Broadcasts reinforced the idea that Muslims were under foreign attack, while stimulating a deeper connection between Muslims resident in diverse states with a larger Islamic community.

Rapidly declining oil prices during the 1980s cut into state balance sheets, exacerbating tensions between secular rulers and Islamists. By the 1990s, Islamist regimes had come into power in Iran, Sudan, and Afghanistan. In Algeria, the army's annulment of a 1991 election that would have given Islamists victory resulted in a brutal civil war that lasted for nearly a decade and killed at least 40,000. Bowing to Islamist pressure, unpopular secular leaders like Qaddafi, Saddam Hussein, and **Hosni Mubarak** increasingly invoked Islamic principles to justify their policies. They also allowed partial Islamization of schools and the courts. State repression and doctored elections prevented Islamists from taking control over the state, but at the local level, Islamists expanded their political base by supporting charities, mutual aid societies, and prayer circles. Politics of the mosque enabled Islamists to advocate *shari'ah* largely free from state repression. This enabled Islamism to coalesce into more focused and robust grassroots movement. This is evident in Turkey in 2002, where Recep Erdoğan led the Justice and Development Party to electoral victory in Turkey. President Erdoğan opted for a gradualist approach of pushing for Islamic reforms at the fringes of Turkish society, while avoiding open confrontation with the officer corps committed to a secular state and defense of Turkey's liberal constitution.

The Soviet War in Afghanistan

Afghanistan's devastation incubated a particularly militant strain of Islamism. In September 1977, riots broke out across Afghanistan's capital of Kabul. Demonstrations united students, state workers, and communists against Afghanistan's king and traditional elites. On April 27, 1978, the Afghan army, backed by communists, led a coup. Moscow applauded, offering support for the fledgling regime, even as Soviet leaders feared becoming stuck in the "graveyard of empires." It is unfair to label Afghanistan a "failed state," because traditionally the Kingdom's monarch lived in Kabul, but his rule never extended very deep into the countryside. There, most Afghans lived in tightly knit rural communities, regionally divided along ethnic, religious, tribal, and linguistic lines inside the rugged Kush Mountains.

The revolutionary regime in Kabul, however, nurtured grand ambitions for building a modern state. They announced a far-reaching set of socialist reforms to cast off "feudalism" and build a modern Afghanistan in five years. Gender equality represented a central thrust for their reform program. Women were encouraged to cast off their veils, Islamic marriage was replaced by the liberal idea of equal rights, and schools were opened for girls. The state also launched literacy and health programs to raise Afghanistan's dismal standard of living. When state reforms met with resistance from rural conservatives, Kabul responded with brutality and terror. The regime targeted enemies of all stripes: village mullahs, tribal leaders, and liberal members of Kabul's traditional elite. Over a span of several months, 18,000 regime opponents were murdered. The Afghan army also launched punitive campaigns into the countryside. Terror created hundreds of thousands of refugees, especially Pashtuns who found shelter among their kin inhabiting the tribal areas of neighboring Pakistan. Rural militants started to identify themselves as the *mujahideen*, or soldiers of God. Islam represented the one transcendent identity local militias, mostly organized along ethnic lines, had in common. By late 1979, Kabul's communist regime reached a critical state. War engulfed the countryside, while Afghan conscripts were deserting in large numbers.

On September 12, 1979, **Hafizullah Amin** seized power following a struggle with his longtime rival Nur Muhammad Taraki. Although Moscow had long fretted about Taraki's competency, megalomania, and alcoholism, Moscow was more worried about Amin fearing he was an American agent. When various KGB assassination plots failed, a reluctant Brezhnev authorized direct intervention. Elite *spetsnaz* gunned down Amin in the Tajbeg Palace while the Red Army rushed in to stabilize Afghanistan's fledgling socialist state. Soviet intervention, however, galvanized popular resistance to the Kabul regime. Foreign invasion allowed Tajiks, Uzbeks, Hazeri, and Pashtuns to cast their struggle as a jihad and plead for external support.

Afghanistan 1979-1996

1978: Coup installs communist regime in Kabul
1979: Soviet special forces assassinate Prime Minister Amin
1979: Red Army intervenes to save unpopular communist government.
1980: Soviets install Babrak Karmal but he fails to restore regime's legitimacy
1980: Conservative opponents to Soviet regime hail themselves as Soldiers of God
1981: Anti-Soviet powers Pakistan, Iran, US and China arm Mujahideen guerrillas
1983: Red Army conducts scorched earth campaigns that fail to uproot the Mujahideen
1985: Half of Afghan population has fled into exile
1986: US supplies mujahideen with Stinger missiles that blunt Soviet military capability.
1986: Soviets install Najibullah as Afghanistan's leader
1988: Peace Accord negotiates end of Soviet Occupation
1989: Last Soviet troops depart
1992: Communist Najibullah regime collapses after Soviet Collapse
1992: Peshawar Accord provides framework for Afghan transition
1992: Competing Mujahideen factions fight for Kabul and begin civil war
1996: Taliban seize control over Kabul

1979 Soviet Coup: USSR fails to stabilize fledgling communist regime in Kabul and stirs emergence of a militant resistance where guerrillas hail themselves as 'Soldiers of God' and call for outside support for their jihad.

1986 Stinger Missile: US introduction of portable anti-aircraft missile erodes Soviet military superiority, increases casualties and incentivizes Gorbachev to find a diplomatic exit strategy from Afghanistan.

1988-1989 Soviet Withdrawal: Soviet troops pull out of Afghanistan.

1996 Taliban Victory: Islamist Afghan Refugees trained in Pakistan Madrassa seize Kabul, end the warlord factionalism and install a radical Salafist state that forces Afghans to live according to a strict fundamentalist code.

1992 Communist Regime Collapse: Najibullah's execution creates a vacuum as various Mujahideen leaders fall out with each other triggering a civil war and fracturing of Afghanistan into warlord factions reflecting ethno-linguistic divisions.

1992 Civil War: Rejecting the Peshawar Accords, Gulbuddin Hekmatyar shells Kabul in a bid to drive rival militias from the capital.

While the Red Army established control over Afghanistan's cities, it struggled to impose authority over the countryside. The *mujahideen* adopted guerrilla tactics, besieging cities, and ambushing Soviet soldiers. While lightly armed, the *mujahideen's* small footprint and intimate knowledge of local terrain enabled them to strike quickly and melt away into the mountains. Like in Vietnam, the Soviet Army won most battles but was steadily losing the war. To combat the insurgents, the Soviet Union relied upon air power and a brutal scorched Earth strategy designed to deprive the guerillas of safe havens. Destroying infrastructure and conducting reprisal attacks, however, rallied Afghani civilians against Soviet soldiers. It also provoked the United States, Pakistan, China, and Saudi Arabia to step up support for the *mujahideen*. Introduction of the US-designed Stinger antiaircraft missile in 1986 crippled the HIND attack helicopter that the Red Army relied upon to fight the mobile guerillas. In 1987, General Secretary Gorbachev—focused on internal reform—announced his intention to withdraw. By 1989, the last Soviet troops evacuated Afghanistan. They left behind **Mohammad Najibullah** to safeguard socialist progress. Najibullah's policy of "national reconciliation" pitted various *mujahideen* factions against each other. This enabled him to remain in power longer than anticipated. Collapse of the Soviet Union in 1991, however, brought aid for Najibullah's regime to a halt. In 1992, **General Dostam** and his Uzbek militia defected from Kabul. Najibullah's regime started to falter. By Christmas, the victorious *mujahideen* entered Kabul and established a new governing council. Celebration proved short lived. The *mujahideen* remained deeply divided over their country's future.

Afghanistan's Civil War, 1992 to 1996

Afghanistan illustrates how proxy war serves as the cradle for failed states. The Soviet War left at least one million Afghans, mostly civilians, dead. Another three million had been wounded and five million rendered refugees. The end of the Soviet occupation, however, did not end Afghani suffering. Afghan children in particular fell victim to the millions of mines that the conflict left behind. The war had also devastated Afghanistan's already insufficient infrastructure, particularly the irrigation works upon which agriculture depended. In 1992, many of Afghanistan's cities were heavily damaged and depopulated. Millions of refugees remained in Pakistan. The war's devastation created a vacuum in which state institutions had all but collapsed. The country's traditional elite had been killed or had fled into exile.

In April 1992, the UN brokered the **Peshawar Accord** in a bid to unite the competing *mujahideen* factions inside an Islamic State. The Accord proposed to install an interim coalition government that would organize national elections and craft a constitution. Afghanistan's most powerful warlord, **Gulbuddin Hekmatyar**, was invited to head this interim government, but he refused. Instead, Hekmatyar launched a campaign to seize absolute power. Pakistan cynically backed Hekmatyar, aiming to expand their regional influence. While Kabul had been an oasis of relative tranquility during the Soviet war, now Pakistani rockets rained down on the city as *mujahideen* factions turned upon each other. Kabul became a war zone as competing factions fired indiscriminately upon civilians and committed countless atrocities. By 1993, Afghanistan's fragile coalition government had split largely along ethnic lines. A second chapter of Afghan's war opened as Iran, Saudi Arabia, and Pakistan backed competing warlords that set up shop in their respective corners of the Afghan realm.

Rise of the Taliban

In 1996, the **Taliban** captured Kabul. The Taliban were a group of religious students named after their white turbans. Their core fighters were young Pashtun Afghan refugees that had studied in Pakistani **madrassas** (religious schools) during the Soviet occupation. Indoctrinated in an extremist Salafist form of Islam, the Taliban sought to reestablish a more pristine form of Islamic society in Afghanistan.

Their vigor, discipline, and valor, combined with Pakistani support, enabled the Taliban to prevail in Kabul and gradually secure most of Afghanistan's territory. Initially, most Afghans accepted the Taliban brutally imposing a strict form of Islam. Female doctors were cast from hospitals, girls were barred from school, popular music was banned, and traditions like kite running were prohibited. While presenting themselves as religious reformers, the Taliban regime was also notoriously corrupt. Many Taliban officials profited personally from the lucrative opium trade, while most Afghans lived under a reign of terror where those accused of "immorality" faced draconian punishments like "stoning" with little juridical recourse.

Sayyid Qutb and Militant Jihadism

The Salafism that emerged inside Afghanistan was influenced by the writings of Egyptian teacher **Sayyid Qutb** (1906–1966). In 1947, Qutb had received a fellowship to study in the United States. This experience shocked the conservative Egyptian. When a Greeley, Colorado pastor invited Qutb to a Church "mixer," he witnessed American teenagers close dancing while a gramophone blared out the risqué lyrics to "Baby its Cold outside." The scene horrified Qutb. It galvanized his repugnant rejection of Western culture. America's decadence was evident in the freedom given women, its consumerist mentality, its jazz music, and the American obsession with manicured lawns. Qutb's immersion experience led him to a sharply different conclusion from Nasser. The West was not worthy of emulation. In fact, Western materialism had corrupted Islamic society, returning Muslims to a state of *jahiliyya* or ignorance. Revival depended on *Salaf*, or purity, stripping out all forms of modern corruption and returning to the purity Qutb imagined Muslims enjoyed during the first three generations following the Prophet's death.

Sayyid Qutb's Salafism to Contemporary Jihadism

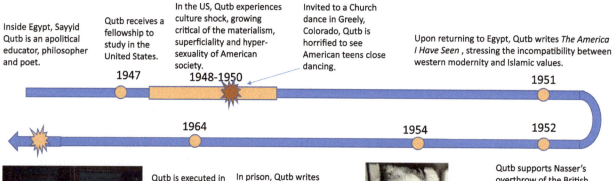

Inside Egypt, Sayyid Qutb is an apolitical educator, philosopher and poet.

Qutb receives a fellowship to study in the United States. **1947**

In the US, Qutb experiences culture shock, growing critical of the materialism, superficiality and hyper-sexuality of American society. **1948-1950**

Invited to a Church dance in Greely, Colorado, Qutb is horrified to see American teens close dancing.

Upon returning to Egypt, Qutb writes *The America I Have Seen*, stressing the incompatibility between western modernity and Islamic values. **1951**

1964   **1954**   **1952**

Qutb's Salafism inspires Afghan's Taliban, Bin Laden, and later ISIS; jihadist movements that sought to create an Islamic State and establish a puritanical Islamic practice they imagined to exist during the lifetime of the Prophet.

Qutb is executed in 1956, but his legacy lives on through *Milestones*, published in 1964

In prison, Qutb writes *Milestones*, a religious tract that develops the doctrine of *al salaf* that posits the incompatibility between Islam and western culture, advocates for a return to the purity of Islamic culture during the eighth century and advocates violent jihad against secular Arab rulers like Nasser that are actively corrupting Islamic society.

Implicated in an assassination plot of Nasser, Qutb is arrested, imprisoned and tortured.

Qutb supports Nasser's overthrow of the British playboy king Furuq, but parts ways after Nasser lays out a path towards secular modernization rather than Islamic rejuvenation.

Upon returning to Egypt, Qutb was initially friendly with Gamal Abdel Nasser, but quickly grew disgruntled with his secular program. After a failed assassination plot against Nasser, Qutb was arrested, tortured, and ultimately executed in 1966. Nasser, however, failed to silence Qutb's ideas. A new generation of Islamic radicals hailed Qutb as a martyr. They read his *Milestones* tract advocating jihad against "apostate" Arab regimes. Qutb's brother lectured in Saudi Arabia where he transmitted Salafism to a new generation that included Osama Bin Laden. For Qutb's followers, the Soviet War in Afghanistan (1979–1989) represented a golden opportunity. Over 30,000 Arabs volunteered to fight in Afghanistan. The Soviet Union's withdrawal and later collapse seemed to vindicate militant jihadism. After the failures of secular nationalism and defeats suffered at the hands of the Zionists, Afghanistan jihadists bested a superpower. Arab Afghanis returned home to spread their jihadist message to a new generation. Exploiting emerging communications technologies, jihadists maintained their network and many veterans went on to fight in Bosnia, Palestine, Algeria, Somalia, and the Kashmir. Others joined local Salafist groups where they put their militarily and logistical skills to use by organizing militant cells against "apostate" regimes that they saw as corrupt and allied to the West.

Postwar Urbanization and Modern Anxieties

Various strains of Islamic radicalism were sourced in the Middle East's transformation from a predominantly rural society where identity was rooted in a network of local ties to extended family, mosque, and tribe to an urban industrial society more deeply integrated to the global economy, reliant upon modern technology and exposed to foreign ideas and practices. For many Arabs, the process of urbanization was disorientating. Older grievances with Western colonialism and discontentment with secular modernizers combined to fuel a more systematic rejection of Western culture, while cementing the perception that modernity conflicted with Islamic traditions. By the 1990s, the *Sahwa* had reinvigorated a sense of Islamic identity, while elevating *shari'ah* as a template for social and state reform.

House of Saud

Saudi Arabia well demonstrates a regional struggle to accommodate tradition with modernity. During the 1930s, the Saud family, supported by the fierce *Ikwan* warriors, prevailed over their Hashemite rivals. King Abdul-Aziz Ibn Saud seized control over the Islamic holy sites of Mecca and Medina and proclaimed a state in Riyadh in 1933. Over subsequent years, the Saud family consolidated their authority over much of the Arabian peninsula, excepting coastal enclaves where Britain backed local Sheiks. Before World War II, most Saudis continued to live as tribal nomads. The Kingdom's future shifted radically when an expedition tasked with discovering water instead found oil.

In 1938, the Standard Oil Company won a Saudi concession and began to build out a petroleum infrastructure. In 1945, Franklin Roosevelt briefly met the Saudi King. Their meeting ratified an informal bargain. The Saudis would trade their oil for US protection. After World War II, Persian Gulf oil assumed tremendous significance as European consumption skyrocketed and traditional oil fields began to peter out. Oil quickly emerged as the Saudi kingdom's principal source of revenue. Creation of an infrastructure to exploit oil, however, necessitated an influx of Western oil men, their families, and modern ways. This foreign presence angered the Wahhabis that strictly adhered to tribal customs and a puritanical form of Islam. Responding to local sentiment, the Saudis sought to contain Western culture by establishing the foreign quarter of Jeddah. Behind its walls, a form of American suburbia blossomed. For Saudis accustomed to the "empty quarter," the ranch houses, green lawns, and Friday Night Football seemed not only alien, but a threat to their way of life. Ghettoizing foreigners limited Saudi contact with the Western world, but it did not alleviate local concerns about cultural contamination.

During the late 1950s, **King Saud** gained notoriety for driving his Mercedes convertible around Jeddah and dispensing wads of dollars to supporters. The king's largesse marked unofficial inauguration of a royal family policy to leverage their oil wealth to buy political support from conservative subjects skeptical about the benefits of modernization. Saud's alcoholism and profligate ways, however, undermined the state's finances and dented the ruling family's prestige. A palace coup in 1958 led to Saud's replacement by his worldlier and more competent brother, **Faisal**. Faisal quickly put the Saudi treasury in order. He also clamped down on Nasserites plotting against his family. Having secured his family's power, Faisal laid the groundwork for the modern Saudi state by negotiating a series of difficult compromises. Faisal required Western expertise to build a modern infrastructure, but he also needed to placate conservative clerics that held tremendous influence among his subjects. Faisal's solution was to coopt the clergy by providing them with generous salaries, funds for new mosques and schools, and giving the clergy a virtual monopoly to dictate the Kingdom's social and religious life. In return for their material comfort and political influence, the clerics supported the royal family's authority and endorsed their controversial policy for economic development. The contradiction between aggressively pursuing modernization, while rejecting Western values grew more intense as more Saudis moved into cities. Televisions, Western products, and foreign workers exposed conservative Wahhabis to radically different ways of living.

After 1973, rising petroleum prices provided windfall profits that enabled the state to pump hundreds of billions into elegant suspension bridges, blacktop roads, state-of-the-art hospitals, and glimmering mosques. A generous Saudi welfare state provided citizens free education and healthcare, subsidized housing, and generous living allotments. While oil wealth introduced Saudis with unimaginable modern luxuries, their society's dramatic transformation proved unsettling to Wahhabis that had long identified material luxury and carnal pleasure as mortal sins. The booming oil economy also brought an influx of hundreds of thousands of foreigners, particularly Palestinians and South Asian whose Islamic ideas and customs conflicted with more austere Saudi traditions.

The tension between modernizing and protecting tradition became embedded at every level of the Saudi state. The royal family appoints the ruling monarch, while 7,000 princes serve leading roles inside the state bureaucracy, regional councils, and municipal governments. This autocracy is checked not by an elected parliament, but by *majlis*, traditional tribal councils where tribesmen pay personal homage to their sheiks, receive gifts, air grievances, and submit petitions. While oil financed a generous welfare state, since the 1980s the standard of living in most Persian Gulf states has fallen because oil prices cannot keep pace with rising birth rates.

By 1990, half of the Middle East's population lived in cities and agriculture's economic role declined sharply. Throughout the Persian Gulf, in a network of hypermodern desert cities, a lost generation of young males drift from one aimless amusement to another during a prolonged adolescence. Many hold degrees in Islamic philosophy that poorly prepares them for the modern workplace. Simultaneously, generous living allotments discourage Saudis from performing manual labor. As a result, Saudi authorities import millions of foreign workers to clean, cook, and perform other menial tasks. Saudi youth can pass hours playing Nintendo or cruising shopping malls, but many fail to land a meaningful job, while struggling to reconcile their modern way of life with their puritanical values. The lavish—often hedonistic—lifestyles of Saudi princes have come under increasing criticism as many Saudis worry that state development programs are failing to diversify the economy for the postoil age. Qatar has proven most successful at training an educated workforce with an emphasis on

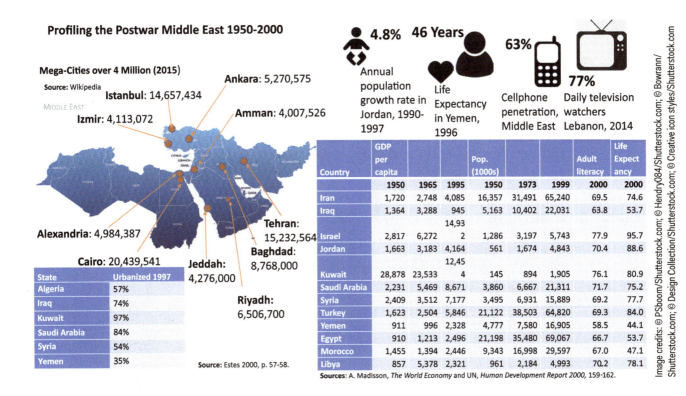

technical skills and female education. Kuwait's ruling family now finances most state spending from its foreign investments. Abu Dhabi has transformed itself into a global financial center. States with fewer oil resources like Bahrain, Yemen, and Tunisia, however, have struggled to maintain traditional subsidies for the urban poor, to generate jobs for university graduates or to accommodate dissidents. As we shall see in Chapter 12, many Middle East states are fragile because ruling families and regional dictators enjoy only marginal legitimacy. The 2011 **Arab Spring** movement showed that regional regimes reliant upon coercion to maintain authority are vulnerable to populist reform movements that exploit emerging digital media to escape traditional censorship.

Oil and Water

Oil shaped postwar Middle Eastern history, but water will determine its future. Water represents a consistent thread running through the Arab-Israeli conflict. Control over this vital resource continues to impede attempts to broker a permanent settlement. After the Six-Day War, Israel gained control over most of the Jordan Watershed. Israel has subsequently used military incursions into Lebanon to prevent Syria, Lebanon, and Jordan from developing tributaries of the Jordan River. Israel has invested heavily in irrigation projects to support its commercial agriculture, with the Israeli parliament commissioning elaborate water works that tap the aquifers affiliated with the Sea of Galilee. Palestinians in the Occupied Territories complain that the Israeli state diverts their water towards illegal settlements. For example, Israeli settlers in the West Bank consume eight times more water than Palestinians. Additionally, Israel siphons water from West Bank aquifers, directing it towards farms inside Israel, while Palestinians are prohibited from drilling deep wells. Palestinians are forced to rely on unreliable shallow wells that often run dry during the summer. When Israeli Prime Minister **Ariel Sharon** established the trajectory of the Separation Wall in 2002, he sought not only to envelope Israeli settlements, but also to secure water resources and infrastructure.

Both Libya and Saudi Arabia have leveraged their oil wealth to build massive water projects. During the 1970s, arid Saudi Arabia feared retaliation for the Organization of Petroleum Exporting Countries (OPEC) embargo. This culminated in a massive irrigation project that pumped water from underground aquifers to nurture a short-lived wheat industry. Since 1988, however, wheat production has plummeted as the aquifers started to dry out. Similarly, Qaddafi spent billions to construct an aqueduct from aquifers in the Southern Libyan Desert to quench thirsty coastal cities. Both projects, however, tapped fossil water from aquifers that were no longer being replenished. With rapidly growing populations, the Middle East faces an uncertain future. As its oil fields pass peak production, its long-term prospects are constrained by a lack of water, the source of life inside this arid region.

Palestinian Intifada and the Oslo Process, 1987 to 2000

For the Palestinians, the Six-Day War erased any realistic chance for refugees to return home. Worse, another 300,000 Palestinians had been driven from their homes, and millions now live under Israeli military rule in what became known as the **Occupied Territories**.

With little chance of defeating Israel, leaders of neighboring Arab states increasingly looked upon Palestinians not as persecuted brothers, but as an economic burden and security threat. Palestinians began to rally around the **Palestinian Liberation Organization** (PLO) that had been founded in 1964. Increasingly, this organization came under **Yasser Arafat's** control as he restructured it into guerilla movement. Israeli control over the Occupied Territories made it difficult to strike the Jewish state directly after 1967. This led Arafat to launch terrorist strikes against Jews abroad. The famed Black September Cell seized international headlines during the 1972 Munich Olympics by taking Jewish athletes hostage, before a botched German rescue attempt ended in disaster.

The PLO's increasing militancy began to worry Arab leaders hosting Palestinian refugee camps. In 1970, Jordan's King Hussein cracked down against PLO militants operating with impunity from his state. In 1971, he expelled the PLO's leadership for scheming against him. Egyptian President Anwar El Sadat similarly turned his back on Palestinians when he negotiated a separate peace with Israel. In 1977, Sadat flew to Tel Aviv and addressed the Israeli parliament in an historic speech. This shuttle diplomacy culminated in the 1978 Camp David Accords where Egypt recognized Israel in return for the Sinai. As part of this deal, Sadat insisted that Israel retain control over the troublesome Gaza strip.

After three decades of conflict, Sadat represented the first Arab leader to accept Israel's existence in 1978. This concession enabled Sadat to secure return of the Sinai and US aid, but also stimulated Arab resentment that culminated in his assassination.

The First Intifada, 1987 to 1992

By 1987, the situation of Palestinians inside the Occupied Territories had grown dire. Economically, the Gaza strip represents a densely populated refugee camp, with insufficient natural resources, including water, to sustain its population. Occupied by the Israeli Defense Forces (IDF), Palestinians have few rights or prospects, while being subject to continual harassment. Many middle-class Palestinians fled the "occupation" during the 1970s, seeking work in the Gulf States or educational opportunities in the West. High birth rates, however, meant that the Arab population in the Occupied Territories kept climbing.

In December 1987, at the Erez Crossing, an Israeli military truck crashed into a Palestinian passenger car killing four. Grief at the funeral brewed into a demonstration that sparked unrest throughout the Occupied Territories. In what would become known as the **First *Intifada***, Palestinians protested their "occupation" by closing their shops, boycotting Israeli goods, painting defiant graffiti, and refusing to pay taxes or use Israeli license plates. The demonstrators constructed barricades, confronted Israeli checkpoints, and young boys tossed stones at Israeli soldiers. Initially, the IDF responded through "nonlethal" tactics, using plastic bullets, "night sticks," and tear gas to break up demonstrations. When "breaking bone," measures failed to subdue the *intifada*, the IDF resorted to harsher methods, including the bulldozing of Palestinian houses to create a "security perimeter," invading Palestinian homes in the middle of the night to search for bombs and confiscating Palestinian property. In November 1988, Arafat offered peace, but Prime Minister Yitzhak Shamir rejected the idea of negotiating with terrorists. The deal breaker was Israel's unwillingness to give up control over the occupied territories where many Jews had settled and upon whose resources Israel had grown dependent.

Despite Israeli "restraint," by 1990, 12,000 Palestinians died compared to 160 Jews. The *intifada* persisted, however, because it united Palestinians like never before and succeeded in grabbing the international spotlight. Western news outlets highlighted the brutality of Israeli troops and the desperate conditions of Palestinians living under occupation. During the 1970s, terrorism had provoked international criticism of Palestinian nationalism. In 1989, the UN General Assembly condemned Israel for "war crimes and an affront to humanity."[4] For Israel, the *intifada* represented a public relations disaster. Domestic liberals joined with international critics, questioning their government's strong-armed tactics that included targeted assassinations of Hamas leaders and beating rock throwing children. Many Israeli hardliners came to realize that security ultimately depended upon a political solution. Palestinian leaders reached the same conclusion after they disastrously supported Saddam Hussein's 1990 invasion of Kuwait. This eroded international sympathy for Palestinians and alienated their Arab backers and supporters. By 1991, the *intifada* lost steam, but both sides had come to appreciate the need for a diplomatic settlement.

The Road to Oslo, 1993 to 1995

In a secret Oslo meeting in 1993, the PLO met Israeli representatives face-to-face for the first time. Both sides accepted that peace required a **two-state solution**. For Israelis to feel secure, Palestinians also needed to achieve a state that could meet their aspirations for a better future. Recognizing deeply rooted animosity, however, the Oslo process resolved on a series of trust-building steps. Each side would make minor concessions in order to accumulate the good will necessary to reach a comprehensive final settlement.

The peace process depended on unlikely partners. Newly elected Israeli Prime Minister Yitzhak Rabin's impeccable military credentials enabled Israelis skeptical of Arafat to trust that their government could engage in diplomacy without compromising their security. Yasser Arafat had to convince Palestinian militants that negotiation with the enemy would deliver major concessions. The Oslo agreement was sealed in famous September 13, 1993, handshake at Camp David. A grim Rabin wondered whether he could trust the mastermind of Palestinian terrorism. A grinning Arafat seemed relieved to escape decades of marginalization. Oslo transformed him into the Arab world's leading statesman destined to take charge over a fledgling Palestinian state.

As leader of the Likud Party, Israeli Prime Minister Netanyahu has played an influential role in unilaterally imposing a settlement upon Palestinians after the assassination of Yitzak Rabin.

From 1993 to 1995, both Arafat and Rabin struggled to push Oslo forward as militant fringes on both sides tried to sabotage the deal. The most visible symbol of Oslo was Arafat's return to take charge of the Palestinian authority, but the momentum behind Oslo dissipated well before Rabin's assassination on November 1995 by a crazed American Zionist that deemed his peace efforts treason. Without Rabin, the Oslo process lacked a champion to bring Israelis to the table. In 1996, the hardliner **Benjamin Netanyahu** became prime minster and froze the Oslo process. From Ramallah, Arafat continued to exercise autonomy over roughly 12 percent of the Occupied Territories, but Netanyahu ruled out further compromises and cynically accelerated Jewish colonization on the West Bank. Palestinians retaliated with a fervent campaign of suicide bombing. Arafat publicly denounced terrorism, claiming he could not control Hamas, while blaming suicide attacks on Israeli provocations and violence by Israeli settlers. Arafat called for reopening Oslo, but after one high-profile meeting, Netanyahu chose to ignore him.

Lost Opportunity for Peace, 1995 to 2000

The virtually unknown Ehud Barak's election in 1999 signalled the Israeli public's fatigue with Palestinian suicide bombing. Prime Minister Barak initiated a dramatic shift in Israeli foreign policy, withdrawing from Southern Lebanon, offering to negotiate with Syria, and seeking out Clinton to revive Oslo. In 2000, Ehud Barak, Bill Clinton, and Yasser Arafat assembled at Camp David. The Israeli Prime Minister surprised Chairman Arafat by unveiling plans for a comprehensive settlement to resolve all outstanding issues. Clinton worked day and night to hammer out a compromise, but Arafat protested that Barak's deal did not go far enough. An exasperated Barak prodded Arafat to consider that Palestinians would never get a better deal. He had already offered Arafat more than he had been authorized. When Clinton failed to break the stalemate, Oslo collapsed. Many blamed Arafat, but the failed summit also hinted at problems in the Oslo framework, which presumed that escalating compromises would enhance trust. In fact, this approach made the peace process vulnerable to extremists. With strong leadership, extremists might have been knuckled down, but leaving the crucial compromises on Jerusalem, Israeli settlements, and the future boundaries of both states to the last stage of the process, neither Barak nor Arafat could muster the necessary support to finalize a deal both sides deemed acceptable.

With the collapse of the Camp David Summit, Barak's government quickly fell. The breaking point came in September 2000 following Sharon's impromptu "visit" to the Temple Mount under armed guard. A second Palestinian *intifada* chased Barak from office and allowed Sharon to win election as Israel's next prime minister. Sharon's peace plan took fragments from Oslo plan and sought to impose a settlement upon Palestinians. The center piece for this strategy was the construction of a **separation wall** between Israeli settlements and Palestinian territory. Ostensibly constructed to interdict suicide bombers, this barrier was erected on occupied territory. By evacuating fledgling Jewish settlements in Gaza and Samaria in 2005, while claiming 17 percent of West Bank for Israel, Sharon effectively imposed the future boundaries for their respective states. Since 2006, there have been violent clashes between Israeli forces and Palestinian militants, including Israeli incursions into areas governed by the Palestinian authority. With living conditions in Gaza deteriorating rapidly, the prospect for an amicable settlement appears grim.

Summary: The Postwar Middle East

At the end of the twentieth century, the Middle East was more urban, more integrated into the world economy, and more comfortable with modern technology and practices. After World War II, secular nationalists had challenged European hegemony and launched ambitious programs for state building and economic modernization. Following the Six-Day War, however, the mantle for reform passed to Islamists. In Iran, the Ayatollah Khomeini overthrew the Shah and established an Islamic Republic. Khomeini's Islamic revolution coincided with a broader spiritual "awakening." The 1970s oil boom had spurred rapid transformation, forcing many Arabs rooted in local communities and traditions to adapt to urban living and "modern" culture. In Persian Gulf cities, the tension between Western cultural norms and tradition proved particularly intense, stimulating various forms of fundamentalism. The Palestinian occupation, Soviet invasion of Afghanistan, and the Iran–Iraq War disrupted regional politics; undermined the legitimacy of the region's authoritarian states; and cultivated a growing sense of Pan-Islamic identity.

Questions for Critical Thought

1. What made Gamal Abdel Nasser such a popular leader? How did his vision of modernization conflict with Islamists, Britain's interests, and the region's conservative monarchs?
2. In what ways did the Six Days War reshape the modern Middle East?

3. What were the principal causes of the Iranian Revolution? In what ways did Khomeini influence Islamists outside Iran?
4. How did Sayyid Qutb and the Soviet War in Afghanistan contribute to the rise of militant Jihadism?
5. In your view, why did the Camp David Summit in 2000 collapse?
6. Is political Islam fundamentally hostile to Western modernity or does it represent a newer version of anti-colonialism?

Suggestions for Further Reading

- Amin, S. *Modern Afghanistan: A History of Struggle and Survival.* 1st ed. London: I.B. Tauris & Co., 2006.
- Cleveland, W. *A History of the Modern Middle East.* 3rd ed. Boulder, CO: Westview Press, 2004.
- Dawisha, A. *Arab Nationalism in the Twentieth Century.* Princeton, NJ: Princeton University Press, 2003.
- Entessar, N. *The Iranian Revolution.* New York: Oxford University Press, 2012.
- Kramer, M. *Arab Awakening and Islamic Revival: The Politics of Ideas in the Middle East.* New Brunswick, NJ: Transaction Publishers, 1996.
- Lacey, R. *Inside the Kingdom: Kings, Clerics, Modernists, Terrorists and the Struggle for Saudi Arabia.* New York: Viking, 2009.
- Morris, B. *Righteous Victims: A History of the Zionist-Arab Conflict, 1881–2001.* New York: Vintage, 2001.
- Pappé, I. *The Modern Middle East.* 2nd ed. Oxon, UK: Routledge, 2010.

Notes

1. Quoted in John Melady, *Pearson's Prize: Canada and the Suez Crisis* (Toronto: Dundurn Group, 2006), 109.
2. Baghdad Pact, February 4, 1955, accessed August 1, 2019, http://avalon.law.yale.edu/20th_century/baghdad.asp.
3. Fordham University, "Statement by Soviet Ministry of Foreign Affairs on Security in the Near and Middle East," April 16, 1955, accessed August 1, 2019, http://legacy.fordham.edu/halsall/mod/1955Soviet-baghdad1.html.
4. UN General Assembly, "Report of the Special Committee to Investigate Israeli Practices Affecting the Human Rights of the Population of the Occupied Territories," December 8, 1988, accessed August 1, 2019, http://www.un.org/documents/ga/res/43/a43r058.htm.

Chapter 8
Sub-Saharan Africa

Chapter Outline

- Introduction: Postcolonial Africa
- Diminishing Hope, 1960 to 1972
- Turn towards Kleptocracy, 1973 to 1986
- Postcolonial Culture and Society
- Democratic Wave, 1987 to 2000
- Rwanda's Tragedy
- Conclusion

Africa Timeline

Hope and Development 1960-1973
- 1948 Establishment of Apartheid
- 1957 Ghana's Independence
- 1960 Sharpeville Massacre
- 1960-1964 Congo Crisis
- 1963 OAU Summit
- 1967-1971 Nigeria's Biafran War

Africa's Lost Decade 1973-1986
- 1971-1979 Idi Amin's Reign
- 1974 Carnation Revolution
- 1975-2002 Angolan Civil War
- 1976 Soweto Uprising
- 1980 Zimbabwe's Independence
- 1982 Start of Debt Crisis
- 1983-1985 Ethiopian Famine

Democratic Wave 1987-Present
- 1987-88 Battle of Cuito Cuanavale
- 1988 Gorbachev's new thinking
- 1990 Namibian Independence
- 1990 De Klerk legalizes ANC
- 1994 Mandela wins South African election
- 1994 Rwandan Genocide
- 1995 Execution of Ken Saro-Wiwa
- 1997 Mobutu's Overthrow

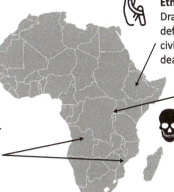

1960 Léopold Sédar Senghor's "non" stance triggers rapid decolonization of French colonial Africa.

1974 Carnation Revolution: triggers collapse of white settler nationalist regimes in Portugal's colonies.

1982 African Debt Crisis: unleashes wave of political instability across Sub-Saharan Africa.

1983-1985 Ethiopian Famine: Draught, deforestation and civil war spur deadly famine.

1994 Rwandan genocide: exposes the dark side of 'democratic' wave

1994 Mandela's election: ends Apartheid in South Africa

Image credits: © Nasi_lemak/Shutterstock.com; © Chippo Medved/Shutterstock.com; © Paramouse/Shutterstock.com; © AVIcon/Shutterstock.com; © Nasi_Lemak/Shutterstock.com; © Zaur Rahimov/Shutterstock.com; © Martial Red/Shutterstock.com; © Zern Liew/Shutterstock.com

Introduction: Postcolonial Africa

Westerners have long imagined Africa as the dark continent. Why does Africa lag other world regions? Geographically, the continent lacks navigable rivers and natural ports. Historically, these disadvantages isolated the continent's communities. Today, insufficient infrastructure still complicates resource extraction and trade. Largely situated inside the tropics, Sub-Saharan Africa's arid climate and mostly marginal soils also leave it poorly suited for large-scale cereal cultivation. Africa is also haunted by a bloody colonial past. The slave trade devastated Africa centuries before its formal conquest. Under Western rule, repression, underinvestment, and ethnic parcelling created political communities that proved fragile after independence. In a 1964 book, Kwame Nkrumah lamented that the African independence movement failed to liberate Africans from a web of "neocolonial" influences that the superpowers, foreign investors, and international lending institutions wove around Africa. These restrained postcolonial policy choices and skewed development towards foreign interests rather than indigenous priorities. First-generation leaders, however, shared part of the blame. Many postcolonial states pursued faulty modernization strategies that culminated in inefficient industries and unsustainable levels of debt.

Africa's postcolonial history divides into three mains eras. Dreams for a better future animated the decade immediately following independence. High commodity prices powered economic growth and social investment throughout the 1960s despite mounting instability. The 1973 Organization of Petroleum Exporting Countries (OPEC) oil shock, however, drove up regional production costs, depressed export prices, and deprived Sub-Saharan states of badly needed investment capital. Throughout Africa, civilian governments succumbed to military coups, corruption, and autocratic rule. By 1982, Africa reached rock bottom as an international debt crisis inaugurated a lost decade punctuated by drought and civil war. Western-imposed structural adjustment programs magnified Africa's problems, spurring the collapse of uncompetitive industries, while driving millions of impoverished peasants to cities lacking services, housing, or jobs. The end of the Cold War offered Africans a fresh start. White settler regimes collapsed in Africa's southern tier, populist movements chased despots from office across the continent. By the twenty-first century, debt relief, foreign investment, and digital technologies rekindled regional growth and restored hope for a better future, even if stability and economic progress remain uneven.

Diminishing Hope, 1960 to 1972

Kwame Nkrumah declared the 1960s Africa's decade. Few witnessing the sudden collapse of European colonial regimes from 1960 to 1966 could disagree. From Leopoldville to Accra, populist coalitions sprung into being, challenging their white rulers and foreign oppression. Lavish independence ceremonies seemed to herald a new age of racial equality, social progress, and economic development. As testified by a Congolese citizen: "Before Independence, we dreamed that it would bring us masses of marvelous things. All of that was to descend upon us from the sky. . . . Deliverance and salvation."[1] To usher in a better future, postcolonial leaders sought to modernize their economies. **African socialism** presented a popular model for development that sought to industrialize local economies, insulate the economy from foreign influences, and align state institutions more closely with local traditions. At the international level, African leaders held conferences aimed at reconfiguring the international system to better represent people of color. Although the 1960s independence movement resulted in a formal transfer of sovereignty, colonial wounds were also deeply etched into African institutions; its political culture, and psyche. Self-rule enabled Africans to invest in schools and hospitals, but the region's underdeveloped economies also required a massive capital infusion to catch up with the rest of the world. During the early 1960s, few Africans appreciated the difficulty of modernizing inside an international system dominated by Western powers, institutions, and investors.

Pan-African Dream

The **Congo Crisis** impressed upon postcolonial African leaders how the Cold War threatened their hard-won sovereignty. At the May 25, 1963, **Conference for African Unity** in Addis Ababa, Ethiopia, thirty-one African heads of state signed a formal declaration pledging to respect each other's territorial integrity, while declaring neutrality in the Cold War. The Addis Ababa Conference gave clearest expression to the **Pan-African** dream. African American intellectuals like Marcus Garvey had decades before stressed the solidarity uniting black Africans with other victims of white racism, slavery, and colonial oppression. The delegates at Addis Ababa, however, struggled to translate Pan-Africanism into coherent policy. Delegates eloquently endorsed racial equality and human rights, but found little agreement in terms of creating a concrete framework for collaborative development. Kwame Nkrumah led the Casablanca bloc advocating for a formal federation to confront the West and orchestrate regional development projects. The Monrovia bloc, led by Senegal's **Léopold Sédar Senghor**, resisted federation. Ultimately, the **Organization for African Unity** never matured beyond a talking shop. Following Nkrumah's fall in 1966, the aspiration for a larger African unity "transcending ethnic and national differences" lost much of its appeal.[2] African leaders became preoccupied with governing their own fractious states. The most tangible legacy of the 1963 summit was acceptance of current boundaries. In the late nineteenth-century European scramble for Africa, the colonial powers had quite arbitrarily grouped ethnic and linguistic groups. African leaders, however, recognized that revisiting these boundaries now would open Pandora's box.

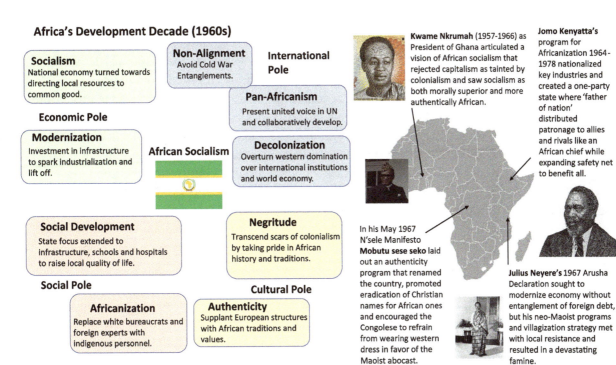

As noted in Chapter 3, African socialism embraced multiple values. Inside Tanzania, Kenya, Ghana, and the Congo, first-generation leaders translated these values into divergent programs for national development.

In their quest to reallocate global resources, Pan-Africanists formed an Afro-Asian Bloc inside the United Nations (UN) that advocated for Western financial atonement for the sins of slavery and colonialism. Nikita Khrushchev emerged as an enthusiastic supporter, infamously bear-hugging several of the fifteen African leaders joining the General Assembly in 1960. The **Non-Aligned Movement** (NAM) informally allied with the USSR to pass UN resolutions condemning Western colonialism, Apartheid, and Zionism. Although anti-imperial resolutions grabbed headlines, they did little to alter the flows of global capital. Institutions of international finance, like the World Bank, remained under the control of Western bankers and continued to disburse aid according to a traditional cost–benefit analysis. Western states mostly refused to increase their level of aid, or divert capital towards "social development" projects like schools and hospitals.

Waning of the Revolutionary State

Postcolonial Africa was born in revolution. During the late 1950s, African demonstrators joined boycotts and stared down police truncheons in their fight for racial equality, social justice, and independence. This revolutionary spirit nurtured postcolonial programs to channel indigenous resources towards the common good and open a road towards a better future. By the mid-1960s, however, African Socialism lost momentum as postcolonial states turned increasingly autocratic. Many postcolonial constitutions had erected parliamentary institutions that required consensus to operate. This proved difficult to maintain inside a postcolonial climate of elevated expectations and sharp sectarian divisions. Europe's colonial powers had inscribed sectional divisions into African states. Reinforcing tribal loyalties, codifying ethnic differences and elevating particular chiefs as colonial surrogates served to keep Africans divided, while augmenting European authority as an indispensable mediator. Although regional independence movements mostly succeeded in uniting Africans against their colonial oppressor, they proved less successful in cultivating a deep sense of national loyalty that transcended a patchwork of local and ethnic identities. As postcolonial leaders braced for the herculean task of economic development, most did not fully appreciate the challenge of nation-building. Inside multiethnic states like the Congo, Nigeria, and Rwanda, democratic elections galvanized sectarian parties with incompatible state visions. Throughout Africa, weak state institutions inherited from the colonial regime struggled to maintain public order or social consensus. Various sectarian groups vied for control over national resources, shares of the state's revenue, or posts inside the government. Inside political communities long conditioned by state violence, and unaccustomed to democratic practice or the rule of law, postcolonial elections often sowed dissension rather than consensus. Managing postcolonial tensions was further complicated by the fact that leaders like **Patrice Lumumba** inherited few indigenous professionals to administer state agencies, maintain order, or provide basic services. In the Congo, almost the entire state bureaucracy was white. There were no high-ranking African bureaucrats inside the government at independence, and only 422 Africans enrolled in local universities in 1959.[3] This made it difficult for first-generation leaders to deliver upon their promise for a better postcolonial future.

Despite the turbulence accompanying the birth of Africa's revolutionary states, throughout the early 1960s, most Africans saw their living standards climb despite the region's structural **underdevelopment**. The colonial state had concentrated on investments in infrastructure that could boost exports. With Africans taking charge, postcolonial regimes now invested in social development projects, particularly education and healthcare. They also borrowed from the World Bank, Western governments, and foreign corporations to construct critical infrastructure: airports, dams, hospitals, and highways. Increased investment brought jobs, electricity, running water, cars, and modern healthcare to Africa. The trappings of modernity particularly transformed colonial capitals. Progress radiated out more slowly to dusty villages where most Africans still lived. Primitive one-room schools opened inside many villages, but they were often cut off from paved roads and electricity. Roving nurses inoculated children against measles, polio, and other infectious diseases spurring a rapid advance in life expectancy. By the 1970s, literacy rates spiked up and mortality rates drifted down. Foreign capital, however, came with strings attached. Loans saddled postcolonial states with interest payments, while bilateral treaties typically forced African states to buy industrial equipment or sell their exports on unfavorable terms.

Nigeria's Disintegration, 1960 to 1978

Nigeria well illustrates the forces of postcolonial disintegration. Like most of its African peers, Nigeria had been cobbled together through European intrigues during the late nineteenth century. In their efforts to control trade along the Niger River, the British had united the Southern Ibo and Eastern Yoruba farmers, who were Christian, with the Northern Islamic Kingdom housing the Hausa and Fulani tribes. By World War II, the British had come to highly regard Nigeria's prospects. But seventy years of British rule had not instilled a deep sense of nation among Nigeria's linguistic, ethnic, and tribal groupings. Southern Nigeria developed a dynamic export economy focused upon cocoa, palm oil, and rubber. The Ibo contributed a class of educated businessmen and professionals that played a particularly prominent role inside the British local administration. A newly discovered petroleum field offered a promising asset for Nigeria's future development. As African nationalism awakened across the continent in the late 1950s, British administrators rushed to prepare Nigeria for independence. In a belated bid to suppress mounting tension among Nigeria's three principal ethnic groups, British officials established a parliamentary system with a federalized structure that conferred considerable regional autonomy. Some British administrators feared this structure would rip Nigerian society apart along sectarian lines, but momentum towards independence could no longer be stopped.

Postcolonial Nigeria confirms that in multiethnic societies, democracy can exacerbate friction. After independence in 1960, three parties emerged to represent each of Nigeria's principal regions. Under Abubakar Balewa, a moderate Northern prime minister, peace initially prevailed. Beneath the surface, however, factional forces were building as ethnic parties resorted to deceit, violence, and illegal means to dispute the census that served as the basis for shares of Nigeria's lucrative oil revenue. In 1966, Balewa was assassinated in an abortive coup by junior officers. This inaugurated a period of intense instability that shattered the fragile political system the British had put into place.

> Is parliamentary decline in postcolonial Africa an indictment of Sub-Saharan tribalism or a reflection of a cynical European strategy of colonial state building?

Nigeria's disintegration climaxed in May 1967 when the Ibo launched a bid for secession and exclusive control of the country's oil wealth. The resulting **Biafran War** would implicate multinational corporations, Britain, the Soviet Union, and several other powers on opposing sides. When the conflict mercifully ended in 1970, over two million Nigerians had lost their lives. Victorious General **Yakubu Gowon** preached reconciliation in his "No victor, no vanquished" speech. This set the stage for the Ibo's mostly peaceful reassimilation into Nigerian society. Gowon, however, had no solution for Nigeria's factionalized political system. In 1975, Gowon was overthrown. Subsequently, multiple successors have proven incapable of uprooting corruption. Since 1975, Nigeria has avoided civil war, but the state has continually veered between constitutions, military coups, and short-lived civilian governments. Africa's most populous state well illustrates how the process of decolonization often culminated in fragile polities that failed to meet popular expectations for development.

Idi Amin's Despotism, 1971 to 1978

"Strong man rule" represented an increasingly common theme in Africa by the early 1970s. Authoritarianism represented a response to internal strife and factionalism. African despots often dispensed patronage among allies like tribal chiefs, while retooling the postcolonial state security apparatus to silence opponents, particularly rival ethnic groups. Arguably, **Jomo Kenyatta** (1963–1978) proved Africa's most benign despot. Over a long career, Kenyatta managed to incorporate the political opposition and rival ethnic groups into a single-party state through an elaborate patronage system. Africa's most colorful dictator during the postcolonial era, Uganda's **Idi Amin Dada** (1971–1979) proved more sadistic. Amin originally joined the British Army's King African's Rifles as a cook. Like many contemporary officers, Amin enjoyed a meteoric rise inside the Ugandan army after independence. Amin's affable personality, ruthlessness, and alliance with Milton Obote keyed his ascension as armed forces chief. To preempt his own arrest for graft in 1971, Amin launched a coup against his boss and former patron Obote. At first, cheering crowds in Kampala gathered to greet the towering 6 feet 4 inch Amin. Charming and gregarious, "Big Daddy" connected well with the common man; cracking jokes, singing, and dancing with the crowd. His charm also enabled him to clown with the international media. To solidify his violent takeover, Amin freed political prisoners and promised elections. Few noticed that in driving Obote into exile Amin also opened up the nondescript State Research Bureau. Suppression and torture constituted its core business. This was revealed in 1972 when Obote's supporters invaded from Tanzania. The invasion triggered deep-seated insecurities inside Amin and awoke his violent nature.

Amin relished in bending intellectuals, arrogant whites, and foreigners to his authority. Uneducated and insecure, Amin placated his ego by inventing grandiose titles like "His Excellency, President for Life, Field Marshal Al Hadji Doctor Idi Amin Dada, VC, DSO, MC, Lord of All the Beasts of the Earth and Fishes of the Seas, and Conqueror of the British Empire in Africa in General and Uganda in Particular."

Highly self-conscious about his fourth-grade education, Amin unleashed a campaign of terror that led to thousands of bodies washing up along the banks of the Nile. Many of Amin's victims were Obote supporters among the Acholi and Lango, but they also included religious leaders and intellectuals Amin judged guilty of condescension. To solidify his power, Amin promoted his own Kakwa tribe and fellow Muslims inside the state and security apparatus. South Sudanese ex-patriots were also recruited into Uganda's army.

Amin's flamboyance was captured in a memorable stunt where he forced British businessmen to carry him around on a throne suspended from their shoulders like a tribal chief.

Amin's fly-by-the-pants leadership style initially entertained Western audiences. The traits of a schoolyard bully, however, did not translate well into managing a modern state. Amin's most memorable initiative was declaring "economic war" upon foreigners. Following his "mentor" Muammar Qaddafi's example, Amin summarily nationalized eighty-five British businesses. This included a boisterous order evicting 80,000 Asians. Despite their longtime residence in Uganda, Asians were given ninety days to leave Uganda with all they could "carry on their backs." Amin's nationalization drive initially proved popular. Despite numbering less than 1 percent of the population, Asians controlled nearly two-thirds of the nonfood economy. Following their summary eviction, however, Uganda's industries grounded to a halt, food rotted away in fields, hospitals were emptied of their staff. Expropriated businesses were handed over to Amin supporters who pillaged and mismanaged them, sending an already fragile economy into a tailspin.

The turning point for Amin's regime came in June 1976. After Palestinian terrorists hijacked an Air France plane, Amin granted them permission to land at Entebbe National Airport. There, Amin kept the terrorists well fed as they menaced 103 hostages in front of international cameras. On the night of July 3 to 4, however, Israeli commandos launched a daring rescue operation. The **Entebbe Raid** freed most of the hostages, destroyed much of Uganda's air force, and exposed Amin as a paper tiger. In a fit of anger, Amin murdered a 75-year-old Jewish hostage who had been taken to a local hospital to treat dehydration. This exemplified his desperate strategy to silence mounting doubt about his rule through bluster. Taking to the radio in 1977, Amin proclaimed himself "conqueror of the British Empire," adding the designation CBE to the panoply of titles and awards he had already showered upon himself including "Lord of all beasts of the land and fish of the seas." The medals weighing down Amin's uniform, however, could not mask his growing unpopularity. In a bid to distract his people from his economic mismanagement, Amin unwisely provoked war with Tanzania in 1978. Within months, Amin's regime had collapsed. The self-proclaimed "King of Scotland" fled to Saudi Arabia, irked that his archenemy Obote had bested him and returned to power. While Amin was a clown, his rule foreshadowed a deeper African trend towards despotism. Junta and autocratic rulers hijacked the revolutionary state and discredited African socialism. Throughout the 1970, African states were often retooled from a vehicle for collective progress into instruments for supporting a strongman and his ruling group. Western observers often invoked the term **kleptocracy**, or government by thieves, to describe this transformation. State collapse was magnified by the 1973 Oil Shock that sent many state balance sheets into deficit. Economic stagnation intensified corruption, slowed further infrastructural investments, and accelerated the evolution of national militaries into instruments for repressing ethnic minorities.

Neocolonial Settlement

Until the 1970s, Sub-Saharan states mostly honored their OAU commitment to respect each other's sovereignty. Initially, this helped most escape the worst effects of proxy war. The 1960 to 1965 Congo Crisis had exposed the Soviet Union's lack of naval and air lift capability. This made the Kremlin wary about supporting African regimes and served warning to postcolonial leaders hoping to rely upon Soviet aid. For the United States, the Congo Crisis illustrated the necessity of supporting unsavory dictators like Mobutu. The West warmed to "strong men" that they believed necessary to keep a lid upon ethnic fissures. Until 1975, however, Sub-Saharan Africa was not considered a strategic priority in either Washington or Moscow.

Relative stability was partially attributable to a phenomenon that Nkrumah derisively labeled **neocolonialism**. As noted in Chapter 3, de Gaulle's grand scheme for keeping the French Empire in Africa alive collapsed in 1960. However, the French Union was unofficially revived over the subsequent decade through a series of bilateral treaties. The precise terms of these treaties varied, but generally a defensive treaty provided modern arms, equipment, and training for African forces in return for a French right to military bases. An associated economic treaty provided the former colony substantial capital in return for a commitment to buy machinery from French industrial firms. After the 1962 Algerian fiasco, this treaty system enabled France to restore its influence over Sub-Saharan Africa. Given, Belgium and Britain's retreat from the continent, French influence increased. For disgruntled nationalists like Nkrumah, the Africa emerging in the early 1970s was a grotesque transfiguration of the liberation they had fought for. Repressive African regimes typically embraced neo-colonialist policies and abandoned comprehensive development in return for foreign arms, technical assistance, and support critical for suppressing internal enemies. The Cold War international environment intensified corruption and extinguished the last embers of Pan-African idealism.

Turn towards Kleptocracy, 1973 to 1986

The 1973 OPEC embargo disrupted the global economy and exposed flaws in the Sub-Saharan strategy for modernization. Over the next two decades, Africa's terms of trade steadily diminished as the prices for commodities Africans sold on world markets declined, while prices for imports ranging from oil to rice and manufactured goods rose on a relative basis. Sub-Saharan Africa hit rock bottom after 1982 when regional economies became mired in a global debt crisis. From 1970 to 1980, Sub-Saharan Africa's debt had steadily climbed from US$6 billion to US$60.9 billion as regional leaders tried to offset inflationary pressures through borrowing. Similar to Latin America, rising interest rates caught African states in a debt trap. Given that African debts were not sufficiently large to threaten the global financial system, however, they were rarely serviced by foreign lenders. Through penalties and accrued interest, African debt levels steadily climbed to $281 billion by 1995, a level equating to 77 percent of regional export earnings.

Debt service, and the inability to raise capital, pushed African economies into a deep recession. Throughout the 1980s, most Sub-Saharan economies contracted year over year. International Monetary Fund (IMF) imposed austerity measures exacerbated this downturn. In return for temporary liquidity, African states were forced to adopt **structural adjustment** mechanisms that redirected large shares of state revenue from education and healthcare to servicing debt. This accelerated a plunge in regional living standards that often wiped out the developmental gains of previous decades. Rapid population growth amplified Africa's woes. From 1954 to 2000, Sub-Saharan Africa's population jumped from 224 million to over 800 million. The combination of population growth and economic contraction pushed one in three Africans into "absolute poverty," defined by the UN as being unable to meet their most "basic needs."

A survey of select national statistics reveals the **Lost Decade's** heavy toll. Another striking feature is the poor correspondence between state size, population, and the value of its natural resources compared to its metrics for development. Small, underdeveloped, and landlocked states like Botswana managed to achieve a middling standard of living through good governance. Meanwhile, giant states with valuable natural resources, like Democratic Republic of the Congo and Nigeria, now rank among the world's bottom in terms of human development. While Africa continues to urbanize rapidly, levels are highly variable, and not necessarily an indicator of prosperity. South Africa is exceptional in having achieved a high level of industrialization, but its post-Apartheid society remains highly stratified between a wealthy, mostly white, upper class and a poor predominantly black underclass, despite redistributive measures.

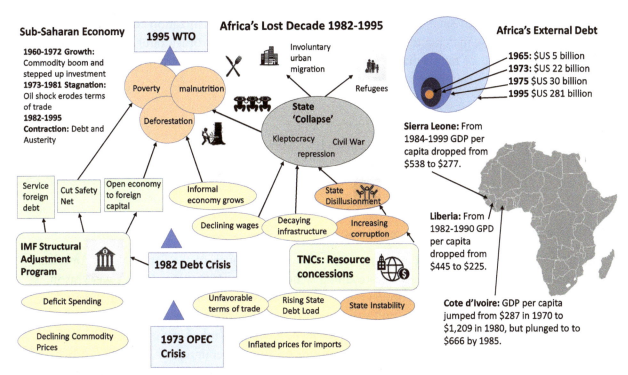

Failed Industrialization

The stage for Africa's **Lost Decade** was set by the failure of regional import substitution policies to spark industrialization during the 1960s. As noted in Chapter 3, following independence, many African governments invested in costly state-managed projects ranging from dams to power plants and steel mills. Megaprojects often relied heavily upon foreign capital, western consultants, and imported skilled laborers. Nearly all failed to increase indigenous technical capacity or to deliver the growth promised. Upon completion, many projects operated inefficiently due to poor national infrastructure and irregular maintenance. Even where properly managed, costly projects were constrained by a domestic market that provided insufficient demand to support the robust growth projections prophesized by Western consultants and technical experts. African industrial projects mostly created shoddy products for the local market that were not competitive abroad. Import substitution policies not only failed to modernize the economy, but also left regional states wracked in debt while soaking up capital desperately needed in rural areas. Initially, Africans had benefited from the **Green Revolution** that transformed India, Thailand, and Southeast Asia into major cereal exporters. Throughout the 1960s, African consumers took advantage of lower food prices to import rice and wheat, but this undercut local farmers specializing in traditional crops like millet, maize, and cassava better adapted to local ecological conditions. When oil prices drifted higher after 1973, Sub-Saharan states had lost domestic production capacity, while poor consumers struggled to pay for imported food.

Throughout Africa, corruption magnified poor state development policies. This was well illustrated in the Congo. Until 1973, the Zairian economy grew at a rapid clip, powered by foreign investment and high copper prices. The 1973 Oil Shock sent copper prices lower and exposed the folly behind Mobutu's white elephant projects like the Maluku steel complex that relied upon imported scrap metal and foreign workers. In desperation, on November 30, 1973, Mobutu issued a localization decree nationalizing foreign owned small- and medium-sized businesses. "Zairianization" of the economy sidelined skilled Lebanese merchants and foreign entrepreneurs in favor of Mobutu cronies. Invariably, they plundered the assets of nationalized firms, creating food shortages and initiating an inflationary cycle that crippled Zaire's economy.

> How could unpopular and incompetent dictators like Mobutu manage to stay in power for so long? Why did locals not overthrow them?

Drought and Urbanization

During the 1970s, a drought settled over the Horn of Africa and much of the Sahel. North American air pollution contributed to the disruption prevailing wind patterns, shortening Africa's wet season. Throughout Central Africa, this transformed hectares of pastures and farms into desiccated wastelands. Desertification was exacerbated by overpopulation. In Ethiopia, deforestation and civil war resulted in a famine from 1983 to 1985 that left over 400,000 dead. In Europe, urbanization had accompanied industrialization with higher city wages attracting migrants from the countryside. In Africa, urbanization accelerated after 1970 mostly because of rural poverty and rising insecurity. Highly indebted states were ill-equipped to handle this influx. Most African cities grew uncontrollably with little infrastructural investment or planning. Today, 70 percent of African town dwellers inhabit slums where families crowd into one-room apartments or self-fabricated shanties. Lagos, Nigeria, typifies a Sub-Saharan pattern of urbanism where two-thirds of residents lack sewage, indoor plumbing, paved roads, or reliable electricity.

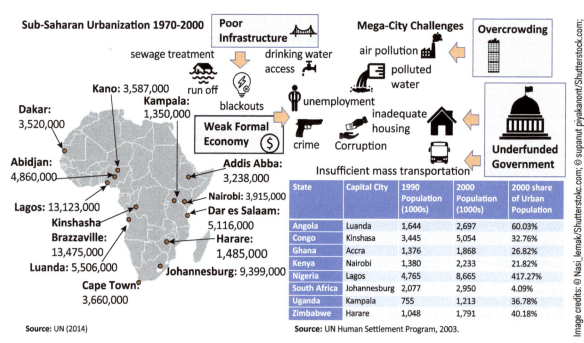

Rapid urbanization and the emergence of megacities in Africa have brought unique developmental challenges linking poverty, environmental hazards, crime, corruption, and inadequate infrastructure.

Rise of Africa's Junta

Flailing modernization programs contributed to a wave of military coups. Throughout Sub-Saharan Africa, the military often represented the most modern and professionally trained institution inside the state. Often African-armed services had originated as colonial institutions. African officers sometimes maintained ties with their former French and English commanders or Russian and American trainers after independence. While African coups invariably had domestic roots, it would have proven difficult for African "strongmen" like the Central African Republic's **Jean-Bédel Bokassa** (1966–1976) to stay in power without French logistical, diplomatic, and military support.

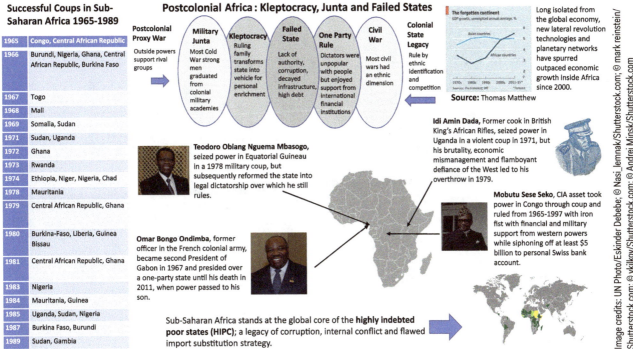

African *junta* transformed the revolutionary state into a vehicle for personal enrichment and sectarian patronage. Military rule represented one manifestation of a larger regional pattern towards corruption, authoritarianism, and nepotism. African *junta* abandoned the idealistic Pan-African language of progress. They mostly avoided ambitious development projects in favor of purchasing military hardware. Deteriorating economic conditions after 1973 also contributed to the collapse of white-minority governments in the southern tier of Africa, while amplifying ethnic, religious, and tribal fissures inside the Horn of Africa. The implosion of postcolonial states into rival factions attracted outsiders scheming for economic or strategic benefit. Not only the superpowers, but the IMF, Cuba, South Africa, China, France, and multinational corporations often financed competing armed factions, amplifying regional strife and state dysfunction. Throughout Africa, the combination of stagnant growth, corruption, and civil war amplified infrastructural decay and disillusionment. By the 1980s, under pressure from structural adjustment mechanisms, the services and support offered by African states had declined, forcing many Africans to build up communal organizations in order to survive.

Mobutu's Kleptocracy, 1973 to 1995

Mobutu Seso Seko donning his leopard skin toque

Throughout his long reign, Joseph Mobutu spent much of his time in an ostentatious marble Palace he dubbed the "Versailles of the Jungle." Privilege kept his family well insulated from the poverty his policies sowed.

Africa's most notorious kleptocrat was the Congo's Joseph Mobutu. Mobutu's instinctive response to mounting economic problems after 1973 was not structural reform, but cracking down on dissent. He purged the army of its ablest officers. In the army's place, Mobutu built an overlapping network of paramilitary units that competed against each other for his favor, while terrorizing local civilians. Mobutu launched elaborate public rituals that called upon his people to celebrate him as the "father of the nation." While the Zaire's infrastructure crumbled, Mobutu jetted around the country in a fleet of Mercedes. Throughout his long reign, Mobutu grew increasingly frustrated with his country's primitiveness. To facilitate periodic escapes from the jungle's oppressive humidity, Mobutu chartered Air France Concordes to shuttle his family on shopping tours in Paris and New York. This luxury necessitated elongating the runway at Gbadolite "International" Airport, constructed around Mobutu's modest natal village at a time when the last public transportation company in Kinshasa had shuttered its doors.

Under Mobutu, Zaire's gross domestic product (GDP) *decreased* 65 percent between independence in 1960 and 1997 despite a booming export sector. By 1990, the formal economy had all but collapsed, forcing ordinary people into survival mode. The resilience of slum dwellers in Kinshasa was often remarkable. For example, female vegetable vendors might rise at 5 a.m. to buy produce at credit from Lebanese merchants. Throughout the morning, they would sell their wares, only to return home between 3 and 5 to cook their family's lone meal. Subsequently, they would return to the streets to hawk unsold produce at half price. Surviving in Kinshasa meant navigating a city without public services, managing a business without credit, and cultivating informal networks with neighbors, peers, and family to supervise children. To the extent that the state existed, it represented a threat. Mobutu's *Forces Armées Zaïroises* (FAZ) were supplied weapons, but paid infrequently. Soldiers were expected to shake down civilians to earn their daily bread.

Despite the Zaire's wealth, its citizens grew progressively poorer, victims of their ruler's greed and a predatory state that sucked up their pennies like a vacuum cleaner. Mobutu's rule paralyzed the state, bankrupted its ministries, and left the country's infrastructure in ruin. Despite this atrocious record, powerful external allies kept Mobutu in power. Following an economic slump in 1977, Mobutu turned to the international community. An array of international sponsors emerged to arrange loans for Zaire. The country's foreign debt steadily mounted to $5 billion. When Mobutu failed to meet interest payments, France and the United States arranged special stabilization measures. Unlike most of the world's debtors, the West proved extraordinarily lenient because they viewed Mobutu as an indispensable strategic ally in central Africa. Unscrupulous foreign investors might have considered Mobutu a miscreant, but they tolerated his despotism so long as he protected their investments and profits.

Postcolonial Society and Culture

Western pundits often attribute Africa's postcolonial struggles to its culture: tribalism, promiscuity, or absence of a work ethic. Such arguments invoke nineteenth-century racial prejudices and ignore Western complicity in supporting African despots. While many postcolonial states struggle to contain ethnic fissures, most sectarian rivalries had colonial roots. In Rwanda, for example, cultural and ethnic differences were transformed into rigid racial identities institutionalized into a structure of state privilege and discrimination. Cynical Belgian cultivation of internal rivalries weakened indigenous resistance to European rule. Rwanda illustrates that the "failed state" label generously applied to postcolonial Africa is difficult to disentangle from their traumatic history, rooted in centuries of slavery, colonial oppression, and neocolonial exploitation after independence.

> Is it fair to attribute contemporary instability in Africa to the sins of colonialism when most of the continent gained independence five decades earlier?

Postcolonial African cultures often nurtured a deep ambivalence concerning the West: Western states represented an oppressive force, but Western institutions and products were often admired. Léopold Sédar Senghor embraced the philosophy of *négritude*, advocating that Africans needed to psychologically transcend the trauma of colonialism by separating from the West and proudly embracing their authentic blackness. Elements of this philosophy influenced many postcolonial leaders and trickled into their development programs. Mobutu rechristened Congolese cities with African names and banned Western attire. Most Congolese, however, viewed Mobutu's authenticity program as superficial and self-serving. At the end of his life, Aimé Césaire mused: "Who am I? Who are we? What are we in this white world?"[4] Césaire could not seemingly devise a clear answer to this question. This dilemma mirrored a central theme in Chinua Achebe's classic 1958 novel *Things Fall Apart*, which offers an allegory for the tragic collision between Western civilization and traditional culture inside a fictional Nigerian village. At the novel's climax, the protagonist, Okonkwo, commits suicide after he realizes that his world has become unglued and that everything that he knew will be washed away. Achebe captures one dimension of postcolonial Africa's struggle to accommodate Western modernity. Most first-generation African leaders were particularly conflicted given their Western education and liberal values. Horrified by white racism, they recognized the importance of modern science and technology that they linked to Western institutions and culture. After various experiments in African socialism failed to uplift Africans from poverty, indigenous enthusiasm for state authenticity programs waned. South African President Thabo Mbeki could still speak about "African renaissance" and "reversing" four hundred years of colonialism, but South Africa's post-apartheid constitution is particularly conspicuous in embracing universal values like liberal freedoms and individual rights rather than African customs.

Historically, Africans have proven cosmopolitan. Religion provides one lens for analyzing Africa's assimilation of foreign institutions, beliefs, and practices. African belief in a supreme being and weak indigenous states left the continent's cultures relatively open to both Christianity and Islam. In 1900, Muslims and Christians remained small minorities in Sub-Saharan Africa, but both faiths grew exponentially after independence. By the twenty first century two hundred million Muslims clustered around the Sahara and East Africa, while 470 million Christians dominated the southern edge of the continent. Organized religion was spread by foreign missionaries, but also expanded rapidly inside the vacuum left by postcolonial states. Islamic charities, independent churches, and a medley of local organizations provided Africans with a range of social services, a sense of community, and hope inside states stricken by conflict, drought, and poverty. Polls consistently reveal that Sub-Saharan Africa represents the world's most pious region. About 90 percent consider spirituality significant in their lives. In most cases, however, organized religion supplements, rather than supplants, traditional religious practice as charms, ancestor worship, and belief in witchcraft persist even among those formally identifying as Muslim or Christian. This syncretic approach to religion is similarly reflected in a high degree of confessional tolerance. In conflict-ridden states like Nigeria and Somalia, extremist Islamic movements like al Shahab and Boko Haram have set up shop, but the more puritanical forms of Christianity and Islam enjoy less support than more moderate branches. Opinion polls reveal clear majorities expressing admiration for Western music, Hollywood movies, and other forms of foreign entertainment. Regional artists, musicians, and chefs readily appropriate foreign ingredients, readily adapting them to local tastes and norms.

African openness to foreign practices is similarly captured in the region's rapid adoption of digital communication technologies. Throughout the 1980s, Africa ranked dead last in terms of phone lines per resident, contributing to the continent's global isolation. Development of cellular phones and communication satellites, however, has enabled African states to leapfrog into the digital age. By 2002, roughly 10 percent of the population in Tanzania, Uganda, Kenya, and Ghana had acquired cell phones. A decade later 83 percent Ghanaians and 74 percent of Ugandan men owned cell phones, penetration rates comparable to that of the developed West.[5] Across the continent cell phones, the Internet, drones, and satellite dishes help to connect Africans to global economy, foreign investors, and Western culture like never before. Deeper integration with the global economy has enabled small farmers to fetch higher prices, empowered women to open businesses, and enabled civil right groups to mobilize against corruption. Some African intellectuals lament that globalization is transforming young people into "coconuts" (black skin, white on the inside) alienated from African traditions and its past. Most millennials growing up in African cities, however, embrace consumer technologies as modern progress. Few reveal any concern that foreign cultural imports will erode their identity, traditions, or sense of self.

Quest for Sustainable Development

Africa's arid climate and marginal soils, combined with explosive population growth, have put pressure upon the natural environment. Two-thirds of Sub-Saharan Africa is comprised by deserts like the Sahara and Kalahari, or dry lands like the Sahel that can support only a minimal number of people and livestock. Already water shortages, deforestation, and land degradation contribute to conflicts inside Darfur, the Niger Delta, and Somalia. Following independence, ecological security ranked low as a developmental priority among postcolonial regimes and external funding agencies like the World Bank. The 1980s debt crisis further marginalized environmental concerns despite pressure from international environmental groups. Following the 1992 Rio Conference, however, the World Bank placed greater emphasis upon environmental sustainability, while tourism emerged as an increasingly powerful driver of economic development in Kenya, Namibia, and Uganda. During the late 1980s, Zimbabwe instituted the innovative CAMPFIRE program that licensed Western trophy hunters. Hunting endangered species like elephants proved controversial, but the program enjoyed local support because state wardens provided villagers with compensation for lost crops, while local village councils received a share of the state tourist budget. In Kenya, by contrast, large tour operators dominate safaris. When local communities benefit little from tourism, poachers flourish by trafficking Ivory to lucrative Asian markets.

For many East Africans, sustainability is not an environmental issue, but a question of survival. The combination of drought, climate change, deforestation, and civil war has wreaked havoc on the land, agriculture, and food distribution.

Despite increased commitment for sustainable development, African ecosystems deteriorated after 1980. The IMF's structural adjustment programs put primary emphasis upon debt repayment rather than conservation. To raise liquidity, Ghana, for example, expanded its timber exports from $16 to 99 million from 1983 to 1988. Africa's recovery during the 1990s was headlined by extractive industries connected to transnational corporations (TNCs) that were frequently linked to bribes, corruption, and environmental pollution. Crony capitalism is well illustrated in Nigeria where discovery of the Oloibiri well in 1956 inaugurated a close partnership between the state and Royal Dutch Shell. From this deal's inception, thousands of barrels of oil have spilled into the fragile Niger delta ecosystem damaging wetlands and fisheries upon which locals depend. Starting in the early 1990s, **Ken Saro-Wiwa** began to organize the Ogoni people in a nonviolent opposition against further oil development. These activities brought Saro-Wiwa into the crosshairs of Shell. In 1995, Shell pressured Nigeria's military government to execute Saro-Wiwa on trumped up charges.[6] Shell's hardball tactics, however, backfired. In 2005, resistance in the Niger Delta evolved into a guerrilla movement that sabotaged pipelines, planted bombs, and kidnapped oil company staff for ransom. The 2010 **Wikileaks scandal** inflamed the insurgency by revealing incestuous ties between Shell and the Nigerian government. While Nigeria's oil has filled state coffers and enriched foreign investors, it has less obviously benefitted local peoples like the Ogoni. Nigeria symbolizes a broader Sub-Saharan trend where corruption ties African elites to corporate officers at the expense of ordinary people and the environment.

Population pressure, however, serves as the principal catalyst for land degradation across dryland Africa. Deforestation is spurred by peasants harvesting wood as a cooking fuel. Forest clearance in dryland valleys rapidly accelerates erosion because roots lock in soil and trap moisture. A persistent problem for conservation in Africa is the weakness of states. Even where parks, reserves, or environmental laws exist, ecological protection can be difficult to enforce by underfunded agencies operating inside highly stratified societies. Cote d'Ivoire typifies a Central African trend where tropical deforestation continues at an unsustainable 7 percent annual clip despite official conservation measures. In Madagascar, only 20 percent of the rainforest remains. The combination of a hilly terrain and high precipitation leaves behind a scarred moonscape that holds little potential for agriculture or livestock.

In a continent where so many people rely upon an informal economy and "subsist" upon two dollars or less a day, sustainable development is crucial. The poor particularly rely upon the bounty of nature for their daily bread and survival. Throughout Africa, the natural systems upon which many depend are reaching critical thresholds, or have plunged to a new less productive normal. For example, Lake Victoria is in danger of eutrophication, transforming its once abundant fisheries into dead zones. From 1966 to 1988, Lake Chad has shrunk from 22,000 km^2 to less than 5,000, leading to the abandonment of irrigation projects and widespread poverty and migration throughout the region. Throughout Africa, ecological stress is a growing contributor to poverty, political radicalization, and civil unrest.

African Women

During the independence struggles of the 1960s, African women played a leading role inside nationalist movements. Following independence, female voices were increasingly marginalized as postcolonial states became dominated by male careerists and increasingly unresponsive to ordinary citizens. No women occupied cabinet posts inside postcolonial states during the 1960s, and few served inside legislative assemblies. Relative marginalization in part reflected Africa's underdevelopment. Inside rural villages traditional patriarchy assigns wives a secondary role. Customary practice also sanctions an unequal distribution of household tasks. Various surveys have shown that on average African women work 20 percent longer than men, while also bearing the burden for household chores like cooking, cleaning, collecting firewood, child care. Africa's lack of infrastructure, for example, can make a simple task like gathering potable water a chore that takes women hours.

Since the 1980s, Western developmental experts have grown increasingly conscious of the implicit gender bias inside developmental theory, which amplifies the "feminization" of African poverty. Studies have shown that every dollar put in the hands of a mother is more powerful because she is more likely to invest it in her children. Accordingly, new programs of microfinance have sought to provide capital directly to female entrepreneurs, recognizing that traditional gender-"blind" policies in their focus upon infrastructure, GDP, or household income could amplify existing gender disparities. In many African states, women continue to have unequal access to education. In the southern cone, women in Botswana and Lesotho, lack legal rights to property. To operate a business, get bank credit, or work outside their family, they need their husband's permission.

Sexist attitudes also contribute to a culture tolerant of domestic violence and sexual abuse. Sexism played into the spread of the HIV epidemic during the 1980s, with Sub-Saharan Africa claiming twenty-three of twenty-five million infections by 2006. Western notions of African "promiscuity," however, fail to account for local poverty or socioeconomic conditions. The spread of HIV was facilitated in part by truck drivers artificially separated from wives because of a restrictive pass system. Prostitution and unsafe sexual practices also flourish inside societies where women have few economic options or rights. In terms of many traditional values, Sub-Saharan Africa appears staunchly conservative, particularly in its boisterous rejection of homosexuality. Heavily influenced by American protestant churches that sponsored local televangelists, Uganda in 2009 imposed a law criminalizing sodomy, including a provision calling for capital punishment for repeat offenders. Only in South Africa is sexual orientation a freedom inscribed inside the constitution.

Liberia's Ellen Johnson Sirleaf

President of Liberia from 2014 to 2018, Ellen Johnson Sirleaf represented one dimension of the democratic wave, increasing female participation in politics even at the highest levels of the state.

With the exception of the Middle East, African women are the most underrepresented in the world in terms of holding political office. Less than 10 percent of the legislative positions inside regional governments today are held by women. Increasing urbanization and growing diffusion of global cultural norms, however, are starting to level such disparities. While opinion polls reveal that a majority of men and women continue to subscribe to traditional beliefs—such that wives should obey their husbands—the number of women inside African parliaments is steadily rising. Headlining this change, in Liberia's 2006 election **Ellen Johnson Sirleaf** became Sub-Saharan Africa's first female head of state.

Democratic Wave, 1987 to 2000

During the late 1980s, after a decade and a half of economic agony—intensified by political corruption—the winds of change once more blew over Africa. Internal and external forces aligned to create conditions for reform. Mikhail Gorbachev's "new thinking" represented one catalyst. The Kremlin lost interest in left wing guerrilla movements in Africa, while improved US–Soviet relations removed much of the oxygen feeding conflicts inside Namibia, Angola, and the Horn of Africa. Collapse of the Soviet Union in 1991 forced Western states to reconsider their traditional support for unsavory African despots and realign their economic relationships with their human rights agenda. Simultaneously, African politics was disrupted by globalization. Nongovernmental organizations (NGOs) promoted local democratic organizations and images of popular demonstrations toppling communist regimes in Eastern Europe lent subtle encouragement to African reformers. International pressure and contingent aid put African despots on the defensive and pressured them to lift censorship of the press and police repression of opponents. Local activists used new media to criticize corruption and injustice and formed broader democratic coalitions uniting Church leaders, international organizations, and trade unions to demand civil rights and multiparty elections.

> Movements for democratic reform appeared across the postcolonial world after 1989. Why do you suppose that such movements were more prominent in Africa and Latin America than inside the Middle East and Asia?

In Zambia, Kenneth Kaunda was swept from power, while in Kenya popular pressure forced Daniel arap Moi to agree to multiparty elections. Malawi's president for life, Hastings Kamuzu Banda lost

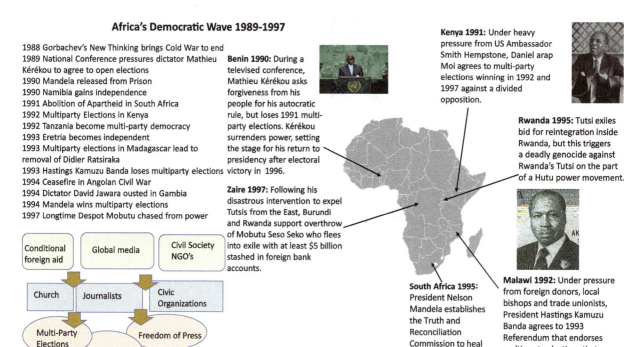

Africa's Democratic Wave 1989-1997

1988 Gorbachev's New Thinking brings Cold War to end
1989 National Conference pressures dictator Mathieu Kérékou to agree to open elections
1990 Mandela released from Prison
1990 Namibia gains independence
1991 Abolition of Apartheid in South Africa
1992 Multiparty Elections in Kenya
1992 Tanzania become multi-party democracy
1993 Eretria becomes independent
1993 Multiparty elections in Madagascar lead to removal of Didier Ratsiraka
1993 Hastings Kamuzu Banda loses multiparty elections
1994 Ceasefire in Angolan Civil War
1994 Dictator David Jawara ousted in Gambia
1994 Mandela wins multiparty elections
1997 Longtime Despot Mobutu chased from power

Benin 1990: During a televised conference, Mathieu Kérékou asks forgiveness from his people for his autocratic rule, but loses 1991 multi-party elections. Kérékou surrenders power, setting the stage for his return to presidency after electoral victory in 1996.

Zaire 1997: Following his disastrous intervention to expel Tutsis from the East, Burundi and Rwanda support overthrow of Mobutu Seso Seko who flees into exile with at least $5 billion stashed in foreign bank accounts.

Kenya 1991: Under heavy pressure from US Ambassador Smith Hempstone, Daniel arap Moi agrees to multi-party elections winning in 1992 and 1997 against a divided opposition.

Rwanda 1995: Tutsi exiles bid for reintegration inside Rwanda, but this triggers a deadly genocide against Rwanda's Tutsi on the part of a Hutu power movement.

South Africa 1995: President Nelson Mandela establishes the Truth and Reconciliation Commission to heal the wounds of Apartheid.

Malawi 1992: Under pressure from foreign donors, local bishops and trade unionists, President Hastings Kamuzu Banda agrees to 1993 Referendum that endorses multi-party elections that he subsequently loses.

office after agreeing to open elections. Inside Benin, an influential national conference forced Mathieu Kérékou to stand for election after initially seizing power in October 1972. Of course, this wave did not produce viable democratic states or accountable regimes everywhere. Seasoned despots like Mobutu buckled down for a fight, while committed revolutionaries like Angola's Jonas Savimbi refused to lay down their arms.

Collapse of Apartheid

The most tangible manifestation of Africa's democratic wave was the collapse of the racist regime in South Africa. In 1948, the **Afrikaner** backed National Party took control over South Africa in a close election. Over the next four decades, they built up **Apartheid**, enshrining racial segregation as the core principle of the country's political system. From 1948 to 1990, various laws separated whites from nonwhites in all spheres of life. Originally passed in 1950, the **Group Areas Act**, variously amended in subsequent decades, forced 3.5 million nonwhites to live in segregated townships until 1983. This odious measure destroyed vibrant black neighborhoods in Johannesburg and Cape Town, while forcing blacks to use passes to travel inside their own country. Passes also forced blacks to commute long distances to work and separated fathers from their families.

Apartheid achieved racial segregation through overlocking mechanisms: physical segregation, disenfranchisement, humiliation, and denial of labor rights. While racial discrimination had various motives, profit served as one rationale. Black miners, for example, were paid one-tenth the wages of whites and this exploitation made the industry profitable. South Africa represented one of the postwar world's most dynamic economies. Its rich soils and mineral reserves, combined with a plentiful supply of cheap African labor, made for a robust export sector during the long postwar boom. The OPEC oil shock did adversely impact South Africa's economy, but this was partially offset by higher gold prices.

During the early 1950s, various black political organizations mobilized for political rights, social justice, and higher wages inside South Africa. One of these nationalists was a young Bantu lawyer of royal lineage, **Nelson Mandela**. He joined the youth league of **African National Congress** (ANC) and participated in various civil disobedience campaigns to pressure the South African government to end racial discrimination. The ANC's 1955 **Freedom Charter** rejected Apartheid by embracing racial equality as the fundamental principle for a future democratic South Africa. After the March 1960 **Sharpeville Massacre** resulted in the death of sixty-nine peaceful demonstrators protesting the pass laws, Mandela realized that Gandhi's peaceful resistance formula would not work in South Africa. Mandela took up armed struggle. His terrorist cell launched a brief campaign of sabotage calculated to destabilize the Apartheid state, but he was quickly arrested in 1962. Mandela remained imprisoned until 1990, but he earned respect from his captors for treating everyone with dignity, even going so far as to memorize the birthdays of his guards' children.

Urged to renounce violence as a condition for release during the 1970s, Mandela steadfastly refused, arguing that Apartheid was its source. Black Africans could not stand down until the state renounced violence. This stand won Mandela acclaim, but during his long imprisonment leadership in the townships steadily shifted towards a younger generation including **Stephen Biko** and the Black Consciousness Movement. This generation had grown up in townships and accustomed to police brutality. Unlike the jailed ANC leaders, many rejected the idea of allying with white liberals against the Apartheid state. Most conceived their struggle as one of black liberation.

Chapter 8: Sub-Saharan Africa

Starting in the mid-1970s, the Apartheid state found itself under increasing pressure. The June 1976 **Soweto Uprising** resulted when the Apartheid government tried to impose Dutch Afrikaans inside Black schools. Students and teachers, who at best had an imperfect grasp of Afrikaans, protested this measure as unfair and impractical. In Soweto, a scheduled three-day protest march was cut short when a police detachment stared down 10,000 protestors making their way towards Orlando Stadium. Unnerved by the size of the demonstration, some members of Colonel Kleingeld's forty-eight-member detachment fired into the crowd, killing two and wounding dozens. The event sparked riots and mass protests across South Africa, created a temporary breakdown in state authority, and undermined faith in Apartheid government among whites and blacks alike.

While the Apartheid regime had effectively interdicted ANC militants infiltrating from neighboring states during the early 1970s, it was blindsided by the collapse of Portugal's dictatorship in 1974. Portugal's Carnation Revolution rapidly transformed South Africa's Northern Frontier. Botha embarked upon a muscular foreign policy to support white-dominated minority regimes in Rhodesia and Namibia, while sponsoring insurgencies against Black nationalist regimes in Angola and Mozambique. While these policies had some effect initially, at the bloody 1987 to 1988 **Battle of Cuito Cuanavale,** South African defense forces suffered heavy casualties, underscoring the need for a political settlement. This culminated in the Trilateral Commission that granted Namibian independence in 1990 and left South Africa's Apartheid regime an isolated anomaly.

End of the Cold War in Africa's Southern Tier

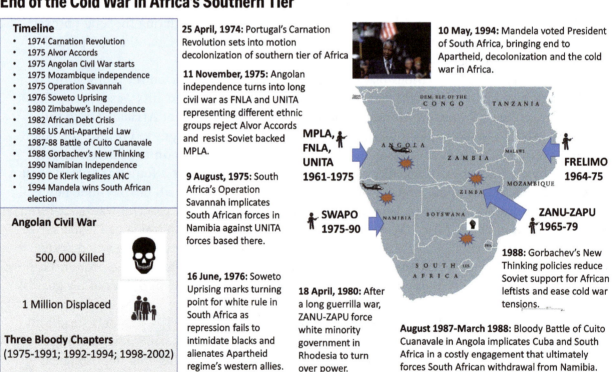

Timeline
- 1974 Carnation Revolution
- 1975 Alvor Accords
- 1975 Angolan Civil War starts
- 1975 Mozambique independence
- 1975 Operation Savannah
- 1976 Soweto Uprising
- 1980 Zimbabwe's Independence
- 1982 African Debt Crisis
- 1986 US Anti-Apartheid Law
- 1987-88 Battle of Cuito Cuanavale
- 1988 Gorbachev's New Thinking
- 1990 Namibian Independence
- 1990 De Klerk legalizes ANC
- 1994 Mandela wins South African election

Angolan Civil War

500,000 Killed

1 Million Displaced

Three Bloody Chapters
(1975-1991; 1992-1994; 1998-2002)

25 April, 1974: Portugal's Carnation Revolution sets into motion decolonization of southern tier of Africa

11 November, 1975: Angolan independence turns into long civil war as FNLA and UNITA representing different ethnic groups reject Alvor Accords and resist Soviet backed MPLA.

9 August, 1975: South Africa's Operation Savannah implicates South African forces in Namibia against UNITA forces based there.

16 June, 1976: Soweto Uprising marks turning point for white rule in South Africa as repression fails to intimidate blacks and alienates Apartheid regime's western allies.

18 April, 1980: After a long guerrilla war, ZANU-ZAPU force white minority government in Rhodesia to turn over power.

10 May, 1994: Mandela voted President of South Africa, bringing end to Apartheid, decolonization and the cold war in Africa.

MPLA, FNLA, UNITA 1961-1975

SWAPO 1975-90

FRELIMO 1964-75

ZANU-ZAPU 1965-79

1988: Gorbachev's New Thinking policies reduce Soviet support for African leftists and ease cold war tensions.

August 1987-March 1988: Bloody Battle of Cuito Cuanavale in Angola implicates Cuba and South Africa in a costly engagement that ultimately forces South African withdrawal from Namibia.

Image credits: © Martial Red/Shutterstock.com; © iconvectorstock/Shutterstock.com; © Leremy/Shutterstock.com; © MuchMania/Shutterstock.com; © Zoart Studio/Shutterstock.com; © Peter Hermes Furian/Shutterstock.com; © mark reinstein/Shutterstock.com

Mounting pressure inside South Africa compelled Prime Minister **Pieter Willem Botha** to institute limited reforms. In 1986, pass laws were abolished, black labor unions were legalized, blacks were allowed to live inside urban areas, and the laws barring interracial intercourse were repealed. This addressed Apartheid's worst inequities, but they did not improve the miserable black standard of living. Most whites inside South Africa began to recognize that Apartheid was no longer viable, but Nationalist politicians lacked an exit strategy. They needed a moderate African with whom to negotiate a political settlement. After years of close observation in prison, they suspected that Mandela might be their man. Botha moved Mandela from Robben Island to Pollsmoor Prison in 1982. They allowed him more freedom and visitors to judge his mettle, but the sticking point remained Mandela's refusal to renounce violence.

Throughout the 1980s, pressure on the Apartheid regime kept mounting. Formation of the **United Democratic Front** (UDF) in 1983 created a 1.5 million strong umbrella organization that united various local organizations against the regime. Simultaneously, international sanctions started to bite into South Africa's industrial economy, dependent upon $13 billion worth of annual trade and $30 billion in foreign investment. As the United States joined the sanctions community in 1986, South Africa declared a state of emergency and began to suffer from shortages. While smuggling, stockpiling, and synthesizing oil from coal enabled the regime to offset some of these hardships, it was becoming increasingly difficult to maintain a modern industrialized state. The strain of sanctions was amplified by an endless array of internal boycotts and strikes. By the 1980s, the Apartheid system had grown inefficient, requiring high overhead costs for policing, transport, and maintaining separate facilities and regulations for various races.

Although Botha realized that Apartheid's days were numbered, he feared to abolish white privilege. After Botha suffered a second stroke, **Frederik de Klerk** inherited power and moved swiftly to open negotiations with Mandela and the ANC to bring Apartheid to an end. Upon taking office as president on February 2 1990, de Klerk delivered a dramatic speech that lifted the ban on the ANC, brought an end to racial segregation, and severely restricted police powers. While de Klerk was consolidating his position among whites, Mandela secured leadership of the ANC. Mandela set about to build a strong party with aim of "securing majority rule." De Klerk's bold diplomacy alienated white supremacists, but during a March 1992 "whites only" referendum, a 68 percent majority supported de Klerk's call for further negotiations with the ANC. The final round of negotiations, from 1992 to 1994, was tense and marred by unprecedented violence, particularly between the Zulu **Inkatha Party** that challenged the Bantu majority inside the ANC. This violence tested the patience of both Mandela and de Klerk given evidence of state support for the Zulu. Neither man fully trusted the other, but ultimately both men weathered the crisis and agreed to a political compromise that paved the way for South Africa's first free and open election on April 27, 1994. The ANC campaigned on "a better life for all" slogan and promised to build a million houses and offer free education and universal access to water and electricity. Mandela and the ANC won 62 percent of the vote, just short of the two-thirds majority needed to amend the constitution. Whites and Zulus each retained control of one province inside South Africa's federal system. Arguably, Mandela's greatest legacy came in healing Apartheid's wounds. As president he worked tirelessly to reassure South Africa's white population that they would be protected and have a voice inside a "Rainbow Nation" to the point that his wife Winnie criticized him for seeming to show more concern for the privileged than his "own" people. Mandela incorporated prominent Afrikaners into his cabinet, pardoned Apartheid figures, and celebrated the victory of the Springbok Rugby team at the 1995 World Cup. At the final over New Zealand, Nelson Mandela jumped onto the field wearing Francois Pienaar's number 6 jersey, a public gesture that expressed his aim to serve as president for the whole nation.

Nelson Mandela

Mandela's Truth and Reconciliation Commission played an influential role in reconciling nonwhites with Afrikaners despite the brutal legacy of the former Apartheid Regime.

Rwanda's Tragedy

The potential for the democratic wave to misfire is best illustrated in Rwanda. The country's 1994 tragedy seemed to come out of nowhere, but closer analysis reveals that Rwanda's genocide was decades in the making. Although "Hutu" and "Tutsi" were identities predating European colonialism, Belgian authorities fixed them into hardened racial categories. Before European arrival, Tutsi and Hutu shared the same language, culture, and religion. In precolonial society, the boundary between the two was fluid—rich Hutu became Tutsi and vice versa. Race in the sense of an immutable barrier represented a European idea. Belgians believed the Tutsis to be genetically different and mentally superior to Hutu. Accordingly, the Belgians bestowed favors upon the Tutsi, giving them greater privileges inside the colonial system including educational opportunities. Not surprisingly, this sparked growing resentment among the Hutu majority that increasingly became an exploited underclass.

Belgian policy experienced a sharp reversal after World War II as the more educated Tutsi tuned in the nationalist wave sweeping across Africa. Tutsi intellectuals began to agitate for independence from Belgium. Some adopted Marxism. The Belgian clergy that had played a leading role in cultivating the Tutsi elite felt betrayed and began to appeal to the Hutu majority. The Belgians stoked Hutu nationalism, warned them about racial domination, and appealed to them as Christian "soldiers" to take arms against the "godless" Tutsi communists. Inside Rwanda, tensions rose during the 1950s, as both the Tutsi and Hutu formed ethnic political parties. After the Tutsi king died in 1957, Hutu mobs attacked their Tutsi neighbors. Belgian authorities did little to discourage ethnic violence, likening mob attacks to a movement for democratic empowerment. In fact, Brussels had cynically cultivated Hutu nationalism as a bet to maximize their postcolonial influence. From 1959 to 1964, Rwandan Tutsi paid the price for this policy. Over 20,000 were massacred and half the Rwandan Tutsi population fled into exile. Until 1973, the Tutsis remaining inside Rwanda were subject to periodic attack, while 300,000 exiles tried to rebuild their lives inside neighboring communities.

Rwandan Civil War, 1990 to 1994

In October 1990, a band of 4,000 Tutsi guerrillas that had fought for **Yoweri Museveni** and Ugandan independence invaded Rwanda. Most of these men were sons of refugees who had fled the violence in Rwanda from 1959 to 1962. They called themselves the **Rwandan Patriotic Front** (RPF), and advanced swiftly until their commander Fred Rwigyema was killed. Subsequently, the RPF attack was blunted as France intervened in favor of their Hutu allies in order to counter a perceived "Anglo-Saxon" advance into their sphere of influence.

The RPF retreated into the rugged north as the conflict slowly settled into a guerrilla war. Mounting casualties on both sides triggered international efforts to broker a ceasefire. The 1993 **Arusha Accords** represented a power-sharing arrangement to end the current fighting and amend an historic injustice by enabling Tutsi exiles to return to their native land. Rwandan President **Juvénal Habyarimana**, backed by Hutu moderates, promised to reintegrate the Tutsi into the Rwandan government and society. Hutu extremists, however, led by Habyarimana's wife and her brothers rejected any compromise. They formed a hardliner coalition known as the *Akazu* or "Little House" after Habyarimana allowed moderate Hutu opposition members into his Cabinet in 1992. Following the Arusha Accords, the *Akuzu* formed a militia called the *Interahamwe*, or "Those Who Attack Together." They gained notoriety for compiling lists of "traitors" and targeting them for violent retribution. The *Akazu* also polluted Rwanda's politics through their flagship *Radio Télévision Libre des Mille Collines*. This evolved into a trumpet for a Hutu power movement that regularly demonized Tutsi citizens as "cockroaches" while spreading Hutu fears about various imaginary conspiracies.

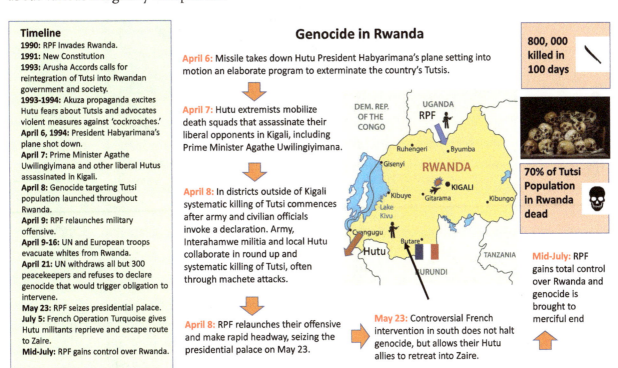

Image credits: © folksterno/Shutterstock.com; © kamnuan/Shutterstock.com; © Martial Red/Shutterstock.com; © pavalena/Shutterstock.com; © Leremy/Shutterstock.com; © MuchMania/Shutterstock.com; © murat Irfan yalcin/Shutterstock.com

On April 6, 1994, Juvénal Habyarimana's airplane was shot down over Kigali. While the perpetrator remains unclear, a well-coordinated genocide of Rwandan Tutsis and Hutu moderates commenced the following day. The *Akuzu* assassinated Rwandan moderates the night of April 6, commencing with Prime Minister Agathe Uwilingiyimana. Having created a political void, Hutu extremists embarked upon a genocide planned months ahead. Their goal was to kill every Tutsi living inside Rwanda.

Window on World History: Romeo Dallaire, Canada, and International Peacekeeping

Roméo Dallaire

In Rwanda in April 1994, United Nations Assistance Mission for Rwanda (UNAMIR) forces were outmanned and outgunned. With only three hundred lightly armed United Nations (UN) soldiers, Dallaire's principal technique for saving Tutsis targeted by *Interahamwe* goons was to confront them with indignant outrage and his booming voice, hoping that defiance and the bluff of the UN flag would send them scurrying away.

Roméo Dallaire was born in the Netherlands in 1945, son of a Canadian sergeant and a Dutch nurse. His life and career would in many ways encapsulate a critical question the world faced after 1991: What role should the UN serve in the post–Cold War world? The great hope of liberals was that the UN might occupy its intended role as preserver of international security that had been derailed by mounting superpower frictions. This dream proved particularly appealing to many Canadians like Dallaire. Canada, after all, had championed the UN's resurrection after the 1950s, with Lester Pearson playing a leading role in developing its peacekeeping mission. During the 1990s, various crises presented the international community with fresh opportunities for humanitarian intervention, nation-building, and peacekeeping. To what extent would the UN fill the international vacuum and would civilized nations contribute soldiers and funding? Following a protracted civil war in Rwanda, international mediators managed to settle the civil war and hammer out a diplomatic settlement that seemed to heal an historic rift between Rwanda's Hutu and Tutsi. Both the RPF and Hutu moderates embraced the 1993 Arusha Accords calling for a ceasefire and gradual reintegration of long-exiled Tutsis into Rwandan society. The agreement resembled a similar bargain that had preceded Namibian independence in 1990. To assist implementation, the Security Council established the **United Nations Assistance Mission for Rwanda** (UNAMIR). For the first time, a Canadian, Lieutenant General Roméo Dallaire was appointed commander of the UN force. From the start, however, UNAMIR was plagued by a lack of funding, troops, and a flawed mission statement. On January 22, 1994, Dallaire was informed of the imminent arrival of a French plane laden with weapons to implement a carefully planned genocide of Tutsi and Hutu moderates. Alarmed, Dallaire sought authorization from New York to seize the weapon cache. Dallaire's superiors, however, refused, telling him that such a mission exceeded his mandate. UNAMIR was not equipped to diffuse a civil war. Ultimately, Dallaire commanded 2,500 personnel, but with the exception of a contingent of four hundred Belgian commandos, his force was only lightly armed. Through the winter of 1993–1994, the international community ignored mounting evidence of a planned genocide. In April 1994, Hutu extremists not only assassinated their political opponents in cold blood, but also targeted UNAMIR, executing ten Belgian soldiers. This precipitated the UN to order UNAMIR's withdrawal, but Dallaire refused to abandon his mission knowing that it would precipitate the murder of thousands of refugees under UN protection. Belgium pulled out its forces, but Dallaire consolidated his remaining 270 Pakistani, Ghanaian, Tunisian, and Bangladeshi soldiers in urban safe zones, ultimately sparing 7,500 Tutsi and Hutu from the murderous bands roving Kigali's streets. When Dallaire's calls for reinforcement were rebuffed, he turned to the media to raise international consciousness. The Western public, however, seemed more captivated by the O. J. Simpson trial than the disaster unfolding in Kigali. Dallaire returned to Canada in July 1994, deeply traumatized and soon retired from the armed forces. In his 2003 autobiography, Dalliare poignantly recounts shaking hands with the commanders of the *Interahamwe* that orchestrated the genocide, likening their lifeless eyes as gazing at the "Devil." Dallaire's experience crystallized into a cynical view of the UN bureaucracy and the West. Dallaire's autobiography harshly criticized contemporary "Canada and other peacekeeping nations" for becoming "accustomed to acting if, and only if, international public opinion will support them."[7] For Dallaire, a rigid moral compass rather than political expediency should inform foreign policy. Under Prime Minister Stephen Harper (2006–2015), the emphasis if not the basic values underlying Canadian foreign policy shifted. Although multilateralism and peacekeeping remained important values, the Canadian forces were revamped into a rapid reaction force that can respond to different types of crises around the world. Harper also lent material support to traditional allies like the United States and Britain fighting the "war on terror." UN peacekeeping and fighting Islamic State in Iraq and Syria (ISIS) present a different Canadian face to the world. They also raise important questions about Canada's role inside the twenty first century international system.

Critical Reflection

1. Can the UN prevent genocides like Rwanda or are there too many humanitarian disasters for the international community to contain?
2. Should Canada continue to support international peacekeeping missions or should Canada take a more active role in support of Western allies fighting ISIS?

Leaders of the *Interahamwe* and Rwandan Armed Forces (FAR) were informed of the President's death, which was blamed on the RPF. Subsequently, they were given the order to begin their work and "spare no one" not even any "baby." With machetes already distributed to militants across the country, a carefully orchestrated genocide began. One horrific aspect of Rwanda's genocide was widespread civilian complicity. The state identified victims then instructed ordinary citizens to hack down and rape their friends, neighbors, and fellow parishioners. Death squads moved block by block with deadly precision, invading homes, repeating the gruesome scene again and again. Given that Rwanda was densely populated and neighborhoods and villages were ethnically integrated, there was little chance for victims to hide or evade capture. Neither women, priests, fetuses nor mixed offspring were spared.

> What does the reluctance of Western states to declare violence in Rwanda a genocide illustrate about liberal internationalism?

Tutsi children seeking sanctuary in schools, churches, or hospitals were often butchered by their teachers, doctors, or priests. Hutu husbands were compelled to kill their Tutsi wives and "bastards" to save their own lives. Those with Hutu papers and flat noses were sometimes killed indiscriminately on the mere suspicion of being Tutsi impersonators. Only in a few villages and districts were reinforcements or pep talks necessary to spur civilians into participating in this orgy of violence. Rape, mutilation, and torture were epidemic, while acts of heroism depressingly rare. Catholic Bishops were mostly mute, and Tutsi priests were often indiscriminately killed with their flock.

As the streets of Kigali drowned in blood, the international community called for a "ceasefire," while steadfastly refusing to utter the term "genocide," a label that would have compelled their intervention according to international convention. In June 1994, when a decisive RPF breakthrough made their victory in Rwanda inevitable, France, which had trained the *Interahamwe*, announced a belated intervention. Supposedly, **Opération Turquoise** was meant to provide a "safe zone," but the genocide had almost run its course. The RPF criticized the French for providing a screen to enable their longtime allies, the remnants the Rwandan army and *Interahamwe* to slip into exile into Zaire. On July 4, 1994, the RPF seized Kigali, ending the genocide and taking control over most of Rwanda by the end of the month. The RPF, particularly its new recruits, had certainly participated in reprisal killings by the end, but of the one million Rwandans estimated to have died in the hundred days of blood, most were Tutsi civilians. Eighty percent of Rwanda's Tutsi population had been wiped out at the hands of a murderous regime the French government had trained, and the Catholic Church had long supported.

Mobutu's Unceremonious Exit, 1995 to 1997

The aftermath of the Rwandan genocide contributed to the downfall of Africa's longest tenured dictator. On May 16, 1997, Mobutu took off from Gbadolite Airport for the last time under a hail of bullet fire. The Marshal's hasty exit left behind a Congo buried in debt. Mobutu had ruled over thirty years, but in the end, he was ousted by intrigues hatched by the Congo's smaller neighbors. Following the Rwandan genocide, over a million Hutus had taken refuge inside the Eastern Congo in July 1994, including many members of the Rwandan Army and *Interahamwe*. In Zaire, these heavily armed forces gradually took over the refugee camps and began to launch guerrilla raids into Rwanda or mount attacks upon Congolese Tutsi. The Tutsi government in Kigali responded by sending arms to aid their brethren.

The Rwandan civil war now spilled into Zaire. In November 1996, in the face of mounting ethnic violence, Mobutu ordered Tutsi to leave. This order backfired. It forced the Congolese Tutsi into open rebellion and spurred Uganda, Burundi, and Rwanda to intervene on their behalf. The Rwandan Army and *Interahamwe* had butchered hundreds of thousands of defenseless civilians in April 1994. In 1996, they proved no match for the battle tested forces of Rwanda and Burundi. As the forces of his Hutu allies melted away, Mobutu was left exposed. For once, the West refused to bail out Mobutu. His army weakened from decades of decay and corruption, rapidly gave up ground to the insurgents. **Laurent-Désiré Kabila**, a previously obscure figure from Katanga, took command over rebel forces. On May 17, 1997, Kabila seized Kinshasa and proclaimed himself president. The first Congo War was over and brought Mobutu's brutal reign to a merciful end. While the 1990s ushered in a decade of restored growth, political reform, and the hope for a better future for many Africans, progress remains uneven. For the people in the Congo, like those in Somalia and Southern Darfur, living conditions did not meaningfully improve over the next decade.

Conclusion

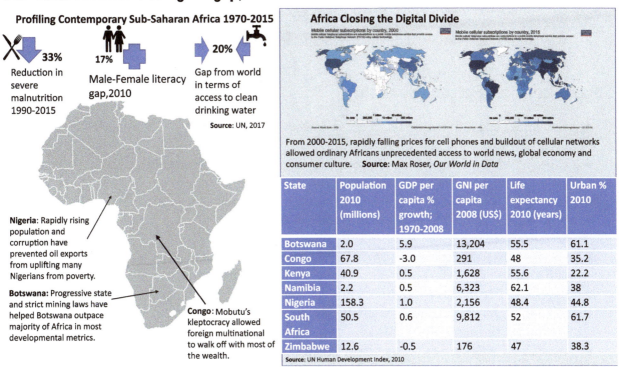

Image credits: © Isared Honghin/Shutterstock.com© Arcady/Shutterstock.com; © Nasi_lemak/Shutterstock.com

After 1960, the dream of African independence collided with harsh postcolonial realities. Import-substitution strategies mostly failed to industrialize Africa, fragile states fell prey to internal strife, external intrigues, and mounting debt. By the 1980s, Sub-Saharan economies cratered, culminating in a lost decade that sunk many into misery and hunger. Since 1998, however, Sub-Saharan African economies have recovered. Heavy multinational investment in mining and increasing trade with China have stimulated economic growth and rising wages in many countries. African states are also rapidly incorporating digital technologies like cell phones lifting the cloud of rural Africa's historic isolation. By the twenty-first century, islands of conspicuous prosperity emerged in cities like Addis Abba and states like Botswana. Africa's future, however, ultimately hinges upon developing a more defined role inside the global economy. Sub-Saharan economies remain highly leveraged to natural resource extraction, commodity exports, and food imports, while Africa's rapidly growing population increasingly depends on a fragile ecology, an inadequate health and educational infrastructure and weak state institutions that often command more suspicion than trust.

Questions for Critical Thought

1. What factors contributed to the decline of parliamentary systems and the rise of autocratic regimes across Africa during the 1960s?
2. Why did the ideals of Pan-Africanism fail to meaningfully transform the international system?
3. How did African despotism marry certain aspects of traditional tribal rule with modern instruments of state?
4. What events and forces triggered Sub-Saharan Africa's lost decade?
5. How did Mobutu stay in power despite presiding over one of the world's most corrupt regimes that sentenced his people to miserable poverty?
6. What African features make sustainability key to its future prosperity?
7. What pressures contributed to the collapse of the Apartheid regime in South Africa?
8. Why is it too simplistic to attribute the Rwandan genocide to ethnic hatreds and tribalism?

Suggestions for Further Reading

- Collins, R., and J. Burns. *A History of Sub-Saharan Africa.* Cambridge: Cambridge University Press, 2013.
- Crowder, M. *Cambridge History of Africa,* Vol. 8 of *1940-1975.* Cambridge, UK: Cambridge University Press, 1984.
- Freund, B. *The African City: A History.* Cambridge: Cambridge University Press, 2007.
- Gordon, A. A., and D. L. Gordon, *Understanding Contemporary Africa.* 5th ed. London: Lynne Rienner, 2013.
- Nzongola-Ntalaja, G. *The Congo from Leopold to Kabila: A People's History.* London: Zed Books, 2002.
- Prunier, G. *The Rwanda Crisis: History of a Genocide.* New York: Columbia University Press, 1995.
- Schmidt, E. *Foreign Intervention in Africa: From the Cold War to the War on Terror.* Cambridge: Cambridge University Press, 2013.
- Welsh, D. *The Rise and Fall of Apartheid.* Charlottesville, VA: University of Virginia Press, 2009.

Notes

1. Quoted in Renee C. Fox, Willy de Craemer, and Jean-Marie Ribeaucourt, "The Second Independence: A Case Study of the Kwilu Rebellion in the Congo," *Comparative Studies in Society and History* 8, no. 1 (1965): 78–109, 91.
2. Organization of African Unity Charter, May, 25, 1963.

3. Didier Gondola, "Chapter 7: 1960-1965," in *History of Congo* (Palo Alto, CA: Greenview, 2002), 116–17.
4. Quoted in A. Césaire, *Nègre je suis nègre je resterai. Entretiens avec Françoise Vergè* (Paris: Albin Michel, 2005), 23.
5. See 2005 Pew Research Center, "Cell Phones in Africa: Communication Lifeline," April 15, accessed August 6, 2019, 2015, http://www.pewglobal.org/2015/04/15/cell-phones-in-africa-communication-lifeline/.
6. Ed Pilkington, "Shell Pays out $15.5m Over Saro-Wiwa Killing," *The Guardian*, June 8, 2009, accessed August 6, 2019, https://www.theguardian.com/world/2009/jun/08/nigeria-usa.
7. Quoted in US Human Rights and Law Sub-Committee, April 25, 2007.

Chapter 9
Postwar Asia

Chapter Outline

- Introduction: Postwar Asia
- Asia's Cold War
- Japan's Postwar Transformation, 1945 to 1991
- Mao and China's Modernization Struggle, 1950 to 1976
- The Asian Miracle
- China: The Wakening Dragon, 1977 to 2001
- Summary: Postwar Asia

Postwar Asia: 1945–2001

1946-1954 French-Indochina War
1947 Partition of India and Pakistan
1949 Mao declares Socialist Republic
1949 Indonesian independence
1950–1953 Korean War
1950 Sino-Soviet Friendship Treaty
1951 Treaty of San Francisco
1954 MITI (Japan)
1955 Bandung Conference
1957 Malaysian independence
1958–1961 China's Great Leap Forward
1960 Sino-Soviet Split
1962 Sino-Indian War
1966 Mao Launches Cultural Revolution
1967 ASEAN formed
1969 Ussuri River Incident
1971 Third Indo-Pakistani War
1972 Nixon visits China
1973 Last US soldiers leave Vietnam
1975 Fall of Saigon
1975 Khmer Rouge seize Phnom Penh
1976 Mao dies
1978 Deng's Open Door Policy
1989 Tiananmen Square Massacre
1989 Japan's Asset Bubble Pops
1998–1999 Asian Financial Crisis
2001 China joins WTO

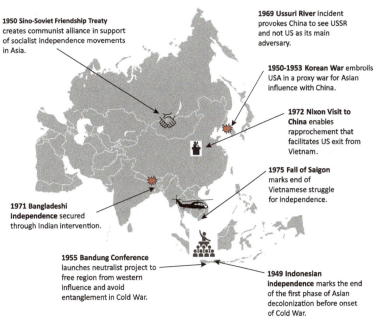

1950 Sino-Soviet Friendship Treaty creates communist alliance in support of socialist independence movements in Asia.

1969 Ussuri River Incident provokes China to see USSR and not US as its main adversary.

1950-1953 Korean War embroils USA in a proxy war for Asian influence with China.

1972 Nixon Visit to China enables rapprochement that facilitates US exit from Vietnam.

1971 Bangladeshi Independence secured through Indian intervention.

1975 Fall of Saigon marks end of Vietnamese struggle for independence.

1955 Bandung Conference launches neutralist project to free region from western influence and avoid entanglement in Cold War.

1949 Indonesian independence marks the end of the first phase of Asian decolonization before onset of Cold War.

Image credits: © Nasi_lemak/Shutterstock.com; © valeriya kozoris/Shutterstock.com; © Chippo Medved/Shutterstock.com; © MuchMania/Shutterstock.com; © Cube29/Shutterstock.com

Introduction: Postwar Asia

The West has long viewed Asian society through the prism of the "Orient." Asia represents an advanced pole of civilization with sophisticated institutions different from, and at odds with, the West. Geographically, Asia constitutes a vast territory stretching from the humid forests and desolate frozen tundra of Siberia to China's densely packed coastal cities. Across its leading edge lie the maritime states of the Pacific Rim featuring dense jungles, thick rice paddies, jagged mountain valleys, isolated hamlets, and now bustling cosmopolitan cities connected to the global economy. South Asia has historically served as a cultural crossroads: a legacy written into multiethnic communities clustering around the river valleys of the Indian subcontinent. Western Asia's mountainous and desert frontier consists of mostly landlocked Islamic states abutting the Central Asian steppe. Chinese civilization once anchored Asian culture and infused regional institutions with Confucian traditions. The Chinese empire's nineteenth-century decline, however, provided an entry point for deeper penetration of Japanese and Western influences into the continent.

Three threads run through Asia's postwar history: the drive for postcolonial independence, the aspiration for modernization, and the quest to unite divergent communities inside a cohesive state. World War II's devastation, combined with European efforts to reassert their colonial authority wracked the region in conflict. By 1948, however, much of Asia had wrestled free from colonial rule. The triumph of Mao's communists in China's Civil War, however, drew the United States more deeply into Asian affairs and seeded deadly proxy wars in Korea and Vietnam that destabilized neighboring states. By the late 1950s, Asia had been effectively partitioned. North of the "Bamboo Curtain" states pursued modernization through state socialism focused upon indigenous industrialization. Southeast Asia pursued a policy of state-guided capitalism focused more on light industries and exports to Western markets.

By the 1970s, the winds of change swept over Asia. Nixon's 1972 visit to China gradually eased Cold War tensions, while the 1973 Oil Shock created an opportunity for Asian manufacturers to expand their market share. By 1980, Japan had evolved into the world's second largest industrial economy. Japan's investment in neighboring Tiger economies also simulated their rapid modernization. Meanwhile, India and China's programs for state socialism faltered. This inspired Deng Xiaoping to change course in 1977 and adopt market reforms. Since 1990, the Asian Pacific has evolved into the world's most dynamic region. High growth and innovation have transformed regional cities into hubs of modernity deeply implicated in the world economy. A critical ingredient powering Asia's miracle, however, was the success of regional states in uniting ethnically and religious diverse communities around a disruptive program of modernization. Rapid industrialization has forced Asians to adapt indigenous institutions and reinvent their identities as they pivot to a more transnational era where their influence on the world stage is growing.

Big Questions

- How did Japan recover from World War II?
- How did Mao's radicalism throw China into turmoil?
- What sparked the Asian Miracle after 1980?
- How is globalization revamping traditional Asian ideas about gender, sexuality, and family?

Asia's Cold War

The origins of Asia's Cold War stretch back to the 1920s, when Soviet agents helped to disseminate Marxist ideas inside a continent experiencing painful transitions. The 1930s Depression Decade convinced many Asian nationalists like Nehru "that capitalism had outlived its day" and that socialism represented a blueprint for Asia's postcolonial future.[1] Colonial repression of communism during the 1930s also forced socialist organizers underground. During World War II, resilient networks survived Japanese occupation. As noted in Chapter 3, communist leaders like Malay's Chin Peng, Korea's Kim Il-Sung, Vietnam's Ho Chi Minh, and Burma's Aung San all acquired nationalist credentials by leading local resistance against Japan's occupation.

Following Japan's surrender in 1945, Asians struggled to thrust off Western rule. Despite ideological differences, Asian socialists, communists, and liberals spoke a similar language of freedom as they partnered inside larger nationalist coalitions. In US-occupied Japan, socialists exploited newly introduced laws to expand their presence inside labor unions and ultimately formed a short-lived government in 1947. In 1948, Kim Il-Sung consolidated his authority over North Korea, launching a comprehensive program for land reform before building up a stalinist workers state. By 1948, much of Asia had broken free from European colonial rule with socialists often occupying a prominent place inside postcolonial states.

China and Asia's Cold War, 1949 to 1962

The Cold War came to Asia when Mao Zedong proclaimed that Beijing would "lean" towards Moscow in 1949. Mao had grown frustrated with US support for Chiang Kai-shek whom he despised and mistrusted. He also believed that the United States would continue to support Chinese nationalists and undermine his socialist state. Establishment of a formal Sino-Soviet alliance led US policy-makers to imagine an unified Communist Bloc and see Asia's security in a new light. When Kim Il-Sung invaded South Korea in a bid to reunify the peninsula, the United States interpreted this act as "communist aggression." When the tide of war shifted in Korea, and United Nations (UN) forces crossed the 38th parallel in October 1950, China saw the American approach to their frontier as an existential threat. The bitter battle with Chinese forces in Korea led the United States to improvise a regional defense perimeter ringing China. It ultimately took the form of a "Bamboo Curtain" stretching from South Korea to Taiwan and Vietnam. The center piece of the United States' containment policy was the 1951 **Treaty of San Francisco**. This rehabilitated Japan from once hated enemy into a bulwark against mainland communism. To reassure Australia and New Zealand—still wary of Japanese militarism—the United States also concluded the 1951 **ANZUS (Australia–New Zealand–United States)** treaty pledging to defend its allies' "territorial integrity."[2] With France pulling out of Indochina in 1954, and communist insurgencies still raging in the Philippines and Malay, the United States created the 1955 **Southeast Asia Treaty Organization (SEATO)** to unite regional allies around containment. Thailand and the Philippines, like Indonesia and Malay, hosted large communities of Chinese descent. These were seen as sources for communist subversion and conduits for Chinese expansion. SEATO never evolved into a formal military organization. However, prominent members like South Korea, Thailand, and the Philippines did ultimately send soldiers to help the American war effort in South Vietnam.

After World War II, a devastated Soviet Union focused on securing Eastern Europe. Relative to Asia, Stalin was mostly cautious, desiring to avoid a direct confrontation with the West. After Mao's victory in China's civil war, however, Stalin warmed to the Asian front. Toasting Mao for his unanticipated victory over Chiang Kai-shek in 1950, Stalin spoke of a "division of labor" where China in the "interest of international revolution" would take "more responsibility" for working the "colonial and semicolonial countries" of the East.[3] These words heralded limited, and mostly covert support for Mao's efforts to stimulate socialist revolution inside Western colonies bordering China. Stalin did not anticipate US intervention in Korea, but

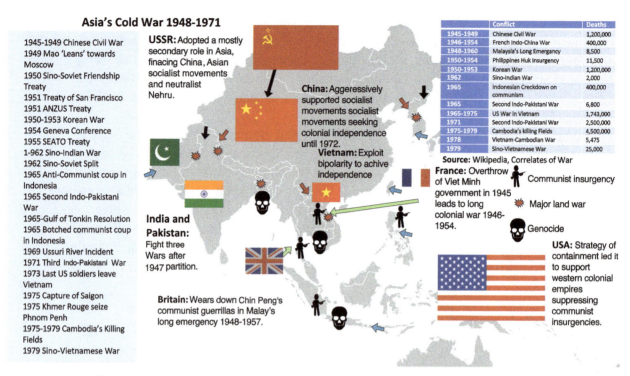

the proxy war between China and the United States suited his efforts to consolidate Eastern Europe into the Soviet Bloc. Soviet policy towards Asia did not evolve substantially under Khrushchev despite his public championing of nationalist liberation movements and the Afro-Asian Bloc inside the UN. Asia remained peripheral to the USSR's security until Khrushchev's 1956 secret speech sparked a rupture with Mao. Over subsequent years, the Chinese grew increasingly vocal in challenging the Soviet policy of "peaceful coexistence," interpreting it as abandoning socialist revolution. In 1959, Khrushchev refused to help Mao build a nuclear bomb. In 1960, the Sino-Soviet split broke into plain sight as Moscow withdrew 1,400 Soviet experts from China. The split widened still further in 1962 after the USSR failed to openly back Mao in China's war with India. Subsequently, Mao challenged the USSR's leadership over the Communist Bloc sending out Chinese advisors, engineers, and weapons to abet socialist movements in Asia and Africa. A border skirmish along the Ussuri River in 1969 brought the Soviets and Chinese into open war and led Mao to seek an accommodation with the United States as a counterweight to the Soviet Red Army.

Western Suppression of Asian Communism, 1948 to 1955

During the 1920s, socialism had acquired a foothold in Asia, particularly among young intellectuals in Asia's lower urban middle classes. Marxism often translated well to Asian societies because its core message resonated with anti-colonialism and indigenous concepts like familial loyalty, communal self-sufficiency, and social harmony. Economic breakdown during the 1930s created an opening for foreign ideologies of all sorts. Communist cadres found fertile soil for expanding their membership inside urban labor unions and rural villages. Colonial suppression of communism forced cadres to develop resilient clandestine networks, while colonial jails often served as universities in Marxist theory. Most Asian communist networks survived Japan's occupation and often played an outsized role during the turbulent process of postwar transition 1945 to 1949.

In the Philippines, the **Hukbong Mapagpalayang Bayan** (henceforth Huks) of Central Luzon originated as a peasant guerrilla movement to resist the Japanese. After liberation, the Huks became increasingly alienated from the US-backed Manuel Roxas regime. Manilla's repression of the Huks enabled communists to seize control over the movement and radicalize it. At its height in 1950, Huk guerrillas numbered over 10,000 fighters and controlled considerable territory in Luzon. Their success, however, also attracted deeper US involvement. The 1952 US–Philippine Mutual Defence Pact provided the Philippine government both economic and military support. US arms and trainers increased the Philippine counterinsurgency capacity, enabling them to wear down the Huk insurgency until its leadership surrendered in 1953.

In British-controlled Malay, communism spread rapidly in 1941 after Japan targeted the ethnic Chinese with murderous Sook Ching "counterinsurgency" missions that often arbitrarily killed men, women, and children. After independence in 1945, the Malayan People's Anti-Japanese Army were celebrated as heroes, but many ethnic Malays remained suspicious of the influence of Malay citizens of Chinese descent. Secretly, Chin Peng reconstituted his guerrilla army into a communist militia, hiding caches of weapons. In 1948, fearing that Britain would move against his supporters, Chin Peng launched a guerrilla war from Malay's sparsely settled northern jungles. The **Malay Emergency** endured because of the dogged resistance of Chin Peng's hardened fighters, but Britain's strategy of political reform, economic development, and systematic village relocation gradually isolated his forces from their civilian supporters. By Malaysia's independence in 1957, Peng's last guerrillas, starved for food and ammunition, had retreated into Thailand. Peng switched tactics and built up a covert communist organization in Singapore. But in February 1963, President Lee Kuan Yew launched Operation Cold Store. This destroyed most of Peng's network. Unlike Vietnam and Korea, Malaysian, Indonesian, and Philippian communists did not share a border with China. The absence of foreign supplies combined with muscular Western intervention wore down three experienced guerrilla movements. Deployment of US ground forces to Korea and South Vietnam, aid to Taiwan and Japan, and suppression of communist insurgencies in Malay, the Philippines, and later Indonesia enabled the United States to establish a security perimeter in Asia by 1955.

Cambodia's Killing Fields, 1950 to 1979

Proxy wars brought terrible suffering to Asia, but nothing compares to the horrors of Cambodia's killing fields. In 1949, the fledgling communist party in Cambodia attracted few supporters. The party's ranks expanded, however, after the North Vietnamese established base camps inside Cambodia to supply their insurgents operating inside South Vietnam. Although North Vietnam provided some logistical support to Cambodian communists, the ranks of the **Khmer Rouge**, named after their distinctive red bandanas, swelled after Nixon's bombing of Cambodia in 1969. While US forces targeted North Vietnamese bases, over 40,000 Cambodian civilians died in the crossfire. Destroyed crops and devastated villages spread suffering and exposed the Cambodian state's many weaknesses. By 1975, many Cambodian peasants had joined the Khmer Rouge as they moved in on Phnom Penh. Collapse of the unpopular American-backed Lon Nol regime enabled the French educated, former school teacher, Saloth Sar (**Pol Pot**), to emerge as Cambodia's head of state. Residents in Phnom Penh initially celebrated the arrival of the Khmer Rouge, believing Cambodia's long civil war over. Town dwellers soon experienced one of the Cold War's worst atrocities. In his long struggle to secure Cambodian independence, Pol Pot had grown disillusioned with his people's "bourgeois attitudes." To Pol Pot's thinking, Cambodia's people displayed insufficient enthusiasm for his grand ideas about agrarian socialism. Believing his revolution superficial, Pol Pot embarked upon a drastic utopian experiment modeled upon Mao's Great Leap Forward. To rip out infectious Western ideas, Pol Pot schemed to return town dwellers to the countryside. Living as peasants would surely cleanse them of foreign customs and cultivate an authentic Cambodian consciousness.

To stimulate mass migration to the countryside, the Khmer Rouge dispensed revolutionary terror. Pushed from their homes, urban refugees, however, found little welcome in the countryside. Local cadres had insufficient resources to feed or house new arrivals and had little interest in "reeducating" migrants already identified as possessing questionable loyalty. Accordingly, refugees "deposited" in the countryside faced persecution, routine beatings, and systematic starvation. At the height of the terror in 1977, hundreds of thousands were buried alive to save the state the cost of an executioner's bullet. From 1975 to 1979, Cambodia's "killing fields" claimed over two million victims before Vietnamese forces intervened to topple the brutal Khmer regime.

The Cold War also triggered a dirty war in Indonesia. President Sukarno had long sought to balance the support from the growing communist party (KPI) against right-wing officers dominating the Indonesian army. During the 1960s, Sukarno had built a close relationship with Beijing, in part to counterbalance clandestine US support for several rebellions. Accordingly, Indonesian communists expanded their presence inside Sukarno's cabinet, creating tensions with conservatives in the army's high command. In 1965, an abortive communist coup launched by junior officers killed many of the Indonesian army's top generals. **General Suharto**, however, survived. He rallied the Indonesian army, seized control over Jakarta and drove Sukarno from power. Subsequently, Suharto's forces fanned out to uproot communism. The Indonesian army, supplemented by death squads covertly organized by the Central Intelligence Agency (CIA), summarily executed known communists. Local civilians sometimes joined vigilante bands that often indiscriminately targeted citizens of Chinese descent. In this brutal crackdown, ethnicity represented sufficient proof of communist leanings and uncorroborated accusations routinely produced summary executions. An orgy of political violence roiled Indonesia for several months, resulting in over half a million deaths. For regional politicians, Vietnam, Cambodia, and Indochina highlighted the deadly potential of the Cold War to ignite internal tensions. Mayhem impressed upon elites the importance of political accommodation and land reform, embracing ethnic minorities and articulating inclusive policies for national integration.

India's Failed Bid for Neutralism, 1947 to 1971

The Cold War's devastation stimulated many Asian leaders to adopt a policy of nonalignment during the 1955 **Bandung Conference**. Arguably the most outspoken advocate for neutralism was Indian President Jawaharlal Nehru. Following Gandhi's death and India's bloody partitioning, he faced the monumental task of forging a democratic polity from a country deeply fractured by ethnic conflict, as well as caste and religious divisions. Nehru needed to establish a new constitution for a secular state that could incorporate various states and diverse ethnic groups inside a parliamentary system of government. Nehru proved unusually successful at maintaining relatively cordial relations with both Moscow and Washington, DC. Public neutralism, however, did not enable Nehru to steer clear from a polarized international system. Despite, Nehru's historical support for Mao's communist regime and his friendship with Zhou Enlai, India became embroiled in a bitter border dispute with China. The 1962 **Sino-Indian** War resulted after Nehru protested China's invasion of their mutual neighbor, Tibet, and gave refuge to its head of state, the Dalai Lama. Mao retaliated by dispatching veteran soldiers to the Sino-Indian frontier. In the Himalayas, the People's Liberation Army (PLA) quickly laid claim to disputed territories and routed India's unprepared forces. Mao's "lesson" forced India to settle the war on unfavorable terms. Nehru subsequently aligned more closely with the Soviet Union, while investing more in national defense.

In 1965, India was dragged into war by neighboring Pakistan. Pakistan harbored deep grievances concerning the perceived unfairness of the 1947 partition lines that left a large Muslim population "trapped" inside Hindi dominated India. India's close ties with the Soviet Union had enabled Pakistani elites to cultivate a close alliance with the United States during the 1950s. This included training and hardware for Pakistan's military. In 1965, Pakistan brashly invaded its much larger neighbor, nursing the belief that Indian forces decimated by the PLA three years before were militarily inferior. Pakistan also presumed that external invasion would stimulate an uprising among the Muslim majority in the disputed Kashmir province. Pakistani troops did catch India by surprise. However, their attack inspired little enthusiasm among Indian Muslims. Following an unanticipated Indian counterattack in the Punjab, Pakistan's overstretched forces were forced to agree to an armistice.

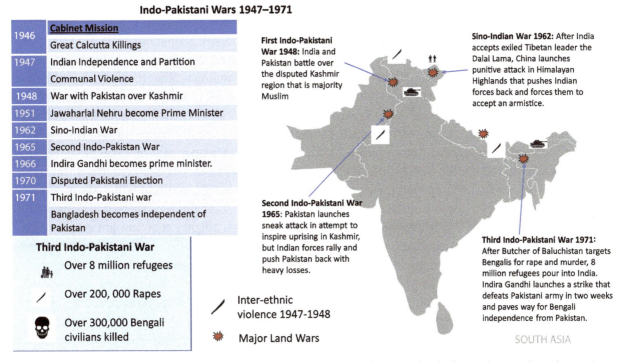

Indo-Pakistani hostilities were renewed on a grander scale after Bengali nationalists in Eastern Pakistan tried to secede from Islamabad following a bitter December 1970 election. Pakistan responded to covert Indian support for Bengali nationalism by dispatching General Tikka Khan, the "butcher of Baluchistan," to restore order. Khan's punitive campaign quickly escalated from systematic rape to genocide. At least 300,000 were killed, while 8 million refugees fled for India. In December 1971, instability in Bengal escalated into formal war. Prime Minister Indira Gandhi invaded East Pakistan in a lightning thirteen-day campaign that battered Pakistan's military forces, secured East Pakistan's independence as Bangladesh, and permanently weakened her archrival. Although India emerged from the Cold War an integral democracy, strife with its neighbors had also compelled the county to step up military investments that distracted from the country's economic development.

> Authoritarianism was a common postcolonial response to internal ethnic fissures. Were there any differences in terms of how Asian, Arab, Latin American, and African states responded to internal tensions?

Waning of Asia's Cold War, 1972 to 1979

In Asia, the Cold War burned hot. US military intervention to contain China's regional influence and repress communist insurgencies left over a million Koreans and three million Vietnamese dead. Even more died in India and Pakistan, although their wars were rooted more squarely in a contested 1947 partitioning arrangement than the Cold War. On both sides of the Bamboo Curtain, abortive insurgencies, dirty wars, and genocides in Bengal, Cambodia, and Indonesia left a grim legacy that steeled the determination of regional leaders to avoid becoming caught in the Cold War crossfire. Authoritarian states focused on maintaining internal security at any cost. US intervention in Asia after 1950 helped to stabilize its allies from the threat of communist subversion. After the 1954 Geneva Conference, Asia had been effectively partitioned into socialist and anti-Communist Blocs. During the April 1955 **Bandung Conference**, many regional leaders embraced the ideal of nonalignment, but peace did not come because local politicians, nationalists, and communists alike remained unsatisfied with this partitioning arrangement and continued to appeal to outside powers to achieve their local objectives. The dynamics powering Asia's Cold War began to shift by the late 1950s, as Mao Zedong became increasingly preoccupied with domestic concerns and more vocally critical of Khrushchev's policy of "peaceful coexistence." Sino-Soviet tensions manifested into open war in 1969 along the Ussuri River. With one million Soviet troops marshalling on China's borders, Mao redefined the USSR as their "main adversary" and opened the door to US rapprochement. Mao found willing partner in President Richard Nixon, eager to gain leverage over China's ally Vietnam in order to withdraw US combat troops. Nixon's 1972 visit to Beijing cemented an informal alliance that brought Asia's Cold War to an end and tilted the international system along a new axis. Formally, the United States agreed to the **One-China policy**, recognizing Beijing as China's legitimate government, with sovereignty over Taiwan, and right to China's permanent seat on the UN Security Council. In return, Mao agreed to pressure the Vietnamese communists to enable US withdrawal. The Beijing–Washington accord represented a working partnership rather than formal alliance. Abatement of Sino-US tensions, however, reduced the fuel for regional conflicts and inaugurated a decade of greater economic cooperation.

Following Mao's death, the **Association of Southeast Asian Nations** (ASEAN), founded in August 1967, reanimated the Non-Aligned Movement (NAM) spirit. During the 1980s, ASEAN evolved into a more robust bloc that united Pacific Rim states on both sides of the Cold War divide around the shared ideals of peace, social progress, and collaborative economic development. While the Cold War had deeply scarred Asians, it also inspired fundamental reforms that laid the foundation for stable postcolonial regimes focused upon social justice, economic modernization, and state-guided industrialization. Like Africa and the Middle East, Asia's ethnic, religious, and linguistic diversity made regional states vulnerable to internal fissures. On both sides of Asia's Bamboo Curtain, authoritarian state structures emerged to suppress internal dissent while promising economic development for all. One dimension of postcolonial Asian state building was land reform. Redistribution was a fundamental characteristic of communist regimes, but it was also carried out in Japan, South Korea, and Taiwan. Diem's resistance to land reform in South Vietnam was a contributing factor in his downfall. Inside Western-aligned states, the threat of communist subversion legitimated martial law as a means to repress civil expression, trade unionism, and political participation. Keeping wages low and guiding private business towards national development goals proved an indispensable element in their export-industrialization strategy for modernization.

While Asian states had a broadly similar political response to the Cold War's disruptive effects, their economic legacy was uneven. The United States' enemies suffered from bombing, embargo, and lack of access to international capital, while client states had their defense subsidized, while gaining privileged access to international capital and the US market. North Vietnam resisted US offers of a settlement and prevailed militarily, but at a high price. Mao's death in 1976, combined with that of Chiang Kai-shek in 1975, and the assassination of longtime Korean dictator Park Chung-hee in 1979 cleared the Cold War slate. This set the stage for regional liberalization measures and the introduction of parliamentary institutions in Taiwan and South Korea.

Japan's Postwar Transformation, 1945 to 1991

Three decades after total defeat, Japan realized its national ambition for modernization and global influence. This triumph was hardly imaginable in September 1945, when a distressed but determined Emperor Hirohito took to the radio to announce Japan's surrender. Japan had waged a bold war for imperial conquest that it justified as Asian liberation. By 1945, eleven million Japanese were homeless, with many on the brink of starvation as Americans disembarked from their troop ships. Truman appointed Douglass MacArthur **Supreme Commander of Allied Powers (SCAP)** with the delicate task of rebuilding Japan. MacArthur needed to demilitarize and democratize an Asian culture that few Americans understood. Initially, SCAP believed that the cure for Japanese militarism was a healthy dose of Americanization. MacArthur sought to curb the influence of the old elites that had dominated Japan's military, government, and industries. From 1945 to 1947, MacArthur broke up Japan's industrial cartels, reformed Japan's schools, legalized labor unions, and conferred women legal equality. The 1947 constitution represented the culmination of SCAP's program to "democratize" Japan. An imposed liberal structure demoted Hirohito from a divine ruler to a mortal figurehead, established a parliamentary system of government, and outlawed war. Rising Cold War tensions, and mounting labor unrest inside Japan, however, provoked a US policy shift. After 1947, Americans came to see communism rather than the "Jap" as their true enemy. This led SCAP to rehabilitate Japan's old elites, deemphasize Americanization, and focus more on economic than political reconstruction. With the Fall of China in 1949, and breakout of Korean War in 1950, America ideas about postwar Japan came full circle. Coming into force in 1952, the 1952 **Treaty of San Francisco** restored Japan's independence and cemented its status as the Western bulwark against mainland communism.

Japan under SCAP 1945-1952

1945 Hirohito announcement
1945 General MacArthur tasked with rebuilding and democratizing Japan
1945 SCAP abolishes Shinto state religion and Thought Police
1945 Legalization of labor unions
1945 Female suffrage established
1946 Land Reform Measure
1946-48 Tokyo War Trials
1947 SCAP suppresses General Strike
1947 Breakup of Japanese zaibatsu
1947 Educational reforms to promote gender equity
1947 MacArthur imposes liberal constitution
1947 MacArthur pares back Americanization liberalization measures
1950 War in Korea
1951 Signing of Treaty of San Francisco

August 15, 1945: Hirohito announces that Japanese people must "endure the unendurable and bear the unbearable." 7 Million Japanese officials and settlers based in their former Asian Empire needed to repatriated to Japanese Home Islands

August 30, 1945: American forces under General Douglass MacArthur arrive in Japan. MacArthur is appointed Supreme Commander Allied Pacific, with the task to demilitarize and democratize Japan. The Japanese people are in a state of shock, kyōdatsu, struggling to get their bearings as they experience an American occupation while 9 million are homeless.

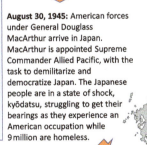

April 28, 1952: Treaty of San Francisco comes into force, ends World War II and restores Japanese sovereignty.

June 1947- June 1950: Economic problems, labor unrest and communist agitation precipitate a shift in SCAP policies as MacArthur scales back liberalization measures, rehabilitates old elites and represses workers in a bid to safeguard Japan from communist infiltration. Outbreak of Korean War underlines the necessity of Japan as corner stone of Western alliance and creates demand for Japanese goods that begins economic recovery.

September 1945-May 1947: During the liberal phase of US occupation, MacArthur adopts broadly New Deal policies to liberalize Japanese society by introducing female suffrage, legalizing labor unions, establishing education equity. Liberal reforms are capstoned by the 1947 Constitution that vests sovereignty in the people, outlaws war, guarantees basic civil rights and establishes a democratic structure of government.

7 million Japanese expatriates awaiting resettlement

 1945
9 million homeless

Rations limited to 1,042 calories per day (65% of minimum)

Image credits: Harry S. Truman Library and Museum © iconvectorstock/Shutterstock.com; © veronchick84/Shutterstock.com; © Zaur Rahimov/Shutterstock.com; © ii-graphics/Shutterstock.com

Supreme Allied Commander posing with Emperor Hirohito, 1945
This famous September 27, 1945, picture sent shockwaves through Japanese society but effectively delivered MacArthur's message that the Emperor was a mortal man, a servant of the American occupation regime, and a partner in Japan's postwar reconstruction.

Postwar Economic Recovery

Although not the beneficiary of Marshall Plan funds, outbreak of war in Korea stimulated Japan's postwar recovery. The United States transformed Japan into a forward staging base. American demand for Japanese products after 1950 also gave Japan's economy a lift at a critical juncture. Another critical actor was the **Ministry of International Trade and Industry (MITI)** that "guided" national recovery during the 1950s by channeling private investment and scarce resources towards strategic heavy industries like shipping, steel, infrastructure, and power plants. Benign US policies certainly facilitated Japan's postwar recovery. The United States demanded no reparations, and while SCAP's postwar reforms were often naïve, they were mostly motivated by a genuine desire to improve Japanese living conditions. As the United States' ally in the Pacific during the 1950s, American leaders championed Japan's membership into General Agreement on Tariffs and Trade (GATT) that provided Japan's industries access to Western markets. Pegging the Japanese Yen at an artificially low rate to the dollar also gave Japanese firms an edge over their Western competitors.

During the 1950s, Japanese recovery was powered principally by domestic investment to rebuild infrastructure, construct housing, and modernize agriculture. The state invested heavily in power plants, roads, and dams, while the countryside reaped productivity gains as farm machinery elevated yields and released rural workers to migrate to Japan's rapidly growing urban centers. By the 1960s, Japan's industries grew in tandem with a global boom. Having invested in modern plants during the 1970s, Japan established global leadership in steel, electronics, and automobile industries. High investment in research and development also gave Japanese products a technological edge by the 1980s that enabled them to expand their foreign market share even further.

Japan's Golden Sixties

Economic growth, urbanization, and modernization transformed Japan's cities, its institutions, and its culture. Until the 1950s, living conditions inside Japan remained tough. *Shikata ga nai* "Nothing can be done about it" characterized the grim but resilient mind-set of many Japanese. Hard work and collective rebuilding provided a pathway for forgetting the war and casting an eye towards a better future. MacArthur's decision to shield Hirohito from prosecution, and the strategic decision to mobilize Japan as a Cold War ally, discouraged SCAP from confronting civilians with Japan's war crimes. Many Japanese felt that the 1946 Tokyo War Crimes Tribunal represented victor's justice. Postwar literature focused upon Japanese suffering and fueled a sense of collective victimization. Shame, determination, and defiance intersected in a deep ambivalence concerning America and the West. The Japanese people relished American cultural innovations from baseball to cars and popular music. They also attributed part of their economic recovery to American guidance and support. The Japanese, however, also resented their unequal partnership and feared the unruly behavior of American servicemen based on their soil.

Japan's war amnesia, and defiant mind-set, emerged as a growing foreign relations problem during the late 1970s as Japan's economic recovery hit high gear. Although Taiwan and Korea were eager to receive Japanese technology and investment, memories of wartime exploitation and abuse remained vivid. Many Asian leaders took offense at Japan's apparent lack of repentance, while others worried that Japanese investments risked transforming their countries into neocolonial outposts for Japan's economically reconstituted empire. Sixty years after World War II, Koreans loudly protested Prime Minister Junichiro Koizumi's 2006 visit to the Yasukuni Shrine, housing the graves of a thousand convicted war criminals.

During the 1960s, many American businessmen had expressed admiration for Japan's "Confucian" culture that promoted hard work, workplace harmony, and company loyalty. As American corporations lost global market share during the 1970s, however, US lawmakers blamed unemployment in the steel and auto sectors on Japanese's subsidies and protectionism. While Japan used various strategies to bar foreign imports, the principal problem confronting US steel mills, electronics manufacturers, and automobile plants was that they had lost their competitive lead through complacency and inadequate investment. After wealthy Japanese investors purchased the iconographic Rockefeller Plaza in New York in 1989, popular fears about **Japan INC** reached high tide. An American fringe imagined Japan as a finely tuned hive conspiring to undermine the US economy and bring down Western civilization.

Japanese Capitalism

Japanese capitalism was distinct from its Western partners in being closely enmeshed with its political system. Politicians, state bureaucrats, bankers, and private businessmen were locked into a political machine that consistently returned the Liberal Democratic Party (LDP) to power from 1951 to 1993. The right-of-center LDP was a conservative party focused on maintaining internal social order by privileging economic growth and exports. This system in part reflected Japan's experience with bitter strikes and social unrest that peaked in 1960 with the controversial renewal of the US–Japan Defense Treaty. Subsequently, turbulence waned as left-wing groups were increasingly incorporated into a new social contract where large Japanese corporations, employing about a third of the workforce, promised their workers' "lifetime" employment in return for accepting lower wages than their Western competitors. In contrast to Western practice, the Japanese government and private businesses also cooperated extensively to achieve national economic goals. MITI served as the principal arbitrator of various interests. Japanese capitalism also featured a cartel system known as the keiretsu, a structure for heavy industry where banks, leading manufacturers, and distributors collaborated in alliances to buy each other's products while holding their allies' stock. Formal price fixing would have been deemed illegal in most Western countries, but this system helped Japan's large industries to become internationally competitive by keeping domestic wages low, protecting internal markets from foreign competition and strategically directing national investment towards key technologies for future growth.

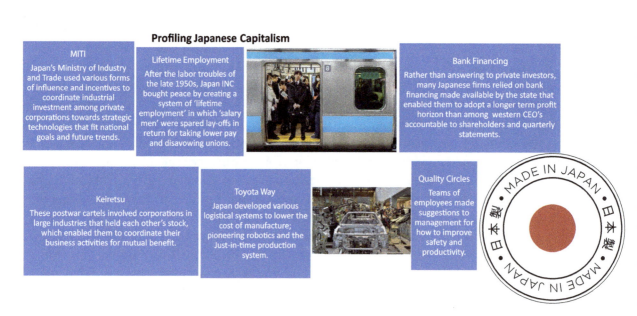

Bright Life and Postwar Anxieties

During the Golden Sixties, Japan's "miracle" provided a framework for the country's peaceful rejuvenation and national redemption. After decades of struggle, suffering, and austerity, ordinary families equated the "three treasures"—a washing machine, television, and refrigerator—with "a bright new life." Throughout the world, modernization and migration of peasants to cities sparked dislocation. In Japan, rising living standards and carefully planned urban centers, however, eased the trauma of transition. The popularity of transistor radios in the 1960s sparked a cultural fascination for electronic gadgets that at a deeper level resonated with the country's struggle to overcome a dark past. Beneath the veneer of modernity embodied in Tokyo's glass skyscrapers, immaculately clean public spaces, and efficient trains, Japanese family life remained dominated by traditional values, particularly a sharp gender division of labor, where the husband served as breadwinner and worked long hours, while the wife was expected to stay at home, mother the children, perform domestic work, rule the household, and care for aging parents. While the economic miracle brought prosperity to Japan, rapid change also sowed anxiety, famously manifested in the popular Godzilla films. This primitive beast, emerging unexpectedly from the murky deep to devastate Yokohama's skyscrapers and elevated highways, manifested a deeper angst. Modern life and postwar prosperity might represent a glittering illusion that could easily be swept away by the tide of older, more elemental forces. The primordial dragon invoked the spirit of old Japan, raising the question of whether Japan's assimilation of Western practices, modernity, and industrial patterns of life had led them astray from the country's traditions and values.

Godzilla Statue lurking over the Tokyo Skyline

In Japanese culture, Godzilla manifests the survival of the old magical world seemingly blotted out by technological modernity.

Minamata Disaster

Environmental pollution represented another challenge to Japan's postwar rejuvenation. In 1908, the Chisso chemical plant had opened in the fishing village of Minamata. After World War II, Chisso evolved into a leading manufacturer of fertilizers. Rising profits drove Minamata's growth into a prosperous industrial city. For years, Minamata's largest employer and taxpayer also dumped waste into the bay. Already in the early 1950s there were reports of birds mysteriously crashing into the sea. In 1956, some local fishermen became afflicted by a strange neurological disorder that impaired motor skills, speech, and brain function. Many blamed Chisso, whose pollution was an open secret. Japan's public health response, however, was notoriously slow and inadequate. Initially, Chisso denied any responsibility for Minamata disease. In fact, the company critiqued disease victims as greedy money grubbers that had failed to assimilate to modern Japan. State officials were complicit in a cover-up that silenced research scientists. Many were paid to claim that there was no conclusive proof that Chisso caused this illness. Minamata disease ran counter to the prevailing national myth that through hard work and successful embrace of technology Japan had transcended a dark past. By the 1960s, it became clear that mercury poisoning was the source for Minamata disease. Chisso, however, leveraged its influence to resist a costly settlement in bitter court wrangling. In 1968, in the wake of national outrage, the federal government stepped in and admitted the link between Minamata disease and mercury poisoning. In 1970, Japan's Parliament passed a wide range of environmental laws that sought to recalibrate Japan's economic growth with public health.

A crippling blow to Japan's redemption narrative came in 1991, as its miracle economy turned to dust. From 1985 to 1991, property prices in Japan had risen over 300 percent. At the height of this bubble, Tokyo's property was theoretically worth more than the entire United States. Japanese property and stock prices had skyrocketed in part because of American pressure to raise the Yen's value. The unintended consequence of this policy was to elevate Japanese purchasing power and to create liquidity that was pumped into real estate. Housing in Tokyo and other metropolitan centers became unaffordable. Most Japanese families lived in very small high-rise apartments that carried generational mortgages spanning ninety-nine years. Japan's property bubble began to deflate in 1989 after the national bank raised interest rates and sent Japan's Nikkei stock market plunging almost 50 percent. Despite a partial stock market recovery in 1990, the real economy turned south again in 1991 after housing prices tanked. Japan never fully recovered from the 1991 crash. While the Bank of Japan closed banks and adopted various initiatives to reinflate the economy, Japan's growth has continued to lag its Organisation for Economic Co-operation and Development (OECD) partners. Japan's high level of national debt, low birth rate, and aging population present a demographic bomb that seems impossible to diffuse.

Mao and China's Modernization Struggle, 1950 to 1976

Despite US and Soviet pressure to reconcile and create a unity government to help war-ravaged China recover, after more than a month of deliberations Mao Zedong and Chiang Kai-shek failed to reach a power-sharing arrangement in 1945.

Mao Zedong and Chiang Kai-shek toast each other in 1946

If any Asian country emerged from World War II more devastated than Japan, it was China. Following victory in China's civil war, Mao declared a People's Socialist Republic in Beijing in September 1949. Chiang's loyalists fled to Formosa where they established the Republic of Taiwan. It took several years for Mao to consolidate his authority. The Korean War disrupted China's process of socialist reform. To reward his peasant supporters, Mao did introduce land reform in 1950. This initiative used intimidation to seize arable land from the powerful landlords that had supported Chiang and had long brutalized the peasantry. Mao mobilized local peasants to confront, shame, and humiliate local landlords. Mob intimidation included insults and often physical beatings. Some landlords were killed on the spot. Others were sent to reeducation camps with their families where a million soon died. A hundred million acres of land was redistributed by 1952. China's long-suffering peasants saw their living standards improve and Mao's campaign helped them to develop a class consciousness. Rather than belonging to a village defined by tradition, patronage, and lineage, peasants were challenged to imagine themselves as agents for creating a more just society.

Mao moved more slowly to reform the Chinese state and urban communities. Until 1956, noncommunist groups continued to participate inside Mao's big tent. Urban factory owners managed their own businesses, shopkeepers ran their shops, and peasants sold their produce at local markets.

The first campaign to modernize China commenced in 1952 when Beijing unveiled a Five-Year Plan that closely followed the Soviet heavy industrialization model. Under terms of the 1950 **Sino-Soviet Treaty of Friendship**, Stalin agreed to supply China with technical assistance, loans, and machinery to facilitate its industrialization. The goal of China's Five-Year Plan was a doubling of the country's gross domestic product (GDP). The plan focused primarily upon expanding steel production and electricity generation. Soviet loans and 10,000 experts supervised the installation of Russian supplied machinery in cities around the country. Mao, however, grew disenchanted with Soviet influence, and suspicious of the emergence of a rich class of peasants in the countryside. To Mao, China seemed only superficially socialist. All around, relicts of old China, Confucian culture, and village tradition remained alive. Mao also worried that Party elites, many who had joined his cause late, were insufficiently committed to socialism. In 1956, Mao introduced his **Hundred Flowers** campaign. This measure invited intellectuals and Party leaders to debate China's best path forward. The criticism of the Party that ensued stung Mao. By late 1956, the Chinese press and police turned against right-wing "revisionists"; code for prominent people that saw China reverting back to more traditional norms. Over half a million people, many of them teachers and party members, were shipped off to harsh "reeducation camps." This repression cemented Mao's grip over the Party and set the stage for a far bolder program to build an authentically socialist society.

The Great Leap Forward

In 1958, Mao, disregarding Soviet experts and orthodox Marxist theory, launched an ambitious program to industrialize China by mobilizing the peasantry. The first step in Mao's plan was rural collectivization. Party cadres bullied villagers into joining large communes that united thousands of peasants into cooperative enterprises tightly run by the state. Chinese farmers were "encouraged" to surrender their land, livestock, and most of their household goods. Henceforth, agricultural decisions and village life would be directed by Party cadres rather than local farmers and village elders.

The theory behind the Great Leap Forward was that larger farms would prove more efficient. Also, rather than investing in expensive heavy machinery with capital China did not possess, Mao would mobilize China's peasant labor to undertake public works projects. Instead of Soviet experts, peasant teams, invigorated with patriotic fervor, would construct irrigation works and backyard furnaces to catch up to the West. Party cadres often approached Mao's bold plan with enthusiasm, but peasants lacked proper tools or engineering expertise. As a result, most of Mao's projects were poorly conceived, many actually lowered agricultural productivity, and many others rapidly fell into disrepair. Rural collectivization also produced food shortages by sidelining peasants and centralizing decision-making in the Party. Some cadres came from towns or secured appointment based on their ideological passion. Cadres were adept at devising ceremonies and slogans that exhorted the peasantry to work day and night ("Catch the Stars") but many lacked the managerial talent or agronomical knowledge to supervise vast enterprises.

Mao envisioned his Great Leap Forward not just as an economic strategy, but a process for creating a "socialist society" by abolishing private property, gender inequality, and the traditional family household. Revolutionary progressivism targeted Chinese traditions as wives were removed from control of their husbands, households were broken up in favor of gender-segregated barracks, and children were placed in village nurseries. This revolutionary leveling of the traditional household manifested most prominently in the establishment of communal canteens where cadres dispensed rations based on work points their assessment of the value of a farmer's work and party enthusiasm.

Utopian Socialism: Breakup the traditional family and village society by separating husbands and wives into gender segregated barracks, establishing communal canteens to supplant household kitchens and nurture children in village creches.

Low-Tech Infrastructure: Peasant laborers and Party cadres rather than engineers and professional construction teams are mobilized to build roads, irrigation works and other infrastructure.

Backyard Furnaces: Promising to catch up with Britain in terms of steel production, Mao orders communes to create primitive smelters that to turn scrap metal and valuable tools into useless pig-iron.

45 million 'premature' deaths
source: Frank Diotter

Cadre Terrorism: With mounting famine in 1959, the authority of cadres who control insufficient food carries life and death leading to widespread abuse of villagers.

Maoist Theory: Great Leap forward overturns orthodox Marxist-Leninism and focuses on industrialization through mobilization of the countryside.

Propaganda Mobilization: Party cadres exhort workers and peasants to work day and night to build a better future.

Cooperative Enterprises: Villages organized into larger cooperative farms run by party cadres rather than local farmers, who often pursue 'non Bourgeois' farming practices at odds with agronomical science.

Great Leap Forward 1957–1962
- 1951 Sino-Soviet Treaty of Friendship
- 1952 First Five Year Plan
- 1956 Mao declares People's Communes are good
- 1956 Hundred Flowers Campaign
- 1957 Great Leap Forward launched
- 1959 Lushan Conference silences Marshall Duhaie and other critics
- 1962 Mao forced into self-criticism

Revolutionary utopianism intersected with corruption to produce the twentieth century's worst famine. What Frank Dikötter has labeled "Mao's great famine" had its origin in a 1957 challenge to village communes to increase their harvest to help finance China's industrialization. Local cadres, whose privileges revolved upon meeting party production targets, responded by announcing continually higher production quotas. To meet these impossible figures, cadres enthusiastically tossed out traditional farming methods that they believed to be tainted by "bourgeois" thinking. In one village, cadres dug out a pit, dumped in their seeds, and layered inches of fertilizer with the hope that the wheat would spring up as thick as concrete. When revolutionary enthusiasm collides with soil science, nature wins. Instead of increasing yields, communist "innovations" mostly reduced harvests and exhausted the soil. Rather than admitting failure and facing sanction, cadres celebrated their success by staging elaborate harvest ceremonies where rice bags were filled with sticks, saw dust, and stalks. When 20 percent of the reported harvest was shipped to Beijing villagers were left to starve.

In 1959, adverse meteorological conditions helped to turn the Great Leap Forward into a humanitarian disaster. The principal source of the famine, however, was Mao's determination to distinguish himself from Khrushchev. Over the fall and winter of 1959, cadres lived well. In some factories, workers ate three square meals a day. In the countryside, starving peasants ate bark, roots, and grass. We will never know how many peasants died as a result of famine, but malnutrition, disease, and Party violence killed between eighteen and forty-five million from 1958 to 1962.[4]

During a Party conference in 1959, mass starvation was impossible to ignore. Defense Minister Peng Dehuai framed his criticisms carefully to avoid blaming Mao personally, but he also pleaded with his old comrade to "think of the people." Mao responded with indignant defiance. His subsequent dismissal of Dehuai, and repression of an "anti-Party clique," silenced criticism. Mao stubbornly pushed forward. By 1961, desperate peasants resorted to cannibalism. One popular technique involved exhuming corpses that were boiled into a broth. Only in 1962, did China's Party leaders step in to end the radical experiment and force Mao to engage in self-criticism.

> Hollywood's fascination with zombies seems to tap a dark historical memory of cannibalism. Zombie films posit the question: When you are starving to death how does the biological drive for food rewire the human brain?

A group of moderates led by Deng Xiaoping and Liu Shaoqi returned state focus towards urban factories, shrunk the size of collective farms, and returned agricultural decision-making to local farmers. This stabilized China's economy and brought the famine to a merciful end. Mao, however, resented his marginalization and the moderate course adopted by his successors.

China's Cultural Revolution, 1966 to 1976

On July 16, 1966, Mao took a "swim" in the Yangtze. Floating 9 miles downstream demonstrated the 70-year-old's virility and set the stage for Mao's triumphal return to Chinese politics. Subsequently, Mao began issuing communiques, while delivering rousing speeches to young students imploring them to save the socialist revolution from "capitalist road graders." These speeches inaugurated the **Great Proletarian Cultural Revolution**. Mao not only cast doubt on China's direction, but the loyalty of his successors. He played to the egos of young students and workers, convincing them they represented the last hope to save socialism from right deviationists. Mao instructed the impressionable youth that they needed to "destroy virtually all state and Party institutions."[5] This intoxicating call to arms stimulated the formation of **Red Guards** throughout China. Soon mobs of militant vigilantes, reciting from the little Red Book containing Maoist sayings, swooped over China. To preserve China's socialist revolution, they attacked the "four olds": customs, culture, habits, and ideas. This included knocking down ancient temples, burning books, and smashing national treasures in their war against old China and poisonous "bourgeoisie" thinking. Red Guards zealously rounded up factory supervisors, professors, Party officials, sometimes even their own family members. Those accused of "right-wing deviation" were subject to public humiliation and extrajudicial beatings. Intellectuals and authority figures were singled out for particular humiliation. Often they were paraded around wearing 3-feet dunce caps and incriminating placards that spelled out their counterrevolutionary crimes. Thousands of Party officials and state officials fell victim to revolutionary terror, their families blacklisted. No one could feel safe after **Liu Shaoqi**, China's head of state, was arrested and labelled the "biggest capitalist roader in the Party."[6] Recanting did not spare Shaoqi, because his real sin was reversing Mao's disastrous policies. In 1969, guards found Shaoqi's corpse sprawled on the dirt floor of his cell.

A culture of fear permeated Chinese society as millions of neighbors turned upon each other, schools closed, and enthusiastic Red Guards decamped to the countryside to sanctify their revolutionary zeal through manual labor. By 1969, Mao was formally restored as head of state and declared the

Cultural Revolution over. The Red Guards had started to target the PLA threatening to spark a civil war. It would take years to quell China's revolutionary fervor, but Mao had engineered his triumphal return to power. The Cultural Revolution left behind a battered state, a broken educational system, and a scarred nation. The country's dramatic embrace of market reforms a decade later attests that it also failed to uproot the deep foundations of Chinese culture or cultivate a new socialist mentality.

State Socialism's Decline

While China's experience was unique, by the early 1980s other Asians increasingly recognized state socialism as a failed modernization strategy. Under Nehru's leadership, India had inaugurated the 1952 **Bombay Plan** to expand the national infrastructure, invest in industry, grow the economy, and "create national awareness" among India's diverse ethnic, linguistic, and religious communities. Nehru's plan invoked the traditional modernization model, nationalizing heavy industries and investing in public work projects ranging from roads to dams and power stations. Following the mixed economies of Western Europe, the lower tiers of the economy and the agricultural sector were left in private hands. Despite his preference for socialism, Nehru was pragmatic enough to realize that radical reforms would have destabilized the state. "Our problem," he said in March 1949, "is to raise the standard of the masses, supply them with their needs, give them the wherewithal to lead a decent life. . . . . I do not care what 'ism' it is that helps me to set them on that road provided I do it. And if one thing fails, we will try another."[7]

Despite impressive gains in steel and electricity production, high birth rates, rural illiteracy, and three separate wars with China and Pakistan derailed Nehru's dream of catching up to the West. Nehru's greatest success lay in the political arena. The Congress Party dominated postwar India and its greatest achievement lay in creating a democratic state, impressive given the country's high degree of diversity. India's federal state system gave individual provinces considerable autonomy, but political stability also reflected the effectiveness of state institutions created under the British Raj and the solidarity Indians built during their long, collective struggle for independence. Under **Indira Gandhi** (1966–1984), some of this democratic consensus eroded away. The Gandhi dynasty, which included her two sons, resorted to a more autocratic style of rule, while sectarian parties grew more influential. Increasing political fragmentation during the 1980s was amplified by growing realization that India had fallen behind other Asian states. State planning had resulted in a massive and corrupt bureaucracy that stifled innovation, discouraged foreign investment, and impeded trade. In comparison to regional neighbors like China, India also lagged far behind in terms of female literacy, education, and healthcare. Despite launching the green revolution to modernize agriculture, rural poverty increased, while the country's high birth rate put extreme pressure on already strained environmental systems.

India's laggard postwar performance was cast into sharp relief by the Pacific Rim's **Tiger** economies that pursued a more liberal development strategy. Although various Indian governments flirted with liberalization measures during the 1980s, only in 1991 did India embark upon systematic program for market reform. By 2007, various reform measures culminated in a GDP growth rate that approached 9 percent, although it declined in the wake of the 2008 Great Global Recession. Like China, India's growth has been concentrated in urban areas and mostly benefitted the urban middle classes. Regional abandonment of state socialism was underscored by communist Vietnam's adoption of liberal reforms. With the fall of Saigon in 1975, the communists finally reunited their country, but developing an economy wracked by intensive bombing and three decades of conflict proved difficult. After independence, Vietnam promoted heavy industry, but like elsewhere, state socialism failed to catalyze growth or meaningfully raise the standard of living. In 1986, Vietnam launched **Doi Moi**, a comprehensive reform program to transition from central planning towards a "socialist market" economy. By 1991, only North Korea still featured a Stalinist economy. The rest of Asia was busily implementing pro-market reforms. Although variant in form, they saw integration with the world economy as key to raising local living standards.

The Asian Miracle

Asia's gradual abandonment of state socialism was influenced by the success of Asia's Tiger economies. Starting in the early 1960s, Singapore, Taiwan, Hong Kong, and South Korea had adopted elements of Japan's export industrialization strategy. After the Oil Shock of 1973, Japanese multinationals increasingly invested in the Tigers as a strategy for outsourcing low margin industries to lower cost regions. Politically, the Tigers mostly featured authoritarian states that were able to keep wages low and direct private investment towards key national objectives. High levels of growth were financed primarily by high rates of internal saving, while corporate profits were channelled back into industry with little state spending diverted towards social welfare programs like healthcare or social insurance. Although the Oil Shock raised production costs, increasing specialization set the stage for the **Asian Miracle** of the 1980s. Two decades of high economic growth enabled Tiger economies to close the developmental gap with the West by the century's close.

Scholars continue to debate the sources for Asia's economic miracle. Initially many analysts praised "Asian values," suggesting that the region's cohesive family structure, tradition of hard work, and Confucian respect for authority provided it a unique competitive advantage. But the Tigers featured divergent societies that could only be superficially reconciled with a generic version of Confucianism. What most united the Tigers was a policy framework. The Tigers financed their own development rather than relying on foreign loans. This freed them from the burden of interest payments that crippled many other developing states. During the 1970s, the Tigers also invested heavily in primary schooling, female literacy, and the build out of robust university systems. This created a skilled workforce necessary for transitioning towards a more sophisticated manufacturing and service economy.

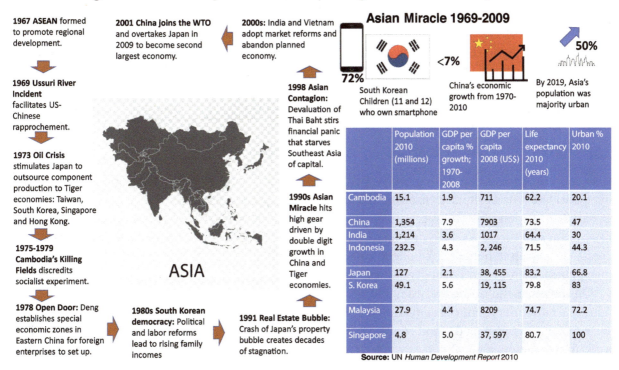

1967 ASEAN formed to promote regional development.

1969 Ussuri River Incident facilitates US-Chinese rapprochement.

1973 Oil Crisis stimulates Japan to outsource component production to Tiger economies: Taiwan, South Korea, Singapore and Hong Kong.

1975-1979 Cambodia's Killing Fields discredits socialist experiment.

1978 Open Door: Deng establishes special economic zones in Eastern China for foreign enterprises to set up.

2001 China joins the WTO and overtakes Japan in 2009 to become second largest economy.

1998 Asian Contagion: Devaluation of Thai Baht stirs financial panic that starves Southeast Asia of capital.

1980s South Korean democracy: Political and labor reforms lead to rising family incomes

2000s: India and Vietnam adopt market reforms and abandon planned economy.

1990s Asian Miracle hits high gear driven by double digit growth in China and Tiger economies.

1991 Real Estate Bubble: Crash of Japan's property bubble creates decades of stagnation.

Asian Miracle 1969-2009

72% South Korean Children (11 and 12) who own smartphone

<7% China's economic growth from 1970-2010

50% By 2019, Asia's population was majority urban

	Population 2010 (millions)	GDP per capita % growth; 1970-2008	GDP per capita 2008 (US$)	Life expectancy 2010 (years)	Urban % 2010
Cambodia	15.1	1.9	711	62.2	20.1
China	1,354	7.9	7903	73.5	47
India	1,214	3.6	1017	64.4	30
Indonesia	232.5	4.3	2,246	71.5	44.3
Japan	127	2.1	38,455	83.2	66.8
S. Korea	49.1	5.6	19,115	79.8	83
Malaysia	27.9	4.4	8209	74.7	72.2
Singapore	4.8	5.0	37,597	80.7	100

Source: UN *Human Development Report* 2010

Image credits: © monaliza0024/Shutterstock.com; © ton Blackmarine/Shutterstock.com; © Globe Turner/Shutterstock.com; © T Lesia/Shutterstock.com; © YasnaTen/Shutterstock.com

Although Western neoliberals lauded the Tiger economies as models worthy for emulation, their economies actually featured a high degree of state guidance. The Cold War also helped to stimulate the Tiger's takeoff. The Korean and Vietnam Wars created robust demand for Asian goods, while the United States rewarded regional allies with economic aid and favorable trade terms inside its vast domestic market. The latter proved an indispensable benefit for states pursuing an export industrialization strategy. Cold War tensions also contributed to development of a corporatist state that suppressed internal tensions by promoting egalitarianism and emphasizing communal wellbeing. While Asia was caught in the crossfire of the Cold War during the 1950s and 1960s, ironically this mayhem also set the stage for state reforms that sought to bridge class and ethnic divisions. Whereas the 1970s introduced turbulence to the Middle East, Africa, and Latin America, the Tigers remained politically stable. This proved essential when pursuing a long-term development strategy geared towards reconfiguring their economies to emerging currents in international trade, global manufacturing, and high technology.

Asian Financial Crisis, 1997 to 1998

The first major challenge to the Asian Miracle arrived in the form of a regionwide financial crisis. Following a democratization wave during the late 1980s, South Asia's economies grew rapidly by liberalizing their financial markets and pegging their currencies to the US dollar. This attracted international investors, led by Western hedge and pension funds. Initially, financial liberalization provided cheap credit for Asian entrepreneurs, while the dollar "peg" provided stability. By the mid-1990s, however, the volume of money pouring into Asia saturated demand. Increasingly, capital was allocated towards speculative investments, especially real estate and the region's hyperinflated stock markets. After Thailand's Central Bank was forced to devalue its Baht in 1997, Southeast Asia's dynamic economies lurched into recession. Regional central banks were forced to devalue their currencies. Stock prices tanked by as much as 60 percent as international investors pulled out their money. By 1999, sparkling high-rise luxury apartments stood empty, the Asian middle classes lost much of their savings, local entrepreneurs were starved for capital, and unemployment spiked higher. Regional currency devaluations left Asian economies laboring under a heavy debt load. By 2000, the Tiger economies entered into recovery. Their industries were mostly owned by domestic investors, which insulated them from volatile foreign capital flows and less burdened by foreign debt. There was, however, a regional divide as Malaysia, Thailand, the Philippines, and Indonesia struggled to regain their former lustre.

Negotiating Between Modernity and Tradition

Asia's miracle suggests that the region has better assimilated to modernity than its regional counterparts. Some attribute Asia's cultural dynamism to the region's geography. Sea lanes and coastal cities contributed to a long history of eclectic mixing. Asia's path to postwar modernization, however, reveals many prongs and setbacks. Mao desired to smash the "feudalism" of old China, not to "modernize" Confucianism. An important component for socialist revolution in China was mobilizing women and liberating them from traditional gender restrictions.

On the other end of the spectrum, India's modernization strategy focused primarily on urban industries rather than gender equity. In India, female literacy continues to lag behind males, spousal abuse remains rampant, and divorced women face a social stigma that isolates them from family and peers. India's gender inequality received international attention following a 2012 incident in Guwahati, where a 23-year-old student endured a 45-minute sexual assault as bystanders filmed her misery rather than intervening. When police eventually arrived, they did not make any arrests until rebroadcasts of the incident prompted national demonstrations among women's groups. Ultimately, the perpetrators were booked for "insulting or outraging the modesty of a woman" because at the time India's arcane laws limited sexual assault to cases of rape.

Window on World History: Japan's Celibacy Syndrome

A 2014 poll revealed that half of Japan's population was single, and that 45 percent of women and 25 percent of men aged 16 to 24 are "not interested in, or despised sexual contact."[8] National leaders had reason to fret about the country's "celibacy syndrome" because Japan's population is shrinking fast, while its birth rate continues to plummet. This represents a security threat to a state laboring with a debt to GDP ratio surpassing 200 percent.

Love Hotel Kabuchiko in Tokyo

Japanese Love Hotels date back to the Edo period, but were reinvented during the late 1960s and have become a prominent feature of the metropolis. Love hotels offer a "rest rate" for customers only wishing to rent a room for a single-hour span.

Many factors contribute to Japan's low birth rate. Japanese women complain that their male counterparts are *soushoku danshi*, or herbivore men, seemingly more interested in videogames than the opposite sex. Japan's low birth rate is also rooted in a cultural expectation that women who marry, or become pregnant, quit work. This leads many professional women to opt for career over family. Professional women seem caught between cultural expectations to serve as care-givers for children and aging parents and the demands of the modern work place that demands a seventy-hour work

(Continued)

week and socialization with colleagues. Not surprisingly, husbands and wives in Japan increasingly live separate lives. In this environment, the sex industry flourishes by transforming sex into an easily obtained commodity, while hostess bars provide lonely wives a feeling of romance. Hard work represented a staple ingredient powering Asia's economic miracle. There are increasing signs, however, that Asia's prosperity has come at a psychological price. In South Korea, two million citizens are estimated to be gaming addicts. Throughout Seoul, cybercafés entice social gaming enthusiasts to embark upon marathon sessions. Addicts escape inside a fantasy world of swashbuckling adventures sometimes forgetting to eat or care for their children. Does Asia's culture provide the West with a model for shaking off the doldrums of stagnant economic growth, or does its culture of hard work create "robots" that have difficulty establishing friendships, maintaining marriages, and staying physically fit?

Critical Reflection

1. Sociologists and psychologists debate the degree to which social media and Internet gaming are transforming social relationships. South Korea has made treatment of Internet addiction a national priority, to what extent does social media contribute to anxiety and depression in a Canada?
2. How do you explain the declining Japanese appetite for sex? Are Canadian marriages more balanced because of greater gender equality?

Throughout Asia, men and women are negotiating the tensions between "modernity" and "tradition." In Malaysia during the 1980s, Minister Tun Mahathir Mohammed enthusiastically labeled the emerging urban middle classes the *Melayu baru*, or New Malay, a vanguard whose cosmopolitan flair and entrepreneurial spirit would invigorate the economy. Rapid change, however, often brings stress and disorientation. For many traditionalists, the hypermodernity of Kuala Lumpur is not something to be admired. It represents the people's alienation from their natal village or *Kampung*. Malay women often find themselves at the crosscurrents of modernization, identifying with a resurgent global Islam and apprehensive about the creeping "Westernism" embedded in Malaysia's "sarong-to-jeans" movement, while also indulging in Indonesian soap operas that chronicle contemporary social problems like divorce, alcoholism, and infidelity. Throughout Asia, ordinary people must reconcile the empowerment offered by new consumer gadgets and the freedoms promised by modern life, with its accompanying problems ranging from addiction, depression, and family breakdown.

There has no uniform pattern characterizing Asia's assimilation of "modernity." Women often bear the brunt of reconciling the contradiction between the demands of the modern workplace with traditional family mores. In Japan, many women chose to forego marriage rather than to endure the gender limitations placed upon their freedom and career aspirations. In Malaysia, traditional women fret about the corrosive influence of modern dysfunction broadcast across their airwaves, while in China young women have embraced the Internet as a liberating platform to develop their unique identity on an equal footing with men. In India, professional women use social media to mobilize against structural misogyny in a culture where female infanticide and domestic violence remain trenchant problems.

In short, Asians are adapting to modernity in discrepant ways. In a society historically marked by diversity, foreign contact, and cultural mixing, however, modernity tends to be embraced mostly as an opportunity rather than construed as an existential threat to tradition. In contrast to those living in rural

Africa or the Persian Gulf States, Asians are more familiar with the West and largely comfortable with modern technology. They seek to accommodate modern progress with traditional mores in order to lead better and fuller lives.

China: The Waking Dragon, 1977 to 2001

President Jimmy Carter and China's "paramount" leader Deng Xiaoping smiling at the Sino-American signing ceremony in 1979. Deng in his personality and approach exemplified the new, post-Maoist China. Rather than waging a crusade against the established world order, under Deng China sought to achieve its national ambitions by adopting liberal reforms and collaborating with the Western powers.

Paramount leader Deng Xiaoping and President Carter

Asia's transition from state planning to capitalism was headlined by China. Following Mao Zedong's death in 1976, a power struggle developed between Mao's followers and a majority in the Party establishment that viewed the Cultural Revolution as a mistake. At the top of the Party, this struggle was exhibited in a duel between the Gang of Four that included Mao's widow versus a rehabilitated **Deng Xiaoping** who served as inspirational leader for China's reformers. By 1977, the Gang of Four had been arrested and marginalized, while Deng initiated the Beijing Spring to enable public criticism of the excesses of the Cultural Revolution. In 1978, after the Third Plenum among. communist delegates, Deng informally took power ruling as paramount leader alongside Party elders. He felt sufficiently secure to inaugurate his **Open Door Policy** inviting in foreign investors and businesses. While Mao had met with Nixon in 1972, at the height of the Sino-Soviet tensions, Deng proposed a more far-reaching rapprochement with the West. Deng understood that better diplomatic ties were a precondition for closer economic collaboration. Deng also believed that under Mao, ideology had gotten in the way of sound policy and common sense. "Seek truth form facts," emerged as a mantra to guide state policy after the Cultural Revolution. Deng also appreciated that Japan's modernization strategy worked, while Mao's socialist experiments had caused great hardships. The challenge China faced revolved around acquiring the technology necessary to achieve economic lift off. For this purpose, Deng championed the establishment of **Special Economic Zones (SEZs)**, unregulated islands of capitalism, private profits, and free trade, where foreign investors flocked to exploit tax subsidies and China's cheap labor. In 1980, communist China set up four SEZs on the coast. Shenzhen, next to British-controlled Hong Kong, enjoyed particularly rapid growth as the primary conduit between China's controlled economy and the rest of the world.

Deng's desire to change his people's attitude towards the economy was counterbalanced by a need to calibrate their expectations. While Deng criticized the excesses of the Cultural Revolution, he also avoided blaming Mao directly. From 1978 to 1981, Deng marginalized Maoists inside the Party, while sketching out his vision for a brighter common future. Deng's allies wrote glowing editorials in official papers debating the merits of a market system with "socialist characteristics." In truth, "market socialism" marked a complete policy reversal that would have made Mao squirm. Deng moved deliberately at first, giving his people time to accept this radical shift from attacking all things "bourgeois," to a system that embraced Western free market principles as key to strengthening China and improving living standards. Deng had few formal powers, but he did wield tremendous influence through strong support among party elders and regional party bosses that had lived through the chaos of the Cultural Revolution. Deng's political future, however, hinged upon successful implementation of his reforms.

In 1980, Deng followed up the Open Door with substantial reforms that loosened various state controls over the economy. By 1981, 73 percent of state farms had been abolished, while 80 percent of state owned enterprises were permitted to retain profits. These reforms created dislocation, particularly high inflation and unemployment. Although Deng's "household responsibility" system returned agricultural decisions to farmers and stimulated an immediate and impressive uptick in agricultural productivity, it also spurred corruption and elevated rural inequality. But improved economic efficiency also raised Chinese living standards, especially in the South. This secured Deng support for extending his pro-market reforms further. By 1988, China transitioned towards a market system, although the state retained significant influence over the economy. Subsequently township and village enterprises (TVEs) functioned for the profit of their owners, state businesses and capital markets remained under close Party supervision. Under the Beijing's guidance, China's per capita GDP increased from less than $500 in 1980 to $8,000 by 2010.

The Tiananmen Incident

Deng's program for economic liberalization—at the hands of the Communist Party—contained many contradictions. These reached a breaking point in April 1989, after the unexpected, but natural, death of reformer Hu Yaobang. Hu had criticized Party corruption, and while hardliners had marginalized him late in his career, reformers and young liberals revered him as a visionary man of the people. During spontaneous mourning, public discontent with the slow pace of political reform intensified into a more formal protest. In Beijing's Tiananmen Square, demonstrators set up camp and a group of students drafted a petition, the *Seven Demands*, for reforming China. Initially, Party leaders were divided on how to respond, but in an April 26 editorial the *People's Daily* deemed the Tiananmen protest a "counterrevolutionary riot."[9] This signalled an imminent response. Following Mikhail Gorbachev's May visit, student leaders erected a styrofoam replica of the Statue of Liberty to highlight their demand for democratic rights. Several student leaders captivated the international press by launching a hunger strike to force Party leaders to acknowledge their petition.

Goddess of Democracy

The Goddess of Democracy monument unveiled on May 30 by students in Tiananmen Square made conscious allusion to the American Revolution. Students in Hong Kong rekindled this memory by erecting a minature replica marking the event's twenty-first anniversary.

In Tiananmen, democracy protestors grew increasingly concerned, but workers and intellectuals all rallied behind the students as the movement radiated out to other cities and campuses. By May 18, the demonstration in Tiananmen had swollen to over a million supporters. On May 20, party authorities declared martial law, dispatching 300,000 soldiers to Beijing. PLA units moving towards Tiananmen found their passage blocked by civilians. Given that many soldiers identified with the reform movement they dared not fire on the crowd. To the embarrassment of Party leaders, the PLA returned to their barracks. The Tiananmen movement had entered a critical stage.

Facing a test to their authority, the Communist Party mobilized loyal troops from the provinces and made a renewed attempt to take control over Tiananmen. This time soldiers were given live rounds and clear instructions to fire at anyone who dared to block their way. On the night of June 3, four armoured columns converged on Tiananmen. In several places, PLA units found their entry blocked by protestors who barricaded bridges with burning busses. Soldiers shot live rounds at demonstrators blocking their passage, igniting bloody street fighting as shocked and overmatched civilians responded with Molotov cocktails, sticks, and insults. News of the street battles reached students in Tiananmen. They nervously debated what to do over the microphone, but most voted to stand their ground.

Around 1:30 a.m., June 4, the first PLA units reached Tiananmen. Some demonstrators had already vacated the square, but at least a hundred thousand defiant activists remained huddled around the Goddess of Democracy. By 4 a.m., the PLA had established control over the four main exits of Tiananmen. When students failed to disburse, authorities cut the lights and moved in. While the Red Army fired low at the feet of demonstrators, many were wounded as bullets ricocheted off the stone pavement. By the next morning, hundreds lay dead, but the Party had cleared the Square. In the subsequent repression of the democracy movement, the state dispensed summary justice, rounding up student leaders and executing labor activists deemed to be trouble makers.

The Tiananmen Square massacre precipitated Deng's retirement. Over the subsequent three years, Jiang Zemin took over the government and rolled back many of Deng's liberal reforms relating to civil society. The Party reasserted its authority and control over the institutions of state. China did suffer an international backlash for the massacre, including various sanctions. By 1992, however, an ailing Deng reappeared on the public stage to launch China on its most ambitious and aggressive program of liberalization to date. In 2001, China's Communist Party symbolically completed their liberalization program when they joined the world's capitalist club, the World Trade Organization (WTO).

Deng did not live to see China's entry into the WTO. By Deng's death in 1997, his liberal reforms, however, had become widely accepted by China's people and the Communist Party. They provided the foundation for China's remarkable transformation from global pariah and isolated basket case to the world's workshop and prominent pillar of the global economy. From 1998 to 2010, China increased its share of global trade from 2 to 10 percent, which in turn facilitated China's remarkable transformation. In the bustling global cities of Coastal China, gargantuan docks were littered with containers heading to Western markets, glass skyscrapers jutted into the smog filled air, and by 2010 a three hundred million strong middle class emerged as the most enthusiastic advocates of consumerism and conspicuous consumption. After Tiananmen, the Party and people had struck an informal bargain. Communist leaders would continue to liberalize the economy and allow prosperity to flow to ordinary people so long as people did not challenge Party hegemony. This implicit contract, rather than any constitution, now underwrites China's civil society. The Party maintains a "great firewall" of Internet censorship that seeks to control information and public debate in the age of social media. While rapid economic growth has brought prosperity for millions of Chinese, it has also come at a price: sharp inequality, rampant pollution, corruption, and the absence of civil rights. It remains to be seen whether China's economic miracle can be sustained, given that its key ingredients were debt, cheap oil, and low Chinese wages.

A Pacific Century?

Some analysts wonder whether China's remarkable transformation and Southeast Asia's rapid economic growth foreshadow a Pacific Century. Generalizing about Asia's future is complicated by the region's incredible cultural and economic diversity. Singapore and Japan have achieved levels of development comparable to the West, but their economies pale in size to India and China. Malaysia and South Korea are growing rapidly, putting them on track to reach or surpass Western levels of prosperity in the next decade. Cambodia and Vietnam, however, feature human development metrics roughly comparable to developing countries in Africa and the Middle East. While China and India's economies are growing rapidly, they continue to suffer from massive levels of rural poverty. Inside their dual economies, a middle class is emerging inside cities while the ranks of an underclass with poor future prospects grow. Incorporating the poor and rural masses represents a key challenge for both countries moving forward.

As Asia's economic footprint inside the global economy has increased, its culture is increasingly shaping global trends, exemplified by the popularity of anime, the martial arts, and Indian cuisine. Asia's growing cultural influence is arguably most evident in the **Korean Wave**. Since the 1990s, the South Korean state has embraced cultural products as vital to its export strategy. Samsung, Hyundai, and LG have emerged as prominent global brands, while Korean soap operas have been exported throughout Asia and the Middle East. This has elevated Korean pop stars like Super Junior to the status of international celebrities and sex symbols. In China, the "K-pop" reached such levels of popularity during the 1990s that it triggered a backlash. For many Chinese nationalists, the United States represents a strategic rival, but Korea, not the West, represents the supreme threat to their identity and culture.

Summary: Postwar Asia

Among all world regions, Asia stands out in terms of the number of states making the leap to Western levels of prosperity. Japan blazed the path, recapturing its earlier modernizing momentum and providing a regional model for modernization. Japanese capitalism copied the West's best practices, but married them to its own distinctive institutions, including pronounced state direction of private investment. By 1970, Japan emerged as a global economic power while China and India's experiments in state socialism faltered. During the 1980s, the Asian Tigers followed Japan's export industrialization strategy to considerable success, leading to a regional shift towards promarket reforms by 1990. China, once a hotbed for radical ideological experiments, led the way under Deng Xiaoping. The key to the Asian Miracle was the region's ability to assimilate to Western norms and modern technology, effective state management of the economy, and high levels of investment in education. Following decades of rapid growth, the "Miracle" has expanded Asia's footprint inside the global economy, while it is increasingly setting cultural trends.

Questions for Critical Thought

1. Why did the Cold War culminate in devastating land wars in Asia rather than proxy conflicts more common in other world regions?
2. How did India's implication in the Cold War illustrate the difficulty for postwar states to pursue a policy of neutralism?
3. What keyed Japan's successful modernization after World War II?
4. What were the objectives and consequences of China's Great Leap Forward? Was Mao an inflexible socialist revolutionary or a brutal narcissist that used socialism to justify his lust for power?
5. Why did Asians increasingly abandon state socialism during the 1980s?
6. What policies and conditions contributed to the Asian Miracle of the 1980s and 1990s?
7. How is the attitude of Asians to modernization different from some of its regional peers?
8. How did Deng Xiaoping set the stage for China's transformation into a global economic power?

Suggestions for Further Reading

- Dillon, M. *China: A Modern History*. New York: I.B. Tauris, 2010.
- Edwards, L. *Women in Asia: Tradition, Modernity and Globalisation*. Ann Arbor, MI: University of Michigan Press, 2000.
- Haggard, S. *The Asian Financial Crisis of 1997-1999*. New York: Columbia University Press, 2001.
- Kingston, J. *Japan in Transformation, 1945-2010*. New York: Longman, 2011.
- Lori, W. *When Empire Comes Home: Repatriation and Reintegration in Postwar Japan*. Cambridge, MA: Harvard University Press, 2009.
- Meisner, M. *Mao's China and After*. New York: Free Press, 1999.
- Owen, N. *The Emergence of Modern Southeast Asia: A New History*. Honolulu, HI: University of Hawaii Press, 2005.
- Owen, N. *Routledge Handbook of Southeast Asian History*. New York: Taylor and Francis, 2014.
- Stein, B. *A History of India*. Chichester, UK: Wiley-Blackwell, 2010.
- Yusuf, S., and Joseph Stiglitz. *Rethinking the East Asian Miracle*. New York: World Bank Publications, 2010.

Notes

1. Quoted in Bal Ram Nanda, *Jawaharlal Nehru: Rebel and Statesman* (New Delhi: Oxford University Press, 1998), 186.
2. ANZUS treaty, September 1, 1951, accessed, August 9, 2019, https://www.aph.gov.au/~/media/wopapub/house/committee/.../appendixb_pdf.ashx.
3. Quoted in John Lewis Gaddis, *What We Now Know*, (New York: Clarendon Press, 1998), 67.
4. Frank Dikötter, *Mao's Great Famine: The History of China's Most Devastating Catastrophe, 1958-62* (New York: Walker, 2011), 333.
5. Quoted in Jin Qiu, *The Culture of Power: The Lin Biao Incident in the Cultural Revolution* (Palo Alto, CA: Stanford University Press, 1999), 45.
6. Robert MacFarquhar, "The succession to Mao and the end of Maoism," in vol. 15 of *The Cambridge History of China*, ed. John Fairbank (Cambridge: Cambridge University Press, 1991), 364.
7. Quoted in Bal, *Nehru*, 191.
8. Jade Adia Harvey, "Single and Sexless: The Celibacy Syndrome," *The Yale Globalist*, September 21, 2014, http://tyglobalist.org/in-the-magazine/features/single-and-sexless-celibacy-syndrome-in-japan/.
9. Frank Tan, "The People's Daily: Politics and Popular Will-Journalistic Defiance in China during the Spring of 1989." *Pacific Affairs* 63, no. 2 (1990): 151–69.

Chapter 10
Life and Death of the Soviet Bloc

Chapter Outline

- Introduction: The Soviet Bloc
- Mysterious Death of Comrade Stalin
- Khrushchev's New Course
- Stability and Stagnation under Brezhnev
- Gorbachev takes the Soviet Helm
- The Revolutions of 1989
- Trauma of Postcommunist Transition
- Conclusion

Post-Stalinist Transition 1953-1963
1953 Stalin Dies
1956 Khrushchev's New Course
1956 Budapest Uprising
1964 Khrushchev's Ouster

Brezhnevian Stagnation 1964-1984
1968 Prague Spring
1979-1989 Soviet-Afghan War
1982 Death of Brezhnev
1983 Jaruzelski bans Solidarity

The Gorbachev Era 1985-1991
1986 Chernobyl Meltdown
1986-87 Glasnost and Perestroika introduced
1989 Fall of the Berlin Wall
1990 Reunification of Germany
1991 Dissolution of USSR

Post-Communist Transition 1992-2000
1992-1995 Bosnian War
1995 Srebrenica Massacre
1996 Yeltsin's Re-election

1989 Polish Elections: first free elections in Soviet Bloc create overwhelming Solidarity majority

1989 Fall of Berlin Wall brings Revolutions of 1989 to their climax.

1986 Chernobyl meltdown leads to evacuation of 200,000

1956 Budapest Uprising crushed by Soviet tanks showing limits of Soviet toleration for national communist reforms.

1995 Srebrenica Massacre ultimately brings Bosnian War to a resolution.

Image credits: © Borhax/Shutterstock.com; © Zoart Studio/Shutterstock.com; © Martial Red/Shutterstock.com; © Zern Liew/Shutterstock.com; © NikolayPetrovich/Shutterstock.com

Introduction: The Soviet Bloc

As ecstatic East Germans clambered onto the graffiti-splashed Berlin Wall in August 1989, their celebration marked the end of an era. For most of the twentieth century, communism had inspired a revolutionary alternative to liberal capitalism. The Red Army's triumph over Hitler had bolstered communism's international prestige and culminated in a Soviet Bloc centered upon Eastern Europe. Ultimately, global communism expanded to encompass twenty-three states and a quarter of the world's population by 1960. Thirty years later, however, festive crowds chiseled away at the most tangible symbol of global partitioning. Around Eastern Europe, bronze statues of Lenin were pulled down, purging decades of Russian domination and mind-numbing state indoctrination sessions. By the dawn of the twenty-first century, communism had nearly ceased to exist. Eastern Europe rushed to transition towards liberal democracy and free market capitalism, while the Soviet Union disintegrated and Chinese communists joined the World Trade Organization (WTO). The world's remaining communist regimes, like North Korea and Cuba, precariously survive as dysfunctional anachronisms.

To contemporaries, communism's "fall" seemed sudden, but it was rooted in decades of stagnation. The Revolutions of 1989 provoking the collapse of the Soviet Bloc might not have been inevitable, but they highlighted a failure among Stalin's successors to revitalize a one-party state and command economy increasingly out of step with modern trends and global logistics. Popular support for Eastern Europe's communist parties had eroded away decades ago, yet these regimes' collapse was closely linked to the Soviet Union's last General Secretary. Mikhail Gorbachev was an ardent socialist, but his aversion to force and inept economic reforms also destabilized a deeply unpopular communist system. When Gorbachev belatedly acknowledged his failure during an anticlimactic 1991 speech, his principal legacy became orchestrating the Soviet Bloc's mostly peaceful collapse.

In Western circles, communism is often remembered as a discredited philosophy. In the former East, many now view the demise of communism with regret and nostalgia. Few taking to the streets in 1989 anticipated the trauma of structural adjustment. Those that had fought most resolutely against communist corruption proved most disillusioned with the "crony" capitalism that blossomed in state socialism's decay. While the twenty-first century brought welcome economic recovery for many Eastern Europeans, postcommunist society fell far short of popular expectations. Today, postcommunist Europe is more prosperous, free, and technologically advanced, but it also manifests many of capitalism's worst excesses, while its standard of living continues to lag behind most industrialized states.

Big Questions

- Why did Stalin's successors struggle to revive the Soviet system?
- Why did Eastern Europeans grow increasingly disenchanted with socialism?
- Did Brezhnev stabilize the Soviet Bloc or squander its last opportunity for reform?
- How did Gorbachev's beliefs and policies contribute to the Revolutions of 1989?

Mysterious Death of Comrade Stalin

Stalin, not Marx or Lenin, was the principal architect of twentieth-century communism. The "man of steel" achieved the ambition of centuries of Russian reformers by using terror to transform the Soviet Union into Europe's foremost military and industrial power. During the Great Depression, Stalin laid the foundation for a modern industrial state that enabled the Soviet Union to weather a furious Nazi onslaught. But Stalin's bureaucratic communism lacked Marx's moral vision, or Lenin's ambition to improve the proletariat's living conditions. Accordingly, Stalin's death in 1953 left a vacuum, a Party elite disconnected from ordinary people and stuck inside a totalitarian system that worked through fear.

After a hard night of drinking on March 1, 1953, Stalin retired to his chambers and left strict instructions not to be roused. When Stalin had not stirred by noon, his orderlies grew concerned. Later that evening, attendants heard a thud. A light had come on in Stalin's quarters, but the orderlies dared not disturb the dictator that had sent millions to the gulags. Only that evening, using the pretext of an arriving cable, did they muster the courage to enter Stalin's bedchamber. There they found the marshal sprawled on the floor in a puddle of his own urine.

Stalin had suffered a stroke and would never regain full consciousness. Some speculate that Stalin was poisoned, but the official autopsy reads "cerebral hemorrhage." Whatever its stimulus, Stalin's death short-circuited a trial of Jewish doctors and imminent purge among top Party leaders. Informed of Stalin's stroke, his closest advisors took considerable time summoning medical help.

After Stalin's death, his adjutants inherited the awesome responsibility of taking over a state that had been ruled for decades by a man many worshipped as a god. Stalin's terror had elevated these men to power, but also scarred them. Stalin loved tormenting his closest associates, getting them drunk to test their loyalty. Now they were free from his grip, but still encumbered by his dark legacy. As Stalin's willing henchmen, they had loyally carried out his orders, while bearing witness to his many failures and ghastly excesses. Huddled over Stalin's body, would they now work together to reform socialism, or compete to replace him?

Stalin's death on March 5, 1953, left his successors facing two simultaneous crises. First, they had the delicate task of announcing the death of the man consummate with the state. Second, much of Eastern Europe was slipping into open revolt against forcefully imposed stalinization. Terror had long defined the Soviet system. Now his successors faced the challenge of managing a repressive bureaucracy accustomed to Stalin's unflinching and often murderous directives.

Given his paranoia, Stalin had not designated a clear successor. At his funeral, Stalin's adjutants took turns eulogizing the fallen hero in a fawning display of public continuity. To the mourning public, Stalin's henchmen presented the idea of collective leadership. **Vyacheslav Molotov**, the old Bolshevik slated for the chopping block, was restored as foreign secretary. **Georgy Malenkov**, the most prominent public figure after Stalin, was installed as premier and head of state. Behind the scenes, **Lavrentiy Beria** expanded his grip over the security establishment. Together, this Troika tackled unrest in the Czechoslovakia, Bulgaria, and East Germany. Stalin's death provided a pretense for Eastern Europeans to resist unpopular reforms. Terror had facilitated state seizure of property, wage cuts, and religious oppression. Through a mixture of force and concessions, the new guard gradually stamped out these revolts inside the Soviet empire.

Khrushchev Wins the Succession Struggle, 1953 to 1957

At Stalin's funeral, Malenkov, Beria, and Molotov delivered the eulogy, laying out the pecking order for the ensuing succession struggle. Mistrusting each other, they initially split Stalin's posts. "Collective leadership" projected stability across the empire, reassured regional party bosses, skittish communist leaders in Eastern Europe, and the grieving Russian people. Behind the scenes, their power struggle heated up. **Nikita Khrushchev** cultivated an alliance with Marshall Georgy Zhukov, hero of World War II. Stalin had sidelined Zhukov, but now the Marshal rallied the Soviet military behind Khrushchev's bid to replace Malenkov as party secretary. Like Stalin before him, Khrushchev used the General Secretary's appointment power to steadily expand the ranks of his supporters among the Party's top rungs.

The sadistic Beria was the first to fall. During Stalin's reign, Beria was notorious for driving around Moscow and directing his chauffeur to apprehend random women for rape. Beria's rivals feared his steady consolidation of the security apparatus. At a June 1953 meeting, Khrushchev ambushed Beria and accused him of treason. Beria protested "are you looking for a flea in my pants?" before turning to his longtime ally Malenkov for support.[1] But Malenkov had switched sides Armed guards burst in. Zhukov placed Beria under arrest. Western observers noted that Beria's box at the opera remained inexplicably vacant. Months later the Soviet Leaders revealed that Beria had been tried and executed before a secret tribunal.

From 1953 to 1957, an uneasy consensus governed the Party's top hierarchy. After sacking Malenkov in 1955, Khrushchev established himself as first among equals, but Stalin's death invariably transformed the Soviet state. The cabinet operated in a climate of frank discussion, mutual mistrust, and compromise. While establishing his primacy, Khrushchev ruled through consensus. This meant that he needed to demonstrate the success of his leadership while warding off rivals as he launched into an ambitious reform program aimed at cultivating a closer partnership between the Party, state and people.

Khrushchev's New Course

In February 1956, Khrushchev boldly set the Soviet Union upon a new course. At the 20th Party Congress, a gathering of top Party leaders, Khrushchev surprised his audience by launching into a blistering indictment of his predecessor. Khrushchev denounced Stalin for establishing a cult of personality and committing "treason against the Party and against the Revolution."[2] Khrushchev reminded delegates of Stalin's lust for power, and how his paranoia led him to imprison and execute many loyal Party members. Over four long hours, Khrushchev detailed Stalin's various crimes and multiple failings. His speech ran deep into the night and shocked Party dignitaries, even if Khrushchev scrupulously avoided insinuations of complicity. Accustomed to working inside a police state, some cheered, but many found Khrushchev's frankness unsettling. How could you indict a corpse embalmed yards away, next to the saintly Lenin? When Khrushchev finished, the audience shuffled out into the chill street disorientated. Top Communist leaders, like most Soviet citizens, found it difficult to grasp Khrushchev's dramatic change of course. When a carefully edited excerpt of the speech was subsequently read out in factories, collective farms, and Party headquarters, some suffered heart attacks. Others bristled and howled. In Tbilisi, local communists rallied around their native son's statue.

Khrushchev's speech was ambitious and reckless. He sought to marginalize his conservative opponents inside the Party and to break the cult Stalin had woven around the Russian people. Khrushchev sincerely believed that Stalin had strangled the Bolshevik Revolution in its cradle by building up a bureaucratic state to serve his ego. To rekindle socialism, Khrushchev launched a program of **destalinization**. Ostensibly, this meant reforming the state by changing the Party's culture. Rather than terrorizing the people, the Party should lead a campaign to "build socialism" and raise living standards.

Already before the 20th Party Congress, Khrushchev had staked out a reform course by encouraging open discussion at party assemblies and rehabilitating some purged party members. **Khrushchev's Thaw** extended abroad. He tried to mend fences with Tito's Yugoslavia, and made a gesture of reconciliation to the West by withdrawing Soviet troops from Austria in 1955 in return for a pledge of neutrality. The Thaw's most tangible embodiment was shuttering Stalin's special courts that had sent millions to Siberian Gulags. Khrushchev's Thaw burned most brightly inside the cultural arena, where Stalin's police state had long stifled artists. Khrushchev did not share Stalin's paranoia about the corruptive influences of Western bourgeois culture or internal dissent. Khrushchev believed so sincerely in socialism's superiority over capitalism that he never tired of boasting about how the Soviet mass production system would overtake the West. This confidence fueled Khrushchev's efforts to liberalize Soviet society. He sponsored cultural festivals, promoted international sports competitions, and hosted foreign film and art exhibitions. The 1957 World Festival of Youth and Students marked the Thaw's high tide. Khrushchev lifted the Iron Curtain and invited curious foreigners to Moscow to witness socialism's achievements.

Soviet artists relished their freedom. They established contact with foreigners and explored genres outside the narrow confines of "socialist realism." Loosening of state control over civic life stimulated a flowering in Soviet poetry, visual arts, film, and literature. It also spurred development of a domestic sphere apart from Party control, rekindling the notoriously dark Russian sense of humor that had traditionally helped people cope with life's hardships.

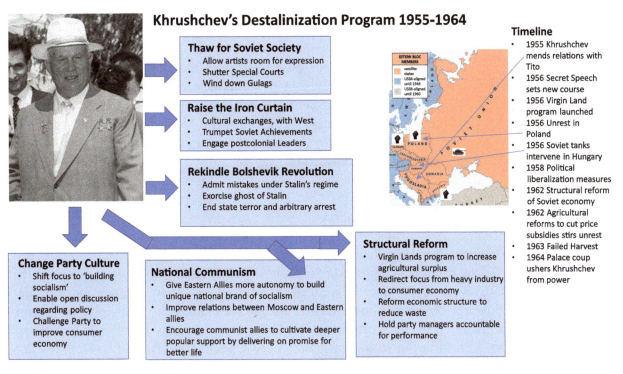

Khrushchev's secret speech marked the pivotal moment in his broader program to destalinize the Soviet Bloc and set the USSR country on a new course.

While Khrushchev's Thaw transformed the state, it did not undercut the Communist Party's monopoly of power, its control over the press, or its management of the economy. In 1958, Khrushchev noisily banned Boris Pasternak's *Doctor Zhivago* for painting an unflattering portrait of the Bolshevik Revolution. Furthermore, Khrushchev demanded that the ailing Pasternak renounce his Nobel Prize following the novel's unauthorized publication abroad. Conversely, Khrushchev allowed Alexander Solzhenitsyn to publish his grueling *One Day in the Life of Ivan Denisovich*. Gulag novels served Khrushchev's political ends by discrediting his Stalinist opponents, but his taste remained conservative. This was famously illustrated in 1962 when hardliners goaded him into visiting a display of *avant-garde* art at the Manzeh Gallery in Moscow. Upon seeing abstract modernist paintings, including faceless figures that a horrified Khrushchev likened to "dog shit," an article appeared in *Pravda* calling for greater artistic purity.[3] This sent a clear message to Soviet intellectuals and artists concerning the limits of state toleration for artistic freedom, even if the exhibit did not prematurely close. The Thaw exemplifies Khrushchev's transformation of the Soviet Bloc. His liberalization measures transformed the state from a totalitarian instrument and saddled the Communist Party with a responsibility of delivering progress to the people, but it did not lay out a clear path for economic and political reform.

The Hungarian Uprising, 1956

Throughout Eastern Europe, Khrushchev's calls for destalinization sparked outbursts of populist anger against the bitter memory of forcefully imposed Stalinization. "Liberalization" created a space for frank discussion that invariably turned towards crimes that local communists had committed during Stalin's reign. In June 1956, a worker's strike in Poznan, Poland, brought to a boil a simmering crisis among various factions inside the Communist Party. Polish reformers ultimately threw their support behind **Władysław Gomułka**, who assumed power from the Stalinist faction. After tense negotiations with the USSR, Gomułka convinced Khrushchev that he had a firm grip over the party and that he could diffuse simmering discontent that threatened to separate Poland from the Warsaw Pact. In Budapest, events took a more radical turn. For months, student groups had been "illegally" forming their own organizations apart from the state. Students issued reform petitions including demands for "general elections in this country, with universal suffrage, secret ballot and the participation of several parties."[4] To Moscow hardliners, the Budapest uprising represented a counterrevolutionary movement that threatened socialism's survival in Eastern Europe. In October 1956, Hungarian security forces opened fire on student demonstrators gathered at a radio station. This event inspired a broader uprising that united students, workers, and complicit state officials to take up arms against the security police. Throughout Budapest, the rebels formed "soviets" that demanded that their government endorse their reforms and liberate them from Soviet domination.

While Khrushchev initially sympathized with Hungarian reformers, he found himself under pressure from Kremlin critics. Budapest illuminated a fatal contradiction embedded in destalinization. Critical examination of the past would not stop at Stalin. It invariably spilled over into criticisms of the Communist Party. Budapest showed how quickly calls for reform could escalate into demands for free elections and independence. The Kremlin watched nervously as the Hungarian government led by **Imre Nagy** gravitated towards accepting rebel petitions. When Nagy announced his intention to withdraw from the Warsaw Pact, Khrushchev intervened. On November 4, Soviet tanks rolled into Hungary. In Budapest, civilians wielding rifles and Molotov cocktails, reinforced by detachments of the Hungarian army, battled the Red Army. A week of fighting left ten thousand dead. This bloodbath "pacified" Hungary and sent a clear message to other Eastern reformers. But Budapest also tarnished communism's international image. Bloody repression contradicted Moscow's claim that communism represented a revolutionary movement for mass liberation.

> Was there a fatal contradiction in Khrushchev's destalinization program? Was it possible to liberalize the socialist system without making party elites accountable to their citizens?

Khrushchev's Erratic Reforms, 1957 to 1964

In public speeches, Khrushchev relished the Marxian saying "the proletariat is the undertaker of capitalism."[5] Stalin had used the state as a bludgeon to industrialize Russia. Khrushchev appealed to patriotism to inspire Russian citizens to build a socialist society. Khrushchev flew across the realm addressing farmers and workers and encouraging them to roll up their sleeves. His main task was to reorient a Stalinist economy focused on heavy industry, cement, mining, and electricity generation to produce more food and better consumer goods so that citizens could enjoy a better life. Khrushchev was determined to overtake the West without falling into the "bourgeois" trap of empty consumerism. In contrast with America's "throw-away" society, Khrushchev focused on producing "durable" goods that served a "functional" purpose. In 1958, Khrushchev launched his ambitious Seven-Year Plan to build twelve million city apartments and over seven million rural houses. Housing represented a pressing need in rural areas where many still lived in hovels without electricity or running water. In Russian cities, many families still lived in one-room apartments sharing kitchen and bathroom facilities. Khrushchev's bold initiative represented a major shift away from heavy industry towards providing the amenities for socialist family life.

Khrushchev Meets Kennedy, 1961

Khrushchev cast a sharply different image from Stalin in his willingness to engage the Russian people and foreign leaders.

> Was destalinization a genuine attempt to reform the Soviet system or a largely superficial approach that Khrushchev pushed mostly to consolidate his grip over the state?

Khrushchev believed that Western capitalism wasted resources by creating different styles of woman's high-heeled shoes and multiple colored toothbrushes. Instead, the socialist economy could mass-produce a single type for every product category. In theory, this would eliminate waste the capitalist economy diverted towards profits, advertising and creating "useless" features. Mass production had worked to pump out large numbers of tanks and rifles during World War II, but the Soviet economy suffered from poor-quality control measures. Communist industries routinely turned out shoddy and frequently unwanted consumer goods. Sometimes the seams of suits unraveled after a single wearing. Irons blew up because of faulty wiring, and families could spend over a decade on a waiting list for the right to purchase the notoriously unreliable "Lada" automobile. From its offices in Moscow, the Soviet planning agency, **Gosplan**, used arcane formulas to estimate consumer demand, but throughout the Soviet Bloc store shelves often ran empty of practical necessities like soap, deodorant, and needles. At other times, stores overflowed with bicycles, frying pans, or platform shoes after Gosplan wildly miscalculated demand or consumer tastes.

Khrushchev liked to see himself as an agricultural reformer. To overcome chronic food shortages inside the USSR, Khrushchev championed the **Virgin Lands** program. The idea was to cultivate marginal land in Kazakhstan and Siberia. At the Kremlin, Khrushchev's colleagues protested his unconventional approach and agronomical experts warned against its ecological infeasibility. Resistance only goaded Khrushchev to carry the program to unfathomable extremes. In 1953, Khrushchev took his bold idea to the people, inspiring hundreds of thousands of young *Komsomol* pioneers to settle the desolate steppe. That first year they reaped a bumper harvest for the motherland, at times heroically lighting bonfires around their fields to stave off the deadly frost pressing down from the Caucuses. Skeptics noted that a record amount of the harvest spoiled due to a lack of silos, inexperienced farmhands, and insufficient railcars. Khrushchev brushed aside such critiques, only to see the next harvest fail spectacularly. From 1955 to 1963, the Virgin Lands program returned uneven results, despite increasingly aggressive state investments of machinery and fertilizer. In the end, Soviet planners acknowledged the ecological reality that Kazakhstan proved unsuitable for industrial **monoculture**. Annual rainfall was insufficient, the harvest period was too short, and crops too vulnerable to early frosts.

The Virgin Lands program highlighted the improvisational nature of Khrushchev's reforms. Khrushchev took pride in a leadership guided by gut instinct, crediting his own tenacity with overcoming the conservative reflex of an entrenched bureaucracy. But Khrushchev's grandiose schemes were poorly conceived and often rammed through without proper preparation. His tendency to ignore experts and embrace programs that disarmed skeptics highlighted a superficial approach to economic policy.

Khrushchev's Fall

Khrushchev's reforms had consistently challenged the bureaucracy's unquestioned authority, the party's privileges, and the elite's traditional way of doing things. Throughout his tenure, Khrushchev clashed with party officials as he introduced reforms to stimulate efficiency inside a bureaucratized planning structure. Successive reforms sought to devolve power from Moscow to regional planning bodies, to split industry from agriculture, and to render factory managers accountable. These initiatives unsettled Party leaders but failed to deliver meaningful results. When successive reforms faltered, Khrushchev, however, failed to accept responsibility, continually shifting blame while abruptly changing course. The year 1962 represented a turning point for the Party. Khrushchev tried to rationalize Soviet agriculture by withdrawing massive state subsidies that distorted costs and disincentivized farmers from increasing production. The resulting price shock, however, stimulated an uprising in the Rostov region that the army quietly put down. Once more, Khrushchev reversed course, but when the Soviet harvest failed again in 1963, Khrushchev was forced to purchase North American grain to feed his people. For someone who had staked his leadership on being an agricultural reformer, Khrushchev's prestige reached low ebb. Thanks to Khrushchev, millions now lived in more comfortable flats, but by 1963 hungry Russians cursed him. Khrushchev had fallen victim to his most tangible achievement: in liberalizing the state he created a socialist system that could hold him accountable.

Following a month's long conspiracy, party leaders summoned Khrushchev back to Moscow from his Crimean vacation. **Leonid Brezhnev**, Khrushchev's protégé, orchestrated a lengthy inquest into his mentor's tenure. After exposing Khrushchev's multiple failings, top party bosses voted for his removal. A heartbroken Khrushchev accepted his ouster pliantly, thankful to escape with his head. Khrushchev retired to his memoirs with a modest pension. Neighbors recall him potting about in his garden, no doubt taking his frustrations out on the soil that thwarted his attempts at reform.

Stability and Stagnation under Brezhnev

Leonid Brezhnev, uncharismatic but pragmatic, was the steady hand the communist party craved following Khrushchev's erratic tenure. For the party, Brezhnev's reign reaffirmed the party's hegemony over the state, while reaffirming the principles of "collectivity of leadership" and "respect for cadres." Party elites no longer worried about arbitrary removal. Brezhnev brought stability to the USSR, but he also ignored deeper structural problems inside the Soviet economy. The "man in the gray flannel suit" did not travel across the realm delivering stirring speeches to crowds of peasants or factory workers. Instead, Brezhnev worked the Kremlin's corridors of power, delegating the business of the state to his allies and party subordinates.

While Brezhnev did not restore Stalin's terror, he also made clear that the Communist Party would not brook any challenge to its authority. Domestically, this message was delivered during the 1965 **Sinyavsky–Daniel Trial**, where two intellectuals were convicted for publicizing tracts in the West exposing contradictions in Soviet life. In reasserting party hegemony, Brezhnev did not seek to reintroduce state dominance over the private sphere that had flourished since Khrushchev's Thaw. "Developed socialism" promised to continue his predecessor's program of managing the economy to improve the ordinary family's standard of living. "Soviet people should receive a normal life," Brezhnev mused, but the Party would crack down on dissidents that dared to challenge their authority publicly.[6]

> Stagnation is not a precise economic term. Could Brezhnev be blamed for the Soviet Union's later collapse because he failed to address shortcomings in the Soviet economy that performed relatively well during most of his reign?

While Brezhnev restored stability, under his tenure socialism also stagnated. Alcoholism became rampant inside a society that provided few opportunities for advancement or leisure. Apathy mounted in a system where Party elites carved out more privileges for themselves, while the living standards for ordinary people plateaued. Officially, the Soviet Union remained a communist state. Under Brezhnev, Soviet foreign policy more aggressively supported foreign allies providing that they dutifully declared themselves "Marxist," but Brezhnev belonged to a generation of technocrats elevated under Stalin. Many were engineers that associated socialism more with a bureaucratic system than the Bolshevik crusade for proletarian liberation. Forced onto the public stage, Brezhnev could mouth Marxist-Leninist platitudes, but his voice carried little conviction. As he privately admitted "who is going to believe that I have read Marx?"[7] Brezhnev reflected a Communist Party that at times aggressively asserted Soviet power in the Third World in defense of international socialism, but increasingly abandoned Bolshevist militancy at home. Inside the Soviet Bloc, living standards rose until the early 1970s, but state surplus also subsidized an increasingly lavish lifestyle for party elites. Throughout the Soviet Bloc, Marxist-Leninism remained the official state ideology and Party membership remained key to promotion, but Party elites focused increasingly on their own careers, opportunities for Western travel, and securing places for their children in elite state academies. Mounting corruption trickled down to workers in factories and cooperative farms. Theft and fraud skyrocketed as ordinary people struggled to cope with an increasingly unmanageable planning system. The young became particularly alienated as ruling elites led inauthentic state rituals like the famous May Day parade in Moscow. Giant billboards blared out socialist slogans in daubs of red ink, but ordinary people learned to tune out Party noise as they focused on bread-and-butter issues. During the 1970s, the productivity inside Soviet Bloc economies leveled, creating shortages while pushing living standards lower. Hardship amplified frustration with the flaws and shortcomings of the socialist system. Discontent flared particularly in regions where poorly conceived state industrial schemes went awry and ravaged local ecosystems.

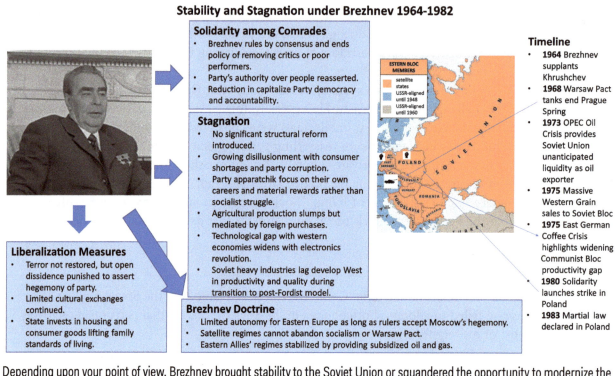

Depending upon your point of view, Brezhnev brought stability to the Soviet Union or squandered the opportunity to modernize the socialist system and keep up with emerging technological and logistical trends.

The hubris of Soviet science, industry, and state planning was exemplified in the draining of the Aral Sea. Since Stalin, the Volga and Dnieper Rivers feeding the sea had been diverted towards various irrigation schemes. Under Khrushchev, however, Soviet planners dreamed up a cotton industry. Massive irrigation works facilitated the launch of an inefficient Soviet cotton farms that slowly strangled the Aral Sea to death. Remarkably, Soviet planners coped with falling water levels by airlifting Baltic fish to keep the indigenous canning industry running, but by the 1980s they abandoned this expensive fix. One of the world's richest fisheries had been reduced to two murky ponds. Today, camels graze on stubble grass among beached fishing trawlers rusting away on desert dunes that once represented the bottom of the famed "Blue Sea."

Destruction of the Aral Sea

The ambition of socialist planners and engineers to use technology and irrigation to make the deserts bloom resulted in the destruction of one of the world's most productive fisheries. Today, the Karakum Desert has appeared from what was once the famed blue Aral Sea.

Life under Communism

The experience of living under communism was not uniform across the Soviet Bloc. Generally, material conditions improved after Khrushchev's reforms. Communist states focused on meeting basic needs for food, clothing, and shelter. In comparison to prewar regimes, communist states expanded the safety net and provided the poor and underprivileged opportunities for education and social advancement. Happiness, however, consists of more than meeting basic needs. One frustration for many living under communism was the lack of freedom, both for personal expression and religion, as well as the stale conformity the Party imposed upon public life. Communism represented a repressive system that operated by keeping its citizens under intense surveillance, while subjecting them to command economy that grew increasingly dysfunctional after 1960.

Under socialism, women were subjected to the "double burden." Socialist liberation tasked women with taking up full-time jobs outside the home, but also failed to liberate them from the societal expectation that they fulfill domestic duties like cleaning, cooking, and nurturing children. Many working mothers spent an hour a day waiting in line for food and basic goods that often ran in short supply. A queue culture developed as women invented an etiquette for standing in line, socializing, and coping with the notoriously rude sales staff that often kept valuable goods aside for customers willing to offer a kickback.

Ordinary people developed various strategies to cope with the system's growing dysfunction. To get meat, pork farmers would bus to nearby cities so that they could fill their satchels with sausages the state had requisitioned from the countryside. For factory workers, theft became an accepted means of supplementing family incomes, while vast black markets flourished to provide consumers with goods otherwise unattainable in state stores. Massive state subsidies distorted prices, encouraging poor resource use and creating shortages. For example, the USSR progressively raised penalties, but never curbed the practice of feeding bread to livestock. This practice evolved because high state subsidies made bread more affordable than feed. Broken light bulbs became a prized commodity given their use as a token to exchange for a working incandescent. In Leningrad, taxi drivers assigned a kilometer quota that routinely cheated the system by running back their odometers.

As living conditions deteriorated during the late 1970s, ordinary people grew increasingly disenchanted with the privileges of connected Party elites. Many youths turned from Lenin to Lennon. For a rebellious minority, all things "Western" represented a foil to communist dysfunction. During the late 1950s, "war of the trousers" party officials forcefully shaved the heads of young men who dared to slick back their pants into tight leggings in imitation of Western styles. By the 1970s, Soviet authorities abandoned radio jamming and mostly tolerated the sale of Levi jeans on black markets. Knockoff bands like Czechoslovakia's Plastic People of the Universe and the USSR's Time Machine built up a steady following in underground bars by the 1970s. By the 1980s, the Iron Curtain has grown so porous that it took less than three months for the latest Rolling Stones tune to be smuggled into the USSR and redistributed using x-ray film canisters.

The Prague Spring

Socialism's prestige received a crippling blow following the Prague Spring. In 1968, Alexander Dubcek with accent on C replaced the hardline communist leader Antonín Novotný, and initiated a series of reforms designed to instill "socialism with a human face." Liberalization of Czechoslovakian life was popular, and reforms quickly gained momentum. Over the summer of 1968, Prague emerged as an island of toleration behind the Iron Curtain. Free speech and freedom of the press flourished in an experiment that explored both the viability of socialism and the limits of Soviet toleration. The Czech Spring, however, worried Brezhnev and Dubcek's less liberal neighbors. They saw his reformed communism morphing into liberal democracy. Moscow feared that a democratic Czechoslovakia would abandon the Warsaw Pact, while neighboring regimes fretted that Dubcek's reforms would spill over their borders to undermine their regimes. During 1968, Brezhnev flew to Prague and tried to reason with Dubcek, while the Warsaw Pact conducted provocative military maneuvers on Czechoslovak soil. When these warnings went mostly unheeded, Brezhnev ordered an invasion of Czechoslovakia to protect "international socialism." Stunned Czechoslovakians watched as their purported allies stamped out their experiment in social reform with naked force. In comparison to Budapest in 1956, there was little bloodshed. Czechoslovakians chose the path of civil resistance, haranguing their "liberators," blocking their tanks and confusing invading troops by repainting road signs. Once more, the Kremlin established the limits of Soviet toleration, but in the process, Brezhnev also shattered the last figment of socialism's legitimacy.

Mounting Pressures Inside the Communist Bloc, 1975 to 1985

By retreating from Khrushchev's reforming ambitions, Brezhnev ignored the sclerosis afflicting Soviet Bloc economies. In agriculture, Soviet productivity lagged so far behind the West that it took 40 percent more land, nine times more labor, as well as more machinery and fertilizer to achieve 12 percent of North America's productivity.[8] In the realm of high technology, Communist Bloc economies that struggled to produce reliable televisions found it impossible to keep up with an accelerating electronics revolution that produced increasingly sophisticated microcircuits. During the 1980s, the Soviet Union cloned the x86 chip, but lacking semiconductor foundries and critically short of computer programmers, the Soviet Bloc had no basis for an indigenous computer revolution. As the pace of technological advance accelerated, the Soviet Union fell more rapidly behind. In terms of brute gross domestic product (GDP), measures like coal and iron production, the Soviet Union remained an economic behemoth. However, by the 1970s, it had become an increasingly backward superpower. Many of its weapon platforms were reverse engineered from stolen US plans, but faulty industrial products could not be exported outside the Soviet Bloc. During the 1970s, Belarus Tractors tried to fill a global niche for inexpensive farm machinery. Canadian resellers, however, had to perform expensive retrofits to replace leaky seals and gaskets in order to meet minimum quality standards. Global trends towards electronics, flexible production, and outsourcing increasingly widened the productivity gap between capitalist economies and the centralized Soviet planning system.

Already in the 1950s, dissidents developed an underground press to disseminate their criticism of repression and to challenge the Party's claims that it served ordinary people. Following Budapest in 1956, however, reformers recognized the futility of openly challenging communist regimes backed by the secret police and Soviet tanks. After Prague in 1968, dissidence broadened into a growing cynicism and apathy, as ordinary people emotionally withdrew from an increasingly dysfunctional system that became increasingly unhinged from its professed values. By the late 1970s, the sluggish performance of Communist Bloc economies forced Eastern European regimes to raise prices, particularly on foodstuffs. In East Germany, a rise in global coffee prices forced the regime to cut back on foreign imports. In 1977, the regime unveiled a barely digestible *Mischkaffee* that blended real coffee beans with licorice and sugar beets. The resulting "Coffee Crisis" well captures the complex political dynamic at play behind the Iron Curtain. While communist regimes were undemocratic and used police repression to crush dissent, they had also staked their legitimacy upon improving living conditions. Price increases, consumer shortages, and environmental disasters dented regime credibility and roused protest. Across the Soviet Bloc, some party elites responded to criticism with liberalization, while others cracked down with police repression. All were constrained by uncompetitive economies that deprived them of badly needed "hard" currency to purchase tropical products, foreign grain, and Western technology. Eastern Europe became increasingly dependent on Soviet subsidies, particularly reselling subsidized Russian oil at below-market prices and pocketing the difference to finance imports for goods their economies could not produce. But Soviet resources and generosity were limited, forcing Eastern European regimes to turn increasingly towards foreign lenders. Détente facilitated a rapid expansion of East–West trade. West Germany emerged as a prominent creditor, routinely including loan provisions that committed socialist lenders to honoring their human rights commitments following the 1975 **Helsinki Conference**. In particular, the West insisted on religious toleration and the curbing of police terror. Growing deficits and dependency on Western credit and imports mired communist regimes not only in debt, but also in a legitimacy trap. This is best exemplified by the emergence of **Solidarity** in Poland during the 1980s. This grassroots trade union movement emerged in response to Poland's flailing economy. Workers paid higher prices for bread, milk, and meat, while their wages remained stagnant. Solidarity's demands, unofficially supported by the Catholic Church, presented a grave challenge to Poland's Communist regime. An "illegal union," Solidarity highlighted the embarrassing reality that, under Brezhnev, the workers' state served party elites far better than ordinary citizens.

Facing mounting pressure to reform, in 1983 Poland's Communist leader, **Wojciech Jaruzelski** arrested **Lech Wałsa** and banned Solidarity by declaring martial law. Jaruzelski cited Prague as his rationale, applauding himself for saving Poland from Soviet invasion. Most of Jaruzelski's neighbors faced similar struggles given the lack of tangible solutions for their economies' deeper structural problems.

With the memory of 1956 still fresh, Hungarians under **János Kádár** sought to reform socialism at the margins. **Goulash Communism** removed many of the subsidies from agriculture, and authorized the formation of small private businesses for profit. These liberal reforms created the most dynamic economy in the Soviet Bloc. Budapest markets were flush with imported Western goods and Hungarians were spared the shortages afflicting their peers, but Kádár was careful to retain an outwardly doctrinaire regime immune from Soviet criticism. In Romania, **Nicolae Ceaușescu's** totalitarian regime marshalled propaganda to glorify his leadership, while the secret police suppressed overt dissent. This hardline policy created superficial tranquility, but silenced rather than tackled popular disillusionment.

By the 1980s, a whole generation had come of age disillusioned with communism. When East German vacationers disembarked on the beaches of Yugoslavia, they met up with young Italians flashing chic clothes and fancy Japanese electronic gadgets that made a mockery of official proclamations about socialist progress. German police dramas and soap operas aired in Hungary, East Germany, and Czechoslovakia. Casual viewers implicitly understood that ordinary families in the West enjoyed far higher living standards. As travel restrictions abroad were relaxed, people inside the Communist Bloc developed a clearer picture of how they were falling behind. Many intellectuals, dissidents, and Christians openly aspired for Western freedoms, but for the majority the "West" beaconed as prosperity and escape from the queue culture, inauthentic state rituals, and the absurdities of an increasingly dysfunctional planning system.

Lech Walesa, November 30, 1989

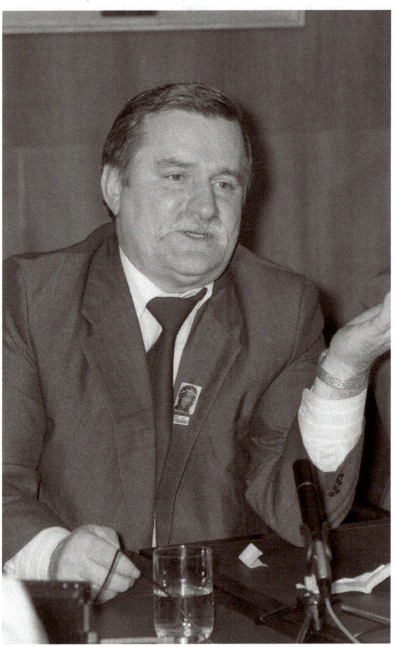

Solidarity leader Lech Wałęsa emerged as the global symbol of indigenous resistance to communist autocracy. Following the Revolutions of 1989, many of the dissidents under communism became leaders of the reformer regimes tasked with dismantling the communist planned economy.

Gorbachev Takes the Soviet Helm

The Communist Party selected Mikhail Gorbachev to lead the Soviet Union in 1985 after two of Brezhnev's geriatric cronies, **Konstantin Chernenko** and **Yuri Andropov**, died in rapid secession. Communism suffered from an acute image crisis, while decades of stagnation had failed to address structural problems in the Soviet economy. Gorbachev's selection marked the Politburo's endorsement of reform. Gorbachev belonged to a younger generation. His fresh face, genuine passion for socialism, and "new thinking" seemed the ideal recipe for resuscitating communism.

As Gorbachev took the helm, however, he faced a daunting task. Half the Soviet state's expenditures went to subsidize food and energy, not only for Russian citizens, but for Eastern European allies. Since the late 1970s, the Party had kept an ailing system afloat by selling natural resources on world markets, but the price of oil had started to level off by 1980 and plunged precipitously after 1985. A year later, the **Chernobyl** nuclear plant meltdown delivered a second shock to the Soviet system. Twenty-eight people died in the immediate aftermath of the blast, but millions were exposed to high levels of radiation. About 25,000 were estimated to have suffered premature deaths, while more than 200,000 citizens were relocated.[9] The cleanup bill drained the treasury and stimulated anger against Party elites that had poorly supervised the plant and subsequently misrepresented the dangers from radioactive fallout. Abroad, Afghanistan was transforming into the Soviet Union's Vietnam. During an era of increasing liberalization, bereaving mothers sent chilling letters to the Kremlin about their missing sons.

Reagan and Gorbachev in Geneva in 1985

Gorbachev became a celebrity in the Western world, both because of his genuine kindness and because of what he represented. For Western citizens, a Soviet leader that smiled and spoke in the language of human rights and basic dignities struck a sharp contrast from the caricatures of Soviet leaders during the Cold War.

Despite the gravity of the crisis facing the Soviet Union, Gorbachev moved deliberately, consolidating his authority and evaluating the modest reforms initiated by his predecessor. Only in 1986 to 1987 did Gorbachev introduce **Glasnost** and **Perestroika** to the global lexicon. They represented the twin pivots for a reform program aimed at resuscitating socialism. *Glasnost* meant openness, and it signaled a return to Khrushchev's program for liberalization. Gorbachev wanted to tackle party corruption by mobilizing ordinary people to restore state accountability. Gradually, the press began to explore previously censored topics. Factory workers were invited to voice their opinions about their managers and Gorbachev launched an aggressive crusade to curb alcoholism that he blamed for eating away socialism's soul. Gorbachev sought to "democratize" society by allowing public debates and having multiple Communist Party members stand for election. *Perestroika* designated restructuring and involved a modest program to improve the efficiency of state industries by creating incentives. While Gorbachev enjoyed some success in mobilizing the Russian people, when his structural reforms failed to revive the Soviet economy, it unleashed turmoil that quickly destabilized the Soviet empire.

Historians debate Gorbachev's failure. His reforms viewed stagnation as a cultural and spiritual problem. Accordingly, *perestroika* introduced mostly cosmetic economic reforms to tackle profound structural problems. For example, Gorbachev allowed state enterprises to fulfill orders for profit, and legalized joint ventures with foreign corporations, but factory managers remained engineers accustomed to promotion by meeting state production targets. They were ill-equipped for innovation, had no experience cutting costs, introducing quality control measures or maximizing profits. *Perestroika* could not revive a system where factories produced shoddy goods with outdated equipment using a bloated and unmotivated work force. In any case, introducing market signals into a command economy only injected chaos into the Soviet system. Gorbachev's reforms undermined the traditional ties binding resource producers, factories, and retail outlets inside the command economy. As the economy began to break down, already endemic corruption intensified with the appearance of a new class of **oligarchs**. This diverse group included ruthless entrepreneurs, criminals, and corrupt Party figures who exploited the chaos of a collapsing system. Most oligarchs made fortunes through fraudulent schemes that involved selling lavishly subsidized state assets on world markets.

> Were Gorbachev's reforms inadequate or did he inherit a Soviet system already beyond resuscitation?

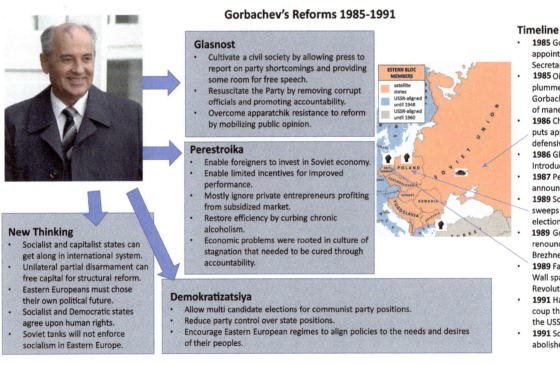

Gorbachev's reform program sought to tackle stagnation by reforming the Party, but Soviet hardliners resisted change and liberal reformers pushed him to abandon socialism in favor of market based reforms.

By 1988, the Soviet economy began to contract, budget deficits mounted, crime and poverty spiked, and food and tobacco shortages increased. The intensifying economic crisis divided the Soviet leadership. Liberals came to doubt Gorbachev's commitment for substantial reform. In 1987, **Boris Yeltsin**, the Moscow Party chief, who had criticized *perestroika*, now attacked Party conservatives and charged Gorbachev of instilling a cult of personality. A stunned Gorbachev sacked Yeltsin and increasingly surrounded himself with conservatives. Gorbachev became conflicted. He had intended to reinvigorate socialism. Instead, *perestroika* was bringing the Soviet system to the brink of collapse. Unable to accept this, or to support his liberal colleagues that advocated for the abolition of "marxism" Gorbachev became increasingly indecisive and isolated.

The Revolutions of 1989

When Gorbachev assumed power, Eastern European dissidents cast a hopeful gaze towards the Kremlin. Gorbachev's overtures to the West, his open discussion of communism's failures, and his reform talk struck a sharp contrast with the hardline regimes that dominated most of Eastern Europe. While a silent majority rejected communism as illegitimate and dysfunctional, reform remained blocked by memories of Prague and the willingness of communist regimes to use military force and police repression. As *perestroika* started to fizzle out in 1988, however, conditions for reform in Eastern Europe ripened. Popular dissident movements had already started to test official tolerance. **Charter 77** in Czechoslovakia endorsed the Helsinki Accords, reminding communist regimes of their failure to respect basic human rights. Internal discontent became conjoined with external pressure, as Gorbachev reached the conclusion that Eastern Europe represented an economic liability the Soviet Union could no longer afford to subsidize. In 1987, Gorbachev initiated a quiet diplomacy aimed at pressuring his European socialist allies to emulate his liberal reforms. In 1988, Jaruzelski responded to Gorbachev's prodding by entering into negotiations with Lech Wałęsa to resolve a debilitating strike. On April 1989, Jaruzelski convinced party hardliners that it was necessary to legalize Solidarity and subject the communist party to a referendum. On June 1989, the first open elections were conducted behind the Iron Curtain since World War II. In two rounds of voting, Solidarity crushed their Communist opposition. Notably, Solidarity candidates captured ninety-nine out of hundred available seats in the Senate. Despite this ringing endorsement, Wałęsa proceeded cautiously, inviting members of the Communist coalition into his government and allowing them to retain control over the sensitive security ministry.

The emergence of Poland's solidarity government coincided with China's brutal crackdown on student demonstrators in Tiananmen Square. A horrified Gorbachev seemingly renounced the Brezhnev doctrine on July 7, 1989, at the Council of Europe deeming "any interference in domestic affairs" of another state "inadmissible."[10] This sent a clear message to dissidents and Communist hardliners in Eastern Europe that Soviet tanks would no longer backstop their regimes.

Hungary's progress towards democratic socialism had been accelerating for months when on May 2, 1989, Hungary promptly decided to dismantle its 230-km long border fence with Austria. This quickly attracted the attention of East German tourists. Over the summer of 1989, a rising tide of Germans and Czechs visited Hungary in order to migrate West. This human flood reached such proportions that West Germany had to arrange special trains and Hungary found it necessary to reclose their border. About 130,000 East Germans exploited the hole in the Iron Curtain. With their escape

Chapter 10: Life and Death of the Soviet Bloc

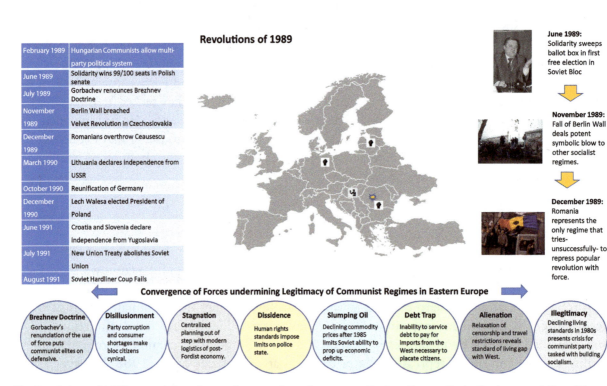

The Revolutions of 1989 spurred the collapse of communist regimes across Eastern Europe. Gorbachev's renunciation of the Brezhnev doctrine was one catalyst, but powerful dissident movements also drew strength from decades of disillusionment with Party corruption, police surveillance, and consumer shortages.

route now cut, mass demonstrations erupted throughout East Germany. In Leipzig, over 100,000 gathered to demand a variety of civil rights. The Communist government struggled to suppress dissent when on October 7, 1989, Gorbachev and other communist dignitaries gathered in Berlin to celebrate the fortieth anniversary of East Germany's government only to be serenaded with muted calls of "Gorby free us!" Realizing that urgent reform was necessary, East German Communists responded to Gorbachev's prodding by sacking General Secretary **Erich Honecker**, who had ruled the country with an iron hand since 1971. His appointed successor, **Egon Krenz**, however, failed to inspire much confidence. Throughout East Germany, popular demonstrations gained in size as they pried ever more concessions from the flailing Communist regime. The fatal blow came during a botched November 9 news conference that lent the mistaken impression that the Party had lifted immigration restrictions. A jubilant crowd descended on "Checkpoint Charlie," where they confronted nervous guards fingering their machine pistols. Ultimately, the Party decided to diffuse the tension by opening the border. A massive crowd surged towards the Brandenburg Gate where they were greeted by their neighbors and countrymen in a raucous celebration. Some jubilant Easter Berliners climbed onto the graffiti clad walls of their former prison. Some brought out pickaxes and took a few symbolic blows. This breaching of the Berlin Wall was rebroadcast, worldwide sending a powerful message about the fragility and unpopularity of Eastern Europe's remaining communist regimes.

> To what extent did globalization contribute to collapse of communist regimes in 1989 by highlighting the gap between Eastern and Western standards of living?

From November to December 1989, the remaining communist regimes in Eastern Europe collapsed like dominos. The **Velvet Revolution** in Czechoslovakia followed an emerging Central European pattern. Popular demonstrations grew steadily in size and audacity over a five-week span, procuring ever more concessions until the tittering Communist regime dissolved itself and returned sovereignty to the people. In Czechoslovakia, demonstrations led to Dubcek's symbolic restoration, and subsequently the longtime dissident Havel's triumphant election as Czechoslovakia's first postcommunist president. Only in Romania did the fall of communism lead to significant bloodshed. The collapse of neighboring regimes had made Ceaușescu increasingly nervous. Returning from a foreign trip, Ceaușescu staged of a mass rally in Bucharest to butress support for his leadership. When he blasted "fascist agitators who want to destroy socialism," the crowd responded with a smattering of boos that soon graduated into jeers and heckling.[11] Despite being surrounded by armed troops, in a brazen act of defiance, the crowd cut out the hammer and sickle from the center of the Romanian flags they had been given. A shaken Ceaușescu retreated from the balcony and ordered an immediate crackdown. Initially, security forces shot some protesters, but then the army intervened on the side of the people. In a hectic four days, Ceaușescu and his wife were arrested, tried, and executed.

Crowd celebrates the revolution of 1989 in Romania

Throughout Eastern Europe in 1989, communist regimes collapsed in rapid succession. With the exception of Romania, the defiant crowds challenging unpopular communist regimes secured more and more concessions until they provoked the final collapse of communist regimes no longer enjoying the support of Soviet tanks.

By December 1989, the Iron Curtain Stalin had imposed upon Eastern Europe had fallen. After embarking upon the socialist experiment with a mixture of ambivalence, trepidation, and hope, people in Eastern Europe celebrated their reintegration with the world community. Many assumed that having thrown out communism, the adaption of Western norms would soon translate into a better life.

Dissolution of the Soviet Union, 1989 to 1992

Gorbachev had urged Kremlin hardliners to acquiesce to Eastern European nationalism in 1989. By 1990, it was clear not only that *perestroika* had failed, but that *glasnost* had unleashed powerful forces that threatened the Soviet Union's own survival. Throughout the USSR, popular demonstrations emerged calling for accelerated reform, while collapse of the Soviet system stimulated the reemergence of long-suppressed ethnic nationalism. This was particularly evident in the Baltic States that Stalin had invaded before World War II. Formally integrated into the USSR, and housing very substantial Russian minority populations, made secession from the USSR problematic. Gorbachev tried to reason with Lithuanian nationalists, trumpeting the benefits of a continued partnership and warning about the dangers of blowback from Kremlin hardliners. When Lithuanian leader Vytautas Landsbergis unilaterally declared independence in March 1990, Gorbachev refused to recognize this. In subsequent months, Soviet security troops moved in to occupy public buildings and round up draft dodgers, arousing protest not only in Lithuania but among other anxious Soviet republics.

In December 1990, longtime Gorbachev ally **Eduard Shevardnadze** resigned in public protest warning that "dictatorship is coming." Gorbachev chided his old friend with abandoning *perestroika* at its most critical hour, while denying rumors of a *coup d'etat*. In truth, Gorbachev had lost control over the liberal revolution he had given birth. This became clear in August 1991. After Gorbachev had embarked for vacation, Soviet hardliners moved to block a new union treaty that spelled the demise of the Soviet Union. Coup leaders confronted Gorbachev in the Crimea and invited him to join their plot to save the USSR. When Gorbachev refused, he was placed under house arrest and the poorly organized coup sputtered forward. Tanks rolled into Moscow and Leningrad, but the conspirators failed to seize the television stations or to arrest Boris Yeltsin. Russian President Yeltsin defiantly mounted on top of a tank surrounding by a swell of supporters as he harangued the conspirators on CNN. The "plot of the doomed" only enjoyed lukewarm support in the army and quickly lost all momentum.

Yeltsin confronts the coup plotters

Yeltsin's August 19, 1991, defiance of the coup in front of the Russian Parliament rallied the public and undermined the resolve of the conspirators.

Gorbachev was liberated and brought back to Moscow, but the baton of reform had passed to Yeltsin. When Gorbachev addressed the Russian Congress of Deputies and criticized the conspirators he had placed into power, some deputies jeered. In December 1991, Yeltsin presided over the USSR's formal dissolution. A new Union Treaty effectively abolished the USSR and vested sovereignty in its constituent republics. This rendered Gorbachev and the Communist state superfluous. The bulk of the Soviet Union would survive as the Russian Federation, containing most of the Soviet landmass, 50 percent of its economy and 60 percent of its population. Hastily brokered agreements ultimately secured the Russian Federation's control over the former Soviet nuclear arsenal, while negotiating leases for military bases outside of Russia's territory, including the strategic Russian naval base at Sevastopol in Crimea.

Trauma of Postcommunist Transition

In 1989, many East Europeans had joined in street demonstrations overthrowing discredited communist regimes. After seizing power, people jubilantly smashed communist idols, concrete hammer and sickle icons, and bronze statues of Stalin. After this ritual purging, however, the real business of postcommunist reconstruction began. The first task lay in removing the communist leadership and punishing those guilty of past crimes. With the exception of Romania, communist regimes handed over power peacefully, which made political transition easier. Eastern Europeans tended to view communism as an unwelcome Russian imposition. Accordingly, only top Communist leaders were tried and imprisoned. Few mid-level party officials were held accountable, and most low-level functionaries remained in office.

A strong consensus and enthusiasm bound the reform movement. This discouraged exploration of the communist past and historical crimes. The release of the internal records, like those of the East German **Stasi**, detailed the extensive scope of state surveillance and discredited communist regimes. Communists reorganized themselves as socialist parties, but enjoyed little support in open elections. Throughout Eastern Europe, constitutional conventions invited various public stakeholders to draft a new political society. The resulting constitutions were not uniform, but most included substantial provisions to protect civil rights, including freedom of speech and the press. Most states in Central Europe also opted for parliamentary democracies that featured bicameral legislatures, consistent with the West European standard. Some Western observers worried whether Eastern Europeans could adjust to democracy after three generations of living under communist rule. Throughout Central Europe in 1989 to 1990, however, popularly elected regimes emerged following peaceful open elections. In Eastern Europe, more authoritarian forms of the state often prevailed, sometimes with former Communist officials rebranding themselves as nationalist politicians.

One overriding concern among reformers was to secure their regime from internal communists, as well as any future threat from Russia. Reformer regimes began the delicate business of negotiating the evacuation of Russian troops from their territory, while also initiating discussions for future membership inside North Atlantic Treaty Organization (NATO) and the European Union (EU). Russian nationalists and communist hardliners were sensitive to former allies and border states joining the Western Bloc, but the chaos of structural adjustment prevented forceful intervention as many former Soviet satellites joined the EU and NATO by 2000.

Western Expansion into the Former Soviet Bloc, 1999 to 2007

1999: North Atlantic Treaty Organization (NATO)	Czech Republic, Hungary, Poland
2004 NATO	Bulgaria, Estonia, Latvia, Lithuania, Romania, Slovakia, Slovenia
2004 European Union (EU)	Czech Republic, Estonia, Hungary, Latvia, Lithuania, Poland, Slovakia, Slovenia
2007 EU	Bulgaria, Romania

The decision not to blacklist rank-and-file Party members and bureaucrats allowed many state functionaries to "switch their hats." Former Communist elites often leveraged their extensive contacts and positions of authority to retain their influence inside reformer regimes. In many places, a select group proved particularly adept at exploiting hasty schemes for privatizing state-owned assets. The political struggle between deposed communists and resurgent democratic forces was most intense inside the Russian Federation, where **Boris Yeltsin** inherited a legislature that had been constituted primarily through indirect elections. The Russian Chamber of Deputies remained dominated by former communists and their conservative allies, hostile to market reforms. This forced Yeltsin to rule by decree and subterfuge. Yeltsin was routinely blocked by the threat of impeachment, while communist-dominated state institutions actively sabotaged his reforms. In 1993, a frustrated Yeltsin illegally abolished the legislature and called for a referendum on a new constitution that would enhance his executive powers. When conservatives responded by occupying the Russian White House, Yeltsin sent in tanks and elite forces to haul out the conspirators, killing 187 and wounding many more.

The most difficult aspect of postcommunist transition involved **structural adjustment**, adapting communist economies predicated up on central planning, price controls, state ownership, and heavy industry. This meant privatizing state property, removing state subsidies, and forcing state industries to compete with more efficient and technologically advanced foreign competitors. Throughout Eastern Europe, reformer regimes grappled with the pain of structural adjustment as they introduced various schemes for privatization and phasing out substantial price controls. **Shock Therapy** emerged as the most popular reform strategy, Proponents of this theory argued that gradually paring back state control over the economy would only prolong the agony of transition. Instead, reformers should focus on dismantling inefficient communist structures and adopting free market institutions as rapidly as possible.

Poland led the former Communist Bloc in shock therapy by cutting all state subsidies for eggs, milk, and meat. Prices immediately shot through the roof. Anger boiled to the surface on the streets of Lublin and Kraków. Young mothers could no longer afford milk for their babies, while pensioners on tight budgets cursed Wałęsa. Within months, however, shock therapy alleviated decades of chronic shortages. Farmers responded to high prices by expanding production and bringing their produce to flourishing urban markets. Throughout the Eastern Bloc, small private farms rapidly supplanted the production coming from giant state enterprises. Prices for most foodstuffs quickly stabilized, quality often improved, and chronic shortages mostly disappeared.

While market reforms were mostly successful in resuscitating agriculture, they often failed to revive heavy industries that had enjoyed substantial state subsidies under communism. Western experts hoped that foreign corporations would invest and modernize communist enterprises, but this occurred only to a minimal extent in Poland, Hungary, and the Czech Republic. As a result, most factories closed within a decade and many unemployed workers found that they lacked the skills to secure jobs inside the burgeoning service sector.

For reformer regimes, the most vexing challenge came with privatizing lucrative state resource corporations. These owned valuable assets, but there was insufficient internal capital to purchase them at full market value. In the USSR, the notorious **loans for shares** scheme, largely concocted at Yeltsin's Spartak Tennis Club, allowed oligarchs to walk away with multibillion dollar assets for pennies on the dollar. At the same time, the state, having shed most of its assets, proved unable to pay wages or honor its pension and welfare commitments.

While most reformer regimes enjoyed tremendous support initially, the trauma of structural adjustment chipped away at their prestige. In Poland, Wałęsa's party was punished at the ballot box in 1993, and he narrowly lost the presidential election in 1995. Throughout Eastern Europe, reconstituted communist parties gained some support as the pain of structural adjustment intensified. From 1993 to 1995, many reformer regimes fell mostly because they failed to meet unrealistic popular expectations for improved living standards. In 1996, Boris Yeltsin launched a reelection campaign enjoying only

10 percent popularity. Momentarily setting the bottle aside, Yeltsin campaigned vigorously despite a chronic heart condition. Yeltsin tabbed support from Russian oligarchs to score an improbable victory that enabled market reforms to inch forward.

Arguably, structural adjustment hit Russia the hardest, in part because Yeltsin became embroiled in a struggle with conservatives that sparked hyperinflation, wiping out the savings of ordinary people. Structural adjustment proved catastrophic to retired workers and widows who often lost their pensions and were left to their own devices. Having shed state assets and unable to collect taxes, the Russian state could no longer afford to pay workers, while the removal of state subsidies sent food and fuel prices higher. This pushed most Russians below the poverty line, with many turning to garden plots to feed themselves. Widows and orphans dependent on the welfare system were hard hit, but factory managers, army officers, and scientists who had been privileged under the old system also struggled. Across the Soviet Bloc older workers struggled to adapt to the frenetic pace of life inside capitalist society or to master the technologies of the modern workplace. East Germans had the great fortune of being assimilated into Europe's most dynamic economy, but despite massive West German subsidies and generous welfare payments, many resented how their society was undemocratically assimilated into the Federal Republic of Germany. Unemployment remained high in East Germany decades after reunification, while older people and manual laborers struggled to adjust to a more competitive society. Elites under the old system discovered that their previous credentials as university professors, musicians, and engineers often failed to carry over. This disillusionment stimulated **Ostalgie** as bitter East Germans embraced a highly romanticized memory of the "quiet life" and the security socialism had once afforded.

Opinion polls following the 2008 Great Recession reveal deep disillusionment with crony capitalism, but also little desire to turn back the clock. The fall of communism has improved food quality, the availability of consumer goods, and guaranteed basic freedoms despite not substantially improved basic living conditions for the majority. Many fighting for change in 1989 were particularly hard hit by industrial decline inside the Eastern Bloc. The difficulties of coping with structural adjustment were magnified by a sense of betrayal on the part of certain groups that profited handsomely from the collapse of the old order. Inside Russian cities, the oligarchs indulged in orgies of conspicuous consumption alienating hungry citizens who had lost their jobs, savings, and pensions.

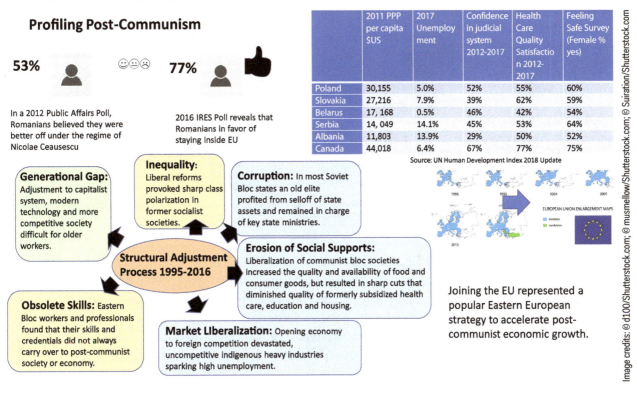

Profiling Post-Communism

53% — In a 2012 Public Affairs Poll, Romanians believed they were better off under the regime of Nicolae Ceausescu

77% — 2016 IRES Poll reveals that Romanians in favor of staying inside EU

	2011 PPP per capita $US	2017 Unemployment	Confidence in judicial system 2012-2017	Health Care Quality Satisfaction 2012-2017	Feeling Safe Survey (Female % yes)
Poland	30,155	5.0%	52%	55%	60%
Slovakia	27,216	7.9%	39%	62%	59%
Belarus	17,168	0.5%	46%	42%	54%
Serbia	14,049	14.1%	45%	53%	64%
Albania	11,803	13.9%	29%	50%	52%
Canada	44,018	6.4%	67%	77%	75%

Source: UN Human Development Index 2018 Update

Structural Adjustment Process 1995-2016

Generational Gap: Adjustment to capitalist system, modern technology and more competitive society difficult for older workers.

Inequality: Liberal reforms provoked sharp class polarization in former socialist societies.

Corruption: In most Soviet Bloc states an old elite profited from selloff of state assets and remained in charge of key state ministries.

Erosion of Social Supports: Liberalization of communist bloc societies increased the quality and availability of food and consumer goods, but resulted in sharp cuts that diminished quality of formerly subsidized health care, education and housing.

Obsolete Skills: Eastern Bloc workers and professionals found that their skills and credentials did not always carry over to post-communist society or economy.

Market Liberalization: Opening economy to foreign competition devastated, uncompetitive indigenous heavy industries sparking high unemployment.

EUROPEAN UNION ENLARGEMENT MAPS

Joining the EU represented a popular Eastern European strategy to accelerate post-communist economic growth.

282   Chapter 10: Life and Death of the Soviet Bloc

The Dissolution of Yugoslavia, 1988 to 1995

In Yugoslavia, the pain of structural adjustment sparked civil war and genocide. From 1989 to 1990, the multiethnic republic that Tito had built entered into a period of prolonged crisis as its constituent republics became dominated by nationalist governments jostling for influence. The principal catalyst for Yugoslav tensions was a former Communist official, **Slobodan Milosevic**. In 1988, Milosevic rebranded himself as a Serbian nationalist. Using his control over the state media, Milosevic unleashed a steady stream of propaganda that dredged up dark Serbian memories about World War II atrocities, while playing up ethnic differences. Economic hardship and ethnic fears galvanized Serbian support for Milosevic, but it also upset the delicate balance inside Yugoslavia's government. By 1990, less than a third identified themselves as Yugoslavs, while Serb minorities painted Bozniaks as "Turks" desiring an Islamic state. As Milosevic moved to consolidate his grip over the federal structure of government, he provoked both Slovenia and Croatia to secede from the Yugoslav Republic in 1991. Slovenia, an ethnically homogenous and mountainous republic on the Western frontier exited with minimal drama, but when Croatia followed suit, the Serb-dominated Yugoslav Army intervened and occupied Western Croatia in the name of protecting its Serb minority. Heavy fighting ensued and the conflict was not resolved until 1993 with full Croatian independence.

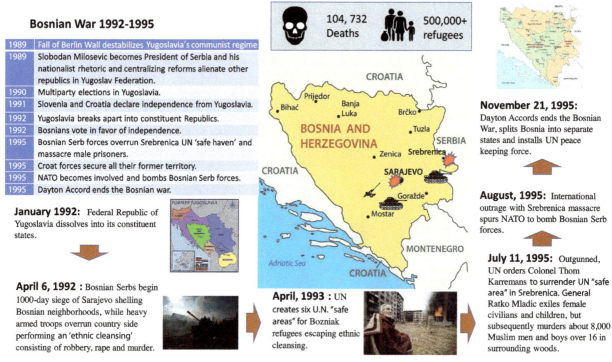

Image credits: © Martial Red/Shutterstock.com; © iconvectorstock.com; © Rainer Lesniewski/Shutterstock.com; © pavalena/Shutterstock.com; © MuchMania/Shutterstock.com; © Northfoto/Shutterstock.com; © Northfoto/Shutterstock.com; © pablofdezr/Shutterstock.com

War in Croatia foreshadowed the potential for civil war in Bosnia and Herzegovina, Yugoslavia's most multiethnic republic. In 1992, the government of Bosnia-Herzegovina staged a referendum on independence boycotted by the minority Serb population. When the Muslim-dominated government used this referendum to declare independence, Bosnian Serbs resisted through armed force and quickly launched a campaign to seize as much territory as possible to build their own state. Bosnian Serb forces enjoyed a military advantage thanks to generous support from Milosevic. In contrast, disorganized Bosnian forces lacked heavy weapons, while an international arms embargo put them at an acute disadvantage. For Europeans, the disintegration of Bosnian society represented an unwelcome introduction to the volatility of postcommunist politics. While Bosnia had been the most heterogeneous of Yugoslavia's republics, with a population 44 percent Muslim Bozniak, 31 percent Orthodox Serb, and 17 percent Croatian Catholic, before 1988 there had been few signs of ethnic tension. During the 1984 Winter Olympics, cosmopolitan Sarajevo served as a global model for multiethnic integration. All Bosnians spoke the same language, and in integrated cities Muslim, Catholic, and Orthodox intermarriage was not uncommon. With the breakup of Yugoslavia, however, the bonds of civil society disintegrated under a barrage of racist propaganda.

Window on the World History: Bosnia's Lessons

Bosnian Serb General Mladić, 1993

General Mladić led the Bosnian Serb forces from 1993 to 1995.

The Srebrenica Massacre brought to horrific culmination Bosnia's brutal civil war, and left many struggling to explain the dissolution of a seemingly well-integrated civil society. By all appearances, Yugoslavia was a successful nation in which people spoke the same language. Despite different ethnic and religious affiliations, there was increasing intermarriage among its three main communities. Yet by 1992, only 5 percent of Bosnia's population identified themselves as "Yugoslav." In 1995, Serbian television thought little about broadcasting grisly images of Serb paramilitaries executing their former neighbors and countrymen. The Bosnian genocide was rooted

(Continued)

less in ancient hatreds or divergent values, than in how unscrupulous politicians exploited the trauma of postcommunist transition. During the late 1980s, Milosevic harnessed state-controlled media to demonize the Muslim population as an enemy group, while invoking painful memories of past atrocities. By 1990, some Bosnian Serbs had become convinced that they were targets of a *jihad* and that their names populated Muslim hit and rape lists. When the Bosnian government declared independence in 1992, it was a foregone conclusion that Serbs would try to form their own state. But Bosnia's civil war quickly escalated into a bloody genocide where Serbs participated in a campaign of "ethnic cleansing" that robbed, raped, and murdered their former neighbors. Croats and Bozniaks responded with atrocities of their own. How could people that had lived peacefully together for decades suddenly turn to each other's throats? The Bosnian tragedy is hardly unique in world history. When a state collapses, ethnicity becomes the lowest common denominator and fear can inspire neighbors to perpetuate the most inhuman atrocities. Bosnia raises troubling questions about the fragility of civil society in multiethnic states. The Quebec sovereignty movement drove home to Canadians how their confederation was founded upon two distinctive national cultures. The 1970 October Crisis exposed deep divisions between French and English Canada and ultimately led Trudeau to redefine Canada as a multiethnic state cemented in shared political values. While it is difficult to imagine a Bosnian tragedy occurring in Canada, recent political history reveals that politicians of various stripes are not averse to labeling certain groups as "un-Canadian" to advance their agenda. Does this constitute free speech or empoison Canadian civil society?

Critical Reflection

1. Canada has never faced pressures comparable to the dissolution of Yugoslavia, but is Canadian society impervious to ethnic conflict?
2. To what extent did the Quebec sovereignty movement spur cultural stereotyping in the media?

The **Bosnian War** (1992–1995) became notorious for its savagery and the indiscriminate killing of civilians. This was best exemplified in the Bosnian Serb strategy for "ethnic cleansing," a euphemism denoting rape, torture, and murder to induce the Muslim population to flee their homes. Serb forces subjected the Bosnian capital of Sarajevo to a different form of terror, placing the city under a 1300-day siege. This cut the population off from food, medical supplies, water, and electricity, while snipers targeted ordinary civilians. Artillery devastated civilian neighborhoods, and progressively leveled urban infrastructure in a calculated move to make life unbearable. In the bleak months of 1993, life in Sarajevo denigrated into an absurdist ritual where young boys dodged sniper fire carrying jerry cans in a hunt for potable water. Haggard old women scurried across street corners littered with the bombed-out hulks of busses. Residents of Sarajevo attained international acclaim for resisting the Serb siege by holding impromptu public concerts, poetry readings, and supporting each other against an enemy determined to strangle life from their city.

The turning point in the Bosnian War came at **Srebrenica**. In 1993, the United Nations (UN) designated this eastern city a safe haven for civilian refugees. In 1995, however, a Bosnian Serb paramilitary group laid siege to the town and tried intimidate its four hundred lightly armed Dutch peacekeepers. The population of Srebrenica had swelled to over 60,000 as Bosnian refugees fled the Serb assault from surrounding hamlets. Bosnian Serb leader **Radovan Karadžić** had grown progressively bolder given muted international reaction to increasingly high-profile atrocities, aiming to achieve a decisive victory in the East, aimed to create "an unbearable situation of total insecurity" around the safe haven.[12] To test international resolve, heavily armed Serb forces attacked UN positions. When UN commander Thomas Karremans requested air support, the Serbian forces threatened French and Dutch soldiers that they held hostage. This ultimatum prompted the UN to back down and evacuate the Dutch forces from Srebrenica. In a haunting image before their evacuation, Karremans toasted General Ratko Mladić before turning over his "Safe Haven." Two days later, the women and children of Srebrenica would be bussed out, but over 8,000 Bosnian men, and boys over 16, that were held captive were led into the neighboring woods. There Serb television broadcast their final agonizing moments as they were humiliated before being shot in cold blood. This atrocity stimulated international outrage at both the Bosnian Serbs and the UN. Srebrenica prompted NATO intervention as the United States led air strikes on Belgrade. This quickly brought Milosevic to the bargaining table, and produced the **1995 Dayton Accords** that brought the Bosnian War to a welcome end roughly along the current lines of territorial control. In the fighting, an estimated 100,000 were killed and over 2 million displaced in the worst genocide to take place in Europe since World War II.

Conclusion

The collapse of the Soviet Union and the fall of communism upset two pillars of the postwar system. The fall of the Berlin Wall precipitated Europe's rapid reunification, the end of the Cold War, and the disappearance of socialism as a viable alternative to liberal capitalism. In this way, the dramatic collapse of communism contributed to global integration and gave momentum to the neoliberal formula for constructing a global economy. Communism's collapse coincided with a democratic wave that washed over Latin America and Sub-Saharan Africa, while South Asian states adopted increasingly liberal market structures as they braced for integration inside the soon to be inaugurated WTO. The fall of communism also ended Eastern Europe's isolation, but for most of the former Soviet Bloc the decade following 1989 proved traumatic. Many people lost their jobs, savings, and safety net. Ironically, many of those that had fought hardest for democracy found themselves most adversely affected by the transition towards liberal capitalism. Structural adjustment pushed many into poverty and deeply disillusioned with the revolution they once championed, even before the 2008 Great Global Recession pared back fragile economic gains.

Questions for Critical Thought

1. Why did Stalin's death ensure major changes across the Communist Bloc?
2. What motivated Khrushchev to deliver his 1956 secret speech and what were the goals of his Thaw?
3. How did the 1956 Budapest uprising and its subsequent repression by Soviet tanks reveal limits with Khrushchev's formula for destalinization?
4. In what ways did Brezhnev both stabilize socialism and create conditions for stagnation?
5. How did Mikhail Gorbachev propose to revitalize the Soviet system and why did his reforms fail?
6. What circumstances and conditions triggered the popular revolutions of 1989 and the fall of communism in Eastern Europe?

7. What difficulties did the process of postcommunist transition impose upon reformer regimes and ordinary people?
8. What triggered the Bosnian War and the subsequent genocide?

Suggestions for Further Reading

- Bacon, E., and Sandle, M. *Brezhnev Reconsidered*. London: Palgrave Macmillan, 2002.
- Brown, A. *The Gorbachev Factor*. Oxford: Oxford University Press, 1996.
- Ellison, H. J. *Boris Yeltsin and Russia's Democratic Transformation*. Seattle: University of Washington Press, 2006.
- Gorsuch, A. E., and Koenker, D. P. *The Socialist Sixties: Crossing Borders in the Second World*. Bloomington, IN: University of Indiana Press, 2013.
- Kenney, P. *A Carnival of Revolution: Central Europe 1989*. Princeton, NJ: Princeton University Press, 2003.
- Kort, M. *The Soviet Colossus: History and Aftermath*. New York: M. E. Sharpe, 2010.
- Stokes, G. *The Walls Came Tumbling Down: Collapse and Rebirth in Eastern Europe*. 2nd ed. Oxford: Oxford University Press, 2012.
- Taubman, W. *Khrushchev: The Man and his Era*. New York: W. W. Norton & Co, 2004.
- Zubok, V. *A Failed Empire: The Soviet Union in the Cold War from Stalin to Gorbachev*. Chapel Hill, NC: University of North Carolina Press, 2008.

Notes

1. Quoted in William Taubman, *Khrushchev: The Man and his Era* (New York: Norton, 2003), 254.
2. Nikita Khrushchev, Speech to the 20th Congress of the CPSU, February 24–25, 1956, accessed August 10, 2019, https://digitalarchive.wilsoncenter.org/document/115995.pdf?v=3c22b71b65bcbbe9fdfadead9419c995.
3. Taubman. *Khrushchev*, 589.
4. Budapest Students, *Sixteen Political, Economic, and Ideological Points Budapest*, October 22, 1956, accessed August 10, 2019, http://www.americanhungarianfederation.org/news_1956_16Points.html.
5. Khrushchev address to Western ambassadors at a reception at the Polish embassy in Moscow, November 18, 1956, accessed August 10, 2019, https://www.cia.gov/library/readingroom/.../CIA-RDP73B00296R000200040087-1.pdf.
6. Quoted in Ian Thatcher, "Brezhnev as Leader," in *Brezhnev Reconsidered*, ed. E. Bacon (New York: Palgrave-MacMillan, 2003), 26.
7. Quoted in R. Suny, *The Soviet Experiment* (New York: Oxford University Press, 2011), 449.
8. Paraphrased from Hebert J. Ellison, *Boris Yeltsin and Russia's Democratic Transformation* (Seattle: University of Washington Press, 2006), 175.
9. UN Scientific Committee on the Effects of Atomic Radiation, "Sources and Effects of Ionizing Radiation," 2011, accessed August 10, 2019, https://www.unscear.org/unscear/en/chernobyl.html. http://www.unscear.org/docs/reports/2008/11-80076_Report_2008_Annex_D.pdf.s

10. Quoted in D. W. Laron and A. Svecehnko, "Redrawing the Soviet Power Line: Gorbachev and the End of the Cold War," in *History and Neorealism*, ed. E. May (Cambridge: Cambridge University Press, 2011), 301.
11. Nicolae Ceauşescu, *Final Speech in Revolution Square Bucharest,* December 21, 1989, accessed August 10, 2019, https://lybio.net/nicolae-ceausescu-final-speech-1989/news-politics/.
12. International Criminal Tribunal for the former Yugoslavia, "Amended Indictment against Radovan Karadzic," April 28, 2000, accessed August 10, 2019, http://www.icty.org/x/cases/karadzic/ind/en/kar-ai000428e.pdf.

Chapter 11
The Globalization of Capitalism

Chapter Outline

- Introduction: Globalization
- Our Shrinking World
- Digitalization of the Economy
- Rise of Transnational Corporations
- Neoliberalism and the WTO
- Globalization's Paradoxes and Discontents
- Conclusion: Globalization and Capitalism

Building Modern World Economy 1944-1970
1944 Bretton Woods Conference
1947 GATT signed
1950s First supertankers
1954 First transistor radio
1956 First container ship
1957 Sputnik
1958 Telstar-1 communication satellite
1959 Microchip invented
1962 Audio cassette invented
1967 ASEAN formed
1970 Boeing Jumbo Jet
1971 Intel microprocessor

Death of Keynesian Economics 1971-1988
1971 Nixon Shock
1973 OPEC Oil Crisis
1973 First cellphone call
1980 Reagan becomes President
1981 IBM personal computer (PC)
1986 IMF forms Structural Adjustment Facility
1986-1994 Uruguay Round of GATT

Neoliberalism Globalization 1989-Present
1989 Fall of communism
1994 NAFTA comes into effect
1994 World Wide Web launch
1995 WTO comes into force
1998 1999 Asian contagion
1999 Introduction of Euro currency
1999 Seattle anti-globalization protest
2001 Doha Round of WTO commences
2001 China joins WTO

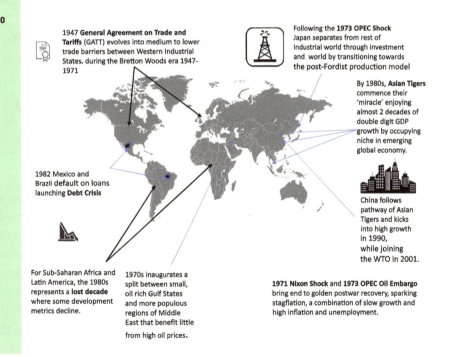

1947 **General Agreement on Trade and Tariffs** (GATT) evolves into medium to lower trade barriers between Western Industrial States. during the Bretton Woods era 1947-1971

1982 Mexico and Brazil default on loans launching **Debt Crisis**

For Sub-Saharan Africa and Latin America, the 1980s represents a **lost decade** where some development metrics decline.

1970s inaugurates a split between small, oil rich Gulf States and more populous regions of Middle East that benefit little from high oil prices.

Following the **1973 OPEC Shock** Japan separates from rest of industrial world through investment and world by transitioning towards the post-Fordist production model

By 1980s, **Asian Tigers** commence their 'miracle' enjoying almost 2 decades of double digit GDP growth by occupying niche in emerging global economy.

China follows pathway of Asian Tigers and kicks into high growth in 1990, while joining the WTO in 2001.

1971 Nixon Shock and **1973 OPEC Oil Embargo** bring end to golden postwar recovery, sparking stagflation, a combination of slow growth and high inflation and unemployment.

Image credits: © Fidart/Shutterstock.com; © Vector/Shutterstock.com; © anthonycz/Shutterstock.com; © 4LUCK/Shutterstock.com

Chapter 11: The Globalization of Capitalism

Introduction: Globalization

Since 1945, our world has progressively "shrunk." Three trends powered postwar integration: a technology-driven information revolution, transnationalization of business activity, and international convergence towards an open market architecture. During the late 1980s, declining costs for computer processing, combined with the build-out of digital networks for exchanging data, reached critical mass culminating in an "information revolution" that transformed social life and disrupted business. Multinational corporations quickly appreciated the opportunity to profit from cross-border investment, trade, and production. Corporate officers championed free market reforms to remove barriers between jurisdictions. They found a receptive audience among Western policy makers. A prolonged economic slump and debt crisis had eroded faith in planning and protectionism. The Uruguay Process commenced in 1986 aiming to reinvigorate the global economy by creating a more open architecture. Despite initial skepticism from non-Western leaders, the **World Trade Organization (WTO)** came into being in 1995. Its liberal rules gave subsequent momentum and structure to economic integration. Globalization intensified in a second stage coinciding with the maturation of digital technologies. By the twenty-first century, social life was increasingly mediated by technology, while the capitalist economy grew increasingly "borderless" and "frictionless," with transactions only minimally referenced to physical geography, state jurisdiction, or culture.

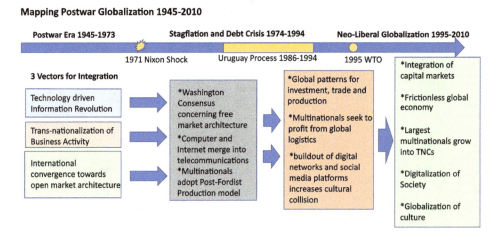

Every revolution is disruptive. It rewards early adopters and punishes stakeholders in the old system. To date, multinational corporations, private investors, western consumers, and high-tech workers have most benefitted from global capitalism. Transition towards more decentralized forms of production, freer trade, and financial deregulation has hurt blue-collar workers, non-western subsistence farmers, and mature industries operating inside protected markets. Since 1995, the paradoxes of "creative destruction" have played out across the world stage. Old industrial centers like Detroit, Norilsk, and Sheffield have decayed. Shenzhen, Dubai, and Silicon Valley have boomed by occupying specialized niches inside a rapidly integrating economy. Family farms that once provisioned local markets are increasingly supplanted by transnational agribusinesses that operate inside global production networks. Everywhere, people living inside rural areas have been forced to adapt their time-honored ways to fit an emerging modernity defined by cell phones, international standards, and consumer expectations.

Globalization is a multidimensional phenomenon. The initial sections of Chapter 11 chart how various postwar technological advances culminated in an information revolution that made globalization possible. The middle sections explore how digital technologies and neoliberal policies combined to restructure the world economy after 1995. The concluding sections chart global capitalism's mostly unintended, noneconomic consequences. How have blue-collar workers, developing states, marginalized groups, fragile ecosystems, and traditional cultures been impacted by economic globalization?

Chapter 11: The Globalization of Capitalism

Big Questions

- What is globalization?
- What technologies seeded the information revolution?
- Why did world leaders reach consensus regarding neoliberal reform?
- What are economic globalization's unintended consequences?

Our Shrinking World

For most of our history, oceans divided continents and mountain ranges separated civilizations. Today, everywhere, distance is dying. In 1990, McDonalds pierced the Iron Curtain by setting up shop inside Moscow's Pushkin Square. Pundits remarked how the Golden Arches had colonized the manger of bolshevism. With the Soviet economy in crisis, long lines of curious Muscovites cued to sample American fast food. An enthusiastic local manager proclaimed that the iconic Big Mac "was perestroika." For Russians, accustomed to consumer shortages, the Big Mac symbolized a brighter future.[1]

Globalization is an old story, but the process of integration accelerated and intensified after World War II. During the 1980s, separate revolutions in transportation, electronics, communications, production, and finance increasingly converged and reached critical mass. This set the stage for a deliberate campaign to integrate national economies into a single capitalist system. The WTO's open market structure dramatically accelerated the flow of ideas, money, people, and goods across the world stage and embedded postcolonial economies more deeply inside its Western core. About a decade later, a second less anticipated chapter of contemporary globalization took hold as digital technologies began to decouple social life, work, and business from territory. Today, for example, an engineer in Shanghai can enter the digital "cloud" to collaborate virtually with a design shop in Pontiac, Michigan, while teenagers look for mates by swiping through Tinder. This "death of distance"' has transformed the physics of the international system, the structure of the economy, and how human live, eat, work, and even think.

Five Revolutions Powering Global Society

	Principal Technologies	Significance	Index
Revolution in Transportation	Containerships, dryships, supertankers, wide-bodied jets	Standardization of containers increased the speed and decreased the cost of global freight.	Volume of world trade has increased 27 fold from $296 billion in 1950 to $8 trillion in 2005.
Revolution in Electronics	Microchip, digital computer, fibre-optic lines, server farms	The electronics revolution facilitated and amplified the scope of other global revolutions.	1963 IBM Gemini mainframe could do 7000 operations per second, while the 2009 Intel I-core7 chip on PCs can perform 932, 000 operations per second.
Revolution in Communications	Communication satellites, cellular networks, Internet, Global Positioning System	Development of overlapping internet, cell, and satellite networks allowed for cheap and instantaneous global communications.	From 1992-2014 cell phone usage increased from 17 million to 6 billion worldwide.
A Revolution in Production	Flexible production, post-Fordism, just-in-time manufacture, global supply chains	The outsourcing of component manufacture and creation of global supply chains has reduced overhead and production costs.	In 1957, 5.7% of Ford's vehicles were produced abroad compared to 2003, when 53% were assembled abroad.
A Revolution in Finance	Deregulation of banking rules, digital stock exchange, derivatives, swaps, and other complex fiscal instruments	Liberalizing capital controls has enabled unprecedented investment flows into the developing world.	From 1990-1997, Foreign Direct Investment (FDI) into China increased from $3,487 billion to $45,463 billion.

Boeing 707 pioneered the wide bodied jet that made trans-oceanic flight affordable.

Intel's x86 architecture powered the **Personal Computer revolution** of the 1980s.

Toyota pioneered the logistics that would give shape to the **Post-Fordist production model** during the late 1980s.

First iPhone in 2007 perfected the smartphone as consumer appliance and personal access node to the network society.

New York's NASDAQ market pioneered computerized trading in 1973 paving way for the integration of capital markets.

Heavy investment in fiber optic lines during the 1990s enabled the Internet to overcome the bandwidth bottleneck and mature into a world wide web and principal conduit for the information revolution.

Image credits: © travellight/Shutterstock.com; © Nor Gal/Shutterstock.com; © Phonlamai Photo/Shutterstock.com; © Vasin Lee/Shutterstock.com; © Eviart/Shutterstock.com; © Fernando Cortes/Shutterstock.com

A Revolution in Transportation

The twentieth century witnessed many remarkable inventions, but the humble shipping container represented a key ingredient catalyzing globalization. Before 1950, docks were bustling places. Global trade for nonbulk goods relied upon brawny longshoremen. On their backs, they hauled canvas sacks and packed wood crates into the holds of ships using grappling hooks, fishnets, and bulging biceps. Before 1960, ship loading proved slow, tedious, and expensive. In 1955, Malcom McLean, a trucking entrepreneur, grew frustrated with the long hours his trucks sat idle waiting for unloading. Then an epiphany struck McLean. What if instead of unloading his truck's contents piece meal, a crane would lift up a truck's entire cargo bay and strap it directly onto a ship deck? That following year, a crane detached a reinforced container directly from his truck chassis. By the early 1960s, shipping containers become uniform in size and basic design. This enabled them to be stacked like Legos. "Inter-modality" enabled their transfer from truck beds onto railcars or ship decks. During the 1970s, global infrastructure was retrofitted to accommodate the container system. This rendered armies of dockworkers obsolete. Today, a single crane operator can lift a shipping container from shore to ship in less than a minute. Containerization spurred efficiencies all along the production chain. It enabled manufacturers to more efficiently load product from assembly plants using forklifts, wood pallets, corrugated fibreboard, and plastic wrap. The container revolution facilitated efficient global transportation at dramatically lower costs. By 1990, shipping product from Hong Kong to Los Angeles was reduced to eleven days. Forty years earlier it could take a month to load a small freighter. Today, 90 percent of manufactured goods—from blue jeans to tooth brushes and televisions—moves from factory floors to retail shelves inside containers. What the shipping container achieved for goods, the supertanker, dry ships, and wide-bodied jets accomplished for oil, bulk commodities, and passengers. Cheap and reliable long-distance transportation networks ushered in conditions favorable for the transnationalization of all sorts of economic activities.

Unloading Chinese Containership in Oakland

Less glamorous then penicillin or the jet engine, globalization would have been impossible without the invention of the humble container. Outsourcing production to low-wage areas would have been impossible without a reliable and cost-efficient mode for global transportation.

Decentralized Production

During the early 1950s, pioneering manufacturers began the shift towards a **post-Fordist** production model by replacing assembly line workers with machines. This improved quality, increased output, and lowered costs. A second phase in post-Fordism commenced during the 1970s when Japanese manufacturers began to outsource component production to lower wage suppliers. In the heyday of mass production, Ford's battery, tire, and mirror suppliers had ringed their flagship River Rouge plant. Containerization and improving global logistics, however, steadily undermined the efficiency gained from geographical proximity. During the early 1980s recession, Chrysler executive Lee Iacocca pleaded with consumers to "buy American." By the late 1990s, however, Detroit's "Big Three" had all shamelessly copied Japan's outsourcing model. The 1994 North American Free Trade Act (NAFTA) agreement accelerated the relocation of American auto plants to Mexico. Other industries followed suit as a global wave of deregulation steadily lowered the costs and hurdles associated with outsourcing production.

From cell phones to jeans and processed foods, nearly all of the consumer products that people buy comes from a post-Fordist production model that leverages telecommunications technologies to create a global supply chains to efficiently tap global labor, commodities and entrepreneurs. Post-Fordism has decoupled the world economy from territory and the jurisdiction of the nation-state.

Transition to Post-Fordist Production Model

Flexible Production Lines to manage inventory and respond to shifts in consumer taste.

Container Revolution facilitates outsourcing to geographically distant places.

Global supply chains lower warehousing costs through Just-In-Time assembly.

Outsourcing component manufacturing to low-cost suppliers.

Information technology communicates exact product standards to ensure quality control among parts suppliers.

Image credits: © Jenson/Shutterstock.com; © Fishman64/Shutterstock.com; © MOLPIX?Shutterstock.com; © Dusan Petkovic/Shutterstock.com; © catastrophe_OL/Shutterstock.com; © servickuz/Shutterstock.com

Outsourcing acquired additional momentum after 2000 when the US Department of Defense opened up its **Global Positioning System (GPS)**, developed for military navigation, to commercial users. This enabled multinationals to more efficiently track product and to construct more sophisticated global supply chains.

A Revolution in Finance

One of the most remarkable shifts of the last two decades has been the sudden transformation of the former periphery of the world economy. The glimmering skyscrapers of Addis Ababa, the plants in

Shenzhen, or the phone kiosks of Lagos offer testament to an unprecedented transfer of wealth from the developed world to the former periphery. From 1970 to 2012, **foreign direct investment** (FDI) to emerging market economies experienced a hundredfold increase. This dwarfed the capital that the World Bank had traditionally supplied postcolonial states for infrastructure projects through low-interest loans. Most FDI however, flowed to BRIC (Brazil, Russia, India, and China) economies rather than those at the periphery that arguably needed development most. Another growing source of capital for emerging economies comes from portfolio investments. Instead of investing in plants or real estate, western mutual, hedge, and pension funds buy stock in foreign corporations. Such investments remained "liquid," enabling Investors to withdraw their capital by selling shares if market conditions soured, or if they believed a more lucrative opportunity existed elsewhere.

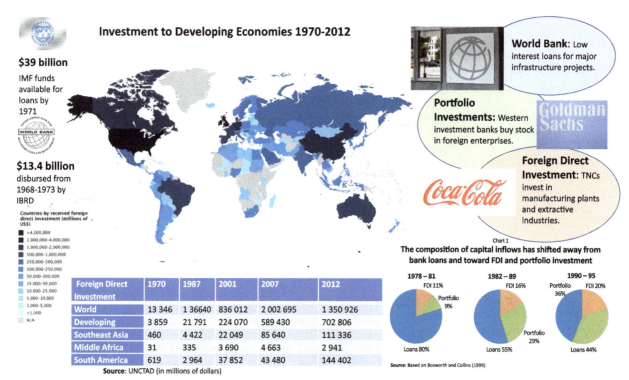

Image credits: © Mark Van Scyoc/Shutterstock.com; © Piotr Swat/Shutterstock.com; © Rose Carson/Shutterstock.com; © Andrei Minsk/Shutterstock.com; © Turn on/Shutterstock.com

Financial capitalism has proven a mixed blessing for developing countries. The high volume of investment has injected badly needed capital, powered growth and raised wages. Private investors, though, prioritize projects focused on short-term returns and large profits. This means that development increasingly reflects the priorities of foreign investors rather than those of the state or local peoples. Investor fickleness also exposes developing economies to volatility. During financial panics like the Asian Contagion of 1998 to 1999, capital was rapidly withdrawn sparking regional unemployment, falling wages and, in the case of Indonesia, regime collapse.

The Electronics Revolution

Contemporary globalization would have been impossible without advances in electronics. During World War II, analog computers ran calculations using metal gears and punch cards. The first transistor was patented in 1947, but they did not replace vacuum tubes until the mid-1960s. In August 1958, Jack

Kilby made a critical breakthrough while tinkering in his Texas Instruments lab by placing transistors on a silicon wafer. This created an integrated circuit. Silicon provided the ideal platform for packing more processing power onto chips, even if it took a decade to perfect the architecture. By the late 1960s, silicon **microchips** rapidly supplanted bulky and fault-prone vacuum tubes in radios and television sets. Microchip sales rose from 8.8 million in 1960 to 934 million in 1969, while their price plummeted nearly 3,000 percent. Subsequently, microprocessor development followed **Moore's Law**: their computational power doubled every eighteen months, while shrinking in size and falling in cost. Today, microprocessors are embedded in all the appliances of modern life, from computers to dishwashers. The flagship Intel 4004 chip of 1971 featured one transistor compared to 70 million on today's 64-bit chips. Incredibly, a modern digital wristwatch packs more processing power than the computers that landed Apollo on the Moon.

Main Stages of the Electronics Revolution

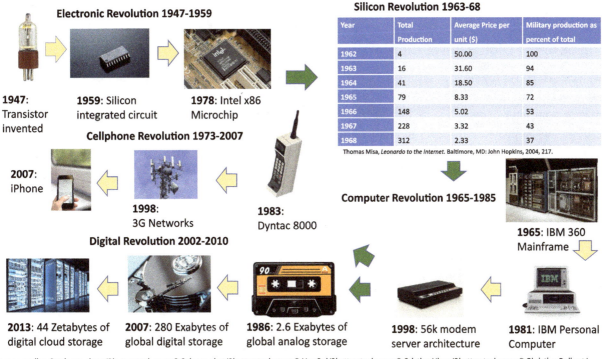

Image credits: © science photo/Shutterstock.com; © Science ohot/Shutterstock.com; © Nor Gal/Shutterstock.com; © Cristina Nixau/Shutterstock.com; © Christian Delbert/Shutterstock.com; © Timur Zima/Shutterstock.com; © icosha/Shutterstock.com; © twin Design/Shutterstock.com; © Doug McLean/Shutterstock.com; © IMOGI graphics/Shutterstock.com; © Aleksandr Grechanyuk/Shutterstock.com; © Tommy Lee Walker/Shutterstock.com

During the 1950s, the Pentagon financed the American electronics industry. Taxpayer money contributed to the development of solid-state microcircuits, RAM memory, and other components of the modern computer. By the late 1960s, however, the consumer market supplanted Pentagon orders and pushed the electronics revolution in new directions, notably in terms of developing communications technology.

A Revolution in Communications

Three years following the 1957 launch of Sputnik, A T&T's *Telstar 1* facilitated the first transatlantic television broadcast. By the 1970s, hundreds of geosynchronous satellites drifted in Earth's orbit facilitating live broadcasts of distant events like the Olympics. The year 1969 marked the dawn of the global telecommunications age as six hundred million witnessed Neil Armstrong's ghostly moon dance. Meteorological satellites transformed the nightly weather broadcast, saving lives by providing early warning for onrushing hurricanes. In remote jungles and drab concrete housing complexes throughout the developing world, satellite dishes began to poke up through slat roofs and rusty porch railings. They tapped into the beams broadcasting Premier League soccer or syndicated reruns of *Dynasty*. For the developing world, the 1970s ushered in the television age. Rising incomes and declining costs for TV sets expanded the ranks of ownership. As television emerged as the principal conduit for global communications, it opened up a window onto the world. Peoples living inside traditional cultures increasingly appreciated how they inhabited a vast world percolating with alien customs, great wealth, and wondrous technologies. Traditional practices, once rooted in place, now became framed against a broader canvass. This marked a revolutionary moment as millions realized both the possibilities of "modern" life and the vast standard of living gap. The television age coincided with rapid migration. Peasants moved to neighboring cities, while skilled workers ventured abroad to benefit from higher wages in developed economies.

Origins of the Digital Revolution

The year 2014 represented a tipping point where Americans spent more time in front of a mobile screen than a television. The origins of today's Internet, however, stretches back to the late 1960s, when three separate computer networks were established in the United States, France, and Britain. Their original purpose was to provide the defense establishment secure communications in the case of attack. By the 1970s, the network acquired a new purpose by allowing researchers to share precious time on expensive mainframes. In 1974, **Arpanet** represented the world's most elaborate computer network linking various US research universities and defense department laboratories.

ARPANET in 1974

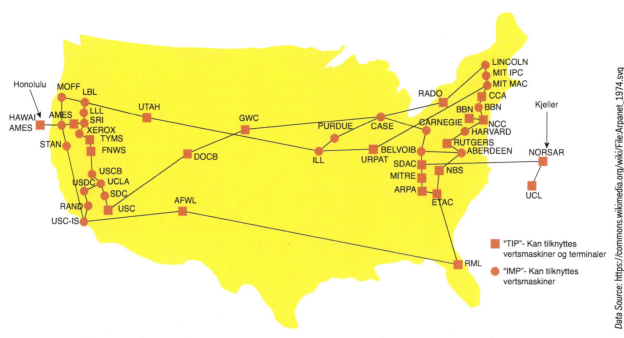

The APRANET computer network provided the foundation for the modern Internet. In 1994, the World Wide Web was launched too much fanfare inaugurating the modern Internet, an open, universally accessible global communications system.

By the late 1970s, various innovations created an official packet-switching "protocol" that facilitated the merger of separate computer networks into a unitary system. Rapid advances in microprocessors spurred a sharp decline in the costs of mainframes, while exploding their user base. Researchers increasingly applied computers to solve a wider range of problems. Fortune 500 companies appropriated computers to manage their inventory, handle their payroll, and balance their books.

The PC Revolution

In his Cupertino garage in 1976, Steve Jobs developed the first Apple. It resembled a clunky typewriter, but it embodied a visionary principle. Jobs imagined a personal computer (PC) that would render the power of microchips accessible to ordinary people. To Jobs' frustration, by 1983 corporate behemoth IBM won the first leg of the PC wars, mass producing the "Wintel" (Microsoft Windows operating system and Intel processor) architecture. By the late 1980s, the PC had become a staple of the American office and a system for home entertainment.

World Wide Web

During the early 1980s, PCs were stand-alone devices whose functionality was limited to their software. Conducive state polices, however, helped to unlock the power of personal computing by connecting them together. Since the 1930s, radio and long-distance telephone service had become regulated monopolies in most Western states. This regulatory model was subsequently applied to television. As state monopolies, these companies focused on expanding reliable service inside protected domestic markets. This conservative mind-set discouraged innovation or adopting new technologies that would undermine the existing infrastructure and customer base. By the late 1960s, national telephone companies managed to bring individual subscriber lines to consumers in rural areas, while building out a reliable long-distance network spanning much of the globe. They had no incentive, however, to invest in digitalisation: a process for transforming information into a code of "1s" and "0s." Instead of investing in a more efficient platform, telephone monopolies lobbied state regulatory bodies to protect them from small upstarts experimenting with disruptive technologies. In 1982, the US federal government made the monumental decision to break up the Bell Telephone monopoly. This landmark case established a model for state—guided for technological innovation that many other states later copied.

Deregulation of the telephone industry paved the way for improved computer networking. The United States' National Science Foundation took the lead in developing technologies, infrastructure, and protocols that allowed PCs to communicate over existing telephone lines. The workstation and local area network soon became obsolete. From 1985 to 1993, the number of PCs connected to the NSF's network exploded from 2,000 to 2 million. However, the narrow bandwidth of dial-up connections constrained functionality. Consumer demand for faster networks spurred a frantic build-out of **fiber optic** lines with digital switches by the 1990s. Like the telegraph build-out a century before, fiber optic lines were laid within cities, between states and across oceans. Digital networks replaced coaxial cables, dramatically increasing the capacity for telecommunications. By the early 1990s, the client–server architecture had become standardized, facilitating various local networks to hook up to the Internet "backbone," gradually transforming it into a universally accessible global communications medium.

Another critical breakthrough in the Internet's evolution came in 1989 when Tim Berners Lee proposed the creation of a "World Wide Web" using **hypertext** as a means to link information stored on various mainframes. This innovation enabled users to "browse" data at will. In 1993, the "World Wide Web" reached critical mass following Marc Andreessen's development of the Mosaic browser that enabled web pages to feature both text and graphics. This enhanced the possibilities for content and improved the browsing experience. From 1993 to 1995 cyberspace grew furiously and became increasingly commercialized. Internet service providers (ISPs) provided access, while businesses set up digital store fronts to sell their products. The number of unique web pages, traffic, and the pool of global users all grew exponentially. By 2000, e-mail had replaced "snail" mail as the principal means for global correspondence. A decade later, social media giant Facebook had over six hundred million daily users. This marked the Internet's maturation into a digital medium that allowed families to share pictures, "gamers" to socialize, and millennials to find mates.

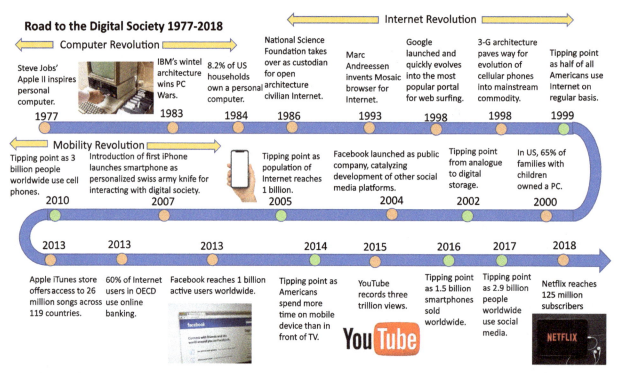

Image credits: © Angelo D'Amico/Shutterstock.com; © guteksk7/Shutterstock.com; © Gil C/Shutterstock.com; © rvlsoft/Shutterstock.com; © Kaspars Grinvalds/Shutterstock.com

During the early 1990s, it became increasingly apparent that the value of the information stored on the Internet was contingent upon its accuracy and accessibility. Search engines emerged to index information on the web and rate its reliability. After 2000, multiple, competing engines were gradually supplanted by a small Silicon Valley start-up, Google. Google's powerful key word search engine became so popular that by 2000 it emerged as the Internet's *de facto* portal. This transformed Google into one of the most lucrative businesses on Earth. Google did not sell consumer products, but information. In particular, Google cornered the market on targeted advertising. Exploiting their sophisticated data about user preferences, Google embeds vendor advertisements into a user's search results.

Mobility Revolution, 1998 to 2017

The second leg in the digital revolution derived from transformation of cellphones into the principal conduit for tapping the Internet. After decades of experimentation with wireless technologies and radio phones, Motorola developed the first mass-produced cellular phone in 1983. The DynaTAC8000 became a status symbol among Wall Street brokers, despite weighing in at 1.3 kg and enjoying less than an hour of battery life. Not until 2G networks emerged during the early 1990s, did cellular phones acquire widespread adoption inside Western countries. By 1998, development of 3G networks spurred some consumers to cut their "landlines." Apple's 2007 introduction of iPhone represented transformed flip-phones used primarily for conversations into smartphones that could take pictures, pat for a cup of coffee, perform Internet banking transactions, navigate streets, or stream movies. Today, smartphones serve as a Swiss Army knife that connect individuals to the "cloud," an ever-expanding virtual real estate that increasingly houses the locales where people collaboratively work, socialize, manage their chores, and seek out entertainment opportunities.

Bridging the Digital Divide

In 1990, the dominant language of the Internet was English, few Africans had cell phones, and only a minority of people in Eastern Europe had Internet connections. This raised concerns about a "digital divide" that would leave poor people, non-western states, and remote regions behind. Since 2000, however, the rapidly diminishing cost of digital networks and personal communication devices has made global telecommunications increasingly accessible. In Africa, from 1998 to 2010, cell phone ownership exploded from 0.53 to 42.82 per 100 residents. Currently, the developing world represents the area of highest growth for Internet use and cell phone adoption, while the amount of non-English content on the Internet has also exploded.

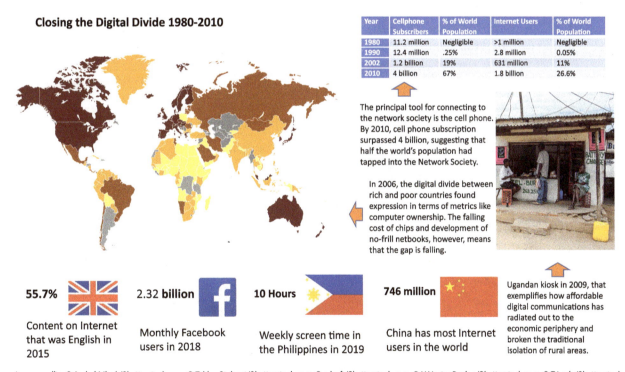

Dawn of the Digital Age

By the twenty-first century, the build-out of fiber optic lines, digital switches, cell towers, communications satellites, and server farms dramatically increased the world's capacity to store and exchange information. The data flowing through planetary telecommunications networks increased exponentially from 281 petabytes in 1986 to 65 exabytes in 2007, roughly equivalent of 6 newspapers per person per day.[2] Digital technologies also began to transform older patterns of work, leisure, and socializing, leading to enthusiasts to speak of a **network society**. Affordable cellular phones and broadband networks have had a particular impact upon poor countries and remote regions. It is not just Internet access, but how such access produces new opportunities. In Central Africa, drones can now deliver blood to trauma victims in roadless areas that might have once died. Networking has also deepened the scope of cultural globalization. JD.com evolved from a humble online electronics store in 2004 to a business with three hundred million active users by bringing the wonders of the global market to isolated homesteads in China. Cell phones allow rural customers to browse JD's catalogue, place orders, and often wait for moped delivery. JD's success highlights how computer networking and consumerism are merging inside a global society where digital technologies increasingly mediate human experience and a global consumer culture defines personal aspirations.

Digitalization of the Economy

Digital technologies have not only transformed social life, they are also disrupting the structure of the economy. Contemporary tech giants like Google, Facebook, and Amazon did not exist as public companies twenty years ago. Today, most of their business focuses on the digital "cloud" that allows consumers to store data, workers to collaborate remotely, retailers to sell products, and professionals to perform services. Increasing bandwidth and the evolution of increasingly sophisticated virtual platforms also enable people to perform routine tasks that once required commuting, face-to-face contact, or physical manipulation of tools and documents.

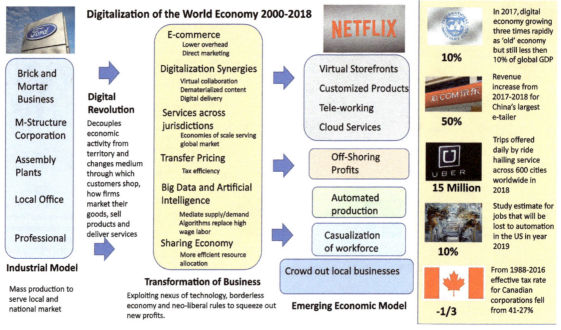

Image credits: © D K Grove/Shutterstock.com; © r classen/Shutterstock.com; © Turn on/Shutterstock.com; © testing/Shutterstock.com; © 360b/Shutterstock.com; © Jenson/Shutterstock.com; © Maximumvector/Shutterstock.com

Disruption of Financial Services

Since the emergence of national exchanges in nineteenth-century Europe, stock and commodity trading remained dominated by brokers who worked the trading floor. During the 1970s, Bloomberg and Reuters developed computer networks that linked stock exchanges to back offices, providing brokers with real-time market data. By 1984, Reuters' Telequote system featured over 40,000 terminals located in over 100 countries. Information technology (IT) also began to transform stock trading. Born in 1971,

National Association of Securities Dealers Automated Quotations (NASDAQ) evolved into an actual exchange, pioneering fully computerized trading by 1987. NASDAQ proved that electronic trading was cheaper and more efficient than the hue and cry of brokers in the "pit." NASDAQ's success forced established exchanges to follow suit. By the early 1990s, fully automated trading became standard across world capital markets, while more relaxed capital rules and deregulation facilitated increasing capital market integration. In 2012, the launch of Euronext united the main European stock exchanges, once prized symbols of national sovereignty. Today, commodities, bonds, stocks, and national currencies can be traded 24/7, while the value and volume of transactions continually rises.

During the 1960s, most banks remained brick-and-mortar businesses. The proverbial "banker" wore a fine suit, lived inside a community and focused on making loans to local entrepreneurs and home buyers by appraising their business plans and credit worthiness. In the United States, Citibank disrupted the banking industry during the 1970s by pioneering the use of computer technology to replace staff, lower the costs, and establish a national network of branches. Similar trends were transforming investment banks that traditionally provided venture capital to national entrepreneurs. The oil shocks of the 1970s left western banks flush with cash and hungry for higher investment returns abroad. When investment bank Goldman Sachs transformed from a partnership into a public company to expand its capital base, other investment banks followed suit. Huge profits could be realized from global deregulation, spurring a merger wave among commercial banks, Wall Street concerns, and insurance companies. Today, a small set of almost a dozen global conglomerates dominates the financial services industry, offering a full spectrum of services ranging from commercial lending, to currency exchange, investment banking, and commodity trading. A recent study estimates that these behemoths collectively control around 40 percent of the shares of the world's "blue chip" corporations.[3]

Bank merger wave, 1996 to 2009

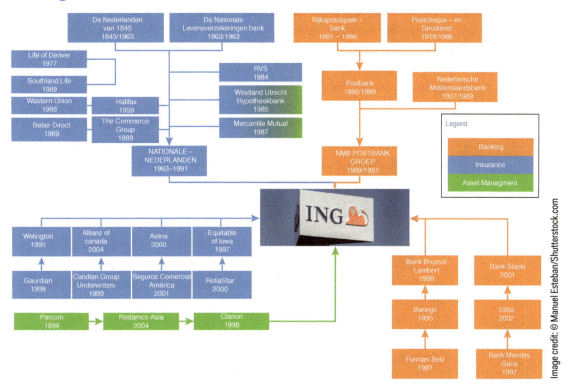

Financial deregulation spurred a merger wave among international banks. Established in 1845 as a Dutch fire insurance firm, the ING group has since emerged as a global financial concern with branches around the globe that marry traditional banking services with insurance and asset management.

As national capital markets merged, New York, Tokyo, and London evolved into hubs for global finance. These banking centers 'floated' bonds that enabled sovereign states to pay their everyday bills. Financial deregulation dramatically accelerated the volume and "velocity" of money sloshing through the global economy. It also spurred the development of derivative instruments and arcane insurance products, like "swaps," to help global banking institutions manage risk.

Flexible Production and E-Commerce

By the century's turn, IT began to disrupt manufacturing and retail. During the 1980s, Toyota executives developed the **Just-in-Time** (JIT) production system to harvest the efficiency of information technologies and transition towards a "leaner" production model. Computers, barcode scanners, and GPS helped Toyota to outsource a much larger share of their component part production to outside suppliers. The JIT model reduced warehousing costs and allowed Toyota to efficiently manage its inventory, while flexibly adapting their product mix to reflect subtle shifts in consumer tastes or demand. By the late 1990s, the JIT model was widely copied, facilitated by neoliberal reforms that removed many of the hurdles for foreign investment. South Asia emerged as a particular beneficiary. China's special economic zones (SEZs) grew rapidly as a global destination for low-margin manufacturing.

Digital Restructuring

By the dawn of the twenty-first century, digital technologies were transforming how things were made, sold, and bought. By 2000, for example, thousands of automated teller machines (ATMs) were deployed across western economies. They replaced the proverbial "bank lady" and enabled consumers to access their financial accounts outside of constricted "banking hours." In the West, merchants adopted various direct payment systems that facilitated electronic transfers using credit and debit cards. By the late 1990s, innovative companies like Dell pioneered a direct retailing model that cut out middlemen. Traditional marketing, like newspaper ads, encouraged prospective clients to visit Dell's website. There, customers could select the components for a custom-built PC that would be shipped directly from the warehouse by parcel post. By the end of 2012, global e-commerce reached $1 trillion with Amazon emerging as the world's leading "e-tailer" by developing a business model that threatens "brick-and–mortar" retail outlets that operate with higher real estate costs. While IT and market liberalization particularly benefited Fortune 500 companies, it also opened opportunities for small businesses. The Internet, social media, and e-commerce enable small companies to serve foreign clients with minimal infrastructure, while many services, software, and digital products can be delivered virtually at little cost.

Rise of Transnational Corporations

The transformation of multinationals into transnational corporations (TNCs) represents one of the most underappreciated dimensions of contemporary globalization. Before 1970, multinationals owned foreign subsidiaries, but their profits remained rooted in their "home" market. The WTO spurred a merger wave that transformed the world's largest multinationals into global conglomerates. Their board of governors, workforce, head offices, and profits no longer meaningfully correspond to their state of origin.

Corporations and Globalization

After World War II, companies like Ford and General Electric (GE) had already saturated their domestic market. Once they had sold an automobile, fridge, or washing machine to every American household, corporations faced the prospect of ever-diminishing sales and lower profits. **Planned obsolescence** represented one solution. Durable goods manufacturers consciously engineered the components of lawn mowers and toasters to wear out after a set time in order to stimulate a replacement cycle.

A second solution lay in expanding foreign market share. The European market proved particularly attractive in the 1960s as family incomes rose. Penetrating foreign markets protected by high tariffs and onerous state regulations proved challenging. For Proctor and Gamble to sell toothpaste in Japan or France, for example, they needed to pass exacting regulatory standards that amounted to an unofficial trade barrier. One technique for breaking into protected markets involved buying out local businesses. This helped consumer conglomerates like GE, Unilever, and Nestle to bypass local regulatory hurdles and acquire preapproved products.

Increasing foreign market share, however, changed corporations. Operating solely inside a domestic market creates a symbiosis between private profits and the national interest. A foreign merger wave during the 1970s began to erode this symmetry. Multinationals began to create complex alliances between private investors, corporate boards, state regulators, and domestic workers. French patriots might protest the buyout of a financially troubled domestic firm by American business interests, but local workers and municipal officials welcomed angel investors who promised to modernize plants and save local jobs.

After 1970, Fortune 500 corporations assumed an increasingly multinational character. Typically, a richly capitalized US corporation acquired a European rival, but the process worked both ways and cut across industries. During the mid-1980s, European states increasingly adopted deregulatory policies and began to divest crown corporations like British Telecom and France's Total. As publicly traded companies, with access to public capital, they now started to buy out foreign competitors. In Asia, Japan's closely held corporations limited foreign takeovers, but rising foreign currency reserves enabled Japan's corporations to buy out western firms and finance foreign subsidiaries, first in Asia, and later through leveraged buy-outs of western corporations.

Sluggish growth during the 1980s created a tough business climate that crimped corporate profits and spurred frustration with protectionism. To open up new market opportunities, corporate officers pressured

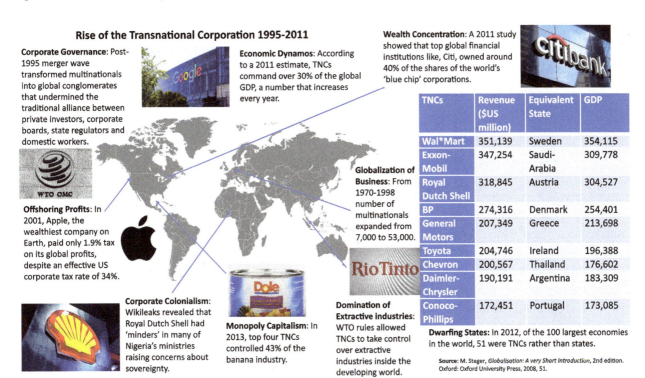

Rise of the Transnational Corporation 1995-2011

Corporate Governance: Post-1995 merger wave transformed multinationals into global conglomerates that undermined the traditional alliance between private investors, corporate boards, state regulators and domestic workers.

Offshoring Profits: In 2001, Apple, the wealthiest company on Earth, paid only 1.9% tax on its global profits, despite an effective US corporate tax rate of 34%.

Corporate Colonialism: Wikileaks revealed that Royal Dutch Shell had 'minders' in many of Nigeria's ministries raising concerns about sovereignty.

Economic Dynamos: According to a 2011 estimate, TNCs command over 30% of the global GDP, a number that increases every year.

Globalization of Business: From 1970-1998 number of multinationals expanded from 7,000 to 53,000.

Monopoly Capitalism: In 2013, top four TNCs controlled 43% of the banana industry.

Domination of Extractive industries: WTO rules allowed TNCs to take control over extractive industries inside the developing world.

Wealth Concentration: A 2011 study showed that top global financial institutions like, Citi, owned around 40% of the shares of the world's 'blue chip' corporations.

TNCs	Revenue ($US million)	Equivalent State	GDP
Wal*Mart	351,139	Sweden	354,115
Exxon-Mobil	347,254	Saudi-Arabia	309,778
Royal Dutch Shell	318,845	Austria	304,527
BP	274,316	Denmark	254,401
General Motors	207,349	Greece	213,698
Toyota	204,746	Ireland	196,388
Chevron	200,567	Thailand	176,602
Daimler-Chrysler	190,191	Argentina	183,309
Conoco-Phillips	172,451	Portugal	173,085

Dwarfing States: In 2012, of the 100 largest economies in the world, 51 were TNCs rather than states.

Source: M. Steger, *Globalisation: A very Short Introduction*, 2nd edition. Oxford: Oxford University Press, 2008, 51.

Image credits: © Valeriya Zankovych/Shutterstock.com; © ricochet64/Shutterstock.com; © Solomon 7/Shutterstock.com; © imwaltersy/Shutterstock.com; © chrisdorney/Shutterstock.com; © Andreri Minsk/Shutterstock.com; © 360b/Shutterstock.com; © TungCheung/Shutterstock.com

Western policy makers to negotiate lower tariffs and to adopt more accommodative business policies. This deregulatory impulse shaped the Uruguay Round of General Agreement on Trade and Tariffs (GATT). US negotiator Carla Hills captured the spirit of reform well in 1990: "We want to abolish the right of nations to impose health and safety standards more stringent than a minimal world standard."[4]

Dawn of the TNC

For multinationals, the WTO's liberal rules marked an emancipation proclamation. After 1995, they exploded in number, size, and influence as they rushed to profit from cross-border opportunities. According to United Nations Conference on Trade and Development (UNCTAD), the number of TNCs has rapidly expanded from 7,000 to 53,000 between 1970 and 1998, employing 73 million people and emerging as the principal conduit for foreign investment.[5] Multinational growth was bipolar, concentrated in small firms that leveraged the e-commerce model to sell goods across national borders and global conglomerates, which voraciously bought out foreign competitors.

The laws governing TNCs were enacted mostly during the nineteenth century when corporations were much smaller entities and operated almost exclusively inside national boundaries. In the contemporary economy, however, TNCs dominate the world's extractive industries, while serving as the principal conduit for foreign investment. Already in 1993, "the 300 largest TNCs own or control at least one-quarter of the entire world's productive assets, worth about US$5 trillion".[6] By 2012, the world reached a tipping point: of the hundred largest economies in the world, fifty-one were TNCs rather than states.[7] The size of TNCs, their global footprint, and supranational outlook make them substantively different from small- and medium-sized businesses. Although the contemporary international system continues to vest sovereignty in states, the world's largest TNCs now dwarf the majority of states. This gives them considerable leverage to pressure developing states for favorable resource concessions and pit developed states against each other for tax subsidies. Deregulation has also made TNCs nimble. They can efficiently relocate plants to escape taxes or undercut the wage demands of labor unions. TNCs have also grown increasingly proficient at exploiting a porous treaty system to "offshore" their profits to tax havens.

> What does democratic government mean in a world where TNCs command such a large role inside the global economy?

Corporate Governance

Despite growing increasingly powerful, as private concerns, TNCs are not subject to much public scrutiny or oversight. Corporate law establishes that the sole fiduciary responsibility of corporate officers is to return profit to their shareholders. This singular commitment pushes corporations to privilege private profit over environmental, social concerns or the public interest. Relocating a profitable GM plant from Oshawa to Tijuana may reward shareholders, but it also harms local union workers and cripples the municipal tax base. While neoliberals often laud the efficiency of the market, in many industries TNCs have grown so large that they operate as *de facto* monopolies, crowding out smaller, less nimble competitors. The concentration of economic power clearly spills over into the political sphere. The US Supreme Court's infamous 2010 citizens united ruling legalized the flow of dark corporate money to flow into national elections. TNCs have also influenced international bodies. For example, during the 1992 Rio Conference, TNCs exerted pressure to remove all proposals concerning corporate regulation from the meeting's agenda.[8]

Neoliberalism and the WTO

Corporate officers played a quietly influential role in shaping the WTO's ultimate configuration. Following the Great Depression in the 1930s, laissez-faire capitalism stood discredited. Around the world, social democrats took charge, arguing that capitalism was unstable and that state regulators needed to counteract market volatility. Liberal economists continued to insist that free markets were essential for economic growth, prosperity, and freedom. Until stagflation hit the world economy in the 1970s, however, liberal economists remained lonely voices in the wilderness. **Keynesians** occupied key positions in state and international financial organizations. All Western states featured mixed economies that combined forms of state planning with private enterprise and secure property rights. The robustness of the global economic recovery after 1950 lent implicit confirmation to the Keynesian model. The Bretton Woods system lent stability to international trade and postwar reconstruction.

During the late 1960s, however, the international economy's underpinnings started to unravel. Robust economic recovery in Europe and Japan put pressure on the Bretton Woods system of fixed currency exchange. Global imbalance manifested in dollar shortages and gold exports from the US Treasury. In 1971, President Nixon abandoned the gold standard. Unilateral devaluation of the US dollar achieved Nixon's immediate goal of lowering the cost of US products. Unilateral devaluation, however, brought the Bretton Woods system crashing down. By 1973, the international community tentatively agreed to allow their currencies to float according to their market price. Demise of Bretton Woods constituted an inflection point for the international economy. Subsequently, developed states began the process of surrendering control over their national economy to global market forces.

While the **Nixon Shock** destabilized the global economy, the 1973 to 1974 Organization of Petroleum Exporting Countries (OPEC) oil embargo knocked it off its moorings. Global dependence on petroleum for electricity, transport and vital products like fertilizers, chemicals, and plastics made it difficult to cope with the inflationary effect of quadrupling oil prices. Cheap oil had fueled the postwar recovery. Without it, Western economies slumped into **stagflation**: stagnant growth, high inflation, and rising unemployment. Higher oil prices hit oil-importing countries like Japan, India, and Singapore hard. But oil importers in the developing world suffered a "double whammy" as the global recession socked commodity prices while elevating the costs of their imports. The oil shocks of the 1970s would ultimately spur a wave of sovereign defaults. The recession of 1980 to 1981 spurred the 1982 Debt Crisis that inaugurated a **Lost Decade** for much of Latin America and Africa. External debt service as a percentage of exports hit 179 percent for Argentina and 129 percent for Mexico.[9] In Africa, the worst hit states saw their metrics for growth and quality of life reverse. This financial crisis, combined with the end of the Cold War, precipitated the collapse of many authoritarian regimes. The more liberal and democratic regimes that emerged scrambled to find a solution for their laggard economies.

Deregulation and Market Reforms

Western stagflation and the Debt Crisis gave ammunition to long-marginalized free market reformers. Now dubbed "neoliberals," they argued that the economic malaise of the 1970s was not the result of higher oil prices, but overregulation. Since World War II, the scope of government interference inside the economy had steadily increased through the expansion of labor unions, welfare entitlements, safety regulations, and various protectionist measures. Individually, these policies might serve a social purpose, but neoliberals argued that collectively they distorted efficient operation of the market. Reigniting growth required a return to the laissez-faire polices of the past. Deregulation would give the economy oxygen and kick-start recovery. States needed to divest crown corporations to facilitate their more efficient operation under private management, to cut back on welfare supports to reduce budget deficits, to eliminate tariffs that promoted economic inefficiency, and to reduce burdensome regulations that constrained entrepreneurial innovation. In Europe, few centrist governments dared to gut welfare measures, but rising budget deficits did spur the adoption of limited market reforms by the mid-1980s. Western European states followed the United States and Britain particularly in deregulating the communications, transport, and mining sectors of their economies.

Clash of Economic Philosophies

Keynesian	Economic Philosophy	Neo-Liberal
John Maynard Keynes 1883-1946	Grand Philosopher	Milton Friedman (1912-2006)
The Great Depression 1929-1939	Crisis provoking theory	Stagflation 1973-1979
Capitalism is fundamentally unstable and states must intervene to modulate the market's boom and bust cycles.	Basic Insight	The market operates according to the law of supply and demand and state intervention distorts its efficiency.
The state must care for the unfortunate and underprivileged.	Moral Vision	Competition promotes progress, self-reliance, and ingenuity.
Fiscal: During a recession the state must adopt fiscal policies that increase spending to nudge the economy back to full employment.	Principal Policy Mechanism	**Monetary:** The state should avoid fiscal policies that will raise the deficit and distort the efficient functioning of the market; instead states should focus on creating low inflation and economic stability.
The Bretton Woods system and its system of fixed currency exchange offered a stability enabling all partners to benefit from international trade while restraining their selfish impulses.	International Trade	Protectionism promotes economic inefficiency. Instead, national economies should liberalize to attract foreign investment and stimulate industries where it holds a comparative advantage.
State planning will prevent major recessions and keep the economy churning at full employment, while providing a level playing field and safety net for all.	Presumed Outcome	Free market policies will ignite growth, improve worker efficiency, and enable states to tackle debt and increase prosperity.

Deregulation Wave, 1986 to 1995

Neoliberal ideas gained traction during the 1980s as Ronald Reagan and Margaret Thatcher championed free market reforms. When Reagan spoke of the 'miracle of the market,' his voice assumed a tone of religious reverence. Reagan linked laissez-faire capitalism to traditional American virtues like self-reliance and ingenuity. Similarly, Thatcher saw capitalism as a cure for flagging British pride and confidence. The "Iron Lady" linked Britain's postwar decline to socialist policies that promoted state dependence, social conformity, and idleness. As heads of state, Reagan and Thatcher served as trail blazers for neoliberal reform inside their own economies, taking on powerful labor unions, paring back state regulation, breaking up public monopolies, and introducing welfare reforms. Internationally, Reagan and Thatcher promoted neoliberal crusaders to prominent posts inside their own governments and international organizations like the World Bank and International Monetary Fund (IMF). This represented a conscious effort to align these agencies more closely with the neoliberal policy agenda.

Thatcher and Reagan outside the White House, 1983

Thatcher and Reagan combined to introduce neoliberal reforms at home, while championing them abroad.

The IMF and Structural Adjustment

The clash between economic philosophies was arguably most pronounced inside Latin America. The 1982 Debt Crisis had spurred a wave of national defaults and set off a crippling spiral of hyperinflation as many states attempted to meet debt obligations by printing money. Under Reagan's sponsorship, neoliberals had gained ascendency inside the IMF. They introduced a **structural adjustment** policy that made emergency cash transfusions and debt renegotiation "contingent" upon their client's willingness to adopt free market reforms. As Tanzania's Joseph Nyerere complained, "the IMF has become largely an instrument for economic and ideological control of poor countries by rich ones."[10] Latin American leaders felt similarly coerced by the IMF, but many former dependency theorists agreed that import substitution policies had failed. After a decade of economic difficulties, they hoped to emulate the success of Asia's Tiger economies and dared not sit out the Uruguay Round of GATT that convened in Punta del Este in 1986. Collapse of the Soviet Bloc in 1989 gave added momentum to the **Washington Consensus**, the presumption that free markets represented the only viable economic system. By 1994, the Uruguay Round culminated in the Marrakesh Agreement that brought the WTO into force in 1995. In one act, 120 states, including most of the world's core industrial regions and a majority of postcolonial states, bound their economies in a single capitalist system. Signatories prayed that neoliberal reforms would power an economic boom.

Assessing Global Capitalism, 1995 to 2007

From the glittering skyscrapers rising up from the sands of Abu Dhabi to Indian peasants forced from their land, neoliberal globalization has proven disruptive, enriching some, impoverishing others, while radically altering the structure of the world economy. The WTO's architects promised not only economic growth, but also social progress. Austerity measures introduced during the 1980s had spurred cuts in healthcare, housing, and education, sometimes translating into declines in the **human development index (HDI)**, which combines income measures with various social and cultural metrics. From 2000 to 2007, however, the HDI rebounded mostly because of the volume of capital flowing into developing economies. This stimulated higher levels of growth and rising wages so that by 2010 poverty and malnutrition had declined inside the developing world as a whole, while their share of global GDP jumped to 50 percent.

Across the world, however, economic and social progress remains uneven. Since 1995, investment has flowed mostly into Southeast Asia, particularly China. This has stimulated high levels of economic growth in Eastern cities, enabling living standards to climb among the rapidly expanding urban middle classes. Until 2000, however, there was little progress in terms of raising living standards for much of Sub-Saharan Africa, Central Asia, rural Latin America, and South Asia, or the nonoil-exporting states of the Middle East. Political instability, combined with poor infrastructure, has discouraged foreign investment in Africa, while rising birth rates in the Middle East have created exorbitant levels of unemployment. For the developing world, land degradation and declining fresh water reserves cap future gains in agricultural productivity. Southwest Africa suffers from a high index of HIV infections that crimps growth and has overwhelmed its inadequate health sector.

Rising global prosperity has also come at an ecological price. China's modernization has created a two hundred million strong middle class, but on most days a dark smog hovers over Beijing, obscuring distant mountains, while darkening the face masks pedestrians wear to cope with an air quality index (AQI) that routinely spikes to the maximal level of 500 (200 is deemed unsafe for children).[11] Growing slums around Jakarta, Islamabad, and Calcutta offer grim testament to a poverty often rooted in the deterioration of marginal farm lands and the bankruptcy of family businesses.

While neoliberal globalization powered economic growth, rising prosperity has not been equally distributed. Today, the richest 8 percent hold as much global wealth as the bottom 92 percent.[12] This disparity actually obscures how the top 1 percent has seen their real incomes rise by more than 60 percent since 1995. Paradoxically, the bottom third has also made significant strides as their real incomes have risen between 40 and 70 percent, except for the world's poorest 5 percent who continue to struggle on less than $2/day. Another loser of neoliberal globalization is the former global middle class. Those with incomes ranging from the 75th to 90th percentile include many blue-collar workers inhabiting the former Communist Bloc, Latin America, and former industrial heartland of the West.

Crisis Capitalism

Since 1995, the global economy has suffered from a series of speculative bubbles followed by financial panics that exposed the global economy to the risk of meltdown. Risk of contagion was first demonstrated during the Asian Crisis of 1997 to 1998. In 1999, bad Asian investments spurred the collapse of a highly leveraged global hedge fund called **Long-Term Capital Management (LTCM)**. Financial deregulation had enabled LTCM to borrow a hundred times its actual reserves. In addition to overstretched leverage, LTCM's trades were highly opaque and implicated multiple global financial institutions, making it difficult to ascertain their losses. Uncertainty precipitated investors to indiscriminately sell shares in all financial institutions. As the sell-off cascaded into a full-blown panic, investors began to offset their losses in banking by liquidating shares in otherwise solid businesses, draining them of liquidity. As global meltdown loomed, the US Treasury intervened by secretly assembling the heads of top Wall Street banks to orchestrate a bailout for LTCM. Their publicly announced rescue plan restored investor confidence and gradually enabled global stock markets to recover, but the LTCM episode foreshadowed the structural vulnerability of financial capitalism. Unfettered capital markets can power rapid growth, but fiscal integration also exposes the global economy to risk to contagion.

> The 2008 Great Global Recession displayed many parallels with the 1999 to 2000 meltdown. What does this say about the stability of our financial system?

While disaster was averted, rescue of the global economy by voluntary intervention from private investors highlighted how deregulation measures had neutered states. Today, central banks and treasury departments have few tools to respond to fiscal crises often rooted in complex instruments that are outside the scrutiny of state regulation and that closely intertwine global financial institutions.

Globalization's Paradoxes and Discontents

The WTO represented the dream of neoliberals and western policy-makers. Many hoped that widespread adoption of free market reforms and closer economic integration would spur growth, improve efficiency, and usher in higher living standards. Integration of national economies invariably spilled over into noneconomic dimensions of life. The NAFTA spurred deindustrialization in the American Rust Belt as factories relocated to the maquiladoras (factories) of Northern Mexico. Expansion of the European Union (EU) precipitated outsourcing to cheaper labor markets in Hungary and the Czech Republic after 1992. The first industries to migrate from the Western core to sweatshops in Asia and the Caribbean were those suffering from low margins. High-tech industries, like semiconductor manufacturing, depended upon a skilled labor force proved more resilient to relocation. While factories in the American Midwest shuttered during the 1980s, San Jose boomed into **Silicon Valley**, a global knowledge center powering innovation in the rapidly growing computer, software, and semiconductor industries. Globally, skilled workers are in high demand. They command not only high wages, but also insist upon a high quality of life. San Jose has joined a network of **global cities** that occupy niches inside the global economy and compete among each other for corporate centers and skilled workers. Global cities benefit from a lucrative tax base to offer a range of amenities from entertainment to quality schools, public services, as well as proximity to scenic natural areas.

On the other side of the global divide, the expanding slums of Manila, Lahore, and La Paz offer grim testament to the vulnerability of local farmers, miners, and foresters to competition from foreign agribusinesses, debt, and environmental degradation. Throughout Eastern Europe, the factories that once anchored the communist economy have wasted away, while Shenzhen and Taipei have boomed into global manufacturing hubs. Relocation of manufacturing plants sparks a downward spiral for local communities as unemployed workers compete for low-wage service jobs that often lack benefits, while young workers migrate to more dynamic regions. Detroit, the "Motor City," well illustrates postindustrial decline, falling from a peak "white" population of 1.5 million in 1950, to 75,000 in 2010. While some Detroiters have fled to the booming economies of the Deep South, the city's demise has mostly come at the expense of neighboring Wayne County. Inside Detroit's city limits once proud Georgian mansions have fallen into decay as a demoralized blue-collar workforce copes with skyrocketing crime rates, squatters that claim abandoned buildings and shuttered libraries and schools.

In 2013, Detroit declared bankruptcy as its shrinking tax base left it unable to meet its commitments to pensioned workers, while Wayne County's prosperous white suburbs have fabricated gates to wall themselves off from the decline of the city where many still work. The Motor City's decay echoes a broader global story. Inside a more competitive global economy where technology drives productivity, unskilled workers struggle to compete against counterparts living inside poorer states. For laid-off workers, loss of a livelihood often triggers an identity crisis. Rather than being "breadwinners," unemployed fathers default on mortgages and struggle to feed their families. Ghettos proliferate across

Abandoned Packard factory

Transition to a Post-Fordist production model and outsourcing manufacturing to Asia and other low-cost areas resulted in deindustrialization and urban plight in the former centers of production like Detroit.

postindustrial landscapes, with racial minorities feeling trapped in decaying neighborhoods, with limited access to jobs, fresh produce, or public transportation. From Detroit's 8 Mile to Rio de Janeiro's *Cidade de Deus* or the *bidonvilles* of Marseille, segregation often manifests in single-parent households. Unemployed mothers raise their families in an environment of crime, underfunded schools, and underemployment that offer few tickets out. Marginalization produces an alienated minority with little stake in the state's political future.

Subsistence Farmers and Tax Havens in the Developing World

Joining the WTO required developing states to progressively lower protectionist measures that once defended local farmers from foreign competition. Since 1995, highly subsidized Western agribusinesses flooded into developing economies, often undercutting local producers. In Jamaica, the native dairy industry was virtually wiped out during the 1990s after foreign multinationals like Nestle dumped powered milk on the market. Once native dairy farmers were forced out of business, the price for powdered milk steadily increased. Such predatory tactics typify how "free trade" liberalization played out across the global economy's uneven playing field. In 2001, the **Doha Round** commenced with the goal of lowering barriers to international trade still further. Boosters claimed a new deal covering more economic sectors would inject trillions into the global economy by capturing new efficiencies. After years of debate, however, Doha has stalled. A bloc of developing states complained that "free trade" does not equal "fair" trade. While multinational corporations have the scale and resources to benefit from the opportunities of a global market place, small businesses and farmers in the developing world often lack the capital and acumen to compete. Local coffee growers in Costa Rica or the Congo might cultivate great beans, but have difficulty getting their product onto western grocery shelves without middlemen that siphon away most of the profit. For the banana industry, for example, only 11 percent of the sale price returns to the locale of production. On the other hand, many software companies, retailers, and small enterprises have benefitted from a frictionless economy that enables them to sell their apps, T-shirts, or services to a global clientele.

Some developing countries like the Bahamas, Bermuda, and the Caymans found a way to compete inside the global economy by establishing themselves as international tax havens. Bermuda features shining office complexes that serve as the "head office" for thousands of Western multinationals. Caribbean addresses feature prominently in the articles of incorporation among the world's largest multinationals. But these "head offices" are empty shells that typically feature little more than a receptionist, telephone, and row of post office boxes. This phenomenon is symptomatic of a tax planning industry that devises complicated structures to siphon corporate profits through a string of holding companies to exploit their divergent tax treatment among national jurisdictions. Drug lords launder money through corrupt bankers. TNCs accomplish this legally by hiring accountants. In 2001, Apple, the wealthiest company on Earth, paid only 1.9 percent tax on its global profits, despite an effective US corporate tax rate of 34 percent.[13] Monetary policies introduced in the wake of the 2008 Global Recession have left TNCs flush with unprecedented levels of cash on their balance sheets, while sovereign states run massive budget deficits trying to stimulate a global economy and finance welfare systems despite a dwindling tax base.

Crony Capitalism and Ecological Sustainability

Although the WTO charter pays lip service to "sustainable development," in practice its regulatory mechanisms dismiss environmental concerns as an illegal trade barrier. A similar anti-ecological bias is present inside the IMF, whose structural adjustment mechanism forces clients to focus on development policies that prioritize debt repayment. During the commodity boom 2000 to 2012, neoliberal policies initiated a spike in growth and jobs, but this came at a high ecological price. Indonesia represents one of the most endowed countries on Earth with abundant reserves of oil, gold, timber, and copper. During the late 1980s, Suharto liberalized Indonesia's economy to attract foreign investment. Indonesian wages and household incomes steadily rose until the 1998 to 1999 Asian Crisis. By December 1999, Indonesia's official unemployment rate had skyrocketed above 20 percent, while devaluation of the national currency wiped out much of the middle class' savings. Riots broke out in Jakarta and other cities, often targeting the more prosperous Chinese minority. Civil unrest, street violence, and exposés of scandalous corruption forced Suharto to resign, but for most Indonesians many of the gains of the earlier decade had evaporated.

Indonesia symbolized **crony capitalism**, a postcolonial economy superficially liberalized by a dictator, without any accompanying political and economic reforms necessary to channel foreign investment towards sound development projects. Indonesia is hardly unique. Throughout the world, a high index of bribery accompanies foreign investment. In Indonesia, state officials and close allies of the Suharto family accumulated billions in Swiss bank accounts from kickbacks offered by foreign multinationals seeking state development licenses. Although neoliberals dismiss bribery as an unfortunate symptom of local corruption, few TNCs have championed democracy or greater corporate transparency. Corruption represents a systemic by-product of a **concession system** where TNCs license the right to harvest natural resources without incurring substantial obligations to hire local workers or respect environmental safeguards. Regardless of whether bribery takes place, the concession system diverts foreign investment towards resource extraction projects that reward shareholders rather than being challenged towards sustainable growth. Inside the developing world, a **debt trap** often fuels unsustainable resource policies as developing states focus on raising liquidity to repay creditors rather than putting the national economy upon a trajectory for sustainable prosperity. Brazil, Ghana, the Congo, and Indonesia exemplify a global trend where debts spur deforestation.

Amazonian Deforestation

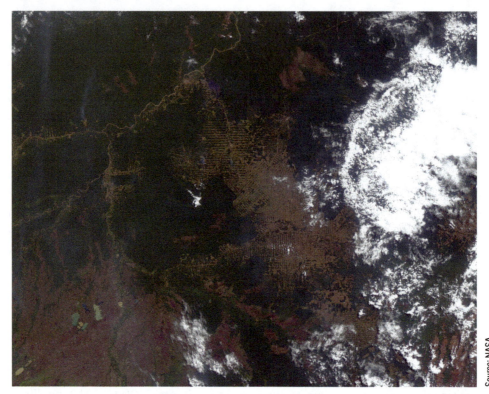

This satellite image of Rondonia, Brazil, reveals a crystalline pattern of deforestation that highlights how since 1960, national policies for development have spurred a cycle of land degradation.

Resistance and the Anti-Globalization Movement

Throughout the world, local groups and indigenous people have mobilized to resist state-promoted development projects that do not benefit them or undermine their resource rights. In 1995, the South Mexican **Zapatista Movement** grabbed international attention when masked Sub-commander Marcos channeled Che Guevara by delivering a passionate rebuke of NAFTA: "In the cabaret of globalization, the state shows itself as a table dancer that strips off everything until it is left with only the minimum indispensable garments: the repressive force."[14] In Nigeria, Royal Dutch Shell routinely calls upon the national army in their decade long battle against Delta insurgents that reap few benefits from their country's lucrative oil industry. In 2001, indigenous tribesmen in Indonesia attacked Freeport McMoRan's Grasberg Mine using bows and arrows to protest the toxic effluent sweeping onto their hunting grounds. From student dormitories and labor offices in the deindustrializing west, to the creeks of Nigeria and jungles of Chiapas, to hackers that inhabit the dark net, local groups have mobilized to oppose neoliberal globalization. The Occupy Movement that spawned in NYC's Zuccotti's park in 2011 protested the million-dollar bonuses dished out by financial firms bailed out by taxpayer money. Subsequently, the "occupy" slogan went global with its meme: "We are the 99%." Still, the accelerating pace of global trade, the growing size of TNCs, and the increasing gap between rich and poor suggests that the fledgling anti-globalization movement is losing the global debate.

Occupy Wall Street

For a few months in 2011 the Occupy Movement set up shop in Zuccotti Park, Manhattan, elevating the "we are the 99%" slogan into a global mantra among anti-globalization activists.

Human Migration and Trafficking

Global integration has launched an unprecedented wave of human migration. In 2013, 3.2 percent of the world population consisted of "migrants" living outside the country of their birth. This represented a 50 percent increase since 1990.[15] Most migration continues to takes place inside states, consisting largely of rural migrants moving to cities. Over the last decade, this trend has been particularly evident in economically booming Southeast Asia where a wide disparity exists between living standards in town and countryside. Most migration between states remains regional. Eastern Europeans have migrated to Western Europe seeking work and educational opportunities, while most Africans and Arab migrants have fled political instability to take refuge in neighboring states. Poverty inhibits transcontinental migration, but sharper awareness of global disparities also increases migration from the global south to more developed industrial states like Japan, Australia, North America, and Western Europe.

While the WTO liberalized trade and investment, it avoided regulating the labor market. This left immigration laws rooted in the territorial jurisdiction of the state, even as the economy increasingly migrated to the global scale, creating a highly polarized international labor market. Inside today's **dual economy**, engineers, scientists, wealth entrepreneurs, and financial analysts from various nationalities easily move between various TNCs, government agencies, and research institutes based inside western states and often benefitting from "fast-track" dispensations that states use to alleviate labor shortages in strategic industries. Talent hungry high-tech companies complain about a lack of skilled workers in the western economies, while sparsely populated developed states like Canada compete for "skilled" workers that can contribute to their economy while acclimating to their national culture.

Canada and Global Migration

Canada's prosperity hinges on immigration. Since 2011, all the growth inside the Canadian labor force has been met by immigrants. In much of the West, globalization has triggered a backlash against "unwanted immigrants" and "economic refugees," while contributing to the rise of nationalist parties demanding that immigrants assimilate to their national culture. Canada is relatively unique in endorsing the principle of multiculturalism, encouraging immigrants to maintain their unique cultural backgrounds, share it with established residents, and participate in building a more prosperous Canada. Canada's liberal immigration policies are partially rooted in our nation's history. The Canadian wilderness attracted British and French colonists who intermarried with each other and first nations' peoples. Since 1945, immigrants were essential for filling needs in the labor market and contributing to a welfare system suffering from declining birth rates and an aging population. Until the early 1960s, however, most immigrants to Canada were of European descent. Europe's postwar recovery stemmed out migration and resulted in Canadian labor shortages. To compensate, the Immigration Act of 1967 ended ethnic and religious discrimination to create a more liberal immigration system predicated on professional and educational credentials. This also stimulated a shift in the ethnic profile of Canadian immigrants. In 2006, the Census identified 16.2 percent of the total population as **visible minorities**, up dramatically from 4.7 percent in 1981. Migration to Canada was also shaped by Prime Minister Pierre Trudeau's endorsement of "Multiculturalism within a Bilingual Framework" in 1971. This represented a bid to compete internationally with the United States and Australia for skilled migrants, while quelling the fires of separatism brewing within Quebec.

Polls consistently reveal that Canadians embrace multiculturalism and that second-generation immigrants tend to identify themselves as "Canadian" first and foremost, yet increasing ethnic diversity is generating tensions. Global communications and social media enable immigrants to remain in contact with their home country and disincentivize cultural integration. Concerns about assimilation have been most pronounced in Quebec, which has in recent decades fought its own battles for national recognition as a "distinctive society." Quebec Premier Pauline Marois' ill-fated 2013 "Charter of Liberties" sought to define legally the limits of "reasonable accommodation" for religious and ethnic minorities, sparking a sharp backlash among Muslims, Jews, and other ethnic groups. More recently, Canadians joining the Islamic State (IS) has raised security concerns, which suggests that the national debate concerning "what is Canadian?" is far from resolved.

Critical Reflection

1. In your view, does Canada's increasing ethnic diversity enrich society or threaten its traditional identity?
2. Should public servants like policemen and judges be allowed to wear religious dress?

On the other end of the spectrum, a tidal wave of farm laborers, political refugees, and indebted peasants dislocated by agricultural modernization, environmental degradation, and political instability desperately sought out opportunities for a better life. As we saw in Chapter 5, stagflation in the 1970s spurred many European states to rewrite their laws for political asylum to deter "economic migrants." The anti-immigrant backlash in the West is often rooted in the rising insecurity of blue-collar workers once protected by welfare measures, union memberships, and tariffs.

Despite a growing trend towards immigration restriction and the militarization of borders, international migration creeps upward because of "push" factors: rising poverty, political instability, and environmental degradation in the global south. **Boat people** represent the prototypical manifestation of this illegal immigration, mounting rickety vessels unfit for ocean travel to escape civil war, persecution, or poverty. Overcrowded vessels routinely succumb to inclement weather, the exhaustion of water reserves, or coast guard interdiction. Heightened restrictions upon legal immigration intensify the criminalization of migration networks. Often viscous "snakeheads" offer illicit passage in truck compartments, tunnels, and cargo containers. Not only on their journey, but after their arrival, illegal migrants are highly vulnerable. Unscrupulous traffickers often confiscate passports, effectively imprisoning migrants in order to profit from their labor. In 2012, the International Labor Organization estimated that over twenty million people fell victim to human trafficking that takes various forms, from forced labor to debt bondage and forced prostitution.[16]

Cultural Collision and Assimilation

For social conservatives, non-western nationalists, and religious fundamentalists, the globalization of the 1990s represented a threat. Inside a "flatter" world, traditionalists needed to compete with an emerging global consumer culture. Multinational fast-food franchises, electronic gadgets, and global brands not only dislodged tradition, they embodied modern ideas, practices, and patterns of thought that challenged traditional notions about the sacred, family, sex, and gender. Conservatives were acutely aware that multinational corporations were sophisticated colonizing agents seeking not only increased market share, but to transform local patterns of consumption. Sleek advertising campaigns, often invoked sexual imagery and presented foreign products as offering a "modern" life of glamor and freedom. Local feelings of invasion were often augmented by the fact that originally most TNCs were American corporations, their officers were predominantly western, and most of their profits are shuttled back to rich investors. Amazon, Google, and Coca-Cola also have the marketing muscle, pricing power, and a global tax structure that enables them to squeeze out local businesses.

Market integration and the proliferation of digital networks have accelerated the velocity of cultural images, ideas, and values flowing across national borders. Canadian law is typical in establishing restrictions on "non-Canadian" content in a bid to preserve cultural heritage. American periodicals, however, found it relatively easy to skirt Canadian content laws by creating subsidiaries. In 2014, over 90 percent of the periodicals in Canada were foreign. Western Europeans experienced a similar "American invasion" following deregulation. Hollywood enjoyed economies of scale that enabled US studios to provide commoditized content like *LA Law* that traveled well across cultures. Since 1990, however, the domestic share of European television content has been rising, while India's Bollywood, Korean soap operas, Latin America *tele-novellas*, and Jap-animation have emerged as Hollywood competitors in a global market.

> Economic deregulation spurred multinational corporations to transplant their franchises across the world stage. Has McDonalds, Netflix, and Facebook made Canada more "American"?

The economic shocks and cultural anxiety that characterized the first chapter of neoliberal globalization seem to be giving way to quieter assimilation of global brands and consumer electronics. A new generation of African and Asian teens is less threatened by foreign ideas and more seamlessly repurposes consumer technologies to fit their own needs. Their adaption mirrors that of early corporate pioneers. McDonalds discovered that translating the fast-food model required adaptation of its restaurants, its menu, and the rules of dining to accommodate local tastes and practices. So today, beer accompanies the Big Mac in Holland, the menu inside the Middle East is halal, and India's golden arches feature the mutton-based Maharaja Mac.

Starbucks in Gyeongju-si, South Korea

To survive, Western franchises like Starbucks needed to assimilate their architecture and menu to fit the local landscape, tastes, and cultural habits.

Amorality Inside the Global Village

In his song *Imagine*, John Lennon pictured humans coming together to embrace their shared differences in recognizing our common humanity. But profits, not love, was the impulse driving the WTO's design. Gordon Gekko, the lead character in Oliver Stone's 1987 classic *Wall Street*, enthusiastically pronounced that "greed is good." Intended as satire, Gekko's creed inspired a generation of Ivy Leaguers to trek off for Wall Street millions. Neoliberals insist that markets, being intrinsically efficient, deliver social benefit in the form of lower costs. Lawrence Summers, a principal works architect of the WTO, argues that globalization's victims, like laid-off factory workers, are highly visible, while the benefits from free trade and the beneficiaries of lower consumer prices escape notice and comments. This might be true, but globalization's efficiencies are also rooted in exploitation. This point was elegantly captured in Summers' infamous 1991 Memo trumpeting the impeccable "economic logic" of dumping toxic western waste onto "underpopulated countries in Africa."[17] TNC profits are intimately connected to exploiting the desperation and weakness of indebted states, nonunionized workers, and hungry people. But global disparities have also benefitted western consumers who pay less for electronics, textiles, and other consumer goods produced in unsafe factories by sweatshop labor. In Bangladesh in 2013, a hastily constructed garment factory collapsed killing 1,129 workers. This tragedy was unique, but hardly an anomaly. While "greedy" corporations offer an easy target for public criticism, Nike Shoes, Apple I-Phones, and Fruit of the Loom undershorts that westerner consumers purchase at big box stores are cheap because they have been outsourced to poor female seamstresses and child laborers. The WTO, by elevating free markets as the principal mechanism for globalization, has made anonymous transactions the basis for human interaction inside the global village. While the "invisible hand" provides some allowance for conscientious investing and green consumption, the complexity of goods moving through global economy makes ethical decision-making prohibitively difficult. With global capitalism, all social, religious, and environmental values have become systematically subordinated to the supreme neoliberal virtue of efficient markets.

Conclusion: Globalization and Capitalism

Globalization has brought people closer together, but profits rather than human rights, environmentalism, and international peace inspired establishment of the WTO. Global capitalism empowered TNCs to harness global synergies from the maturing information revolution. Neoliberals promised that free markets would diffuse economic opportunity, political freedom, and human rights around the world. Since 1995, market integration and technological advances have stimulated growth, while lowering poverty and malnutrition inside the developing world. But TNCs pursue profits at the expense of other values, sowing ecological deterioration, rural security, and volatility inside financial markets. The digital revolution will continue to transform how people work, consume, invest, and socialize with others, regardless of their physical location or culture. Globalization represents a multidimensional phenomenon. This makes it difficult to bring into focus. The rising influence of TNCs is eroding the power of states, mature industries, and interest groups wedded to the national economy, the mass production model, brick-and-mortar businesses, or traditional culture. At the same time, the global economy is enriching skilled workers and the urban middle classes in Asia. Technology is empowering the rural poor and international advocacy groups like Green Peace. The decay of Detroit and Gdansk is offset by mountains of shipping containers piling up on the docks of Shanghai. The proliferation of global brands and Western franchises transmits the implicit values of a generic consumer culture, but digital technologies also create opportunities for non-Western entrepreneurs, and empower creative peoples to reach new audiences with sophisticated products. Around the world, local peoples are adapting to the diet of industrial agriculture, Facebook, and cell phones, while a never-ending array of gadgets and virtual platforms continues to emerge for linking people across oceans and cultures. Whether the infrastructure of global capitalism is sufficiently stable, sustainable, or socially responsible to reflect the values of future generations remains to be seen. Currently, the pace and scope of global integration continues to intensify, along with a sharper polarization between the 1 percent and the "bottom billion" that represent a global underclass with few prospects for a better future.

Questions for Critical Thought

1. How did the container revolution facilitate cross-border economic activity?
2. How did invention of the microprocessor set the stage for the electronic revolution, the information age, and digital technologies?
3. How did improving global logistics and state deregulation contribute to the evolution of TNCs?
4. What events, beliefs, and policies set the stage for the deregulatory wave of the 1980s?
5. Who were the neoliberals and what particular reforms did they advocate for resuscitating stagnant economies during the 1980s?

6. How had economic globalization according under the auspices of the WTO impacted global growth, poverty, and investment?
7. How did the LTCM episode reveal the fragility of global financial markets?
8. What patterns have characterized human migration in the age of globalization?

Suggestions for Further Reading

- Bales, K. *Disposable People: New Slavery in the Global Economy*. Berkeley, CA: University of California Press, 1999.
- Berger, P., and Samuel Huntington, eds. *Many Globalizations Cultural Diversity in the Contemporary World*. Oxford: Oxford University Press, 2002.
- Harvey, D. *A Brief History of Neoliberalism*. New York: Oxford University Press, 2005.
- Mason, M. *Development and Disorder: A History of the Third World since 1945*. New York: Between the Lines, 1997.
- Ritzer, G. *Globalization a Basic Text*. New York: Wiley-Blackwell, 2010.
- Singer, P. *One World: The Ethics of Globalization*. New Haven: Yale University Press, 2002.
- Stearns, P., ed. *Consumerism in World History: The Global Transformation of Desire*. New York: Routledge, 2006.
- Stiglitz, J. *Globalization and its Discontents*. New York: W.W. Norton, 2003.
- Tapscott, D. *The Digital Economy: Promise and Peril in the Age of Networked Intelligence*. New York: McGraw-Hill, 1997.

Notes

1. Thomas Misa, *Leonardo to the Internet* (Baltimore, MD: John Hopkins, 2004), 243.
2. Martin Hilbert and Priscilla López, "The World's Technological Capacity to Store, Communicate, and Compute Information," *Science* 332, no. 6025 (2011): 60–65.
3. S. Vitali, J. B. Glattfelder, and S. Battiston, "The Network of Global Corporate Control," *PLOS ONE* 6, no. 10 (2011): e25995, accessed August 12, 2019, http://journals.plos.org/plosone/article?id=10.1371/journal.pone.0025995.
4. Quoted in Chris Lewis, "Global Industrial Civilization," in *On The Edge of Scarcity: Environment, Resources, Population, Sustainability, and Conflict*, eds. Michael N. Dobkowski and Isidor Wallimann (Syracuse, NY: Syracuse University Press, 2002), 16.
5. United Nations Conference on Trade and Development, "World Investment Report 1998 Trends and Determinants," Geneva, 1998, accessed April 7, 2019, http://unctad.org/en/docs/wir1998_en.pdf.
6. Bill Emmott, "Everybody's Favourite Monsters," *The Economist*, 326, March 27, 1993.
7. Sarah Anderson and John Cvanagh, "Top 200: The Rise of Global Corporate Power," *Global Policy Forum*, 2000, accessed April 7, 2019, https://www.globalpolicy.org/component/content/article/221/47211.html.
8. Kenny Bruno, *The Greenpeace Book on Greenwash* (Amsterdam: Greenpeace International, 1992), 5 and John Madeley, *Big Business, Poor Peoples* (New York: Zed Books, 2001), 159.
9. Mike Mason, *Development and Disorder: A History of the Third World since 1945* (New York: Between the Lines, 1997), 426.

10. Quoted in Mason, *Development and Disorder*, 429.
11. Dominic Barton, Yougang Chen, and Amy Jin, "Mapping China's Middle Class," *McKinsey Quarterly*, June 2013. Accessed April 7, 2019, http://www.mckinsey.com/industries/retail/our-insights/mapping-chinas-middle-class
12. Branko Milanovic, "Global Income Inequality by the Numbers: In History and Now," *World Bank, Policy Research Working Paper 6259*, 8, accessed, June 3, 2015, http://elibrary.worldbank.org/doi/pdf/10.1596/1813-9450-6259.
13. Daily Mail Reporter, "How Apple Paid a Tax Bill of just 1.9% on its Overseas Profits by using Complex Avoidance Schemes," *Daily Mail*, November 4, 2012, accessed April 7, 2019, http://www.dailymail.co.uk/news/article-2227939/How-Apple-paid-tax-just-1-9-overseas-profits-using-complex-avoidance-schemes.html.
14. Martin Urbina, *Twenty-First Century Dynamics of Multiculturalism* (New York: Charles C. Thomas, 2014), 223.
15. See http://www.unis.unvienna.org/unis/en/pressrels/2013/unisinf488.html.
16. International Labour Office (ILO), Special Action Programme to Combat Forced Labour (SAP-FL), 2012, https://www.ilo.org/global/topics/forced-labour/publications/WCMS_182004/lang–en/index.htm.
17. Jim Valette, "Lawrence Summers' War against the Earth," Global Policy Forum, accessed August, 12, 2019, https://www.globalpolicy.org/component/content/article/212/45462.html.

Chapter 12
Bridge to the Twenty-First Century

Chapter Outline

- Introduction: New World Order?
- Triumphant Liberalism
- 9-11 and Security in the New Millennium
- Kyoto and the Tragedy of the Global Commons
- Crisis Capitalism and the Great Global Recession of 2008
- The Arab Spring and Digital Populism
- Multipolarity and the New Cold War
- Conclusion: Bridge to the Twenty-First Century

Timeline: Transition to the twenty-first century

Timeline
1987 Montreal Protocol
1990-1991 First Gulf War
1991 Breakup of USSR
1992 Rio Earth Summit
1993-1995 Bosnian War
1995 Rwanda Genocide
1996 Bin Laden *fatwa*
1997 Kyoto Protocol
2000 George W. Bush's election
2001 9-11 Terrorist Attack
2001 China joins WTO
2003 US invades Iraq
2008 Putin invades Georgia
2011 Arab Spring
2011 US withdraws from Iraq

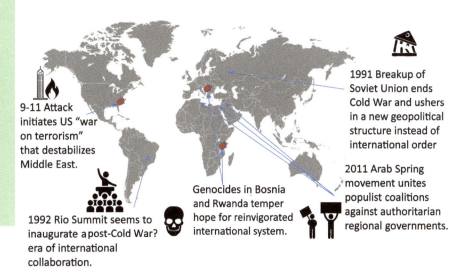

9-11 Attack initiates US "war on terrorism" that destabilizes Middle East.

1992 Rio Summit seems to inaugurate a post-Cold War? era of international collaboration.

Genocides in Bosnia and Rwanda temper hope for reinvigorated international system.

1991 Breakup of Soviet Union ends Cold War and ushers in a new geopolitical structure instead of international order

2011 Arab Spring movement unites populist coalitions against authoritarian regional governments.

Image credits: © Andrei Minsk/Shutterstock.com; © Nist and Victor Z/Shutterstock.com; Shutterstock.com; © Martial Red/Shutterstock.com; © Leremy//Shutterstock.comCube29/Breakup; © suesse/Shutterstock.com

Introduction: New World Order?

In January 1991, US President George Herbert Walker Bush proposed construction of a "New World Order" predicated upon "the rule of law ... govern[ing] the conduct of nations." The collapse of the Berlin Wall still fresh in his mind, Bush hoped that a "credible United Nations" would live up to the idealism of its founders and fulfill its international peacekeeping mission.[1] Bush, Western hardliners, and neoliberals were united in seeing the collapse of the Soviet Bloc as an historic moment. End to the twentieth century's bitter ideological conflict paved the way for a brighter future. Nations were rallying to America's "Atlantic vision"; a world united by the ideals of democracy, international collaboration, free markets, and human rights. In hindsight, Bush's address represented liberal optimism's high tide. A decade later, the 9-11 attacks, collapse of the Kyoto Accord, and the 2008 Great Global Recession soured the international mood and highlighted the inadequacy of international institutions to cope with emerging threats.

Through eleven chapters, this book has chronicled the events, people, and trends that shaped the postwar world. Although history has no end, this chapter seeks to bring this study to a conclusion by surveying the last two decades. So far, the salient events of new century remain consistent with longer twentieth-century trends. The forces spurring global integration continue to accelerate. Transnational corporations have grown in size, digital networks are proliferating even into remote regions, and a global consumer culture is both empowering and challenging local traditions. Human civilization still relies upon cheap oil, its materialistic ideals of prosperity poorly align to ecological limits and unregulated integration of financial markets has made the world economy vulnerable to crises. This chapter revisits many of this book's key themes, while highlighting some of the events that have shaped the early twenty-first century: the 9-11 attacks, global inaction on climate change, the 2008 Great Global Recession, and the Arab Spring. Each case study illustrates a different dimension of the twenty-first century and the challenges outlining our common future.

Big Questions

- How did the Cold War's end change the international system?
- How did the 9-11 attack illuminate the risk of asymmetric threats?
- What are the structural weaknesses of the global economy?
- Does the Arab Spring movement foreshadow a golden era of digital populism?

Triumphant Liberalism

With the collapse of the Soviet Bloc, Western liberals felt triumphant. Contemporary idealism was exemplified in the 1992 **Rio Conference**. Quickly dubbed the "Earth Summit," this conference convened to unite the international community around tackling shared environmental problems. The groundwork for collaboration had been laid with the 1987 **Montreal Protocol** that cut production of chlorofluorocarbons eating away at the earth's protective ozone layer. Enthusiasm for Rio flagged when President Bush announced that he would not support stringent carbon caps to address climate change. Ultimately, Rio delegates signed **Agenda 21**. This "action plan" boldly endorsed sustainability as the model for the twenty-first century development. At the surface, the Rio Conference exemplified the post–Cold War spirit. Having buried divisive dogmas, the world community could now unite around a brighter future.

> Rio delegates viewed sustainability as a revolutionary concept, but to what extent has this idea translated into meaningful reform to align economic growth with ecological limits?

Agenda 21 reaffirmed the 1987 Brundtland Report's definition of sustainability as "development which meets the needs of current generations without compromising the ability of future generations to meet their own needs."[2] In essence, Rio married sustainability to the neoliberal efficient market hypothesis. Rejecting the conventional trade-off between economic growth and environmental conservation, the **Sustainable Development (SD)** model argued that natural systems, like free markets, were inherently "efficient." Rio delegates saw the twenty-first century's key challenge as developing green technology and reshaping international policy to recalibrate human needs to nature's limits. Despite failing to address climate change, most participants judged Rio success. The conference endorsed an emerging consensus that environmental concerns transcend culture, class, and generations. Notably, industrial lobbies did not oppose Agenda 21, since it imposed no concrete sanctions upon corporations. The SD model also met approval from many postcolonial leaders, frustrated with a modernization strategy that had resulted in inefficient industries, high levels of debt, and extensive environmental degradation.

Solidarity at Rio was mirrored by international collaboration in the security sphere. On August 2, 1990, Iraqi President **Saddam Hussein** invaded Kuwait, accusing them of slant drilling into his oil fields. Few in the West knew much about the tiny oil kingdom that Britain had carved from the Ottoman Empire following World War I. Lackluster public interest alarmed President George H. W. Bush. Hussein had once served as an informal ally against Revolutionary Iran, but struggled to manage debts accumulated during the **Iran–Iraq War** (1980–1988). Annexing Kuwait concentrated tremendous wealth and power in Hussein's hands. It also brought Iraqi tanks to the doorstep of Saudi Arabia's oil fields.

To mobilize public support for war, President Bush deployed a campaign of deception. He trumpeted the democratic aspirations of the Kuwaiti kingdom, while shamelessly accusing Iraqi soldiers of tossing newborn babies from incubators. Demonizing Hussein mobilized public support for military action. With Saudi permission, Bush first deployed a small US force to screen the kingdom's northern border. Subsequently, Bush reached out to Gorbachev and his Middle Eastern allies to slap an international embargo upon Iraq. Working through the United Nations (UN), Bush constructed a multinational coalition for Kuwaiti liberation. When Hussein refused to leave Kuwait, a UN coalition, led by US forces, struck on January 1991. As advance US units approached Baghdad, President Bush called a halt to **Operation Desert Storm**. After only a hundred hours, coalition forces had evicted Hussein from Kuwait and decimated his Republican Guard. Stopping short of Baghdad proved controversial when a weakened Hussein managed to cling to power. Over the next decade, he continued to menace his neighbors.

> Defense Secretary Dick Cheney justified the hasty armistice in the First Gulf War as necessary during a 1991 interview. If the UN had "gotten rid of Saddam Hussein and his government, then we'd have had to put another government in its place. What kind of government? Should it be a Sunni government or Shi'i government or a Kurdish government or Ba'athist regime? Or maybe we want to bring in some of the Islamic fundamentalists? How long would we have had to stay in Baghdad to keep that government in place?"[3] Why did Cheney fail to heed his own advice in 2003?

Saddam Hussein

Saddam Hussein posing in modern Western garb. As ruler over multiethnic Iraq, Saddam was known for frequently changing costume to appeal to various Iraqi constituencies, most famously by riding into Baghdad in 1990 on a white horse in a transparent effort to evoke legendary hero Saladin.

The Rio Conference and the Gulf War suggested that Soviet collapse could usher in an era where the former superpowers might collaborate inside a revitalized UN. For President Bush, western liberals, and non-western leaders, the United States unprecedented strength was an asset for nudging the world towards adopting western norms for democracy, free markets, and respect for human rights.

Wavering Optimism, 1992 to 2000

In 1995, the World Trade Organization (WTO) brought to realization the dream of western liberals that deeper economic integration would diffuse liberalism and democracy around the world stage. Many believed that democracies and trading partners did not wage war on each other. Liberal optimism lost much of its luster in November 1999 as a rainbow coalition of labor, student, human rights, and environmental groups descended upon Seattle during a seemingly routine meeting of the World Economic Forum. As the demonstration turned violent, policemen donned combat helmets, transparent shields, and black tankards. As riot police squared off against masked demonstrators, stones, batteries, and Molotov cocktails rained down among their ranks. Behind the barricades, conference delegates, accustomed to negotiating the arcane rules of international finance in relative obscurity, watched the acrid smoke rising up from burned out cars and spent tear gas canisters. The scene hinted that the unique 1989 moment had passed. Whatever consensus had underpinned liberal optimism in the wake of communism's collapse, it washed away on the debris-choked streets of Seattle. A cohesive anti-globalization movement uniting labor groups, human rights activists, student organizations, and environmentalists now opposed the emerging international order. Anti-globalization activists blamed the WTO for unemployment, injustice, and inequality. Protestors saw free markets not as instruments for progress, but as mechanisms that enabled transnational corporations to outsource jobs, exploit developing states, and degrade the environment. After another bloody encounter at the 2001 Summit of the Americas in Quebec, subsequent meetings among international bankers and economic policy-makers moved to more remote and defensible locations like Jackson Hole, Wyoming, and Doha, Qatar.

Violence in Seattle

In hindsight, Seattle represented a turning point. Economic globalization driven by financial deregulation, free trade zones, and the WTO gave rise to a capitalism that undermined the older mass production model, brick-and-mortar stores, family farms, and labor unions. By the twenty-first century, accelerating market integration had intensified globalization's disruptive effects. Old centers for heavy industry like Detroit decayed. Multinational franchises like McDonalds set up shop across the world stage, low-margin manufacturing plants relocated to low-wage areas, and peasant small holders struggled to compete with subsidized Western agribusinesses. Seattle had for the first time mobilized diverse losers of globalization around a common cause. Subsequently, a coherent anti-globalization movement would represent a feature of the international landscape, drawing support from wavering public commitment for grand liberal projects like global security, state building, and human rights.

Another root of disillusionment lay in the 1992 to 1995 war in Bosnia. France and Britain led a UN peacekeeping mission, eager to reassert a United Europe's influence inside the post–Cold War world. From the start, however, the UN mission was thwarted by insufficient resources. European leaders were reluctant to intervene inside what they considered the Balkan "tinderbox." The UN did not step up its commitment as graphic accounts concerning the Siege of Sarajevo and "ethnic cleansing" began to saturate the international media.

Only after the July 1995 **Srebrenica Massacre**, did public outcry stimulate a more vigorous response. US President Clinton led North Atlantic Treaty Organization (NATO) airstrikes on Serbia that had been actively supporting Bosnian Serb separatists. This brought the Serbs to the negotiating table at Dayton in 1995. Bosnia seemed to demonstrate the continuing importance of US power in brokering international settlements. It also ended talk about NATO's irrelevance. Subsequently, this Cold War outfit was progressively retooled into a western instrument for international intervention, especially in cases like Bosnia where a Russian or Chinese veto stymied the UN. On the other hand, the Bosnian War also highlighted the superficiality underpinning international commitment to human rights and peace. Western hypocrisy had already been laid bare in Rwanda in 1994. Top statesmen had colluded to not label the escalating violence a "genocide," a term that would have triggered a formal UN obligation to intervene.

Siege of Sarajevo

Bosnian Serb shelling and deadly snipers were part of a coordinated campaign to make life impossible in Sarajevo. Bosniaks defied this intimidation, collaborating to provide basic services and holding impromptu concerts to raise spirits.

9-11 and Security in the New Millennium

The end of the Cold War spurred global disarmament. American public attention veered towards domestic problems and economic security. On September 11, 2001, two hijacked airliners slammed into the World Trade Center (WTC). The impact unleashed a thundering fireball and a shower of glass shards upon shocked commuters below. Hundreds of passengers and office workers were killed instantly. The crash also trapped thousands working in the Twin Towers' upper floors. Forty minutes later, American Airlines 175 crashed into white colonnades of the Pentagon. Shortly later, United Airlines 93 nosedived into a Pennsylvanian field after passengers overwhelmed their abductors in the doomed plane's cockpit. The climax of 9-11 came at 9:58 a.m. when the South Tower collapsed in a plume of toxic ash. Its metal core had melted under the extreme heat generated by aviation fuel. This initiated a deadly cascade that would send observers scurrying for cover and leave a gash in the New York skyline.

> In a September 20, 2001, address before Congress George Bush argued that "this is not, however, just America's fight … This is the world's fight. This is civilization's fight. This is the fight of all who believe in progress and pluralism, tolerance and freedom."[4] Have subsequent events confirmed Bush's assessment that militant jihadism represents an existential threat to Western civilization?

Ground Zero in Manhattan, September 11, 2001

The collapse of the Twin Towers delivered a blow to the American psyche. Throughout most of its history, the United States has been insulated from enemy attack by vast oceans. On September 11, the United States was hit on its home turf by a previously obscure enemy.

9-11 represented a coordinated attack by Islamic extremists that exploited the United States' lax visa and airport security system. Box cutters, basic martial arts training, and rudimentary piloting skills had enabled the hijackers to "weaponize" transcontinental commercial aircraft, laden with fuel, into guided missiles. Together, the 9-11 attacks killed 2,977, rung up $10 billion in property damage, sent the stock market into a nosedive, and incited widespread panic.

Bush's War on Terrorism

Before September 2001, few Americans had heard of **Osama bin Laden** or **Al Qaeda**. Terrorism seemed a distant threat that challenged Western outposts abroad. On September 20, before a joint session of Congress, Bush made his administration's case that "9-11 changed everything." Addressing not only a domestic, but an international audience, Bush unveiled his "war on terrorism." The **Bush Doctrine** argued that in the age of globalization, where stateless enemies attacked without warning, the United States could not afford to abide by international law. Instead, the United States needed to "pre-empt" enemies before they emerged as tangible threats. In the months following 9-11, the Bush administration ramped up fear concerning a successor attack, while sounding dire warnings about "mushroom clouds" blooming over American cities. A compliant mainstream media steadily broadcast unsubstantiated rumors concerning sleeper cells, imminent attacks, and nuclear plots. Public angst bred acquiescence to a radical set of policies to "keep Americans safe." From 2001 to 2003, the Bush administration gutted the core values of the international system that the United States had played a key role in establishing after World War II. Some worried that the 2001 **Patriot Act** undermined civil liberties in the name of heightened state surveillance and police powers, but it ultimately passed the US Senate by a resounding 98 to 1 vote.

> Edward Snowden's 2013 revelations about National Security Administration (NSA) wiretapping sparked a global debate about state surveillance in a democratic society. Does the threat presented by terrorism merit some restraint upon civil liberties?

Neoconservatives and the Project for the New American Century

After 9-11, President Bush complained that the WTC attack could not have been anticipated, a surprising claim given Al Qaeda's escalating string of attacks on US targets from 1998 to 2000. US intelligence had also intercepted chatter suggesting an imminent Al Qaeda attack on the US mainland. In 2001, the Central Intelligence Agency (CIA) identified two of the 9-11 hijackers in Los Angeles, but turf battles discouraged them from sharing this information with the Federal Bureau of Investigation (FBI). In August 2001, the FBI arrested Zacarias Moussaoui following errant behavior in a Minnesota flight school. The interrogator sounded the alarm but was ignored. Despite electronic intercepts recording "buzz" concerning a terrorist plot using airplanes as missiles, for almost a year, the Bush Administration failed to heed warnings from its own intelligence establishment.

While 9-11 "truthers" claim that the WTC attack was an "inside job," the real conspiracy involved the Bush administration's cover-up of their intelligence failures. The roots for George W. Bush's "war on terrorism" stretched back to the Cold War. In 1991, George Herbert Walker Bush declared the Cold War over. Many working inside his administration anticipated putting their distinctive stamp on the post–Cold War world during his second presidential term. But despite a triumphant victory in Iraq in 1991, the first President Bush lost his reelection bid to a scandal plagued, but charismatic governor from Arkansas, William Jefferson Clinton. The Clinton years represented a bitter pill for officials in

328 Chapter 12: Bridge to the Twenty-First Century

the Bush administration to swallow. Not only were **neoconservatives** like Dick Cheney and Richard Perle swept from office, but they were also forced to watch Clinton scuttle their carefully laid plans for extending US power. As a "new Democrat," Clinton proved conservative on social and economic issues, but with the collapse of the Soviet Union he saw little need for maintaining the military arsenal of a global superpower. Clinton's military cutbacks drew the ire of neoconservatives who believed he was squandering a historic opportunity.

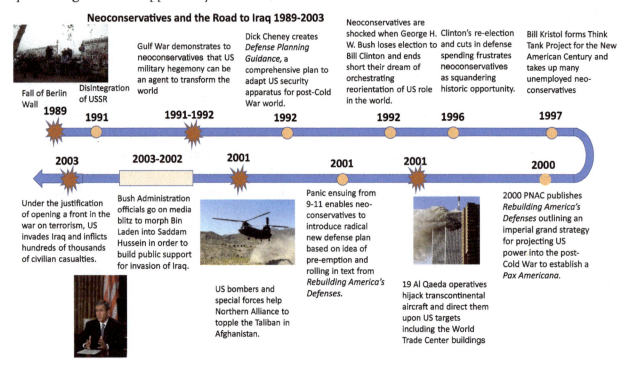

Image credits: National Archives Catalog © Ken Tannenbaum/Shutterstock.com; Courtesy George W. Bush Presidential Library and Museum

During the Clinton years, various think tanks emerged to employ disillusioned Bush 41 officials. The **Project for the New American Century (PNAC)** brought together an A-list of neoconservatives that would play a key role in the future George W. Bush administration, including Dick Cheney and Paul Wolfowitz. In an innocent sounding document entitled *Restoring America's Defenses*, neoconservatives laid out an ambitious plan for leveraging US power to reshape the international system. Establishing an "American Century" required investment in next-generation weapon systems. This would enhance America's military superiority to such a degree that it would evolve into a **hyperpower** capable of filling the vacuum left by the USSR's collapse. Military rearmament would enable the United States to intimidate **rogue states** and discourage rising powers like China from challenging US hegemony. Neoconservatives believed that military power, unilateralism, and military force were key ingredients for creating a better world.

US Plan of Attack, 2001 to 2005

The conspiracy of 9-11 involved the Bush administration's hijacking of a national tragedy. *Restoring America's Defenses* constituted a blueprint for transforming the United States into a global empire. Among its various objectives, the plan mentions unilaterally withdrawing from the **Anti-Ballistic Missile (ABM)** Treaty, increasing military spending, building forward military bases, and securing strategic resources. PNAC also identified Iran, North Korea, and Iraq—the future "Axis of Evil"—as rogue states needing regime change. The parallels between PNAC and Bush administration initiatives from 2001 to 2005 is not surprising given that nearly all of the plan's authors assumed senior posts in the Bush administration after 2000. In their plan, neoconservatives lamented that barring a "Pearl Harbor" event, Americans were unlikely to endorse rearmament. As Defense Secretary Donald Rumsfeld pulled victims from the burning hulk of the Pentagon, he realized that 9-11 presented a golden opportunity to revive PNAC. To mobilize public support, the Bush administration that had all but ignored Al Qaeda before 9-11 now inflated them into a menace threatening the American way of life. In particular, they traveled the press circuit sounding dire warnings about jihadists seeking weapons of mass destruction. Vice President Dick Cheney repeatedly insinuated Saddam Hussein's involvement in 9-11 despite the absence of any credible evidence. Morphing bin Laden into Hussein mobilized public support around a key PNAC objective: regime change in Iraq. Establishment of military bases in Iraq would enable the United States to replace those being lost in Saudi Arabia while allowing US forces to keep watch over Persian Gulf oil fields.

In October 2001, the United States launched airstrikes on Afghanistan, while funneling arms to the Tajik-backed **Northern Alliance**. Nine weeks later the Taliban regime had collapsed, but the Bush administration inexplicably allowed a surrounded bin Laden to escape from his mountain fortress in **Tora Bora**. Bin Laden's escape underscored how invading Iraq constituted the Bush administration's core objective. The "war on terrorism" merely represented a slogan to unite public support for the administration's radical grand strategy. In March 2003, the Bush administration launched their long-planned invasion of Iraq, despite the fact that UN weapons inspectors had failed to turn up any trace of weapons of mass destruction. Although the UN Security Council balked at authorizing an attack on Iraq, President George W. Bush cobbled together a "coalition of the willing." This included Britain, modest contingents from a few European allies, as well as many Latin American states that participated mostly in name.

Initially, American troops made rapid headway following a devastating air assault that killed thousands of Iraqi soldiers and even more civilians. The toppling of Saddam Hussein's statue in Firdos Square in April 2003 was globally broadcast. It seemed to affirm the Bush administration's narrative that Iraqis were embracing American soldiers as liberators. While many oppressed Shia did welcome Saddam's demise, they quickly turned hostile as Western contractors descended on Iraq and began to survey the country's oil fields. On May 1, 2003, a triumphant President Bush rode shotgun as a Lockheed Viking touched down on the *USS Abraham Lincoln*. Behind a banner pronouncing "Mission Accomplished," Bush boasted that "we do not know the day of final victory, but we have seen the turning of the tide."[5] Shortly later, a suicide bomb ripped through the UN mission in Baghdad. This ignited what the Bush administration termed the "insurgency." Initially, resistance to the US occupation authority came from Saddam Hussein loyalists. In May 2003, Paul Bremer, leader of the US occupation authority inexplicably banned former Baathists from participating in the post-Saddam state, forcing them into armed resistance. Shia militants soon joined in attacks on US soldiers. In December 2004, a year after Bush declared victory, the fiercest battle of the war raged through the streets of Fallujah. By 2005, US soldiers had restored control over the restive Sunni Triangle, but US soldiers faced unrelenting improvised explosive device (IED) attacks.

Iraq's insurgency intensified after 2004 when **Abu Musab al-Zarqawi** established Al Qaeda in Iraq. This Salafist group was comprised mostly of foreign volunteers, angry at the US occupation, and the killing of Iraqi civilians. Al-Zarqawi adopted a cynical strategy of launching suicide bombings targeting Iraq's Shias. Al-Zarqawi reasoned that intensifying sectarian divisions would destabilize Iraq and keep US troops pinned down. Civil war would also undermine the Bush administration's claim that they had brought "democracy" to the Middle East. US military leaders struggled to pacify an insurgency that had broad support and fighters who blended in with the civilian population. A rushed 2005 election only cemented the divergent aspirations between Iraq's Shia, Sunni, and Kurd communities. Only in 2007, when the Bush administration sent in a "surge" of US combat troops that allied with local Sunnis alienated by al-Zarqawi's puritanical form of Islam, was Al Qaeda in Iraq rolled up. Slowly, Iraqi stabilized.

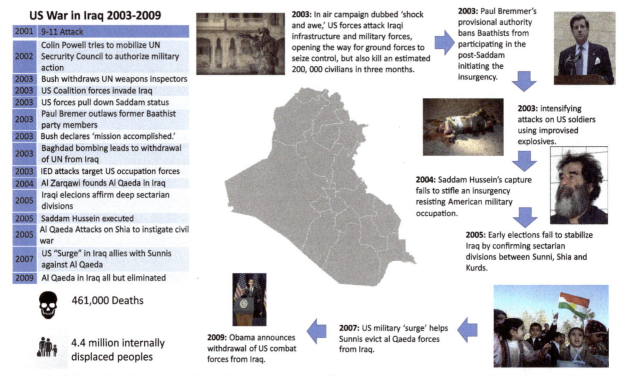

Image credits: © Schwabenblitza/Shutterstock.com; © BPTU/Shutterstock.com; National Archives Catalog; National Archives Catalog; © serkan senturk/Shutterstock.com; © Christopher Halloran/Shutterstock.com; © Martial Red/Shutterstock.com; © iconvectorstock/Shutterstock.com

The Iraqi occupation fiasco forced neoconservatives to abandon their grander ambition for regime change in Iran. During Bush's second term, his popularity sagged. Neoconservatives were increasingly replaced by moderates and realists were more skeptical about brazen use of US power. In 2008, discredited Republicans lost the White House to a young African American senator that had openly campaigned on revoking the Bush doctrine. Barack Obama proposed withdrawal from Iraq and return to a more multilateral foreign policy. Ultimately, President Obama would disappoint his most liberal supporters by continuing key elements of the Bush administration's national security strategy. Proclaiming an end to the war on terrorism, however, did change the tone coming from Washington, DC.

Demise of US Unilateralism

PNAC represented a bold strategy for transforming the international system. Like neoliberals, the neoconservatives recognized that the fall of communism represented a historic opportunity, but they drew different conclusions. Disdaining multilateralism, the neoconservatives sought to revoke international treaties and alliances to free the United States to leverage its unprecedented power to reshape the world. Neoliberals were progressives who believed that free societies and open markets would diffuse liberal values, modern technology, and democratic practices throughout the world. Over the long run, global integration would inspire stronger states, greater tolerance, and higher living standards. Neoconservatives were more cynical about human nature. They saw military force rather than free markets as the best mechanism for international restructuring. They argued that rogue states like Iran, Iraq, and North Korea threatened US allies, sponsored terrorists, and were developing nuclear technology. They believed it naive to assume that hardened enemies actively undermining the international order would fade away.

Although neoconservatives succeeded in toppling Saddam, in the broken alleys of Iraq their imperial dream suffered an ugly death. Bush's dismissal of the UN undermined the international cooperation necessary to tackle global challenges like jihadism. The occupation fiasco also revealed that PNAC was rooted in twentieth-century doctrines increasingly out of step with the emerging realities.

Asymmetric Threats

The 9-11 attacks shifted the course of twenty-first century. Subsequently, securing the "border" became a preoccupation in an open society where millions of foreign students attended North American universities under lax visa regulations, European Union (EU) residents moved unchecked across national frontiers and millions of containers flowed through the global economy. Al Qaeda had shown that nonstate actors, with modest means, could threaten national security by targeting soft targets. National defense now needed to protect the food supply, safeguard the power grid, and defend private financial institutions from cyberattacks. Accelerating virtualization of society continually extended the state's defensive perimeter, while increasing the velocity of capital, people, and filtering through the world economy undermined traditional state tools for tracking terrorists, illegal financial transactions, or communications flowing across global networks. The 2001 US **Patriot Act** had many corollaries across the Western world. National policy-makers revamped intelligence agencies to leverage new surveillance technology and share time critical data with allies. In the wake of 9-11, the United States' NSA patched into the servers running the Internet backbone. This enabled them to track terror suspects abroad and gather metadata in the hope of sniffing out terror plots. Revelations of domestic spying, however, raised concern about the "security state." How do you balance security from terrorism with privacy and the protection of constitutionally guaranteed civil freedoms?

A central irony of Bush's war on terrorism is that the United States' supposed ally in the war on terrorism, Pakistan, played a critical role in exporting nuclear technology. In 1970, the Great Powers had introduced the **Non-Proliferation Treaty (NPT)**, recognizing the diminishing financial and technological barriers for achieving nuclear fission. This treaty aimed to create an international environment that would limit diffusion of sensitive technology to minor powers, but many nonnuclear states looked at the NPT with skepticism, especially with regional rivals covertly developing nuclear capability. In 1974, India publicly broke the nuclear monopoly that had existed among the five permanent powers of the UN. This spurred Pakistan to develop its only nuclear deterrent. In 1998, Pakistan successfully tested a nuclear device in the remote Ras Koh Hills. Subsequently, program administrator **Abdul Qadeer Khan** covertly exported nuclear technology to North Korea and Iran.

> Security experts warn that Iran's development of nuclear weapons would spur a regional arms race. Is it fair to apply sanctions to Iran while ignoring Israel's nuclear program?

Iran's desire to acquire a nuclear bomb alarmed Israel and the West. Recognizing the risk posed by an enemy air strike, Tehran situated most of their nuclear infrastructure in underground bunkers around Natanz, making them impervious to a conventional air attack. Since 1993, the United States had led a Five Power Coalition to dissuade Iran from developing nuclear weapons. Iran countered that its nuclear ambitions were purely civilian and necessary for the country's energy security. In 2006, the UN Security Council demanded that Iran suspend its enrichment programs. When Iran refused, the UN imposed sanctions. Iran pointed to other states with enrichment programs, including Israel's unacknowledged program. Iran's position found backing among the Non-Aligned Movement, while the Bush administrations struggled to reconcile their hardline stance against Iran with their 2005 nuclear treaty with NPT violator India. This highlighted how US concerns with proliferation focused arbitrarily on states it deemed hostile. At the same time, the United States' muted response to continual North Korean provocations confirmed to Iran's mullahs that nuclear weapons provided deterrence against those publicly identified as "rogue states."

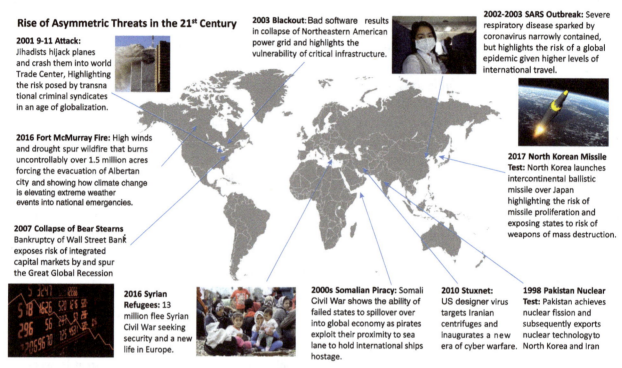

Image credits: © KeKen Tannenbaum/Shutterstock.com; © swissmacky/Shutterstock.com; © 3Dsculptor/Shutterstock.com; © Ververidis Vasilis/Shutterstock.com; © interstid/Shutterstock.com; © Andrei Minsk/Shutterstock.com

To set back Iran's program, the United States and Israel allegedly developed the **Stuxnet** computer virus. In 2010, this malware was first identified by Russian Internet Security firm Kaspersky. This "worm" piggybacked on the Internet and through infected Universal Serial Bus (USB) keys, slowly infiltrated the Siemens programmable logic controllers on Iranian subterfuges. Once embedded, Stuxnet released a malicious code that subtly disrupted the calibration of Iranian subterfuges, ultimately damaging 20 percent of them. Iran retaliated to this cyberattack by exporting medium range missiles and military experts to Hamas in Palestine and Hezbollah in Lebanon. These alliances provide Iran with deterrence were Israel or the United States to strike the country.

Iran reveals the challenges the international community faces in slowing nuclear proliferation. Despite various international programs inaugurated during the 1990s to secure Soviet nuclear materials, diminishing technical barriers increase the probability that weapons of mass destruction will land in unscrupulous hands. Pakistan represents a nightmare scenario. The fragility of the state, combined with the presence of various jihadist groups, has raised concerns about the vulnerability of Pakistan's nuclear arsenal. Jihadists have shown themselves to be both determined and extreme in their use of violence to achieve political goals. Radical groups might be more inclined to use nuclear weapons given their extremist beliefs and limited potential for western retaliation.

Nuclear proliferation, Stuxnet, and jihadism highlight how proliferation of transnational networks and increasing virtualization of society have transformed security. In the twenty-first century, conventional ideas about defensible borders and national defense are adapting to a new international environment, a more global society and an emerging digital economy. The 2014 declaration of an **Islamic State** inside Iraq and Syria (ISIS) highlighted how jihadists can exploit the fragility of failed states and the power of global networks to establish a unique hybrid organization combining features of a terrorist cell, fundamentalist movement, criminal syndicate, and rogue state. The traditional security establishment built upon twentieth-century ideas like deterrence, tactical air superiority, and economic sanctions needs to revamp its infrastructure to deal with an increasingly borderless and digitally linked world. Today, forensic accountants, drone pilots, hackers, spy satellites, data mining, and special forces soldiers are replacing the "grunts," tanks, and aircraft carriers that offered security in previous decades.

Kyoto and Tragedy of the Global Commons

Jihadists hardly represent the greatest threat facing human civilization. In 2013, NASA's chief climatologist James Hansen warned that climate change represented a "planetary emergency." Hansen lamented the gap between what scientists know versus what most citizens understand. Since 1900, the human impact on the earth's ecosystems has steadily increased. Throughout the world, water tables are falling, soil is being eroded faster than it can be created, forests are falling to chainsaws, livestock grind grasslands into deserts, while high-tech trawlers deplete ocean fisheries. A slew of recent reports from the UN, Organisation for Economic Co-operation and Development (OECD), and World Bank all warn that global civilization is hurtling towards disaster. In 2012, the Bulletin of Atomic Scientists set their famous doomsday clock to five minutes before midnight citing the risk of petroleum-fueled climate change and "new developments in the life sciences that could inflict irrevocable harm."[6]

The notion of environmental fragility runs counter to human experience. After emerging from the savannahs of Africa, *Homo sapiens* evolved inside an environment with recurring famines. Still today, volcanoes, tsunamis, and earthquakes demonstrate the force behind nature's awesome ravages. Yet, the human population has climbed from one to seven billion in less than a century, mostly by using technology to transform the natural environment. While humans have manipulated nature for millennia, industrialization represents a geological tipping point. Irrigation and artificial fertilizers in particular have enabled humans to make the deserts bloom to feed our growing masses. Twentieth-century conquest of nature, however, has limits and comes at a price. Nearly all the indexes for environmental health are flashing red, raising troubling questions about the viability of modern civilization.

> Could contemporary civilization collapse, or will rapid technological advances enable us to adapt to diminishing resources and ecosystem degradation?

The WTO has spurred increasing levels of prosperity, but consumer capitalism also threatens planetary life. The waste generated by consumption is washing up in the world's oceans, already acidifying from agricultural waste. Ecological collapse cuts against ingrained societal assumptions about unlimited growth. The western public finds it difficult to quantify environmental threats in part because they increasingly live divorced from nature. By the twenty-first century, most people inhabited cities, increasingly hypermodern bubbles where humans connect to each other digitally. This alienation is visible in the polarized debates concerning climate change. Although the scientific community reached consensus that **anthropogenic** forces were transforming the biosphere, many citizens have difficulty conceptualizing the "real-world" consequences posed by a seemingly modest 1.5°C rise in global temperatures.

To those not growing their own food and socializing through virtual networks, extinction of some creepy arachnid like the *Dicrogonatus gardineri* hardly seems cause for alarm. Scientists, however, warn that we are at the cusp of the sixth major extinction event. Global **biodiversity** loss represents a growing threat to human survival. Past history demonstrates that ecosystems are resilient but complex. They possess indiscernible thresholds that, once crossed, trigger a rapid downward spiral in productive capacity to a new normal. Historically, ecological degradation plays a major role in the collapse of human civilization.

> "Climate change is not a pollution problem. It's not like any environmental problem we've faced before. In some sense, it's not an environmental problem but a planetary transition. We've already pushed the earth into it. We're going to have to evolve a new way of being a civilization, fundamentally."
> Adam Frank, Astrophysicist[7]

Current degradation is linked to a capitalist economy that presumes that nature's value lies in extractable commodities like timber, bushels of grain, and barrels of oil. Planetary life, however, is predicated upon supplies of fresh air and flows clean water. By assigning no monetary value to ecological services, our market system promotes unsustainable resource use. It also levies an invisible, but often astronomical price tag on the world economy in the form of crop failures, lost soil productivity, shortened life spans, and devastating storms. Already the World Bank estimates that climate change alone has created a 1 percent drag on global growth. Also, cities around the world are struggling to cope with extreme meteorological events. Global degradation is also rapidly diminishing the productive capacity of global

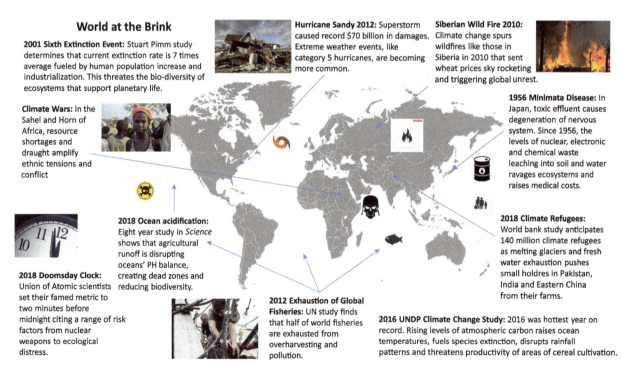

World at the Brink

2001 Sixth Extinction Event: Stuart Pimm study determines that current extinction rate is 7 times average fueled by human population increase and industrialization. This threatens the bio-diversity of ecosystems that support planetary life.

Climate Wars: In the Sahel and Horn of Africa, resource shortages and draught amplify ethnic tensions and conflict

2018 Doomsday Clock: Union of Atomic scientists set their famed metric to two minutes before midnight citing a range of risk factors from nuclear weapons to ecological distress.

2018 Ocean acidification: Eight year study in *Science* shows that agricultural runoff is disrupting oceans' PH balance, creating dead zones and reducing biodiversity.

Hurricane Sandy 2012: Superstorm caused record $70 billion in damages. Extreme weather events, like category 5 hurricanes, are becoming more common.

2012 Exhaustion of Global Fisheries: UN study finds that half of world fisheries are exhausted from overharvesting and pollution.

Siberian Wild Fire 2010: Climate change spurs wildfires like those in Siberia in 2010 that sent wheat prices sky rocketing and triggering global unrest.

1956 Minimata Disease: In Japan, toxic effluent causes degeneration of nervous system. Since 1956, the levels of nuclear, electronic and chemical waste leaching into soil and water ravages ecosystems and raises medical costs.

2018 Climate Refugees: World bank study anticipates 140 million climate refugees as melting glaciers and fresh water exhaustion pushes small holdres in Pakistan, India and Eastern China from their farms.

2016 UNDP Climate Change Study: 2016 was hottest year on record. Rising levels of atmospheric carbon raises ocean temperatures, fuels species extinction, disrupts rainfall patterns and threatens productivity of areas of cereal cultivation.

Image credits: © Adriana Mahdalova/Shutterstock.com; © Leonard zhukovsky/Shutterstock.com; © ressormat/Shutterstock.com; © Lucky Graphic/Shutterstock.com; © AF studio/Shutterstock.com; © VoodooDot/Shutterstock.com; © Martial Red/Shutterstock.com; © iconvectorstock/Shutterstock.com; © FARBAI/Shutterstock.com; © John Wollwerth/Shutterstock.com; © Andrei Minsk/Shutterstock.com; © Parrot Ivan/Shutterstock.com; © Linda Parton/Shutterstock.com

ecosystems despite more intensive technological and capital inputs. Often degradation proves irreversible. In the Amazon, deforestation results in a hard-baked tarmac that ecologists estimate might take 500,000 years to regenerate. While most subtropical environments are less fragile, rainforests and coral reefs represent centers of global biodiversity containing most of the Earth's species. Accelerating degradation there tears the web of life that nourishes us. The modern myth of progress preaches that technology can save us, but this optimism is not confirmed by the historical record. For modern civilization to remain viable, technological development must focus on recalibrating human needs to ecological limits.

Demise of the Kyoto Protocol, 1997 to 2008

Over the last decade, the climate models developed by the **International Panel on Climate Change (IPCC)** have been continually revised upward. The IPCC models correspond with studies of wildlife biologists and ecologists that reveal multiple stressors acting upon our biosphere. Scientists warn that we are at the brink of the Earth's sixth major extinction event. This time, the stimulus is not some super volcano or asteroid impact, but industrial civilization itself. According to some estimates, humanity claims nearly 40 percent of the biosphere and our consumption crowds out other species.

Recognizing the danger of climate change, the international community agreed to the **Kyoto Protocol** in 1997, creating a framework for nation-states to limit, freeze, and ultimately cap their carbon emissions. Kyoto relied on two controversial features. First, developing countries argued that poverty left them unable to pay for the pollution caused by rich countries so they needed to be left out of any international agreement that curbed their ability to modernize. Another controversy surrounded a system of carbon credits, whereby developed countries failing to reach their assigned targets would compensate developing countries for any "credit" beneath the cap. Economists calculated that this mechanism would incentivize states like Brazil to curtail deforestation and placated critics in developing states that argued that sustainable development was not affordable.

Passed in 1997, the Kyoto Protocol was not slated to come into force until 2005. However, the global consensus accompanying its passage dissolved after 2000. In the United States, newly elected President Bush never hid his hostility for the "theory" of climate change. He withdrew from Kyoto after the treaty failed to achieve Senate ratification. Subsequently, the Bush administration sabotaged further international efforts to tackle this threat. Nothing was less appealing to neoconservatives than Kyoto, which gave China *carte blanche* to economically develop using cheap carbon, while imposing an effective tax on profitable US petroleum companies. Other developed states had similar reservations about the carbon credit mechanism, feeling that Kyoto needed to embrace sacrifices from all states to succeed. During the 2008 Great Global Recession and its aftermath, embattled European governments fended off a **Sovereign Debt Crisis**. Austerity and popular demonstrations sapped their resolve for hard targets that might derail a fragile economic recovery. The final nail in the Kyoto Coffin came in 2011 when Canadian Prime Minister Stephen Harper withdrew from the treaty because of designs to develop the Canadian Oil Sands.

Kyoto's death ensures that human carbon emissions will continue to accelerate. In 2013, the Mauna Lao observatory in Hawaii detected atmospheric carbon levels above 400 part per million (ppm) for the first time in history. Scientists had long maintained that allowing carbon levels to glide above the 370 ppm ceiling would pose substantial risk. Some hope that an unknown corrective mechanism might kick in and reverse current warming. For instance, higher temperatures would seed more clouds that block out solar radiation. Volcanoes can put up immense amounts of particulate matter that dim the sun and cool the earth for a short period of time. To date, however, climate researchers have not identified any mechanism capable of counteracting the anthropogenic effects of climate change. On the contrary, they have discovered positive feedback mechanisms. In 2012, for example, a Russian expedition in the Arctic was surprised to find huge bubbles percolating to the surface as rising global temperatures released methane long trapped in the Arctic ice.

> Although criticized by environmentalists for rescinding Kyoto, Prime Minister Stephen Harper won several subsequent elections including a majority government in 2011. Opinion polls reveal strong public support for environmentalism, but consumer habits and voting patterns often reveal the opposite inclination. How do you explain this?

The slow demise of the Kyoto Accord stimulated a popular backlash, especially after new climate studies kept upping the range for future temperature projections. This confirmed that climate change was not just a threat to future generations; it was already exacting a formidable, though largely unmeasured, cost in the form of natural disasters and crop failures. Albert Gore's *Inconvenient Truth*, and Hurricane Katrina that flooded New Orleans in 2006, convinced many skeptical Americans that climate change was real. Internationally, the 2007 Bali Summit featured an extraordinary reversal as the Bush administration was shamed into ending its obstruction and following international consensus for climate action. Conservative economic bodies like the UN, World Bank, and OECD started to price the costs of climate change into their economic models, highlighting how it creates a drag on global growth, while contributing to ethnic conflict and a global tide of refugees. These fears increased anticipation that the 2010 **Copenhagen Summit** might lead to a substantial agreement. But at Copenhagen, once more, cash-strapped states managed only to agree to aspirational goals that will not translate into meaningful reform over the near term.

Satellite image of Hurricane Sandy

Hurricane Sandy hit the highly urbanized East unleashing an unprecedented level of property damage. Throughout the world, insurance companies are taking note of increasingly frequent "extreme" events and rising premium represents one drag on the global economy, but this is not priced into the carbon-centered economy.

Explaining International Paralysis

Given the overwhelming evidence that climate change represents a clear and present danger, why has the international community proven so slow to act on it? One compelling reason remains our civilization's dependence on petroleum for much of its transportation, electricity, as well as petrochemical products like fertilizers, textiles, and plastics. Given this addiction, there is no ready substitute for oil.

The threat of climate change, and our dependence on fossil fuels, places human civilization in a double bind. Our consumption contributes towards climate change that is already wreaking havoc on coastal areas, food crops, and tropical environments making the transition towards a greener infrastructure urgent. Yet, there is no Manhattan Project underway to develop renewable energy or implement a sustainable system for agriculture. The rising price of oil has stimulated corporate research to develop green technologies that will profit their balance sheets. To date, solar technology has been the largest beneficiary of green investment. The cost for generating electricity from the sun will soon dip below oil, creating a tipping point that could lead to a rapid phase out of many oil technologies.

Unfortunately, lack of a revolutionary technological breakthrough, like cold fusion, means that human civilization remains stuck with the petro-industrial complex over the near term. There is no alternative to replace the energy load carried by petroleum or for its use in such a wide range of industrial products. Any effort to build out a nonoil infrastructure would prove to be an extenuated and expensive process. While shale oil and fracking will provide a temporary reprieve from peak oil over the next decade, they cannot alter the basic pattern of declining stocks of easily accessible oil reserves. Meanwhile any delay in the transition towards a green economy will amplify the negative impacts of climate change that already carry an astronomical price tag.

Another explanation for global inaction is provided by Garrett Hardin's **Tragedy of the Commons Model**. The capitalist structure of the world economy has created a disjunction between the benefits of economic growth versus its ecological costs. The global environment represents a "commons" that all humans rely upon, but inside an international system of competing nation-states, there is incentive to exploit natural resources because their benefits accrue to one's own people, while the costs of pollution are distributed to everyone. China exploits coal to industrialize and expand the ranks of its middle class, but much of its air pollution drifts across the Pacific and creates smog in Los Angeles and Vancouver. The Canadian Oil Sands produces an economic boom in Alberta and strengthens the finances other Canadian provinces through the procuration formula, but it also contributes to global warming that is decimating the Amazon and polar ecosystems. Similarly, the world's fisheries are nearing exhaustion, as various states compete to extract their share of a diminishing resource.

The scary math of climate change suggests that the biosphere is hurtling towards a dangerous tipping point. While scientists are getting better at forecasting what global temperatures will look like in 2100, they cannot predict the ecological consequences of blowing past the 400 ppm threshold. The World Bank in its 2012 study *Turn Down the Heat* shows that global warming is already imposing itself upon many poor people living in marginal areas. Environmental degradation and securing access to diminishing resources is also a major contributing factor in civil conflicts like the war in Darfur. Few Westerners appreciate the costs of climate change because our typical metrics for measuring prosperity disregard ecological health. The pollution generated from coal-fired power plants may damage marine ecosystems and generate lung cancer, but gross domestic product (GDP) limits itself to measuring the economic benefits of any development project.

In terms of climate change, many scientists fear that the Earth has already reached a tipping point where humanity will no longer see incremental warming, but rather a radical acceleration of temperatures and a spike in extreme meteorological events as ocean currents, the jet stream, and global weather patterns reset. This new normal will permanently disrupt global rainfall patterns and consequently rewrite the history of the Earth. Some put hope in geoengineering. Humanity has the ability to seed the oceans to absorb more carbon and clouds to block out more solar radiation, but these technological approaches carry considerable risk. The history of human intervention in natural systems shows that the cure often proved worse than the disease. In the case of geoengineering, the principal danger lies in diverting rainfall from the Earth's richest agricultural lands.

The basic rules for the global economy were established by the WTO. Despite paying lip service to sustainable development, its dispute resolution mechanisms ignore environmental concerns. The international economy remains largely unregulated and constructed upon laissez-faire principles that incentivize poor resource use. Global capitalism elevates the "market" as the medium that ties consumers, corporations, and fragile ecosystems together. But the market is not really "free"; rather it is conditioned by corporate law that elevates profit as the system's primary goal. Under global capitalism, economic activity shows up as profit on corporate balance sheets, but its social, ecological, and economic costs are not priced into products we buy on store shelves. Accordingly, the costs of ecological degradation remain hidden in the form of low economic growth, high debts, sluggish labor markets, underfunded state universities, and higher insurance premiums.

Global Futures and Ecological Limits

Climate change headlines the most visible threat to our biosphere, but many ecologists believe that ocean acidification and biodiversity loss pose an even graver risk to human civilization. Various ecological assessments are in rough agreement that during the 1970s human civilization began to exceed the Earth's **carrying capacity**. A 1999 David Pimentel Study put the earth's carrying capacity at two billion, while in 2013 the Global Food Network estimated that we currently stand at 40 percent overshoot, meaning that we are diminishing the Earth's carrying capacity over the longer run by extracting nonrenewable resources and employing "cost-effective" extractive methods that permanently degrade soils, forests, and the oceans.

Window on World History: Last of His Kind

Lonesome George died on the Galapagos on June 24, 2012. Every day, dozens of species perish too little fanfare. George, however, was an international celebrity feted by the international media as the "last of his kind." *National Geographic* chronicled the story of the last known Pinta Island tortoise and the failure of conservationists to find him a suitable mate among other subspecies. News of George's passing was presented as a lamentable tragedy with environmentalists indicting humanity's failing conservation efforts. Tabloids speculated that George died of a broken heart. Decimation of local tortoise populations stretches back to the eighteenth century when western sailors took them aboard their ships as stores of fresh meat. A second blow came during the 1970s, when human settlers arrived and introduced pigs and goats that devastated the native fauna. Two centuries ago, 300,000 giant tortoises inhabited the Galapagos. Today, fewer than 40,000 remain in this Pacific archipelago.

Lonesome George on Santa Cruz Island

Lonesome George viewed in his pen at the Charles Darwin Research Center in the Galapagos Islands.

Very few mourning George related his death to a planetary extinction crisis. During the long twentieth century, human prosperity has rapidly accelerated, with other species paying the price as their habitat has been transformed into farmland and beach homes. Environmentalists suspect we are approaching the brink of the Earth's sixth major extinction event. This time the stimulus is not some supervolcano or asteroid impact, but the boundless human appetite for larger homes and increasingly sophisticated gadgets. Global biodiversity loss is accelerating, the systematic by-product of capitalist system that transforms ecosystems into commodities to be harvested for human benefit. Yet contemporary society rests upon a hollow foundation because our metrics for prosperity fail to price in the costs of "free" environmental services. The World Conservation Union estimates that the monetary value of the goods and services provided by global ecosystems equals US$33 trillion per year, considerably more than the US GDP of $14 trillion in 2008. We know from history that ecosystem collapse often comes suddenly when pressures surpass an intangible threshold spurring a rapid crash to a new, less productive normal. What is unprecedented today is the level of ecological impact exercised by human modern industrial civilization. This suggests that the tragedy of Lonesome George is not the loss of another species, but humanity's stubborn refusal to acknowledge its fundamental cause; the emergence of a global consumer society.

(Continued)

> **Critical Reflection**
>
> 1. How do you explain public mourning for lonesome George? What types of species seem to attract human conservation efforts?
> 2. Many ecologists believe that the biodiversity loss represents the supreme threat facing humanity moving forward. Why do many Canadians have difficulty appreciating this?

Food production constitutes another limit facing human civilization. During the last decade, food prices have climbed as China and India have become food importers and incorporated more meat into their diets. Meat production, particularly beef, is ecologically inefficient in terms of calorie output per unit of land. Western agriculture compensates for declining soil fertility through irrigation and industrial fertilizers and pesticides. Industrial agriculture is focused on maximizing output per unit of labor, but it depletes the soil and harvests a massive share of the world's fresh water store. Already, agriculture in many marginal areas is threatened by acute water shortages, particularly in Dryland Africa, the American Southwest, Northern India, and Southwestern China. **Peak water** represents an immediate challenge because of commercial agriculture's reliance upon irrigation. Throughout the globe, fresh water reserves are being tapped out. Climate change contributes to peak water by altering rainfall patterns, while melting glaciers threaten many riverine systems like those in Northern India. Throughout the world, rivers no longer reach the sea, farms in marginal areas are being abandoned, and aquifers are being drawn down. This represents a considerable headwind considering the high rate of human population growth particularly in arid areas like India and the Middle East. But agriculture represents just one limit confronting human civilization. Around the world, giant steam shovels work open pit mines literally consuming the Earth's crust as they chase miniscule concentrations of copper, gold, and nickel. This highlights how the world's store of easily accessible mineral resources is rapidly dwindling, forcing mining companies to tap poorer deposits at a higher economic and environmental cost.

The transition away from the petro-industrial complex that dominated the second half of the twentieth century is already underway, from green technologies to the smart design of cities and lower impact models for farming and manufacture. A complex of more efficient technologies is emerging from electric cars to distributed smart grids that incorporate renewable energy sources, Leadership in Energy and Environmental Design (LEED) buildings that drastically improve efficiency, and telecommuting that reduces congestion and air pollution. There are manifold technologies capable of addressing the diverse problems inherited from the twentieth century. Advances in synthetic materials, biochemistry, and genetic medicine continue to advance rapidly. This holds the promise of elevating the Earth's carrying capacity, raising human longevity, and lowering the human footprint. To date, however, the pace of such advances is inadequate to meeting the world's interlinked problems. Agenda 21 proposed to create a civilization living in balance with environmental limits, but currently the gap between human consumption and environmental limits continues to expand.

Crisis Capitalism and the Great Recession of 2008

The year before the 2007 financial meltdown, the global economy resembled a runaway train. Many observers saw that the global economy rumbling down the track to briskly, but they could not anticipate when it would run off the rails or what would happen when it crashed. The failure of Bear

Stearns in July 2007 triggered a global recession. This venerable Wall Street Bank had been a pioneer in developing a financial product called **mortgage-backed securities (MBS)**. Previously, brick-and-mortar banks had offered loans to homebuyers based on their evaluation of credit risk. In 2000, Wall Street began buying up thousands of mortgages from local banks, and reselling them to global investors from Dubai to Narvik. Wall Street argued that this "innovation," packaging shares of diverse mortgages together, reduced the risk of default. By late 2006, however, the US housing market cooled. In cities like Detroit, thousands of first-time minority homebuyers had been lured into subprime mortgages that offered an initial "teaser" interest rate that seemed to offer a ticket to the American Dream and participation in a booming national property market. Subprime mortgages, however, were toxic products. Their rates reset within a year or two at a much higher rate that the lenders often knew their buyers could not afford. The unscrupulous brokers selling no income, no job, no asset (NINJA) loans did not care because they were paid on commission. The risk of default was passed on to unwitting investors that bought up Wall Street's MBSs. Investors failed to appreciate the risk of MBSs because they were complex products that official rating agencies deemed them safe. As the US economy lurched into recession in 2007, savvy investors started to unload their MBSs. This put pressure on Bear Stearns and other banks holding these instruments. Bear Stearns had borrowed heavily to buy MBSs and over the course of 2007 their share price plummeted from $78 to $2. In July 2007, citing risks of contagion, US Treasury Secretary Henry Paulson intervened and bailed out the venerable Wall Street bank. While this relieved Bear Stearns investors, it also focused attention on the toxic loans on the balance sheet of other banks. Over the next few months, the crisis played out in both Washington, DC, and New York. Paulson and his crisis team met in the Federal Reserve building with the CEOs of the top Wall Street banks in a desperate attempt to stem a deepening crisis. When the buyout of Lehman Brothers failed in September 2008, the investment bank was forced into bankruptcy. The next day the crisis engulfed AIG, an insurance firm that had made a fortune unwisely insuring MBSs to investors around the world. Deeming AIG "too big to fail," Paulson decided to bail it out to the lofty tune of $85 billion. The subprime crisis had now escalated into a global contagion. AIG spooked investors. They engaged in panic selling as they realized they could not ascertain the size of the massive losses of MBSs hidden on the balance sheets of banks. Many European banks now required massive bailouts as "runs" on the bank in England, Ireland, and Iceland had depositors queuing up around the street to withdraw their life savings. At the height of the financial crisis, the global economy neared total meltdown and credit markets froze up. Short-term credit represents the lifeblood of the capitalist economy. Not only small and medium businesses, but Fortune 500 companies borrow trillions to cover the ordinary costs of running their operations. In the summer of 2008, however, even corporations with iron clad balance sheets, like General Electric, could no longer borrow overnight to keep their plants running. This threatened to push the global economy into a depressionary spiral like the 1930s.

Understanding the need for urgent action, Paulson dreamed up the **Toxic Asset Relief Program (TARP)** in attempt to contain the crisis. The plan called for injecting an unprecedented sum of $700 billion into the financial system. The sheer size of the bailout had its desired effect. This measure restored confidence and slowly credit markets unfroze. At the G-8 in Washington, DC, China, the United States, and their European partners tentatively agreed to inject stimulus to spur global economic recovery. While the ultimate policy measures adopted proved modest and uncoordinated, it changed the international mood and prevented total economic collapse.

By late 2009, the world economy entered into a fragile recovery. Europe suffered the worst owing to high state debt levels. The structurally unsound economies of Ireland, Greece, Cyprus, and Portugal required bailouts after their governments failed to sell bonds to pay for their everyday expenditures. By 2014, the global economy appeared to have weathered the global recession of 2008, but the crisis continues to raise troubling questions. The recurrence of speculative bubbles, followed by devastating crashes, as well as the high costs of bailouts cast doubt upon the current model of minimally regulated financial markets. Since the Nixon Shock of 1971, steady financial deregulation has shifted control over the global economy from state governments that directed economic activity towards the national interest, towards investors and speculators seeking individual profits. While MBS might have represented a novel product, stock market bubbles are hardly unprecedented. They have occurred in roughly fifteen-year intervals, most recently during the 1997 to 1998 Asian Financial Crisis.

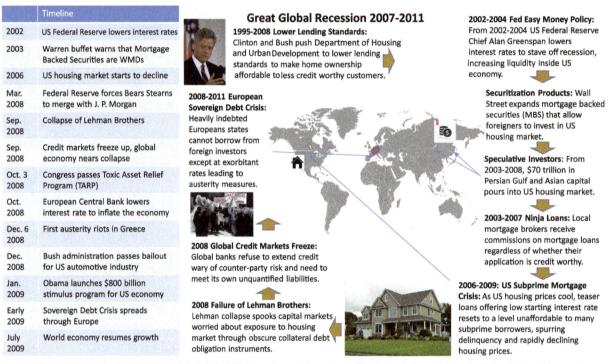

Image credits: © mark reinstein/Shutterstock.com; © Andrei Minsk/Shutterstock.com; © Kostas Koutsafikis/Shutterstock.com; © rSnapshotPhotos/Shutterstock.com; © veronichick84/Shutterstock.com; © Irina Adamovich/Shutterstock.com

Although swift action on the part of the US Treasury Department, certain investment banks, and the IMF and G9 prevented a total meltdown, the world brushed awfully close to disaster. Subsequent reforms have sought to curtail the worst abuses in the US mortgage industry that created the housing meltdown, but they have been less successful in bringing regulation to Wall Street. The 2010 US **Dodd-Frank** law sought to limit speculation among international banks that during the crisis were bailed out after being deemed "too big to fail," but this modest reform measure has seen its regulatory teeth progressively stripped down by corporate lobbyists and colluding legislators. One central problem confronting the global economy is that business has become international, but most regulatory authority remains vested inside states. This gap represents a particular problem as the volume of financial transactions that take place outside the scope of traditional regulatory bodies like the United States' Security and Exchange Commission (SEC) increases. It is very difficult to estimate the size of the global derivatives market, but their nominal value is likely 20 times the gross output of the world economy and 1,000 times greater than the TARP bailout passed by the US Congress in 2007. The presence of such massive **black pools** of capital sloshing through the global economy, largely outside the infrastructure of traditional regulation, exposes the global economy to substantial risk. Although an individual derivate might enable an investor to "hedge" a particular investment, the combined effect of millions of investors hedging creates a complex system whose dynamics cannot be measured or anticipated. According to chaos theory, inside complex systems a small input has the potential to produce a dramatic outcome. This is precisely what misfired in 2007, when trillions in derivatives were priced based on faulty assumptions about risk. Despite the massive damage to the global economy subsequent reforms have not brought greater regulation to derivative instruments. In fact, the number and value of these instruments have only increased since 2007. This means that the global economy has become more volatile, nearly impossible to govern, and even more vulnerable to a future shock.

The Arab Spring and Digital Populism

On December 17, 2010, street vendor **Mohamed Bouazizi** set himself alight outside a police station in Tunis. Earlier in the day, Bouazizi had refused to pay a bribe for operating his vegetable cart. In retaliation, a police woman confiscated the scales Mohammad used to measure his produce. Humiliated, and desperate after struggling to support his widowed mother for many years, Bouazizi reached a break point. When police authorities refused to return his property, Bouazizi ventured to the neighboring gas station. There he purchased a can of petrol, sprinkled it over his head and defiantly lit a match.

Sometimes extraordinary acts inspire sweeping changes. Around the world people routinely suffer and die, but Bouazizi's story went viral on social media. It resonated in the Middle East, where unemployment remains dreadfully high, and a lost generation of highly educated young people remains stuck in their parents' home, idle, bored, and anxious about the future. For the disgruntled, Bouazizi's story touched a nerve. Since the late 1960s, most Arab states have relied upon censorship and a brutal security establishment to quell dissidence, making the region the most "unfree" in the world according to indexes like the Freedom House survey. News of Bouazizi's death, however, spread through the Middle East thanks to widespread penetration of cell phones, social media, and satellite television. Within weeks, empathy galvanized into national protests that forced the abrupt resignation of Tunisia's unpopular dictator **Zine El Abidine Ben Ali** in January 2011. By then, discontent had spilled over Tunisia's borders, triggering the **Arab Spring**. Throughout Middle Eastern cities, demonstrators used social media to rally supporters in public squares to challenge unpopular regimes and demand greater voice in the political process.

> Since World War II there have been many protestors that set themselves alight in front of international cameras without stimulating a protest movement. Are global media platforms like Facebook, CNN, and YouTube inaugurating a golden age of democracy?

Bouazizi represented only one catalyst for the Arab Spring. Global warming had contributed to wildfires in Siberia in 2010 that destroyed over 30 percent of the wheat crop. This translated into higher prices that hit the Arab poor in urban slums particularly hard. Another catalyst was the **WikiLeaks scandal**. In 2010, Julian Assange published confidential US diplomatic dispatches that painted an unflattering portrait of Arab leaders and rampant corruption. The protests were also shaped by a new global media environment. Access to the Internet, social media, and ubiquitous cellular phones provided the young and unemployed access to news repressive governments had earlier managed to censor, while also enabling this more technologically savvy generation to organize protests that quickly overwhelmed traditional mechanisms of state repression. Satellite television coverage of protests in places like Tahrir Square in Cairo provided a platform for demonstrators to air their grievances to a global audience while restraining the state's use of repressive violence.

Cairo's Tahrir Square, 2012

In Egypt, a populist movement demanding reform and regime change set up camp inside Tahrir Square. Ultimately, a split would emerge between liberal reformers and Islamists over the country's future.

Across the Middle East the desire for reform cut across religious, demographic, ethnic, and class lines, culminating in populist coalitions that toppled repressive governments in Tunisia, Egypt, Yemen, and Libya by 2012. However, the ultimate ramifications of the Arab Spring remain unclear. Despite early optimism that populist movements would bring representative governments to the Middle East, many of the newly installed regimes have proven unpopular, unstable, or both. In Syria and Libya, popular protest resulted in civil wars between competing factions. In Libya, NATO bombers supported local groups that overthrew longtime dictator Myanmar Qaddafi. Qaddafi's summary execution in 2012 resulted in a fledgling regime that failed to fill the ensuing vacuum, sparking a conflict among competing regional and religious factions. In Egypt, street protests led to the resignation and imprisonment of Hosni Mubarak and Egypt's first free elections in 2012. The Islamic Brotherhood's candidate **Mohamed Morsi** was briefly sworn in as President, but his determination to impose an islamic constitution, virulently opposed by many in Egypt, led to his arrest and imprisonment by the army in July 2013. In Syria, resistance to the **Bashar al-Assad** regime triggered a civil war between the majority Sunni and Assad's **Alawites**, often supported by other fearful religious and ethnic minorities. The collapse of civil society in Syria provided an avenue for more extremist opponents of the Assad regime, particularly foreign jihadists, to prosper. Syria's civil war has already spilled over to its fragile neighbors Iraq and Lebanon. While it is too early to know how the Arab Spring will turn out, to date it has brought more instability than freedom in its wake.

The Arab Spring offers a cautionary tale to liberals who believed that digital technology would usher in a golden age of public engagement and government accountability. On the other hand, the Arab Spring also demonstrates the potential for international populism. Social media and the diffusion of cell phones not only facilitated local protests, but showed that local groups could dynamically respond to external events and surf on broader geopolitical currents. States and corporations have adapted to digital technologies and popular mobilization techniques to preserve their own interests.

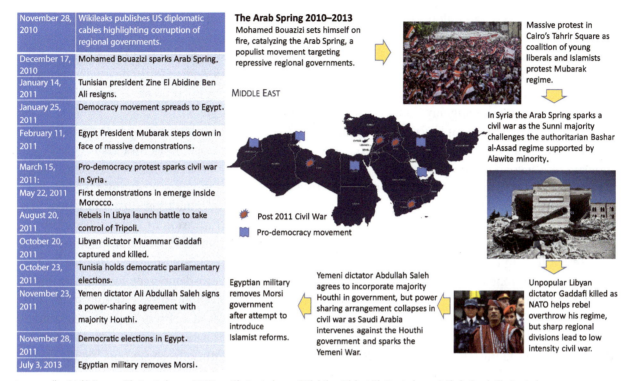

China's Communist Party monitors and censors the Internet, corporations have launched social media campaigns to respond to consumer boycotts, and states infiltrate populist movements to discredit demonstrations and push them towards violence. While the Arab Spring seems unlikely to culminate in a democratic Middle East, it has proven that digital technologies have become inextricably interwound with contemporary politics.

Multipolarity and the New Cold War

The Bush administration's muscular unilateralism provoked resistance from traditional rivals and some of the United States' most important allies. Many observers had interpreted 1991 as a "unipolar moment" where the United States would expand its global influence and spread liberal freedoms across the world stage. The political dissolution of the USSR, and the country's subsequent economic problems, precipitated a rapid erosion in Russia's military capacity. Under Gorbachev, and later Yeltsin, the Russian Federation assumed a new international role, mostly aligning with the West and collaborating inside the UN to tackle collective security concerns. *Ad hoc* incorporation of Yeltsin into the G-9 and NATO represented a transparent attempt to mollify angry Russian nationalists bristling at their state's declining power and diminishing influence.

In 1999, during his last year in office, Boris Yeltsin appointed a previously obscure former KGB agent, **Vladimir Putin**, as his designated successor. Upon Yeltsin's death, Putin took over the Presidency and quickly consolidated his authority inside the Russian Federation. Putin quickly brought Russian oligarchs under his thumb. He also gradually rolled back Yeltsin era liberal reforms and press freedoms. Rising oil prices contributed to a robust Russian recovery following the sharp 2000 to 2001 recession. Stabilization of state revenues enabled Putin to build public support and reinvest in a battered security apparatus. Putin also began to articulate his "New Russia" vision that asserted an aspiration to restore Russian power and global influence. Buoyed by high popularity, Putin progressively gutted Russian democracy from within, jailing opponents, harassing journalists, assassinating foreign critics, and closing opposition newspapers, while building up a patronage network that tied industrialists to the state security apparatus. Russian democracy's official death came in 2008 after Putin devised a stratagem to subvert constitutional term limits. President Putin changed seats with his protégé, Prime Minister Dmitry Medvedev, not leaving any doubt as to who was really in charge.

When Putin tried to return to Russian Presidency in 2012, however, domestic liberals challenged his despotism. Members of the punk band Pussy Riot were jailed for mocking Putin Public demonstrations were quelled by security forces and armed goons. The incarceration of dissidents and orchestration of a fraudulent election restored Putin to the Presidency, but also left him weakened. In a bid to restore public support, Putin resumed his long-term strategy of rebuilding Russian's global prestige and regional influence. In 2008, Putin orchestrated the covert invasion of Georgia, ostensibly to protect ethnic Russians, but in fact to prevent the former Soviet Republic's incorporation into NATO. The Ossetia campaign sent a clear warning to other former Soviet republics with ethnic Russian citizens. Putin had long complained about covert foreign support for pro-democracy movements inside the former Soviet Bloc, as well as the West's aggressive efforts to incorporate Russian border states into the EU and NATO. After Kremlin ally **Victor Yanukovych** was displaced as President of the Ukraine in the Revolution of 2014, Putin retaliated by annexing the Crimea, inhabited primarily by Russians and also home to the Russian Navy's Black Sea fleet. Subsequently, Putin offered support for Russian separatists inside the Ukraine, triggering international sanctions.

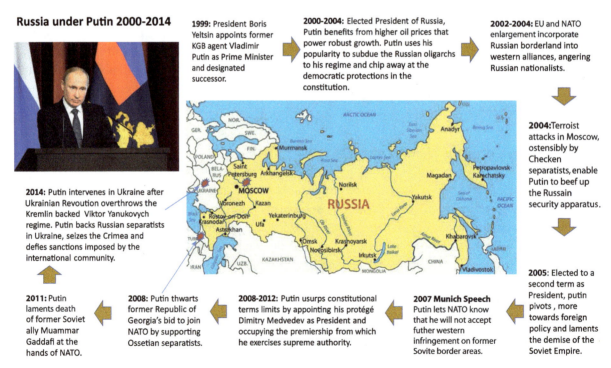

Image credits: © Free Wind 2014/Shutterstock.com; © pavalena/Shutterstock.com

Putin's bellicose challenge of the West represents an effort to mollify domestic dissidents, reassert Russian power, and maintain control over traditional borderlands. Challenging the international community, however, represents a risky strategy that exposes Russia's oil-dependent economy to international sanctions. Putin's bid to revive the Cold War by sending bombers and submarines into western airspace and waters constitutes more of an annoyance than a tangible military threat. But Russia's depleted military still maintains control over the world's second largest nuclear arsenal, ensuring that it cannot be ignored.

The principal rival to US military power and Western influence comes from China. In 2012, China emerged as the world's second largest economy with some estimates projecting that its GDP will overtake the United States around 2030. Unlike Putin's improvisational strategy, China has crafted a deliberate plan to expand its global influence. China's more muted approach is not surprising given its economic interdependence with the United States. From 1990 to 2007, the two countries' economic fortunes were so closely aligned that some economists dubbed the phenomenon "Chimerica." The United States outsourced factories to China, cheap Chinese goods flooded western markets, and China purchased US treasuries to keep interest rates artificially low in order to stimulate US consumption. The Great Global Recession, however, destabilized this symbiosis. US consumers cut back spending, while rising Chinese wages led to an exodus of western factories. Both the United States and China accused each other of currency manipulation. As the US–China partnership resets, the Chinese Communist Party has pursued a deliberate plan to offset US global dominance by stealing western technology, strategically investing in next-generation weapons platforms, and subtly challenging US control over international finance organizations. The Communist leadership is highly conscious of its military inferiority, but it has responded by modernizing the People Liberation Army and developing advanced anti-satellite weapons, anti-ship missiles, and hypersonic fighters that counteract key elements of the US arsenal. Since the 1990s, China's growing currency reserves have powered a low key economic diplomacy that has built up key clients in South Asia and Eastern Africa. China's massive Silk Road initiative, investing in infrastructure that ties postcolonial states to its economy, represents a bold ploy to reorient the world economy towards Beijing. This also fulfill a longer objective of securing control over strategic resources like oil, water, and farm land, critical to the country's future growth.

Since 1989, China and Russia have assumed new roles inside the international system. The former communist powers have traded in state planning and revolutionary socialism for capitalist market structures. While acquiescing to the new global order, both are also suspicious of US power and its geopolitical motives. The former communist powers envision themselves as world powers that operate in an international system still dominated by the West. Their policies reveal a willingness to interact with the West economically and engage the United States internationally for mutual benefit, but also suspicious regarding western interference in what they consider their sphere of interest. The strategic threat presented by US military power has diminished Cold War era tensions between Russian and China. They increasingly see themselves as strategic partners, along with other emerging economies, to create a more representative international system. Russian power is declining, while China's economic influence and military power continues to increase. As a result, how China will be incorporated inside the international system will serve as a key variable to how the immediate future plays out.

Conclusion: Bridge to the Twenty-First Century

The collapse of communism paved the way for a more integrated world. Observers in 1991 entertained rosy dreams about a more peaceful future, but the following two decades gave way to mounting pessimism. While our world continues to shrink and economically expand, neoliberal integration results in a world system unshaped by any humanitarian impulse, while ignoring fundamental ecological limits. As a result, global financial markets are fragile, while the international community has shown little willingness to tackle genocides, nuclear proliferation, global poverty, or climate change. Although technological advance continues at a brisk pace, currently most investment is conducted by multinational corporations and focused on profit rather than planetary survival. Meanwhile, states suffer from high debt loads that limit funding for research focused on meeting future food needs, ecological sustainability, or human health.

The proliferation of global networks is creating a more intimately connected world system. Although networks are inherently efficient, they also suffer from a structural weakness: problems arising in the periphery can rapidly infect the entire system. The 2008 Great Global Recession has revealed the fragility of capital markets and the erosion of the power of state regulatory bodies. Demise of the Kyoto Protocol and accelerating ecological degradation have highlighted the weakness of international institutions and the inability of contemporary civilization to direct its resources to pressing threats and future challenges. Many contemporary problems are closely interwoven. Climate change accelerates land degradation, which sows poverty and spurs migration to megacities with inadequate infrastructure, which in turn generates political instability. Over the last decade, the global system has grown less stable and resilient. Seemingly small events like a lucky terrorist strike, or the immolation of Bouazizi, has triggered major episodes of geopolitical disruption. This suggests that the world system requires a better structure for sharing the costs and benefits of economic growth and promoting collaboration to tackle clear and present dangers. Humanity has already developed technologies and practices for coping with many of contemporary problems, but planetary transition towards green architecture, renewable energy, financial regulation, and sustainable farming practices has proven inadequate in addressing the accelerating rate of resource exhaustion, climate change, and derivatives. While we cannot predict the future course of the twenty-first century, considerable challenges lie ahead.

Questions for Critical Thought

1. Why did the collapse of communism generate so much optimism about a better future?
2. What contributed to wavering liberal optimism from 1992 to 1995?
3. How did the 9-11 attacks reveal the darker side of globalization?
4. How did neoconservatives look at the post–Cold War world and in what ways did they propose to transform US foreign policy?
5. Why did the neoconservatives insist on regime change in Iraq and how did this ultimately undermine their grand ambitions for reshaping the world?
6. Why did the Kyoto Protocol fail to mobilize global action on climate change?
7. Why did the global economy lurch into a recession in 2008? How does this highlight the vulnerability of global financial markets?
8. In what ways have China and Russia challenged the United States? How do they propose to reform the international system?

Suggestions for Further Reading

- Berberoglu, B. *Beyond the Global Capitalist Crisis*. London: Routledge, 2016.
- Brown, L. *World on Edge*. New York: World Policy Institute, 2011.
- Cronin, J. *Global Rules: America, Britain and a Disordered World*. New Haven: Yale University Press, 2014.

- Geisen, M. *The Man without a Face: The Unlikely Rise of Vladimir Putin.* New York: Riverhead Books, 2013.
- Guzman, A. *Overheated: The Human Cost of Climate Change.* Oxford: Oxford University Press, 2013.
- Kiely, R. *The Clash of Globalisations: Neo-liberalism, the Third Way, and Anti-globalisation.* New York: Brill, 2005.
- Koshrokhavar, F. *Inside Jihadism.* New York: Routledge, 2013.
- Wright, L. *The Looming Tower: Al-Qaeda and the Road to 9/11.* New York: Vintage, 2007.

Notes

1. John Ehrenberg, *Iraq Papers* (New York: Oxford University Press, 2010), 6.
2. United Nations, "Report of the World Commission on Environment and Development: Our Common Future," 1987, accessed August 13, 2019, http://www.un-documents.net/our-common-future.pdf.
3. Robert Geyer and Samir Rihani, *Complexity and Public Policy: A New Approach to 21st Century Politics, Policy and Society* (New York: Routledge, 2010), 149.
4. Televised Presidential address. "Selected Speeches of George W. Bush 2001-2008," September 21, 2001, 66, accessed August 12, 2019, http://www.cnn.com/2001/US/09/20/gen.bush.transcript/.
5. Brian Steed, ed. *Voices of the Iraq War: Contemporary Accounts of Daily Life* (New York: Greenwood, 2016), 61.
6. Bulletin of the Atomic Scientists, "Doomsday Clock." http://thebulletin.org/multimedia/timeline-conflict-culture-and-change.
7. https://www.commondreams.org/views/2018/08/20/saying-goodbye-planet-earth Chris Hedges, "Saying Good bye to Planet Earth," Common Dreams, August 20, 2018. Accessed August 12, 2019.

Index

A

Abdul Qadeer Khan, 331
ACC. *See* Allied Control Council
Accra Conference, 67, 72
Acheson, Dean, 91
Ad Council, 120
Addis Ababa Conference, 203
Admiral's Revolt, 90
Afghanistan's Civil War, 191
African National Congress (ANC), 219
African Socialism, 69, 202
Afrikaner, 219
Afro-Asian Bloc, 60
Agenda 21, 322
Agricultural modernization, 123
Akuzu, 223
Alawites, 344
Alfonsín, Raúl Ricardo, 168
Algerian nationalism, 64
Algerian National Liberation Front (FLN), 62
Algerian War of Independence, 1954 to 1962, 66
Algiers Conference 1967, 21
All African People's Conference, 67
Allende, Salvador, 154–155
Alliance for Progress, 152
Allied Control Council (ACC), 53
Al Nakbah, 175
Al Qaeda, 4, 327, 329, 331
Amazon apocalypse, 168–169
American Free Enterprise system, 133
Amin Dada, Idi, 206
Amin, Hafizullah, 190
Anderson, Rudolf, 99
Andropov, Yuri, 272
Anglo-American agreement, 32
Anglo-Iranian Oil Corporation (AIOC), 81, 182
Anglo-Saxon traditions, 116
Anthropogenic forces, 333–334
Anti-Ballistic Missile (ABM) Treaty, 328

Anti-Bolshevist sentiments, 47
Anti-communism, 95
Anti-globalization activists, 324
Anti-globalization movement, 312
Anti-Japanese Malay People's Army (MPAJA), 39
Anti-Zionism, 181
Anxious 1960s, 124–133
Apartheid, 219–221
    regime, 68
Arab forces, 51
Arab Liberation Army, 51
Arab nationalism, 175
    after Suez, 179–180
Arab Revolt 1936 to 1939, 50
Arab Socialism, 21, 175–176
Arab Spring, 343–345
    movement, 195
Arab summit, 180
Arafat, Yasser, 196–199
Árbenz, Jacobo, 20, 102, 153–154
Arden-Clarke, Charles, 67
Argentina's dirty war, 156
Arkhipov, Vasili, 99
Armas, Carlos Castillo, 154
ARPANET, 296–299
Arusha Accords, 223
"Asia for Asians" slogan, 38
Asian Communism, 234–235
Asian Miracle, 82, 249–253
Asian modernity, 18
Asia's Cold War, 238–239
al-Assad, Bashar, 344
al Assad, Hafiz, 182
Association of Southeast Asian Nations (ASEAN), 238
Atlantic Charter, 32, 36, 37, 61
Atlantic Dream, 1941 to 1949, 32
    Bretton Woods and postwar economy, 35
    new International System, 32–33
    Nuremberg Tribunals and International Law, 33–34
Atlantic Settlement, 1947 to 1955, 117–118

(Nine)9-11 attack, 4, 28, 326–333
Attlee, Clement, 43, 89
Aung San, 38, 40
Australia–New Zealand–United States (ANZUS) treaty, 233

B

Baby boomers, 130
Baghdad Pact, 179
Bamboo Curtain, 76, 232, 233
Bandung Conference, 60, 62, 101, 176, 236, 238
Bani-Sadr, 186
Barak, Ehud, 198, 199
Batista, Fulgencio, 96–97, 147
Battle of Algiers (1956 to 1957), 66
Battle of Cuito Cuanavale, 220
Battle of Surabaya 1945, 38
Bay of Pigs, 97
Belgian policy, 221
Belgrade Conference 1961, 101
Benelux, 118
Ben-Gurion, David, 51
Beria, Lavrentiy, 89, 261
Berlin, 96
   crisis, 42, 56, 88, 117, 152
Berlin Blockade and Airlift, 55–56
Bernays, Edward, 120
Beveridge, William, 43
Biafran War, 205
Big Three, 32
Biko, Stephen, 219
bin Laden, Osama, 327
Birth of Israel, 1945 to 1949, 49–52
Black Consciousness Movement, 219
Black Friday Massacre, 184–186
Black Lives Matter movement, 127
Black Panthers, 127
Black pools, 342
Blair, Tony, 138
Boatpeople, 315
Bokassa, Jean-Bédel, 211
Bolshevik dogma, 32
Bolsheviks seized power in 1917, 88
Bolshoi speech 1946, 53
Bombay Plan, 248
Borlaug, Norman, 78–79
Born Again movement, 134
Bosnian War, 284
Botha, Pieter Willem, 221
Bouazizi, Mohamed, 343
Bové, Shepherd Juan, 3
Branco, Humberto Castelo, 169
Brandt, Willy, 132

Braudel, Ferdinand, 8
Brazil's national integration program, 12
Bremer, Paul, 329
Bretton System, 36
Bretton Woods Accord, 11, 35
Brezhnev, Leonid, 267
Britain's council housing system, 121
British-controlled Malay, 235
British Labour Party, 43, 46, 89
Brussels Roundtable, 73
Bundeswehr, 117
Bungalow, 121
Burma, 38
Bush, George, 323, 324, 329, 330
   war on terrorism, 327
Bush, Herbert Walker, 327

C

Cabinet Mission, 41
Cairo Declaration, 186
Calderón, Felipe, 170
Cambodia, 235–236
Camp David Summit, 199
Canada and global migration, 314
Canada–US free trade pact of 1987, 139
Canadian perspective, 24–27
Canadian school system, 26
Capitalism
   crisis, 308–309
   crony, 311
   global, 307–308
   globalization of. *See* Globalization of capitalism
The Captive Wife (Gavron), 130
Carson, Rachel, 128
Carter, Jimmy, 136, 184
Castro, Fidel, 63, 96, 97, 155
Castro's Cuban Revolution, 62
Catroux, Georges, 61
Ceausescu, Nicolae, 272, 277
CFM. *See* Council of Foreign Ministers
Charismatic leaders, 20
Cheney, Dick, 328, 329
Chernenko, Konstantin, 272
Chernobyl nuclear plant, 273
Chiang Kai-shek, 42, 92, 233, 238, 244–245
Chicago Boys, 165
Children of Berlin, 55
Chile's Shock Therapy, 165–166
China's Civil War, 1945 to 1949, 42
China's Cultural Revolution, 247–248
China's offensive, 93–94
Chinese civilization, 232

Chinese Communist Party, 347
Chinese-Vietnam War 1979, 105
Chin Peng, 235
Chirac, Jacques, 139
Christian Democratic coalitions, 118
Church Committee 1975, 105
Churchill, Winston, 8, 32, 36, 43, 52, 53, 118
Church leaders, 162
Civil War 1948, 150
    in El Salvador, 158–159
Clark, Mark, 159
Clashing expectations for decolonization, 1945 to 1955, 61–64
Clay, Lucius, 53
Clinton, Bill, 198, 199, 325
Clinton, William Jefferson, 137, 327–328
Cold War, 8, 20, 84, 88
    distortive effects, 106
    in popular culture, 106–110
    postwar Latin America, 152–160
Cold War era (1949–1991), 23
Colonial Development and Welfare Act 1945, 61
Colonial retrenchment, 63–64
Communications, 295–296
Communism, 269–270
Communist Bloc, 270–272
Communist leadership, 347
Communist Party, 255
Concession system, 311
Conference for African Unity, 203
Congo Crisis, 70, 72–75, 95, 203
Conservative Resurgence, 1980s, 135–137
Consumerism, 19
Containment, Congress, 89
Contemporary globalization, 294
Contemporary integration, 2
Contemporary students, 28
Contemporary Western society, 137–142
Contras, 157
Copenhagen Summit, 336
Corporate governance, 304
Council of Foreign Ministers (CFM), 53
Counter-Reformation Catholicism, 146
Coup in Guatemala, 153–154
Cripps Mission, 40
Crony capitalism, 311
Cuban Crisis, 98, 100
Cuban Missile Crisis, 88, 96, 97, 99, 100, 107
Cuban Revolution, 21, 96–97, 151, 152, 154
"Cubs," 82
Cultural collision and assimilation, 315–316
Cultural globalization, 17–18
Culture wars, 139–140

D

Dallaire, Roméo, 224–225
Dallas or *Dynasty* episodes, 15
d'Aubuisson, Roberto, 151, 158
Dayton Accords 1995, 285
DDT, 128
Debt Crisis, 60, 82–84
    postwar Latin America, 164–166
Debt Crisisto, 10
Debt trap, 311
Decentralized production, 293
Decentralized production model, 14
Decolonization, 22
Deeper West European Integration, 1951 to 1967, 118–119
Deep state, 21, 76, 182
de Gaulle, Charles, 36, 37, 61, 131
Deindustrialization, 139
Deir Yassin massacre, 51
de Klerk, Frederik, 221
Democratic National Convention 1968, 129
Democratic Republic of the Congo, 73
Democratic wave, 167–169
Democratic West, 34
Deng Xiaoping, 232, 247, 253–254
Deng's market socialism, 18
de Oliveira Salazar, António, 64
Dependency theorists, 148
Deregulation, 305–306
Desaparecidos, 156
Despotic rule, 83
Destalinization, 262
"Developed socialism," 267
Dicrogonatus gardineri, 334
Diem, Ngo Dinh, 104
Dien Bien Phu, 64
Digital age, 299–300
    dawn of, 299–300
Digital divide, 299
Digitalization of economy, 300–302
Digital populism, 343–345
Digital restructuring, 302
Digital Revolution, 296
Dirty wars, 76, 156
Dissolution of the Grand Alliance, 1945 to 1949, 52–56
Doha Round, 310
Doi Moi, 248
Dollar diplomacy, 152
Domino theory, 92
Dorman-Smith, Reginald, 38
Dostam, 191
Drafting process, 34

Drought, 210
Dryden, Ken, 108
Dual economy, 313
Dubcek, Alexander, 270
Dulles, John Foster, 154
Dumbarton Oaks Conference 1944, 32
DuPont, 128

E

Earth Day, 128
ECLAC. *See* Economic Commission for Latin America and the Caribbean
Ecological sustainability, 311
E-commerce, 302
Economic Commission for Latin America and the Caribbean (ECLAC), 148
Economic cycles, 9–11
Economic frustrations, 149
ECSC. *See* European Coal and Steel Community
Eden, Anthony, 177–179
EEC. *See* European Economic Community
Egyptian refugee camps, 180
Eisenhower, Dwight, 102, 109, 126, 153, 177, 179, 180
Electronics revolution, 294–295
El Norte, 165
El Salvador, civil war in, 158–159
Entebbe Raid, 207
Environmental pollution, 243
Equal Rights Amendment, 130
Era of Coalition Governments, 1944 to 1947, 47–48
Ernesto Guevara, 62
Erratic reforms, 264–266
Euro-centric, 24
European Coal and Steel Community (ECSC), 118
European colonialism, 64, 101
European colonial rule, 233
European Community, 138
European Economic Community (EEC), 118
European empires, 60
"European-like" Tutsi minority, 64
European social democracy, 117
Europe's campaign for colonial restoration, 38
Europe's Counterculture Movement, 130–133
Europe's Golden Age, 1950 to 1973, 121–122
Evans, Gareth, 120
Export industrialization strategy, 82

F

Faisal, 194
Fall of the Iron Curtain, 1945 to 1949, 47
    Era of Coalition Governments, 1944 to 1947, 47–48
    Soviet Hammer, 1948 to 1953, 48–49

Falwell, Jerry, 134
Fanon, Frantz, 63
Fashion model syndrome, 164
"Fatherland liberation" war, 91
"Father of the bomb," 99
"Father of the Nation," 77
FDR. *See* Franklin Delano Roosevelt
Federal Republic of Germany (FRG), 56
Feminine Mystique (Friedan), 125
Feudalism, 190
Fiber optic lines, 297
Fifth Pan-African Congress, 61
Finance, revolution in, 293–294
Financial services, 300–301
First Arab-Israeli War, 52
First *Intifada*, 197
Fischer, Bobby, 108
Flexible production, 302
Force Publique, 73
Forces Armées Zaïroises (FAZ), 213
Fordist model, 11
Foreign capital, 205
Foreign direct investment (FDI), 294
Four-Power Treaty, 53
France's Unceremonious Exit, 1957 to 1962, 66
Franklin Delano Roosevelt (FDR), 32
Freedom Charter, 219
Freedom Riders, 126
Free trade blocs, 138–139
"Free world" in 1947, 88
French authorities, 131
French Union 1946, 61
FRG. *See* Federal Republic of Germany
Friedan, Betty, 125
Front Nationale, 139
Fulbright, William, 160

G

G7, 27
Gandhi, Indira, 237, 248
Gastarbeiter system, 123
Gavron, Hannah, 130
General Agreement on Trade and Tariffs (GATT), 11, 35, 240
General Theory of Employment, Interest and Money (Keynes), 43, 46
Geneva Accords 1954, 65
Geneva Conference, 65
Geneva Conventions, 180
Genocide, 33
    convention, 34
George, Lonesome, 338, 339
German Democratic Republic (DDR), 56

German Miracle, 121
German refugee camps, 49
Ghana, 67–68
  economy, 70
Giáp, Nguyên, 63–64
GI Bills, 117
Glasnost, 274
Glenn, John, 1
Global Age, dawning of, 1–3
Global biodiversity, 334
Global capitalism, 338
  assessing, 307–308
Global cities, 309
Global Cold War, 1949 to 1991, 88. *See also* Cold War
  Global Spillover, 1949 to 1953, 89–91
  Gorbachev's End Game, 1985 to 1991, 110–111
  Nuclear Brink, 1954 to 1963, 94–100
  popular culture, 106–110
  Third World in Cross Fire, 100–106
  war in Korea, 91–94
Global history, 26
Global integration, 3
Globalization, 2, 3, 19
Globalization of capitalism
  ARPANET in 1974, 296–299
  communications, 295–296
  dawn of digital age, 299–300
  decentralized production, 293
  digitalization of economy, 300–302
  electronics revolution, 294–295
  globalization's paradoxes and discontents, 309–317
  neoliberalism and WTO, 305–309
  revolution in finance, 293–294
  rise of transnational corporations, 302–304
  transportation, 292
  World Trade Organization (WTO), 290
Globaloney, 3
Global Positioning System (GPS), 293
Global rich list, 24
Global Spillover, 1949 to 1953, 89–91
Glocalization, 3
Golden Postwar Recovery, 1950 to 1972, 11
Golden Sixties, 241
Gomulka, Władysaw, 48, 264
Gorbachev, Mikhail, 110–111, 191, 274, 275, 278
  and Eastern Europe, 111
  End Game, 1985 to 1991, 110–111
  liberal reform, 13
Gosplan, 266
Goulash Communism, 271
Gowon, Yakubu, 205
Gracey, Dick, 39
Grand Alliance, 36
Granma, 96
Great Depression, 8, 32, 43, 49, 61, 122

Great Global Recession, 4, 28
Great Leap Forward, 245–247
Great Proletarian Cultural Revolution, 247
Great Society program 1964, 123
Great Unraveling, 1956 to 1966, 64–68
Great War, 35
Green Revolution, 78–79, 209
Group Areas Act, 219
Group of 77 for New International Economic Order, 21
Guevara, Che, 151, 160
"Guided democracy," 183
Gulf of Tonkin Incident 1964, 105
Gulf sheikhs, 12, 13

H

Habyarimana, Juvénal, 223
Haider, Jörg, 139
Hammarskjöld, Dag, 74, 95
Harper, Stephen, 225
"Hedgehog" strategy, 64
Hekmatyar, Gulbuddin, 191
Helsinki Accords 1975, 106
Helsinki Conference, 271
Hendrix, Jimmy, 130
Hispanic immigrants, 137
History's new physics, 4–6
Ho Chi Minh, 20, 40, 63, 101, 105
Homo sapiens, 333
Honecker, Erich, 276
"Household responsibility" system, 254
House Un-American Activities Committee, 107
Hudud law, 187
Hukbong Mapagpalayang Bayan, 235
Human development index (HDI), 307
"Human dignity," 186
Human migration and trafficking, 313–315
Hundred Flowers campaign, 245
Hungarian Uprising, 264
Hussein, Saddam, 185–186, 188, 323, 324
Hybrid approach, 23–24
Hypermodernity, 141
  global march towards, 141–142
Hyperpower, 328
Hypertext, 297

I

IBRD. *See* International Bank of Reconstruction and Development
ICBMs. *See* Intercontinental ballistic missiles
Ideological flexibility, 70
Idi Amin's despotism, 206–207
IMF. *See* International Monetary Fund
Import substitution industrialization (ISI), 148

Inchon landing, 92
India's independence, 40–41
Indigenous communists, 47
Industrialization, 209–210
Industrial monoculture, 266
Institutional Revolutionary Party, 150
Interahamwe, 225–227
Intercontinental ballistic missiles (ICBMs), 94, 95
"Inter-modality," 292
International Bank of Reconstruction and Development (IBRD), 35
Internationalization of the independence struggle, 61–63
International law, 33–34
International Monetary Fund (IMF), 13, 82, 165, 307
International Monetary System, 35
International Panel on Climate Change (IPCC), 335
International paralysis, 337
Internet service providers (ISPs), 298
Intifada, 197
Iranian Revolution, 174, 182–189
Iran–Iraq War, 188, 323
Iran's Revolution, 19
Iron Curtain, 48, 52
ISI. *See* Import substitution industrialization
Islamic law, 185, 186
Islamic revival movement, 174
"Islamic Revolution," 187
Islamic State, 333
Islamism, rise of, 187–189
Islamist movements, 187
Islamist reform program, 182
Islamization of society, 189
Israeli troops, 180
Istiqlal Party, 61

J

Japanese Capitalism, 241–242
Japan, Golden Sixties, 241
Japan INC, 241
Japan's Postwar Transformation, 239–244
Jaruzelski, Wojciech, 271, 275
Jawaharlal Nehru, 41
Jewish Agency, 51
Jewish forces, 51
Jim Crow laws, 125
Jinnah, Muhammad Ali, 41
Johnson, Lyndon B., 104–105, 123, 124, 128, 153
Joplin, Janis, 130
Judeo-Christian traditions, 116
Junta, 146, 150–151, 155, 165, 211
    fall of, 166
    and state terrorism, 159–160
Justice and reconciliation, 167–168
Just-in-Time (JIT) production system, 302

K

Kabila, Laurent-Désiré, 227
Kádár, János, 271
Karadžic, Radovan, 285
Kasa-vubu, Joseph, 73
Kennan, George, 90
Kennedy, John F., 97, 99, 100, 152
Kenyatta, Jomo, 206
Keynesians, 305
Keynes, John Maynard, 35, 43
Khmer Rouge, 235, 236
Khomeini, Ayatollah, 18–19, 183–188
Khrushchev, Nikita, 94–97, 99, 107, 177, 179, 204, 262–267
Khrushchev's Thaw, 262
Kim Il Sung, 91
King David Hotel bombing 1946, 50
King, Martin Luther, Jr., 126–127
King Saud, 194
Kissinger, Henry, 132
Kleptocracy, 76, 207, 208–213
Kondratieff, Nikolai, 10
    model, 10
    theory, 15
Korean War, 10, 91–94, 102
Korean Wave, 256
Krenz, Egon, 276
Kubrick, Stanley, 107
Kuomintang, 42
Kwame Nkrumah, 67–70
Kyoto Protocol, 335–338, 348

L

Labour Party, 117, 135
Laffer, Arthur, 137
Land redistribution, 183
Laporte, Pierre, 132
Latin America
    Debt Crisis, 1982 to 1989, 164–166
    neoliberal turn, 168
Latin American society
    women, 162–164
Lee Kuan Yew, 235
Leftist organizers, 60
Lenin, Vladimir, 38
Lennon, John, 316
Le Pen, Jean-Marie, 139
Levitt, William, 122
Liberal Democratic Party (LDP), 241
Liberalization, 264
Liberal optimism, 324–325
Liberal regional immigration laws, 137
Liberation, strategies for, 63

Liberation theology, 162
Limited Test Ban Treaty 1963, 100
Limited war, 94
Liquidity trap, 165
Liu Shaoqi, 247
Loans for shares scheme, 280
London Conference 1947, 55
Long-Term Capital Management (LTCM), 308
Longue durée, 8
Lord Mountbatten, 39
Lost Decade, 82–84, 165, 166, 208, 209, 305
Lumumba, Patrice, 20, 72–73, 95, 101–102, 204

M

Maastricht Treaty 1992, 138
MacArthur, Douglass, 92, 93 94, 239
Macmillan, Harold, 65, 119
Madrassas, 191
Magna Carta, 34
Mahathir, Mohamad, 18, 141
"Malaise speech," 136
Malay Emergency, 235
Malcolm X, 127
Malenkov, Georgy, 261
Malinovksy, Rodion, 42
Management skills, 75
Manchester Conference 1945, 37
Mandela, Nelson, 219, 221, 222
Mao Zedong, 8, 40, 42, 89, 92, 96, 107, 233, 236, 244–245
Marcuse, Herbert, 130
Market reforms, 305–306
Marrakesh Agreement, 307
Marshall, Andrew, 106
Marshall, Elsie, 106
Marshall, George, 42, 53, 152
Marshall Plan, 36, 40, 54, 64, 152
Marsh of Blackpool, 106
Martial law, 151
Marxist Tudeh Party, 182
Mass media, 187
McCarthy, Joseph, 89, 107
Megacities, 79
Meron, Theodor, 180
Microchips, 295
"Middle East," 174
Mikołajczyk, Stanisław, 48
Militant Jihadism, 192–193
Milosevic, Slobodan, 282, 284
Minamata disaster, 243–244
Mindszenty, Jozsef, 48
Minh, Viet, 104
Ministry of International Trade and Industry (MITI), 240
Mitterand, François, 136

Mladic, 283–284
Mobility Revolution, 298–299
Mobutu, Joseph Désiré, 75, 95, 212–213, 226–227
Modernization model, 68, 75
Modernization theory, 68
Mohammad Reza Shah, 182
Molotov, Vyacheslav, 261
Mondale, Walter, 137
Monetary policy, 46
Monnet Plan, 46
Monoculture, 266
Monolithic communism, 90
Monroe Doctrine 1823, 152
Montreal Protocol, 322
Moore's Law, 295
Morsi, Mohamed, 344
Mortgage-backed securities (MBS), 341
Moscow Declaration 1943, 32
Moscow Treaty 1970, 132
Mossadegh, Mohammad, 81, 182, 183
Mothers of the Plaza de Mayo, 163
Mountbatten, Louis, 41
Mountbatten Plan, 41
Mouvement National Congolais (Lumumba), 73
MPAJA. *See* Anti-Japanese Malay People's Army
Mubarak, Hosni, 189
Mujahideen, 190, 191
Munich Olympics 1972, 81
Museveni, Yoweri, 223
Muslim Brotherhood, 175
Mutually assured destruction, 106
Myanmar Qaddafi, 181, 343

N

NAACP. *See* National Association for the Advancement of Colored Peoples
NAFTA. *See* North American Free Trade Agreement
Nagy, Imre, 264
Najibullah, Mohammad, 191
NAM. *See* Non-aligned movement
Nasser, Gamal Abdel, 16, 65, 101, 174
and revolutionary nationalism, 175–182
Nasserism, 181–182
National Association for the Advancement of Colored Peoples (NAACP), 125
National Association of Securities Dealers Automated Quotations (NASDAQ), 301
National communism, 95
National Front, 182
National Health Service, 46
Nationalism, 37
Nationalization, 78
schemes, 78
National Liberation Front (NLF), 104

National Security Council, 90
National security doctrine, 150
Nation of Islam, 127
NATO. *See* North Atlantic Treaty Organization
Nehru, Jawaharlal, 101, 236
Neocolonialism, 103, 207
Neocolonialism: The Last Stage of Imperialism, 72
Neocolonial settlement, 207–208
Neocolonial structure, 72
Neoconservatives, 328, 330, 331
Neoliberal Globalization, 1986 to 2007, 13–15
Neoliberalism, 305–309
Neoliberal reforms, 134
Neoliberal World Trade Organization, 84
Netanyahu, Benjamin, 198
Network society, 299
Neutralism, 236–237
"NEVER AGAIN," 32
New Cold War, 345–347
New International System, 32–33
New Look Doctrine, 102, 153
"New World Order," 322
NGOs. *See* Nongovernmental organizations
Nguyên Giáp, 63
Nigeria, 5
    disintegration, 205–206
Nixon, Richard, 11, 14, 105, 110, 133, 154
Nkrumah, Kwame, 101, 103, 202, 203
    development program, 69–72
    downfall, 70–72
NLF. *See* National Liberation Front
"No-fault" divorce policies, 134
Non-aligned movement (NAM), 20, 21, 84, 95, 101–102, 204, 332
Nongovernmental organizations (NGOs), 4, 218
Non-Proliferation Treaty (NPT), 331
Non-Western nationalism, 43
Non-Western societies, 43
NORAD. *See* North American Aerospace Defense Command
Nordic Bloc, 138
North American Aerospace Defense Command (NORAD), 119
North American Counterculture Movement, 1965 to 1975, 128–130
North American Free Trade Agreement (NAFTA), 137, 169–170, 293
North American suburbanization, 124
North Atlantic Treaty Organization (NATO), 27, 36, 64, 117
Northern Alliance, 329
North Vietnamese government, 104
Novel fiscal instruments, 4
NSC-68, 90
Nuclear Brink, 1954 to 1963, 94–100
Nuremberg Tribunals, 33–34
Nyerere, Joseph, 307

O

OAS. *See* Organization of American States
Obama, Barack, 127, 330
"Objectivity," 26
Occupied Territories, 196
October Crisis in Quebec, 132
OECD. *See* Organisation for Economic Co-operation and Development
OEEC. *See* Organization for European Economic Cooperation
Oil and water, 195–196
Oil Crisis 1973, 81
Oligarchs, 274
One-China policy, 238
One-Dimensional Man (Marcuse), 130
OPEC. *See* Organization of Petroleum Exporting Countries
OPEC Embargo and the Lost Decade, 1973 to 1985, 12–13
Open Door Policy, 181, 253
Operation Amazonia, 169
Operation Condor, 156
Operation Desert Storm, 323
Opération Turquoise, 226
Oppenheimer, Robert, 99
Organisation for Economic Co-operation and Development (OECD), 5, 27, 119
Organization for African Unity, 203
Organization for European Economic Cooperation (OEEC), 118
Organization of American States (OAS), 152
Organization of Petroleum Exporting Countries (OPEC), 10, 81–82, 133
    oil shock, 202
Ortega, Daniel, 157, 158
Oslo Process, 196–199
Ostalgie, 281
Ostpolitik (Brandt), 132–133

P

Pacific War crimes, 34
Pahlavi dynasty, 183
Palestinian Intifada, 196–199
Palestinian Liberation Organization (PLO), 196
Pan-African dream, 203–204
Pan-American Conference 1948, 152
Pan-Arabism, 175–176
Pasternak, Boris, 262
Patrice Lumumba, 67, 70
Patriot Act, 327
PDAM. *See* Program for Amazon Development
Peaceful coexistence, 94
Peak water, 340
Pearson, Lester, 4, 71, 177–178

Pele, 164
Pemuda, 40
Peng Dehuai, 247
People's democracies, 48
People's Liberation Army (PLA), 91
Perestroika, 274, 275
Perle, Richard, 328
Perón, Isabel, 156
Perón, Juan, 76, 147
Persian Gulf States, 81–82
Personal computer (PC) revolution, 297
Peshawar Accord, 191
Petrodollars, 12, 82
Peurifoy, John, 154
Philippeville Massacre 1955, 66
Pieds-Noirs, 64
Pink Tide, 168
Pinochet, Augusto, 151, 155, 167–168
Pinochet's Coup, 155–156
PLA. *See* People's Liberation Army
Plan Dalet, 51
Planned obsolescence, 302–303
Polarization of Latin American society, 150
"Political Islam," 188
Pompidou, Georges, 131–132
Pope John Paul II, 162
Popular Unity, 154
Populism, postwar experiment in, 147–151
Postcolonial Africa, 202
Postcolonial African cultures, 213
Postcolonial challenges, 1973 to 1982, 75–80
Postcolonial modernization schemes, 80
Postcolonial Nigeria, 205
Postcolonial World, 15
Post-Fordist production, 293
Postindependence disintegration, 73–75
Postindustrial economy, 134
Postwar Asia
    Asian Miracle, 249–253
    Asia's Cold War, 238–239
    Japan's Postwar Transformation, 239–244
    Mao and China's modernization struggle, 244–249
    Waking Dragon, 253–256
Postwar Asian Nationalism, 1945 to 1949, 39–40
Postwar culture and society, 160–164
Postwar decolonization wave, 1945 to 1949, 36–38
    Burma, 38
    China's Civil War, 1945 to 1949, 42
    India's independence, 40–41
    postwar Indonesia, 40
Postwar economic recovery, 240–241
Postwar economy, 35
Postwar era, 1945 to 2010, 6–7
    economic cycles and regional discrepancies, 9–11
    Golden Postwar Recovery, 1950 to 1972, 11

    Neoliberal Globalization, 1986 to 2007, 13–15
    OPEC Embargo and the Lost Decade, 1973 to 1985, 12–13
    shape of the long twentieth century, 8–9
Postwar feminism, 44–45
Postwar Indonesia, 40
Postwar international system, 35–36
Postwar Latin America, 146–147
    Cold War, 152–160
    at crossroads, 170–171
    culture and society, 160–164
    Debt Crisis, 1982 to 1989, 164–166
    democratic wave, 167–169
    experiment in populism, 147–151
Postwar Middle East, 174
    Iranian Revolution, 182–189
    Nasser and revolutionary nationalism, 175–182
    Palestinian Intifada and Oslo Process, 196–199
    postwar urbanization and modern anxieties, 193–196
    Soviet War in Afghanistan, 189–193
Postwar West, 116
    Anxious 1960s, 124–133
    Conservative Resurgence, 1980s, 135–137
    Contemporary Western Society, 137–142
    Golden Recovery, 116–119
    Society of Affluence, 1950 to 1969, 120–124
    Stagflation Crisis, 1973 to 1980, 133–135
    in twenty-first century, 142
Potsdam Agreement, 53
Potsdam Conference, 37, 91
Powell, Lewis, 133
Prague Spring, 270
Prebisch, Raúl, 69, 148
Primitive one-room schools, 205
Process of National Reorganization, 156
Program for Amazon Development (PDAM), 169
Progressive postwar reforms, 146
Project for the New American Century (PNAC), 328
Protectionism, 148
Proxy wars, 102
Putin, Vladimir, 345, 346

Q

Qaddafi, Muammar, 78, 181, 182, 196, 207, 343
Quebec sovereignty movement, 284
Quebec's Quiet Revolution, 124
Quest for National Development, 1960 to 1975, 68–75
Quiet Revolution of the 1960s, 124
Qutb, Sayyid, 192, 193
al-Quwatli, Shukri, 37

R

Rabin, Yitzhak, 198
Radical fringe of the counterculture movement, 132
Rapid integration, 2
Reagan, Ronald, 110, 111, 116, 134, 157, 165
    and conservative resurgence in the United States, 136–137
Real Politik, 153
Reconciliation, justice and, 167–168
Red Guards, 247
Red Scare, 89, 95, 107
Reformer regimes, 280
Regional central banks, 250
Regional discrepancies, 9–11
Resolution 181, 50, 51
Revolutionary Council, 185
Revolutionary Nationalist Movement, 153
Revolutionary state, 204–205
Revolutionary utopianism, 245
Revolutionary wave, 21–23, 149–150
    clashing expectations for decolonization, 1945 to 1955, 61–64
    decolonization and development, 60
    Great Unraveling, 1956 to 1966, 64–68
    postcolonial challenges, 1973 to 1982, 75–80
    quest for National Development, 1960 to 1975, 68–75
    waning of, 80–84
Revolution of 1968, 81
Revolutions of 1989, 13
Reykjavik Summit 1986, 111
Rhee, Syngman, 91
Ridgeway, Matthew, 93
Right Wing parties, 139
Rio Conference, 322
Rio Pact 1947, 152
Robeson, Paul, 89, 90
Robust economic growth, 123
Robust nuclear disarmament movement, 106
Robust postwar economic growth, 119
Rockefeller Foundation, 79
Roe v. Wade, 135
Rogue states, 328
Romero, Oscar, 158, 159
Roosevelt, Eleanor, 34
Roosevelt, Franklin D., 32, 36, 120, 152
Roser, Max, 6
Rumsfeld, Donald, 329
Rural collectivization, 245
Rural insecurity and developing world urbanization, 79–80
Russian–German hostilities, 33
Rwandan Civil War, 223–226
Rwandan Patriotic Front (RPF), 223
Rwanda's tragedy, 222–227

S

Sagan, Carl, 99
Sahwa, 188, 193
SALT. *See* Strategic Arms Limitations Talks
Sandinistas in Nicaragua, 157–158
Santayana, George, 27
Sarney, José, 168
Saro-Wiwa, Ken, 216
SARS. *See* Severe acute respiratory syndrome
Saudi Arabia, 3, 193–195
SAVAK, 183
Sayyid Qutb, 192–193
Schengen Convention 1985, 138
Schneider, Rene, 156
School of the Americas, 160
Schuman, Robert, 118
SDI. *See* Strategic Defense Initiative
Second wave feminism, 130
Secular modernization schemes, 188
Security Council, 32, 36
Senghor, Léopold Sédar, 203, 213
Severe acute respiratory syndrome (SARS), 4, 28
Shari'ah law, 19
Sharon, Ariel, 195, 199
Sharpeville Massacre, 219
Shevardnadze, Eduard, 278
Shock, Nixon, 305
Shock Therapy, 280
Silicon Valley, 309
Silva-Herzog, Jesus, 164
Sino-Indian War, 236
Sino-Soviet Treaty of Friendship, 245
Sinyavsky–Daniel Trial, 267
Sirleaf, Ellen Johnson, 217
Sit-ins, 126
Six-Day War, 76
Social democracy, 46, 117
"Social development" projects, 78
Socialism, 69
Socialist allies, 106
"Socialist Hegemon," 105
"Socialist market," 248
Social movements, 60
Society of Affluence, 1950 to 1969, 120–124
Society, postwar culture and, 160–164
Solidarity, 271
Somoza, Anastasio, 157
Soros, George, 5
South Africa's National Party, 63
Southeast Asia Treaty Organization (SEATO), 233
Southern Baptist Convention, 134
Sovereign Debt Crisis, 335
Sovereign Debt Crisis 2008, 139

Soviet aggression, 34
Soviet Bloc, 22, 167, 260
    Gorbachev takes the Soviet Helm, 272–275
    mysterious death of Comrade Stalin, 260–267
    revolutions of 1989, 275–279
    stability and stagnation under Brezhnev, 267–272
    trauma of postcommunist transition, 279–285
Soviet confiscations, 47
Soviet Hammer, 1948 to 1953, 48–49
Soviet ICBMs, 97
Soviet soldiers, 47
Soviet Union, 32, 34, 47, 277–279
Soviet War in Afghanistan, 189–193
Soweto Uprising, 220
Spassky, Boris, 108
Special Economic Zones (SEZs), 254
Sputnik 1957, 95
Srebrenica, 284
Srebrenica Massacre, 325
Stagflation, 81, 305
Stagflation Crisis, 1973 to 1980, 133–135
Stalinized, 48
Stalin, Joseph, 32, 33, 36, 42, 47, 48, 52–54, 89, 91, 92, 94, 117
    Red Terror, 107
Stasi, 279
State terrorism, *Junta* and, 159–160
Stephenson, Adlai, 99
Strategic Arms Limitations Talks (SALT), 106
Strategic Defense Initiative (SDI), 110
Structural adjustment, 280
    mechanisms, 208
    policy, 307
Structural adjustment mechanisms, 165
Structural reforms, 13
Structural underdevelopment, 204
Stuxnet computer virus, 332
Sub-Saharan Africa, 76
    African socialism, 202
    democratic wave, 218–222
    Idi Amin's despotism, 206–207
    Kleptocracy, 208–213
    neocolonial settlement, 207–208
    Nigeria's disintegration, 205–206
    Nkrumah, Kwame, 202
    Pan-African dream, 203–204
    postcolonial Africa, 202
    postcolonial society and culture, 213–217
    revolutionary state, 204–205
    Rwanda's tragedy, 222–227
Suez Crisis, 63, 71, 94, 177–179
Suharto, 236
Sukarno, 40, 62, 101
Summit Series, 27, 108

Supreme Commander of Allied Powers (SCAP), 239
Sustainable Development (SD) model, 323

T

Taiwan Straights Crisis 1958, 96
Taliban, 191–192
Tanzania's postcolonial development program, 17
Taraki, Nur Muhammad, 190
Technology and industrialization, Canadians, 7
"Territorial integrity," 233
Tet Offensive 1968, 105, 129
Thatcherism, 135
Thatcher, Margaret, 110, 116, 135, 166
Third and Fourth Geneva Conventions, 34
"Third International Theory," 182
Third World, 60, 62, 70, 88
    in cross fire, 100–106
Thirteen Days in October, 97–100
Thompson, Llewelyn, 99–100
Tiananmen incident, 254–256
Tiananmen Massacre 1989, 18
Tiger economies, 232, 248–250
Tito, Josip Broz, 101
TNCs. *See* Transnational corporations
Tora Bora, 329
Toxic Asset Relief Program (TARP), 341
Tragedy of the Commons Model, 337
Trans-Amazonian Highway, 169
Transformation of Western Society, 1955 to 1979, 123–124
Transnational corporations (TNCs), 4–5, 141, 142, 216, 304
Transportation, 292
Treaty of Asunción, 168
Treaty of Rome 1957, 118
Treaty of San Francisco, 233, 239
Trudeau, Pierre Elliot, 71, 120
Trujillo, Rafael L., 147
Truman Doctrine, 53
Truman, Harry S., 33, 50, 53, 88–94
Tshombe, Moïse, 74
Tudeh Party, 183
Tun Mahathir Mohammed, 252
Twenty-first century
    9-11 and security in new millennium, 326–333
    Arab spring and digital populism, 343–345
    crisis capitalism and great recession, 340–343
    Kyoto and tragedy of global commons, 333–340
    liberalism, 322–325
    New Cold War, 345–347
    "New World Order," 322
Two-state solution, 197
Tyranny of Debt, 78

U

UFCO. *See* United Fruit Company
Uhura, 38
Ulbricht, Walter, 96
UN-brokered peace treaty, 168
UN Charter, 34, 94
UN General Assembly, 21, 34, 84, 101
UN intervention, 92
United Arab Republic (UAR), 180
United Democratic Front (UDF), 221
United Fruit Company (UFCO), 153–154
United Nations (UN), 5, 61
United Nations Assistance Mission for Rwanda (UNAMIR), 225
United Nations Emergency Force (UNEF), 178
United States' global containment strategy, 64
Universal Declaration of Human Rights 1948, 34
UN "Trusts," 38
Urbanization, 123, 210
Uruguay Process, 13, 290
Uruguay Round of General Agreement on Tariffs and Trade, 168
US Civil Rights Movement, 62, 125–126
US Declaration of Independence, 67
US Department of Agriculture, 79
US Dodd-Frank law, 342
US Empire, 90–91
US foreign policy, 53
US–Japan Defense Treaty, 242
US Marshall Plan, 117, 118
US National Housing Act 1934, 121
US Patriot Act, 331
US–Philippine Mutual Defence Pact, 235
US plan of attack, 328–331
US policy-makers, 97
US unilateralism, 330–331
Uwilingiyimana, Agathe, 223

V

van Bilsen, A. J., 64
Vanished Dream, 75
Velvet Revolution, 277
Versailles Conference 1919, 8, 32
Versailles system, 35
Veteran's Administration, 121
"Viet Cong" (Diem), 104, 105
Viet Minh, 63
Vietnam War, 104–105
Violence in Seattle, 325
Virgin Lands program, 266
Visible minorities, 314

Volcker, Paul, 137
Volta River Project, 70
Voting Rights Act, 127

W

Walsa, Lech, 271
Waning liberalism, 133
War Powers Act 1973, 105
Washington Consensus, 84, 307
Watts Riot, 127
Wehrmacht, 53
Western counterculture movement, 131
Western economies, 116
Western European social democracy, 46
Western Feminism, 130
Western optimism, 116
West European Social Democracy, 1945 to 1949, 43, 46
Westmoreland, William, 105
White, Henry Dexter, 35
White Revolution, 183
WikiLeaks 2010, 5
WikiLeaks scandal, 216, 343
Wilsonian idealism, 35
Wizard of Oz, 4
Woodstock in 1969, 130
World Bank, 35, 78, 79
World Trade Organization (WTO), 2, 17, 22, 60, 146, 290, 305–309, 324
World War II, 21, 25, 32, 35, 49, 56, 60–61, 71, 78, 88, 112, 116, 121, 123, 125, 128, 146, 147
World Wide Web, 297–298

Y

Yalta Accords, 47, 52, 54
Yalta Conference 1945, 38
Yalu Mountains, 93
Yanukovych, Victor, 346
Yeltsin, Boris, 275, 280–281
Yom Kippur War, 12, 81, 181

Z

Zairianization, 210
Zapatista Movement, 312
al-Zarqawi, Abu Musab, 329, 330
Zhou Enlai, 92
Zine El Abidine Ben Ali, 343
Zionism, 49
Zulu Inkatha Party, 221

CPSIA information can be obtained
at www.ICGtesting.com
Printed in the USA
FSHW021254250819
61374FS

9 781524 986926